Career Development

CAREER DEVELOPMENT

Counseling Through the Life Stages

CHARLES C. HEALY

*University of California,
Los Angeles*

Allyn and Bacon, Inc.

Boston   London   Sydney   Toronto

Library of Congress Cataloging in Publication Data

Healy, Charles C.
    Career development.

    Bibliography: p.
    Includes index.
    1. Vocational guidance.   I. Title.
HF5381.H338   331.7'02   81–8056
ISBN 0–205–07557–6   AACR2

10 9 8 7 6 5 4 3 2 1   87 86 85 84 83 82

Printed in the United States of America

CONTENTS

2182082

Preface   *vii*

part one   Careers and the World of Work   1

    1.   The Nature of Career   3
    2.   Relating to Work   28
    3.   Characteristics Related to Career   64
    4.   Careers and our Educational-Work System   113

part two   Career Counseling and Evaluation   163

    5.   A Career Counseling Framework   165
    6.   Evaluation and Research in Counseling   196

part three   Career Counseling Procedures Through the Life Stages   239

    7.   Growth Stage Career Counseling   241
    8.   Exploratory Stage Career Counseling   287
    9.   Transition From Exploration to Establishment   365
   10.   Career Choice Counseling   414
   11.   Counseling For Career Establishment   475
   12.   Maintenance Stage Career Counseling   529

part four   Career Counseling and the Future   573

   13.   Auspicious Developments and Dark Clouds   575

Contents

Appendices   593

   A.   Descriptions of Five Career Development Tests   595
   B.   Excerpts from *Foresight*   599
   C.   Excerpts from *Overview*   601
   D.   Excerpts from *Captain's Introduction*   604
   E.   Excerpts from *Alternate Specialty*   605
   F.   Excerpts from *Self-Assessment*   606
   G.   Excerpts from *Career Strategies*   608

Bibliography   611

Name Index   650

Subject Index   659

PREFACE

Career Development: Counseling through the Life Stages presents detailed descriptions of multiple career counseling procedures, organizes them according to career developmental stages, and examines the research that has been done on each of the procedures. This presentation will enable counselors to identify the counseling actions that have contributed to resolving particular career problems and permit them to examine the empirical evidence that has accrued for particular procedures. Such knowledge is essential for accountable practice.

The detailed descriptions are not meant as recipes to be applied mechanically or uncritically. Rather, readers should view the techniques as examples of how client needs and principles of learning have been synthesized into particular counseling actions. An understanding of the framework of career counseling presented in this text and a familiarity with different career counseling techniques will increase professional counselors' capacity to create individualized treatments for their clients.

The book has four parts. Part I presents key concepts and facts about careers and introduces the worlds of work and education in which these concepts and facts unfold. Chapter 1 covers the concept of career. Chapter 2 reviews major ways of conceptualizing people in relation to careers. Chapter 3 examines our knowledge of the major human characteristics associated with different careers. Then Chapter 4, the last chapter in Part I, reviews aspects of the worlds of work and education that are important in shaping careers and in developing methods of informing people about work.

Part II describes career counseling and offers important factors to consider concerning its evaluation. First, chapter 5 shows how counseling is a special kind of teaching, delineates a procedure for individualizing such teaching, and indicates how career counseling applies general wisdom to improve careers. Chapter 6 describes summative and formative evaluation and tells how to make career counseling repeatable. Counseling is an art. But, by delineating the essential elements of our practice, we can advance counseling through replication just as scientists have advanced other kinds of knowledge and technology. The hallmark of a professional is the ability to improve service through practice. The exposition of formative evaluation in chapter 6 will help counselors to discharge this professional obligation.

Part III (Chapters 7–12) describes counseling procedures that have been used successfully to assist people at different stages of their careers. Chapter 7 presents procedures for people in the growth stage—usually elementary school children; Chapter 8, techniques for those in the exploratory stage—usually adolescents and adults who are substantially redirecting their careers. Chapter 9 provides methods for people moving from one stage to another—especially from school to work. Next, chapter 10 details and critiques procedures for those seeking to integrate their experiences and preferences into a career choice. Chapter 11 then presents ways for those coping with the tasks of establishing themselves in work. Finally, Chapter 12 delineates methods for the tasks of the maintenance stage. In Part IV, the closing chapter (13) reviews the current status of career counseling and offers suggestions for its improvement.

Chapters 7–12 each summarize the needs of clients at a particular career stage, describe the appropriate counseling practices in detail, and review the research pertinent to these practices. The career stages are assumed to be hierarchical, e.g., a person in the establishment stage should successfully have completed the tasks of all previous stages. Often, of course, one will confront tasks at a later stage, before having resolved fully those from an earlier stage. In this case, the counselor may have to start with tasks of an earlier stage or undertake those from different stages concomitantly. Of course, a most important step with such clients is to convince them that they need to work on tasks from the earlier stage and to verify that the current situation permits such an undertaking.

There are few studies that demonstrate the validity of using certain career counseling procedures for different life stages. By delineating treatments clearly, bringing together much of the past research, and pinpointing many evaluation needs, this text should encourage more such studies. Even after a decade that proclaimed the need for evaluation to establish accountability, the limited amount of empirical verification suggests that counselors are accepting other evidence to validate their practices. Indeed, they appear to operate on the common sense of their actions. In presenting each method, therefore, the author has explained the heuristic principles of teaching or learning that underlie that procedure. Because each technique is based on these common-sense beliefs about human interactions, one can partially judge the probable efficacy of any method by learning whether it builds on appropriate heuristic principles.

In a second response to the limited empirical study of counseling procedures, the author has described the "human intelligence or adversary" method of evaluation in chapter 6 and illustrated how it might be used to study counseling. Conversations with many counselors indicate that they now use at least parts of this procedure as they struggle to improve and verify their own effectiveness. Formalizing and making the process more public should enable these operations to be even more productive.

The contributions of many people helped make this book a reality. I would like to take this opportunity to acknowledge their generosity and express my gratitude. Professors Donald Super and Garth Sorenson stimulated my examination of career development and counseling, and Professor Roger Myers, who had guided my initial counseling efforts, again offered timely assistance by alerting me to developments in computer counseling. Many students at UCLA have joined me in developing replicable counseling procedures; especially Drs. Ann Fogel, Louis Markert, Ann Marshall, Victor Ogilvie, Linda Phillips-Jones, Frank Santoro, Gregory Snodgrass, Sheila Vaughan, and Edna Zinar, helped create the framework for replicable counseling offered here, and their enthusiasm has helped sustain me in this effort.

Friends and colleagues such as Professors Gordon Berry, Fred Ellett, Ann Phelps, Romeria Tidwell, and Mr. Benett Dolin also offered constructive suggestions for illuminating key points. Moreover, very comprehensive reviews by Professors Bruce Shertzer and Earl Moore pinpointed ways of refining the presentation and encouraged persistence in completing it. Not to be forgotten is the superb copyediting of Grace Sheldrick, which smoothed many bumpy passages. Finally, special gratitude is owed my wife, Margaret, for ongoing editorial assistance and patience and to Mrs. Ida Lees for her faithful typing, editorial advice, and constant encouragement.

C.C.H.

CAREERS AND THE WORLD OF WORK

part one

Most people devote many hours to training and working. Their efforts can delight or frustrate, challenge or bore, injure or heal, ennoble or degrade. Often the outcomes are predictable; if people learn about themselves in relation to work and stay vigilant, they can influence the results of their training and working activities. To provide counselors with background for helping people take charge of their careers, Part One of this text, which includes Chapters 1 through 4, examines the nature of careers and the education-work system in which careers unfold. (Career is used in the sense of a person's on-going relation to work.)

Before undertaking to help people with their careers, a counselor must define his or her theory of career. Chapter 1 introduces the concept of career as work-related positions, including all jobs and all training and honorary positions stemming from or leading to those jobs. This definition takes account of both the objective and subjective realities that encompass the particular positions as well as of the person's thoughts and beliefs about those positions. The exposition shows that career is one means most people must pursue to express personhood. After reminding the reader that complex but partially predictable forces influence a person's career, the chapter elaborates on principles such as "careers develop people" and "a person creates a concept of self in relation to working that can increasingly guide the career" in order to help the reader articulate a personal theory of career.

Chapter 2 continues to examine the concept of career by deducing the implications of seven models of a human being for pursuing a career. Each model has inspired research, generated knowledge, and helped some people in their careers. To help a client use these different views of "person" to fashion a career, the chapter closes by illustrating how each perspective leads to a somewhat different self-appraisal operation. By using each operation in turn, the client can form a more comprehensive career self-concept.

Chapter 3 introduces technical concepts of ability, interest, value, personality, gender, social class, and race; it reviews how these attributes are measured and have related to career; and it shows how using our current understanding of these attributes can enable people to have more control over their careers. Based on data from vocational psychology research, the chapter proposes that counselors move beyond using these concepts only to generate a series of possible options for clients to showing them how understanding of these concepts and systematic effort can enable them to develop particular abilities and interests and lessen the obstacles of race and social class. The chapter closes with a reminder about the limitations of measurement, admonishing the reader to support efforts to train youngsters early in accurate self-appraisal so that they can better interpret their experiences and expand their prospects.

Chapter 4 highlights aspects of our educational work system, suggests what is important to learn through career information seeking, and notes recent advances in dissemination of career information. Many aspects of occupations are fixed for most workers since society collectively shapes and sanctions these occupations. Nevertheless, the reader need not accept the view that a client or even most clients must adjust. Rather, a counselor should remember that current work and education practices are consequences of human policy established in reaction to changing possibilities and demands. Change is inevitable, and new policies about working and training will be forthcoming. By considering the forces that are likely to affect careers, the counselor will be better able to help clients anticipate changes and better equipped to participate constructively in establishing new policy. The chapter highlights existing work-education structures with the hope of stimulating the reader to think about "what might be" in the tradition of the late Robert F. Kennedy.

The Nature of Career

1

The Concept and Power of Career

Natural endowment, social class, the state of the economy, national policy, and even chance itself influence an individual's career. Together their influence is substantial, and each of these factors is beyond the individual's control. Why, then, a book on methods of helping people to create their careers? Would not a text on career adjustment be more appropriate, since one can argue that only a fool will expend energy trying to plan and create who he or she wants to be, when the outcome is already determined?

Clearly, expressing oneself through a career is, and probably always will be, a challenging undertaking, for it requires continuing effort, vigilance, and adaptability. Fortunately, however, people can choose the abilities and interests they build and use at work, even though nature puts some constraints on the degree of such development. They can understand the world of work, including economic cycles, access routes to opportunities, and manpower programs. Furthermore, they can even learn to cope with chance.

People who are handicapped, victims of discrimination, or from disadvantaged families and communities will have to strive harder to take charge of their careers. At times, their efforts may have to be even heroic, but people such as Helen Keller, Ralph Bunche, Abraham Lincoln, and countless others have shown that self-expressive careers can be created. And, as these people have shown, the career then reflects the human capacity to meet and master adversity rather than be overwhelmed by it.

In most careers, there will be points where compromise and adjustment are necessary, even desirable; but at other times, one will want to alter the self and/or the situation. Only occasionally may these efforts be feats of public notice and acclaim, but nonetheless they will reflect human determination and ingenuity in improving rather than merely in "coping" and "adjusting."

Many careers appear to happen, but this book is written in the belief that most careers can be created. The key ingredients are understanding, determination, and ability. Every person, barring a major handicap, has multiple, continual options. In order to exercise these options, the career-ist must: (a) stay alert to recognize the options, (b) pick those for which one possesses or can build the necessary abilities, and (c) apply oneself energetically and persistently after choosing. Moreover, since there are multiple options, the person, like a stock trader, should accept that although some career influences are beyond prediction and control and that some efforts will fail, nevertheless one can succeed by being correct more often than incorrect. To do so, one must work vigorously to ensure that neglect is not the reason for failure.

"Sense of agency" is a term coined by Tiedeman (1972) that effec-tively communicates the personal perspective needed to take charge of one's own career. The concept communicates energy, ongoing applica-tion, and struggle. First and foremost, the person continually strives to understand himself and the forces that are creating him. According to Thoresen and Ewart (1976), the careerist must struggle persistently to win control of the career. The career seeker has many arduous tasks, including: "analyzing the environment; committing oneself to take action and maintain action; identifying and altering faulty perceptions, beliefs and attributes; trying out new ways of acting; and restructuring the environment to promote change and foster encouragement." Perhaps even more demanding is the need identified by Ginzberg et al. (1951) to know when and how to compromise.

Although there are more career opportunities and more ways of achieving them than ever before, and although our financial resources force fewer people to work purely to survive, Americans are having many problems with their careers. One recent federally commissioned report stated that workers in every occupational strata are suffering tension, illness, and general dissatisfaction because their work has lost its chal-lenge and opportunity for personal development (O'Toole, 1973). For many of these workers, the report continued, satisfaction would require radical changes in work design and substantial increases in access to new training programs. Many other observers have also noted this malaise. In *Working*, journalist Studs Terkel presented interviews with a broad cross-section of workers. Almost invariably these typical em-ployees were dissatisfied due to repetitiveness and lack of challenge. Work was not meeting their expectations, and they felt trapped by rigid salary and pension systems and lack of transfer opportunities. A Nader report of an intensive study of nine blue-collar workers revealed similar feelings of worker dissatisfaction and lack of hope (Lasson, 1971).

The discontent is not limited to lower-level workers as Sarason and his colleagues (1975) confirmed, reporting on high-level professionals. Physicians, lawyers, dentists, engineers, scientists, and college pro-fessors may suffer boredom after several successful years of work, and they feel the same powerlessness to correct the situation. Following up 240 clinical psychology students after 25 years, E. L. Kelley et al. (1978) found that nearly half of the 80 percent who responded would not have become clinical psychologists if they had it to do again. Apparently, however, most of these workers were doing little to change their situation, and the O'Toole (1973) report suggested that there was little that they could do. Implicitly, most had not learned to "engineer their career" (Thoresen & Ewart, 1976), and reports such as Nader's, Terkel's, and O'Toole's suggest that many observers do not believe that careers can be engineered by the worker.

Even though there may be disagreement about the extent to which it is possible for a person to direct his or her own career, there is no disagreement that steering a career is difficult and that pursuit of a career is fraught with emotion. A career can bring happiness, excitement, accomplishment, and tranquillity; but it can also bring sadness, frustration, and anxiety. Terkel's work implies that professionals promoting another's career development will often meet clients when they are anxious, bewildered, apathetic, and frustrated. That very distress will make it more difficult for them to build the skills necessary for directing their careers. Because he or she will be called on to help another person who is under stress to grow, but who feels unable to succeed, the career helper must be a professional.

Career: A Perspective

Career can be defined as the sequence of major positions occupied by a person throughout his or her pre-occupational, occupational, and post-occupational life. It includes all work-related positions such as those of student, employee (or employer or self-employed worker), and pensioner, together with complementary avocational, familial, and civic positions. Careers exist only as persons pursue them; they are person-centered (Super, 1976). A position becomes part of a career if it is a work position, if it prepares the person for a work position or enhances the person's work, or if it is a direct consequence of working. An avocation, therefore, may or may not be part of a career depending on whether it contributes to work directly, as when a stamp collector manages a hobby shop; or indirectly, as when model railroading relieves the tensions of management or when the hobby arises from the career, as in the case of the executive who takes up golf in order to meet the bosses. Positions as volunteer or extracurricular participant are career positions for some but not all people, and in some cases, one will be able to recognize that such a position was part of the career only in retrospect.

By this definition, there are more than two hundred twenty million careers in progress in the United States. One defines the career by how an individual acts in each position. Many careers are comparable because they include similar positions in a similar sequence, but each is distinguishable because of how the person performs the position. For example, two well-known contemporaries, Presidents Lyndon Johnson and Gerald Ford, compiled very different congressional and presidential records even though both rose from the working class to commissions in the United States Navy, to congressional seats, to party leadership in Congress, and eventually to the Presidency. The personal character of a career means that understanding a particular career requires attending to the unique characteristics of the careerist; that is, awareness of individual differences is essential to capturing the essence of particular careers.

Career is both an objective and a subjective reality. Each position has observable duties and prerogatives, and opens or closes future options. It requires, exercises, and refines measurable skills, interests, and values as it provides particular background and establishes contacts. At the same time, encumbency in a position produces personal thoughts, feelings, and aspirations. Often a position is more than the series of duties and expectations set by family, school, or employer. The police officer, for example, is "the new centurion"; the immigrant's child entering the MBA program feels she is her parents' hope of realizing the American dream. Both aspects of career are important in understanding a person's behavior.

Understanding career requires recognizing that it is essentially a response to the need to work. The need to work or to produce goods and services is a natural and a societal need: human beings by nature, must acquire goods and services from other people in order to survive, and societies exist in part because their members believe that they expand or ensure the availability of goods and services.

In our society, all people are expected to work in order to compensate for the goods and services they receive, and as a consequence everyone is expected to prepare for working. Nevertheless, in our society the prominence of the work role varies, principally in terms of sex, age, and social class.

Many middle-class American males act as if the career embodied their major efforts to fulfill a calling or vocation. They expend substantial personal and material resources in preparing for, and advancing in, their career. On the other hand, men who are not middle class and many women attribute less significance to their careers.

Children devote little attention to careers, and young adolescents give it only slightly more thought, even though the skills and habits acquired in childhood and the choices made at the start of adolescence have profound effects on the career. By late adolescence and early adulthood, career becomes and remains for many years a focal point for most men and for increasing numbers of women. As young adulthood turns into middle adulthood, women who had foregone careers in order to raise families turn their energies to paid employment, while the veteran worker has begun rethinking his or her approach to working. Finally, as old age approaches and career involvement declines because of institutional customs and declining energies, the prominence of career fades. Yet the success and satisfaction of the career continue to influence the quality of life, for in retirement society provides rewards commensurate with career attainment.

Career possibilities vary according to social class. For most, there are careers, but for the lower class, only leftover work. The middle and upper classes can look forward to careers of relatively stable, continually challenging, and satisfying work in what is termed the primary labor market. In contrast, lower-class persons are far more likely to find themselves in the "secondary labor market" in a series of unsteady, menial jobs, with prospects no brighter than those proclaimed in the coal miner's ballad about working hard loading sixteen tons of coal but only increasing one's debt.

Throughout the book, several common words referring to careers will be used with very specific meanings. Table 1–1 presents the terms and their meanings for this text. The table represents an attempt by Super (1976), in concert with several vocational psychologists, to establish conceptual uniformity for the study of the phenomenon of career.

Careers Are Mandated, Not Chosen

The linkage of careers to human production and to societal existence renders careers subject to economic, sociological, political, and psychological forces. As a consequence, a career cannot be whatever a person wants it to be.

Most people create their careers as they do only because at some point in their lives, usually throughout most of their adulthood, they must pursue one or more occupations in order to earn a living. Nearly everyone anticipates pursuing an occupation; the Bureau of Labor Statistics predicts that more than 90 percent of the boys and girls born today will work, on the average, more than forty and twenty-five years, respectively. Few people, however, would work at their current jobs or at least as steadily as they do, if they did not need the earnings their jobs produce. People would react in this way because in every job there are involuntary components. In some jobs, the amount of personal subordination to the dictates of others is less than in others. But even in the most attractive professions such as medicine, law, athletics, and entertainment, the worker usually would produce differently, or not at all, if not motivated by wage concerns. The involuntary character of work is sometimes obscured as other aspects of work gain attention. Recognition that most people obtain most of their income by working has underscored work's strong influences on life style, both its material character and availability of time. The realization that community and civic organizations seek high-status persons to guide and promote them has prompted social scientists to note that working, especially in prestigious occupations, becomes almost a *sine qua non* for meaningful participation in the governance of one's own community.

In equipping people for their work role, one must not obscure the compulsory character of work. Yet society's need for work has led to emphasizing the pleasurable activities that comprise working and preparing for work and to de-emphasizing its somewhat arbitrary nature and tedium. The knowledge that a few people can meet the demand for

Table 1–1. A Career Development Glossary for Career Education

Time and Effort

Work
The systematic pursuit of an objective valued by oneself (even if only for survival) and desired by others; directed and consecutive, it requires the expenditure of effort. It may be compensated (paid work) or uncompensated (volunteer work or an avocation). The objective may be intrinsic enjoyment of the work itself, the structure given to life by the work role, the economic support which work makes possible, or the type of leisure which it facilitates.

Labor
Productive work for survival or support, requiring physical or mental effort.

Employment
Time spent in paid work or in indirectly paid work such as homemaking.

Leisure
Time free of required paid or unpaid work, in rest, play, or avocations.

Play
Activity which is primarily recreational and relaxing; engaged in for its own sake; it may be unsystematic or systematic, without objective or with an objective which is of temporary and personal consequence; it may involve the expenditure of effort, but that effort is voluntary and easily avoided by the player.

Content

Task
A performance required at work or in play.

Position
A group of tasks to be performed by one person; in industry, performed for pay. Positions exist whether vacant or occupied; they are task- and outcome, not person, defined.

Role
A set of behaviors associated with a position. The *role concepts* of persons occupying positions may be so called; those of persons surrounding the position *role expectations.*

Job
A group of similar, paid, positions requiring some similar attributes in a single organization. Jobs are task-, outcome-, and organization-centered.

Occupation
A group of similar jobs found in various organizations. Occupations are task-, economy-, and society-oriented.

Vocation
An occupation with commitment, distinguished primarily by its psychological as contrasted with its economic meaning: ego-involving, meaningful to the individual as an activity, not solely for its productive, distributive, or service outcome and its economic rewards although these too are valued. Vocations are task-, outcome-, and person-centered.

Avocation
An activity pursued systematically and consecutively for its own sake with an objective other than monetary gain, although it may incidentally result in gain. Avocations are task-, outcome-, and person-centered.

Career
The sequence of major positions occupied by a person throughout his preoccupational, occupational, and postoccupational life: includes work-related roles such as those of student, employee, and pensioner, together with complementary avocational familial, and civic roles. Careers exist only as people pursue them; they are person-centered.

Structure

Organization
A specific institution, company, or other independent or autonomous entity producing or distributing goods or services.

Industry
A branch of an art or trade which employs people to produce or distribute goods or to provide services; a group of similar organizations.

SOURCE: D. E. Super. *Career education and the meanings of work. Monographs on Career Education.* Washington, D.C.: U.S. Office of Education, 1976.

work through activities that they generally enjoy, and that most jobs have at least some components that are potentially pleasurable, has spurred people to discount the involuntary aspects of all work and instead to strive to locate and enter fantasy work positions. Such beliefs, unfortunately, are often taught to people who do not fully understand that their chances of achieving the desirable occupation are slim. They may not even recognize that they are gambling, nor appreciate that they will have to defer many of life's pleasures to achieve the occupational goal and then to maintain themselves in it. In the long run, a distorted presentation of employment is more likely to turn people against working. It seems unethical, therefore, to encourage all people to focus large amounts of their energy on preparing for work with the expectation that their jobs can be tailored to their needs for self-realization. More ethical is the acknowledgement that work will be required, although not as much as in the past, and that jobs requiring personal commitment and competition will probably be more rewarding than less demanding jobs. Human actualization, as always, will require additional achievements in the family, social, civic, religious, artistic, and recreational spheres. For many people, achievements in these noncareer roles may be more satisfying.

In economic terms, the available resources—including raw materials, capital equipment, existing technology (both apparatus and organization)—and the supply and demand for particular goods and services influence what can be produced and how it can be produced. For example, most of our transportation and communication equipment could not have been produced one hundred years ago because of the lack of resources; so, of course, most communication and transportation occupations were unknown then. Today, lack of demand is limiting the use of horses; consequently, there are few blacksmiths. Similarly, lack of capital goods such as farm machinery and fertilizers are restricting adoption of modern agricultural methods in third world countries; therefore, agriculturists with advanced specialized training from our agricultural colleges cannot find employment readily in underdeveloped nations.

Reduced labor costs in the third world, of course, are forcing American industries, such as steel and textiles, to increase automation in order to remain competitive. Since limited assets prompt consumers to seek the lowest possible prices, work must be performed in a manner that maximizes efficiency. As such, work differs from leisure in that demands of the market dictate how work is to be done.

From a sociological perspective, existing institutions influence the nature of work and careers directly and indirectly. A society's institutions define roles and positions, thereby limiting how a person can act in a particular career. The family, regardless of its form, is a person's first institution and generally influences the work its offspring perform. Many studies show that parental social status relates to a person's eventual educational and occupational level, and to a lesser degree, studies indicate that a father's occupational field influences a son's area of work. Although the explanation of the relation between parental status and children's work is still under study, it is evident that families equip children for particular kinds of work but not for others; that is, high status families prepare children for professions but not for crafts or unskilled work, and low status families socialize offspring for low-level occupations. In regard to the manner of working, cultural anthropologists point out many differences attributable to familial socialization. For example, white, Anglo families tend to instill expectations and preference for autonomous, competitive work, whereas American Indian families tend to inculcate an expectation of communal, cooperative work.

More visible, perhaps in shaping a society's work are large employers such as corporations and governments. The positions they define influence what their employees and other workers will do as work. For example, national and international corporations are notorious for demanding middle managers to relocate periodically in order to move up the corporate ladder, and at times modern bureaucracies drive people to amass more power and responsibility than they can manage (Peter, 1974).

Apprenticeship, licensing, and credentialing laws define avenues of access to and codes of behavior for particular occupations. In a less direct manner, labor unions and professional and vocational schools influence how many people with what backgrounds and experiences will enter an occupation. Moreover, they influence what workers will do on their jobs by their work rules and training. In academia, for example, the scholarly organizations with their journals sustain professors' commitment to publishable research in the face of administrators' and students' demands for increased attention to teaching. These organizations have this power because they influence professional prestige, and promotion in reputable universities depends more on individual visibility among peers than on the calibre of one's former students.

Institutional interfaces such as labor-management negotiations, corporate-professional organization lobbying of government, and even international treaties influence the existence and execution of many occupations. There are many examples of such activity, but one apt reminder for the reader is the fact that the counseling and clinical psychology professions came into existence as a consequence of the GI benefits programs following World War II.

Institutions not only influence the nature of particular jobs and occupations, but they also dictate their interrelationships and actually create careers. Glaser (1968) has adopted the term "organizational career" for this phenomenon. He has noted:

> Some organizational careers advance persons in different—usually more skilled—work; some merely advance the career while the work stays the same; and some make the work easier or less skilled. . . . Organizational careers guide the person into kinds of interpretations, perspectives or meanings of his work and his performance of it, his responsibilities, his powers, his rights and privileges and his identity, and they guide other appraisals of the person on these dimensions. Further, the organizational career structures each stage, the various people within and outside the organization that a person will work and

"associate with. . . . The organizational career literally moves the person through the organizational structure or freezes him in one place. . . ." (p. 14)

In view of institutional influences on careers, workers need to understand a job's context as well as its content; that is, they must "avoid missing the forest by concentrating on the trees." In opting to pursue a particular education or occupation, one not only affirms the legitimacy of the immediate office that one enters, but also tacitly supports the policies that brought it about and sustain it. The tragic Nazi holocaust and subsequent Nuremberg judgments illustrate mankind's belief in our responsibility to be aware of the context and consequences of our actions. Certainly, people who are aware of the institutional forces controlling jobs will better understand the likely consequences of occupying a position and therefore will be better able to control the chosen positions. People who regard only the visible demands on position, while ignoring institutional influences, risk the delusion that they are creating a career rather than merely adjusting to institutional dictates.

In terms of political influences, such societal decisions as those about distribution of wealth, public ownership, taxes, regulation of work and commerce significantly affect the kinds of careers that are possible over the short-, intermediate-, and long-term. The emergence of the modern corporation and of large government agencies are the results of a series of political decisions. Shorter term, more visible effects on careers are seen in legislation about minimum wages (increases tend to eliminate low-level service jobs), safety and pollution regulations (creating ecology jobs and eliminating hazardous occupations or at least altering how occupations are performed), gambling (creating jobs such as blackjack dealer), and so forth. Taxing and funding policies relating to education, on the other hand, illustrate intermediate-term effects on possible career options. In this country, for example, extensive support of higher education has multiplied the number of professional/technical/managerial workers, and the system of research and development grants has supported the maintenance of an elitist system of medical training.

Psychologically, a person's abilities, values, experiences, and capacity to know and ponder self and the world influence the work he or she will do. Our civilization is built on many capacities—speaking, writing, reading, counting, acquiring, and processing information, planning, building, and so forth. Even though we have built machines with such capacities, the continued evolution of humanity requires individuals to have such skills and to generate new ways of employing them. Without goals, whether hedonistic, aesthetic, or altruistic, however, human talents would lie dormant. And without opportunities to learn and exercise them, the abilities would not emerge.

Perhaps most important is one's capacity to envision oneself and a world as the reality in which to act and thereby define and become aware of oneself. This capacity to know oneself and one's world and eventually to use that knowledge in guiding one's passage through life explains why people, unlike all other animals, have adapted the world rather than adapted to it and why economic, sociological, political, and even psychological, forces will influence careers but will not annihilate human beings as a species in the manner that they have rendered other species extinct.

Humanity's ability to define and modify self and the world is the reason that the preliminary chapters of this anthology of methods for promoting career progress are psychological rather than sociological, economic, or even political in perspective. The task for the reader is to understand how people can view career so as to acquire and apply social science knowledge to improving career. As a consequence, this chapter focuses on explaining a model of how people relate to work over a lifetime and develop a career self-concept which, in time, guides that relationship; of how society acts to shape the career self-concept, and ideas about careers generally, and of the intertwining of career satisfaction with life satisfaction.

This text cannot teach the many sociological, economic, political science, and psychology concepts and principles that relate to careers, but counselors who wish to help clients to understand their career worlds will be aided considerably in that task by acquiring such knowledge. At the minimum, every counselor should have the equivalent of a basic college course in each of these disciplines.

The linkage of careers to work also alerts us to expect that careers will be different in content and connotation over time as economic, social, political, and psychological factors change. Limited capital and technology, for example, required eighteenth and nineteenth century workers to toil long to produce enough for survival. Rigid class structures of feudal times limited the work particular people could do, thus interfering with the development of banking. Today, political intolerance in countries such as the U.S.S.R. restricts distribution of goods and services, curtailing development of service jobs and occupations. Closer to home, our beliefs about the importance of a person's selecting his or her own occupation have extended the time required for Americans to prepare for working beyond that of their European counterparts. Perhaps the fact most certain about careers in the future is that their content and connotations are likely to be different, and those differences will, in part, be due to economic, societal, political, and psychological changes.

Before concluding this elucidation of the compulsory, constricted nature of work, it is important for the reader to remember that people of every rank and station have and continue to turn working into an ennobling experience. They selflessly concern themselves with the welfare of others, committing their energies to benefiting other people rather than worrying about how their work will profit themselves. Modest laborers, janitors, and clerks toil to feed and educate children, unconcerned with their station and taxing, onerous or tedious labors. Artesians and entertainers craft and perform to illuminate human powers and to share beauty, unwilling to sacrifice quality for either more money or fame. Medical missionaries and public defenders brave hardship and rebuke to bring health and justice to the improverished and foresaken. Although such selflessness sometimes verges on the heroic, folk wisdom embodied in adages such as "It is better to give than receive" suggest that recognizing the serving potential of working and/or one's job can enable every worker to render working at least somewhat ennobling.

Career Includes One's Vocation and One's Occupation

Career is not just another word for vocation or occupation, which refer respectively to a person's calling to a special life's work and to a set of jobs with similar duties and prerogatives. Rather, the concept of career stands for the belief that there is consistency over a lifetime in a person's relation to work. The continuity and coherence over a lifetime stem from the facts that people seek out and repeat the familiar, that our education work systems encourage specialization, and that many occupations and training positions have similar requirements: to follow written and oral directives, meet time schedules, travel to and from work, cooperate and accept interdependence, and complete assignments. Of course, the anticipation of similarity among work positions helps people to face the prospect of multiple occupational changes without fear. Indeed, within a career context, changing occupations can be a virtue, for different occupations may develop different facets of the self without radically altering the person's challenges. From such a perspective, career becomes the path for self-development and assumes the positive connotation of the vocation.

Similarity across career positions, in turn, assures that different workers approach working in the same ways because it demands like accommodations. This is especially true as youngsters share increasingly more hours of the same general formal education and the same media socialization about working and consuming. Moreover, as more people work for large corporations and large government, which are growing more monolithic in organization and administration, their careers become less distinguishable.

The concept of career captures the sameness of people's schooling and work positions, but it supports our society ideals of equal training and work opportunities. By emphasizing the similarity of responsibilities, the concept of career shows that people deserve similar entitlement to meet their obligations rather than special prerogatives because of a distinctive calling. Every person's career has its unique personal and situational aspects, but if its expression is important to all persons, in fairness, an egalitarian society must strive to provide each individual the opportunity to work to maximum self-development.

The concept of career, therefore, is useful in characterizing a democratic people's relation to work in twentieth century America, just as the concept of vocation was useful in describing pursuit of a particular kind of work in earlier times.

Of course, to the degree that a person's relation to work alters drastically over a lifetime or to the extent that people's work differs greatly, the concept of career is less useful and may even be harmful. For example, the civil service clerk who becomes an inventor-entrepreneur and necessarily exercises new skills and attitudes and seeks new work satisfactions is now relating to work in such a radically different manner that she might better be considered as having two careers. Similarly, toll bridge collectors and architects are in occupations that overlap so minimally in duties, training, and work satisfactions that identifying both as careers may obscure their differences. The concept of career is really a theory about the human connection to work rather than an established fact. Over time, the definition and utility of the concept of career will change to accord with new understanding and new ways of relating to work.

Propositions Related to Guiding a Career

The following propositions about career help guide career progress: Careers develop people; a person creates a self-concept in relation to work that increasingly can guide the career; career satisfaction is inextricably linked to life satisfaction; and careers manifest human interdependence and are shaped through socialization. Each proposition is discussed below.

Careers Develop People

The view that careers develop people, who in turn develop their careers, is widely used by educators in designing programs to assist people concerning work. Pioneered by Super and his colleagues (Super et al., 1957, 1960, 1969), the postulate affirms that a career is a lifelong process of adaptation related to preparing for work, working, moving among work positions, and leaving the world of work. It involves, according to Super et al. (1957), "the progressive increase and modifications of [a person's] capacities and dispositions for particular behaviors related to work."

The concept of career development postulates that a career builds on what a person has done, is doing, and hopes to do and that its evolution can be thought of as progressing through stages. The development of careers is continuous, but not necessarily unalterable. A person's past is part of the present, and the present influences the future, but present actions and future aspirations can sometimes correct earlier errors in development (Allport, 1937). Some research on career traits and work habits shows they are consistent over time and place (Holland, 1966; Strong, 1955; Brenner, 1968); but other studies show that traits change (Strong, 1955; Sears, 1977) and work habits can be altered (Oetting & Miller, 1977). People's career positions and performance influence eligibility for subsequent positions. Yet, some people who have not taken science and mathematics in high school have eventually entered science and engineering, even though *Project Talent* data (Cooley & Lohnes, 1968) suggest that they would be the exceptions. Likewise, people who have occupied a series of unskilled and semiskilled jobs occasionally enter executive suites or become professionals, even though Warner & Abegglen (1955) have shown that these are exceptional careers.

Career development signifies focusing energy and refining assets, but it also implies foreclosing some options, as Tyler (1969) has pointed out and as Robert Frost has expressed so poignantly in "The Road Not Taken." Unfortunately, the development is not always positive. O'Toole et al. (1973) have documented how some jobs can stifle ambition and depreciate skills and self-confidence. People are fortunate, however; often the likely consequences of a career position can be predicted.

Psychologists and counselors have found a five-stage model of careers useful. The titles of the stages—growth, exploration, establishment, maintenance, and decline—characterize the major effort of the person in that period, although the functions expressed by these titles continue throughout the career. More specifically, theorists such as Super (1957) characterize the stages as follows. In the growth stage, the child acquires the tools, habits, attitudes, and awareness of opportunities needed for a career in his culture. Exploration, in turn, is the time when the adolescent examines the appropriateness of different options and prepares for particular options through tryout. Next is establishment, when the young adult follows through on an appropriate option and improves the required skills and/or contacts in order to advance and secure the position. This leads into the maintenance period, wherein middle age signals the time to start consolidating and rounding-off accomplishments rather than opening new vistas. In time, aging necessitates decreasing activity and preparing to leave work activity in order to be able to reserve energies for the more basic activities of life.

Super (1953) noted that the ages at which Americans could expect to experience these career stages were approximately:

Growth	0–14
Exploration	15–24
Establishment	25–44
Maintenance	45–64
Decline	65

As changes in work accelerated during the 1960s and 1970s, Super (1976) re-emphasized the dynamic aspect of stages, noting, for example, that many people in the establishment or even maintenance stages might appropriately re-engage in activities of the exploration or even growth stages. For example, a plumber, conscious of the declining number of plumbing jobs due to increased use of prefabricated materials, might appropriately be pursuing a business degree while plying his trade. Similarly, a homemaker who had been a teacher of French and was preparing to re-enter work after raising children might try out several courses, including a career appraisal course, in order to identify occupations that were now compatible with her characteristics and aspirations.

Each career stage has broad, distinctive tasks that must be accomplished in order to succeed in that stage and move on to the next. The tasks and particular accomplishments of every stage necessarily change with alterations in our educational-work system. Identifying these tasks requires ongoing observation of successful careers. Super (1957) and

Table 1–2. Super's Career Development Stages and Selected Tasks

Stage	Age	Task
Growth	0–14	Try multiple experiences Form self-concept Develop an understanding of the meaning and purpose of work
Exploration	14–24	Recognize and accept need to make career decisions and obtain relevant information Become aware of interests and abilities and how they relate to work opportunities Identify possible fields and levels of work consistent with these abilities and interests Secure training to develop skills and advance occupational entry and/or enter occupations fulfilling interests and abilities
Establishment	25–44	Achieve full competence in occupation through experience/training Consolidate and improve status in the occupation Advance vertically or horizontally
Maintenance	45–65	Preserve skills through inservice/continual training Develop retirement resources/plans
Decline	65+	Adapt work to physical capacity Manage resources to sustain independence

SOURCE: Adapted from pages 73–74 and 77–78 in THE PSYCHOLOGY OF CAREERS by Donald E. Super. Copyright © 1957 by Donald E. Super. Reprinted by permission of Harper & Row, Publishers, Inc.

others have indicated some of the tasks in Table 1–2. The list is based on limited time and geographic observations and, therefore, is necessarily incomplete. Possibly some of these tasks are even outdated for people in our society generally. Consequently, counselors will systematically have to observe and verify or even identify tasks. For particular subgroups such as minorities, women, or the handicapped, observation and identification are even more essential.

The career stages are ongoing and overlapping. Each continues throughout life, but generally one stage is dominant at each point in life. The timing of each stage is determined both by the society's educational and work systems and by human nature. Every society evolves its own organization so that its members in the same age cohort tend to act similarly. The parameters of the organization are dictated by universal factors such as physical and mental maturation, but the particulars of the stage vary across cultures. In agrarian societies, for example, thirteen- or fourteen-year-old adolescents are well along in mastering the duties and knowledge of farming, whereas American adolescents only begin to master occupational duties toward the end of their teens after they have explored their compatibility with several occupations.

The structure of society creates the different career stages. The separation of family, school, and work in our society requires a person making career progress to move from home to school, from school to work, and then among distinctive types of work such as production and managerial work. Finally, one passes out of work back into the core of the community. These movements alter one's manner of living and, hence, impose a new stage of living. Moreover, our education and work systems are vast and complex, but interdependent and somewhat hierarchical. Although there are thousands of training programs, and nearly a hundred million jobs, one needs educational and sometimes work prerequisites to enter most jobs and advanced training programs. Even for unskilled jobs, one often needs at least ten to twelve years of successful schooling. Such prerequisites are an ordered set of accomplishments, whose existence attests to the fact that modern career progress requires passage from one way of functioning to another.

The concept of stages also is supported by our knowledge of human development. The thesis begins with the recognition that human beings, as members of one species, share similar growth patterns. Many observers have conceptualized the human growth pattern as progressing through stages. On the physical side, for example, infants make random sounds before combining them into words and then they gradually combine words into two-, three-, four-, and five-word sentences. Similar passages occur in movement and thinking capabilities, leading observers to infer that, for many accomplishments, a person's physiology and experience must reach a particular level and the environment must afford the opportunity, and perhaps even the stimulation and modeling for the task. Moreover, the more complex accomplishments are frequently combinations of simpler achievements. In other words, accomplishments build upon one another and one activity may be impossible until a person completes prerequisite simpler actions. Although the area of study is very new, evidence is accumulating that if the environmental supports are not available within a certain period after appropriate physiological maturation, the person may never be able to achieve the particular competence. As a consequence, failure to achieve simple competencies may impede acquisition of more complex ones.

Counselors can establish particular accomplishments as necessary to career development by showing that their achievement permits career progress while their neglect or failure retards it. There are five kinds of evidence: (1) controlled experimentation that demonstrates persons improve their career development after accomplishing the career task, (2) consensus among expert observers that a particular task is requisite for career development, (3) consistent testimony by persons progressing in their career that a particular accomplishment promoted their career, (4) verification that persons who have accomplished the career task lead people who have not done the task in career development, and (5) task analysis of the career challenges faced by the target population.

The idea of career development generates a matrix of broad achievements related to career progress. These accomplishments are necessarily more abstract than are achievements for an occupation or school because they must incorporate attainments in different occupations and schools. For example, Table 1–2 shows that a career development task of the early establishment stage is achieving eligibility to perform one's work. It does not specify whether that eligibility means achieving journeyman status in a trade; passing a licensing examination for one's profession; or securing the required permits, premises, stock, and credit lines for one's own business.

Analysis of particular tasks can indicate the necessary competencies; in turn, their identification can provide guidance in building a career curriculum (Herr, 1980). By targeting instruction toward such competencies and periodically assessing student progress, educators can ensure that students have career-related experiences. Moreover, they can test student accomplishment of the tasks in order to identify those having career difficulties before serious impairment occurs. For example, establishing eligibility to teach in high school can be divided into the subaccomplishments of securing a bachelor's degree, successfully completing ten semester units of student teaching, passing courses in the Constitution and the history of the licensing state, receiving at least a certain grade on a teaching test in one's subject, and passing an oral interview. Delineation of these components allows the identification of the competencies that are required to teach. These would include scholastic reasoning ability, perseverance in academic pursuits, and the ability to communicate ideas to children.

Recent career education legislation (Public Law 95–207) has mandated that states prepare plans for systematically directing and monitoring student career growth in order to be eligible for federal career education monies. As a consequence, most states have adopted curriculum goal matrices composed of career development tasks.

Without doubt, competence specification can become lengthy, depending on how precisely one defines the competence. For example, efforts to define the required competencies for elementary school students led the American Institute of Research to list more than nine thousand measurable objectives. The enormous number of these competencies plus the fact that changes in our educational-work systems are likely to alter the developmental tasks makes it unlikely that individuals will be assessed on the full spectrum of competence in order to pinpoint all areas needing remediation.

The broad career development matrix can be the starting point in establishing career development programs and in setting goals for individual clients. But since clients are likely to have unique tasks depending on their circumstances, needs, and resources, the counselor should not expect that a career development matrix will soon be the basis for a directory linking career objectives to counseling strategies. There will simply be too many entries, especially for people more advanced in their career development.

The concept of career development stages, nonetheless, provides one reasonable way of organizing counseling strategies because people in a particular stage, by definition, share common past accomplishments and present challenges. Moreover, counselors have traditionally served people at one or two stages (students in the exploration stage or young adults struggling with establishment) and therefore are likely to concentrate on strategies appropriate to these stages. Thus, the strategies in this text are clustered in terms of developmental stages.

The Career Contributes to the Self-Concept

People are not passive observers of their careers. As they grow, youngsters acquire an emerging consciousness of themselves and increasingly choose from among alternative experiences. Observing this, vocational psychologists have posited that youngsters develop self-concepts or egos, which begin to control their experiences. That aspect of the self-concept concerning work can be considered the *career self-concept*. The self-concept is who the person believes he or she is; it includes one's perceived abilities, interests, and values. The ideas are initially concrete, but become more abstract with maturation. Over time, this self-guiding mechanism expands and becomes more differentiated, enabling the person to exercise control over more of one's own experiences. For example, the six-year-old ice cream lover who disdained spinach becomes the adolescent who values a balanced diet including green vegetables, but periodically rewards this dietary discipline by enjoying an ice cream sundae.

People start creating their careers in childhood through reactions to parental expectations and home and community opportunities. Home furnishings and activities, household conversation and entertainment, family outings, and toys and games provide models and materials for role play, practice of skills, and development of interests. With increased skills and mobility, the child becomes proactive as well as reactive. Fun in growing and identifying house plants leads the budding horticulturist to the library in search of books for erecting and outfitting a backyard hothouse. Over time, patterns of style, energy level, skills, and interest begin to emerge. As one pursues postsecondary schooling and enters an occupation, personal style is more consistent and predictable. These positions in turn shape the individual. What teacher, for instance, is not at least somewhat pedantic, what lawyer not officious, or what truck driver not rough and ready? For most people, this process of defining self in terms of career continues throughout life, for every career remains capable of, and even requires, further expression. Indeed, no one can ever fully control one's experiences and no life contains enough hours to express all of a person's potentials.

A self-concept reflects expectations. People expect to have careers because their family and community expect them to work and expect them to behave in certain ways as a consequence of the career they are pursuing. People may not define "career" in exactly the same manner as the social scientist, but they recognize that careers are that part of their identity connected with the occupation they will do, are doing, or have done. Indeed, for most people, the career self-concept becomes a classification for selecting and organizing experiences relevant to working. The maturing individual accumulates a repertoire of expectations, habits, and attitudes in relation to working, creating a "psychological set." This "set," which can be termed the *career self-concept*, in turn influences how one reacts to phenomena that one labels career. Over the years, the set becomes strengthened, and complex changes in it require ever greater expenditures of energy.

The performance of career positions helps to create identity and in turn reflects unique interests, abilities, and values. An individual cannot put on and take off career habits with the nine o'clock bell or the five o'clock whistle. One's speech, ideas, acquaintances, and very lifestyle signal one's career. The very selection of an occupation has long been considered as implementing a self-concept (Super, 1953); several researchers have shown that professional aspirants characterize themselves more like the stereotype of their own profession than of others (Bingham, 1966; Healy, 1968). Some people regard occupational membership as a means of creating a desirable self; they prefer occupations in which the workers are most like their ideal person (Healy, 1973; Wheeler & Carnes, 1968).

"What kind of work do you do?" is usually one of the first things asked when getting acquainted. The answer provides strong clues about the past experiences of the new acquaintance, indicates what the person is doing at the moment, and hints at aspirations. Even more, the response suggests the person's interests, abilities, values, and status in the community. Certainly, no other single datum provides as much information and basis for speculation.

Career Involvement Affects and is Affected by Life Satisfaction

Part of the career self-concept concerns the individual's beliefs about career success. A society offers general guidelines about work success, and theoretically its rewards (prestige and money) are distributed to compensate achievement. One's own interpretation of what constitutes career success, however, is mediated by one's immediate group's views and by personal experiences relative to career. Therefore, people of different sexes and from different social and ethnic groups often define career success differently.

The person's concept of success and ensuing estimate of personal success are very important because they influence career satisfaction; that satisfaction in turn influences self-esteem and willingness to commit oneself to a career. Table 1–3 presents seven propositions regarding the interrelation of self-esteem, career satisfaction, and career commitment formulated by Hall (1976) to represent how these attributes interact.

The propositions in Table 1–3 tend to be supported by the ongoing research of Korman on self-esteem (Korman, 1970). They suggest that people who have minimal career success will not invest effort in locating a career position congruent with their capacities and goals nor exert themselves in seeking and pursuing challenging career goals. To the

Table 1–3. The Interrelation of Self-Esteem, Career Satisfaction,
         and Career Commitment

Proposition I:	In an attempt to experience psychological success in the career, the person will tend to select career roles congruent with present or potential subidentities which are (a) potentially or presently competent, and (b) highly valued.
Proposition II:	The higher the individual's level of self-esteem, the more extensive his search will be for information about (1) available career roles, and (2) the value he attaches to the relevant subidentities, and (3) his present or potential competence in these areas.
Proposition III:	The more the individual searches for information about available career roles, personal values, and competencies, the more aware he is likely to be of these entities.
Proposition IV:	The more aware the person is of his subidentities and available career roles, the closer the match will be between the selected career subidentity and role.
Proposition V:	(Derived from II–IV) The higher the individual's level of self-esteem, the closer the congruence will be between the selected career subidentity and career role.
Proposition VI:	The higher the individual's self-esteem, the greater the likelihood that he would risk committing himself to a career role providing challenge to a highly valued subidentity.
Proposition VII:	The higher the individual's self-esteem, the higher will be the difficulty level at which the role–subidentity match occurs.

extent, therefore, that a person believes schooling and working are connected—as they increasingly are in our society—he must experience successful schooling to exert himself in order to have a successful career.

Signs of school difficulty manifest themselves early, long before youngsters can appreciate the consequences of school failure on their careers. Unless parents and educators act on these danger signals, children's careers are at risk. Providing alternative forms of education as early as possible to assure more possibilities for successful school experiences is, therefore, important.

Career and Life Satisfaction

Career satisfaction is related inextricably to life satisfaction. Logically, a person pleased with living will approach work more positively, and a person satisfied with work should feel more positively toward other life roles. Since career has been as important an aspect of life as being a son or daughter, a neighbor, friend, spouse, parent, or citizen, its privileges continuously must be balanced with the other privileges and responsibilities of life. Overemphasizing or neglecting career leads to frustration and unhappiness as surely as misbalancing other facets of personhood.

The changing quality of career and the need to accommodate it over one's lifetime have led scholars such as Super (1975) and Ginzberg (1972) to speculate that the appropriate life objective concerning career is to balance it with other life roles. Such a balance entails both seeking career demands and rewards compatible with the person's abilities and values and distributing the available time and energy reasonably among the varying roles.

In a dynamic world, such a balance will be neither static nor tranquil. Changes in the education and work systems, ongoing maturation, experience, and alterations in the immediate lifespace will lead to performing and defining the career role differently over time. Fortunately, society has recognized this dynamism by providing schools and training programs to foster growth in specific occupational and general career skills and, increasingly, by encouraging people to avail themselves of such training throughout adulthood. Recently, as occupations have become more specialized and volatile due to technological advances, society has endorsed downward vertical and expanded horizontal mobility across occupations, assuming that such mobility increases productivity by redistributing workers to areas of need and by providing workers with new challenges and opportunity for expression. Nevertheless, career and personal opportunities and frustrations will repeatedly disturb the balance and challenge the careerist to re-establish it. Over the course of a career, therefore, the careerist who succeeds can expect to feel alternately satisfied and dissatisfied with the balance, and both apprehensive and optimistic about new directions. The successful worker will recognize the inherent fluctuations in a career but, nevertheless, will enjoy the challenge of moving the career forward by persevering and producing under varying degrees of stress. The satisfied careerist should not expect a personal Shangri-La, but will understand and will accept that life's relationship to work provides uncertain challenges. Over time, these demands can be mastered sufficiently to provide some sense of accomplishment and to permit attention to the other tasks of life.

The fulfilled worker is not necessarily the most successful person in an occupation or school class (Bray, 1977; Sears, 1977). Achieving balance among life roles may preclude the intense commitment of energy that reaching the very top in competitive occupations and schools requires. The successful, satisfied careerist, however, should enjoy greater mental and physical health than the apparently successful one.

Career Management and Satisfaction

The recognition that career is a dynamic adaptation to one's work-educational systems based on unfolding skills and opportunities cautions against rigid, long-term occupational goals and planning. Career management involves evaluating improvement of one's career positions as well as movement toward prespecified achievement. Super, Kowalski, and Gotkin (1969) have found that long-term planning increased career equity—reflected in higher salary, prestige, and responsibility—during adolescence and young adulthood, but Jordaan and Heyde (1979) noted that these planners changed their goals frequently during high school, suggesting the importance of flexibility.

The fluidity of the educational-work system and personal malleability create the need for, and even the desirability of, compromise over the career. Ginzberg and his associates (1951) noted this long ago. The knowledge produced by moving toward the goal enables refinement or even alteration of the goal and plan. Static goals and plans would deny the dynamism of people and their situations. For example, Mary Jones, an apprentice maintenance electrician who turns to electrical appliance repair after she has been laid off from the auto plant, may have advanced her career even though she originally planned to be an industrial electrician. Her new position pays more, carries more responsibility, and offers more time to dabble in design, an area that interests her. It is not that one should not plan, but rather that one should recognize that plans must be flexible since they are aids for improving one's situation.

Likewise, compromises do not necessarily mean settling for less. Rather, they involve substituting goals based upon the exigencies of the situation. Sometimes they can lead to fuller personal realization than the original goal. Here, for instance, the layoff spurred Ms. Jones to an alternative that was more promising. Although she will not become proficient in industrial machine repair and maintenance, she can develop skills that will enable her to become a technician or even an inventor.

As one moves closer to realizing a planned career goal, situational constraints often exert greater influence. The real opportunities are compared to the goal and the planner must compromise because he or she usually cannot control the nature of the options. If Ms. Jones is worried about another layoff, she may choose an established firm that has prospects for a stable future instead of a firm that is more venturesome. Of course, desire for stability may possibly reduce her chances of becoming an inventor. Realizing that plan implementation is moving from thought to actuality, most people choose and pursue an acceptable, available option, almost unaware of the compromises they make. One's starting goal is typically general enough for several options of varying desirability to be acceptable. Nonetheless, career counselors should recognize this general readiness to compromise in regard to career implementation in order to understand accurately our own and clients' career management.

Characteristics of Work Related to Satisfaction

In spite of the demands of a career, workers should not despair. Over the last twenty years, Gallup polls (1973) have found 80 percent or more of American workers report satisfaction with their jobs, indicating that at least some aspects of working are satisfying. Moreover, national policy is committed to equipping citizens for satisfying, productive work and to encouraging development of job opportunities. Large-scale programs have been initiated to provide special help for veterans, the handicapped, and impoverished mothers trying to prepare for work or secure suitable employment.

Conceptually, career satisfaction subsumes satisfaction with current job and occupation, current prospects and aspirations, and past achievements. How these combine into one feeling will vary among individuals and over time. One task of counselors may be to help people recognize that viewing career as a passage enables them to stabilize their feelings about their work.

Although career satisfaction is, by definition, a subjective evaluation of the desirability of the return in relation to personal expenditures, all people can apply similar criteria to measure satisfaction. Consequently, it is not surprising that surveys of workers in many occupations regularly indicate that work satisfaction is due to the challenge of using one's ability, the absence of routine, autonomy, decent pay, and suitable supervision. Surveys also show, however, that some workers in occupations with many satisfiers are not as gratified as workers in occupations with fewer rewards, suggesting that satisfaction is not simply a function of the number of satisfiers. Clearly, satisfaction also depends on how one interprets return from work. For example, a person earning $150 a week for secretarial work, who has learned the requisite skills as part of a high school program and who associates with other workers earning comparable wages, is likely to be more satisfied than a secretary with the same salary who invested two years in an AA degree to obtain the requisite skills and whose associates earn $200 a week. Similarly, if the $150 a week secretaries find that secretaries typically earn only $125 a week, their satisfaction is likely to increase if they feel their work is of high quality, but it may decrease if they do not feel they are doing their jobs well.

More than twenty thousand different occupations and hundreds of different training programs in the United States offer many different kinds of career satisfaction. These rewards range from the opportunity for intellectual and aesthetic stimulation to the chance to serve and interact with others or the opportunity to earn high income and enjoy prestige and comfortable surroundings. Of course, no job or program offers every satisfaction, and there is keen competition for occupations with more satisfiers. Nearly 50 percent of graduating high school students, for example, aspire to be physicians, and even by college graduation there are three or four times more aspirants for medical schools than are accepted. Yet, since not every person will seek the same satisfactions, many opportunities exist to obtain some gratification from one's career. Certainly, those who help people to chart their careers should make them aware of the many different satisfiers and to the facts that occupations differ in the rewards they offer and in the prices they exact.

Clearly, understanding the mechanisms underlying career satisfaction will help counselors to understand and to direct careers. But a comprehensive explanation of career satisfaction, which fits the findings of the thousands of work-satisfaction studies, has not yet been formulated.

Promising formulations of career-satisfaction theory and helpful overviews of the current literature are available in works by Lofquist and Dawis (1969), Lawler (1973), Crites (1969), and Dubin (1976).

Careers Manifest Humanity's Interdependence

The career sets parameters for human expression. Colleagues, occupational norms and ethics, and the expectations of the general public prescribe what is acceptable in particular career positions and sometimes even what is appropriate for the incumbents when they are acting outside their positions. Occupancy of particular career positions entitle the incumbents to certain societal resources and prerogatives that otherwise are likely to be denied. On the other hand, those positions demand at least 50 to 60 hours of an adult's 112 waking hours a week and 40 or more hours of a student's. These people, therefore, have little time for extra-career activities. Unfortunately, our society's allocation of so much time to work implicitly precludes other major achievements. This heavy commitment to work is part of twentieth century living (Dubin, 1976), despite the fact that our folk wisdom argues convincingly for balance among life's undertakings.

Even while it proclaims our uniqueness, the career reflects our interdependence. The positions that comprise a career are influenced by others in the society who prescribe the nature of the duties and prerogatives. We depend on others to equip us to perform career duties and to move from career position to position. Relationships such as student-teacher, apprentice-master, employee-employer, protégé-mentor, and client-counselor reflect the ongoing interdependence of careers. Paradoxically, one can increase individual control over the career by recognizing the limits of one's power.

Present careers build on past human achievement and influence future human potential. The accumulated wisdom and resources of our ancestors enable us to enjoy the career positions of our modern age, and our performance of those tasks will determine what our progeny can do. Careers are personal; yet their use of mankind's legacy demands that they be enacted responsibly, with attention to what they will do for others as well as how they will enhance the self. The O'Toole (1973) task force found that workers suffered if they did not believe their productions contributed to societal welfare and ecology. In an age of individualism and nationalism, we must be alert to our career legacy lest we overlook our connection and our obligations to other people and other societies as we work. Clearly, the recognition that a career taps mankind's common inheritance alerts us to the fact that workers will be at peace with themselves only when they are accountable for that common legacy. The widespread acclaim for President Kennedy's inaugural injunction, "Ask not what your country can do for you, but instead ask what you can do for your country!" should not be forgotten.

Without doubt, the recognition that careers draw upon a common human inheritance and that they develop people positively or negatively

requires the effort to afford every person an opportunity to have work
that will be self-enhancing.

By necessity, careers are both the targets and means of socialization,
the process by which society teaches people what is appropriate. The
media, family, community, school, peer, church, and, eventually, work
groups socialize us. Well before we join a work group, these other groups
have taught us an approach to living and working.

Socialization is both formal and informal, direct and indirect, but
not necessarily a coordinated process, for different sources often give
different messages. A parent or teacher may each offer a demonstration/
lecture on table manners, but each presents different rules or patterns
of etiquette. Our multicultural and multiclass society produces different
approaches to living and to working, while the pervasiveness of the
media and universal schooling create ever more similarities. As an example of difference, consider how many lower-class workers expect
daily or weekly pay in cash, whereas upper-middle-class persons are
surprised with anything other than a bimonthly or monthly check; or
recall that a Samoan will treat work tools as community property,
whereas an American will expect each to use personal tools.

Many common messages clearly support the Establishment: "Work
hard to learn and to produce, and you will earn and deserve material
comfort"; "Stay loose, roll with the punches, and you will succeed." Yet
other messages, not as supportive of the Establishment, proclaim "Do
your own thing" and "Only the presently visible and sensational are real
and worthy of attention."

To some degree, each person incorporates the messages that per-
vade the general culture and especially his or her subculture. American
workers, therefore, differ markedly from one another, but they will
differ even more significantly from Russian or Japanese workers or from
American workers of a different era.

Work ethic is the term that designates the set of beliefs about how
and why to work and what to expect from working. Many observers
have noted that the American work ethic is changing. That change
reflects the move from an industrial to postindustrial era as well as
increased schooling and the pervasive influence of radio and television
that enable all to experience more socialization messages. Certainly the
character of the new work ethic will have profound effects on the careers
that develop in the 1980s and 1990s, whether or not it includes pre-
cepts such as: (a) participate in designing your own job and periodically negotiate output, and (b) alternate from supervisor to supervisee
or from teacher to learner.

Career and the Layman

Many people will not regard career as it is presented in this text.
The fact that there are several different definitions of career in Webster's *New World Dictionary* (College edition), ranging from the career
as "one's progress through life," or "one's advancement or achievement

in a particular vocation," to "a life work, profession, occupation" attests to its variety of meanings. Similarly, review of scholars' definitions of career will show disagreement among them as well.

These differences underscore the fact that all views of career are essentially *theories* designed to communicate and to explain facts economically. Thus every person is entitled to hold the theory that is personally useful. But, operating with a career theory that excludes realities is likely to decrease one's ability to manage a career. The counselor who believes that this author's framework of career fits reality will, therefore, often want to expand the client's view to include those parts of this formulation that are not now part of the client's theory.

On the other hand, the counselor should review a client's career theory carefully, for it may reveal aspects of that person's connection to work not included in a broad theory, and may even uncover facts about careers that have been omitted from this framework.

Although definitions may differ, the layman has a strong interest in career. Witness the bestseller status of books such as *Working* (Terkel, 1974), *Passages* (Sheehy, 1976), *The Managerial Woman* (Hennig & Jardim, 1976), and the conversion of *Working* into a musical. Note the repeated call for more "career guidance" in surveys of parents and students (Campbell, 1968; Garbin, 1970; Educational Testing Service, 1979a); and recall that nearly 20 million Americans are enrolled in education programs for career purposes. Clearly, many potential clients await the help of competent counseling in pursuing their careers.

Relating to Work

2

This chapter describes seven models of a human being that are useful in understanding how people relate to work: trait-factor, intelligent, developmental, behavioral, sociological, psychodynamic, and economic being. Each model pinpoints career and personal information that should be considered in directing a career. As White (1952, 1966) and Hewer (1963) have pointed out, every model contributes something different to our understanding of an individual's potential relation to work and, as such, needs to be appreciated by counselors. More recently, Crites (1974b, 1976) reiterated the importance of five models and formulated a comprehensive method of career counseling that reflects their contributions. As yet, however, his comprehensive method has not been refined nor tested widely.

Trait-Factor Model

The trait-factor person is a set of enduring tendencies and predispositions—called traits—that result from heredity and learning, in varying, but as yet undetermined mixes. At least to some degree, a person's traits are variable across situations (Mischel, 1968); yet nearly everyone can be assigned with considerable reliability a percentile on multiple characteristics—abilities, interests, values, and such. These traits are useful in establishing selection criteria for educational and occupational positions and, to a lesser degree, in helping individuals to predict their performance in educational and training programs and in certain occupations (Goldman, 1972; Ghiselli, 1966).

Educational and work environments can be portrayed in terms of certain traits by sampling people in them and ascertaining their mean or modal trait percentiles (Strong, 1927, 1955; Holland, 1973; U.S. Department of Labor, 1978). Noting that people of similar traits clustered by occupation and that people tend to move from occupations less consistent to ones more consistent with their traits, trait-factor theorists posited that occupational adjustment and, more recently, occupational actualization mean being in an environment that fits, or is at least compatible with, one's traits (Parsons, 1909; Williamson, 1939, Holland, 1973).

The trait-factor model tends to support the status quo, although one of its most prominent originators, Gordon Allport (1960), emphasized the notion of becoming. The model relies on biased measures to define traits and on criteria generated from existing worker and student populations to define occupational possibilities. It therefore promotes accommodation to who we are now and to what now exists. Only limited attention has been given to identifying how incumbency in a particular career position changes one's traits, and that examination generally has been restricted to college positions (Stern, 1970). The fact that some clients making occupational choices are doing so more in terms of who they want to be than in terms of who they now are (Wheeler and Carnes, 1968; Healy, 1973a) has not stimulated research of the effect of career positions on traits. If career options become defined more by the tasks they require and assessment of potential for these tasks relies less on measures that reflect the past, then the trait-factor model may become more supportive of change.

For trait-factor person, career is a set of positions that are enacted productively and with personal satisfaction to the extent that they fit the person's traits. The implications about self and informational needs and how to relate self and career information to career options are clear. Experts must first discover the traits that are related significantly to education and working and then compose scales to categorize people and occupations. Then a person can be assessed on the traits, learn individual scores, and identify educational and training positions that accommodate this pattern of scores. Accommodation is required for ability traits, if not for interest, value, and other personality traits. The matching procedure will produce a number of options for most people, enabling them to narrow their choices further by weighing the attractiveness of other factors such as supply and demand, distance from home, hours of work, and contacts to facilitate entry.

There are many aids to help the person in matching. These aids include self-instructional programs, such as Holland's (1970) *Self-Directed Search* and Maagoon's (1969) *Effective Problem Solving* programs; computer programs, such as those for *Project Talent* data (Flanagan et al., 1973) and for *Differential Aptitude Test* (Psychological Corporation, 1975); and counseling programs with specific methods such as Williamson's (1939) content analysis and Healy's (1974a, b) self-concept-translation procedure. Through these aids, the client can use subjective estimates of individual and a career position's attributes to locate suitable occupations for in-depth exploration or can obtain leads to occupations based on the similarity of personal test scores to composite scores of different occupational groups. These matching aids also enable one to account for one's own attitude toward risk-taking since they include expectancy table data or subjective estimates of the like-lihood of achieving entry to particular positions. Excerpts from Williamson (1939) in Chapter 10 illustrate how he offered estimates of the likelihood of achieving different objectives.

Although the computer matching procedures are generally based on objective estimates of client and position attributes, even they do not match people directly with jobs. The result is the possibility of error, especially for members of groups who have not been represented in an occupation. At present, direct job assessments of work are made in terms of functions or worker actions, which are conceptually different from attributes. Occupational profiles now used in computer matching are based on job validation studies, which establish correlates of perform-ance; contrasts of high- and low-performing workers on the attributes as, for example, in *The Occupational Aptitude Profiles of the Dictionary of Occupational Titles;* or from expert judgments about the attributes required of workers in a particular job. These estimates about worker attributes are indirect because they involve analyzing worker differences rather than directly measuring the work tasks. Inevitably, these esti-mates include nonessential worker characteristics in a job profile. For-tunately a solution may soon be found. Dunnette (1976) reported that the work of McCormick and his colleagues on equating work function factors from their *Position Analysis Questionnaire* with aptitude factors suggests that direct person-occupation linkages may be possible.

Using trait-position matching should identify an occupation or edu-cational program that employs people with characteristics similar to one's own, that is somewhat more likely to be satisfying (Crites, 1969), and that is likely to be pursued for a longer period than less compatible occupations (Campbell, 1971). The model implies that people who want to pursue an occupation incompatible with their characteristics should either change characteristics or be prepared to perform the occupation in an unusual way if they expect to remain in the occupation. For example, the adventuresome physician could be an astronaut flight surgeon rather than a general practitioner or traditional specialist. The model, however, is silent about how to change one's characteristics.

In terms of career changes, the trait-factor model underscores the need for accurate information about attributes required by one's options. Theoretically, people contemplating a sequence of positions would scru-tinize their compatibility with higher positions on each alternative occu-pational ladder, not just the fit of the entry positions. For example, the ambitious, money-conscious college student with mathematical aptitude would not only compare engineer, mathematics teacher, and accountant, but would also contrast senior engineer, project supervisor and middle manager with mathematics department chairperson and vice principal; and both these ladders with certified public accountant and accounting firm partner. With slight software modifications, computer counseling programs such as the *System of Interactive Guidance Instruction* (SIGI) should be able to provide such exploration today, although no research on sequential matching has been reported.

Current career counseling practice based on the trait-factor model, however, is for people periodically to recompute the compatibility of alternative options. They may do this routinely, as part of their career management, or when they feel the need to change positions. The theory says little about what might motivate a desire to change, although developmental theory and the limited research, such as that of Levinson (1978), suggest that there are points in the career when the individual feels a need to change the career role or the manner in which he or she is rendering it. Therefore, it would appear useful for trait-factor counselors to have data about whether various career positions require incumbents to make different accommodations at different ages. Certainly, the fact that several occupational scales of the *Strong Campbell Interest Inventory* are not the same for men and women suggests that those occupations permit, or even require, different accommodations for men and women. Thus, they support the possibility that an occupation's role demands vary according to age. Likewise, change in other life roles is likely to alter expectations of the career role. For instance, increased financial demands are probable when one's children reach adolescence and possibly when one's parents retire and/or sustain illness. Certainly, many teachers and scientists lament that they rejected more enterprising career directions, which might have been only somewhat less compatible at entry, but would be more fitting when family and social demands make them more aware of their low salaries.

The Intelligent Model

Intelligent, scientific, or rational people are learners, planners, and problem solvers (Dewey, 1933). They live to learn about self and the world, to tease out of experience principles for guiding action, and to formulate and strive for goals, whether they be financial gain, discovery of knowledge, or decisions for God. Increasingly an interpretation of who they are and want to be (self-concept) and how their world could be (ideal self-concept) guide their living. They proceed as social scientists, systematically gathering and processing information in order to understand themselves and their world and in order to create purposes (Kelly, 1955). They then opt for some and commit to them, accepting that they are deciding what they will and will not be by the choices.

As these people learn about the world and their relation to it and establish and achieve goals, they continue to become more aware of themselves and their world and to generate new goals, thereby achieving even more of their potential. This process may involve increasing specialization that provides opportunities to refine and exploit one facet of self, or it may involve more general but less refined development. Success depends on the individual's continuing willingness to expand and modify interpretations as new evidence presents itself.

Ideally, rational or scientific people perceive and consider emotions as merely one kind of data. They seek to understand them rather than to savor or be propelled by them. They acknowledge the value of emotions to alert them to needs and dangers and to make living pleasurable. However, rational people's emphasis on comprehending sometimes leads to their subordinating the awareness of emotion so they cannot sense the feeling part of the emotion or admit that its propulsion is causing non-logical action. These errors have long been recognized as intellectualization and rationalization respectively.

Intelligent people recognize and relish the need continually to process information and to update self understanding. In terms of self-knowledge, they ask how well they are learning particular subjects and skills, how much wisdom and tolerance they are acquiring, what values they are identifying and expressing, what modes of instruction are more helpful than others, whether and how they can improve their information gathering, processing, and decision making in general as well as in particular areas. They examine achievement, aptitude and diagnostic data from the perspective of their own experiences and goals rather than only in comparison to people of their age or those pursuing a similar educational or occupational goal. Ipsative, as well, as normative and criterion-referenced assessments are integrated into their self-appraisals. Their approach is that of clinicians' constructing a case study rather than that of a psychometrician's entering test and inventory scores on a profile. They generate hypothetical images of themselves to guide them and they continually refine those images based on the information from their new experiences.

For rational people, career is a series of connected experiences that emanate from working or learning to work. They hope to grow through working rather than simply to "fit in." They scrutinize occupations and training positions in terms of whether these will expand and refine their talents and capability to become aware of themselves and their relations to the world, and whether these positions will strengthen their zest for life and confidence in their ability to direct that life. They want not only to know the required qualifications, duties, and salary, but also the time and energy the occupation will require, and the range of people and ideas to which it will provide access.

Intelligent people want to learn about both the modal and atypical workers in an occupation and how each type performs. Their curiosity extends not only to occupational advancement opportunities open as a consequence of performing a job, but also to the personal impacts that one can expect from five, ten, fifteen, or even more years in the occupation.

Rational people connect knowledge of self and occupations through the planning paradigms explicated by Dewey (1910) and exemplified in Sorenson's (1967) guided inquiry counseling and in the computer counseling program of Katz and his colleagues (System of Interactive Guidance, 1972). These careerists derive goals from what they have learned to value through career and other life experiences and what they understand is, or could be, available within society's structure.

Ideally, early experience provided an overview of a broad range of work values and constructive models.

By observing their own and others' performances and by task analysis and problem solving, rational careerists generate alternatives to achieve their goals. To choose alternatives correctly, career seekers need to gather accurate and comprehensive information about self and careers to evaluate the advantages and disadvantages of each alternative; to learn and try out career skills, to make decisions, and to receive feedback; and to meet and to identify with effective models.

Awareness of one's own competence and capacity to improve, as well as recognition that disciplined perseverance is necessary to succeed, increase the likelihood of success. This evaluation must include rational formulation of criteria for success. For example, the pre-med student realizes, from previous self-monitoring, that difficulty with several organic chemistry assignments before the first exam is a warning signal. Knowing that survival in pre-med requires consistently high grades, the student hires a tutor.

For intelligent people, career decision making is likely to be a collaborative developmental process that is reversible until completed, as described by Tiedeman and O'Hara (1963). In this process, *exploration* becomes *crystalization*, or acceptance of direction, which becomes an affirmation of an objective or a choice. This choice leads to *clarification*, or reduction of doubt which, in turn, leads to implementation of trial plans. The implementation includes *induction* or acceptance of the decision maker into the career position, *reformulation* of self and position in light of passing induction, and then *integration* of new personal characteristics in light of the new position. The individual will rarely make decisions in the manner of a case exercise but will engage in an apparently "muddling through" process that Heller (1976) has noted is how decision making appears to occur in corporations. Clearly, observations by Perry (1968) of Harvard students and research on Harren's (1966) *Vocational Decision-Making Checklist* support this "muddling through" interpretation of how college students decide on college majors and occupational choices. Moreover, Hilton's (1962) observations that graduating engineering students rarely used an explicit problem-solving framework to make their job choices but somehow selected an option that became compatible, and Hall's (1976) description of managers' career decision making, both support a "muddling through" view of decision making.

Recognizing that planning is how intelligent people meld career and self-knowledge alerts counselors to the need to provide clients with feedback on the effectiveness of their decision making and information about the nature of different career paths. Since rational people view the traits as potentially changing entities, they will be as interested in evaluating their current traits as in learning how to pinpoint them and to estimate their change by using moderator variables (Anastasi, 1976). Similarly, they not only will want to find out what the modal worker in a particular occupation is like, but will also wish to learn job analysis in order to be able to judge what a successful worker might be like and to ascertain the typical growth patterns of workers within that occupation. Since they expect continually to monitor their own careers, they also seek out benchmarks against which to measure the career. In other words, they want to know what is typical, as well as what is possible after five, ten, and twenty years in an occupation. And since their goals may lead them off the beaten career paths, they will appreciate support and opportunity to review their experiences with a mature career observer.

The hope of rational people is that attentive, flexible, self-directed energetic approach to working and living will provide them with challenges, which will enable them to grow and to end life with a sense of accomplishment and contribution. Like developmental people (to be described next) they want to have work when they want it and to be advancing to more satisfying work, but are more willing than developmental people to risk innovating rather than to abide by what have been the developmental tasks of their predecessors.

Developmental Being

Developmental people are evolutionary; they are unfolding predictably in accord with maturation of inherent capacities and external stimulation. With proper stimulation and support, growth will be optimal, although their achievement cannot outstrip the maturation of their requisite physical and mental capacities. Abstract thinking, for example, will be out of the reach of most seven-year-olds, regardless of the stimulation and support offered by an environment, but most thirteen- and fourteen-year-olds will acquire the capability, except under very restrictive conditions. Our nature provides the potential, but ongoing nurturance and success are necessary for people's realization of their potential. Future successes build on past accomplishments. The grade-schooler, for instance, who learns to ignore external distractions and accept but not be distracted by physiological signs of stress in a testing situation, will blossom more fully through schooling than the peer who has not acquired such test taking competence. The developmental human being is Darwin's, Piaget's, Kohlberg's person, being what survives, what works.

Developmental people's humanity unfolds as they are stimulated by the tasks of living and supported in mastering them. Free societies move to organize themselves so that their citizens' development is optimal; that is, so that commensurate with resources, people are called upon to learn and to perform the tasks of living at a time and in a manner that will bring out the best in them. Of course, if a people is denied information and participation in societal decision making, totalitarianism will result, and optimal human development will not be approached.

Scholars and scientists pursuing the developmental model assume that there is a discoverable standard analogous to Plato's ideal against which to measure a person's life and career progress. Vocational psychology has set out as one objective to define the career tasks comprising that standard and to alert people to them. In line with this, Super et al. (1957, 1961, 1969) and Gribbons and Lohnes (1968) have studied longitudinally the career development of representative boys and girls from adolescence into adulthood. Synthesizing several theories guiding such studies, Jordaan (1974) has suggested that careers in our society should proceed in several predictable directions as indicated in Figure 2–1.

Table 2 in Chapter 1 outlined both the stages that characterize the career and some of the tasks that are typical of each stage. In theory, sequential mastery of these tasks will bring optimum development. Since living in a complex, changing system continually increases what people believe is necessary and possible regarding working and living, they can expect to be continually stimulated to new career accomplishment. The society needs continually to identify the evolving chal-

Figure 2–1. Directions In Career Growth

1. Greater familiarity with and more effective use of environmental resources and opportunities.
2. Greater awareness of and concern with impending and eventual choices.
3. More effective and more systematic exploration of one's self and one's environment.
4. More extensive and more specific educational and occupational information.
5. Better understanding of the factors to be considered in making various kinds of choices.
6. Greater awareness of factors which might upset or delay one's plans and of ways of circumventing or coping with these contingencies.
7. Greater willingness to assume personal responsibility for one's decisions.
8. Greater awareness of one's ability to determine the course and outcomes of events through the kinds of decisions one makes.
9. Greater awareness of personal assets and deficits and of their implications for choice.
10. A clearer, more complete, better integrated, and more realistic self-concept.
11. The translation of this self-concept first into general and then into more specific occupational terms.
12. Greater commitment to one's goals and subsequently to one's occupation.
13. More specific, stable, and realistic objectives.
14. More specific plans for achieving these objectives.
15. Goals, and eventually an occupation, which are more in accord with one's interests, abilities, values, personality traits, self-concept, work experience, and job skills.
16. Ability to compromise between desire and reality, between the hoped for and the feasible.
17. The selection of educational and occupational environments which are more compatible with one's personality and life-style.
18. Stable employment offering job security and prospects of a decent livelihood.

lenges and opportunities in order to devise new supports to enable its people to accomplish these evolving tasks. Chapters 7 through 12 delineate more fully the tasks of the major life stages in presenting counseling methods for assisting with them.

Our understanding of the components of career development is still limited, but theorists are pursuing several hunches. Super (1974) and Crites (1969) have offered the models of the structure of career development that appear in Figures 2–2 and 2–3. These models indicate some of the broad competences that are likely to be important in careering and even today might be used by the individual to initiate an evaluation of his or her career development. Notice, for example, that Super implies the person should review self in terms of planning, acquired information, exploration, accomplishment, decision making, and realism.

Recently, test developers such as Super et al. (1971), Crites (1965, 1973), Healy and Klein (1973), and the College Entrance Examination Board (1977) have composed tests based on these career development models in order to measure people's career task achievement. These measures are useful as benchmarks in comparing groups' career accomplishments and in suggesting need for assistance in problem solving and planning.

Career Information Needs

In terms of career, the developmental perspective suggests that people should understand the overall organization of the society's education and work institutions and their relation to them as well as the physiological and psychological maturation curves of the human species. Since the perspective posits that career is a process unfolding over distinctive stages, people ought to recognize that past and present actions and aspirations are connected and will combine with personal and environmental changes in determining future work roles. Career biographies can supplement traditional occupational descriptive literature in showing how people grow into sequences of positions as a consequence of capacities they nurture and opportunities society extends as they fulfill prerequisite requirements. Especially desirable is that youngsters learn to consider career as a sequence of positions rather than as only one position and to contrast careers in order to identify both the competences related to career success and the ways and times in which people like them have built those competences. Moreover, by examining and contrasting people in different life stages, people can learn to isolate the challenges that career is likely to pose at particular stages.

In terms of human maturation, people should understand how physical and mental capacities unfold and may be strengthened or obstructed, as described later in Chapter 3. They should also become acquainted with current theories of interest and value development referred to in Chapter 3. Likewise, they will profit from reflecting about the changing demands and responsibilities which are likely in moving

Figure 2–2. Donald Super's Model of Career Development for the Midcareer

I. Planfulness or Time perspective
  A. Past: Exploration
    1. Crystallizing
    2. Specifying
    3. Implementing
  B. Present and immediate future: establishment
    4. Stabilizing
    5. Consolidation
    6. Advancement
  C. Intermediate future: Maintenance
    7. Holding one's own
    8. Keeping up with developments
    9. Breaking new ground
  D. Distant future: Decline
    10. Tapering off
    11. Preparing for retirement
    12. Retiring

II. Exploration
  E. Querying
    1. Self
      a. in time perspective
      b. in space (organizational, geographic)
    2. Situation
      a. in time perspective
      b. in space (organizational, geographic)
  F. Resources (attitudes toward)
    1. Awareness of
    2. Valuation of

  G. Participation (use of resources)
    1. In-house resources (sponsored)
    2. Community resources (sought-out)

III. Information
  H. Life stages
    1. Time spans
    2. Characteristics
    3. Developmental tasks
  I. Coping behaviors: Repertoire

    4. Options in coping with vocational development tasks
    5. Appropriateness of options for self-in-situation
  J. Occupational outlets for self-in-situation
  K. Job outlets for self-in-situation
  L. Implementation: Means of access to opportunities
  M. Outcome probabilities

IV. Decision-making
  N. Principles
    1. Knowledge of
    2. Valuation of (utility)
  O. Practice
    3. Use of in past
    4. Use of at present

V. Reality Orientation
  P. Self-knowledge
    1. Agreement self-estimated and measured traits
    2. Agreement self-estimated and other estimated traits
  Q. Realism
    3. Agreement self and employer-evaluated proficiency
    4. Agreement self and employer-evaluated prospects

  R. Consistency of occupational preferences
    5. Current
    6. Over time
  S. Crystallization
    7. Clarity of vocational self-concept
    8. Certainty of career goals
  T. Work experience
    9. Floundering vs. stabilizing in mid-career
    10. Stabilizing or maintaining vs. declining in mid-career

SOURCE: From Super, D. E. Vocational maturity in mid career. *The Vocational Guidance Quarterly*, 1977, 25, 294–302. Copyright 1977 American Personnel and Guidance Association. Reprinted with permission.

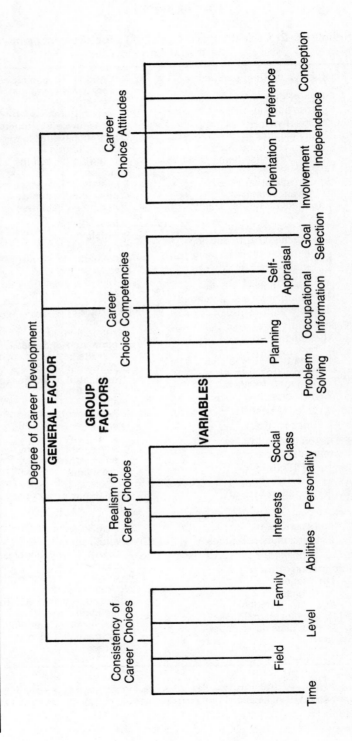

Figure 2-3. John Crites's Model of Career Maturity in Adolescence

SOURCE: J. O. Crites. The career maturity inventory. In D. E. Super (ed.). *Measuring vocational maturity for counseling and evaluation.* Copyright 1974 American Personnel and Guidance Association. Reprinted with permission.

38

from studenthood to full-time worker, from single to married and very probably a dual career family, and from childlessness to parenthood. The developmental perspective reminds us that a person can probably predict future personal assets and constraints and societal demands. To awaken this perspective in clients, counselors can alert them to information and instruction about human development and the arrangement of a society's institutions and challenge them to project themselves into the futures that trends in their own and their society's development are likely to bring forth.

More immediately, the developmental perspective calls for pinpointing one's career stage and how well one is doing on the stage's tasks. Consequently, the adolescent who learns of the need to be aware of the duties, requirements, and supply/demand projections for occupations of interest, needs to verify personal interests and acquire information about occupations that are compatible with those interests. In the same manner, the management trainee who finds that mentors are a *sine quo non* of management advancement must judge whether existing relationships qualify as mentoring and must judge whether their mentoring is likely to be effective.

Assisting developmental people's career calls for actions such as these: 1) providing current information about evolving career challenges and possibilities, and the resources that can help in mastering them; 2) teaching or supporting teaching about the structure and workings of educational and economic systems; 3) creating opportunities to obtain feedback from valid tests of career skills and from caring educators; 4) locating and directing clients to good skill development programs; 5) introducing careerists to concerned mentors and sponsors who will advise and support them as they use the programs and create their careers (for example, big brother and sister programs, and some of the women's consciousness raising programs, have moved to fill the dearth of mentoring for some of the people in our society); 6) challenging people to anticipate their reactions to future scenarios wherein their assets and responsibilities are predictable, although different from their current ones; and 7) helping students to use information gathering and processing operations such as job analysis, successful-nonsuccessful person comparisons, decision trees, and consultation. Indeed, the developmental counselor, in recognizing the developmental character of career, will strive to increase a client's willingness to confer about career in the future.

Behavioral Beings

Behavioral people are creatures of needs who acquire or learn a set of responses to meet these needs. The responses to environmental and internal stimuli, which endure and are likely to be repeated, are those that satisfy needs (operant or instrumental learning) or those that have been associated with satisfying needs (conditioned learning). As ongoing growth in a changing world elicits new needs, and as people mature, new responses develop and old ones become refined or extinguish, depending on their efficacy.

Behavioral beings strive for continual need satisfaction. They thrive to the degree that they can distinguish familiar from unfamiliar stimuli, so they can alter responses to the new stimuli, can discern when a response is or is not productive, and can develop new responses to alter unproductive behavior. In other words, more adept learners and more favorable learning conditions create more impressive performances.

Behaviorists such as Krumboltz (1976), who combine the behavioral and rational being paradigms, posit that behavioral people create "*self-observation generalizations (SOG)*" or sets of propositions about self, especially preferences that are the outcome of experience, in order to become more predictable and hence more able to identify and then to act to meet their needs. For instance, youngsters may have learned from their soccer experience that they like the applause of peers and possess soccer skills that produce applause. When they transfer to a new high school and recognize the desire for admiration in the new school, they predictably will turn to soccer or another sport such as field hockey in which their prowess can elicit peer approbation. The SOG is a person's record of learning experiences that is brought to bear in deciding courses of action. The concept of SOG approaches the self-concept of the intelligent being, although SOG does not stress the phenomenal character of the rational being, and its self-knowledge is used in reaction to the challenges of the environment, whereas the rational person's self-knowledge is applied more proactively.

When a need of the behavioral person is not being met, the paradigm indicates that the person can change responses; reduce, alter, or substitute needs; restructure the environment; or move to a new environment. Considerable information on changing behavior is available. Among the more general discoveries are that change is easier when anxiety is low or moderate, when the nature of the new behavior is explicit, and when quality instruction for the new behavior and suitable models of it are available, and expected reward is forthcoming. Desensitization and reinforcement-modeling counseling exemplify application of such principles; and they have proved successful in increasing information seeking, deliberation about plans, interview performance, and test taking, as indicated in later chapters. Rules relating to need reduction are less clear, although the so-called secondary needs (social approval, money, status), which are acquired because of their association with primary needs (food, drink, shelter, sex, exploration), would appear easier to reduce than are the primary needs. In terms of environmental alteration, writers such as Thoresen and Mahoney (1974) have indicated how people can analyze the environment in order to pinpoint contingencies that are not supporting the desired behavior and then proceed to organize and add contingencies to encourage desired behavior. Likewise, many behavioral consultation models have been applied successfully in assisting classroom teachers and institutional personnel, such as nurses and prison guards, to restructure their environments to elicit desirable student and inmate responses.

In regard to environmental change, behavioral people would identify their needs and appropriate environments, perhaps using instruments such as the *Personal Preference Schedule* (Edwards, 1959). Certainly, data on occupational migration by Roe et al. (1966) and Gottfredson (1977) support the thesis that people will move to an environment that is more compatible with their needs. In the realm of careers, the Dawis et al. (1964) propositions about occupational satisfaction and occupational satisfactoriness provide a scheme for assisting people in locating need-satisfying occupations.

From the behavioral perspective, the career is a connected series of problems. Their ongoing resolution is rewarding but requires careerists to obtain information about such things as the needs that different activities and positions meet, the performances that they require, or the obstacles that must be surmounted to gain entry. Concurrently, they must also identify their ever emerging needs and the assets they have developed or might develop for removing the obstacles and meeting the position demands. When solutions are not forthcoming, people become anxious and may need assistance in reducing anxiety to a level that permits problem solving. Careerists will profit especially from learning task and situational analysis procedures and from learning methods of controlling their own anxiety and their acquisition of rewards. Moreover, they need to be acquainted with information resources (Ryan, 1968) and habituated in using the steps of decision making, problem solving, and planning.

Sociological Human Beings

Sociological beings are products of their institutions, which are sets of group made, noncodified, tacit policies guiding how group members will cooperatively achieve human ends such as family life, production and education. Families sustain fathering, mothering, grandparenting, brothering and sistering. Privileged family circumstances combined with quality education produce high achieving youth likely to attain high occupational status. Compulsory, age-segregated schooling through age eighteen in a curriculum remote from daily life within a society that prizes personal freedom begets adolescents who invariably challenge adult society. In terms of work, readers will recognize that unspoken policies such as: award a responsible position after a youth reaches the early 20s, men have first call on jobs, and the competent dress and talk in accord with their job station have helped sustain unfair employment practices. On the other hand, tacit guidelines such as: subordinate your wants to cooperative production and a fair wage warrants a full day's work have helped build a great nation.

Society's institutions affect people differentially, on the basis of their status. One's status derives from family's background, sex, prestige of schools and career, and in the case of women, their husband's occupation. Rich and poor children receive differential treatment in schools, churches, courts, and even families. Families, schools and employers, despite Title IX, have different expectations of boys and girls, men and women. Prep schoolers and Ivy Leaguers have an entree to opportunities, both social and career, which public school and state college students of comparable ability are denied. Similar advantages occur throughout life.

Institutions influence a person through the positions they confer and the roles a person assumes and develops to discharge the positions. Since a sociological perspective defines a person's career as the sequence of work-related positions occupied by that person over the lifetime, it follows that one can appreciate a sociological interpretation of career and ascertain its implications for career assistance by understanding the concepts of position and role and examining propositions related to these concepts. This section, therefore, develops these concepts and propositions.

As introduced in Chapter 1, a position designates a group of tasks to be performed by one person. The tasks comprising traditional positions such as family member, student, and professional evolve from a culture's judgment about what has been adaptive. When change is rapid, however, institutional leadership such as school boards and employers set up positions to meet particular tasks on the basis of goal analyses. Some positions such as child in a family or student in elementary school are birthrights, but others such as employee or employer must be earned by demonstrating the capability of discharging the position. Still other positions are imposed, as, for example, when parenthood follows procreation and the new parents are given the rights of parenthood and held liable for the discharge of the responsibilities, unless they relinquish custody of their offspring.

A position's responsibilities and prerogatives derive from folkways and the expectations of those directly affected by them rather than from detailed, fixed codes. Those people directly affected by a position help to shape it by how they guide and interact with new incumbents. A position's evolving definition tends to accommodate incumbent idiosyncracies that manifest themselves in discharging the position. Position definition, in other words, usually allows some give and take between incumbents and those linked to it. There are few contracts detailing position tasks, even for work positions. Marriage and other covenants tend to be general. This kind of agreement allows most people to discharge their positions in a distinctive way and to adapt performance to changing circumstances, and it explains why a variety of performances in similar positions is usually satisfactory. Observation of families with twins will show this for our most basic institution, and reflection about how different workers such as auto mechanics, grocery clerks, secretaries, police officers discharge the same job will establish this for most work positions.

Even though most positions tolerate a range of acceptable behaviors, they exert a powerful influence on what one does and learns. Incumbents of similar positions exhibit many commonalities and act in the same fashion because positions directly prescribe certain actions and access to societal resources and indirectly affect possible allocation of time and energy and one's interpersonal network. Moreover, deviancy is punished by incumbents of related positions and societal institutions. For instance, a restaurant patron who submits her order and turns to read her paper, will be surprised and chagrined if her waiter sits down beside her and strikes up a conversation. The waiting cook may be even angrier. Recall, too, how courts, churches, and schools uphold parental and child and employer and employee rights and responsibilities.

Predictably, people linked directly to a position can exert considerable influence on an incumbent's behavior. Sometimes the expectations of different persons and their groups are contradictory, and this fact makes discharging the position difficult, regardless of the incumbent's talents. By identifying various involved groups' expectations for a position and the predispositions of the incumbent, one can predict his or her behavior, as Gross, Mason, and McEachern (1959) did in studying the influence of teachers, parents, and school boards on school principals. When diverging groups have legitimate demands on a position, conflicts are likely to arise, and the more conflicts in their demands, the more stressful and difficult the position is likely to become. Firing a principal from a school undergoing crises because of a changing community, therefore, might be foolhardy, since structural failures rather than worker defects are obstructing performance.

Many positions are complex, involving different actions with different persons and groups. As a consequence, the set of behaviors associated with the position, defined as its role, is often more understandable and communicable when the behavior subsets have distinctive labels. One position, in other words, may confer multiple roles. By way of illustration, recall how a university professorship confers the roles of instructor, scholar/researcher, colleague, committee member, text/equipment purchasing agent, and perhaps subordinate of a dean.

The more complex a position and numerous its roles, the more difficult it is to be clear about the responsibilities, the more challenging it is to discharge, the more likely it is that internal conflicts will arise among the roles, and the more likely the incumbent will encounter conflict in discharging it. Moreover, since throughout life people occupy several positions concomitantly, and since these positions sometimes involve noncomplementary or even contradictory roles, it is almost inevitable that a person will encounter role conflict. Undoubtedly, people have a continuing need to decide how to allocate energy and time in discharging their multiple positions and to ascertain how to reconcile opposing pressures across and within their positions.

The place of a position in an organization and its linkages to positions in other organizations may be as important as are its duties in shaping its incumbent. The linkages form the communication network through which a person can learn, receive support, and manifest talent. Isolated and "dead end" are perjorative terms when applied to schools, businesses, governmental agencies or to positions in general because their isolation and lack of connection to higher positions curtails aspiration and thwarts growth.

Desirable positions often require candidates to serve time in prerequisite positions and/or to be endorsed by incumbents of desirable positions. For example, prestigious law and public accounting firms and prestigious government agencies such as the State Department favor applicants from prestigious universities, which in turn favor students from quality high schools and may even require recommendations from professionals. It is not always as simple as saying that who you know is more important than what you know. Perhaps more often, and at times with some legitimacy, successful firms and agencies insure the continued quality of their recruits by selecting candidates who have shown their capabilities to persons who can evaluate fitness and in so doing have acquired a sense of the behavioral style that the organization expects. The people without linkages and prerequisites who believe that they have the capacity for the position may not appreciate the position's total function, since they have not established themselves with those governing its entry and discharge.

Institutional Influences on Career

Schools and colleges move students among a fixed series of positions, and in so doing increase the likelihood of their having particular qualities. Each position has prescribed entry ways and definite prerogatives, responsibilities, and restraints. College sophomores must have been freshmen, they can play varsity sports and exhibit sophomoritis, but they must reflect the sophistication of the initiated. Socialization in and out of the school supports their privilege of experimentation, autonomy, and reflection, even at points of "town-gown" conflict, often to the chagrin of nonstudents. Educators, as gatekeepers and credential awarders, have a considerable power in a person's career development.

As noted in Chapter 1, Glaser (1968) proposed that corporations have similar and perhaps even more power. He contended that they mold careers by organizing sequences of positions and moving people through them, so that the workers acquire the skills and attitudes the corporation desires. According to Glaser, corporations develop people as deliberately as they produce their products or services.

Even when persons work for themselves, consumers' demands, constraints of land, materials, equipment and labor, and government regulations more or less delimit how the person may enter and ply a trade. These forces influence the positions that can be pursued and the roles that are viable. Indeed, these demands, constraints, and regulations operate to socialize nonorganizational workers informally, whereas the organization socialized its workers formally.

Many jobs, perhaps unfortunately, are not embedded in organizations and thus do not fit Glaser's model. Employers of these workers do not feel a need to develop the employee. These jobs tend to be the unskilled and semi-skilled occupations, casual or temporary positions, and other jobs outside the primary labor market. Workers are paid for their current performance; their compensation does not include promises about the future. Although these jobs do not offer hierarchical, functional, or inclusive mobility, continuation in them requires role compliance. Implicitly, satisfaction from nonembedded jobs will be lower than from embedded jobs because fewer satisfiers are available.

Further explicating the organization-individual relationship in career development, Schein (1971) constructed the processes shown in Table 2–1 to portray how the organizational structure and a person interact as the worker passes through the work organization. According to Schein (1971), workers can make hierarchical movements (up or down in rank), inclusive or central moves (more involved in decision making), and functional moves (working in different activities). He proposed the following set of hypotheses to account for the series of interchanges between organization and individual during the organizational passage.

Hypothesis 1. Organizational *socialization* will occur primarily in connection with the passage through hierarchical and inclusion boundaries; efforts at *education* and *training* will occur primarily in connection with the passage through functional boundaries. In both instances, the amount of effort at socialization and/or training will be at a maximum just prior to boundary passage, but will continue for some time after boundary passage.

The underlying assumption behind this hypothesis is that (1) the organization is most concerned about correct values and attitudes at the point where it is granting a member more authority and/or centrality, and (2) the individual is most vulnerable to socialization pressures just before and after boundary passage. . . .

Hypothesis 2. Innovation, or the individual's influence on the organization, will occur *in the middle* of a given stage of the career, at a maximum distance from boundary passage.

The person must be far enough from the earlier boundary passage to have learned the requirements of the new position and to have earned centrality in the new out-culture, yet must be far enough from his next boundary passage to be fully involved in the present job without being concerned about preparing himself for the future. Also, his power to induce change is lower if he is perceived as about preparing himself for the future. Also, his power to induce change is lower if he is perceived as about to leave (the lame duck phenomenon). . . .

Hypothesis 3. In general, the processes of socialization will be more prevalent in the early stages of a career and the process of innovation late in the career, *but both processes occur* at all stages.

Hypothesis 4. Socialization or influence will involve primarily the more labile [changeable] social selves of the individual, while innovation will involve primarily the more stable social selves of the individual, provided the individual is not held captive in the organization. . . .

Hypothesis 5. A change in the more stable social selves as a result of socialization will occur only under conditions of coercive persuasion, i.e., where the individual cannot or does not psychologically feel free to leave the organization. Conditions under which coercive persuasion would operate can be produced by a variety of factors: a tight labor market . . . ; an employment contract which involves a legal or moral obligation to remain with the organization; a reward system which subtly but firmly entraps the individual through stock options, pension plans, deferred compensation plans, and the like (Ibid., pp. 414–16).[1]

Passage through school and work means that people must accommodate to prescribed linkages, predictable role expectations, and extant customs. People can accommodate and have done so in the following six ways.

1. Accepting the organizational system and purposes as their own, agreeing to its demands in exchange for its rewards (identity, security, prestige, predictability), and socializing others into the system directly by coaching, teaching, and sponsoring, and indirectly by abiding and therefore supporting the system.

2. Minimizing the work role by locating and performing jobs that provide subsistence income for small commitment of time and energy. (Society thwarts this option by encouraging consumption needs.)

3. Trying to express self through work to the greatest degree (intelligent or trait factor person) by locating those occupations, usually professions or self-employment positions, which offer latitude for working or by working for oneself to gain this opportunity. (This option often requires considerable commitment to career, and in universities it may require a dean who assumes a patron role toward the actualizing scholar.)

4. Joining in redesigning one's job so that it can better express one's individuality. (The human resource theory Y model of management [McGreggor, 1960] suggests that this will promote production and satisfaction. Widespread implementation of the job redesign option, however, may require that society as a whole, especially people as consumers, adjust their expectations about work output; that is, they will have to be willing to pay for worker growth in addition to worker output. Certainly Katzell, Yankelovich et al.'s (1975), review of work redesign projects suggests that some workers are skeptical about the benefits of work redesign and prefer to minimize their involvement in work.

5. Rejecting "the system" through alternatives such as communal living, welfare, panhandling, or perennial studenthood.

6. Opposing "the system" through criminal or revolutionary activity.

[1] Reproduced by permission from *The Journal of Applied Behavioral Science*, "The Individual, the Organization, and the Career: A Conceptual Scheme," by Edgar H. Schein, Volume 7, Number 4, pp. 415–416, and 421–424, Copyright 1971, NTL Institute.

Table 2–1. Interaction of Worker and Organization in Career

Basic Stages and Transitions	Statuses or Positions	Psychological and Organizational Processes: Transactions between Individual and Organization
1. Pre-entry	Aspirant, applicant, rushee	Preparation, education, anticipatory socialization.
Entry (trans.)	Entrant, postulant, recruit	Recruitment, rushing, testing screening, selection, acceptance ("hiding"); passage through external inclusion boundary; rites of entry; induction and orientation.
2. Basic training novitiate	Trainee, novice, pledge	Training, indoctrination, socialization, testing of the man by the organization, tentative acceptance into group.
Initiation, first vows (trans.)	Initiate, graduate	Passage through first inner inclusion boundary, acceptance as member and conferring of organizational status, rite of passage and acceptance.
3. First regular assignment	New member	First testing by the person of his own capacity to function; granting of real responsibility (playing for keeps); passage through functional boundary with assignment to specific job or department.
Substages 3a. Learning the job 3b. Maximum performance 3c. Becoming obsolete 3d. Learning new skills, etc.		Indoctrination and testing of person by immediate work group leading to acceptance or rejection; if accepted further education and socialization (learning the ropes); preparation for higher status through coaching, seeking visibility, finding sponsors, etc.
Promotion or leveling off (trans.)		Preparation, testing, passage through hierarchical boundary, rite of passage; may involve passage through functional boundary as well (rotation).
4. Second assignment Substages	Legitimate member (fully accepted)	Processes under no. 3 repeat.
5. Granting of tenure	Permanent member	Passage through another inclusion boundary.
Termination and exit (trans.)	Old-timer, senior citizen	Preparation for exit, cooling the mark out, rites of exit (testimonial dinners, etc.).
6. Post-exit	Alumnus emeritus retired	Granting of peripheral status.

SOURCE: Reproduced by permission from The Journal of Applied Behavioral Science, "The Individual, the Organization, and the Career: A Conceptual Scheme," by Edgar H. Schein, Volume 7, Number 4, pp. 415–416 and 421–424, copyright 1971, NTL Institute.

Implications of Positions for Future Career

Not only do one's positions influence present behavior, but they also enable predictions about the future. Several principles help to explain this. For example, it is logical that the longer one is in a position, the more one becomes habituated to its roles. Similarly, the more one expects a new position to be like a current position, the more likely one is to act in the new position as one has acted in the old. These two propositions combined with the tendency for people to study for longer periods and increasingly to consider studenthood as a career position suggests an explanation of why students become disillusioned with their first jobs and why employers complain about their "prima donna" attitudes (Shein, 1965). For although the student position prepares one for work, its goal is person development not production for others. As a consequence, the student position is allowed much wider tolerances than are permitted in most jobs. Inevitably, therefore, after experiencing the liberation of a paycheck, new workers chafe under the restrictions of the job regimen, and their employers are likely to resent their slowness in adopting the work group's customary behavior.

Although many complex interactions will determine the character of future work roles, the role expectations learned in schools and elsewhere will contribute to how future work is approached. It is noteworthy, therefore, that today's youth are learning to expect more autonomy and challenge in work, because they take more advanced, challenging schooling with greater autonomy; they want more for less production, expecting college admissions for lower grades and test scores; and they are learning that status is acquired as much by consumption as by production. Demand for greater challenge and autonomy in work and a higher return for less work supports innovation and increased efficiency and productivity, which should be beneficial in an increasingly competitive economic world, but inculcation of extended material needs seems at odds with predictions about limits on physical resources.

Necessity of a Sociological Perspective

Many human problems stem from shortcomings of human institutions and their positions rather than from personal deficits (Weinberg, 1969). The principalship described above exemplifies this. Another example of institutional salaciousness occurs when society expects a position to meet particular goals without providing sufficient resources and societal support. One too common example is the position of student in a disjointed, authoritarian educational system with high teacher and peer transiency and low attendance and performance standards. Such a position promises development of competence and independence, but instead it breeds dependency and fatalism. Fortunately, many incumbents of these positions have managed to build a sense of agency and skills in spite of the defects of their position. Nevertheless, the structure of the position itself has created unnecessary stress for members of society.

Once one recognizes the power of positions, especially their negative potential, it is hard to be content with trying to help particular unfortunate incumbents. Instead, one looks to correct the position. Observing from a sociological perspective is essential to do this effectively, for that perspective alerts us to look at how positions are defined, provisioned, and linked to one another. It encourages tracing problems to institutional deficiencies and then correcting the deficiency to benefit people generally.

A sociological perspective complements the behavioral in suggesting ways of resolving career problems. Whereas the behavioral emphasizes the impact of the rewards and expectation of a particular situation on the individual's adaptability, the sociological focuses on whether the resources and linkages of a class of positions are proportional to the demands of the mission. The behavioral perspective leads to ways of adapting incumbents or reorganizing the position so that the special individual's performance increases, while the sociological suggests change in allocations of resources for the position or changes in the interrelation of the position with others so that it can be discharged more effectively by the current incumbents in accord with the society's overall welfare. Since early career positions, especially school positions, affect future positions substantially and are amenable to societal upgrading, it is important to scrutinize such positions from a sociological perspective in addition to assisting people to adjust to them. More particularly, a sociological perspective elucidates that such problems as youth unemployment require structural change. Not only must job seekers be equipped, but access to entry positions also must be opened. Society must alter views about the eligibility of youth for responsible positions, perhaps by restructuring the final years of school so that youth and employers have more chances to become acquainted.

Institutional corrections are so important that individuals are expected to abide them rather than to press for more immediate personal adjustments that might restrict institutional improvement. Indeed, at times individuals may have to defer personal benefit in order to assist institutional improvement. This perspective recognizes people's common specie bond and responsibility, whereas individualistic psychology models do not. Support for busing of white children to inner-city schools, for instance, is based in part on sociological notions, although the cross-cultural experience provided the bused youngsters can be argued to be fair compensation for the travel time and possibly slowed academic development (Coleman, 1977).

Implications for Career Information and Assistance

In regard to career information, a sociological perspective suggests the need to understand the lifestyles and requirements of the roles one's status permits and the lifestyles and requirements of alternative statuses that may be open. People need to understand where the transitions between and among school and work are and how they are accomplished.

They should examine successful people in their status in order to determine what they know and are doing that is different from people who are failing. By identifying how institutions such as family, school, work, church, media, and government aid or hinder people in their status to make transitions and learn roles, they can begin to take charge of their own training.

To decide whether to try to maintain their class or move to another through career, people must recognize their social class and strata and then examine the lifestyles and requirements of acceptable classes and strata, including their own, in order to determine their competence and comfort with the respective lifestyles. Whenever career choice involves a class move, more than the typical transit support may be needed, since studies indicate that interclass mobility is more the exception than the rule. Indeed, limited knowledge of changing suggests that people find the class change difficult and often experience anomie.

Ignoring class differences blurs the process of career transition, especially from school to work and job to job, and this may explain why extra confusion and disruption of careers exist at transition points. The methods and institutions involved in transition vary by class. Jameson (1978) has pointed out that most jobs are secured through family and personal contacts. Since people tend to associate by class, even from their school days (Coleman, 1961), they will have more entries to positions in their own class than to positions in other social classes. Although schools are thought to ignore class, and therefore one might expect their formal placement and work study programs to counter class barriers, examination of career program assignments by Cicourel and Kitsuse (1963) showed that these assignments were influenced by social class, thus increasing the likelihood that youngsters would leave school with credentials commensurate with their class. Moreover, the fact that class is a powerful mediator in school progress and achievements reduces the school's potential for reducing class barriers. Similarly, the federal government's extensive employment service in each state, which places millions of workers yearly, does not counter class influence in job acquisition appreciably because the large majority of its placements are working-class level or below. At best, it facilitates access of lower-class people to the working class.

Acknowledgment of the linkages of occupational levels to socioeconomic origins need not lead lower class persons to eschew efforts at occupational mobility. Rather this knowledge can alert society to the desirability of providing more supports for such movement. In addition, it should prompt a reexamination of differences in compensation and privilege across occupational levels.

The sociological model indicates at least three ways by which counselors can aid career development. First, the fact that society has a stake in the success of every career means that eventually it will exert pressure for change on groups or policies that thwart the career development of individuals. Consequently, counselors can aid current or perhaps prospective clients by documenting obstacles to careers and by bringing the existence of such obstacles to the attention of society's leaders and members. Dickson and Roethlisberger (1965) reported that the provision of counseling in industry originally envisioned counselors giving such feedback to management.

Second, since a changing society enables and requires many workers to change work positions regularly, many people will need assistance in moving from position to position and in learning their new roles. This aid often will require either administrators who build linkages among a society's institutions and minimize obstacles such as nontransportable pensions and unnecessary entry requirements, or teachers or counselors to teach the person both the means of moving from position to position and the skills required by new roles. Among the necessary linkages are those from home to school, school to school, school to work, occupation to occupation, and work to retirement. Programs for building such linkages include headstart programs, work-study programs, and placement, and outplacement programs.

Teaching assistance should involve alerting a person to both the duties of new positions and to possible conflicting role expectations such as the discrepant expectations for school superintendents identified by Gross, Mason, and McEachern (1958). It should introduce people to the functions of accrediting and licensing agencies that help to define new position duties and assure uniformity of expectations and should inform them of the ones related to their work aspirations. In addition, instruction should address the competition of career with a person's other life positions, such as spouse, friend, and citizen, and point out models who have exemplified different ways of balancing roles. Especially useful will be models exemplifying alternate ways of avoiding and resolving conflicts.

Third, by redesigning or teaching people to redesign their jobs, we may help the sociological being reduce the conflict between work role expectations and other life roles. For this, counselors might explore collaboration with unions and management. Discussion of project assignments in school and work study programs would seem to be a feasible arena wherein students can begin to see themselves as persons who engineer their own job and consequently will learn the structure of a work organization in order to judge which alterations in a particular position are feasible.

The Psychodynamic Human Being

The psychodynamic person can be pictured as a being with an emerging set of innate, initially unconscious, needs linked to survival of the species. This being has an expanding, though finite, energy system for discharging these needs. Murray (1938) has suggested the list of needs (see Figure 2–4). This list adequately communicates the range of gratifications psychodynamic persons must have.

As these needs arise, they draw energy; that is, they propel the person to act, with or without awareness. Ideally the individual begins to recognize particular needs, such as hunger and warmth, and learns

Figure 2–4. A Spectrum of Needs Proposed by H. A. Murray

Abasement	Exhibition
Achievement	Harm avoidance
Affiliation	Avoid humiliation
Aggression	Nurturance
Autonomy	Order
Counteraction	Play
Defendance	Rejection
Understanding	Sentience
Deference	Sex
Dominance	Succorance

SOURCE: From *Explorations in Personality*, edited by Henry A. Murray. Copyright 1938 by Oxford University Press, Inc.; renewed 1966 by Henry A. Murray. Reprinted by permission of the publisher.

actions, such as securing and eating food and finding a thermostat, to relieve these needs without creating anxiety. If need awareness and relief learning do not occur, the needs still stir the person; but instead of providing pleasure through their fulfillment, they create anxiety and sap the person's energy. Children's initial reactions to need frustration are often to deny or to suppress awareness of (repress) the need, and this manner of dealing with frustration persists throughout life. The person, therefore, often does not know the cause of the anxiety, and is constrained in relieving the tension. Thus, the individual becomes propelled by unconscious, irrational forces.

The psychodynamic perspective recognizes feelings as manifestations of a person to be experienced, explored, and appreciated rather than only known and controlled or manipulated. Family, social, school or work roles that interfere with perceiving emotions are dysfunctional and need to be restructured. Persons who intellectualize or in other ways stifle and repress emotions are likely to be dissatisfied, as are those who act impulsively, without regard to the consequences of such expression.

As an individual matures, the growth elicits more needs and society expects the person to become more self-sufficient in satisfying them. The person, therefore, must develop new behaviors for meeting needs and a finer capacity to discriminate among them. A baby, for instance, will cry appropriately when in need of nourishment or warmth and will receive gratification from the discerning parents; but the teenager in need of rejuvenation is expected to ascertain whether the need is food or warmth and to take appropriate actions, such as preparing a sandwich or securing a blanket.

During these transformations, people are sometimes overwhelmed and adopt strategies that are not completely effectual in discharging their needs. These insufficient strategies are the defense mechanisms, such as rationalizing, denying, and projecting. Their operation "bottles up" the person's energy, and their extensive use eventually renders the person immobile.

Once the individual starts employing defense mechanisms in one or more areas of life, less energy remains for all other tasks, since one's energy system is unitary. When a client presents a particular problem, therefore, the psychodynamic therapist first reviews the person's overall adjustment to ascertain whether the presenting problem is symptomatic of more general personality disintegration. In such a reconnaissance (Sullivan, 1953b), the therapist also learns the client's pattern of defense mechanism usage and notes strengths that might be used to resolve the particular frustration.

From the psychodynamic perspective, the career is the connected set of accommodations that the person makes to education and work. In theory, one learns to study and work effectively if these tasks are presented in a nonthreatening manner consistent with emerging skills and if there are suitable models with whom to identify. All people possess the propensity for these competences. What is required is a propitious environment that stimulates and gratifies their manifestation.

Career accommodations meet some of the person's needs. Consequently, difficulty in the career can interfere with other aspects of living, while other frustrations can be expected to spill over into the career. One must continually refine and reintegrate approaches to accommodate career demands. And, as in all aspects of life, the transformations will be easier when the situation is challenging but not stressful, when the other people involved are coping effectively, and when one's general life situation is not anxious. More specific to career, one's likelihood of success will be higher to the degree that one has been able to learn in school and to perform effectively in past employment, and, therefore, has had minimal occasion to use defense mechanisms in coping with career.

In terms of understanding one's career, the individual wants insight about the needs being gratified through career, the assets and activities enabling him or her to discharge these needs, and both the frustrations that trigger defensiveness and the defense mechanisms typically employed when anxiety is high.

In regard to educational and occupational information, the client seeks to know the need that can be gratified in particular occupations. Bordin, Nachmann, and Segal (1963) proposed examining occupations with regard to the following dimensions: nurturant (feeding and fostering), oral (aggressive–cutting, biting, devouring), manipulative (physical and interpersonal), sensual (sight, sound, touch), anal (acquiring, timing, ordering, hoarding, smearing), genital (erection, penetration, impregnation, producing, exploratory sight, exploratory touch, exploratory sound, flowing-quenching, and exhibiting), and rhythmic movement. Furthermore, they recommend estimating, for each dimension, the degree of involvement of each need-gratifying activity, the mode of acting, the object of action, the male-femaleness of the mode, and the type of effect provided. As examples, they rated accounting on the dimension of nurturant fostering as follows: Accounting has some involvement with nurturant fostering through the activity of giving financial advice and safeguards; the objects of this activity are the financial affairs of the clients, the mode of activity is masculine, and the action permits feeling that one is nurturing. In contrast, they described social work's involvement in nurturant fostering as very important. This involvement occurs through encouragement and protection; the object is the client's growth and health; the mode is feminine; and the effect offered is reaction formation as well as direct experience.

In addition to information about the occupation, the psychodynamically oriented client will want to seek out information about the emotional quality of particular education and work settings, recognizing that impoverished environments are likely to be more frustrating. The client will ask, for example, whether suitable mentoring is available, whether quality performance is given due recognition, and whether expectations are realistic in terms of resources.

Unfortunately, little information has been gathered systematically about the degree to which existing career positions meet psychodynamic needs and rarely do informational publications comment on the mental hygiene of existing career positions. As a result, a counselor following this model will have to guide clients in securing extensive information on their own.

Career Assistance Suggested by Psychodynamic Model

To contribute to the psychodynamic person's career, a counselor can help: a) to bring into consciousness the needs the individual can satisfy through career, and the manner and activities through which one can meet these needs; b) to enter educational and work situations that promote growth; c) to discover and to imitate successful models; d) to anticipate one's changing needs and priorities, and to change career commitments and directions accordingly. This help can be offered through individual or group insight counseling or through directed reading.

The Economic Human Being

Recognizing the scarcity of personal and environmental resources, the economic individual acts, therefore, to be efficient . . . , to maximize benefits and to minimize costs. This person is concerned with ideas such as capital development and depreciation of things and people, elasticity of supply and demand, diminishing marginal utility, expected rates of return, opportunity costs, and profit. Economic person is a planner and decision maker. This individual identifies life goals and reviews internal and external assets available or potentially available for securing those goals, allocates resources for their acquisition, and then reviews success to determine necessary adjustment. This individual expects continually to alter resource allocations, for goals and resource availability change.

Taking an economic perspective reminds a person that a career springs from the need to earn goods and services and requires understanding the operation of a market. The careerist appreciates people's need to identify or even to create a demand for the labor or commodity that they will sell and to package it in order to be able to secure a fair return for it. Furthermore, the orientation helps the person to recognize that one can limit the obligation of career by reducing one's use of goods and services but will increase the obligation through heavy consumption. In addition, the perspective reminds people that they are capable of laboring in a variety of ways; that each way will differ in terms of income and costs on factors such as energy, concentration, time, and preparation; and that some ways of working will yield benefits in addition to purchasing rights for other goods and services.

The economic orientation underscores the value of human and capital development. The economic being recognizes that one's options about working increase when there is income from investments and/or when one has a scarce and refined competence. As a consequence, this person will accept a position to gain access to others, even though it is not the most rewarding in the short term. The perspective, moreover, underscores the importance of learning about career ladders and developing networks of people ready to support one's career progress. Abiding the perspective, one might take a position merely to secure funds to train for a totally unrelated position or might volunteer in an organization to meet/interact with potential contacts. But regardless of the options available, the economically oriented person estimates both the present compatibility of a position with personal goals and its impact on future assets. Developing and maintaining a competitive advantage in the market is important, for it is a major index by which one can gauge one's well being.

The economic perspective heralds the importance of general career skills such as bartering and negotiating, market analysis and merchandizing, identifying growth situations, ongoing information gathering, decision making, planning and forecasting. It proclaims that anyone who will not be a slave must develop entrepreneurial capability. Human dependence on goods and services binds people to work, but our entrepreneurial capability allows us to control many of the parameters of work such as place, kind, and duration. Accepting the responsibility for, and learning how to recognize demand, initiate work contracts, secure appropriate compensation, and keep abreast of changing demands and opportunities is a logical consequence of understanding the economic perspective and should provide the person a definite advantage in our educational-work system.

Information Needs Suggested by an Economic Perspective

The economic person needs extensive information about different methods of achieving goals and their costs and availability. Likewise, the person requires extensive self-knowledge and experiences to discover the personal worth of goals. To obtain these, one can examine how people have lived, are living, and might live; one can identify the skills they develop and judge how costly developing different skills are, based in part on the competition involved in developing those skills; one can try out and reflect on different activities; and finally, one can consider how much satisfaction different degrees of parenting, socializing, civic involvement, and career advancement are likely to provide in order to judge how to allocate available time.

In regard to the characteristics of career positions, the person will want to know about necessary preparation, likely competition and risk, skill and time requirements, constraints (travel, relocations, weekend work), rewards (salary, status, resource access and accumulation), and avenues of advancement afforded. A careerist will ask about the chances of succeeding in different positions or moving along particular paths. As a consequence, the person is likely to consider contingency table data, whereby one can learn the probability of a person with similar grades and characteristics succeeding in a particular training program or firm. Yabroff (1969) has, for instance, developed these tables for high school students. To help establish goals the careerist will also scrutinize the relation of occupations to one another in terms of factors such as prestige, financial return, and hours, and note the merits of different educational programs in terms of access to occupations, costs, and skills developed. Wilms (1975), as a matter of fact, has pressed for legislation requiring proprietary schools to furnish these kinds of data relative to their vocational training.

In terms of self-knowledge relating to career, the economic perspective indicates knowing one's learning capacities, skills and shortcomings, one's relative competitive advantages, both now and after different kinds of learning, the extent of one's desires for purchasable goods and services, status needs, and the dependence of one's self-expression on access to special societal assets. Likewise, the person will want to know about the demands on his or her internal and external assets and about options for satisfaction independent of career. This kind of self-awareness needs to continue to grow and be refined as a person matures and as new options become available.

For economic being, career is a cost-benefit proposition. On the benefit side, it provides opportunity to earn entitlement to desirable goods and services, to an esteemed social status, and to privileged, legitimized access to societal resources such as university libraries, computers, resource people. On the cost side, a career consumes a large proportion of one's waking hours and energy; it requires performances that meet other people's specifications; and it restricts associations, life style, and place of residence.

This person is likely to use a balance-sheet approach to decisions, such as exemplified in Figure 2–5. Note that Janis and Wheeler's (1978) sheet permits considering how a decision affects other people besides the decider. Moreover, as the cost of career satisfactions increases, their marginal utility will lead the person to considering seeking at least some self-expression through noncareer activities. As a consequence, the careerist will seek information about such possibilities as writers like Warnath (1975) have suggested.

Figure 2–5. A Manager's Balance Sheet

The grid lays out the pros and cons of one alternative facing a production manager at a large manufacturing plant who is contemplating a job change: whether or not to remain in his present position. Balance sheets would be filled out for all other alternatives as well—for example, whether to seek a lateral transfer within the company. (The information comes from Decision-Making, *by Irving Janis and Leon Mann.)*

	Positive Anticipations	Negative Anticipations
Tangible gains and losses for *self*	1. Satisfactory pay. 2. Plenty of opportunities to use my skills and competencies. 3. For the present, my status in the organization is okay (but it won't be for long if I am not promoted in the next year).	1. Long hours. 2. Constant time pressures—deadlines too short. 3. Unpleasant paper work. 4. Poor prospects for advancement to a higher-level position. 5. Repeated reorganizations make my work chaotic. 6. Constant disruption from high turnover of other executives I deal with.
Tangible gains and losses for *others*	1. Adequate income for family. 2. Wife and children get special privileges because of my position in the firm.	1. Not enough time free to spend with my family. 2. Wife often has to put up with my irritability when I come home after bad days at work.
Self-approval or self-disapproval	1. This position allows me to make full use of my potentialities. 2. Proud of my achievements. 3. Proud of the competent team I have shaped up. 4. Sense of meaningful accomplishment when I see the products for which we are responsible.	1. Sometimes feel I'm a fool to continue putting up with the unreasonable deadlines and other stupid demands made by the top managers.
Social approval or disapproval	1. Approval of men on my team, who look up to me as their leader and who are good friends. 2. Approval of my superior who is a friend and wants me to stay.	1. Very slight skeptical reaction of my wife—she asks me if I might be better off in a different firm. 2. A friend in another firm who has been wanting to wangle something for me will be disappointed.

SOURCE: Janis, I. and Wheeler, D. Thinking clearly about career choices. *Psychology Today*, 1978, 11(12), 67–76, 121–122. Reprinted from PSYCHOLOGY TODAY MAGAZINE. Copyright © 1978 Ziff-Davis Publishing Company.

Counseling Assistance Suggested by the Economic Model

The economic being model suggests helping people in careers by: 1) aiding them in securing current career information and in integrating it into their planning; 2) providing frameworks such as those in Figure 2–5 to help them plan systematically and to periodically replan; 3) joining them in reviewing career progress in order to pinpoint inefficient use of resources and weigh the utility of new options; 4) providing exercises for clarifying their work and life values and current and likely future assets so that they can determine how much energy to invest in career at particular times in life. Expansion of computer information systems such as the CVIS by the Department of Labor (1976) make this first counselor contribution much easier. The traditional career choice counseling interactions described in Chapter 10 address the second and third types of assistance, and the futuring indicated in the fourth contribution will be more feasible with use of computer counseling systems such as SIGI and the use of new value clarification exercises such as values auctions.

Models of Human Beings and Self-Concept

Now consider these seven models of human beings and their implications for self-concept, the set of images and ideas one has about oneself. Clearly, each model suggests a differently structured self-image. Table 2–2 contains the author's views about the kind of structure that each implies and the kinds of goal criteria each structure would accommodate. One can broaden one's self-awareness by viewing oneself and possible goals from the perspective of each model. Many of the counseling procedures described in later chapters would accommodate a multiple-perspective, self-conceptualization.

To see how the models complement one another and yet overlap, consider the following self-pictures of the same person from several of the perspectives.

Exemplifying the *trait factor perspective,* Sandy is task-oriented and performs academic work ably, enjoys studying the social sciences, dates and socializes frequently, works out regularly in track, enjoys both the opportunity of interacting with customers in a campus store clerkship and the financial independence the job bestows.

From the *sociological perspective,* Sandy is an upper-middle-class, college student with a GPA in the upper 25th percentile who is single and majoring in social science at UCLA and who is also a member of Alpha Gamma Beta, the track team, and a part-time clerk in the ASUCLA bookstore.

In terms of a *scientific perspective,* Sandy realizes the shaping influence that the desire for a professional lifestyle has had and perceives having the desire and talent to actualize self by accepting the challenges of studying social sciences, engaging in organized athletics, especially ones involving track skills, and integrating these with part-time clerking and an active social life.

Table 2–2. The Self-Concept Structures Suggested by the Seven Models of a Human Being

Model	Structure	Goal
Trait factor	Estimates of self on career attributes	Estimates of ideal on career attributes
Intelligent	Estimates of present and predictions about future self in terms of structural constructs used in construing the world, strategies used in striving and coping, and traits and roles	Set of desired discoveries, accomplishments, and expanded capacities and their attendant probabilities of occurring
Developmental	Ratings of past and present achievements of stage-appropriate tasks and estimates of future tasks and probability of mastery	Complete achievement of appropriate stage tasks
Psychodynamic	Set of needs with corresponding behavior repertoires that have satisfied these needs	Spontaneous awareness, acceptance, and resolution of emerging needs
Behavioral	Set of situation memberships and repertoire of behaviors for ascertaining and mastering situation demands, plus a hierarchy of preferred reinforcers	Memberships in environments that operate rationally, afford opportunity for learning, and specify available reinforcers and behavior mastery required
Sociological	Set of institutional memberships with mandatory and optional roles, and set of rights, responsibilities, supports and linkages for performing or learning the roles or altering the role expectations	Set of roles that can be performed with distinction and without strain and that will develop and sustain rights, supports, and responsibilities.
Economic	Set of goals and ledger of assets and liabilities, plus experience-based expectations about particular situations with regard to their effects on particular assets and liabilities	Realizing goals and/or expanding preferred assets, while not depleting valued resources or assets

From the *developmental perspective*, Sandy is a person who has successfully mastered the tasks of career exploration and adolescence and who is now addressing the tasks of career establishment and young adulthood. Predictably, Sandy is in a social science major congruent with measured abilities and interests and is working part time in order to increase self-dependence. At the same time, Sandy is balancing study and work with an active social life and energetic exercise through participating in track. These activities are laying the groundwork for tasks of Erickson's (1963) intimacy stage and a lifelong habit of balanced leisure and physical exercise, which are required for a fully functioning adult.

From the *behavioral perspective*, Sandy is pursuing a social science major, which requires the same scholastic skills and interest in how people live that high school and friends and parents had nurtured. Finding that disciplined study and effort produced success and satisfaction in college as they had in high school encouraged Sandy to continue developing track prowess, while carrying on an active social life, and holding a part-time job. The habits and skills fostered in the quality suburban high school are serving Sandy well in college.

The *psychodynamic* model emphasizes Sandy's needs and repertoire of coping strategies. Growing up in a supportive, stable family and identifying with positive aspects of both parents and then having multiple professional models and succeeding older youngsters to emulate, Sandy developed strong needs for achievement, affiliation, understanding, nurturance, sex, play, and exhibition and low need for abasement, aggression, defendance, and dominance. Concomitantly, in high school and college, Sandy found that parties, peer socializing, intellectual exploration and production, exhibiting self through rhythmic athletic performance were gratifying. The need for autonomy was growing; Sandy secured part-time work with opportunity for socializing. The work added energy for Sandy's balanced, but full schedule. Although succeeding athletically and academically, Sandy limited participation to one sport and declined to accelerate in college by taking extra courses.

In contrast, the economic perspective shows Sandy as a person who numbers among her assets scholastic aptitude, study skills, ability to delay gratification, partial parental support for four or more years of higher education, prowess and liking for social science, track, and sorority/fraternity living. On the liabilities side are restrictions of a very tolerable part-time clerkship and a structured, demanding schedule with high performance expectations. The professional future and enhanced marketability that this promises to provide is an asset.

In examining self-concept, Super (1963) has pointed out that one need not only focus on the scope and content of concepts, but one also can consider the accuracy of different ascriptions, one's satisfaction with the different attributes, one's sense of control over oneself, the stability of one's different factors, and the importance of one's different ascriptions. He termed these dimensions of self-concepts *metadimensions*. *Self-esteem* is the metadimension that has received most research attention. That research has suggested that self-esteem, which refers to how a person evaluates his attributes, mediates success. More specifically, research has found that high-esteem people are more likely to accept challenges involving moderate risk (Korman, 1970), are more likely to excel than are low-esteem equals (Oden, 1968), are more likely to select occupations that build on their strengths and interests (Korman, 1970) and differentiate more sharply among occupations (Healy, Bailey, & Anderson, 1973), are more effective as counselors (Carkhuff, 1971), are more likely to benefit from counseling (Rogers, 1967), and are more likely to choose prestigious occupations (Korman, 1970).

Human Models and the Organization
of this Book

The models described in the preceding sections portray people's connection to work from different yet not completely distinctive perspectives and lead to different emphases in counseling. A balanced counseling approach, of course, requires consideration of all perspectives. Here, the counseling implications of the models are summarized briefly.

The trait factor model leads one to obtain expert appraisal and assistance in matching one's own and educational or occupational traits in order to narrow career choices and then to permit further narrowing based on personal preferences and economic conditions. Once the choice is made or verified, the person makes and carries out a plan for its realization. The process can be repeated several times over the career to deal with changes in oneself and in the world of education and work.

From the intelligent human being model, it follows that the counselor will help the individual develop or verify the understanding of oneself and one's world, expanding one's store of heuristic principles, and improving one's planning skills. Or, the counselor will identify particular obstacles and then indicate, and perhaps provide instruction, to overcome the obstacles in the career passage. Emphasis will be on equipping intelligent people for managing career tasks with their own resources. The counselor will encourage the intelligent person to reflect on the process of self-creation, to evaluate career and life growth, to verify the accuracy of one's guiding principles, and to tolerate different values as one identifies one's own.

Following the developmental being model, a counselor will provide check-ups and instruction on challenges to be expected. The counselor will ascertain the client's developmental stage and relative progress within the stage. When deficits are found, the counselor will prescribe exercises and/or bring to bear resources that have been found helpful to clients in coping with similar tasks. The counselor will help the client develop information-seeking and processing habits that enable one to remain alert to upcoming tasks.

Pursuing a behavioral perspective, the counselor would join the client in a task and environmental analysis to determine the obstacle to performance. Especially important are factors such as clarity of expectations, arrangement of rewards, availability of models and instruction, client's skills, and client's anxiety level. If anxiety is excessive, the counselor would prescribe anxiety reduction. Once the obstacle and probable sustaining influence have been identified, the counselor would either consult with those controlling the environment or arrange a sequence of activities by which the client could overcome or bypass the obstacle. Some behaviorists, such as Krumboltz and Thoresen (1976), would, as part of the process, teach the client how to proceed in this fashion without the counselor when future obstacles arise.

Following a sociological model, the counselor would determine whether the client is having difficulty determining appropriate role behaviors or moving among positions. To improve role behaviors, the counselor would work with the client individually, or in collaboration with others, to identify and practice correct role behavior, using techniques such as role play and role reversal. The counselor would recruit and secure models and sponsors for the client, or arrange assignments to a special learning situation, such as a work-study or subsidized on-the-job program, or a special training program, such as those used in rehabilitation of veterans. In the latter case, the counselor might also provide assistance in learning about options. Perhaps the counselor would refer the client to reading materials such as Lovejoy's *College Guide*, or to a testing program geared to identify educational options such as the *ACT* in order to pinpoint alternatives, or to the *USES* job bank to locate possible jobs. On the other hand, for a job seeker, the counselor might provide placement counseling; for a student searching for a college, college advisement counseling. Turning to institutional correction, the counselor would move to create policy, to provide models and sponsors, and to establish linkages between school and work roles.

Following a psychodynamic model, the counselor would first ascertain the client's overall available energy, the person's insight about personal actions, and the typical manner of coping with career difficulty. If the career impasse appeared to manifest more widespread personality dysfunction or if the client were unaware of the significance of his or her actions, the counselor would recommend psychotherapy. If reasonable overall personality integration existed, the counselor would help the client to generate and to implement strategies for resolving the difficulty, without major personal reintegration (Hummel, 1962).

Operating from an economic model, the counselor will assist the client in evaluating the allocations of time and energy in terms of professed career and life goals. Then the counselor will guide the client in securing and interpreting information and in adjusting goals or reallocating resources to enable the desired achievement.

This book organizes counseling methods primarily from the intelligent and developmental being perspectives; that is, it presents methods as teaching strategies for performing tasks associated with a particular stage. As will become clearer in Chapter 5, the counseling methods tend to be components of counseling procedures, since most lack both the diagnostic and evaluation components that would make them full methods. (Chapter 5 describes a diagnostic and an evaluation component that can be used to make the methods complete procedures.) Although some of the methods clearly presume a particular model, all can be encompassed in a rational or developmental person perspective. Of course, the counselor employing a particular method needs to remember the model it supports, in order to modify the method, if needed, to include concepts and principles about self and career that the underlying model does not consider. For example, career problem-solving that follows the behavioral or developmental being model may draw excessive client energies or resources to a career task that would imbalance other life commitments. This problem may not be apparent unless the counselor is cognizant of the tenets the psychodynamic and economic models posit about possible unconscious motivations and the importance of balanced resource allocation, respectively. Or a behaviorist guiding a client through problem solving might not be concerned with the client's understanding or interpretation of the approach. On the other hand, since each model also portrays a facet of human beings not emphasized in the others, a counselor using an intelligent being model logically would acquaint clients with all the models.

Characteristics Related to Career

3

This chapter reviews the definitions and measurement of the major attributes linked to careers and comments on their implications for career development and counseling. "Know thyself" is an injunction nearly as old as speech itself. Yet what to know and how to learn it are questions that people ponder in every era.

Career Attributes

Vocational psychologists have found that certain human attributes relate to the pursuit and performance of particular occupations. Use of this knowledge has improved selection of trainees and workers in terms of training costs and time. In terms of counseling, directing people to occupations and training programs consistent with their measured attributes has improved their career achievement somewhat (Williamson & Bordin, 1940; Campbell, 1963), although client benefits are not as extensive as selector benefits (Goldman, 1967).

Counselors long have believed that knowing oneself in terms of career-relevant attributes would facilitate career choice (Parsons, 1909; Williamson, 1939). And one of the most sought and most expected outcomes of career counseling has been increased self-awareness in terms of career attributes (Myers, 1971). However, this author is not aware of a study that shows that increasing self-understanding per se has led to an improved career, even though there is undeniable evidence that people's adult occupational choices are predictable by career attributes assessed in high school or early adulthood (Flanagan, Tiedeman, Willis, McLaughlin, 1973; Thorndike & Hagen, 1959).

Although most personality theorists endorse increasing self-understanding, for many years George Kelly (1955) was one of the few prominent personality theorists who explicated a model of how self-knowledge developed and affected behavior. More recently, attribution theorists such as Weiner (1972) and Meichenbaum (1975) have focused on the process and consequences of self-attributions. Although much remains to be learned, already it is clear that selected self-characteristics can have powerful positive or negative consequences for a person.

Research repeatedly shows that individuals often do not describe themselves on particular attributes in the same manner that a test or inventory does (Super & Crites, 1962). Sherwood (1966) has shown that describing the attribute carefully for a person increases the correspondence between a self-estimate and "objective" measure, but clearly the description does not make them congruent. Since most of the research that relates attributes to the pursuit and performance of an occupation is based on "objectively" measured attributes, an individual must know his or her objective score in order to use that information. Nevertheless, the "objective" score represents only one perspective of reality, and, at times, that perspective has not been as predictive of career behavior as the person's subjective estimate of personal attributes (Holland, 1976b).

Before proceeding to consider career-relevant psychological and demographic attributes, the reader should recall that their "objectivity" is not usually similar to the objectivity of height, weight, or blood type. Rather, the measures of these constructs do not have comparable reliability, and they refer to domains of behaviors or experiences about which there are disagreements among experts. Moreover, measures of these constructs sample the domains unevenly so that one measure of a construct will often correlate only moderately with another measure of the same construct. Also, realize that the psychological attributes are, by construction, factors, designed to explain only part of the most performances. For example, a verbal aptitude score is designed to contribute to predictions about performance in activities such as reading comprehension, but it is expected that other factors, such as quality of instruction and motivation, will combine with I.Q. in producing actual performance. Other potential self attributions described in Chapter 2, such as a series of implemented plans and solved problems that scientific people create for construing themselves, are more holistic. They involve a Gestalt of interactions and predict future planning and problem solving in similar contexts directly, without having to be combined with other factors. Logically, one could portray occupations as requiring solutions for predictable sets of problems, and then a careerist could choose the most compatible set of problems rather than selecting the most compatible set of factors. Extrapolating from the fact that past school performance is the best predictor of future performance, decisions based on the fit of holistic experiences might be as, or more, effective than those based on the fit of trait factors. Indeed, writers such as Bolles (1974) are following this reasoning in urging people, especially women, to expand their occupational options by remembering the problems they have solved and the scenarios they have mastered, rather than by attending slavishly to the factors in job specifications. For example, the homemaker with an R.N., who is considering sales occupations, should not only recall her assertiveness ratings, grades in speech courses, and similarity to sales professionals as indicated by her *Strong-Campbell Interest Inventory*, but she should also include her effectiveness and satisfaction with activities such as soliciting advertisers for her college paper and launching a scout troop and sustaining parent commitment to it.

At the same time, the widespread use of factors in human language suggests that our self-concepts are at least partially organized as a set of factors. Yet, clearly we conceptualize ourselves in other ways, too. Consequently, even though the major career-choice counseling procedures now used (Chapter 10) reduce to trait-factor models, a counselor will want to avoid using only a factors structure to guide a client's career choice making.

Abilities

Want ads indicate clearly that ability is a prime consideration in obtaining a job. An *ability* can be defined as the capacity to perform successfully. The term *ability* may refer to the performance of one task, typing, or it can designate a capacity to perform a series of complex tasks, as in computer programming. Abilities are products of experience and natural endowment (termed an *aptitude* for one task). Their emergence depends on maturation, on mastery of requisite simpler skills, and on an environment that is challenging and affords opportunity for learning and practice of the elements of the ability.

A person's experience in developing abilities is very important. Success creates an attitude of self-confidence, which encourages the person to accept more challenges and develop new abilities. In contrast, consistent failure produces fear of new challenges, consequently diminishing the person's capacity far beyond the loss of the unmastered abilities (Korman, 1970).

Abilities are dynamic; they grow or decline with exercise. Most people can strengthen their abilities by working systematically to do so. They can observe effective models and obtain clear instructions about what the task performance involves; they can obtain feedback on performance, continuing what they are doing properly and correcting their errors; and then they can practice. Surprisingly, the NVGA–AMEG (National Vocational Guidance Association–Association for Measurement and Evaluation in Guidance) Commission on National Assessment of Career and Occupational Development concluded that many adolescents and some adults do not apply these principles to improve their abilities (Aubrey, 1977; Mitchell, 1977; Westbrook, 1977).

All people have many similar abilities. For most human abilities, a range of performance can be established, and the distribution of performance will approximate a normal distribution. On such a distribution, therefore, some people score high, some low, most average. High and low, of course, are relative terms, indicating the person's standing compared to others. For many occupations, the performance standard is below the median on particular ability continuums. In other words, most occupational duties can be performed adequately by people who rank lower than most people in the requisite ability. This paradox occurs because ability distributions derive from norm-referenced tests, designed to distinguish people rather than to indicate the percentage of the tasks comprising the ability a person can perform. An individual may be able to do the tasks but may take longer than others; therefore, he or she will rank lower on the ability. The more desirable occupations, of course, require people on the high end of the ability continuum. Even for these occupations, however, the amount of ability required for entry and continuation in the occupation will be a function of worker supply and demand.

People acquire abilities by doing. Schooling and other kinds of training, such as apprenticeship and do-it-yourself manuals, offer formal direction in acquiring skills; but many informal learning situations, such as family chores, hobbies, travel, working itself, and playing, enable a person to acquire and to expand abilities. Although human learning capacity appears to be maximum from the mid-teens to mid-twenties, research indicates considerable learning capacity before and after those years. Indeed, the aged retain great capacity until death (Knox, 1978).

Of course, like interest, value, need, and personality, ability is a concept used to organize perceptions. The concept actually embodies a theory of what causes particular performance. One achieves success in a task, and observers ascribe to that person the capacity to do the task, to have the ability. Implicitly, they affirm that it is his or her acting— a series of internally initiated operations—rather than externally based operations, that produced achievement. The performance and achievement are visible, but ability can only be inferred.

Those who examine abilities group together tasks with similar requirements, such as adding, subtracting, dividing, and multiplying one-, two-, three-digit numbers, and ascertain whether persons who can do some of these tasks can do most of them. A label for the commonality of these achievements is designated; in the example, computational ability. The ascription is arbitrary, but the operations are manifest. The value of the ascriptions depends on their contribution to comprehension of the world and transmission of that understanding; in other words, like any theory, their utility is not judged on the basis of their inherent truth or falseness (Hall & Lindzey, 1970).

The almost limitless number of human abilities necessitates categorization, but there is no universal taxonomy. Laymen tend to think of abilities in terms of broad school subjects, leisure activity groupings, and occupational groupings such as math ability, art ability, science ability, selling ability, tennis ability, social ability, engineering ability, or mechanical ability. These categories facilitate communication because most adults have a general awareness of the subject or occupation; but the categories are not mutually exclusive, nor is there agreement about the specific elements that constitute one category. Math ability, for instance, may simply mean capacity to balance a checkbook or it may refer to the ability to derive calculus theorems.

Aptitude

Some experts use *aptitudes* and *worker functions* as the basis for grouping abilities in order to achieve fewer categories and to increase reliability and precision. As noted above, an *aptitude* refers to the inherited, innate component of ability. An aptitude signifies a person's potential for acquiring an ability. Aptitudes cannot be measured directly because they mature over time as a function of experience. Instead, professionals infer a given aptitude from samples of a person's performance on a range of tasks deemed to require that aptitude. Since performance on such tasks is influenced by experience, the aptitude attributed to the performance is recognized as an estimate. Unfortunately, no indisputable method of estimating how much of the resulting aptitude score is due to aptitude and how much is due to experience yet exists.

A widely used aptitude classification is the *General Aptitude Test Battery* (USES, 1958) of the United States Employment Service. The eleven aptitudes of that classification are listed in Table 3–1. Those aptitudes represent an arbitrary judgment of qualities that relate to the capacity to learn a broad range of occupational duties. Aptitudes such as music and art are not included in the *GATB* because these qualities relate directly to only a few occupations.

Table 3–1. Aptitudes of the General Aptitude Test Battery

Specific capacities and abilities required of an individual in order to learn or perform adequately a task or job duty.

G	INTELLIGENCE: General learning ability. The ability to "catch on" or understand instructions and underlying principles. Ability to reason and make judgments. Closely related to doing well in school.
V	VERBAL: Ability to understand meanings of words and ideas associated with them, and to use them effectively. To comprehend language, to understand relationships between words, and to understand meanings of whole sentences and paragraphs. To present information or ideas clearly.
N	NUMERICAL: Ability to perform arithmetic operations quickly and accurately.
S	SPATIAL: Ability to comprehend forms in space and understand relationships of plane and solid objects. May be used in such tasks as blueprint reading and in solving geometry problems. Frequently described as the ability to "visualize" objects of two or three dimensions, or to think visually of geometric forms.
P	FORM PERCEPTION: Ability to perceive pertinent detail in objects or in pictorial or graphic material; To make visual comparisons and discriminations and see slight differences in shapes and shadings of figures and widths and lengths of lines.

Table 3–1. (*Continued*)

Q	CLERICAL PERCEPTION: Ability to perceive pertinent detail in verbal or tabular material. To observe differences in copy, to proofread words and numbers, and to avoid perceptual errors in arithmetic computation.
K	MOTOR COORDINATION: Ability to coordinate eyes and hands or fingers rapidly and accurately in making precise movements with speed. Ability to make a movement response accurately and quickly.
F	FINGER DEXTERITY: Ability to move the fingers and manipulate small objects with the fingers rapidly or accurately.
M	MANUAL DEXTERITY: Ability to move the hands easily and skillfully. To work with the hands in placing and turning motions.
E	EYE-HAND-FOOT COORDINATION: Ability to move the hand and foot co-ordinately with each other in accordance with visual stimuli.
C	COLOR DISCRIMINATION: Ability to perceive or recognize similarities or differences in colors, or in shades or other values of the same color; to identify a particular color, or to recognize harmonious or contrasting color combinations, or to match colors accurately.

Explanation of Levels

The digits indicate how much of each aptitude the job requires for satisfactory (average) performance. The average requirements, rather than maximum or minimum, are cited. The amount required is expressed in terms of equivalent amounts possessed by segments of the general working population.

The following scale is used:

1   The top 10 percent of the population. This segment of the population possesses an extremely high degree of the aptitude.

2   The highest third exclusive of the top 10 percent of the population. This segment of the population possesses an above average or high degree of the aptitude.

3   The middle third of the population. This segment of ·the population possesses a medium degree of the aptitude, ranging from slightly below to slightly above average.

4   The lowest third exclusive of the bottom 10 percent of the population. This segment of the population possesses a below average or low degree of the aptitude.

5   The lowest 10 percent of the population. This segment of the population possesses a negligible degree of the aptitude.

Significant Aptitudes

Certain aptitudes appear in boldface type on the qualifications profiles for the worker trait groups. These aptitudes are considered to be occupationally significant for the specific group; i.e., essential for average successful job performance. All boldface aptitudes are not necessarily required of a worker for each individual job within a worker trait group, but some combination of them is essential in every case.

SOURCE: *The Dictionary of Occupational Titles* (Vol. II) (3rd ed.). Washington, D.C.: U.S. Government Printing Office, 1965. P. 653.

Table 3–2. Work Functions Used to Classify Occupations in
Dictionary of Occupational Titles

A job's relationship to Data, People and Things can be expressed in terms of the lowest numbered function in each sequence. These functions taken together indicate the total level of complexity at which the worker performs. The fourth, fifth and sixth digits of the occupational code numbers reflect relationships to Data, People and Things, respectively. These digits express a job's relationship to Data, People and Things by identifying the highest appropriate function in each listing as reflected by the following table:

DATA (4th digit)	PEOPLE (5th digit)	THINGS (6th digit)
0 Synthesizing	0 Mentoring	0 Setting-Up
1 Coordinating	1 Negotiating	1 Precision Working
2 Analyzing	2 Instructing	2 Operating-Controlling
3 Compiling	3 Supervising	3 Driving-Operating
4 Computing	4 Diverting	4 Manipulating
5 Copying	5 Persuading	5 Tending
6 Comparing	6 Speaking-Signaling	6 Feeding-Offbearing
	7 Serving	7 Handling
	8 Taking Instructions-Helping	

SOURCE: U.S. Department of Labor, *The Dictionary of Occupational Titles* (4th ed.). Washington, D.C.: U.S. Government Printing Office, 1977, p. 1369.

The U.S. Employment Service also has defined the Major Worker Function Classification, which consists of the twenty-four worker actions in Table 3–2. These functions are organized under the categories of "People," "Data," and "Things," to indicate that each action can be conceptualized as concerned primarily with one of the three domains.

Other aptitude classifications include those provided by the *Differential Aptitude Test (DAT)* and by Guilford (1967). The *DAT* classification, which parallels the *GATB*, includes verbal reasoning, numerical reasoning, abstract reasoning, space relations, mechanical reasoning, clerical speed and accuracy, spelling, language usage, and general intelligence. Guilford (1967) presented a theory of intelligence that delineated four kinds of intellectual content, five operations, and six products. The cube in Figure 3–1 is Guilford's portrayal of intelligence. Theoretically, one should be able to devise a distinctive intellectual exercise for every cell of the cube.

Intelligence

Intelligence or scholastic aptitude is the one factor reflecting experience and aptitude that repeatedly predicts achievement in academic and occupational training (Anastasi, 1976; Cronbach, 1970; Stewart, 1947), in occupational level attained (Thorndike & Hagen, 1959; U.S. Department of Labor, 1965), and, more recently, in overall career maturity

Figure 3–1. Model of the Structure of Intellect

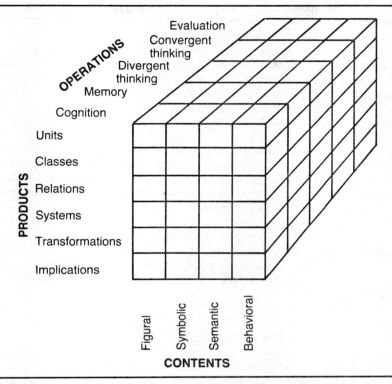

SOURCE: J. P. Guilford. *The nature of human intelligence*, p. 63. New York: McGraw-Hill, 1967. Reprinted by permission of the publisher.

(Super, Kowalski, & Gotkin, 1969; Crites, 1973). In theory, intelligence is the ability to comprehend, to make judgments, to maintain a mental set, and to perceive and correct errors (Binet & Simon, 1908). It is a person's general learning and adaptability capacity. Construct validity studies indicate that intelligence scores relate to succeeding and persevering in school and to entering and pursuing prestigious occupations. Although intelligence and scholastic aptitude are not always equated, some theorists propose that intelligence is a more general learning aptitude than scholastic aptitude; each is the operational ability to solve problems by manipulating verbal, numerical, and spatial configurations. These problems include identifying synonyms, answering questions about a reading passage, anagrams, computation, counting blocks, mathematical word problems, and determining three-dimensional figures from two-dimensional drawings.

Intelligence has been, and continues to be, important in setting goals and in obtaining access to educational and occupational opportunities. Logically, whether intelligence is regarded as general learning capacity (Spearman, 1927) or as the distinctive verbal and numerical reasoning aptitudes (Thurstone, 1938) that are the mainstays of formal instruction, one's intelligence needs to be weighed when deciding on a particular career option. Not surprisingly, therefore, both the level of a child's occupational aspirations and the career advice received are related to intelligence. Even clients applying to the Veterans Administration or to a state rehabilitation agency must surpass particular cutoffs on intelligence tests in order to receive benefits for skilled and professional training programs. Furthermore, civil service and many private sector corporations still use intelligence tests to select candidates for higher-level occupations. For example, the *PATH* test, which is a form of intelligence test, is the general screening instrument of the federal government for most managerial and administrative entry positions.

Although intelligence is often a factor in securing entry to an occupation, workers who excel in the occupation itself generally do not have significantly higher intelligence scores than others in their occupation (Ghiselli, 1966; Thorndike & Hagen, 1959). Nevertheless, persons who move to higher-level occupations do have higher intelligence than those who do not move; for example, accountants who become treasurers, engineers who earn Ph.D.s, and managers who become corporate officers. Evidently, intelligence gives an edge in securing additional training and perhaps in acquiring the broader perspective needed for higher-level management.

Intelligence Testing is Controversial

With the growing recognition that the tests are biased against minorities and possibly against women, using intelligence test scores for selection and even for guidance has become controversial. In the employment arena, the *Griggs vs. Duke Power* 1971 Supreme Court ruling declared that it is unconstitutional to base selection for an occupation on a test unless the skills assessed by the test are those skills used directly in the job. More recently, court decisions have declared that even where tests relate to job skills, their use must be restricted if a minority group is expected to score considerably lower on the test. In the educational arena, criticism of such tests is increasing because many minority persons are put at a disadvantage by the intrinsic character of the tests. When a minority person's scores are referenced to the total applicant sample, the ensuing ranking is not as accurate a predictor of academic performance as is a white applicant's ranking predictive of performance. The accuracy of prediction increases for blacks when they are compared only with black's, but using the equations from these comparisons would often lead to setting lower cutoff scores for blacks than for whites and possibly lead to admission quotas. These quotas appear unacceptable under the 1978 Supreme Court ruling on *Bakke vs. Regents of the University of California*. Doubtlessly, the notion of lower scores would also be difficult to promote.

A second difficulty with intelligence scores and even with past academic grades as selection criteria arises from the realization that above a cutoff score, these scores and grades add little in predicting achievement in professional schools, especially in graduate, law, and medical schools. Observers such as Ellett (1980), therefore, have suggested that applicants above a cutoff score and below the very top end of the distribution be selected on the basis of a lottery rather than according to their exact rank. Since slightly higher test scores and grades would not give advantage, the effects of wealth and cultural advantage would then be reduced in awarding opportunities.

At the other end of the educational spectrum, recent court decisions have precluded assigning minority youngsters to remedial education programs on the basis of I.Q. tests alone. Again, the courts have noted that, regardless of their true ability, persons outside the mainstream culture are disadvantaged by these tests. Moreover, the courts recognize that assignment to such remedial programs labels a person in a manner that often affects one adversely.

Intelligence and Education

Intelligence is considered a relatively stable ability that we inherit (Torrance, 1975). Correlations of intelligence scores across time are typically high, and testing specialists interpret variations in scores over time as being due to test unreliability rather than to instability in the capacity (Anastasi, 1976). Injury, drug usage, or environmental deprivation, of course, retards intelligence and may well prevent its expression. On the other hand, Anastasi (1976) reported that positive family environments may bolster I.Q.

In general, education is designed to increase intelligence. But since I.Q. or scholastic aptitude scores are normative rather than criterion-referenced measures, one's intelligence may expand with age and schooling; but most people's position relative to peers with comparable schooling is unlikely to change appreciably. Research consistently shows that intelligence scores correlate with amount of schooling (Anastasi, 1976), but these correlational data do not indicate whether schooling per se increases intelligence or whether the more intelligent seek more schooling. The new statistical procedure of *PATH* analysis may be able to clarify this question in the future.

On the other hand, findings such as those of Tuddenham (1948) that World War II military conscripts scored substantially higher on I.Q. tests than did World War I conscripts provide strong support for the inference that schooling has increased intelligence, since the average World War II soldier had completed several more years of schooling. Whether the differential scores or signs of intelligence actually reflect increased intellectual capacity, of course, can be argued.

Educators have argued, and will continue to argue, about the kinds of education most effective in expanding intelligence. Volumes have been devoted to the issue, but still there is no consensus. The reader concerned with this question should consult Guilford (1967) and Hunt (1961).

Two issues about intelligence testing, however, often concern the career counselor and are treated here briefly. First is the issue of declining intelligence or scholastic aptitude scores. Clearly, high school students' average scores on the standardized tests of scholastic aptitude (Educational Testing Service, 1979) have been declining since 1964. One may argue that these declines are due to the fact that a larger percentage of students are taking the tests, so that more marginal performers now in the sample pool cause the means to decline. Likewise, a larger percentage of the test pool is now from outside the mainstream culture, since mainstream families are not producing proportionately as many children as those outside the mainstream. Since those outside the mainstream are at a disadvantage on the scholastic aptitude tests, larger proportions of such examinees reduce the test score means.

Certainly these facts explain some of the decline, but they do not refute the conclusion that the current generation of college students is, on the average, not as well equipped for college work as the preceding one. Since 1964, the decline in scholastic aptitude test scores is nearly half a standard deviation. If the scores do correspond to capacity for intellectual learning, then that decline shows that the generation now leaving high school does not have as great a capacity to learn as the preceding generation had when graduating from high school in the 1950s and early 1960s.

The second issue concerns elevating scores on intelligence tests or scholastic aptitude tests through special preparation. Clearly, people can be educated to be more "test wise." At least for less carefully designed tests, such sophistication can raise scores (Chase, 1978). Examples of "test-wise" strategies are these:

1. Move expeditiously through items you know, deferring difficult items until you have completed items you know.
2. For multiple choice items, guess wisely by eliminating foils that are clearly wrong and then estimate your chance of a correct answer. If it exceeds the test penalty for guessing, guess.
3. To eliminate foils in a multiple choice exam that requires one correct answer, ascertain if two foils are equivalent and then eliminate both.
4. Through prestudy of the test, determine the type of foils. For example, in vocabulary tests, foils often are words that are spelled like the correct word but have different meanings. Reject these unless you are sure what they mean.

Part of test wiseness, no doubt, is a "set" to deal expeditiously with the kind of questions on the test, whether anagrams or reading passages. In implicit recognition of the facts that previous experience with the kind of question on the test and a "set" to answer expeditiously also improve scores, large testing corporations such as the Educational Testing Service and the American Council on Education urge examinees to practice sample questions before taking the test. Similarly, many counselors recommend that students complete the *Preliminary Scholastic Aptitude Test (PSAT)* in their second or third years of high school in order to become familiar with the testing format.

Similarly, multiple studies support the proposition that reducing an examinee's anxiety about taking a test and teaching study skills improves performance on the test (Anton, 1976). Indeed, many colleges now routinely offer such treatments through their counseling centers. This type of counseling is presented in Chapter 9 as one career counseling technique. Thus careful preparation does appear to be able to improve somewhat the typical person's performance on an I.Q. test.

Career Skills

Knowledge of a person's aptitudes and work function skills is very useful in suggesting suitable occupations and training programs for exploration. Logically, a person will not succeed in an occupation without a minimum of the requisite aptitudes and work function abilities. Yet, successful creation and development of a career also requires self-management, a sense of agency, information acquisition and processing skills, decision making, interpersonal cooperation, and the abilities to be at work on time and to complete work when expected. These capabilities or habits are requisite in all careers and are therefore labeled career skills. Typically, these career skills are omitted from discussions of abilities or aptitudes; but Oetting and Miller (1977) have said, in describing experiences with hardcore unemployed, that their absence prevents persons from securing employment.

Recently, Fine (1974), a pioneer in job classification, has emphasized the importance of these habits. He suggested that work requires three types of skills: functional, specific content, and adaptive. Functional skills are competencies that enable one to relate to things, data, and people in some combination according to personal preference and, to some degree of complexity, according to abilities. Examples are operating machines or supervising people. Specific content skills, in contrast, refer to competencies that permit "an individual to perform a specific job according to the standards set by the market." An example would be operating an IBM Selectric at 90 wpm. Finally, adaptive skills are the capacities to manage the demands for conformity or change in relation to the physical, interpersonal, and organizational arrangements and conditions on which a job exists. The latter appear to be the career skills discussed above; according to Fine, they are the most crucial skills for career success.

Limited observation suggests that general career skills develop in the same manner as other abilities; that is, these skills grow when they are expected to be learned and when modeled correctly and reinforced appropriately. Yet they appear to have an attitude component and are sometimes called work habits (Shartle, 1959). Today, many proponents of career education, who do not believe general career skills are being developed as effectively as they might be in the school systems, are seeking changes in the educational curriculum to develop these skills.

Ability Measurement

Ability is measured primarily by school grades, paper-pencil tests, and ratings of performance on tasks. Scores from paper-pencil tests and school grades are the prime indices of ability considered in the admission of students to postsecondary colleges and training programs, in the selection and assignment of recruits and inductees in the Armed Forces, and in the hiring of employees for entry positions. As employees advance in industry and even in civil service, much greater weight is given to supervisors' ratings or to evaluations of performance in preceding jobs. Occasionally, in admitting students and more often in hiring and promoting employees, abilities are also measured by interview. The interview assessment, however, is notoriously unreliable and of dubious validity. Because of its potential for bias, applications of the Supreme Court decision (*Griggs* vs. *Duke Power,* 1971) against discriminatory selection practices are likely to limit use of the interview as an ability assessment device in the future.

Grades. The manner in which abilities are assessed is likely to leave many people with an unclear idea about their abilities. School grades often lack objectivity and are not comparable from school to school. They are not even comparable among teachers within a school. Frequently, one's grade is based on the teacher's subjective estimate of the student's mastery of the subject matter compared with that of classmates. Most teachers construct and administer tests to aid in grading, but rarely are these tests criterion referenced. Consequently, even though test grades are expressed in percentages, a particular grade is not likely to mean that a student has mastered that percentage of the subject matter. Rather, the grade means only that the student has answered correctly that proportion of test items on the test, a particular set of items that has some unknown amount of bias in it.

Similarly, the class or cohort ranking is not readily interpretable. This ranking is based on grades of confused meaning and on who happens to be in the class. Perhaps the best indicator of whether one is gaining mastery of a subject or series of subjects, therefore, is whether one is able to progress in the subject. Not surprisingly, grades have related minimally, if at all, to occupational achievement (Thorndike & Hagen, 1959; Ghiselli, 1966). But amount of education completed satisfactorily has related consistently to occupational status achieved (Stewart, 1947; Thorndike & Hagen, 1959).

Tests. Standardized paper-pencil tests are more reliable measures of ability, and the basis of their scores is defined. They provide useful estimates about how a person's ability compares with the ability of others. Generally, these are norm-referenced tests, designed to provide an estimate of how a person compares to others with regard to the particular ability. They do not indicate how much of the ability the person has mastered as a criterion-referenced test would. Many of the norm-referenced tests sample specified domains, and criterion-referenced tests could be developed from the item pools. For a criterion-referenced test, however, items would be selected to span the domain rather than to provide a normal distribution.

Test scores are only estimates. First, a test is a sample of items from a larger domain of items so that some error is likely in estimating the ability because all facets of it have not been examined. Secondly, test items are frequently signs of the ability rather than direct samples of the ability. For example, a comprehension test purporting to measure the effectiveness of a person's reading will present a paragraph followed by a set of multiple-choice questions. The number of the examinee's correct responses is the test's estimate of reading ability. The test, however, does not ask the examinee to tell what was understood in the reading; instead, it asks the test taker to select one of four or five possible answers to particular questions. These questions and answers limit what the examinee can express as the understanding, and they cue the reading of the passage. Although the examinee's performance on the questions probably correlates highly with the comprehension of the passage, the task is not the same as understanding the passage. Since the task is only an approximation, some error in extrapolating from the simulation to the real situation is likely. The test, therefore, is called a sign test, in contrast to a work sample test, which samples actual performance. A work sample reading comprehension test might involve an examinee reading a passage on carburator repair and then describing the steps in his or her own words.

There are many ability and aptitude tests. Reviews and bibliography of the major ones appear in the eight *Mental Measurement* yearbooks edited by O. K. Buros (1978). Although testing is often an important element of career counseling, it is beyond the scope of this work to treat the myriad of technical details in test development, administration, and interpretation. Basic texts on ability and aptitude tests include: Anastasi, A., *Psychological Testing;* Cronbach, L. G., *Essentials of Psychological Testing;* Goldman, L., *Using Tests in Counseling;* and Super, D. E., and Crites, J. O., *Appraising Vocational Fitness.*

Ratings. Ratings are the third major assessment device. Like grades and tests, they are problematic. At first glance, ratings seem easy: one only has to decide which trait to rate and then to think about what the person is like in terms of that trait. Unfortunately, this attitude has prevented ratings from realizing their potential in clarifying abilities.

Ratings have great promise because they are easy to construct, to use, and to understand. Proper use, however, requires recognition that they are judgments about observations and that certain principles must be followed to increase the accuracy of these observations and to minimize error. Table 3–3 presents principles for constructing and conducting effective ratings.

Table 3–3. Rules for Improving Self-Ratings

1. Define the attribute to be rated in concrete, observable terms and specify the contexts in which you manifest and can observe it.

2. Anchor the rating scale with examples illustrating different degrees of the attribute.

3. Compare your ratings with those of other observers, and discuss agreements and disagreements to understand better the attribute and context.

4. Distinguish normative from criterion comparisons; that is, be explicit about whether you are comparing yourself to a particular population or are judging your performance according to standard criterion, such as percentage of vocabulary words you can define or percentage of carburetor problems you can solve.

5. When you are comparing yourself to some population, specify the population and identify the bases of your estimate of their distribution on the attribute you are rating. Remember that a general population tends to have a normal distribution, whereas special groups often have skewed distributions. For a high-achiever group, for instance, more than half will score above the mean, and the scores above the median will be more spread out because you are sampling the extremes of a normal distribution.

6. When comparing yourself against a criterion of performance, establish the components of the criterion and rate yourself on the subcomponents in proportion to their representation in the criterion. For example, if the criterion is the ability to do computations with counting numbers or positive integers, take proportionate samples of multiplication, addition, subtraction, and division.

7. Practice using the rating scale in a situation as close to the rating context as possible in order to be comfortable using the instrument. That will give you more time to focus on the attribute. If feasible compare your ratings with an expert or standardized rating. For example, counselors might rate taped counseling films for rater training and compare their ratings with the standard before rating themselves.

8. Limit observation to a manageable number of attributes. Before observing, establish the number of attributes you can accurately monitor in the situation.

9. Record ratings during the observation or as soon as possible thereafter.

10. Observe and rate the attribute in the various situations where it is manifest, preferably selecting the contexts randomly.

11. Position yourself to observe and to rate with minimal distraction, and rate yourself when you are calm and feeling comfortable.

12. Periodically verify that your ratings continue to be accurate by comparing them with those of independent observers.

13. Discard observations obtained under extremes, such as unusual ratee stress or situation distraction, unless you are trying to predict behavior under such extremes.

Although many rating forms exist, few have been standardized or validated. An exception is the set of ratings scales produced by Dawis and his colleagues (1964) in the Minnesota Rehabilitation Project. Manuals describe the dimensions to be rated and report the studies that validate the ratings.

Much counseling activity and evaluation relies on self-ratings. Few reports of these practices, however, indicate that clients are assisted in making more accurate ratings. Research by Sherwood (1966), showing that agreeing on terms significantly increases correlation between self-ratings and inventory score, and research by Healy (1971), showing that instructions influence rating, indicates that counselors need to provide instructions before having clients undertake ratings. Especially, one would think that instruction on rating would be an important prelude to discovering self through depth introspection.

Interests

Everyone likes some activities better than others, and all are more curious about some things than about others. These preferences act as motivators and reinforcers. Labeling one's preferences permits predictions about that person. A preference cultivated during leisure time or during working is called an *interest*. Attributing an "interest" to a person summarizes information about the person and implicitly makes assumptions about his or her future behavior.

Since interests act as motivators and reinforcers, they are very important in careers. They should be fun to discover and develop. Surprisingly, however, little research has been done in actually guiding people to discover and to develop interests. Most work has focused on studies of interest inventories, which represent only one way of discovering interests. Although empirical evidence is minimal, most assume one can discover interests by:

1. Trying out a series of activities under conditions that provide positive regard, appropriate instruction, proper materials and equipment, constructive feedback, and adequate opportunity for practice. The activities that prove enjoyable are the ones likely to become interests.

2. Reviewing past activities in order to pinpoint those that were enjoyable and have been repeated.

3. Observing activities of immediate relatives and persons one admires to isolate those activities one wishes to imitate. Activities that others like us enjoy may well be enjoyable for us also.

4. Reviewing a broad set of activities to identify those that are appealing. The activities in the survey or inventory are generally clustered on empirical or logical grounds, and the clusters with a high percentage of preferences are likely to be potential interest areas. Of course, the meaning of a high interest on such an inventory will depend on the person's familiarity with the range of activities. The more one has sampled the activities under conditions described in #1 above, the more one's interest scores should accurately represent one's interests.

Interest expansion and cultivation have been studied only minimally. Yet clinical observation suggests that an activity is more likely to become an interest if the person:

1. Is properly equipped when undertaking the activity
2. Receives proper instruction and feedback
3. Undertakes the activity under pleasant circumstances
4. Sees others rewarded for doing it
5. Is helped to recognize the challenge in the activity
6. Is aided to learn the activity at a pace commensurate with ability
7. Has time to recognize and to feel satisfaction in the accomplishment
8. Recognizes how the activity contributes to particular life goals.

Origin of Interests

The origin of interests is still a scientific mystery. Children tend to have interests similar to their parents and siblings, but no one knows how much of the similarity is due to such factors as hereditary predispositions, to family modeling, to being rewarded for imitating family members, or to occupying a position where the accoutrements of the interests are prominent.

Understanding the malleability of human interests is very important now that people need to be increasingly adaptive in their careers. Great flexibility in the interests one may develop would expand significantly the number of potentially satisfying occupations for the person.

Interest Inventories and Expressed Interests

A counselor's knowledge of client's interests derives largely from the use of interest inventories. These measures are summations of self-reported preferences for different activities, subjects, and occupations. Items are assigned to the inventory either because they distinguish persons in a particular occupation from others (*Strong Vocational Interest Blank*) and/or because they elicit parallel responses to items that logically are related (*Kuder Preference Record*). Consequently, scores on an interest inventory indicate whether a person responded to the inventory's items in a way comparable to that of particular occupational groups or whether the person has many or few preferences for activities, subjects, and occupations in areas such as aesthetics, mechanics, or science. This useful information is only part of what one needs to consider about interests when making career choices.

Clearly, interest inventories provide only limited information about interests; they do not measure the intensity of a person's interest nor the priority among the person's interests. Neither do they assess the percentage of activities in a particular interest domain. In part, this problem occurs because such domains are not defined; in part, because the measures are designed to distinguish among people in terms of one's preferences for a set of activities rather than to reflect the percentage of those activities that appeal to the person. Also, interest inventories can be confusing if one's experiences with the activities they sample is limited or occurred under unfavorable circumstances. In such instances, scores on inventories may lead to forsaking possibly attractive pursuits.

Since a standard list of interests does not exist and since the domain of particular interests has not been established, an interest scale on one inventory is not equal to a similarly titled scale on another (Cronbach, 1970). Therefore, to use the findings from a particular inventory, one must complete that inventory so that one's measured interests are defined in that inventory's terms. Table 3–4 lists the interest categories of major inventories.

Table 3–4. Names of Interest Scales from Four Major Inventories Arranged by Title Similarity

Strong Campbell Interest Inventory (23 scales)	Kuder General Interest Survey (10 scales)	Ohio Vocational Interest Survey (24 scales)	Career Assessment Inventory (22 scales)
Agriculture		Agriculture	Agriculture
			Animal service
Nature			Nature/outdoors
	Outdoor		
Adventure			
Military activities			
			Carpentry
		Manual work	manual/skills/ trades
Mechanical activities	Mechanical		mechanical/fixing
		Machine work	
		Applied technology	
		Inspecting/testing	
			Electronics
Science	Scientific		Science
Mathematics			
	Computational	Numerical	Numbers
Medical science		Medical	
Medical service			Medical service
		Nursing and related technical services	
Music	Music	Music	
		Entertainment and performing arts	Performing/ entertaining
			Arts and crafts
Art	Artistic		

Table 3–4. (*Continued*)

Strong Campbell Interest Inventory (23 scales)	Kuder General Interest Survey (10 scales)	Ohio Vocational Interest Survey (24 scales)	Career Assessment Inventory (22 scales)
Writing			Writing
	Literary	Literary	
Teaching		Teaching, counseling, social work	Teaching
			Child care
		Skilled personal services	
Social service	Social service		Social service
		Caring for people or animals	
		Personal services	
Athletics			
Domestic arts			
			Food service
Religious activities			Religious activities
Public speaking			
	Persuasive		
		Promotional communication	
Law/politics			
		Appraisal	
Merchandising			
Sales		Sales representative	Sales
Business management		Customer service management and supervision	
			Business
Office practices			Office practices
	Clerical	Clerical work	Clerical/clerking

The research on interest inventories is too extensive to be summarized or referenced here. A complete research bibliography for each instrument, along with at least one critical review, can be found in the eight editions of the *Mental Measurement Yearbook* (Buros, 1978). Critical reviews of some or all of the inventories also appear in Anastasi (1976), Cronbach (1970), and Super and Crites (1962).

Expressed interests—that is, one's answer to such questions as "What are your interests?"; "What areas arouse your curiosity?"—are important in career but correlate only moderately with inventoried interests. The limited correlation probably reflects the facts that expressed interest involves felt intensity for activities, whereas the inventory does not consider intensity; and also that the individual's definition of the interest domain differs somewhat from the inventory maker's. By late adolescence and in adulthood, expressed interests are as useful, or more so, than inventoried interests in predicting future career behavior (Whitney, 1970; Holland, 1976a). Data from Terman's gifted child follow-up indicate that people with expressed interests are happier and healthier than people without interests (Sears, 1977). Having "interesting work" repeatedly is one of the major goals of Americans (Yankelovich, 1978), and persons who do not satisfy their interests in work often require an avocation (Super, 1942).

Inventoried interests can be assessed with some reliability by adolescence, and some of these interests tend to persist throughout life. Interests identified by inventory, however, do not appear to stabilize until early adulthood (Campbell, 1971), and even after that new interests emerge and old ones recede.

Particular inventoried and expressed interests are associated with particular occupational groups in the manner one would expect. For instance, persons in science curricula or occupations are more likely than other workers or students to have science interests (Holland, 1966, 1973; Campbell, 1971; Strong, 1955). Likewise, persons with such interests are more likely to enter and remain in the associated occupations than people without such interests.

Holland (1959, 1966) has pioneered extensive research suggesting that there are six broad interest categories, each of which is associated with a distinctive lifestyle. He suggests that identification of a person's leading two or three areas permits accurate predictions about the person's general career and life behavior. Holland's six categories and associated lifestyles appear in Table 3–5.

Interest Counseling

Interest inventorying and discussion typically have been a major part of traditional vocational counseling. A person's interests are inventoried and identified in order to suggest educational and occupational goals and to increase commitment to such goals. Rarely have vocational counselors used inventories to stimulate a person to explore unfamiliar activities and perhaps to uncover latent interests. Although many inventory authors urge counselors to use interest inventories to stimulate exploration, evidence on the effect of completing interest inventories suggests that this task actually discourages exploration (Zenner & Schnuelle, 1972; Zytowski, 1977).

Recognition that career development is a process that can be positively influenced makes it likely that future career counseling will incorporate strategies to expand and to create interests, rather than strategies that only label them. Accompanying this development will be a need for a new type of interest measure to assess a person's direct exposure and relative intensity of attraction to the interest area. The notion of an

Table 3–5. John Holland's Six Personality Types and Their
                 Characteristics

Realistic	A person who is interested in mechanical activities and in developing coordination and physical strength. These people manipulate tools and other concrete objects. They describe themselves as concrete, strong and masculine rather than social skilled or sensitive.
Investigative	A person who engages in thinking, organizing and understanding. These people engage in scientific and scholarly activities and describe themselves as analytical, intellectual, curious, reserved and scientific rather than persuasive or social.
Social	A person who finds satisfaction in helping, teaching, and serving. These people describe themselves as gregarious, friendly, cooperative and tactful rather than mechanical or technical.
Conventional	A person who prefers orderly, structured situations with clear guidelines. These engage in clerical and computational activities and describe themselves as precise and accurate, clerical and conforming.
Enterprising	A person who enjoys organizing, directing or persuading other people and exercising authority. These people describe themselves as persuasive, possessing leadership, ambitious, and optimistic.
Artistic	A person who enjoys performing athletically or artistically. These people describe themselves as emotional aesthetic, autonomous, unconventional, impulsive and imaginative.

"interest test" is likely to be revived, as Super and Crites (1962) predicted when they reviewed the limited area of interest investigation twenty years ago. Likewise, counselors will want inventories that sample clearly defined interest domains, and they will employ those inventories in the manner that stimulates exploration.

Work Values

Work values are the short- and long-range goals sought by a person through working and the means a person accepts as appropriate for achieving those goals. They are complex, abstract concepts that include means and ends as well as their interrelationships. Often means become short-term and then long-term goals. For instance, the means "work hygienically" often becomes "have a job in pleasant surroundings."

Blurring of means and ends can create problems for a society. Once a society accepts working hygienically, honestly, or in accord with ecology as a desirable goal for many, but not all, occupations, the demand for these ways of working becomes fragmented, even though these conditions are essential to society's long-term survival.

Values are attributed to a person on the basis of what one says is worthwhile and on the basis of the actions of which one is proud. These attributions are assumed to be the personal criteria by which one weighs personal actions. An adult who lacks values is deemed pathological.

Moreover, values are assumed to become more differentiated as a person matures, integrating new experiences and digesting the feedback from them. Thus, a person's values presumably become less egotistic with increasing age. Certain values are expected of adults, and those who do not manifest them are criticized. Note, for instance, the general disdain for the "playboy."

A person's values reflect aspirations and give direction to actions. When actions are congruent with values, one should feel happiness for being true to oneself, whereas when actions contradict values one should feel distress because one is contradicting what one represents. Judgments about whether work is meaningful, challenging and honest and the concommitant positive or negative feelings depend on one's awareness of what one values.

People must develop, recognize, and implement constructive work values if a society is to serve its members well. Especially in a free society where a person can work or withhold work, socialization must impart a willingness to work cooperatively and energetically for the advancement of society. Recent widespread concern about the erosion of the *Protestant work ethic* in our society (Hoyt *et al.*, 1972) and the support this concern has generated for career education indicate growing awareness about need for such socialization in our society.

Until recently, concern with work values had focused almost exclusively on the ends of working, that is, on the rewards and benefits that working produces. These ends include creativity, adventure, and prestige. In recent years, however, emphasis on the pluralism of our society, the growing competition for limited high-status positions and resources, and the discovery of a self-perpetuating, hard-core underclass have demonstrated that people can vary significantly regarding the means they deem acceptable, as well as the ends they hope to achieve. Consequently, education is being called on to reemphasize such instrumental values as "winning is unacceptable unless it is accomplished honestly," "the discomfort of hard physical and mental effort is compensated by achievement," and "team achievements require and justify self constraints," while continuing to announce the "good life" goals available in our society. There are no standard lists of either kinds of values, but Table 3-6 provides a list of some widely accepted as values.

The family, school, peer, and work groups are major forces in shaping one's values; the influence of religious organizations seems dependent on the family's receptivity (Greeley & Rossi, 1966). These primary groups direct a person's energies by providing resources, instruction, and models and by differentially rewarding and punishing particular behaviors and beliefs. Human survival requires interdependence; consequently, human beings seek inclusion in at least some of these groups. The price of such inclusion is accepting at least some of the values of the groups.

Work values become clearer as one moves from youth into adulthood. Crites (1971) indicates that a youngster's awareness of societal values increases with age. Knowledge of one's own work values appears to unfold slowly. Tiedeman and O'Hara (1959) found that adolescents

Table 3–6. Work Values: Goals and Acceptable Means of
            Pursuing Them

Work Goals

Companionship	Creative outlet
Wide ranging activities	Management
Prestige	Autonomy-teamwork
Physical activity	Tangible products
Security (physical-economic)	Expansion of talents and interests
Economic returns	Advancement potential
Surroundings	Altruism
Compatibility with interests/abilities	Expansion of knowledge

Instrumental Work Values

1. Follow instructions and regulations of legitimate authority.
2. Produce to a standard of which you can feel proud.
3. Do your job efficiently without wasting time or material.
4. Work enthusiastically and cooperatively.
5. Safeguard personnel, equipment, and materials as you work.
6. Give work your full attention and the energy needed to produce a good quality product.
7. Subordinate yourself to production to the degree your contract requires it.
8. Be loyal to the company to the degree that this is fair.
9. Work in a manner that reflects, rather than debases, human dignity.
10. Work in a manner that supports, rather than flouts, ecology.
11. Report for work unless you are too sick to work, affirming that sick leave is for illness; it's not another form of vacation leave.

were not nearly as aware of their inventoried values by high school graduation as they were of their inventoried interests or tested abilities. Neither the manner in which values grow nor how parents and others affect them is clear. Each model offers a somewhat different explanation. These explanations rely extensively on philosophical rather than empirical arguments. Counselors should reflect on the ways in which different philosophies have approached values, so that they will be better able to help clients identify and develop constructive values.

Assessment of Work Values

Work values scales are of two types: those that elicit views about desirable work goals, such as the opportunity to manage, to add to knowledge and beauty, and to become wealthy; and those that elicit sentiments about working and about acceptable means of working. The former inventories are very similar to interest inventories and often can be distinguished from them only by their intent, since values and interests correlate moderately or highly (Osipow, 1973). These working goals scales traditionally are called values scales. Research has shown these scales usually do distinguish among different professionals in the direction predicted. The latter inventories are often dubbed attitude scales and can be considered cognitive tests because they indicate the respondent's awareness of society's judgments about work. Since these judgments reflect the society's common wisdom, education should be able to increase this knowledge among students. Research, therefore, has employed these inventories primarily as indices of whether *career education* alters students' *career maturity*, as operationalized or represented by these measures. Extensive studies of the Crites's (1965) *CMI* Work Attitude scale show that career education has improved its mean scores.

Other means of assessing work values are possible, but researchers have not yet studied them. One might, for instance, test whether a person can identify correctly the values likely to be realized in an occupation (expert judgments can provide the criteria); or one could test whether a person could give cogent pro and con arguments for a professed value. (The latter assumes that one having a firm value is aware of the reasons for and against it.) On the behavioral level, one might ascertain a person's values by charting time expenditures in terms of different values.

Values Clarification

Many means are available for consciously building and clarifying values (Simon et al., 1972). These techniques stimulate examination of one's means and purposes and sensitize a person to the values implicit in the actions of others. Persons using the exercises tend to be pleased, but the lack of objective methods of assessing values has hampered their critical evaluation. A major exception concerns efforts assessed by the Crites (1965) *Vocational Attitudes Scale*. Using that scale, research has shown that complex career education programs involving examination of worker's and adolescent client's values lead the young people to endorse statements about working that are more in accord with those of adults in the society.

Only limited research is available to suggest that knowing one's career values or that having values consistent with one's occupation or educational endeavors increases productivity or career satisfaction. Career Pattern study correlations (Super, Kowalski, & Gotkin, 1969) suggest a relation between awareness of values and successful careers, and reviews of work productivity and satisfaction studies suggest some relation between those variables and value consistency.

The argument for career value clarification depends essentially on logic. One's purpose is likely to be more enhancing and realizable if one has examined its consequences, has contrasted it with other possible purposes, and has scrutinized one's own actions to assure that they are consistent with the purpose or that one wants to change so that the behavior becomes consistent. The examination should increase motivation, either by leading to affirmation of the goal or by encouraging its abandonment and the selection of a more attractive alternative.

Work Values and Needs

Logically, values derive at least in part from *needs*, which are internal states of want that require satisfaction for continued living. Values involve judgments about the desirability of a means or an end, and logically an end that corresponds to a need would tend to become a value. In themselves, needs may propel without cognitive affirmation. Both values and needs, of course, are explanatory constructs whose properties are delineated by the explainer and affirmed by study of the measures that bring the constructs into operation. Surprisingly, the conceptual linkage of career values and needs has not been explored, and findings of high intercorrelations among purported measures of interests, values, and needs has led to disputes about the utility of considering these three concepts as separate constructs (Osipow, 1973).

Clearly, the physiological needs of water, sleep, food, shelter and the psychological needs of nurture and affiliation must be gratified before other needs can be attended. Building on the idea of priorities among needs, Maslow (1954) suggested that needs are ordered in decreasing potency as follows: physiological needs; safety needs; belongingness and love; need for importance, respect, self-esteem, and independence; information need; understanding need; need for beauty; and need for self-actualization. Of course, many great artists and leaders, such as Vincent van Gogh, Edgar Allen Poe, and Ghandi, are notable exceptions to this order.

There are many classifications of needs. Murray's list (1938), portrayed in Chapter 2, is one of the more comprehensive; it has spurred research, especially because the *Personal Preference Schedule* (Edwards, 1959) was derived from it.

Major research on the relation of need achievement to occupational and school progress has been pioneered by McClelland (1967, 1978). The accumulating evidence shows that measured need achievement relates to performance in school and work, even when intelligence is controlled. Moreover, McClelland (1978) and de Charms (1976), among others, have shown that increasing people's need achievement leads to improved school and work performance. In addition, Korman (1977) noted that occupational research suggests that the needs for power and affiliation may also be useful in understanding differences in occupational preferences and career behavior.

Research on needs has also shown that some occupations are differentiable in terms of the needs they are likely to gratify, and that people in some occupations have higher need for such gratification than those in other fields (Bordin, Nachmann & Segal, 1963; Nachmann, 1960;

Schaffer, 1976; Segal, 1961). But research generally has been unable to establish the relation between the inferred need state of childhood and adults' career behavior and occupational preferences that Roe (1957) postulated (Osipow, 1973).

Personality

Personality is the hypothetical construct referring to the aggregation and integration of all the person's qualities. Unfolding nature, the immediate environment, experienced pasts, and anticipated futures render every personality a dynamic, complex, unique entity.

Survival requires people continually to adapt and to remain flexible. Not surprisingly, similar challenges are met regularly by various people through somewhat different combinations of attributes. In regard to careers, most positions can be played in one of several ways by persons with unlike characteristics. Often a person of moderate academic ability parlays that ability into an outstanding performance in college or graduate school through excellent study habits and motivation. Similarly, the quiet, detail-conscious sales representative who learns his customers' particular needs and conscientiously arranges timely deliveries outperforms outgoing, persuasive colleagues.

Abilities, interests, and values—all part of personality—were described above. Other facets of the person, such as temperament (cheerfulness, energy level, anxiousness, conscientiousness, sociability, or independence) and perceptual/cognitive style (introspectiveness, risk-taking preferences, perceived locus of control, self confidence, or achievement drive), also relate to career. Describing a person in terms of each of these characteristics helps to predict that individual's performance in a career.

By definition, personality is not simply the sum of qualities but the integration of their interactions (Allport, 1937). Not surprisingly, no one understands how an individual synthesizes these attributes into apparently rational patterns of action. Like abilities, interests, and values, other personality traits are a consequence of nature and nurture. The personality continually is emerging and being refined as Allport (1937) noted long ago. Its essence is ongoing integration; that integration is awesome yet difficult to capture, requiring extensive, ongoing observation and model building (Allport, 1960; White, 1966). Artists have been far more effective in capturing the synthesis than social scientists.

Personality in Vocational Guidance

For career counselors, personality is largely a profile of traits derived from an inventory, ratings of these traits by the client or others, inferences from projective tests, or perhaps, in the future, expert judgments of *assessment center* performance (Bray et al., 1966). These assessment techniques are described briefly below.

Inventory. The inventory is a set of aspirations, behaviors, preferences, and so forth, which the respondent identifies as characteristic or not characteristic of himself or herself. Typically the inventories employ true-false, forced-choice, or Likert scale formats. The stimuli are selected because logically or statistically they cluster to reflect a particular attribute or, less often, because they have related to some external event. For example, endorsing words such as energetic, initiating, assured, adventuresome, and persevering can be considered as indicating achievement motivation because these words logically relate to that characteristic and/or because people who check one tend to check the others. In contrast, adjectives such as withdrawing, sensitive, cautious, and guarded might be clustered together because persons endorsing them were judged by experts to be anxious.

On an inventory, the person's responses to a set of items are aggregated, either by theoretically or by empirically determined weighting, into a score for the quality represented by the scale. Usually a high score means that the individual is more likely to manifest the quality than a low-scoring person, not that one has more of the quality. For example, a low score on the *16PF* scale of trusting-suspicious means a person is likely to trust a wider range of people although the score does not predict how much trust he or she invests in people.

The meanings of the scores are a function of their established correlates. The traits are often labeled by a common adjective or adjectives, such as aggressive, nurturant, affiliative, introverted, but they rarely equate with a dictionary definition of the adjective. Their meaning is a function of the studies made of persons with particular scores on those scales. Thus, scoring "high aggressive" on the *Personal Preference Schedule (PPS)* does not mean that a person is inclined to physical fighting, but rather that the person is more likely than most people to "attack contrary points of view, to tell others what one thinks about them, to criticize others publicly . . . , to read newspaper accounts of violence" (*Personal Preference Schedule Manual,* Edwards, 1959, p. 11).

Since extensive data exist for some trait scores, clients are urged to complete inventories so that they can identify groups to which their answers are similar or dissimilar. Unfortunately, some counselors then hypothesize, often without a rationale for estimating the probability of being accurate, that the person will act, think, feel, or want to be like the groups whose members answered the questions in a comparable manner. Surprisingly, little research has focused on how the counselor and client together might make these predictions more accurate.

As in the case of abilities, interests, and values, no standard list of personality traits exists. In 1936 Allport and Odbert extracted more than 18,000 words representing different traits from a Webster's *Unabridged Dictionary* and, by analysis, reduced the list to slightly more than 200. That list, however, has not been used widely. Starting with that list and using content analysis and factor analysis, Cattell (1946) did extensive work to assemble a list of traits that would represent a large portion of the variance in human character. His work has resulted in the scales of the *16 Personality Factor test (16PF)* described in Table 3–7, and this

Table 3–7. Primary Bipolar Traits of the 16 PF Test

1. Reserved	Outgoing
2. Dull	Bright
3. Affected by feelings	Emotionally stable
4. Humble	Assertive
5. Sober	Happy-go-lucky
6. Expedient	Conscientious
7. Shy	Venturesome
8. Tough-minded	Tender-minded
9. Trusting	Suspicious
10. Practical	Imaginative
11. Forthright	Astute
12. Self-assured	Apprehensive
13. Conservative	Experimenting
14. Group dependent	Self-sufficient
15. Undisciplined	Controlled
16. Relaxed	Tense

SOURCE: The *Administrator's Manual for the 16 PF*, 1972, 1979 Champaign, Ill.: Institute for Personality and Ability Testing, 1972, 1979. Reproduced by permission of the copyright owner: The Institute for Personality and Ability Testing, Inc.

instrument has been widely used, although few believe it spans all human characteristics (Thomson, 1949). Another attempt at a taxonomy of traits is the work of Guilford (1959), who, through analysis of factor analytic studies, arrived at eighty "primary traits" grouped in four modalities: somatic, temperament, aptitude and motivation.

Projectives. Another common method of assessing personality is the projective test, despite the fact that research on projectives generally has not been promising. Projectives require a person to interpret ambiguous stimuli and assume that the interpretation is an expression of the person or some facet thereof. These tests provide a stream of data that enable construction of a more dynamic model of a person than do traits. But extensive research of the *Rorschach Inkblots* and the *Thematic Apperception Test (TAT)* drawings has not consistently found relations between total personality models derived from the protocols and real life behavior, although there are promising developments in relating pretherapy projective scores to psychotherapy outcomes. One promising development in projectives for careers is the finding that subscores on selected *TAT* cards consistently have related moderately to indices of achievement motivations (Klopfer & Taulbee, 1976).

Ratings. Self- or observer-ratings in natural or contrived situations are also used in personality measurement. Generally within a natural setting, and often from memory, a rater describes the subject in terms of the frequency of specific behaviors, such as comes to class on time, or responds when spoken to, or on the degree to which the person has qualities such as punctual or friendly. The ratings are aggregated or considered singly.

Most of these ratings produce trait scores for particular qualities. Generalization is limited, to an unknown degree, by the context of the assessment. Strictly speaking, the interpretations of the ratings beyond behavioral description must depend on the research concerning the particular measure. Comparable scores on traits with the same or similar names can have radically different meanings. Mischel (1968), for example, in summarizing research on trait assessment, notes there is only limited-to-moderate correlation between behavior and rating in one situation and behavior and rating in a different situation. As a result, a trait score without a description of the context within which it is assessed is virtually useless.

One can improve personality ratings in the same manner as improving ability ratings. (See Table 3–3.) In addition, since personality is a more pervasive entity than is ability, practices such as multiple independent observations, assessment by different methods and observers, examination of residuals such as the size and content of a personal library to index a person's intellectuality or a review of records or detailed descriptions of time usage and interpersonal activities, will elucidate the personality of counselor or client. Certainly the fact that novelists and playwrights employ these devices to create personality lends support to using them to discover and to verify personality.

Assessment Centers. Increasingly, business is turning to simulation exercises to evaluate and, more recently, to provide appraisal data for managerial and technical personnel. Earlier, during World War II, the Office of Strategic Services, the forerunner of the Central Intelligency Agency, successfully used simulation to evaluate personnel. Today, military training routinely includes multiple simulations for training and evaluation.

Assessment center refers to exposing a person to a series of simulations wherein he or she is systematically observed on a series of traits deemed relative to particular jobs and duties. The simulations include activities such as the "in basket technique," in which the examinee encounters a series of assignments that can be completed within a time frame only by proper allocation of time, delegation, coordination, and setting priorities; and the "leaderless group," in which the assessees, as members of a team with given tasks, interact to reveal skills in cooperating, organizing, persuading, listening, and the like (Bray et al., 1966).

Connecting Career and Personality

Holland (1959, 1966, 1973) offered a very comprehensive and economical theory of how personality and educational-occupational positions are related. He pointed out how studies support the proposition that occupations and education programs can be clustered into six relatively distinct groups on the basis of their incumbents' personality characteristics. Then he argued that these occupations were independently distinguishable by the nature of their demands; that is, the duties required and the conditions of work. Multiple studies that differentiate educational and occupational groups have offered moderate support for the contention that incumbents and aspirants of different occupational and educational groups are distinguishable as proposed. In terms of work demands, the few available studies offer both support and challenge to the view that the six career environments are distinguishable in the terms hypothesized by Holland (1973).

The personality types are described in Table 3–5 and the career clusters in Table 4–3. A description of guidance practice following the Holland theory appears in Chapter 8. The theory has also been used in suggesting career directions for the Career Planning Program (American College Testing Program, 1972) and the new *Strong Campbell Interest Inventory.*

The third edition of the *Dictionary of Occupational Titles* provides the most comprehensive grouping of occupations by personality characteristics. In the *D.O.T.*, occupations are grouped into *Occupational Aptitude Profiles (OAP),* and profiles are provided for each OAP. Table 3–8 shows a page from the *D.O.T.* The 1965 *OAPS* are being updated and will appear as supplements to the fourth edition of the *D.O.T.* issued in 1977.

Personality profiles have been used mainly to direct clients to career options. They have not been related to different treatments, although Holland (1976a), among others, has suggested that the different types may plan career differently and, by inference, would require different assistance. Nor have personality profiles been set as career counseling outcomes, even though a treatment might be imagined that would seek to help a client become more like the modal personality of a preferred or intended occupation.

Personality Research Related to Careers

Most personality research related to careers is quantitative and analytic. Its purpose has been to discover differences among people in occupations rather than to understand modes of functioning in the positions. Regression and discriminant analyses have been used to locate a best fit for an occupation rather than isolating several personality patterns for the occupation. These studies have identified characteristics and clusters of characteristics associated with occupancy and performance in particular educational and occupational roles. Most of these characteristics are abilities, interests, or values, but some are temperament qualities such as energetic, taciturn, sociable, assertive, docile, cheerful, while others are perceptual and cognitive styles such as confident, risk-taking, intro-

Table 3–8. Example of Occupational Aptitude Profile from
Dictionary of Occupational Titles

Guidance and Counseling .108; .208

Work Performed

Work activities in this group primarily involve guiding and/or counseling indi-viduals or groups in the solution of occupational, educational, personal, or social problems. Typical situations would be assisting prison parolees in gaining employ-ment and adjusting to society; counseling high school students about college ad-mission requirements and curricula; counseling unhappy or frustrated workers or jobseekers into more fulfilling work; and assisting troubled individuals or families toward normal social adjustment and development.

Worker Requirements

An occupationally significant combination of: Sympathetic attitude toward the welfare of others; capacity to absorb training and apply knowledge to the solution of diverse problems; verbal facility to relate to people at all levels; organizational ability in order to plan and direct guidance programs; tact, poise, and general de-meanor that tend to inspire confidence and esteem.

Clues for Relating Applicants and Requirements

Volunteer welfare work for local church group.
Expressed preference for public contact work.
Membership in school debating club.
Successful academic record in pertinent courses, such as psychology or education.
Poise and self-confidence exhibited in an interview.
Elective office in school.

Training and Methods of Entry

A college degree is the minimum requirement for entry into this field. In most cases, education beyond the 4-year college is required, varying according to the individual situation.

Most municipal and State governments and private organizations require 2 years of graduate study from applicants who are interested in pursuing social work as a career.

Openings in school-counseling work are usually available to individuals who have State teaching certificates and special certificates for school counseling. Most States issue counselor certificates only to people with a master's degree or the equivalent in counselor education, as well as actual teaching experience.

A graduate degree in psychology serves as an excellent qualification for entry into numerous positions, particularly those in industry.

Related Classifications

Administration (.118 .168) p. 237
Interviewing, Information-Giving, and Related Work
(Vocational, Educational, and Related Activities)
(.168; .268) p. 250
High School, College, University, and Related Educa-
tion (.228) p. 341
Social Science, Psychological, and Related Research
(.088) p. 294

Qualifications Profile

GED:	5	6		
SVP:	7	8		
Apt:	GVN	SPQ	KFM	EC
	1 1 3	4 4 4	4 4 4	5 5
	2 2			
Int:	4 6 5 8			
Temp:	5 9 4			
Phys. Dem:	S L 4 5 6			

SOURCE: U.S. Department of Labor, *The Dictionary of Occupational Titles* (Vol. II) (3rd ed.). Washington, D.C.: U.S. Government Printing Office, 1965, p. 296.

spective, internal locus of control and need-achievement. Holland (1966) and Pietrofesa and Splete (1975) have summarized many of the relationships among personality traits and occupations.

Personality research has implicitly assumed that career roles are selected because they somehow fit the personality, rather than because they are a means for constructing a particular personality; or because they are entered without attention to personality compatibility, but after entry require certain personality adaptations. If the latter possibilities concerned personality researchers, they would examine the range of qualities possible within a particular curriculum or occupation and would seek to understand how different kinds of people are able to perform in the same position. They would study how exemplars of different patterns perform the occupation. Even the work of Bordin and his colleagues (1963), which centers on developing and validating prototype personalities for professions such as artist, accountants, and social workers, has not proceeded beyond distinguishing among occupations.

Many personality studies arose from the selection needs of the Armed Forces and private business and industry. This employer's perspective carried over into the development of measures for personal guidance. For this reason, persons working to expand or to adapt themselves to particular roles will not receive clear direction from personality testing. Instead, on their own or under the guidance of a counselor, they will have to study the parameters of the career roles directly and be cautious not to overestimate the meaning of any assessed "compatibility" or "incompatibility" with the particular role. This need to make direct observation of the fit of one's attributes with an occupation also applies, to a lesser extent, to the areas of abilities, interests, and values.

Surprisingly, there is little research concerning the impact that particular occupations or school experiences exert on personality. Pace (1964) and others have shown that colleges impose different "presses" for particular personality styles, and correlational data suggest that people staying in a school alter their personality, at least temporarily, to accord more with that "press." Newcomb's work (1967) suggests, however, that the alteration may be temporary.

Clearly the dictum that "you are what you do" affirms that the pursuit of an occupation alters personality. This belief is a central tenet of the theory that one can create oneself by one's choice. If various occupations have different effects on people and if there are alternative occupations to select among, then one's occupational choice is, in part, a decision to create a particular kind of person. But this author is not aware of studies that document the effects of different occupations on personality.

Moreover, this author is not aware of research that has shown that strengthening or altering particular personality characteristics or patterns, other than abilities, has influenced occupational or academic performance. Certainly, strengthening abilities through formal education has enhanced performance. Furthermore, many therapists claim that their treatments improve particular work performance, although evaluations of therapies are problematic in pinpointing specific gains even when

evidence does support the proposition that therapies provide some benefits (Smith & Glass, 1977; Bergin, 1971). In addition, Dale Carnegie-
type programs and sensitivity groups have claimed to improve personality with the consequence of bolstering careers, but these organizations
have not documented their claims empirically. Perhaps the dearth of
evidence stems from the lack of necessity to establish causality because
the proposition is self-evident, the cost of the undertaking too high, or
the state of the art of evaluation research too primitive. But techniques
such as path analysis, coupled with increasing concern for accountability, may soon facilitate collection of pertinent evidence.

Socioeconomic Status

SES not only looks like sex, but many Americans avoid discussing it as
steadfastly as they avoid discussing sex. Newspapers have their social
pages and communities their social registers and country clubs. Regardless of the political party in power, the majority of our ambassadors and
high-ranking appointed officials share similar background and memberships in the same social and country clubs. Yet 95 percent of Americans
identify themselves as middle class, although they do not attribute
middle-class status to that percentage of their fellow citizens (Hollingshead, 1949).

By definition, class is the status of a person in the community. Class
depends on wealth, family background, education, and eventually, on
one's economic pursuits. Birth bestows independent biological life and
lower-, working-, middle-, upper-middle-, or upper-class status. That class
level tends to remain throughout life, probably because the accomplishments of youth are closely related to accomplishments of adulthood,
and youthful achievement relates to class.

People in the same class share many habits, beliefs, and expectations. Their material resources and security are comparable; they tend
to reside near one another, attend school together, socialize with and
marry one another, work and do business with each other, and even
attend church together. They have similar lifestyles and aspirations, and
tend to vote in the same manner. Most Americans do not associate exclusively with members of their class, and there are many members of
every class who differ markedly from others in their class in some or
even most of the foregoing qualities. Nevertheless, many characteristics are attributable to class, and most people recognize what these
qualities are.

Upper and Lower Classes

The upper classes, by definition, own a larger share of a society's resources, enjoy more esteem, are better educated, healthier, longer lived,
and more secure. To the degree that income confers advantage, they
clearly are more privileged, as reflected in Table 3–9. Compared to per-

Table 3–9. 1978 Distribution of Money Income Among
Households in the United States

	Percentage of income	Cumulative
Lowest fifth of households under $6,391	4.3 percent	4.3 percent
Second fifth of households $6,392–11,955	10.3 percent	14.6 percent
Third fifth of households $11,956–18,121	16.9 percent	31.5 percent
Fourth fifth of households $18,122–26,334	24.7 percent	56.2 percent
Highest fifth of households $26,335–and over	43.9 percent	100.0 percent

SOURCE: U.S. Department of Commerce, Bureau of Census. *Consumer Income.* Washington, D.C.: Government Printing, 1980.

sons from lower classes, they delay gratification longer, and some evidence suggests that their career preferences are more often based on congruence between self and occupation (Healy, 1973a).

In contrast, the lower classes live in precarious conditions. They own little, are almost totally dependent on wages or public welfare, and are members of families whose head is often unemployed or underemployed. Even when the breadwinner has work, these jobs are marginal and transitional. Persons of these classes often have no personal acquaintances who are employers or who can hire them. The work system has not rewarded such people, and many of them feel it never will. Perhaps this attitude explains why they have difficulty delaying gratification and acting on plans. Certainly, few of them feel that they control their careers, and many lack the basic knowledge and career skills needed for launching and sustaining a career (Oetting & Miller, 1977). Recently, *Time* magazine (1977) dubbed the persons in the bottom of the lower class the "underclass" and suggested their lack of hope, coupled with their awareness of the advantages of others, was creating a time bomb waiting to explode.

Career Advantages and Social Class

Repeatedly, social class relates to career maturity, to levels of educational or occupational aspiration, and to educational and occupational attainment itself. Indeed, class relates positively to almost all abilities (Super, Kowalski, & Gotkin, 1969; Thorndike & Hagen, 1959). Super (1969), in noting the relation of class to achievement, indicated that this correlation at least showed that the upper classes were using their advantages productively.

Although nominally our society is classless, with equal opportunity for all, social standing and family wealth clearly make an upper-class youngster "more equal" than others. Unquestionably, one can secure a tuition-free education through twelfth grade and generally can pursue some college degree for a minimal tuition. Without family financial support, however, it is very difficult to pursue higher education in the more prestigious universities and Ivy League colleges, whose graduates outstrip graduates of other colleges in their career attainments (A. W. Astin, 1977). Similarly, without wealth or a patron, medical school or a quality law school is likely to be beyond one's reach, although public funds of $12,000–$15,000 supplement each student's direct $6,000– $8,000 cost of medical school each year. (Of course, admission to medical school often raises one's credit rating, enabling some aspiring physicians to borrow funds for their own postcollege schooling. Loans to medical students are popular; the average amount owed at graduation is approximately $36,000). Likewise, only the subsidized are likely to have the "dowry" required for many judicial appointments.

Other factors beside material wealth contribute to the advantages conferred by class. Among these are many achievement-oriented, successful models; easy access to career information and informational resources; privileged access to opportunities for exploring and developing skills, (such as an arranged summer job or the telephone call to a prospective employer who happens to be a former fraternity brother); expectation of achievement by the school and community (Cicourel & Kitsuse, 1963), and association with peers who aspire and are expected to achieve. In *The Managerial Woman*, Hennig and Jardim (1976) have cogently shown how socialization prepares upper-middle class and higher males to be effective managers, whereas socialization of women thwarts their acquisition of managerial skills. In other words, sex socialization teaches ways of operating in sex-related occupations. Similarly, and perhaps more effectively, class socialization teaches the person the "ropes" of class-related occupations.

The concept of class socialization suggests that working acquires different meanings for different classes. This idea does not negate the importance of occupation in fixing social class. But workers at one level of work may not be expecting and seeking the same rewards from their occupations as workers at another level.

Surveys of American workers and students have not found marked differences among classes in the satisfaction they report seeking from work. Repeatedly, however, studies of job satisfaction show that professional and technical work provides intrinsic and extrinsic rewards, whereas lower-level work provides primarily extrinsic rewards. Partially in response to these two observations, personnel and industrial psychologists are increasingly redesigning some lower-level jobs, hoping that such jobs can begin to be intrinsically satisfying. In reviewing many of these efforts, Katzell and Yankelovich (1975) came to the surprising conclusion that making a job more intrinsically satisfying frequently is not a priority of the workers.

At least two explanations are tenable. First, wages and job security of these workers are low and, therefore, these bread-and-butter issues— the traditional issues of organized labor—may be their major priority. Second, these workers may have reconciled themselves to obtaining only extrinsic satisfiers in work, while hoping for intrinsic satisfaction from non-job pursuits and, therefore, are giving their attention and energy to the latter. Consequently, they do not wish to revise their work, lest revision reduce the time and energy available for non-job pursuits. This latter explanation becomes more plausible if the workers and the members of their class regard their jobs as the acceptable way of supporting self and family, but not as a major means of achieving status. Indeed researchers have indicated that status within the working class is achieved by sports prowess or sports knowledge, regularity at the tavern or lodge, children's achievements, and visibility or leadership in church or community affairs more than by one's job.

Upward Mobility: The Unspoken Career Goal

Class is a major determinant of career attainment, and class advancement or maintenance are career goals of many persons, although not loudly proclaimed. Super (1957) pointed out that upper-class men focused on high-level professions rather than following their mechanical interests, which they instead satisfied as hobbies. Many people still speak of getting out of blue-collar work and into white-collar work. Likewise, in our leisure-focused society, life style is often a major career objective, and life style is an indicator of one's class more than it is a distinguishing characteristic of occupations at the same level.

Sociologists point out that many Americans have suffered *anomie*, a chronic, painful condition of aloneness, rejection, and isolation experienced by persons moving from one group to another, usually from lower to higher socioeconomic status. These social climbers adopt the ways of the new group, who are often not especially welcoming, and they abandon the ways of the former group, thereby alienating themselves.

Western civilization requires some upward mobility because increasing numbers of leaders and skilled personnel are required for its complex organization and expanding technology and because the upper classes do not have enough children to replace themselves. Consequently, it is not surprising that our educational system and other socializing institutions foster an upward mobility goal. The question that has not been answered, however, is: "Should the upwardly mobile be assisted in overcoming or avoiding anomie by societal provision of services such as interim support groups of the upwardly mobile or a clearinghouse of sponsors for the upwardly mobile?"

Schooling has been the traditional route of upward mobility. When there were relatively few schools and few students in higher education, where a student earned a degree may not have influenced achievement of upward mobility. With the rapid expansion of higher education and the widespread availability of financing for higher education, upward mobility may be available only through attendance at prestigious schools. Widespread opportunities have not been available long enough to tell, but studies of higher education financing by A. W. Astin (1977) certainly suggest that graduates of prestige institutions are more advantaged than others. Certainly, previous studies have shown that graduates of such schools achieve more than do graduates of other schools.

Sex

Sex in career is often the basis of jokes, but the discrimination against women in education and in occupations is no laughing matter. Women are underrepresented in higher-level occupations and more prestigious schools and overrepresented in lower occupations and less prestigious colleges (*Manpower Report to President*, 1975; A. W. Astin, 1977). They have been systematically denied access to educational and occupational training programs (Farmer & Backer, 1977). They have been paid as much as 60 percent less for the same work as men in the same occupations and with comparable education, as shown in Table 3–10. Although the Equal Pay Act of 1972 was designed to correct wage inequities and has led companies such as Corning Glass and AT&T to pay large amounts of back pay to women for unequal past treatment, the discriminatory situation is not likely to be reversed soon. In part, this inequity exists because women are crowded into a limited number of low-paying occupations. As Hedges and Bemis (1974) noted, 50 percent of female workers are in sixteen occupations, whereas 50 percent of the male workers are in sixty-four occupations.

Today, predictions are that 90 percent of women will participate in the labor force twenty-five or more years. Many will hold jobs while they

Table 3–10. Comparison of Male and Female Wages Based Upon Full-Time Workers Over Age 25

Educational Attainment and Sex		Median Income 1974	1970
Women			
Total, 25 years and over		$ 7,370	$ 5,616
Elementary:	Less than 8 years	5,022	3,798
	8 years	5,606	4,181
High School:	1 to 3 years	5,919	4,655
	4 years	7,150	5,580
College:	1 to 3 years	8,072	6,604
	4 years or more	10,357	8,719
Men			
Total, 25 years and over		$12,786	$ 9,521
Elementary:	Less than 8 years	7,912	6,043
	8 years	9,891	7,535
High School:	1 to 3 years	11,225	8,514
	4 years	12,642	9,567
College:	1 to 3 years	13,718	11,183
	4 years or more	17,188	13,871

SOURCE: U.S. Department of Commerce, Bureau of the Census, *Current Population Reports, Series P-60, Nos. 99 and 80.*

are raising small children. In 1974, 43 percent of married women were working, including 34.4 percent of those with children ages 0–5, and 51.2 percent of those whose children were at least six and less than seventeen (*Manpower Report to President,* 1975). Not always acknowledged, many women have to work either because they are single, are heads of households, or because their husband's incomes are inadequate to support their families. Farmer and Backer (1977) estimated that at least 42 percent of working women need their earnings for basic support.

The uneven distribution of men and of women in occupations, generally, and in high-level occupations, particularly, is not justified by biological differences between the sexes (Bem & Bem, 1971). Women are physically slighter, but such a difference is a factor in few jobs. This fact is exemplified by the wide array of occupations performed by women during the World War II mobilization. After age ten, American women exhibit less numerical and spatial ability (A. W. Astin, 1973) and more verbal and clerical ability than males (Maccoby & Jocklin, 1974), but such differences may reflect socialization rather than nature. These differences have not been established in non-western cultures, and occupational distributions in countries such as Russia, where more than half the engineers and scientists are women, call into question the linkage of mathematical and spatial aptitude to the sex gene. Furthermore, in 1970 less than 5 percent of the lawyers and judges, and less than 25 percent of the editors and reporters were women, although test results suggest that women have higher verbal abilities than do men (Farmer & Backer, 1977).

Social Expectation and Female Career

Social career expectations for women are different from those of men. A woman's social status does not depend nearly as much on her career as does a man's. Society expects a woman to subordinate her career to her husband and family and allots status to a woman based on her husband's achievement. Until recently, many considered education to be a woman's insurance against not marrying or against an unfavorable marriage rather than a means of self-enhancement. Moreover, the custom was that as a girl approached graduation, she put aside her career plans, located a suitable spouse, and then deferred career until after childrearing. Indeed Gray-Shellberg, Villarel, and Stone (1972) found that in resolving career conflicts, women would subordinate their interest to the interest of a fiancé or husband. Even the new generation and well-educated males find it hard to question these expectations. McMillan (1972), for instance, in studying the attitudes of single college males, found that more than 49 percent did not consider that their wives would pursue careers, even ones allowing an interruption for children. High school boys, in contrast, were willing to accept the wives of other men working but balked at accepting that status for their wives (Nelson and

Goldman, 1969). In sampling professional men and women's attitudes about women pursuing the "doubletrack" career (that is, work and homemaker/mother), Daley (1971) found that men held negative attitudes, but women were more positive.

After finding that women's responses to the *SVIB* changed considerably with instruction to imagine the home-career conflict reduced, Farmer and Bohn (1970) concluded that level of vocational interest in women would rise considerably if the home-career conflict were reduced. Hawley (1972) reached a similar conclusion about the negative impact of expectations on women's careers. She found that twenty-three women pursuing nontraditional occupations were less likely than thirty-three homemakers and thirty women in traditional occupations to have ideas about proper female career behavior. She surmised, therefore, that women's guesses about what men, and more generally their society, expected did influence their career behavior substantially.

More impressive evidence about the constraining effects of perceived male reaction to female careers was found by Mathews and Tiedeman (1964). Studying 1,237 women ranging in age from 11 to 26, they detected a pervasive expectation of negativism from men to their use of intelligence. Similar findings about competition with males among various groups of college women spurred Horner (1970) to hypothesize that women are socialized to avoid success, in contrast to men's development of a motive to achieve; and Lipman-Blumen (1972) to hypothesize that women achieve vicariously through the success of important males in their lives. Clearly, avoiding success or achieving vicariously portends serious strain for women in this career-oriented society.

Counselors have supported, rather than challenged, societal restrictions of women's careers. Thomas and Stewart (1971), for instance, found that counselors who listened to records of girls with plans to enter either traditional or nontraditional occupations tended to rate the traditional girls as less deviant and less in need of counseling. Schlossberg and Pietrofesa (1973) found that counselors viewed occupations as male or female rather than in terms of job requirements. Friedersdorf (1969) found counselors more receptive to the male need for career planning than to female need for planning.

Many counselors still may not be encouraging women to aspire as highly or widely as men. Donahue and Costar (1977), for instance, found that 228 of 300 randomly selected male and female Michigan counselors tended to recommend to women occupations that paid less, required less education, and were supervised more closely. The different recommendations were made for six cases that differed only in the sex of the fictitious students. Conflicting, albeit more encouraging, results were reported by Smith (1974) in the same journal, although not referenced by Donahue and Costar (1977). Smith asked the 507 high school counselors in the Denver area to make predictions about the academic success of two of four cases, identical except for sex and ethnicity. Analysis of the 198 usable responses (39 percent of the sample) did not show differential prediction attributable to client sex or ethnicity (Chicano versus Anglo) or to rater's sex The difference in these two analogue studies may stem from the limited percentage of respondents to Smith or to the amount of data in the cases. Smith's cases appeared to have considerably more information, and graduate students had judged that respondents would not recognize concerns about sex and ethnicity as the motivators of the study. A possible explanation of the discrepant findings is that with multiple data about a person, counselors treat men and women equally. When limited data are available, sex becomes a major consideration, to the disadvantage of women.

Another recent study of counselor attitudes toward females' careers suggests that counselors have become more favorable, although not completely unbiased, toward expanded career roles for women. Based on a cross-sectional sampling of Minnesota guidance counselors in 1968, 1971 and 1974, Engelhard, Jones and Stiggins (1976) obtained responses about women's careers from 139, 143, and 179 counselors, which comprised 100 percent, 82 percent, and 90 percent of the polled samples, respectively. Examining the changes in attitude over time and between sexes (males comprised 74 percent or more of these samples), they found that male and female counselors increased their acceptance of mothers with young children pursuing careers and their acceptance of women working in occupations that have traditionally employed few women. Female counselors, not surprisingly, held more liberal views on these issues than did male counselors.

Many authors claim that career development is different for men than for women. In one of the few data-based presentations, Angrist and Almquist (1975) proposed that women weigh life-style options primarily and occupational options secondarily as career goals during college. In contrast, men focus primarily on occupations. Their proposition is based on the relative stability during college of a life-style index measuring importance of employment in contrast to the instability of occupational choice in that period. Based on their study of eighty-seven women over four years of college, they identified five career types for women: careerist (career intertwined with marriage/family), noncareerist (employment not salient), defectors (change from careerist to noncareerist), convert (change from noncareerist to careerist) and shifter (waivering between the two). This typology showed high internal consistency and increasing reliability from year to year as the group approached graduation. On the other hand, the occupational choices of the women were unstable over the four-year period.

The authors further contended that women choose occupations differently from men because half the women did not hone in on a choice during college, nor did their aggregate work values change to reflect their changes in occupational choice. The conclusion, however, is arguable because the authors defined occupational field so narrowly that history and law were classified as different fields and because they did not show that men change their work values in accord with changes in occupation. Indeed, inspection of the values scale used in their study suggests that its values do not differentiate dramatically among professional-level occupations and consequently would not be sensitive to occupational changes of college students.

Girls Experience Career Bias From an Early Age

Societal restrictions on female careers are communicated early in life. Tyler (1951, 1955) found first-grade girls pursuing fewer activities than their male agemates, and she noted that their activities were less likely to coincide with their abilities. By age ten, the career choices of these children followed the traditional sex stereotypes. In another study of how youngsters view careers, Schlossberg and Goodman (1972) discovered that kindergarteners designated different work activities as appropriate for one sex or another even though their physical-intellectual development did not support the difference.

Sex stereotyping is taught early, and through many sources, with unfortunate consequences. Busby (1975) documented extensive work role stereotyping in television programming; and Miller and Reese (1976) found that a child's rate of television watching correlated with acceptance of traditional work roles for women. Indeed, O'Bryant and Corder-Bolz (1978) demonstrated that showing five to ten-year-old children commercials featuring women in nontraditional work roles reduced stereotyping and expanded girls' range of occupations. Even standard government and major publishers' literature is biased against women, as Birk, Cooper and Tanney (1973) indicated in their review of publications such as the *Occupational Outlook Handbook*. By the age of nine, and more clearly by thirteen, the national assessment of career maturity showed that girls feel less confident in career development skills than do boys (Miller, 1978; Aubrey, 1977; Mitchell, 1977).

Bingham and House (1973) have documented that as girls move forward into junior and senior high school, many counselors provide prejudicial career counseling. Even in testing, Diamond (1975) showed that technical errors in existing interest inventories discourage girls from exploring the "traditional male" occupations.

By the time women are ready to attend college, many have excluded themselves from careers in science and management because they have omitted the prerequisite mathematics, science, and economic courses (Solomon, 1977). Counselors are moving to correct this situation by offering programs to desensitize women to their fear of mathematics (Hendel & Davis, 1978). Table 3–11 shows the low proportion of women in physical science, engineering, business curricula in 1972 and 1974. But changes are occurring. A recent report by the American Assembly of Collegiate Schools of Business showed matriculated female MBA candidates increased from 10.8 percent in 1973 to 18.4 percent in 1976.

Image of Career Women

Successful career women have, in the past, been portrayed as different, often somewhat less feminine. This image, however, appears to be changing. Hennig and Jardim (1976), studying a small sample of high-achieving women who started the work portion of their careers in the

Table 3–11. Percentage of Women Aged Fourteen to Thirty-four in Different Curriculum in 1972 and 1974

Major field of study	1974	1972
Total enrolled	44.2	41.6
Agriculture forestry	13.5	11.3
Biological sciences	41.0	36.6
Business or commerce	31.7	23.2
Education	72.6	72.3
Engineering	6.8	2.0
English or journalism	59.1	51.5
Other humanities	48.0	47.3
Health or medical profession	64.2	56.5
Law	23.2	17.7
Mathematics or statistics	44.6	34.3
Physical sciences	26.9	27.4
Social sciences	44.4	47.5
Vocation-technical studies	25.4	(NA)
Computer science	20.0	(NA)
Other	41.0	39.7
None and not reported	44.7	41.9

NA Not available.

SOURCE: U.S. Department of Commerce, Bureau of the Census, *Current Population Reports*, Series P-20, No. 260 and unpublished data.

1930s and 1940s, found that these women tended to be first-born children with close ties to fathers, often had been "tomboys," and were aided in their career progress by male mentors. Phillips (1977), in contrast, studying more than 300 females with prominent achievement, who started their work careers from the 1930s through 1960s, found that only about 25 percent of her sample fit the Hennig-Jardim model. Moreover, these 300 respondents listed competence, drive and determination, personality, and appropriate schooling, and experience as sources of their career success as often or more often than "male mentoring."

Even though expectations about working are changing, women still have negative or mixed views about career women. Wilkinson (1979), for instance, found that nineteen career aspirants, matched in age, social class, and education with nineteen career women at the supervisory and middle-management level, had several negative beliefs about career women that the career women did not have. Furthermore, twenty other career aspirants and twenty women who were working, but had not advanced in their work, also rated career women somewhat less positively. Studying college women's ratings of authors, Goldberg (1968) found that they rated women authors inferior to men even though there was no basis for this difference. He concluded that they were prejudiced against career women.

Correcting the Discrimination

The federal government has moved to correct unfair treatment of women in work and education with the *Equal Pay Act* of 1972, the *Equal Employment Opportunity Act of 1964* and as expanded by *Executive Order, 11246,* and by *Title IX of the Education Amendments of 1972.* These authorize the Office of Civil Rights to bring suit against employers or colleges or universities that deny equal rights to women, and they require "affirmative action" policies to expedite equal treatment. Farmer and Backer (1977) have included these regulations in their text and have listed court cases relating to them.

Federal policy has also prompted publishers of textbooks, tests, inventories, and educational and occupational materials to eliminate sex bias in educational materials. Books, tests, and audio-visuals produced since the mid 1970s present women and minorities in a wider, more balanced range of contexts and levels. Even the pronoun *he* is no longer used exclusively to refer to human agents.

Society is revising, even revolutionizing, its view of female careers. Clearly everyone can contribute to expanding women's career options. Among other things, counselors can help women look beyond traditional stereotypes when they are setting goals and making career plans. They can direct women to appropriate information and models. They can assist women in finding support for pioneering ventures. Employers can adopt a truly "affirmative action" posture, rather than merely complying with affirmative action mandates; can provide access for thirty-five to forty-five-year-old women and men to enter ladder traineeships; and can allow "mainline" jobs to be filled on a half-time basis or shared basis by half-time workers.

Husbands can plan careers jointly with wives, giving attention to the career wishes of both parties, and they can accept more responsibility for homemaking and parenting. Children, likewise, can contribute more to homemaking and take greater responsibility for arranging their own activities and transportation and secure more assistance from other resource people such as teachers, librarians, fathers, older siblings, grandparents, and neighbors. But especially, women themselves can accept the possibility of a new relationship to work with its accompanying responsibilities and advantages. They can redefine commitments and establish plans for meeting the responsibilities and realizing the benefits. Women should take initiative in examining possibilities, locating educational and work opportunities, establishing supports for their growth, and assuring that their efforts are creating a person they and their society can respect. Certainly, many specific opportunities and strategies can be identified by contrasting successful with unsuccessful women. Authors, such as Farmer and Backer (1977), Bolles (1974), and countless others, are now suggesting specific opportunities and strategies for women.

Racial and Ethnic Background

Unquestionably, minority Americans have been and continue to be denied equal access to educational and occupational opportunities because of their racial or ethnic background. Until 1954, blacks and other minorities could not attend some tax-supported and private schools. Major universities, including prestigious Ivy League schools, restricted admissions of minorities until the 1950s. As late as World War II, the armed services segregated white and minority servicemen, and until 1963 there was no effective federal support of minorities suffering discrimination in employment. Even until 1971, employers, government agencies, and the armed forces could use screening devices biased against minorities.

Today, federal legislation has established means of safeguarding the rights of minorities, and many states have enacted similar and complementary legislation and established similar civil rights agencies for safeguarding career rights. The problem of unequal treatment, however, is a long way from resolution. Because of past discrimination, blacks and other minority people have grown up in disadvantaged circumstances and must raise their children in similar conditions. Nearly half the American black population, for instance, lives below the official poverty level. Many black children attend schools that receive substantially lower funds per pupil (Serrano & Priest, 1971) than white children in their state. Their schoolmates score lower on tests and drop out of school earlier than students in mainstream schools, and their school faculties are likely to have lower educational qualifications than those in schools populated primarily by white students. Moreover, minorities are more likely than whites to live in impoverished areas underserviced by the government. They have less access to successful career models and less acquaintance with persons who can get them jobs.

Table 3–12 shows that blacks are underrepresented in higher-level occupations. Only 1 percent of our engineers, for example, are black. Blacks own a very small percentage of businesses. Estimates reported in the December 7, 1977, *Wall Street Journal* indicate that black-controlled businesses obtain less than 1 percent of the subcontracts from major American industry. Certainly, a black director of a *Fortune 500* corporation is a news item. Yet, in spite of professed energetic recruitment, relatively few blacks are enrolled in Master's of Business Administration Programs (*Los Angeles Times*, 1978). On the other hand, black unemployment rates typically are nearly double those of whites. Among a recent random sample of seventy-five blacks who had graduated from California State University between 1973 and 1977, Obinna (1979) found fewer than half reported full-time employment and fewer than

Table 3–12. Percentage Distribution of White and Black and Other Workers in Each Occupational Group: 1958 and 1977

	White		Black and Other	
	1958	1977	1958	1977
Professional and technical workers	11.8	15.5	4.1	11.8
Managers and administrators	11.7	11.4	2.4	4.8
Sales workers	6.9	6.8	1.2	2.6
Clerical workers	15.4	18.0	6.1	16.1
Craft workers	14.3	13.6	5.9	9.0
Operators	17.9	14.7	20.1	20.3
Nonfarm laborers	4.5	4.6	14.7	8.3
Private household workers	1.7	.9	15.4	4.2
Other service workers	7.7	11.4	17.7	20.8
Farmers/farm managers	5.0	1.8	3.7	.4
Farm laborers/supervisors	3.0	1.4	8.8	1.8

SOURCE: Table A–16, *Employment and Training Report of the President*. Washington, D.C.: U.S. Department of Labor, 1978, p. 208.

half were satisfied in their careers. The career problems of minorities are widespread, yet the reasons for them are not fully understood and the solutions are sometimes controversial.

Minorities and Access to Work

Father-son and uncle-nephew unions, both in the crafts and in the professions, and "old boy" networks indicate that entering a decent job, training program, or school requires sponsorship. Although these concepts herald the extremes in preferential treatment for in-group members, they underscore the fact that many people obtain employment through personal and family contacts (Jameson, 1978), and that many schools and training programs give preference to sons and daughters of former graduates. Such practices may not be intended to disadvantage blacks and other minorities; they probably reflect that people in the system take care of their own first. The effect, however, is to disadvantage minorities especially, since they had deliberately been excluded and even expelled from the system until the recent past.

Differences between Whites and Minorities

Some people have argued stridently that minorities, especially blacks, are less able intellectually (Jensen, 1969), and that this "fact" accounts for the underrepresentation of blacks in the mainstream of the American economy. Others, however, have pointed out that the intrinsic, probably inestimable, bias of intellectual tests against disadvantaged persons precludes establishing the relative intellectual abilities of the races. Many comparisons of blacks and whites on intellectual tasks have been made, but few, if any, of these comparisons have been fair. Consequently, judgments about racial differences based on these comparisons are not justified. But even if the races differed intellectually and if it were possible to designate people as black or white, the hypothesized intellectual differences among races (½ standard deviation) would not explain why 50 percent of the American black population lives below the poverty level. Clearly, blacks and most other minorities face more obstacles to career development than mainstream Americans. Realistically, they do not expect to achieve as much educationally or occupationally as their white counterparts.

Disappointingly, however, minorities encounter a school and guidance establishment that has been less effective in meeting their needs than those of mainstream white Americans. Both the guidance instruments—informational material and tests—and the counselors and teachers have been subtly, although not necessarily intentionally, biased in favor of whites. For instance, many studies have shown that occupational literature depicts minorities in less prestigious positions and that educational and occupational tests put applicants from outside the mainstream at a disadvantage. At any rate, mainstream whites have benefited more from counseling than have other groups.

The greater benefit from counseling by mainstream whites may of course reflect that they are advantaged in their environments and as a consequence better able to implement the teachings of counseling. Certainly, the failure of multiple researches to establish that counselors of the same racial or ethnic group are significantly more effective with members of their group suggests that the bias is not due to personal prejudice. For, even though failure to reject the null hypothesis does not prove it, the fact that differences were not established at least implies that any differences are not large. Instead of a prejudice explanation, the source of probable bias suggested by Blocher et al. (1971) encompasses both observations. They hypothesized that the strategies used in counseling and the solutions taught therein favor the mainstream white because of the resources they require and the style of coping they presume.

By implication, their hypothesis requires a counselor to establish clearly the kind of assistance minority clients expect and to ascertain the actions that are most likely to work for minority persons in resolving their problem. The counselor must be careful not to presume that the actions most likely to help mainstream whites also will aid those outside the mainstream. Instead, the counselor needs to observe successful members of the minority group to ascertain what has been working for them.

The Blocher et al. (1971) view, of course, does not necessarily support establishing corps of minority counselors to give minority communities greater control over their youngsters' counseling. Nevertheless, experience of immigrant groups indicates that political power has contributed to social progress in the United States (Fitzpatrick, 1961). This author, therefore, believes more minority people should become career counselors so the minority community may have more influence in counseling its youth. Furthermore, efforts to improve counseling for minorities should explore new methods of teaching solutions to new problems, rather than continue to seek out small racial and ethnic differences that, at best, are likely to be minimally important.

Correcting the career disadvantages of minority group members will not be easy. Even massive "war on poverty" programs have not seemed able to provide the early career nurturance, secure environment, models, and contacts with the career world they lack. Although the 1964 civil rights laws and their amendments permit government to intervene on behalf of workers who are the object of discrimination, and suits have been pursued successfully, correction of discriminatory practices is slow.

In 1972, therefore, the government moved to implement a more active program—Affirmative Action. Essentially, this program asks employers to seek out qualified minority people and women for positions and promotions, not merely to avoid discriminating against them. Implementation of this program is increasingly controversial, and several counter lawsuits have been filed.

Certainly a very fine line exists between seeking out qualified candidates of a particular race or sex and affording preferential treatment to candidates because of their race, sex, or ethnic background. Support for the former position should become more widespread when people recognize the detrimental effect that past discrimination has had and continues to have throughout a minority person's career, and when they recognize that such injustice cheats all society as well as the individual. To date, however, little has been done to educate Americans about the extent of the obstacles facing minorities. School administrators, for instance, often hide inner-city school disruptions and their consequent damage to the careers of many innocent minority students in such schools. Moreover, statistics about high dropout rates among minority students are often downplayed by some people who naively believe they are promoting a positive minority image by not focusing on them. Yet, such statistics indict the school system rather than the minority dropout, and underscore the fact that better school services for minority children are needed.

A Word of Caution

Blacks and other minorities are not monolithic groups, except in the sense that they have been victims of discrimination and injustice. They have diverse cultures just as Europeans have many cultures. Not all blacks come from matriarchial families or the inner city. They have a wide range of talents, aspirations, and accomplishment. Moreover, they profess different religious and political beliefs. Obviously, each minority member is a distinctive person who merits the same individualized consideration as any other person.

One very helpful development in recent years is the American resurgence of racial and ethnic pride. For racial or ethnic pride is a component of self-confidence, and total self-confidence is a powerful moderator of achievement. Black and Hispanic youngsters who accept that "Black is beautiful" and that the Hispanic culture merits esteem are more able to master career challenges and to contribute to society. Development of such consciousness need not emphasize minority persons' separation from the mainstream or accentuate ethnic or racial membership, but rather it can illuminate their distinctive history to equip them for full participation in the mainstream culture.

Career Counselors' Responses to the Racially and Ethnically Disadvantaged

As professionals, career counselors can take several actions to aid the career development of minorities.

First, they can scrutinize counseling and educational programs to ascertain what is and is not working; not to find fault or to curtail funding, but to expedite improvement by identifying and multiplying effective programs.

Second, counselors can encourage and conduct programs that educate mainstream Americans about how minorities, through no fault of their own, encounter innumerable obstacles to their careers, and how those injustices cheat the entire society, not just the minorities.

Third, counselors can support programs and legislation that provide tuition, models, mentors, and other resources that help minorities take advantage of educational and occupational options that have recently become available through civil rights legislation.

Fourth, on a more personal level, career counselors can become aware of the context within which their minority clients operate in order to be cognizant of what successful peers of these clients are doing and of what is appropriate for their clients to learn and to do with their own resources.

Fifth, they should encourage minority youngsters to set appropriately high goals, and should tell them that the law now supports their legitimate entitlement to opportunities that were recently denied their parents and older siblings. In addition, counselors should realize that minority students may abandon realistic goals when temporarily frustrated. Counselors should remember that minority persons may find it harder to believe that perseverance will pay off because they have been victims so long and still encounter personal prejudice.

A Final Word

This chapter has reviewed attributes that research and tradition suggest are important to career. Implicitly, the review shows gaps in the knowledge about people in relation to work.

Yet, recognition of these informational gaps can be helpful. For example, the difficulties with current methods of assessing abilities, interests, values, and other personality traits should indicate clearly that people must understand more about basic appraisal so they can be better able to clarify who they are. Early in one's development, each person should be taught concepts such as reliability, validity, and over-generalization. Most children recognize that one "20 percent day" on the basketball "free-throw" line does not mean that they are poor foul shooters; they need to apply the same principle to judgments about their other qualities too. Similarly, one who recognizes that a teasing younger brother cannot accurately estimate one's mechanical prowess also must learn to expect accurate appraisals of one's qualities only from people who are qualified to judge and who have had enough time to observe them. Also, one needs to recognize that the appraisal of one's ability improves with evidence from different sources, such as a coach, a test, and "buddy" ratings. Likewise, one probably will recognize that winning the fifth-grade award for best essay does not necessarily mean that one is the fifth grade's best writer. Self-awareness potential will improve by appreciating that generalization about any quality will be more accurate if one has sampled several activities within the range of the particular quality. The adage that "one swallow doesn't make a summer" exemplifies this fact.

But, not only can people learn assessment concepts, they also can recognize their need to locate and to create situations by which they can understand who they are or can become. Due to the emphasis in guidance and personnel selection on testing and record keeping, many people do not know or believe in their potential for change.

America is the land of "instants" and labor savers, so many people offer instant personality discovery and creation. Early in their careers, however, youngsters need to recognize that society expects people to initiate exploration of the many aspects of themselves not addressed in the school curriculum. Moreover, they need to realize that such exploration takes time and often considerable energy, and they should have the opportunity to see how instant, easy gimmicks lead to inaccurate self-appraisals.

Many implications for viewing and guiding careers can be derived from the models of man described above, and from considering how factors such as ability, interests, values, personality, social class, sex, and race influence career opportunity. This chapter has reviewed important aspects of these concepts. Now the reader should ponder and discuss their implications with colleagues; such thought is necessary to formulate one's own approach to guiding people in their careers.

Careers and Our Education-Work System

4

Careers unfold in the education-work system of a society, and that system affects what work will be like. Our system has become an industrial, or perhaps a postindustrial complex with more than 20,000 occupations, 100,000,000 workers, and thousands of college and post-high school programs that train people for those occupations.

This chapter reviews the structure of our education-work system and examines the information processes available to help people negotiate their careers within this system. The world of work and, to a lesser degree, the world of schools have changed and are changing rapidly; but, barring a revolution or cataclysm, the changes will take place within the broad parameters of education-work that exist today. Certainly, existing education and work institutions have a commitment to such stability. Understanding our present structures, therefore, will enable one to anticipate future careers and will suggest means for helping people become more aware of career possibilities.

Work, Education and Societal Direction are Dynamically Interrelated

The institutions of education and work affect and are affected by developments in the total society. The nature of schooling and the activities called work reflect society's intentions and resources; once established, the structures around these activities seek to perpetuate themselves.

America's large, formal education structure, legally mandatory for most people until age eighteen, is not the only system that might have evolved to support an industrial society, according to analysts who are designing education systems for third world nations that wish to enter the industrial age. Nor did this education system just happen to evolve.

Rather, the growing power of organized labor supported longer schooling to reduce the competition for jobs and to increase the mobility potential of their children. Business and industry supported extended training that shift some of the occupational training expense from their budgets to the public expense and provided a credentialing service for them. Naturally, the educational establishment welcomed the opportunity to expand.

America's corporate work world is also traceable to special interests. An exposé of Ralph Nader et al. (1976) reveals that a small number of corporations bribed and cajolled a few state legislators at the turn of the century into enacting a legal structure that favors a corporate work system rather than one of small owners. In Western Europe and Japan, in contrast, small firms have become more important. Clearly, a different kind of private work sector might have come into existence to support America's industrial expansion. If one accepts that the educational-work institutions have been created by people with specific motives, beliefs, and knowledge, then today's citizens have an obligation continually to re-examine whether existing systems should be reaffirmed or changed in light of current motives, beliefs, and knowledge.

Work is Evolving, but Still Necessary

Although some onerous aspects of work have been removed as civilization has advanced, work still involves effort, drudgery, lack of control, and dependence. Like the ancestral hunters, gatherers, and shepherds, today's workers must expand energy and time to produce goods and services. All too often, that uninteresting or unenjoyable effort tires these laborers who yearn for its end. Generally, the start, pace, and termination of work are not decided by the laborer. Frequently, workers cannot even decide how to do the job or what materials to use. They often must coordinate their actions with those of other people or machines; hence, changes in their work depend on the desires of other people. These negative aspects of work readily bring to mind jobs, such as waiter, elevator operator, assembler, and grocery clerk; but, even professions, such as lawyer, dentist, and teacher, contain these negative elements to some degree. Certainly, the lawyer must pore over law passages long after they have ceased to be interesting. And, of course, clients, judges, or legislators—not the individual lawyers—determine the kind of brief to be produced.

On the other hand, work has become somewhat easier. Machines, such as tractors and air conditioners, have reduced the need for human physical energy and have improved working conditions. Likewise, advances, such as irrigation and automation, enable workers to use resources more easily and predictably and to achieve greater, more precise output.

But people still must produce the goods and services needed to sustain society. Machines contribute more than ever before, but human beings have to design, build, manage, and maintain the machines.

Furthermore, many jobs still exist for which machines have not yet been invented. Currently, science fiction is the only domain where people do not have to work.

Americans assume that every able-bodied adult works. Every politician knows that even the suggestion that a small percentage of able-bodied people are accepting idleness and welfare rather than meeting their work obligation angers the citizenry. Even most mothers with children feel exempt from the obligation to work only until their children are old enough to attend school. Then they, too, must join the labor force, begin volunteer work, or return to school in order to prepare for work. Otherwise, they lose status in the community and welfare benefits if they are on public assistance.

Work (*Manpower Report to the President*, 1975) is, in fact, a person's dues to the society, the fruits of which enrich the society and add to its gross national product. Few adults are exempted from these dues. Work binds the people of a society together because the products and services of one citizen assist others, who in turn produce in order to receive these benefits; as a consequence, these workers help still others. Without work, society could not meet the needs and wants of its citizenry, and would eventually die.

Work also has many other functions. Economically, it is a major factor in production; as such, work influences the kind and quantity of goods and services available. Sociologically, work confers status and legitimizes activity. One's prerogatives and recognition in the community are a function of one's work role or anticipated work role. Moreover, actions performed according to the job specifications are deemed useful and adult if not self-enhancing, since working affirms one's support of societal institutions and purposes. Indeed, refusing to work is tantamount to rejecting society. Psychologically, work is one manner of self-expression. Effective performance of challenging, socially meaningful work enhances self-esteem and overall mental health, while laboring in unchallenging, undesirable jobs reduces self-esteem and correlates with many physical and mental disorders (O'Toole, 1973).

Once survival needs are met, society seeks other ends in work. The amount of time necessary to work for survival depends on the available other resources: land, energy, capital goods, and capital. In China and India, the scarcity of these other assets necessitates more people working longer hours to meet the basic needs of food, clothing, and shelter.

America and Work

Production and consumption have been nearly deified in America. A larger percentage of adults work outside the home in America than in any other Western civilization, and Americans save less of their income than citizens in other developed countries. Veteran demographers predict that the percentage of Americans working would grow even larger if more jobs were available (Yankelovich, 1978). Surprisingly, not nearly as many Americans vote as work. It is therefore predictable that America leads the world in sheer production and in consumption. Nor is it surprising that American advertising, which promotes consumption, is more developed and given more power over the public media than in any other country. Moreover, "GNP," "unemployment rate," and "inflation rate" command more attention in the American press than other possible indices of societal well-being such as birth, mortality, divorce, church and education participation rates. Clearly, *"Stop the World I Want to Get Off"* achieved such acclaim in America because it poignantly parodied our worship of production and consumption.

Status in America depends on consumption of goods and services, including education. Since most people's incomes depend almost totally on wages, occupational advancement is one of the major routes of upward social mobility. Wealth dominates politics and community organizations in America. Workers are expected to sacrifice health, integrity, family, community, and ecology to earn more so that they can consume more.

Exemplary Americans are active in career and in leisure. They work and play hard, conspicuously taking advantage of computers, expensive cars, and other luxury items. These paragons of success have busy, well-arranged schedules featuring quick production and decisions that express individuality and autonomy.

Paid work commands the best hours, and in other, less obvious ways, influences how one plays life's other roles. In America we do not eat midday meals with family because that practice would interfere with production and formal education, even though it might enable less-tired family members to enjoy one another more. Promotion and even employment are denied if workers are not available for overtime or relocation. Moreover, corporate policy and occupational demands influence even one's community involvement and political posture.

Individuals and society regard volunteer work as of secondary importance, even though it is often more creative and more directly beneficial to society. For example, people are excused from their volunteer commitments readily, especially to meet their work commitments. Successful volunteer work, moreover, does not appear to bolster self-esteem as much as paid work. Certainly, volunteer workers are not employed nearly as efficiently or systematically as paid workers. Although authors, such as Bolles (1974), implore people to inform potential employers of talents developed through volunteer work, those hiring do not regard volunteer experience as important as paid work experience. Not surprisingly, women, therefore, have felt the need to engage more fully in paid employment. They and the minorities have recognized that, without equal access and opportunity to work in our society, they become second-class citizens.

Benefits for Modern Workers

Many modern workers feel confident that they will secure their basic food, clothing, and shelter needs as long as they work. As output expands, society can redistribute profits from a successful sector to one that temporarily has failed.

Working has improved in other ways, too. The number of hours workers must toil in order to earn a living has decreased, while the production of the individual worker has multiplied through modern work methods. As a consequence, today's worker earns much more from significantly reduced effort than did great grandparents or parents. Within the last century, the work week has shrunk from sixty to forty hours, while the worker's purchasing power and the goods and services available have multiplied. Most American workers now own their own cars, receive nearly a month of paid holidays, have medical, dental, retirement, and survivor benefits, and can afford to dine out regularly. These benefits were unknown fifty years ago. Similarly, workers are better dressed and better housed in heated and often air-conditioned quarters. Many own their own homes, televisions, hi-fi sets, refrigerators, campers, swimming pools, and increasingly, membership in a local country or athletic club. The late George Meany, long-time leader of the AFL-CIO, claimed that this affluence explains the decline in union militancy over the last fifty years.

Perhaps the major improvement in work is the diversification of jobs. The modern worker can pay societal dues in one of many ways. Increasingly, a person can leave a job that has become taxing or dull for one that is more compatible. In fact, society underwrites many job training and retraining programs. Table 4–1 shows the expansion of occupations and changes in distribution of workers. The figures indicate the great diversity of modern employment and the immensity of our work force. They do not, however, point out that the shift from farming, mining, construction, and manufacturing, to service and professional occupations was possible because of technological developments that allowed production industries to operate more efficiently with significantly reduced human toil and risk for those who continued in them.

Nor, do the numbers show that technological developments improved the quality of work in many occupations and reduced their noxious elements. But recent discoveries by the Office of Occupational Health and Safety indicate much still remains to be improved. Our awareness of work hazards must be put into perspective, however; physical and psychological hazards can and must be reduced, although much has already been done to improve the quality of work.

Trends That Will Influence Work

Many trends will affect the nature of future work. One major influence will be resource availability. Predicted shortages of resources, such as fossil fuels and capital, would require more workers to do more physical work and would reduce the quantity of goods and services available.

Another factor that affects work is knowledge. New discoveries suggest new needs and new potentials for improving life, thereby spurring job creation and commitment of resources. Advances in chemistry, for

Table 4–1. Distribution of Nonagricultural Workers by Industry
(Figures are in thousands)

	1919	1939	1960	1977	1990
Mining	1,124	845	748	867	1,072
	4.2%	2.8%	1.1%	.9%	.9%
Contract construction	1,021	1,150	3,654	4,672	5,748
	3.8%	3.8%	5.3%	5.0%	4.8%
Manufacturing	10,534	10,078	17,197	19,844	23,882
	39.2%	33.2%	25.0%	21.2%	20.1%
Transportation and public utilities	3,711	2,912	4,214	8,173	9,189
	13.8%	9.6%	6.1%	8.7%	7.7%
Wholesale/retail trade	4,664	6,705	14,177	20,908	27,370
	17.4%	22.1%	20.6%	22.3%	23.1%
Finance and others	1,050	1,382	2,985	4,888	6,695
	3.9%	4.6%	4.3%	5.2%	5.6%
Service[a]	2,054	3,228	12,152	17,674	26,742
	7.7%	10.7%	17.6%	18.9%	22.5%
Government	2,671	3,987	8,353	15,189	17,507
	10.0%	13.2%	12.1%	16.2%	14.8%

[a] Domestic occupations, such as housekeeper, contributed substantially to the 1919 and 1939 service groups, but not to the 1960, 1977, or projected 1990 groups.

SOURCE: U.S. Bureau of Labor Statistics, *Employment training Report of the President*. Washington, D.C.: U.S. Government Printing, 1979.

example, have given rise to the pollution prevention industry. Knowledge of what others are doing and enjoying increases demand for existing goods and services. More leisure time will undoubtedly focus greater attention on philosophy, the arts, and cultural exchange. Ultimately, the inevitable comparisons of current life styles with alternative life styles may well lead to changes in the work people are willing to do.

Closely related are advances in technology. To a degree, society has done what its technology would permit. With continuing technological development surely will come the tendency to do what technology will allow. Automation continues to alter and to eliminate many jobs, displacing thousands of workers yearly. The jobs that are becoming available through automation require more technological sophistication (e.g. design and maintenance jobs) or routine observation and alertness (e.g. operator jobs).

Linked to increased automation are advances in microprocessors, which are likely to accelerate the use of computers. By 1990, computers could easily be a typical household appliance as the calculator is now. Advances in communication technology, too, will surely enable more workers to interact with larger networks of people without direct contact, and perhaps in a less personal way. New technologies probably will allow working from home, thereby saving transportation fuels and using home (a capital resource) more fully. The larger communication networks also will increase the need for precision in language.

Changes in social, political, and economic beliefs and customs will, in turn, shape the future education and work systems. Demands by younger people that work be intrinsically satisfying and require less time and commitment will diminish the attractiveness of some occupations and influence the design of new occupations. Even now, high-skill trades, such as tool and die making, are anticipating worker shortages at a time of rising unemployment. Two probable reasons are that the intrinsic rewards of precision work are not manifest and that the craft's demanding character does not fit the expectations of limited commitment to work. On the other hand, youth's concern with ecology may lead to changing living styles that emphasize conserving rather than consuming. According to the American Institute of Architects, such a turnaround can create hundreds of thousands of jobs to make homes and other buildings more energy efficient. Moreover, Long (1977), in a 1977 Los Angeles *Times* article proclaiming how conservation could create construction work, noted that these jobs would accommodate low and moderately skilled workers—the people who now suffer high unemployment.

Turning to political and economic trends, acceptance of increased federal regulation clearly is leading to more equitable educational opportunity for all citizens, regardless of sex or race, and to more uniform health and safety standards for all workers. On the other hand, minimal involvement of workers in their unions and professional associations suggests that job redesigning efforts in America will remain largely the province of management, whether the employers' or the workers' organization.

On the economic side, increased consumption and reduced saving are making private capital accumulation more difficult. At the same time, greater consciousness about consumer rights is leading to greater attention to product and service quality. These combined developments may slow down innovation, lead to emphasis on upgrading existing goods and services, and elevate prices for these products.

Demographic changes are a fifth trend that will alter the education and work systems. Demographic characteristics of a population refer to its frequency distribution of variables such as age, sex, years of working, family composition, education, literacy, ethnicity, social status, and residence in rural, urban, and suburban communities. Alterations in these characteristics affect many aspects of a society (Wolfbein, 1968). For instance, the large increase in the number of children in the 1960s led to the expansion of the educational system, high demand for teachers, increase in delinquency and crime, and development of many youth-oriented products and services. Similarly, the upsurge in the proportion of disadvantaged persons in the large youth group spurred many remedial and special assistance programs in education and manpower.

As demographers look toward the late 1980s and early 1990s, they see that the bulge in population will move to the thirty-five to fifty-year-old range. Since this adult population will be better educated than ever before, many demographers predict expanded productivity in America. They reason that since the work force will have a proportionally larger number of mature workers with a higher education level, new surges in productivity are inevitable. Looking even further into the future as this surge in population moves into retirement after the year 2000, Social Security Administration actuarians have become worried about the solvency of the system under the strain of so many retirees. They antici- pate that there will then be one annuitant for every 2½ workers, whereas now there are four workers to one annuitant. Certainly, raising man- datory retirement to age 70 had the support of these trend watchers.

The sixth trend likely to affect work is increased centralization. The growing population and the demands on resources have to be coordinated and articulated in terms of broad societal intention. Centralization and bureaucracy increasingly have been the answer to the need for coordina- tion; yet bureaucracy often stifles individual initiative and inventiveness that move a society forward and keep it vital. Certainly, how the chal- lenge of interdependence is managed will affect significantly the char- acter of future work.

Linked with centralization is the trend of specialization. The bureau- crats required by centralization divide administration into a myriad of distinctive functions, leading to many different jobs. Concomitantly, knowledge advances in administration and other fields are making it increasingly difficult for workers to avoid specialization, whether their occupation is medicine, engineering, law, accounting, laboratory tech- nology, auto repair, or law enforcement. Specialization increases inter- dependence while accentuating differences among people by leading them to perform different activities and build distinctive identities. As a consequence, workers now can engage relatively fewer of their neighbors in "shop talk," and there is danger that larger numbers of workers will feel that an ordinary person will not be able to appreciate their work.

The eighth and last trend is individualized education, which is part of Toffler's (1980) broader individualized production trend. Such educa- tion may hasten specialization, but it will definitely expedite learning and enable people to acquire the educational prerequisites for occupa- tions more quickly and therefore facilitate occupational change. In- creased use of self-instructional materials and computers to assemble and guide learning will soon enable people to create individualized learning programs electronically for use in their own homes. This will enable students to be more efficient, learning only what they need and starting at the appropriate level, rather than having to attend to super- fluous material because it is part of a standard program or part of a class. Likewise, learners will be able to move at their own pace and study when it is convenient. Fortuitously, expanded learning may counter the societal divisiveness that Dubin (1976) predicts will result from specialization. Knowing more and being able to learn faster will permit people to keep up with what their neighbors are discovering. That should be more positive for survival than would be matching neighbors in consumption.

Researching the factors behind each of these trends and speculating about their probable impacts can be fun and can alert clients to what they should do to be able to manage their careers. Therefore, examining trends and imagining their personal implications are likely to become important components of career counseling. Surprisingly, no research has been reported relative to such examination and speculation in counseling. However, exploration is underway. For example, Len Steinberg has established a course at California State University, Los Angeles, in which prospective counselors engage in deliberation about trends and their impact on career.

Occupational Differences

Even though more than 20,000 different occupations exist in the United States, more than 90 percent of the work force is in less than one hundred occupations (Holland, 1971). Some occupations, such as harness makers and coopers, number only a few workers; others, such as truck drivers, assemblers, waitresses, janitors, typists, and elementary school teachers, engage over a million people. Nevertheless, more than another 20,000 occupations exist for people who wish to work at something out of the ordinary.

An occupation is distinct primarily because it involves a unique set of duties that contribute in a special way to the production of a good or service. Other distinguishing factors, however, include required skills and training, previous occupation, working conditions, entry or leaving age, prestige, salary, equipment used, amount of routine, degree of autonomy, and isolation.

Systematic study of occupations requires a rational and simple classification system. One system, the field by level classification of Roe (1956), outlined below in Table 4–2, is widely used by researchers because of its simplicity and comprehensiveness. There are, of course, other possible classification systems, including the United States Census Classification of Edwards (professional, proprietary and managerial, clerical and sales, skilled and supervisory, semiskilled, and unskilled), the fifteen career clusters of the United States Department of Education (consumer and homemaking, transportation, health, personal service, public service, manufacturing, construction, fine arts and humanities, marketing and distribution, agribusiness and natural resources, environmental, marine science, communications and media, business and office, hospitality and recreation), and the standard industrial classifications (agriculture-forest, mining, construction, manufacture, trade, finance, transport, service, and government). The relative merits of such systems have been discussed by Super (1957) and Isaacson (1977).

Occupational Field

Roe defined occupational fields as foci of activity and interest. Her fields approximated several of the clusters that were apparent in the *Strong*

Table 4-2. Two-Way Classification of Occupations

Level	I. Service	II. Business Contact	III. Organization	IV. Technology	V. Outdoor	VI. Science	VII. General Cultural	VIII. Arts and Entertainment
								Group
1	Personal therapists Social work supervisors Counselors	Promoters	United States President and Cabinet officers Industrial tycoons International bankers	Inventive geniuses Consulting or chief engineers Ships' commanders	Consulting specialists	Research scientists University, college faculties Medical specialists Museum curators	Supreme Court Justices University, college faculties Prophets Scholars	Creative artists Performers, great Teachers, university equivalent Museum curators
2	Social workers Occupational therapists Probation, truant officers (with training)	Promoters Public relations counselors	Certified public accountants Business and government executives Union officials Brokers, average	Applied scientists Factory managers Ships' officers Engineers	Applied scientists Landowners and operators, large Landscape architects	Scientists, semi-independent Nurses Pharmacists Veterinarians	Editors Teachers, high school and elementary	Athletes Art critics Designers Music arrangers
3	YMCA officials Detectives, police sergeants Welfare workers City inspectors	Salesmen: auto, bond, insurance, etc. Dealers, retail and wholesale Confidence men	Accountants, average Employment managers Owners, catering, dry-cleaning, etc.	Aviators Contractors Foremen (DOT I) Radio operators	County agents Farm owners Forest rangers Fish, game wardens	Technicians, medical, X-ray, museum Weather observers Chiropractors	Justices of the Peace Radio announcers Reporters Librarians	Ad writers Designers Interior decorators Showmen

Group

Level	I. Service	II. Business Contact	III. Organization	IV. Technology	V. Outdoor	VI. Science	VII. General Cultural	VIII. Arts and Entertainment
4	Barbers Chefs Practical nurses Policemen	Auctioneers Buyers (DOT I) House canvassers Interviewers, poll	Cashiers Clerks, credit, express, etc. Foremen, warehouse Salesclerks	Blacksmiths Electricians Foremen (DOT II) Mechanics, average	Laboratory testers, dairy products, etc. Miners Oil well drillers	Technical assistants	Law clerks	Advertising artists Decorators, window, etc. Photographers Racing car drivers
5	Taxi drivers General houseworkers Waiters City firemen	Peddlers	Clerks, file, stock, etc. Notaries Runners Typists	Bulldozer operators Deliverymen Smelter workers Truck drivers	Gardeners Farm tenants Teamsters, cowpunchers Miner's helpers	Veterinary hospital attendants		Illustrators, greeting cards Showcard writers Stagehands
6	Chambermaids Hospital attendants Elevator operators Watchmen		Messenger boys	Helpers Laborers Wrappers Yardmen	Dairy hands Farm laborers Lumberjacks	Nontechnical helpers in scientific organization		

SOURCE: A. Roe, *The psychology of occupations*, p. 151. New York: John Wiley and Sons, 1956. Reprinted by permission of the publisher and the author.

123

Vocational Interest Blank (Strong, 1955). Each field represents a relatively distinct approach to production, illustrated in Table 4–2. More specifically, occupations in a field at the same level use similar tools and equipment, produce similar goods or services, and often employ the same modes of dealing with people, things, and data. Workers in these occupations, especially at the higher level, satisfy and pursue similar interests and work values. Their training has involved related experiences and school subjects, and their previous, full-time employment after completing formal schooling is similar. Training for science occupations, for example, generally includes laboratory experience, science courses, and mathematics or statistical methodology courses. At the upper levels, many scientists have been "post docs." In contrast, incumbents of general cultural occupations frequently study the humanities and psychology, sociology, or anthropology, and, at the upper level, practitioners complete internships and require mentors.

When workers change occupations, they are more likely to enter another occupation in the same or in an adjoining field (Roe, Hubbard, Hutchinson, & Bateman, 1966; Gottfredson, 1977). This fact is readily explainable by the similarity in duties and preparation, since occupational changes within a field or to an adjoining field require minimal retraining, while migration to a distant field is likely to involve extensive changes in occupational duties and thus require considerable retraining.

Holland (1959, 1973) and those testing his propositions have amassed substantial evidence that at least the higher level occupations fall into six broad categories. These categories were developed, in large part, from work on the *Strong Vocational Interest Blank*, and essentially they condense Roe's eight fields into six. When the interrelationships among the Holland fields are graphed, their relationship approximates a hexagon (Figure 4–1), in which those cells closer to one another are more alike. Moreover, Holland's theory, which is closely linked to empirical evidence, suggests a distinct personality style relates to each environment. Many studies have supported this environmental typology and have established that a distinct constellation of abilities and personality traits are associated with each. For example, the realistic personality prefers outdoors, working with tools and tangible materials, and tends to avoid interpersonal relationships. Table 4–3 presents Holland's description of the six environments.

Distribution of Occupations

Occupations are not distributed evenly among the eight occupational fields or six environments. The approximate percentage of jobs in each environment is indicated in Table 4–3. Contrasting these percentages with Holland's (1977) estimate of the percentages of people preferring particular environments suggests that many persons will not be able to work in their preferred environments unless the distribution of jobs is altered radically.

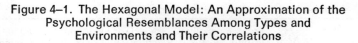

Figure 4–1. The Hexagonal Model: An Approximation of the
Psychological Resemblances Among Types and
Environments and Their Correlations

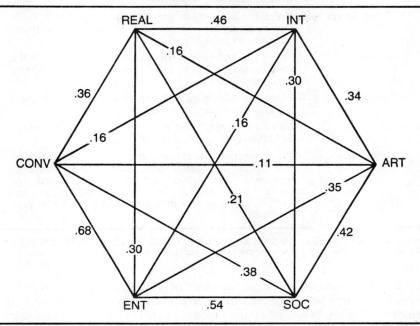

SOURCE: J. L. Holland, D. R. Whitney, W. S. Cole, and G. M. Richards, Jr. *The empirical occupation classification derived from theory of personality and intended for practice and research.* Research Report #29. Copyright 1969 by the American College Testing Program. Reprinted with permission.

Within fields and environments, jobs are not equally distributed among levels. For the artistic, enterprising, and investigative environments, the majority of jobs are in the professional-technical level, but in the conventional and the social environments, most jobs are at the skilled or lower levels.

Occupational Level

Roe (1956) defines six occupational levels to represent distinctive degrees of responsibility, capacity, skill, education, and prestige. Clearly, occupations differ in terms of amount of training required, challenge, opportunity for creativity and substantive community contribution, potential interest of work, opportunity for recognition and advancement, commitment to work demanded, independence afforded in one's work, prestige, and salary. Not unexpectedly, all of these factors are correlated highly with one another, as well as with the amount of schooling obtained and social class. Consequently, even though judges, dentists, scientists, and certified public accountants perform radically different

Table 4–3. John Holland's Six Environments

Realistic:	Press for explicit, ordered, or systematic manipulation of objects, tools, machines and animals predominate.
Investigative:	Press for observation and symbolic, systematic, creative, investigation of physical, biological, or cultural phenomena predominate.
Artistic:	Press for ambiguous, free unsystematized activities and competencies to create art forms or products predominate.
Social:	Press for informing, training, developing, caring, enlightening, or serving others predominate.
Enterprising:	Press for manipulating others to attain organizational or self-interest goals predominate.
Conventional:	Press for the explicit, ordered systematic manipulation of data, such as keeping records, filing materials, reproducing materials, organizing written and numerical data according to a prescribed plan, and operating business and data processing machines predominate.

SOURCE: John L. Holland. MAKING VOCATIONAL CHOICES: A THEORY OF CAREERS (pp. 29–33). © 1973. Adapted by permission of Prentice-Hall, Inc., Englewood Cliffs, New Jersey.

tasks, their salaries, prestige, amount of training, job challenge, and amount of independence are more like each other than these professionals' jobs are like legal stenographers', dental technicians', laboratory technicians', or bookkeepers' jobs, respectively. In addition, professionals are more likely to socialize with one another than with persons at lower rungs of their own occupational area.

Training and Occupational Level

At first glance, occupational field may appear to determine methods of training. But, although the subject matter in training depends significantly on occupational field, the methods and duration of training are more a function of occupational level. Figure 4–2, which describes the different kinds of training programs, including their duration and training methods, illustrates this relationship. Most low-level jobs are taught by brief demonstration, oral instruction, or by having the entry worker coached by a veteran worker in *On-the-Job Training* (OJT). By contrast, professionals, technicians, and managers are taught through extensive formal course work involving lectures, extensive reading, paper-and-pencil testing, and lengthy internship or simulated internships. Even though almost every worker receives some OJT, the scope and duration correlate with the worker's level. Consequently, low-level entry workers are coached in a few simple operations for a short period, while the business executive's OJT will often cover multiple aspects of supervision and coordination and may last months.

Figure 4–2. Thumbnail Descriptions of Work Training Programs
for Use with Junior and Senior High School Students

High School Programs

Vocational and technical programs enable you to learn basic occupational skills while earning a high school diploma. Most high schools have some vocational programs that you can elect to take if you choose. There are some high schools offering vocational and technical programs exclusively. These schools are designed for students who want to learn a trade and who will probably go to work soon after graduation.

Some of the programs offered in vocational and technical schools are given in the following list:

- Auto repair
- Bookkeeping
- Carpentry
- Data processing
- Dress making and design
- Drafting
- Electricity and electronics

- Food preparation
- Machine shop
- Metalwork
- Nursing care
- Plumbing
- Printing
- Secretarial services

In some vocational programs, students enjoy the advantage of being able to work part time, for a salary, in local industries and businesses while still going to school. For more information about vocational and technical training programs, see *Lovejoy's Career and Vocational School Guide* by Clarence E. Lovejoy, Simon and Schuster, New York, 1973; *Technician Education Yearbook, 1973–74*, 6th edition, edited by Lawrence W. Prakken and Jerome C. Patterson, Ann Arbor, Michigan. You can probably find these books in your school or public library.

Many high schools offer academic, or college-preparatory programs. These programs offer courses that are needed for admission to college. Such courses teach students the skills and knowledge necessary to succeed in college. After graduation from a college-preparatory program, you can go on to a junior or senior college, or to a business or technical school. These schools are discussed later in the chapter.

If you are interested in a college-preparatory program, ask your guidance counselor or school librarian for information on the programs offered in local high schools.

Apprenticeship Programs

Apprenticeship programs are 2- to 6-year training programs in which the apprentice learns a craft under the guidance of a skilled worker. Apprentices are paid about half the wages that an experienced worker receives. Apprentices must be at least 16 years old, usually high school graduates, and take at least 144 hours of classes in occupational courses each year of their apprenticeship. Labor unions and company management jointly administer apprenticeships under the regulation of the state government.

There are apprenticeship programs in more than 300 trades and crafts. Some of the occupations that offer apprenticeship programs are given in the following list:

- Airplane and auto mechanic
- Baker
- Barber
- Bookbinder
- Bricklayer
- Carpenter
- Cement mason

- Electrician
- Engraver
- Ironwroker
- Jeweler
- Painter
- Photographer
- Upholsterer

Figure 4–2. (*Continued*)

For a complete list of the occupations for which apprenticeships are available, write to the U.S. Government Printing Office, Washington, DC 20402. Your local labor council, the state bureau of apprenticeships, and the chamber of commerce will be able to tell you about apprenticeship opportunities available in your community.

On-the-job-training Programs

On-the-job training programs are just what their name says they are. They are programs in which you learn while you're employed in a particular job. Usually, you work with experienced workers, observing what they do and helping them. Sometimes there is formal classroom training as well. On-the-job-training programs are generally offered for jobs that can be mastered in a short period of time. Some of the jobs that offer on the-job-training programs are given in the following list:

- Assembler
- Bank teller
- Cashier
- Construction worker
- Elevator operator
- Factory worker
- Gas station attendant
- Grocery clerk
- Janitor
- Mail carrier
- Miner
- Nursing aide and orderly

To find out about on-the-job training programs, look in the classified section of your local newspaper for want ads for trainees or helpers. Contact the local state employment office. Ask your counselor or school's work-study coordinator about opportunities in your town.

The United States Armed Forces

The services offer training and experience in many occupations. These range from computer programmer to foreign-language translator, from aircraft mechanic to aircraft pilot. They all have the advantage of paying a fair salary while giving you the opportunity to serve your country and to gain valuable career experiences. The best training opportunities go to those who learn quickly and have earned high school diplomas and college degrees, but non-high school graduates may also qualify. Check with your local armed forces recruiters.

Junior and Community Colleges

Junior and community colleges offer 2-year programs. After completing the program, some students decide to go on to a 4-year college. Others start to work in jobs for which the school has prepared them. A few junior colleges are residential, that is, students live in dormitories and participate in the full round of campus life. Community colleges, on the other hand, are for day students who live at home. Both kinds of colleges offer training in skilled occupations. Some of the programs junior and community colleges usually offer are given in the following list:

- Accounting
- Auto repair
- Construction technology
- Cosmetology
- Electronics
- Fire and police technology
- Information processing
- Journalism
- Mechanics
- Merchandising
- Music
- Nursing

Figure 4–2. (*Continued*)

You can find out about the courses, costs, and requirements of junior and community colleges in *American Junior Colleges,* 8th edition, edited by Edmund J. Gleazer, Jr., American Council on Education, Ace, Division of Charter Communications, New York, 1971; and *Lovejoy's College Guide,* 12th revision, by Clarence E. Lovejoy, Simon and Schuster, New York, 1973; *Barron's Guide to the Two-Year Colleges,* 2 volumes, revised edition edited by R. William Graham. Volume 1, *One Thousand Two Hundred Thirty College Descriptions;* volume 2, *Occupational Program Selector,* Barron, New York, 1974; and *Ferguson Guide to Two-Year College Programs,* J. G. Ferguson Editorial Staff, Doubleday, New York, 1971. These books will probably be available in your school or public library.

You can also obtain a catalog by writing to the college in which you're interested. Catalogs of local junior and community colleges may also be on hand at your local library as well.

Adult Education Programs

Adult education programs are offered by high schools, colleges, community colleges, and church groups. You can find out about particular programs in your community through your high school counselors.

Business and Technical Schools

Usually, business and technical schools require a high school diploma (or other qualifications based on work experience and ability). They specialize in skills and crafts requiring 6 months or more of training. Some of the jobs in which these schools offer training are given in the following list:

- Bookkeeper
- Computer programmer
- Dental or medical technician
- Drafting technician
- Machinist
- Printing machine operator
- Secretary

Books to consult are *Directory of Business Schools in the United States,* National Association of Business Schools, Washington DC, 1963; *Lovejoy's Career and Vocational School Guide* by Clarence E. Lovejoy, Simon and Schuster, New York, 1973.

Colleges, Universities, and Professional Schools

Agriculture, the arts, business, engineering, English, languages, life sciences, mathematics natural sciences social sciences—these are a few of the broad categories of educational offerings at the college level. At least 4 years of college training are required for many careers. The professions such as law and medicine, require additional education after college. Scientists, teachers, engineers, business executives, and journalists almost always are college graduates and often have advanced degrees.

For information about colleges, universities, and professional schools, see *Lovejoy's College Guide* 12th revision by Clarence E. Lovejoy; and *American Universities and Colleges* by O. A. Singletary, 11th edition, American Council on Education, Washington DC, 1973. You can also write to the colleges that interest you and ask them to send you their catalogs.

Since World War I, training requirements for occupations have been rising along with the increase in educational attainment of youth. Apparently this trend will continue due to the use of ever more sophisticated equipment and processes, as well as the desire of occupational groups to enhance their occupational status and control of entrants by imposing higher training requirements. Demands for greater preparation are likely to continue, despite the observation by Berg (1975), in *Education and Jobs: The Great Training Robbery*, that the inflated requirements do not necessarily improve productivity. Even knowledge that inflated requirements are a subtle way of discriminating against minorities and women, who tend to have less training, is unlikely to reverse the trend. Certainly additional licensing and training requirements will make job changes more difficult.

Job Satisfaction and Job Level

Workers in higher-level occupations report more job satisfaction than do workers in lower levels. The advantages are clear—more money, prestige, job challenge. Higher-level occupations also have disadvantages, however, that are sometimes forgotten. These include: 1) long job preparation without income; 2) specialization that limits where one works, (for example, one can only be an anthropology professor or a brain surgeon or even a corporate lawyer in certain locations); 3) greater immersion in work, (for many university professors, executives, physicians, and professional entertainers, for instance, the fifty to sixty-hour week is normal); 4) greater liability and/or risk of financial loss (unlike many employees, high-level workers more frequently are victims of mergers and economy drives, or as self-employed persons they are more vulnerable to the vagaries of the economy and liability lawsuits). In spite of the disadvantages, workers in higher-level work tend to live longer and to have better health and to enjoy retirement more (O'Toole, 1977).

Distribution of Workers by Level

Table 4–4 presents the current distribution of workers by occupational level and projected distributions. Note that the expected changes are not drastic. Since job satisfaction relates highly to occupational level, and since higher school attainment increases expectation of work satisfaction, more than half the work force, who will still be in low-level jobs, will have difficulty achieving work satisfaction over the next thirty years within the existing education-work structure. This fact has led to ominous forecasts about the future of work (O'Toole, 1977).

The dire predictions about shortages of satisfying work assume several things: (1) little mobility exists among occupations so that working in a low-level occupation does not help one to qualify for a higher-level occupation; (2) low-level occupations cannot be satisfying even if performed for only a limited time; (3) most low-level occupa-

Table 4–4. Distribution of Workers and Projected Requirements, According to U.S. Census Classification

	1910	1940	1976	1985
Professional workers	1,632 4.4%	3,382 6.5%	13,329 15.2%	15,800 15.1%
Managers; administrators[a]	1,201 3.2%	1,921 3.6%	9,315 10.7%	11,300 10.8%
Sales workers	1,246 3.3%	2,038 3.9%	5,497 6.3%	6,400 6.1%
Clerical workers	3,804[b] 10.2%	8,924[b] 17.2%	15,558 17.8%	20,000 19.2%
Craft and kindred workers	4,367 11.7%	6,105 11.7%	11,278 12.9%	13,700 13.2%
Operatives	5,489 14.7%	10,918 21.0%	13,356 15.3%	15,600 15.0%
Nonfarm laborers	5,462 14.7%	5,566 10.7%	4,325 4.9%	4,800 4.6%
Service workers	2,533 6.8%	4,182 8.0%	12,005 13.7%	14,800 14.2%
Farmers/farm laborers	11,539 31.0%	8,923 17.2%	2,823 3.2%	1,900 1.8%

[a] In 1910 and 1940 managers and administrators included farm owners and tenants, wholesale/retail dealers and others. The figures under managers; administrators in this table are the others; the wholesale/retail dealers are under sales; the farmers are combined with farm laborers.
[b] The clerical workers 1910 and 1940 included clerks now listed under sales; consequently, the 1910 and 1940 figures for clerical workers are based on more occupations than the 1976 figures and 1985 projection.

SOURCES: For 1910 and 1940 figures, A. M. Edwards. *Comparative occupation statistics for the United States, 1879 to 1970.* For 1976 and 1985 figures, *Employment and training report of the President.* Washington, D.C., U.S. Government Printing Office, 1978.

tions cannot be redesigned into challenging jobs; (4) most workers cannot learn how to obtain satisfaction from low-level jobs, since they will be seeking intrinsic satisfaction from work.

But, considerable vertical and horizontal mobility do appear to exist. Whether mobility is due to workers' acquiring more education or to being rewarded for loyalty, hard work, and competence is not clear. Furthermore, exact figures on mobility are not available. Many workers have moved from so-called "entry" occupations, and the possibility of movement would seem to contribute to work satisfaction. Unfortunately, some professional associations and unions increasingly are interfering with such movement by inflating training requirements and through contracts and laws demarcating areas of practice.

The assumption that low-level work is, by its nature, not satisfying has not been verified. In fact, high and average aptitude workers manage to achieve satisfaction from jobs that others consider boring and even demeaning. Perhaps these workers have learned how to make at least some of these jobs rewarding. Studies of these workers and their jobs might be very revealing, since many low-level jobs have characteristics such as independence (taxi driver), self-regulation (housekeeper, gardener), and potential for challenge (a waiter can try to serve so many customers or a retail clerk sell so many items) that are associated with so-called satisfying jobs. But, the low wages and status these jobs command may mask their intrinsic gratifications. Salary is a satisfier, for example, which has intrinsic and extrinsic connotations (Crites, 1976), and in many low-level occupations salaries are very close to the subsistence level. Such low salaries would certainly weaken other satisfactions of work.

In regard to work redesign, many business and industry initiatives are underway, but surprisingly few efforts in the United States have been initiated by workers or by worker associations. Katzell and Yankelovich (1975), in evaluating the research in work redesign, indicated that such redesign can sometimes, but not always, improve worker satisfaction. Most redesign efforts are company-initiated. Since company redesigners are likely to consider a limited number of job variations because they support the current work system (Nord, 1977), increased success in redesigning jobs seems to require that workers take more initiative and exercise more control over the changes to be made. Otherwise, Dubin's (1976) projection that widespread job redesign will take many years is likely to be accurate.

Surveys such as those of Yankelovich (1978) suggest that many Americans value intrinsic satisfaction from work. With increasing education, an even larger percentage are likely to expect such satisfaction. As long as people must continue to spend a major portion of their lives in career pursuits, such work should be meaningful, challenging, and self-enhancing.

Nevertheless, much remains to be learned about how work becomes challenging and self-enhancing, and about what percentage of one's work must be intrinsically gratifying to render the job fulfilling. Individual differences certainly lead some people to like particular work that others dislike, but possibly personal interests are much more maleable than has been assumed. If most people could learn to expand their interests, they would find a wider range of work activities intrinsically stimulating.

But, some work-redesign efforts have found that workers do not wish to put in the extra effort and commitment required to expand their job's intrinsic satisfaction (Katzell & Yankelovich, 1975). This fact is understandable since the gains in work satisfaction might require foregoing the pleasures of leisure and family pursuits that may be more gratifying than those related to work, since they are more voluntary. Certainly, every worker should regularly review whether the life achievements forgone to achieve intrinsic career fulfillment outweigh the benefits of career satisfaction.

On the other hand, the nature of work needs continued attention. Assuredly, there are people who would choose intrinsic career satisfaction but whose education and experiences have not equipped them to obtain it. With greater self and occupational knowledge, with exposure to models who are experiencing intrinsic gratification, and with fairer access to opportunities, such people would probably seek more intrinsic career satisfaction.

Solutions to Shortages of Satisfying Jobs

Observers, such as Warnath (1975), have suggested that counselors alert people to the keen competition for the limited number of jobs likely to provide intrinsic satisfaction, and encourage clients to direct some energies and part of their education to defining and pursuing nonwork goals that will be fulfilling. Others, such as O'Toole (1973, 1977), believe that the solution lies in redesign of jobs; but Dubin (1976), after examining the role of change in work practices, believes that the needed extensive redesign of work will take many years.

Other possible remedies might include requiring incumbency in minimally satisfying jobs for a given number of years to qualify for a satisfying job. Many students now endure and even enjoy part-time jobs with minimal satisfiers, other than salary, as they pursue advanced study. Generally, they consider these jobs to be temporary. Unfortunately, evidence is not available on how such a scheme might affect subsequent work productivity or overall career development. For occupations such as physical science, mathematics, and poetry, where the height of productivity occurs relatively early, the policy could be disastrous.

Another solution is to limit the number of hours per week for which people can receive salary from satisfying jobs so that more people can have these jobs. Again, however, this approach might reduce individual productivity, and might increase costs if workers had to be paid for more hours than they worked.

Other possibilities include the establishment of fellowships for college or technical study patterned after the G.I. education bill for people who have held low-level jobs for ten or fifteen years. Or, continuing education programs that now tend to draw highly educated and high-level workers might be altered to serve the interests of low-level workers.

Relation of Occupations to One Another

Occupations not only relate to one another in terms of field and level, but also in terms of the industry in which they occur. Industrial clusters of occupations reflect the fact that every occupation in a particular industry contributes to producing the same goods or services.

Many new occupations come into existence as production requires a distinct set of tasks to make operations more effective. Often the characteristics of the new occupations are defined in the process of production by workers who had been producing the particular product or service. Recruits for these new occupations may be in related occupations, but frequently they come from workers in a completely different area. For instance, a typist in a chemical firm producing a new battery shifted into a battery technician's job in the firm because of production information acquired while typing and courtesy explanations received while verifying the typewritten material.

Most craft-to-supervisor or supervisor-to-manager transfers and most occupational advancements, except those obtained through formal education, are within the same industry. This internal mobility occurs, in part, because advancement usually requires a broad appreciation of the business or industry. Also, the insider's knowledge of job openings, job specifications, and acquaintance with employers provide an advantage in obtaining a job. Finally, many large firms and civil service promote primarily from within their organizations.

Career Ladders

When one occupation is a prerequisite for another or one is ordinarily performed in order to move up to another, the two or more related jobs constitute a career ladder. There are many career ladders in large corporations and in civil service, but occupations at different levels in the same field and industry are not necessarily linked in career ladders. For example, registered nurses ordinarily have not been practical or vocational nurses and rarely become physicians; vocational or practical nurses normally have not been nurse's aides or orderlies; and electricians rarely become electrical engineers or physicists.

Generally, vertical mobility on most career ladders involves moving from a semiskilled, skilled, technical, or professional job into positions of supervision and managerial responsibility. Rarely does a career ladder link semiskilled occupations to skilled occupations, or skilled occupations to technical occupations, or technical occupations to professional occupations, other than administrative ones. Entry to skilled, technical, and professional occupations increasingly requires specialized schooling and internships or apprenticeships.

Career Patterns

The sequence of educational and occupational positions one occupies is termed the person's *career pattern*. Career patterns can be divided into eight broad categories: stable, conventional, unstable, multitrial, stable homemaking, double track, interrupted, conventional becoming homemaking. The stable and conventional patterns are characteristic of persons in professional, technical, or skilled occupations, and the multitrial and unstable typify workers in low-level occupations.

Most male careers follow one of four broad patterns, whereas female careers will follow one of those patterns or one of the four distinctly female patterns. The female patterns reflect the accommodation of working to childrearing and homemaking. Super's description of the patterns appears in Table 4–5.

Table 4-5. Donald Super's Description of Career Patterns

Stable pattern	The person goes directly from school or college into work in which they persist.
Conventional pattern	The sequence of jobs follows the progression from initial through trial to stable employment.
Unstable pattern	The sequence is trial, stable, trial; the worker does not succeed in establishing himself permanently in an occupation, but shifts around.
Multiple trial pattern	This pattern reflects frequent change of employment, with no one job sufficiently permanent to justify calling the person established.
Stable homemaking pattern	Person who marries during or shortly after school without ever having significant work experience.
Conventional becoming homemaking pattern	Person works for several months or years in an occupation not requiring training beyond formal education and stops the work after marrying.
Double-track pattern	Person pursues double roles of work and homemaking.
Interrupted pattern	Person enters work, stops for homemaking duties and child care. Then several years later returns to work in answer to financial needs or occupational aspirations.

SOURCE: Condensed from D. E. Super, *The Psychology of Careers.* New York: Harper & Row, 1957, pp. 73–74, 77–78.

Industries vary in the degree to which they promote different career patterns. For example, an analysis of 1 percent of the 1974 Social Security returns by the University of Michigan's Institute of Labor and Industrial Relations ranked eight industries in terms of new hires as follows: construction 51 percent, retail trade 34 percent, services 28 percent, mining 23 percent, wholesale trade 19 percent, finance 19 percent, manufacturing 16 percent, transportation 15 percent. (New hires are employees who had not worked for the firm the previous year.) Turnover rates also vary by geographic area and by size of firm. Workers in the South, Southwest, and West are more likely to change employers than are those in New England and the Midwest. The small firms, surprisingly, experience higher turnover rates than large ones (Cohen & Schwarz, 1979).

Miller and Form (1951) pointed out that career patterns are closely associated with the amount of education completed and the level of one's occupation, both of which relate to social class. Persons who persist in school longer and are from middle- and upper-class backgrounds are more likely to have stable or conventional careers. Such careers are preferred, in part, because many of the high-status occupations outside the arts field have such patterns and, in part, because such work and its place in life are more predictable. Of course, the changing work tasks and environments and lack of commitment to work associated with the unstable career are preferable to some people. Path analysis, such as that used in status attainment studies by Blau and Duncan (1967), allows some estimation of the kind of pattern a person is likely to have. To date, however, individuals have not received such estimates as part of their guidance.

The number of persons whose careers follow a particular pattern is not known, but vocational guidance has encouraged the expectation of stable or conventional careers. Counselors have offered little help to the many people who will have other career patterns, in spite of Super's (1957) recommendation that counselors need to expand their awareness of these groups and the world of work in order to aid such clients with decision making.

Clearly, an important career education task will be to alert youngsters to the existence of the different career patterns, to the factors associated with particular patterns, and to the likelihood of their pursuing a specific pattern. Such information may spur them to continue in school and to compete for entry into occupations likely to offer a stable, conventional career pattern; this knowledge may also create demand for education needed to perform many occupations and establishment of a government employment service responsive to the needs of workers in unstable or interrupted careers.

Occupational Supply and Working Conditions

Supply and demand of workers for an occupation and its working conditions are crucial aspects of occupations that are independent of occupational level. These factors vary widely among occupations and are major considerations when one is choosing a field. They are discussed below.

Supply and Demand

For the last one hundred years, demand for high-level workers in our economy has been growing; but the absolute number of unskilled and semiskilled openings still exceeds the number of skilled, technical, and professional jobs available. This apparent contradiction arises because there are nearly twice as many low-skilled jobs as high-skilled ones, so that while high-skilled jobs are increasing at a faster rate than low-skilled positions, their absolute increase is not so large that their openings approach the number of low-skilled jobs available.

The entry requirements of high-skilled jobs, of course, are much more extensive and specific than those of lower-skilled ones. As a consequence of the specificity, a professional or skilled worker in a specialty often cannot qualify for another specialty within that present occupation. For example, in the early 1970s when there was a surplus of electrical and mechanical aeronautical engineers, there was a slight shortage of sewage engineers, but few of the unemployed electrical and aeronautical engineers qualified for sewage engineer positions. Therefore, high-level workers do not necessarily have an easier time locating appropriate work, for their employability depends on the number of jobs available in their particular occupation, not on the number of high-skilled openings in general. Nevertheless, unemployment tends to relate inversely to the amount of schooling completed. Better educated workers may not always obtain the job for which they are equipped, but, if necessary, they appear to take lower-level jobs, replacing those with less education.

Factors regulating supply and demand of jobs in an occupation are complex, especially in a mixed economy. The supply and demand of workers for an occupation indicates the competition a prospective worker will face in obtaining work. Therefore, a career seeker should consider supply and demand projections in deciding among occupational training programs, for such data will enable predictions about chances of employment and advancement. Indeed, the correlational data from *The Career Pattern Study* (Super et al., 1969) and the *Career Development Study* (Gribbons & Lohnes, 1968) show that adolescent knowledge of supply and demand factors relates to their later career success.

The Bureau of Labor Statistics regularly accumulates supply and demand data for major occupations; from these data the Bureau projects trends, and estimates future supply and demand figures. In the past, the BLS surveyed employers for estimates of supply, but since 1976 it relies on extrapolations from past figures. Their projections appear annually in the *Manpower Report to the President,* now called *Employment and Training Report of the President,* and are integrated biannually into the *Occupational Outlook Handbook.*

As government has become larger, its taxation and disbursement decisions substantially affect the supply and demand of jobs and workers with particular training. Large corporations and large labor unions are aware of this fact and naturally try to influence government to act in a manner beneficial to them. Therefore, a profession that seeks to promote career development must learn about the likely outcomes of any government action in order to help assure that such action is as equitable as possible to all people pursuing careers.

In 1972, this author suggested that the American Personnel and Guidance Association occasionally rally its membership to declare a position on federal legislation or policy that would have major impact on career development opportunities (Healy, 1972b) and pointed out that government policies were sometimes affecting the supply of jobs adversely (Healy, 1972a). Since 1972, APGA has become more active in presenting its views to Congress about federal educational policy and in keeping its membership informed about some legislation, but it has not moved to bring member power to bear on any issue and is surprisingly silent about noneducational legislation that affects career options.

Manpower Programs

Except for the peak years of World War II, the American economy has had a substantial number of unemployed and underemployed workers (the underemployed are those who work in part-time, occasional, or casual jobs). In addition, millions of workers labor in jobs that do not pay them a subsistence wage. This chronic *structural unemployment* is unlikely to abate in the near future, since experts such as Yankelovich (1978) estimate that, if more decent jobs were available, job seekers would increase by 25 percent. Many homemakers and other persons not now seeking work would then decide to seek employment.

Since the mid-1960s the United States government, primarily through the Department of Labor, has operated a series of manpower and training programs to combat poverty and to reduce unemployment. The early and current programs have included paid academic training, paid short-term job training, subsidized on-the-job training, and employment in public and nonprofit agencies. Current programs also contain some incentives for private industry to create jobs. The 1960s programs were often restricted to the disadvantaged, but 1970s programs often served nonpoverty groups. Generally, training and the employment opportunities have been for semiskilled jobs. The latest program is the 1973 *Comprehensive Employment and Training Act (CETA)* as amended in 1978, which includes the Youth Employment and Demonstration Projects Act of 1977. It is summarized in Figure 4–3.

As Figure 4–3 shows, the act provides a wide array of services to combat unemployment and inadequate career development. As in previous programs, services are often restricted to special categories of disadvantaged workers.

At first glance, such extensive programs appear to provide a substantial boost to the career development of American workers. To date, however, the Department of Labor programs have not been dramatically successful in upgrading participants' work skills, occupational status, or job-holding power. Typically, participants do not acquire skilled or higher-level job abilities, nor do they garner jobs that enable them to move far beyond the brink of poverty. Clearly, the programs have transferred substantial monies to poor people, although the amount to individuals is miniscule in comparison to farm subsidy payments to individual farmers and ranchers. Whether these income transfers have forestalled participation in illegal activities or have sustained health is unknown from the Department of Labor research. No evidence is available to show that the programs have not harmed the beneficiaries, possibly depriving them of the motivation to break out of poverty on their own.

Some critics point out that the programs have emphasized molding workers to employees' demands. The programs offer the disadvantaged another chance to accept "the system," but do not attempt to equip the worker with the ability to negotiate with employers in order to modify jobs to better accommodate the worker's talents and needs. Even though adult career maturity in America envisions a modicum of self-direction and job control, federal manpower programs have not scrutinized the job side of work-adjustment problems, nor have they funded programs to redesign jobs. Quinn, Levitin, and Eden (1975), indeed, noted how disregarding the nature of the jobs doomed a typical adjustment workshop to failure in one manpower program. Although job redesign is sometimes arranged in rehabilitation, surprisingly, it has not been attempted as part of Department of Labor programs.

Figure 4–3. Fact Sheet on Comprehensive Employment and
Training Act (CETA) and the Youth Employment
and Demonstration Project Acts of 1977

CETA—A Thumbnail Sketch by Titles

The Comprehensive Employment and Training Act Amendments of 1978, approved
by the President Oct. 27 (PL 95–524), extended public service employment (PSE)
and job training and initiated several new program services through FY 1982. FY
1979 operating funds were provided by a continuing resolution approved Oct. 18.
Following is a title-by-title summary of the reauthorized CETA.

Title I—Administrative Provisions: General provisions applicable to the act. Authorizes programs through FY 1982 except for three youth programs (Part A of
Title IV) and the private sector initiatives (Title VII) which are authorized only
through FY 1980.

Directs the Secretary of Labor to establish an Office of Management Assistance
to provide prime sponsors with management and technical services to help them
improve program administration.

Limits participation: (1) No one can be in any CETA program longer than 2½
years in a five-year preiod; and (2) No one can be in PSE longer than 78 weeks
in a five-year period. There also is a waiver for on-board enrollees at the Secretary's discretion if a prime sponsor is having extreme hardship in placing PSE
enrollees in unsubsidized jobs, or if the area has 7% or more unemployment.

PSE wages may not exceed $10,000 per year, adjusted upward by the ratio that
local wage rates bear to the national average, but not to exceed 20% of the
maximum (no more than $12,000), with some exceptions. Further, average wages
in each prime sponsor area may not exceed $7,200, adjusted by the ratio that the
local wage bears to the national average.

Title II—Comprehensive Employment and Training Services: Training, education,
work experience, upgrading, retraining, and other services (Parts A, B, and C), and
counter structural public service employment (Part D) to prepare jobless persons
for unsubsidized employment.

Participants in training programs and services (except upgrading and retraining)
must have been economically disadvantaged and either unemployed, underemployed, or in school. Participants in PSE must have been economically disadvantaged and unemployed 15 or more weeks or on welfare. PSE must be entry level
and combined with training and supportive services, if available. Supplementation
of wages under this title is specifically prohibited.

Authorization: Parts A, B, and C, $2 billion in FY '79, and such sums as may be
necessary thereafter; Part D (PSE), $3 billion in FY '79, and such sums as neces-
sary thereafter, but not more than 60% of the entire title for Part D.

Funds Available For FY 1979: Parts A, B, and C, $1,914,100,000; Part D, $2,516,-
930,000.

Title III—Special Federal Responsibilities: Programs for persons who have a particular disadvantage in the labor market, including Native Americans, migrants and
other seasonal farmworkers, the handicapped, women, displaced homemakers,
public assistance recipients, and other special target groups.

Authorizes welfare demonstration projects, projects for middle-aged and older
workers, and a program for better coordination between prime sponsors and state
employment security agencies. Voucher demonstration projects are now mandated.

Authorization: Twenty percent of the total funds for CETA minus Titles II-D
and VI.

Funds Available For FY 1979: $371,632,000.

Title IV—Youth Programs: The Job Corps, Summer Youth Programs, and programs
enacted in the Youth Employment and Demonstration Projects Act of 1977 (except
the Young Adult Conservation Corps which is still Title VIII), namely, Youth Incentive Entitlement Pilot Projects, Youth Community Conservation and Improve-

Figure 4–3. (*Continued*)

ment Projects, and Youth Employment and Training Programs. The Job Corps and Summer Youth Program are authorized for 4 years, and the 3 new youth programs for 2.

Authorization: $2.25 billion in FY '79; $2.4 billion in FY '80; open-ended authorization in FY '81 and '82 for Job Corps and the Summer Youth Program.

Funds Available For FY 1979: $1,750,196,000.

Title V—National Commission for Employment Policy: Renames and reconstitutes the National Commission on Manpower Policy. Cabinet participation on the Commission is reduced.

Title VI—Countercyclical Public Service Employment Program: Temporary public service employment opportunities during periods of high unemployment, in sufficient number to employ 20 percent of the unemployed in excess of 4 percent unemployment, and 25 percent of the excess when national unemployment is 7 percent or higher. Participants must be unemployed at least 10 of the last 12 weeks or on welfare, and from a family whose income does not exceed the BLS lower living standard budget.

At least 50 percent of the Title VI funds must be used for the employment of persons in projects. These must be limited to 18 months, but can be extended in some circumstances. Persons not employed in projects must be hired at the entry level. Funds are to be distributed to prime sponsors by formula, which for at least 85% of the title's funds is as follows: 50% based on total unemployment in a sponsor's area, 25% on unemployment over 4.5%, and 25% on unemployment over 6.5%. Of the title's total funds, 2% must be reserved for programs for Native Americans. Remainder: at Secretary's discretion.

Wage supplementation under this title cannot exceed 10% of the total grant to any prime sponsor, except in areas where the average wage is between 125% and 150% of the national average, in which case supplementation may not exceed 20%.

Authorization: Enough funds to support jobs for 20% of the unemployed in excess of 4%; except when the national unemployment rate exceeds 7%, jobs are authorized for 25% of the excess.

Funds Available For FY 1979: $3,474,954,000.

Title VII—Private Sector Opportunities for the Economically Disadvantaged: Authorizes a Private Sector Initiative Program (PSIP) to demonstrate the effectiveness of ways of increasing the involvement of the business community, including minority and small businesses, in employment and training activities supported by CETA, and increase private sector jobs for the economically disadvantaged.

Provides funds for the establishment of private industry councils (a majority of whose members must be from the business community) which shall participate with prime sponsors in developing opportunities for economically disadvantaged persons in the private sector.

Of the funds appropriated under this title, 95% is to be allocated among prime sponsors, taking into account the factors in the formula for parts A, B, and C of Title II. The remainder of the funds shall be used by the Secretary for distribution to prime sponsors who join together to establish a single private industry council, and to Native American entities. Authorized for 2 years.

Authorization: $500 million for FY '79; $525 million for FY '80. *FY 1979 Funding:*

Title VIII—Young Adult Conservation Corps: Provides employment and experience in various occupational skills to out-of-school young people from all social and economic backgrounds through work on conservation and other projects on federal and non-federal public lands and waters. Participants may be hired for a maximum of 12 months. Operated under agreement by Departments of Labor, Agriculture, and Interior. Authorized for 4 years, through FY 1982.

Figure 4–3. (*Continued*)

Authorization: $350 million for FY '79; $400 million for FY '80; open-ended for FY '81 and '82.
Funds Available For FY 1979: $216,900,000.

Timetable for implementation: (1) Provisions throughout the act aimed at preventing fraud and abuse: as soon as possible. (2) Supplementation, maximum federal wage, and eligibility: within 90 days (by January 25, 1979), and (3) All others: by April 1, 1979.

For Further Information: Office of Information, Employment and Training Administration, U.S. Department of Labor, Room 10410, 601 D Street, N.W., Washington, D.C. 20213. (Phone: 202-376-6905).

Youth Employment and Demonstration Projects Act

Background: The President signed the Youth Employment and Demonstration Projects Act of 1977 (PL 95–93) on August 5. It authorizes four new programs under the Comprehensive Employment and Training Act (CETA), three of them under a new Part C of Title III, and one under a new Title VIII. The $1 billion in initial funding for the four programs was provided by the Economic Stimulus Appropriations Act (PL 95–29), approved May 13, in anticipation of the youth legislation. An important purpose of these programs is to provide a basis of knowledge and experience so results can be studied and improvements made before a nationwide youth employment policy is established.
    All of the new youth programs plus Job Corps and the Summer Program for Economically Disadvantaged Youth are administered by ETA's newly established Office of Youth Program. Young people seeking to apply for any of these programs should be referred to the nearest Job Service office (state employment service) or CETA prime sponsor. Following are program summaries:

Youth Incentive Entitlement Pilot Projects

Short Name: Entitlement Projects (YIEPP)
Authority: CETA Title III, Part C, Subpart I
Objective: To help economically disadvantaged youth complete high school as a foundation for career success.
Eligible: Youth, 16 through 19, from families that are economically disadvantaged, as defined by the Office of Management and Budget's poverty income guidelines, residing within the designated entitlement area, who are in school or willing to return to school.
Capacity: About 20,000 jobs will be provided during an 18-month period.
Funding: $115 million.
Duration: Funded for 18 months, January 1, 1978 through June 30, 1979.
Design: Every eligible youth in a selected geographic area is guaranteed a year-round job if he or she agrees to return to or remain in high school. Jobs are for up to an average of 20 hours a week during the school year and for up to 40 hours during the summer. Participants may be given career counseling, academic tutoring, and other services.
Operation: Projects covering areas with 3,500–12,000 eligible youth are operated by 7 CETA prime sponsors. Smaller projects with up to 1,500 eligible youth are operated by 10 sponsors. Projects are scheduled to operate from January 1978 through June 1979.

Youth Community Conservation and Improvement Projects

Short Name: Community Improvement Program (YCCIP)
Authority: CETA Title III, Part C, Subpart 2

Figure 4–3. (*Continued*)

Objective: To develop the vocational potential of jobless youth through well-supervised work of tangible benefit to the community.
Eligible: Youth, 16 through 19, who are unemployed, with preference given to out-of-school youth with the severest problems in finding employment.
Capacity: About 22,000 year-round openings.
Funding: $115 million, of which $86.25 million, or 75 percent, goes to CETA prime sponsors for basic program operations. Of the remainder, two percent is for Native American youth, two percent for migrant and seasonal farmworker youth, and 21 percent for the Secretary's discretionary use.
Duration: Funded for no more than 12 months. Most projects are expected to operate between January 1, 1978 and September 30, 1978.
Design: Youth are employed on community-planned projects lasting up to one year and producing tangible benefits for the community. Supervision is by skilled tradesmen who are good instructors and sensitive to the needs of youth. To make sure youth get individual attention, no more than 12 are assigned to each supervisor. Community-based organizations such as YMCAs, the Red Cross, and other private non-profit agencies organize projects. Youth advisory councils and prime sponsor planning councils consult in project design. Labor organizations consult on wage rates and possible worker displacement. Schools are asked to grant credit for experience, thus encouraging youth to return to school and complete their education.
Operation: Of funds available, 75 percent is allocated among the states based on the number of unemployed. Each state's share is apportioned among its prime sponsors on the same basis. Sponsors select projects in their area competitively. Sponsors may use up to five percent for administration, leaving 95 percent for the projects, of which at least 65 percent must be used for participant wages and fringe benefits, no more than 10 percent for project administrative costs, and the remainder for equipment, supplies, and supervisor's wages.

Youth Employment and Training Programs

Short Name: Youth Employment and Training (YETP)
Authority: CETA Title III, Part C, Subpart 3
Objective: To enhance job prospects and career preparation of low-income youth who have the severest problems in entering the labor market.
Eligible: Youth, 14 through 21, in families with income at or below 85 percent of the Bureau of Labor Statistics lower living standard income level, with preference going to economically disadvantaged youth with severest problems in finding employment.
Capacity: About 150,000 year-round openings.
Funding: Seventy-five percent of YETP funds, or $402.5 million, is currently available by formula to CETA prime sponsors of which at least $88.5 million, or 22 percent, must be for in-school projects. Five percent of funds are used for grants to states, two percent for Native American youth, and two percent for migrant and seasonal farmworker youth. The remaining $69.8 million, or 16 percent, is for the Secretary's discretionary use.
Duration: Most projects are expected to operate between January 1, 1978 and September 30, 1978.
Design: YETP authorizes the same kinds of activities for youth as are allowed under Title I of CETA with the exception of public service employment. The intent of the program is to improve the quality and coordination of such services. Annual plans, prime sponsor planning councils, and newly formed youth councils are tools for achieving this. Gaining practical experience on a job is an essential part of the training, and related education is provided through close liaison with local educational agencies. Participants are paid a wage or training allowance depending on whether they spend most of their time on the job or in training. Wherever possible, job information, job counseling, and placement services are provided. Of funds available up to 10 percent may be used for programs that include youth

Figure 4–3. (*Continued*)

of all economic backgrounds, as a test of whether the disadvantaged benefit from being in "untargeted" programs. At least 22 percent of each prime sponsor's funds must be used for in-school-youth programs carried out with local educational agencies. Arrangements may be flexible, and the educational agencies may contract with junior colleges, post-secondary schools, and other community agencies serving low-income or in-school youth. School-based counselors advise YETP in-school participants as to the relevance of their career and educational programs. Labor organizations counsel on wage rates and possible displacement of regular workers. Community organizations have an activist role in the planning and delivering of services.

Operation: All CETA prime sponsors are eligible for a share of the funds, calculated by a formula based on the extent of unemployment and numbers of low-income individuals in their area. ETA's regional administrators send application forms to sponsors, review them, and approve those that meet the requirements.

Young Adult Conservation Corps

Short Name: Young Adult Conservation Corps (YACC)
Authority: CETA Title VIII.
Objective: To give young people experience in various occupational skills through productive work on conservation and other projects on federal and non-federal lands and waters.
Eligible: Youth, 16 through 23, from all economic and racial backgrounds who are legal residents of the U.S., unemployed, out of school, and capable of working. Those under 18 must not have left school to join YACC. No one is eligible for enrollment solely between normal school terms.
Capacity: About 25,500 openings during FY 1978.
Funding: $233.3 million, of which 30 percent is for state conservation programs providing about 6,600 openings (see "Operation" below).
Duration: Authorized for three years, FY 1977 through 1979. Funded for FY 1978. Participants may be hired for a maximum of 12 months. First jobs began in late October 1977.
Design: YACC is operated under a tripartite agreement between the Department of Labor (DOL), Agriculture (USDA), and Interior (USDI). Enrollees are involved in all types of conservation work: preservation, management, and improvement of vegetation and wildlife; development, rehabilitation, and maintenance of recreational facilities; prevention and control of insects and disease; and natural disaster damage control and cleanup. They also do clerical and other work to support conservation efforts. Enrollees are generally paid at least the federal minimum wage. Higher rates will be paid those assigned more responsibility, such as leading a work crew. Where necessary, enrollees may use payroll deduction to pay their transportation to residential camp sites. Residential enrollees will be charged for food and lodging. State Job Services may assist youth to find other employment when they leave. YACC has nonresidential projects to which enrollees commute daily and are given work assignments, and residential camps that provide food, lodging, and supportive services seven days a week, 24 hours a day, and from which work projects are assigned. During FY 1978 most openings will be nonresidential, but some residential camps will be activated. Residential camps will vary in capacity up to 250 youth, who will be assigned as near to their homes as practicable, without regard to State boundaries.

SOURCE: *Program Fact Sheets,* Washington, D.C.; U.S. Department of Labor, Employment and Training Administration, 1978.

Other critics have noted that the federal programs do not address the problem of an insufficient number of decent jobs. No coordinated government policy relates manpower development, public and private sector production, and taxation. One can wonder, for instance, whether steel tariffs and government subsides for transportation have not enabled unionized steel and transport workers to receive considerably higher wages than workers in hospitals, who often must work in situations that are also noxious and demanding. Tax credits or direct subsidies could enable incumbents of such necessary jobs to receive adequate compensation.

A full analysis of the federal unemployment policy is beyond the purview of this text, but the reader is urged to consult *CETA-YEDPA Education Policy: Issues and Recommendations*, National Association of State Boards of Education, 1979. Clearly, career counselors will want to learn the assumptions and implications of programs such as CETA in order to inform their clients about possible benefits from them. Likewise, they will want to judge whether to lobby for CETA-type programs to combat other probable causes of unemployment.

Career counselors and their professional associations have had little influence in structuring Department of Labor programs. Perhaps this fact explains why career counselors in CETA are typically compensated at a level far below counselors in the United States Employment Service or the Veteran's Administration. Nevertheless, there may well be a role for counselors and their professional associations in CETA and other future programs. Indeed, CETA mandates provision for counseling services. What counselors must do, however, is not wait to be called. Instead, they must acquaint themselves with local programs and propose promising counseling operations to the prime sponsors and contractors who have the authority and responsibility of providing quality career counseling services.

Work Conditions

Table 4–6 lists the major work conditions identified by the Department of Labor. The presence or absence of these conditions in an occupation can be ascertained by consulting the *D.O.T.* and the *Occupational Outlook Handbook* for the major occupations. Ascription of work conditions to an occupation are based on periodic job analyses (now every six years) of samples of jobs within key occupations of the *D.O.T.* clusters. Work conditions, of course, vary from job to job and, in many cases, may be modified. In the future, adjustments in conditions such as hours, split shifts, work environment, and physical activities, are likely to permit women and handicapped persons to enter a wider range of occupations and to assure greater worker safety.

The work condition descriptions enable assignment of occupations to broad categories, thus permitting people to identify what might be clearly inappropriate; but the descriptions are too abstract to communicate the actual nature of a particular job. The *Dictionary of Occupational Titles and Occupational Outlook Handbook* descriptions in Figures 4–4 and 4–5, for example, do not state either the amount of worktime under certain conditions nor the variation in particular conditions among jobs in the occupation. Even if such information were provided, how-

Table 4–6. Working Conditions

1. Inside, Outside, or Both:
   I   Inside: Protection from weather conditions but not necessarily from tempera-
       ture changes.
   O   Outside: No effective protection from weather.
   B   Both: Inside and outside.
   A job is considered "inside" if the worker spends approximately seventy-five
   percent or more of his time inside, and "outside" if he spends approximately
   seventy-five percent or more of his time outside. A job is considered "both" if
   activities occur inside or outside in approximately equal amounts.
2. Extremes of Cold Plus Temperature Changes:
   1. *Extremes of Cold:* Temperature sufficiently low to cause marked bodily dis-
      comfort unless the worker is provided with exceptional protection.
   2. *Temperature Changes:* Variations in temperature which are sufficiently marked
      and abrupt to cause noticeable bodily reactions.
3. Extremes of Heat Plus Temperature Changes:
   1. *Extremes of Heat:* Temperature sufficiently high to cause marked bodily dis-
      comfort unless the worker is provided with exceptional protection.
   2. *Temperature Changes:* Same as 2 (2).
4. Wet and Humid:
   1. *Wet:* Contact with water or other liquids.
   2. *Humid:* Atmospheric conditions with moisture content sufficiently high to
      cause marked bodily discomfort.
5. Noise and Vibration:
   Sufficient noise, either constant or intermittent, to cause marked distraction or
   possible injury to the sense of hearing and/or sufficient vibration (production
   of an oscillating movement or strain on the body or its extremities from repeated motion or shock) to cause bodily harm if endured day after day.
6. Hazards:
   Situations in which the individual is exposed to the definite risk of bodily injury.
7. Fumes, Odors, Toxic Conditions, Dust, and Poor Ventilation:
   1. *Fumes:* Smoky or vaporous exhalations, usually odorous, thrown off as a re-
      sult of combustion or chemical reaction.
   2. *Odors:* Noxious smells, either toxic or non-toxic.
   3. *Toxic Conditions:* Exposure to toxic dust, fumes, gases, vapors, mists, or
      liquids which cause general or localized disabling conditions as a result of
      inhalation or action on the skin.
   4. *Dust:* Air filled with small particles of any kind, such as textile dust, flour,
      wood, leather, feathers, etc., and inorganic dust, including silica and asbestos,
      which make the workplace unpleasant or are the source of occupational
      diseases.
   5. *Poor Ventilation:* Insufficient movement of air causing a feeling of suffoca-
      tion, or exposure to drafts.

SOURCE: U.S. Department of Labor, *Dictionary of Occupational Titles* (Vol. 2) (3rd ed.).
Washington, D.C.: U.S. Government Printing Office, 1965, p. 656.

ever, the descriptions would still miss much of the flavor of the work
setting. Yet, the work ambiance is often precisely what a prospective
worker *wants* to learn. New occupational information, for example
Careers in Focus (Winn, 1976) and *Vocational Biographies* (1978),
therefore, is presenting job descriptions within an action scenario. But
even these materials fail to capture the sense of the work situation as
realistically as literature has. Consequently, educators concerned with
career development are using literature more and more to help persons
obtain a better appreciation of what working is really like.

Figure 4–4. Job Description from *Dictionary of Occupational Titles*

045.107-042 Vocational-Rehabilitation Counselor (gov. ser.) counselor, vocational rehabilitation.

Counsels handicapped individuals to provide vocational rehabilitation services: Interviews and evaluates handicapped applicants to determine degrees of handicap, eligibility for service, and feasibility of vocational rehabilitation. Accepts or recommends acceptance of suitable candidates. Determines suitable job or business consistent with applicant's desires, aptitude, and physical limitations. Plans and arranges for applicant to study or train for job opening. Assists applicant with personal adjustment throughout rehabilitation program. Aids applicant in obtaining medical service during training. Promotes and develops job openings and places qualified applicant in employment. May refer qualified applicant to BUSINESS-ENTERPRISE OFFICER (gov. ser.) for placement in business enterprise.

SOURCE: U.S. Department of Labor, *Dictionary of Occupational Titles.* Washington, D.C.: U.S. Government Printing Office, 1977, p. 49.

Figure 4–5. Description of Rehabilitation Counselor in *Occupation Outlook Handbook for 1976–77*

Rehabilitation Counselors

Nature of the Work

Rehabilitation counselors help people with physical, mental, or social disabilities to adjust their vocational plans and personal lives. Counselors learn about clients' interests, abilities, and limitations. They then use this information, along with available medical and psychological data, to help disabled persons evaluate themselves for the purpose of pairing their physical and mental capacity and interests with suitable work.

Together, the counselor and client develop a plan of rehabilitation, with the aid of other specialists responsible for the medical care and occupational training of the handicapped person. As the plan is put into effect, the counselor meets regularly with the disabled person to discuss his progress in the rehabilitation program and help resolve any problems that have been encountered. When the client is ready to begin work, the counselor helps him find a suitable job, and usually makes followup checks to insure that the placement has been successful.

Rehabilitation counselors must maintain close contact with the families of their handicapped clients, other professionals who work with handicapped people, agencies and civic groups, and private employers who hire the disabled. Counselors in this field often perform related activities, such as informing employers of the abilities of the handicapped and arranging for publicizing the rehabilitation program in the community.

An increasing number of counselors specialize in a particular area of rehabilitation; some may work almost exclusively with blind people, alcoholics or drug addicts, the mentally ill, or retarded persons. Others may work almost entirely with persons living in poverty areas.

The amount of time spent in counseling each client varies with the severity of the disabled person's problems as well as with the size of the counselor's caseload. Some rehabilitation counselors are responsible for many persons in various stages of rehabilitation; on the other hand, less experienced counselors or those working with the severely disabled may work with relatively few cases at a time.

Places of Employment

About 19,000 persons, one-third of them women, worked as rehabilitation counselors in 1974. About 70 percent worked in State and local rehabilitation agencies

Figure 4–5. (*Continued*)

financed cooperatively with Federal and State funds. Some rehabilitation counselors and counseling psychologists worked for the Veterans Administration. Rehabilitation centers, sheltered workshops, hospitals, labor unions, insurance companies, special schools, and other public and private agencies with rehabilitation
programs and job placement services for the disabled employ the rest.

Training, Other Qualifications, and Advancement

A bachelor's degree with courses in counseling, psychology, and related fields is
the minimum educational requirement for rehabilitation counselors. However, employers are placing increasing emphasis on the master's degree in vocational
counseling or rehabilitation counseling, or in related subjects such as psychology,
education, and social work. Work experience in fields such as vocational counseling and placement, psychology, education, and social work is an asset for
securing employment as a rehabilitation counselor. Most agencies have work-
study programs whereby employed counselors can earn graduate degrees in the
field.

Usually, 2 years of study are required for the master's degree in the fields preferred for rehabilitation counseling. Included is a semester of actual work experience as a rehabilitation counselor under the close supervision of an instructor.
Besides a basic foundation in psychology, courses generally included in master's
degree programs are counseling theory and techniques, occupational and educational information, and community resources. Other requirements may include
courses in placement and followup, tests and measurements, cultural and psychological effects of disability, and medical and legislative aspects of therapy and
rehabilitation. About 85 schools offered graduate training in rehabilitation counseling in 1974.

To earn the doctorate in rehabilitation counseling or in counseling psychology
may require a total of 4 to 6 years of graduate study. Intensive training in psychology and other social sciences, as well as in research methods, is required.

Many States require that rehabilitation counselors be hired in accordance with
State civil service and merit system rules. In most cases, these regulations require applicants to pass a competitive written test, sometimes supplemented by
an individual interview and evaluation by a board of examiners.

Since rehabilitation counselors deal with the welfare of individuals, the ability
to accept responsibility is important. It also is essential that they be able to work
independently and be able to motivate and guide the activity of others.

Counselors who have limited experience usually are assigned the less difficult
cases. As they gain experience, their caseloads are increased and they are assigned clients with more complex rehabilitation problems. After obtaining considerable experience and more graduate education, rehabilitation counselors may
advance to supervisory positions or top administrative jobs.

Employment Outlook

Employment opportunities for rehabilitation counselors are expected to be favorable through the mid-1980's. Persons who have graduate work in rehabilitation
counseling or in related fields are expected to have the best employment prospects.

Contributing to the long-run demand for rehabilitation counselors will be population growth and the extension of service to a greater number of the severely
disabled, together with increased public awareness that the vocational rehabilitation approach helps the disabled to become self-supporting. The extent of growth
in employment of counselors, however, will depend largely on levels of government funding for vocational rehabilitation. In addition to growth needs, many counselors will be required annually to replace those who die, retire, or leave the
field for other reasons.

Figure 4–5. (*Continued*)

Earnings and Working Conditions

Salaries of beginning rehabilitation counselors in State agencies averaged $9,300 a year in 1974. Experienced counselors earned average salaries of $12,200 a year; the range was $9,800 to $16,400 among the States.

The Veterans Administration paid counseling psychologists with a 2-year master's degree and 1 year of subsequent experience—and those with a Ph.D.—starting salaries of $15,481 in late 1974. Those with a Ph.D. and a year of experience, and those with a 2-year master's degree and much experience, started at $18,463. Some rehabilitation counselors with a bachelor's degree were hired at starting salaries of $10,520 and $12,841. In general, salaries of rehabilitation counselors are above the average earnings for all nonsupervisory workers in private industry, except farming.

Counselors may spend only part of their time in their offices counseling and performing necessary paperwork. The remainder of their time is spent in the field, working with prospective employers, training agencies, and the disabled person's family. The ability to drive a car often is necessary for fieldwork.

Rehabilitation counselors generally work a 40-hour week or less, with some overtime work required to attend community and civic meetings in the evening. They usually are covered by sick and annual leave benefits, and pension and health plans.

Sources of Additional Information

For information about rehabilitation counseling as a career, contact:

American Psychological Association, Inc., 1200 17th St. NW., Washington, D.C. 20036.
American Rehabilitation Counseling Association, 1607 New Hampshire Ave. NW., Washington, D.C. 20009.
National Rehabilitation Counseling Association, 1522 K St. NW., Washington, D.C. 20005.

SOURCE: U.S. Department of Labor, *Occupational Outlook Handbook.* Washington, D.C.: U.S. Government Printing Office, 1976, pp. 515–517.

Part-time Employment

Millions of people work in part-time jobs, which are positions averaging less than thirty-five hours per week. During 1979, about fifteen million workers held such jobs exclusively, and another four million were moonlighting in addition to their full-time jobs. Most part-time work is in the finance and service sector (48.9 percent) and wholesale and retail trade (37.6 percent), with less than 6 percent being in manufacturing and only 3.1 percent in transportation and public utilities, 2.6 percent in public administration and 1.8 percent construction (*Employment and Training Report of the President,* 1979).

Voluntary part-timers average eighteen hours of work a week. Their limited work hours enable them to attend school, manage family responsibilities, abide physical limitations, or enjoy more leisure. A complaint of more than half the full-time working women, both professional and managerial and skilled and semiskilled, is insufficient time for leisure (National Commission on Working Women, 1979); and one can assume that many male workers have similar feelings.

About 80 percent of part-timers prefer shorter hours, and indications are that more people, especially women, would work part-time rather than working full-time or remaining unemployed if suitable part-time opportunities were available. Approximately 70 percent of the part-timers are women, and about 30 percent of working women are employed part-time. In their recent survey of 110,780 women, the National Commission on Working Women (1979) found that 25 percent of the full-time women workers would prefer to work part-time, and 50 percent of those seeking work were looking for part-time employment, whereas only 20 percent of the part-timers wanted full-time jobs. Also supporting the thesis of greater demand for part-time jobs is the experience of Santa Clara County in California. In 1976–1977, the county initiated a voluntary work-week reduction program to prevent layoffs threatened by fiscal problems. The fiscal situation improved in 1977 and 1978, but nearly half (seven hundred) of the fifteen hundred workers who had voluntarily accepted reduced work weeks from among the county's ten thousand employees sought to continue their reduced work schedules.

Regretably, part-time work is often not compensated proportionately to full-time work. The Bureau of Labor Statistics estimates that part-timers average 29 percent less in hourly wages than their full-time colleagues, and many part-timers do not obtain proportional fringe benefits, although many firms and the federal government are now providing proportional fringe benefits (*Employment and Training Report of the President*, 1979).

Efforts are underway to create more opportunities for challenging work on a part-time basis, but these attempts are not likely to alter the outlook for such jobs dramatically for some time to come. Corporations and government are studying job sharing, in which two workers divide a single job; and work sharing, in which workers reduce their number of hours in order to enable more persons to work. In addition, federal legislation (Federal Employees Part-time Career Employment Act) enabled part-time permanent positions to be counted as the appropriate fraction of a position in an agency's allotment, thereby enabling agencies to hire part-timers without being penalized. Still, less than 5 percent of permanent federal employment is part-time.

One alternate way of expanding opportunity for part-time, challenging work involves increasing the number of independent contractors. Instead of seeking a job, a contractor contracts with employers to produce a certain amount of product or service. Many people already work in this way to create computer programs, architectural drawings, advertising copy, typed manuscripts, instruction, delivery service, nursing, coaching, catering, cleaning services, and other things. What seems to be needed is promoting an entrepreneural attitude among more people and teaching them how to contract their services. The provision of service as needed is inviting to many businesses and agencies, which have fluctuations in demand and prefer to avoid tying up resources for temporary or seasonal jobs.

Availability of more and better work situations on a part-time basis would be a boon to career development for many, especially homemakers.

Counselors can contribute in at least three ways. First, they can alert students to the possibility of contracting and being one's own boss in a range of occupations and industries, and they can help their students to identify and to explore contracting opportunities. Second, they can support curriculum changes that develop and sustain an entrepreneural attitude and build such skills as marketing, job estimation, and contract negotiation. Dr. Marilyn Kourilsky, who has developed and studied economic simulation exercises for kindergarteners through business executives, believes about 25 percent of American kindergarteners have an entrepreneural attitude, but that by the time they graduate from high school less than 5 percent can still be considered entrepreneural. In part, she believes this change is due to the bias against entrepreneural activity in the school curriculum. Similarly, workshops and adult education programs increasingly are featuring instruction on starting one's own consulting firm or business, but such a course is almost never found in the regular high school or even community college and college curriculum. Third, counselors can offer placement services to contractors in the same way they assist regular job seekers. Although the traditional institutional bases of placement services make it undesirable for counselors to continue to be clients' agents; initial, neutral assistance in launching a contracting career should receive subsidized assistance from school or government placement services. Indeed, other agents are not likely to become available to the client who has not yet demonstrated promise in the field.

Employment and Entry to Work

Most people still do not work for large corporations or government, and many still work for themselves. Of the approximately 100 million jobs in our labor market, 16 percent are federal, state, and local government; 30 percent in private companies employing 100 or more workers; and approximately eight million are self-employed positions (*Employment and Training Report of President,* 1978).

Persons seeking entry and advancement in small firms or even in small government offices undergo considerably different screening and selection procedures than those entering large firms. The former are much less likely to encounter employment tests or formal appraisal. Instead, their references and sponsors' recommendations count more. If they are interviewed, the interviews will be more variable than they are for large corporations or businesses because the prospective employers are not professional personnel workers.

In contrast, employment selection and advancement in large corporations and governments have become more standardized. In part, this trend reflects pressure of court action for equal opportunity. Ordinarily, the applicant to a large organization takes paper-pencil tests for clerical and technical jobs and undergoes screening interviews with the probable supervisor. Increasingly, management candidates encounter simulation tests and intensive interviews. Professionals, too, undergo extensive interviews so that potential colleagues can judge their compatibility in addition to screening of their credentials. In contrast, unskilled and semi-skilled workers will be screened by a personnel technician and asked to complete applications, documenting education, past experience, and references, but less often given tests. The personnel screening interview will evaluate appearance, oral communication, and attitude.

The skilled, technical, managerial and professional workers are expected to communicate their qualifications in brief, pointed résumés. Some professionals, especially academics, often provide fuller credentials through vitae. Semi-skilled and unskilled workers have no need of résumés. The formats and contents of résumés vary across occupations and decade. Candidates, therefore, should consult placement service to determine what is in vogue for their field.

Promotions, too, are more formal. Increasingly skilled, technical, lower managerial, and some professional personnel receive supervisory or collegial reviews of their work, which often are to be communicated to them. These are used alone or in combination with formal appraisals to rank the person for promotion. Civil rights legislation is increasingly requiring the process to be public.

There are few studies of the psychological factors that might be manipulated to enable workers who have been laid off to reenter work. One study by Sheppard and Belitsky (1965), however, provides several leads. They analyzed structured interview responses from 450 blue-collar and 80 white-collar workers drawn from the unemployment roles in Erie, Pennsylvania. Among other things, they found that younger and higher skilled male workers were able to return to work sooner than others during a period when industries employing higher skilled workers were increasing activity more than others. They also found that early search for new work, wide-ranging job inquiries, and willingness to change occupations related to higher success, especially for workers who were more than thirty-eight years old. In contrast, the expectation of being called back to their old jobs diminished search for new work, but often the expectations were realized.

Interlinked with these behaviors for males are sociopsychological variables of "achievement motivation" (defined by McCleland) "motivation," "achievement value," and "reported job interview anxiety." High achievement motivation and achievement values were related to success in reentering work, to looking for work sooner after layoff, to using more methods of obtaining work, to contacting firms advertising and not advertising for work and to making more job inquiries. Interview anxiety in turn is associated with less job seeking for all workers and lower success in getting employed for older workers. Interview anxiety was higher among younger workers and those with more dependents. The relevance of psychological variables was clearer for workers over thirty-eight years of age who tended to have more difficulty returning to work.

In terms of effectiveness of methods, personal contacts appeared to be the most productive source of new jobs, although workers rated this third in usefulness. Other useful sources were unions, employment service, and direct contact with the employer. Those applicants of the employment service who received direct referrals as part of their employment service interaction obtained jobs more often than enrollees who were not referred to employers.

Sheppard and Belitsky (1965) ended their report with multiple recommendations, including:

1. Increase the unemployed's achievement motivation and achievement values.
2. Assist workers adopt a more flexible posture on changing occupations and alter employment service practices to accommodate that flexibility.
3. Alert the unemployed to the importance of contacting friends about securing job leads and referrals.
4. Assist the unemployed in mastering job interviewing techniques.

The value and relative use of different job search and acquisition are becoming of more concern. The *Manpower and Training Report of the President* now contains data on differential use of job search techniques by different age groups.

Worker Organizations

There are many worker organizations with millions of workers in the United States. These organizations enable workers collectively to express their views about what their jobs should be and how they should perform them. They have, and will continue to have, profound influence on the nature of work in America. Since World War II, approximately 25 percent of nonfarm workers have been members of unions, and nearly half the twenty million managerial and professional workers are members of professional associations.

Professional associations and unions influence work in several ways. Many set standards for entering training. Through training and sponsorship requirements they regulate who can enter an occupation. Professional associations and craft unions often accredit schools; and their officers serve on licensing boards and apprenticeship councils in order to regulate the training content. Through codes of conduct and contractual bargaining, they establish how work will be performed. Moreover, many professional groups and craft unions lobby for credentialing and licensing legislation. Most unions influence salaries by direct negotiation, and many professional associations establish informal pay standards. Professional associations sponsor development of particular kinds of new knowledge pertinent to their members' work and promulgate this information through publications and educational programs.

People are generally aware that professional organizations and unions are responsible for such things as restricting American midwifery almost exclusively to physicians and to limiting the use of pre-fabricated units of construction. They have heard television performers joke about their need for a union worker to move a chair and have listened to colorful labor officials denounce automated innovations. As a consequence, most people recognize the fact that worker organizations try to control job boundaries and work processes. Fewer people may recognize that these associations, by controlling worker selection and training, actually affect the definition of many jobs. For example, counselor education programs in which trainees work individually to develop themselves, rather than collectively to develop a team, do not encourage the trainees to become coordinators and collaborators. Likewise, the absence of the study of nutrition in medical schools has led many physicians to prescribe drugs and even surgery for some conditions correctable or preventable through diet change.

Workers should be aware of regulations and precedents about worker organizations so they can benefit from their organizations. Certain union and professional association activities are regulated by the Wagner Act of 1935, the Taft-Hartley Act of 1948, and the Landrum-Griffith Act of 1959. Established by the Wagner Act, the National Labor Relations Board of the federal government acts to assure fair labor practices by worker groups and employers. Although not as closely regulated as unions, professional associations influence work conditions and salary by promulgating information about typical hours, duties, and salaries of their members and by testifying on the appropriateness of insurance company and government payments for particular services. Moreover, these associations often represent members against employers when a member is upholding professional standards, much as unions defend their members in the grievance procedure process.

Unfortunately, high schools and colleges do little to prepare students for membership in worker organizations. Technical and professional schools socialize the student into their respective occupations, but often do not provide a person with a full perspective of the worker organization. In a 1966 survey of high school social science curricula, Scoggins (1966) found minimal treatment of the National Labor Relations Board, the major union legislation, or the history of union and professional organization development.

Another disappointing fact about worker organizations is that the percentage of the membership shaping their policy and practice is small. Hagburg and Levine (1978), in writing about unions, and Moore (1970), in writing about professional associations, have noted that these groups tend to be nominally democratic, but oligarchic in actual operation. Perhaps career education activities, such as classroom simulations of collective bargaining and internships on union and professional association governing boards, can increase worker participation in these organizations. Clearly, such associations will have to sanction many job redesign attempts. Consequently, persons who want to be able to have job design available to them for managing their careers will want to learn how worker associations do and could operate.

Occupational Information

Creating a career requires understanding our educational-work system and its range of options and requires continuing information procurement and processing. As important as knowledge about the total system and specific occupations is an understanding of the strengths and weaknesses of the different ways of obtaining that information. Also vital are accumulated successes in using the different information gathering and processing methods. This information gathering and processing knowledge is so important for several reasons: 1) most people will be changing their occupations several times over their careers; 2) their implementation of early career choices will change who they are, necessitating re-examination of their goals and career paths; 3) occupational and educational options will be changing in number and kind over time; and 4) continued information acquisition and processing can be expected only if a person has been reinforced regularly for such efforts.

What to Teach About the Career World

First, an understanding of the society's economic workings is essential; that is, one needs to know how owning, investing, training, producing, and consuming are interrelated. Disappointed with American youth's lack of appreciation of these interrelationships, economic educators such as Kourilsky (1975) and Darcy (1968) have developed instructional materials to help elementary and junior high school students acquire such knowledge.

In addition to understanding economic forces, careerists need an awareness of the range of occupations and education programs, including a general appreciation of how they are related and how they are different. In other words, youngsters should be developing their own versions of classification systems such as Roe's (1956). This broad appreciation is deemed important for youngsters nine years and older, according to tests of career development such as the *Career Maturity Inventory* (Crites, 1973), the *New Mexico Career Education Test Series* (Healy & Klein, 1973), the *Career Skills Assessment Program* (College Entrance Examination Board, 1977), and the *Assessment of Career Development* (American College Testing Program, 1974).

Although the models used to conceptualize careers differ in the information they imply one needs, careerists and career counselors have tended to employ mixed models. There is, indeed, general agreement about the kinds of occupational and educational information that is desirable. Hoppock (1976), for instance, claims that people should know the following facts in order to relate themselves to occupations: work duties, skill requirements, supply-and-demand outlook, salary, other work satisfactions, work conditions, relation of the occupation to other occupations, and the school curricula needed for the occupations. The U.S. Department of Labor (1976) claimed an ideal career guidance information system would include descriptive information about the occupation, especially its requirements and economic aspects. Thus, one should learn the costs of training, the factors associated with being on the high or low end of the occupation's salary distribution (for example, graduates of prestigious law schools who are in the upper quarter of their graduating class and on their law review are much more likely to enter a prestigious law firm and, therefore, have a better chance for a large income), and the social status and life styles enjoyed by members of the occupation. Likewise, recognizing that an occupation or training position is a choice within a broader context, Tyler's (1969) decision paradigm implies that the careerist should consider factors such as the alternatives opened or closed by the choice, the personal adjustments that are likely from incumbency in the educational program or occupation, the amount of time and energy required by the choice, and the waiting period to be endured before realizing the fruits of the choice. Physicians anticipate a substantial income, for instance, but typically spend four years in medical school without earnings and two to six years in residency with minimal incomes and very long hours in training and in work. Similarly, apprentices endure several years of intensive training before being able to perform the full range of their craft for a full wage.

Finally, the growing realization that satisfied workers often redesign their jobs, or are in redesigned jobs, should lead students to examine how workers in a particular occupation have altered or plan to alter their work. They should examine the factors that caused the job to be as it is, noting how prospective changes would have to be managed in light of such factors.

How many occupations to learn about in order to choose a career direction is an important content issue that has not received direct research attention. Logically, a person needs a broad sampling, but how to obtain it has not been explicitly defined. Crites (1973) assumes that youth need to learn about many occupations, for his *Career Maturity Inventory Information Test* samples knowledge of occupations in a manner to cover the Roe classification. Likewise, the exploratory phase of career education is targeted at providing youngsters with a broad sampling of occupational knowledge. Moreover, the Holland thesis that new occupations are likely to emerge within existing areas provides another reason for acquainting oneself with all areas, for by acquiring such knowledge one is likely to have a general understanding of what the yet-to-evolve occupations will be like. One approach to gaining this knowledge advocated by this author (Healy & Quinn, 1977) is that during the first ten grades of school the person should examine and experience three or four occupations from each category in the Roe classification. Or one might sample occupations from the USOE Career Clusters. This sampling approach, indeed, is the rationale of the *Careers in Focus* program of Winn (1976).

Acknowledging the rapidly changing nature of modern work, however, also emphasizes the importance of research findings, such as those of Gupta (1976) that teenagers have a different activity structure from adults. Their structure differentiates several recreational areas and does not distinguish between work areas that are typically differentiated in adult structures. As automation increases time for leisure, occupations may develop in leisure and service areas, that are not now in our work scheme. In any event, it is especially important that people learn about occupations that may not be categorizable in the current framework, since these fields may be the vanguard of many future occupations.

So far, research on career development has shown most support for a person acquiring specific occupational knowledge rather than information processing skills or successful information utilization experiences. This conclusion is due, in part, to the fact that these latter variables have been assessed only occasionally in studies of career development, perhaps because there are few existing measures of them.

Instinctively, educators have recognized that information alone is not enough; therefore, many efforts are aimed at developing skills such as the ability to conduct an interview with a worker doing a specific job and the ability to pinpoint skill requirements of particular jobs by rotating through a series of job stations. One Detroit counselor, for instance, had third graders develop interviewing skills in a career education project. As a byproduct, they also acquired occupational knowledge and learned to use a tape recorder. First she guided the third graders to identify the information they wanted; then she helped them to develop a structured interview and to decide which parents or family acquaintances to interview; finally, she provided a form for showing the interview results (Wellington & Olechowski, 1966).

This kind of direct information gathering seems most important for students to learn, since occupations are increasing in number and changing rapidly. Indeed, as important as any fact about an occupation, by adolescence one should know how to do a job analysis in order to be able to discover the characteristics of possible occupations. Hoppock (1976), the dean of occupational information, has provided clear guidelines for doing a job analysis and repeatedly has stressed the importance of keeping occupational information updated; but the literature on career guidance is unclear about how many students know how to do a field job analysis. Unfortunately, the major career maturity measures do not test such ability.

Information Delivery

Clearly, expanding the objectives of society's, and especially the school's, occupational information program requires changing the traditional career information service which has relied heavily on one course in occupational information, extensive independent reading, and uncoordinated dispensations by concerned teachers or counselors. Even though the new program's content and methods are not yet clear, the varied efforts at developing career awareness by the career education movement should suggest acceptable approaches.

Reading is likely to continue to be the major method of obtaining general information about occupational and educational opportunities; it is simply the most efficient method. Thus, publications such as the

Occupational Outlook Handbook, the *Dictionary of Occupational Titles, Baron's Profiles of American Colleges, Lovejoy's College Guides,* and *American Universities and Colleges* are apt to remain the basic references of a career information service. Many other informational materials—books, occupational briefs, pamphlets, school catalogues, audio-visuals, simulation kits, and decision games—are becoming available and should become a part of a career information center. To help the counselor choose among new materials, the *Vocational Guidance Quarterly,* which is the journal of the National Vocational Guidance Association, regularly lists and evaluates new guidance materials.

An important effect of the 1970s concern with career development has been a substantial upgrading of schools' career information programs, including the creation of career information centers. An effective career center is an important adjunct to career counseling; counselors should support establishment of such centers in the school and in the community. Reardon and Burck (1975) have described the organization and equipage of a college career center, and the American Institute of Research has developed a set of materials to guide the organization and operation of such centers (Wood, Rogers, & Klinge, 1979). In addition, the counselor setting up such a center can consult texts such as Lee Isaacson's *Career Information in Teaching and Counseling* (1977) and Robert Hoppock's *Occupational Information* (1976) for a broad overview of establishing a career information service.

Even now, two new ideas about career information promulgation are very promising: 1) infusing career information into the instruction of the traditional disciplines; and 2) involving parents, business and industry, labor, and community persons more deliberately and more extensively, even collaboratively (Hoyt, 1976), in the career awareness effort.

Logically, some occupational awareness should be developed within classroom instruction of traditional disciplines to help the student appreciate how the discipline relates to working. Infusing career awareness means either targeting conventional lessons to teach career awareness in addition to traditional objectives, or redesigning lessons to accomplish both the career awareness and traditional objectives.

Figures 4–6, 4–7, and 4–8 present three infusion lessons. The lesson in Figure 4–6 might be altered to have students work in teams and to receive feedback about their product from a cartoonist. Many infusion activities, such as Figures 4–7 and 4–8, can approximate a real work task, can provide rich material for discussing strengths and weakness of different informational gathering methods, and can increase the likelihood of a student's being successful. Thousands of infusion lessons have been produced and tried by teachers. Many are available through the National Clearinghouse for Career Education in Missoula, Montana.

The classroom, vital as it is to provide opportunity for analysis, deliberation, and reflection about feedback, must be complemented by direct experience with working in order for its instruction to foster appreciation of work. Certainly, Piaget's notion that conceptual learning and thinking require linkage of the concepts to concrete instances, and

Figure 4–6. Example of Lesson to Infuse Career Awareness
through Subjects Such as Art or Social Studies

Career Awareness through Caricature

Rationale:

Students should be familiar with careers in many fields.

Objectives:

1. Each student will do research on a particular job assigned. Student will be able to describe duties, conditions, wages, method of entry and requirements for the assigned job.
2. Each student will draw a caricature of someone working on that job.

Description:

1. Assign a particular job to each student in the class to research.
2. After research, have students draw a caricature of someone working at that job.
3. Display caricatures and discuss what information was most useful for facilitating the drawing. In the discussion, bring out how well they must know what they are drawing before they pick up their materials and start; point out that, to be good, the drawing must be instantly recognizable by almost anyone.

Personnel required: teacher
Cost: none
Time: 1 period for initial discussion and assigning jobs; 1 period for research; 1 period for drawing caricatures; possibly 1 period for exhibiting caricatures and further discussion
Impact on community: caricatures might be used for a display
Resources: information on jobs

SOURCE: Healy, C. C., and Quinn, J. *Final Report of Project Cadre.* Los Angeles: UCLA Graduate School of Education, 1977.

Dewey's (1910) view of understanding argue for direct experience. Thompson (1970) has proposed that informational activities order themselves in terms of their distance from actual experience as follows: publications, audio-visuals, programmed instruction, computer systems, interviews with experts, simulations, synthetically created work environments, direct observation, directed exploration, and on-the-job try-out. Recognizing this continuum, educators and adult collaborators can identify actual work activities, construct lessons, supervise youngsters, and provide feedback and opportunity for review so the activities foster career development. Many examples of activities and lessons are also becoming available through the National Clearinghouse for Career Education.

Computer-Based Information

One long-term problem in educational and occupational information has been the difficulty of obtaining accurate, up-to-date local information

Figure 4–7. Example of Lesson to Infuse Self-Awareness
through Subjects such as Mathematics or Social Studies

Opinion Surveying to Bolster Self-Awareness

Rationale:

Students should have an understanding of how to measure people's opinions and preferences and what part the results play in determining production of society.

Objectives:

1. Students will identify three implications of public opinion on production, including amount of product available in store, company profit, recognition of product by households surveyed, etc.
2. Students will describe in one paragraph whether they liked or disliked their role as researchers and the reasons why.

Description:

1. Assist students to identify five survey questions, each one designed such as the following:

    Which laundry product do you prefer?

      a. Tide
      b. Cheer
      c. Fab
      d. Oxydol
      e. Other _____

    Use vegetables, dairy products, sporting equipment, entertainment, etc., for the other questions.
2. Have each student survey ten households, being sure to keep addresses, or to work only in an assigned area in one evening.
3. Remove duplicate data (if any) by using addresses.
4. Have students tabulate data.
5. Have students divide into groups (five) or individually calculate:
      mean
      mode
      median
      range
      standard deviation (optional)
6. Have students graph results using a histogram.
7. Share results, discuss implications for products (first, second, and last in each category)
8. Discuss the effects this might have on jobs in various cities where products are made.
9. Summarize by reviewing purposes of activity, including students' role as researchers. How did they like it?

Personnel required: teacher
Cost: none
Time: questions, 1 period; tabulation and calculation, 1 period; discussion, 1 period
Impact on community: students survey households in the community

SOURCE: *Ideas for Activities.* Lansing, Mich.: Office of Career Education of the Michigan State Board of Education, undated, Lesson 26. Used with permission.

Figure 4–8. Example of Lesson to Infuse Career Awareness
through Subjects such as Mathematics or Economics

Follow-Up of Graduates

Rationale:

Students should have the opportunity to know what happens to the graduates of their high school, in order to learn more about individual differences in training needs.

Objective:

Each student will predict where he/she will be in two years, five years, and 10 years in a 3-page essay, in terms of job, education, living situation (where living, leisure activities), and the student will indicate why his future will be the same or different from that of past graduates.

Description:

Using the counselor as a resource, obtain figures on what has happened to graduates for the last three (five, ten, etc.) years. Tabulate figures and make a bar graph which indicates percentages for the following:

1. Going to 4-year colleges
2. 2-year colleges
3. technical schools
4. job training programs
5. armed services
6. marriage and house work, etc.
7. leisure activities
8. city of residence

Discuss meaning of figures. Compare with other classes, area schools, expectations of present students, etc.

Personnel required: teacher, counselor
Cost: none
Time: 1 or 2 periods
Resources: counselor's records of graduates; graph paper

SOURCE: Healy, C. C., and Quinn, J. *Final Report of Project Cadre.* Los Angeles: UCLA Graduate School of Education, 1977.

---

about educational programs and occupations. With widespread computerization, this problem is being resolved. Computer systems such as IBM's *Educational and Career Exploration System* (Minor, Myers, & Super, 1969), *Computer Vocational Information System* (CVIS, 1977), the *System of Interactive Guidance and Information* (Katz, Chapman, & Godwin, 1972), and *Guidance Information System* (Guide, 1972), enable students to obtain leads to educational and occupational opportunities commensurate with their tested and expressed abilities and interests; and these systems provide, or direct users to, current information about these opportunities. Beginning in 1976, the Department of Labor has provided start-up grants to eight states—Alabama, Colorado, Massachusetts, Michigan, Minnesota, Ohio, Washington, and Wisconsin—to develop statewide career information systems that will provide up-to-date local information in a form that will be useful to people planning their careers. The model for the organization of these programs is the Career Information System of Oregon, which provides for cooperation among state and private agencies that need to disseminate career information (McKinley, 1974). Overseeing the development in these states and serving as a clearinghouse for occupational information dissemination is the Employment and Training Administration, United States Department of Labor, Washington, D.C.

Adult Informational Needs

Even though career education is increasing youngsters' career awareness, little progress has been made to address the informational needs of workers changing occupations or about to enter work immediately. Instead of broad information about occupations, these adults are seeking specific details about such items as equipment, and processes used in jobs. The computer programmer, for example, will want to know the particular computer language and computer model in use and will want to know whether a prospective employer contracts the system analysis tasks or has opportunities for programmers to develop that competence. The manager will be interested in the firm's organization and management philosophy as well as in the career patterns of managerial personnel within the firm. The secretary will be curious about time among typing, dictation, and administrative duties. In other words, adult workers want to know what they are expected to be able to do when reporting for work and what they can expect to learn on the job. They want to know the resources available to help them in doing their job and in enriching and enlarging their occupational skill repertoires. Many professionals, such as college teachers or lawyers, will want to know the calibre and collegiality of colleagues and the college's or firm's support of occupational development activities such as securing research grants and accepting leadership in the professional organization. These workers are also concerned with overall employer policies in regard to working hours and travel demands, economic condition and image of the firm, worker morale and fringe benefits, expectations about relocation, and vertical and horizontal mobility. They even weigh costs of living and nature of the community where the firm is located, including data about local and state taxes, in deciding whether to pursue or accept a position. But, government publications, the United States Employment Service, and most occupational publications do not directly address these informational needs of adults. Even the recruiting literature of major corporations and civil service offer little information beyond the descriptions found in the *Occupational Outlook Handbook*.

But, some very promising innovations have been made in career information pertinent to these adult information needs. Hoyt (1965), for instance, initiated an *SOS* program in which local high school counselors and their students periodically surveyed their school's graduates about their post-high-school training programs. Surveys covered concerns of most interest to graduates, and the results were published in an easy-to-comprehend format. In audiovisuals, Magoon (1968) had experts from the University of Maryland interviewed about their professions and job prospects. He then made tape recordings of these interviews available through a jukebox in the counseling center. Of course, the content of the tapes can be updated.

In regard to expert informants, several career placement and career information centers have established directories of workers who will discuss their work with interested students and prospective workers. Many adult career questions refer to particulars that either change periodically, such as operating procedures and benefits, or are subjective judgments, such as employee morale and collegiality. As a consequence, interviews with nonpersonnel workers in a nonevaluation situation, are helpful before deciding about whether to apply for a position. After being hired, the worker can usually make contacts with future colleagues and gather such information, but having such information before making the employment decision would benefit both employers and employees.

CAREER COUNSELING AND EVALUATION

part two

This text is designed primarily to illuminate a comprehensive model of career counseling, which will enable counselors to be accountable. Recognition that career is an integral part of the life passage indicates that career development requires many different kinds of accomplishments. Morrill and Forest (1970) pointed out this fact more than a decade ago. Since people have been helping one another with their careers for many years, professional counselors and lay advisers must have devised a variety of useful methods to help people overcome obstacles at different stages of their careers.

To tap this experience base and to add to it, a professional career counselor needs an operating model that guides selection, use, and monitoring of such methods. Part two, which includes Chapters 5 and 6, delineates such a model and highlights selected research and evaluation concepts to prepare counselors to use the model. Part three then presents counseling methods for use and adaptation within the framework of this model.

Chapter 5 considers counseling as the creation and implementation of a learning program for mastering the challenges of everyday living and views counselors as program managers. The chapter details broad strategies that counselors and other teachers have traditionally used to help clients to execute a learning program. Amplifying the notion that counseling is individualized instruction to meet problems in living, the text describes how a counseling (learning) program proceeds through four stages: 1) establishing client needs, goals, obstacles, and strengths; 2) identifying and selecting solution strategies; 3) teaching and otherwise assisting the client to implement solutions; and 4) evaluating the effectiveness of the effort. Then the text explains how heuristic principles or rules of thumb for teaching and living, such as "you can catch more bees with honey than with vinegar," provide both a rationale for counseling methods and the concepts and principles of the counseling curriculum.

Viewing counseling as creation and management of a learning program suggests several ways of improving it. Especially important is the observation that one can increase counseling's potency by integrating teachers other than the counselor into the operation. Although few career counselors now incorporate other people into their counseling, the success of some career education programs suggests that collaboration will improve counseling.

Chapter 6 focuses on research and evaluation concepts in order to acquaint counselors with tools that can help them establish accountability. Before describing particular counseling methods and research, the chapter points out the difficulties of examining counseling and some common faults in counseling studies. This introduction tries to prepare the reader to approach subsequent presentations both critically and sympathetically, knowing that systematic study of counseling is difficult and aware that many commendable studies have limitations, which reduce the reliability and generalizability of their findings.

The text then describes tools for achieving accountability: it explains and illustrates the widely recommended formative evaluation methods; details how to describe counseling methods so they can be replicated; and describes the adversary or human intelligence method of inquiry, which can complement quantitative research methods. Then, the chapter closes with suggestions for professional organizations to follow to promote and upgrade counseling research and evaluation.

A Career Counseling
Framework

5

This chapter presents the author's definition of counseling so that the reader can appreciate the perspective used in examining the counseling strategies presented in Chapters 6 through 12. Career counseling is individualized instruction proceeding through some or all of four stages. This chapter identifies the important properties of counseling, delineates the four counseling stages and their corresponding tasks, describes the responses that counselors use in guiding clients through the stages, explicates the notion of heuristic principles (which are the bases for how and what counselors teach in counseling), and shows how individualized instruction is compatible with group counseling. In closing, the author notes that the differences between counseling and other forms of career development assistance are blurred, and suggests that the lack of a precise definition of counseling is helpful because it enables continual adaptation in light of new knowledge about human development and about teaching.

Most people have a need to work, but assuredly, societies require their citizens to pursue careers energetically. To reconcile the need of citizens to work with the cherished heritage of the individual's right to be free, our society has commissioned a profession to help people to identify and to enter satisfying work. Termed *counselors*, members of this profession work in schools and colleges, governmental and private agencies concerned with work and manpower, and occasionally in private practice. When these counselors specialize in career development, they are termed *career counselors*, to distinguish them from counselors who work with the general range of human development concerns.

Nature of Counseling

Counseling is helping by teaching. Counselors empower a client to use knowledge to develop the skills and attitudes needed for mastering daily living. Many disciplines treat topics related to human development. Psychology deals with human learning and motivation; sociology clarifies the impact of human groups and institutions; drama and poetry depict human character and emotion; and economics studies the distribution of resources. Counseling differs from such disciplines primarily because its goal is to help the client relate pertinent principles from these disciplines to his or her own life. The objective of counseling is that the person master personal developmental tasks rather than master a discipline. The counselor assists the client in selecting and applying the knowledge of such disciplines to his own circumstances.

Counselors are commissioned by the client, or the client's family or community group, to share with the client principles and rules from the behavioral sciences for solving a problem or mastering a developmental task. Many life problems and attendant emotional distress stem from ignorance or erroneous information and beliefs. Some husbands and wives do not communicate their feelings and intentions clearly, and they always become upset when their spouse reacts differently than they wanted because they interpret the spouse as deliberately thwarting them rather than as misunderstanding them. Lonely people do not know where to meet people who are likely to be compatible, and their ensuing distress interferes with their initiating and sustaining social contacts (Szabo, 1973). In regard to careers, many persons have not learned to appraise their attributes and goals and to relate them to working. They have not acquired the habit of gathering information about career opportunities and changes occurring in themselves; nor have they learned to resolve problems, profit from mistakes, and improve their own confidence. These people feel the frustration of such deficits, but often they do not relate it to their ignorance or their erroneous information and beliefs.

The implications of conceptualizing counseling as teaching are that a counselor helps a person who is having difficulty coping with everyday concerns by creating an atmosphere conducive to learning and by guiding the person through a sequence of exercises that provide information, teach skills, or develop habits. The exercises actually constitute a learning program in which counselor and client establish the client's goals and the steps needed for achieving the goals. Then, from the counselor's knowledge of how people solve that type of problem, and with the client's assistance, they set up one or more exercises that will expose the client to the ideas or will teach the skills needed for achieving the goal.

As an example of how a set of exercises might be arranged for a client, suppose a twelfth grader wanted to obtain a position as teller in the local bank. Since others also would be seeking the job, the student would need to impress the bank manager with his or her potential. Together, the student and counselor would analyze the objective and decide that the student needed to learn about the duties of a teller, how the student's skills related to those duties, and how to show the bank manager that the student has the abilities needed for the teller's job. Reading about the occupation of bank teller and then observing a teller and asking specific questions will teach the student about the duties of a teller. The client and counselor can discuss the client's skills and a teller's duties to clarify for the client how his or her skills relate to a teller's duties. To learn how to demonstrate the skills required of a teller, the client can first fill out a practice application and obtain feedback from the counselor. Then the student and counselor can role play the upcoming interview with the manager and make corrections with the help of the counselor. Finally, they would meet to review the outcome of the interview and to plan the next steps. The counseling, therefore, consists of these exercises: an initial discussion to set the objectives, information-seeking exercises by the client, a discussion of that information and the client's abilities, completion of a practice job application and feedback, role playing of a job interview with corrective feedback, and an evaluation of the effort.

Counseling Is Personal

Its objectives and the learning exercises needed to accomplish them emanate from and focus on the client as an individual. Counseling helps clients to change their situation and feel better about it. Skills, attitudes, and insights are developed for the sake of the client. The learning program is individualized for the particular client. Counseling succeeds when the clients realize their goals, not when they achieve some standard of knowledge.

Media and Techniques

Counselors use a broad spectrum of media and techniques to teach clients. Direct face-to-face communication is still most common, but counselors also have integrated audio and videotaping, computers, slides, filmstrips, records, and movies into counseling. Traditionally, career counseling has included testing and interpretation, role playing or rehearsal, and extra counseling assignments to acquire information. More recently, counselors have added self-directed exploration manuals and programs, simulations, and relaxation exercises to their repertoire of techniques.

Counseling Requires Trusting Relationship

Counseling distinguishes itself from other teaching in its development and use of a trusting interpersonal relationship to facilitate a client's learning or change. The hallmark of counselors is their ability to persuade clients that they are interested in knowing them and are committed to helping them with their concerns. Counselors accept clients nonjudgmentally without necessarily approving particular behaviors or motives. This trust enables clients to examine their situations honestly and deliberately and to employ varied strategies for improving their situations. To warrant trust, counselors must accept only clients they expect they can help, must offer quality services and verify their quality, and must uphold the welfare of both client and community in counseling.

Counseling Goals

Counseling must have goals. These goals limit the scope of the counselor-client relationship. The goal may be to improve a domestic relationship, to reduce phobic behavior, or to acquire greater career self-awareness. Whatever the goal, it limits the information to be sought about the client, as well as the commitment of the counselor to the client. In stating goals, it is important that the counselor not covertly suggest broader goals by the questions asked or the responses made to a client. Multiple goals can, of course, characterize a particular counseling, thus expanding the scope of the relationship, as well as counselor responsibility. Even with multiple goals, however, client and counselor prerogatives and responsibilities are limited by the nature of the accepted goals. A counselor, for example, who is assisting a group of ninth graders in improving their career self-esteem should inform them that improvement of self-esteem is their purpose. Then, if in the course of the group session, one student asks for help in relating better to parents, the counselor need not assume responsibility for providing such help. It would be appropriate to acknowledge the request and to state that, though this goal is important, it is beyond the realm of the group's purpose. Ideally, the counselor would suggest another source of help or even offer to help outside the group, if competent. Of course, if the counselor or group will not provide help, then encouraging the youngster to bare concerns and details about the family situation would be unfair and confusing. But, an objective and understanding acknowledgment of the problem and a reminder of the limits of counseling are appropriate, and will maintain the career counseling relationship.

Counseling Contracts

Establishing goals in counseling and agreeing about what each party will do to achieve them is tantamount to establishing a learning contract. Social psychology suggests that the actual declaration of a goal increases client commitment to its achievement, and makes clearer the expectations of counseling. Formalizing the counseling contract has the advantage of making explicit the fact that both parties will work cooperatively until the goal is achieved. This agreement is especially important since counseling is an educational process in which some false starts and recycling are the norm. Although few counselors now use formal written contracts, many studies support the use of contracts in individualized instruction. Therefore, counselors should seriously consider using formal contracts.

The counseling contract is a major way of distinguishing counseling from other instructional activities of a counselor. By contracting, the client and counselor commit themselves to work toward a goal, and at least implicitly both agree to the means whereby the goal will be achieved. When counselors give information, interpret tests, teach a problem solving strategy, or review a person's plans without a contract, neither party is committed to achieving a particular outcome. Without the commitment and explicitness about the intended outcome, the outcome is less likely to occur. Doubtlessly, the activities are valuable in themselves, and providing them without a counseling relationship may enable the counselor to offer them to more people. Yet, in themselves they are not counseling. For, in providing them without a counseling contract, neither counselor nor learner are obligating themselves to personalize the information, nor to relate the problem solving strategy to a real problem, nor to support implementation of a personal plan.

Counseling Will Be Differentially Effective

Defining counseling as a special kind of teaching highlights the fact that growth through counseling depends on the content and learning skills which the client brings to counseling. Thus, the client who historically is an effective student is likely to derive more from counseling in a shorter time. The client who is effective in information acquisition and processing and knows how colleges operate, for example, is more likely to obtain accurate information about particular programs, than the client deficient in these skills. Accordingly, the counseling program for the latter must include exercises for developing such competencies, and, even with such exercises, the counselor should not be surprised to find the former client progressing more rapidly than the latter.

Similarly, counselors should expect a client overwhelmed with self-doubt or beset with multiple problems to have a poorer prognosis. Such feelings limit the client's capacity to examine fully and to learn about one's problem and may precipitate premature action. The distress usually stems from the client's sense of failure at tasks peers are managing. The concerns that prompt counseling are generally not physical ailments nor external threats, but rather interpretations of everyday problems. Such perceived failures threaten one's sense of mastery and make one feel less than a person in our society, which idealizes the autonomous, coping individual. As a consequence, the client may be inclined to flee, panic, cry, give up, or lash out, all of which interfere with putting personal problems into a perspective that would enable their resolution.

Counseling Techniques

Specific communications and social learning strategies or techniques are the recognized tools of counselors. These techniques foster trust and facilitate completion of the counseling exercises. The counselor selects particular exercises through task analysis of the client's goals. Although many of these teaching techniques derive from client-centered counseling and behavioral psychology, counselors of most orientations use them. Indeed, classroom teachers also employ many of the same techniques. This author has classified these techniques into the six broad areas described below. The counselor should use some or all of these techniques in counseling for each of the career developmental goals described later in this book.

1. *Explaining the Task and Procedures.* Counselors explain their objectives and the operation of a procedure by speaking clearly and slowly, by giving examples familiar to a client, by illustrating or modeling what they want a client to do, and, by drawing the client's attention to suitable models or by showing films of appropriate models. If modeling is used, research suggests that counselors select as models those who are the same sex as the client, have high status, are peers with high social power, and are similar to the client (Hosford, 1969). Counselors also encourage questions. They answer them cordially and as directly as possible, and sometimes they give clients a written description of counseling or even show films to make sure their expectations are clear.

2. *Involving Clients in Counseling.* Counselors invite clients to talk, ask open-ended questions, and wait for the client to respond, thereby encouraging participation. A counselor's posture, expression, and total attention to clients show clients that they are expected to talk. Periodically, the counselor paraphrases what is being said, reflecting the feeling as well as the content of the client's communication. In group counseling, the counselor calls clients by their names; redirects one client's question to another; points out similarities among clients' work experiences, interests, talents, and aspirations, and encourages them to do the same; and guides clients to discover how their backgrounds relate to the group discussion.

Recognizing that everyone wants to be on a "winning team," a counselor subtly tells clients that they are in "goods hands" and will become winners through counseling. The counselor exudes enthusiasm, and may disclose personal success experiences in pursuits similar to the clients or in counseling. In groups, counselors involve clients by eliciting testimonials about their benefits from counseling.

Ownership of counseling is also shared to promote client involvement. Client contributions, such as theme songs for groups, assistance in setting up exercises or equipment, explanations to one another, and elaboration and extension of concepts are welcomed to the degree that time constraints permit. The periodic request for the client to summarize not only aids evaluation but also promotes client ownership of counseling.

3. *Diagnosing the Need for, or Evaluating, Progress in Counseling.* Counselors weigh the data received from and about a client before and during counseling both to determine an appropriate learning (counseling) program for the client and to pace counseling. If information about client's need and progress are forthcoming, as one would expect from effective use of explanation, involvement, and reinforcement techniques, the counselor has only to process information. If needed data are not

forthcoming, the counselor asks direct questions; or, if client's understanding is unclear, asks the client to demonstrate progress by giving examples. After discussing a strategy for improving communication with a work-study supervisor, for example, the counselor might ask the client to describe what he or she will do in the next meeting with the supervisor. The counselor asks for this description to be sure that the client can say what to do before moving to the next step.

In evaluating progress, the counselor may use written tests or periodically can restate the situation and ask the client to make needed corrections. Ongoing verification may seem superfluous, but interview communication, especially the nonverbal element, lead to many misinterpretations, which such verification can prevent. Indeed, counseling research suggests that in successful counseling, counselor and client language converges and counselor and client are in agreement about what transpired.

Clients, of course, evaluate their counseling progress, too, and their judgments in part reflect their interpretations of the counselor's assessment. Client's positive evaluation of progress and the contribution of counseling should increase the client's commitment to counseling, whereas the client's negative evaluation may lead to withdrawal or may obstruct further learning. Counselors, therefore, should monitor clients' evaluations of counseling continually. They should share with clients their evaluation matrix so that clients are more aware of how to judge their own progress. They might even wish to share their evaluations with clients directly in order to preclude misunderstanding. Clearly, Rogers's (1951) early admonitions against evaluation are, in part, directed at the dampening effect of counselor's negative evaluations of the client's progress. Counselors cannot avoid evaluations, but perhaps they can be more explicit and open about them.

Since continuing a client in counseling itself reflects optimism about outcome, the counselor's input into the counselor-client review of progress is likely to be positive. Even when the progress seen by the counselor is not as great as that hoped for by the client, joint review will enable the client to be more realistic. This review will alert the client sooner to the probable needs for patience and perseverance. On the other hand, eliciting the client's negative evaluations early through joint review can alert the counselor to failure to communicate reasons for optimism or to neglected aspects of the problem. In either case, the early warning may enable the counselor to correct the difficulty before the client withdraws.

More and more counselors now collect ratings from clients at termination of counseling. Perhaps even more valuable would be to collect such ratings after every session in order to enable communication problems to be identified quickly. Certainly, the notion that a client is an aware, responsible partner in counseling supports the practice of closing each session with a mutual review of accomplishments and next steps. The input into the review might be oral or written.

4. *Reinforcing Constructive Counseling Behavior.* Counselors believe that behavior that is reinforced is more likely to recur, and thus they reinforce positively a client's efforts to cooperate in establishing a trust-

ing counseling atmosphere, and in accomplishing the counseling exercises. Counselors praise constructive actions and elicit group praise for them. They also encourage a client to feel the gratification that comes from learning and achievement of a goal by such simple mechanisms as suggesting that the person take a moment to consider how it feels to be successful. When client statements are only partially correct, the counselor modifies or completes them, rather than labeling them as erroneous. In addition, the counselor rewards clients by listening attentively to them.

Counselors remember that what is reinforcing for one client may not reward another, that rewards loose their potency with repetition, and that variation is itself rewarding. In initial client contracts, counselors ascertain what is rewarding to the client. In particular, counselors respond to the universal "Let me try!" or "let me say it!" of learners, pacing instruction so that clients can practice new skills or demonstrate new knowledge and feel the inherent satisfaction of succeeding.

5. *Clarifying and Confronting Resistance.* Counselors must sometimes make explicit a client's noncompliance with the counseling program. Several tactics are useful. A counselor can reflect the difficulty the client is manifesting, or can focus the client's attention on contradictory actions. For example, the counselor who directs the reluctant client to consider if facial expression and tone of voice correspond with trying to "let go" in the role play exercise. An even more direct approach is to point out the noncompliance and engage the client in telling personal feeling about noncompliance. Sometimes, counselors can guide clients in examining their feelings by interpreting what the noncompliance means. For example, to the client resisting involvement in role play, the counselor might say; "You are finding it hard to let yourself act as if this were real, just as you found it hard to ask for assistance in using our library and in securing a suitable job. It is as if you feel getting assistance in securing a job raises doubt about your capability of handling a job."

As clarification emphasizes the contradiction in the client's behavior and becomes confrontative and even interpretative, the counselor increases the client's anxiety. Either this anxiety will lead the client into a defensive posture, which can obstruct learning, or it will encourage more openness to reduce the tension arising from the confrontation. Before using confrontation, therefore, a counselor must judge whether the confrontation can be tolerated by the client and is more likely to aid progress than are other actions, such as focusing on another topic, attempting to shape a noncompliant response without direct acknowledgement of its noncompliance, or delaying the problem until the next session.

Confrontation is risky; to be professional in its use, a counselor must be especially sensitive to the interaction with the client. Brammer (1979) calls this being sensitive to "fine shades of feeling in oneself." In his examination of confrontation, Brammer (1979) distinguishes among several types of confrontation, and suggests seven guidelines for giving "feedback," which he termed a strong type of confrontation. These guidelines appear related to all confrontations and therefore are modified for confrontation in general and summarized here.

1. Confront only after the counseling relationship is strong enough for the client to tolerate the stress confrontation produces and appears ready to examine the contradiction it brings into awareness.

2. Describe the client's behavior, which is the object or source of confrontation, as part of confrontation.

3. Confront the behavior, giving opinions about it, rather than judgments about the person.

4. Confront those actions that can be changed by the client within the context of counseling.

5. Confront small amounts of behavior so the client can react without being overwhelmed.

6. Confront current behavior.

7. Elicit and observe the client's responses to confrontation in order to prevent misunderstanding and to assure that one deals with potential client resentment.

6. *Problem Solving.* Counselors employ specific strategies to help clients who are unable to keep up with the counseling (learning) program. Most counselors provide additional information or models if they judge that clients need such information, and they teach or have taught concepts and skills that will assist clients in the program. For example, to help a client profit from group counseling, a counselor might teach assertive or listening skill to a client on an individual basis. Routinely, counselors alter the pace of counseling to prevent procrastination or to enable full comprehension. When clients resist progress, the counselor helps them by using such techniques as: a) encouraging them to examine the consequences of not proceeding; b) refocusing counseling to enable clients to see where an unlearned concept or skill fits into solving a problem; and c) increasing clients' motivation by pointing out others who are going, or have gone, through the same process and are being rewarded as a result. In a group, counselors can bypass resistance by ignoring distracting or unproductive behavior and redirecting attention to a client whose behavior is productive. In problem solving, counselors can advise clients directly about how to proceed or can help them to discover how.

Nature of Career Counseling

Career counseling is specialized counseling focused on career implementation and planning. The career counselor helps a client to generate and to use personal and career information, to obtain and to interpret experiences relevant to careers, to set goals and to solve problems, and to evaluate progress. Typically, career counselors join clients in developing the client's motivation to acquire self and career understanding, in establishing frameworks for organizing and synthesizing information, and in formulating and enacting problem-solving strategies and plans. The clients of career counselors are individuals who have failed to learn what is needed for their career development through existing informational materials and educational programs; persons who wish expert advice and reaction to their career development; or those who lack access to appropriate information, experiences, and career positions.

Information giving, class scheduling, testing, and test interpretation are often considered the main activities of career counseling, but in fact they are only elements and sometimes are not included. Indeed, such activities only become a part of counseling if they are integrated into a learning program for achieving a goal for which the client and counselor contract. If these activities are done without direct attention to their relevance for the client, they are not counseling, but merely services, which a counselor instead of a clerk happens to offer.

First of all, a career counselor should determine that the client lacks information, skill, or access to resources needed to create an effective career. The problem is educational rather than medical, and the help is teaching rather than therapy. If the client is anxious because he is not progressing in his career, effective career counseling requires that the counselor establish that the anxiety stems from failure to progress, rather than from underlying personality confusion or dysfunctional thinking. Necessarily, the counselor judges whether to reduce anxiety immediately by augmenting anxiety reduction activities in counseling, or more slowly by adapting the teaching strategies so they will be effective with an anxious learner. The counselor might also refer the acutely anxious client for concomitant anxiety reduction exercises. Progress in career counseling should itself reduce career-related anxiety, but it is unlikely to change a client's personality radically (Tyler, 1969).

Even with the physically and mentally ill, educational deficits are the major component of the problem addressed by career counseling. Thus, a career counselor working with a handicapped client will identify strengths and learning capabilities not paralyzed by the handicap, and will guide the client in using those assets to define and to achieve meaningful career goals. For instance, a carpenter suffering severe psoriasis, which precluded further shop or construction work, was helped to recognize the selling ability he was developing through his church work. He was guided to select training that refined that ability, and later the counselor assisted him in entering a sales position in a firm that handled carpentry-related products. Identification and development of selling skills restored his capacity to support his family and sense of adequacy.

Emergence of Career Counseling

From its beginning around 1900, formal assistance with career development has been offered as an educational undertaking. Pioneers, such as Parsons (1909), used the interview to clarify a client's goals and attributes, to verify the client's accurate interpretation of assigned observation and reading, and to guide the client's selection of an appropriate course of action. These pioneers had clients do individualized homework assignments, including reading and job analyses, in order to clarify self-attributes and work opportunities. We can infer that they facilitated these assignments by coordinating with employers. They probably even arranged job tryouts similar to the ones available in the vestibule schools of World War II.

As advances were made in ability and interest measurement and as career assistance moved into schools, the helpers, by then termed *counselors*, added testing, record review, activity try-out, modeling and advising to their set of strategies (Williamson, 1939). During the same period, interest in physical and mental hygiene supported the establishment of courses and homeroom activities for assisting youngsters in their development, including their career development.

The number of counselors was small in the years before World War II. Often counselors served several schools from a district office; hence, they acted as consultants and coordinators. They welcomed the proliferation of self-development manuals and vocational guides, using these resources to strengthen their consultation and the teaching they coordinated.

As understanding of learning and communication technology expanded in the 1950s and 1960s, simulation and role play exercises, computer counseling programs, and peer and paraprofessional coaching exercises were added to the array of counselors' strategies. In addition, vocational measurement and career materials were upgraded, and counselors started receiving systematic training in interviewing and counseling, resulting in improvement of these strategies. By the 1970s, counselors were employing a broad array of increasingly improved strategies to facilitate the career development of their clients.

Individualizing Career Counseling

The essence of counseling is individualizing. Counselors prescribe individual learning strategies and join clients in making the strategies work. The process of individualizing has four stages: (1) establishing client needs, goals, and the obstacles to them; (2) identifying and then selecting particular strategies; (3) teaching and assisting the client in implementing solutions; and (4) verifying accomplishment of the solution and achievement of the goal. Sorenson (1967) has developed a counseling method following these stages, but the stages themselves provide a useful overlay for understanding individualization. Many counseling procedures described in this book emphasize Stage 3, and have given minimal attention to Stages 1 and 2, with only somewhat more attention to Stage 4.

Stage 1: Establishing Client Individuality

The uniqueness of each career requires understanding the individual nature of the person and his or her situation. For this author, the seven overlapping dimensions of individuality below facilitate understanding. Counselors have long recognized the importance of helping clients to use and to develop their assets to resolve their everyday problems (Tyler, 1969). The first dimension of individuality, therefore, is comprised of the aptitudes, abilities, interests, values, and personality, as well as the client's social network and support system, past accomplishments, and general aspirations. The other six dimensions are the client's (2) particular goals; (3) perceived obstacles; (4) beliefs about means of achieving goals and removing obstacles, including ideas about what constitutes appropriate risks and effort, and how a counselor should help; (5) actions already taken; (6) feelings about the goal, including confidence and motivation in succeeding; and (7) learning style. Ongoing research of systematic counseling by Sorenson (1967) and his students, such as Hawkins (1967), Bates (1971), and Farmer (1972), as well as other proponents of systematic counseling, such as Krumboltz and Baker (1973) and Stewart et al. (1978), have shown the utility of such information for designing individualized counseling treatments. Jim's case below offers concrete examples of elements from each of the seven dimensions and shows how each contributes to the counseling program fashioned for Jim. Following the introduction of Jim, dimensions of individuality 1–7 are reviewed.

Jim was a graduating mathematics major who had done well in mathematics and science courses, but only fair in social sciences and English. He was sensitive about his working-class origins and having to work throughout college in a series of semi- and unskilled jobs. He had never tried to get employment related to becoming a programmer or business executive, the occupations he might enter. Perhaps this was because he was shy and he did not have the connections needed to get good jobs. At intake, Jim clarified that he wanted to become financially independent as soon as possible, and to advance into management. To get the proper connections, he was thinking of going to a prestigious graduate school for an MBA. When asked to elaborate on how the MBA would secure him a high quality job, he acknowledged he was not sure, but acquaintances had told him a two-year MBA was the only sure ticket to management. He was worried that his $3,000 savings would not be sufficient to support him and to pay tuition, and he did not like the prospect of continuing his part-time work as a grocery checker. He had applied to two major schools, but now was also considering interviewing for a programmer's job, since a professor told him he had high potential for such work. The placement counselor, he hoped, would help him set up interviews and perhaps put in a good word for him with employers. He was receptive to the counselor's offer of sorting things through, for he was good at problem solving but had not thought of his concerns as something on which to apply problem solving. He was pleased the counselor was recommending some readings because he learned well on his own from reading and mapping out things. He wanted to be sure, however, that it would not take too long, since he had to agree with the counselor that his growing uncertainty was making him tense and irritable and was probably the reason he was not sleeping well nor able to concentrate on his studies. The text will return to Jim's counseling experience in illustrating these four phases of counseling.

Goals

The goals are the end states that the client wants to realize. They are amalgams of interactions, perceptions, cognitions, and feelings. Jim, in the example, wants to be in a position challenging his analytical abilities and offering opportunity for exchange with like-interested colleagues. The position should not only be aiding him to grow intellectually and develop his marketability, but it also should offer an income sufficient to sustain him at a level appropriate to a new professional, or if it is a training or apprentice program, it should at least not deplete his cash reserves.

At the start of counseling, many clients can only declare vague outcomes such as a better career or fewer hassles with school or work. Helping clients specify what they and others involved in their difficulty might be doing when it is resolved often requires detailed probing and may require both client and counselor to do data gathering between counseling sessions. Pinpointing the elements of the desired end states, however, gives direction to ensuing counseling and reassures the client that progress can occur.

The need to recognize a client's uniqueness in goal setting and its difficulty for clients are widely recognized. Krumboltz (1966) has been especially helpful in making these points. He pointed out that counseling goals should be "capable of being stated differently for each individual client . . . compatible with, although not necessarily identical to the values of the counselor, and . . . their degree of accomplishment capable of observation." Elsewhere, he and Baker (1973) noted that initially the client can be expected to be less concerned about goal setting than the counselor, but they suggested that by "probing, restating, conjecturing," a counselor can increase the client's commitment to the process and eventually the client's ability to monitor counseling. Of course, even though formulating an explicit goal takes extensive effort, the client must, as Krumboltz and Baker (1973) observed, be permitted to change goals when he or she wishes.

Obstacles

The barriers preventing a client from realizing the desired end state are the obstacles to the goal. They can be internal or external. Among the internal obstacles are perceptual problems such as ignoring or misreading aspects of the problem and its context; cognitive deficiencies, such as lack of knowledge and ability or obstructive beliefs; and affective troubles, such as disruptive emotion or lack of motivation. (Ultimately, this author believes, affective obstacles are rooted in cognitive deficits.) External obstacles, on the other hand, include positions in the education and work systems that either have inadequate resources for meeting the position's responsibilities and developing the incumbent or are rent by competing, apparently legitimate expectations of different groups.

Once goals are defined, obstacle identification becomes easier. Then, there is a standard against which to estimate whether a correction of a personal deficit or exit from a faulty position would move the client closer to the goal. In Jim's case, for instance, pinpointing his goal made it evident that inexperience in securing professional level work and the attendant anxiety interfering with problem solving were primary obstacles, whereas vague beliefs about the need for sponsorship for an entry to a professional position and lack of related work experience were secondary obstacles.

Assets for Securing Goal

Adaptability of people and adaptation of their environment are keys to human survival and prosperity. Every person has an array of assets for coping; yet many philosophers and scientists believe that human beings exercise only a small portion of their coping powers. As a goal emerges and its meaningfulness becomes apparent and as the obstacles are identified, counselors help clients to enumerate assets relative to the goal and then to plan ways of bringing those assets to bear on the problem.

The attribute categories of ability, interest, values, personality, and positions discussed in Chapter 3 offer an array of assets that can contribute to goal achievement. One's many abilities, especially the learning and general career abilities and one's personality, make possible the solution strategies. Interests and values especially help to sustain action and generate energy for extra effort. One's linkages or networks and the other prerogatives of one's position also can facilitate action. In Jim's case, for example, the student position entitled him to free placement services, which did not strain his marginal financial position; it enabled him to acknowledge confusion about career without questioning his adequacy as an adult; and it had introduced him to professors who had contacts with employers looking for promising professionals like Jim.

Beliefs About Problem Resolution and Counseling

One's culture instills ideas about what is proper and not proper, feasible and not feasible for resolving different situations. When confronted with problems, almost automatically people are guided by these cultural beliefs.

Like the feelings discussed below, these beliefs can be either assets or liabilities. They embody wisdom from past generations, and they may represent viable solutions of the problem. Jim, for example, had only a vague idea of why he sought counseling. Yet a person well acquainted with him and his family could point out that he had seen parents and neighbors seek the counsel of spiritual and community leaders when problems arose.

On the other hand, past solutions may not apply to present problems, and relying too heavily on them can thwart development of new, appropriate solutions. Jim was fortunate, for example, because he was willing to question the belief that an MBA or graduate degree would advance a career more than would working right after college.

Clients, of course, also have beliefs about what counseling will do, and these beliefs appear to be related to their preferred mode of learning. Internally controlled, self-confident clients make more progress in counseling than do others. Perhaps these clients and the counselors share the same perception of what a client is supposed to do as a consequence of counseling. Clients with a different perspective, however, will not know what is expected of them and therefore may not use the help provided.

Counselors are concerned about what professional peers think their role should be, as suggested by the many professional articles on the topic; but their literature gives surprisingly little attention to what clients expect of counselors. Certainly, clinical impressions suggest that many working-class clients expect their middle-class counselor to tell them what educational program or occupation to enter, or to find them a suitable job, or even to rearrange their environment so that the bothersome conflict is eliminated, or in some other way to intervene for them. After all, the counselor has the power of the establishment. Such clients may not realize that the counselor expects to help primarily by equipping them with new skills and courage. Moreover, these clients may not believe that they really can improve their own situation, for they know few people who have been thus empowered through counseling.

Action Already Taken

Few clients bring anticipated problems to counseling. Instead, clients come after they have failed to improve their situation. Review of their efforts to resolve the problem not only clarifies the goal and obstacles but also saves the counselor from endorsing solutions that the client had found ineffectual. Of course, review of precounseling problem-solving efforts often illuminates errors in the effort, which if corrected, would enable the effort to be effective. Yet a counselor who guides a client to generate alternative solution possibilities without first ascertaining why past efforts had failed risks losing the client's trust and surely will find it difficult to have the client correct and reapply the formerly unsuccessful strategy.

Feelings

Client feelings about the goal and means for realizing it may be either an asset or liability and must be taken into account in planning a learning program. Recognizing that there is a more satisfying end state that one can realistically hope to attain engenders positive feeling and motivation. Even identifying irritations stemming from being frustrated by the problem should stimulate goal pursuit, while not recognizing the relation of the irritants to the frustration may distract the person from focusing on the goal's attainment.

The reader will recognize that although the tension and the sleeping and concentrating difficulties are symptomatic of the problem and were not addressed directly in Jim's counseling, they prompted Jim to get and to continue counseling. Not surprisingly, only their alleviation convinced him that counseling had been worthwhile. Even though it is well known that noxious work or schooling can produce serious disorders such as ulcers, headaches, and high blood pressure and can lead to destructive behaviors such as barroom brawls, family disputes, and substance abuse, counselors clarifying vocational or educational concerns rarely guide clients to enumerate their unwanted feelings and behaviors and link them to career problems. Yet, unless counselors ascertain the related symptoms, they are not likely to sense a client's situation accurately nor communicate their appreciation of it, and therefore, they will not be as effective in developing the counseling program the client needs.

Learning Style

Since counseling is a special kind of teaching, the counselor must consider how the client learns and expects to learn through counseling. Some people learn easily from reading, others benefit more by observing and imitating a model, and still others profit most from oral discussion in interviews. Inasmuch as the counselor is putting together an individualized learning program, the methods that have been effective for that particular client are important data.

The new emphasis on cognitive learning theory underscores the need to ascertain one's learning strategies and to create conditions that allow one to give meaning to the material to be learned (Wittrock, 1978b). Witkins, Moore, Goodenough, and Cox (1977), for instance, have differentiated between a field-independent, or differentiated style, and a field-dependent, or global cognitive style. Their evidence indicates that field-independent people learn better by self-definition of goals, self-reinforcement, and intrinsic motivation. In contrast, externally set goals and reinforcement, well-defined structure, and minimal criticism increase learning by field-dependent people. Wittrock (1978a) and other researchers have shown that designing instruction to interact with children's developmental stages and information-processing strategies can expedite various kinds of learning. Still other research supporting the proposition that learning involves a person imposing meaning on subject matter has shown that vocabulary retention can be increased by having subjects embed unfamiliar words in a story context of their own choosing (Wittrock, Marks, & Doctorow, 1973) and by having them represent the unfamiliar words with drawings. Moreover, evidence also shows that aptitude and treatment interact in learning (Cranbach & Snow, 1977).

Each of the seven dimensions of individuality affects the content and method of delivery of the prospective counseling program. Juxtaposing impediments with previously demonstrated strengths should suggest approaches for a client to acquire the necessary competence and should suggest how difficult solving the problem will be. For example, an avid reader can fill information deficits by direct library research, and a sorority member's wrenching conflict about studying for a "man's profession" because she lacks experience in technical pursuits will suggest work-experience exploration.

By clarifying the seven elements, one concrete goal should stand out as primary or as the first of a series of goals. Identifying a specific goal and realizing that the counselor understands that goal will reassure the client. Jim, for instance, acknowledged that the intensive intake gave him the feeling that counseling would be worthwhile, since the counselor was helping him organize his thinking. Nevertheless, he was still distressed when the initial interview ended. On the other hand, discounting any one of the seven dimensions may create a learning program of a type that has already failed, or conflict with client beliefs, or ignore learning styles.

Goal Impediments

A counselor will know that stage one of counseling is complete when one or more of the following emerge as impediments to client accomplishment of goals. Although these categories have not been tested empirically by cluster or factor analysis, reviewing them assures a counselor and client of considering a broad spectrum of obstacles before closing Stage 1.

1. *The client has unrealistic or unclear goals.*
   American society rightfully boasts of unlimited opportunity. But that does not mean that each person can be anything he or she wants. More correctly, one can compete for many opportunities. We strive to make the competition equal, although wealth and connection operate against equality. Youth quickly learns the status of different occupations and, not surprisingly, many wish to pursue prestigious occupations until they realize they cannot. This society assumes citizens should strive for high career achievement, and its socialization confers more status on those who aspire to greater achievement. Surely a teenager or adult who settles for a medium or low occupation may lose self-esteem. As pointed out above, such a decision cuts a person off from many privileges and lessens prestige as well. To reduce the strain on long-term career goal-setting, society must find means of awarding prestige and privilege for achievements in other life areas, so a decision to pursue a limited-status occupation does not deny full citizenship.

The injunction of the society to aim high, coupled with its other-directedness (Riesman, 1957), nonreflectiveness, and reliance upon validation through external achievements, makes decision making difficult at particular points in a career. These influences lead many people to aspire unrealistically above their competence, as suggested by popular books such as *The Peter Principle*. At the same time, the complexity of the opportunity system, the growing separation of society's basic institutions (Dubin, 1976), and age segregation through childhood and adolescence make it difficult for a young person to know the achievements possible at different career points.

Aspire high does not give clear direction. Parents want their children to "get ahead," but they do not know enough about the work system to tell them how to get ahead—other than to say: "Stay in school!" Educators also urge youth to stay in school in order to get ahead, but they, too, are vague about what one is to accomplish by staying in school. Although specificity and concreteness facilitate direction setting and planning, many people do not define carefully what they want to be doing. Once they can do so, of course, a proper course of action becomes easier to determine.

2. *The client has insufficient knowledge, ability, interest, training or resources, to reach the goal.*
    The career role entails production: first one's own talents and interests, and then goods and services for others. Such production requires knowledge, ability, interest, training, and resources. One cannot produce whatever one wants whenever one wants; one must have the skills, the motivation, the resources, and the status necessary for obtaining the goods and services used in production. Specification of a career goal helps to pinpoint the assets needed to achieve it. Then one can review one's accomplishments and use attribute tests and facts about resources such as scholarships, loans, and so forth, to judge whether one has the required assets or can hope to obtain them.

    Since career is a developmental phenomenon, many asset deficits are not recognized until they have existed for a while. Redressing the difficulty, consequently, requires a sustained series of achievements. In concert, client and counselor have to devise a plan that not only includes a series of subjectives such as passing particular courses, mastering skills, and building work habits, but also provides for ongoing psychological and material support for accomplishing the subobjectives.

3. *The client does not try long or hard enough to succeed.*
    People are creatures of habit. Even in this rapidly changing world, many forces affect actions. Altering our actions and the ways others react to us often takes time. So one major source of frustration for a client can be that changed behavior takes a long time to produce desired results even though the new approach

is an effective strategy. Perseverance, then, becomes an essential element of success.

4. *The client has misconcepts about how the system operates.*
Exclusion of people from the work system and specialization and isolation within the system leads to many misconceptions about what is possible and how to achieve it. Especially in a quickly changing and many-faceted system, becoming out of date or misconstruing the context is easy. Aberations, such as grade inflation, have obstructed accurate self-appraisal, and a constant diet of television and movie dramatizations have promulgated fantasy solutions to problems and instilled unrealizable expectations for careers.

Beliefs develop over time and influence one's perceptions of reality. As Festinger (1957) has noted, one tends to select aspects of reality consistent with one's beliefs and to interpret reality to be consistent with them. Long-held beliefs can be quite resistant to change. Of course, beliefs embedded in a culture have been adaptive. In challenging such beliefs because they appear to frustrate development, therefore, a counselor must recognize their adaptive function. For example, the candidate for high school science teacher who has substantial research potential but aspires to return to his rural community because of family commitments, should be told not only about the opportunities in different research careers, but also the advantages of serving rural peoples immediately and of returning to the nurturant family community.

5. *The client's goals are thwarted by system defects or obstruction.*
Education and work systems are only as effective as their creators. As knowledge expands, systems are likely to improve in the number, quality, and equity of options open to their citizens. But limited, fluctuating capital resources and economic cycles are always likely to prevent some qualified persons from entering the training or jobs for which their talents and skills suit them.

Although society moves toward realization of human development ideals, obstructions still impede individual career development. Some obstacles are faults in the system, which may require action by the system to correct. The recent ruling by the U.S. Supreme Court on affirmative action in the workplace (*Weber vs. Kaiser Aluminum and Chemical,* 1979), for example, illustrates supreme court recognition that special action by corporations is appropriate to give minority workers a fair chance for career development.

In clarifying career obstructions, therefore, counselor and client need to recognize that unfair employment or promotion policies can create frustration in career development. The client may want to act individually to surmount discrimination, but should not deny that the difficulty is an injustice. Consequently, the person should not feel the problem reflects a personal shortcoming. Likewise, counselors need to be prepared to act to alter the system.

At the minimum, they can refer clients to legal and government services that can rectify system injustices.

6. *The client is unable to decide and commit to one alternative.*
Career choices often require relinquishing something desirable to gain something more desirable, and often they involve people gambling that they will succeed at a new challenge and better their situations. Forsaking something desirable is not pleasant, even to go in something more desirable, especially when one is not certain of achieving the more desirable end. Examples come to mind: the successful technician taking a supervisory position with former colleagues, the liberal arts student choosing a major that restricts the kind and number of courses instead of selecting on the basis of interest, the executive trainee deciding between pursuing a MBA at night or socializing with singles.

Some apprehension about career choices is normal and indeed healthy. It signals the need for deliberation. After one follows a decision-making paradigm systematically, however, action is needed. Not that concern should vanish, for vigilance in implementation is warranted, but the decider must act even though a decision can never be guaranteed fully. When action does not follow deliberation, choice anxiety is generally indicated.

7. *The client's problem has been formulated incompletely or inaccurately.*
In the throes of the personal frustration produced by career obstructions, the client often neglects to analyze the dilemma calmly and to pinpoint the contributing factors. The calm, deliberative counseling intake enables such an overview. Not surprisingly, this overview itself may produce sudden insight, enabling a client quickly to formulate a feasible, promising course of action, or the overview may even reveal that the problem is not a difficulty. For instance, the policewoman graduating with a bachelor's degree in accounting, wrenched by a desire to continue in law enforcement and also to pursue accounting, recognizes when she formulates the problem that her desires are not incompatible. Internal Revenue Service agent and Federal Bureau of Investigation agent, among other positions, satisfy both desires.

8. *Interpersonal conflict.*
People are interdependent. Other people's actions affect them, and they in turn influence others' lives. One's actions and plans often require the direct or indirect cooperation and support of others. Of most consequence are the views and actions of significant others, such as parents, spouses, siblings, children, relatives, friends, teachers, supervisors, and work and student colleagues. Opposition from, or conflict with, one or more of these people can dissipate the energy needed for career progress.

9. *The client's affect is inappropriate for his problem.*
Career obstructions are distressing and merit the concern needed to prompt action. Were there no concern, the client may not have

accepted ownership of the problem and would be unwilling to commit the time and energy required to resolve it. Before proceeding, therefore, the counselor will have to assist the client to recognize the dilemma and to experience distress. Likewise, a client should approach a goal with optimism. Review of related past accomplishments and enumeration of assets should help to arm the client with requisite self-confidence, enabling him or her to acknowledge concern while marshalling assets appropriate to the challenge.

Excessive emotion, on the other hand, will thwart counseling as surely as not admitting the problem. Consequently, for clients paralyzed by distress, the counselor will first have to try to help them gain perspective about their problems in order to reduce their anxiety to manageable limits, or if this approach fails, will want to refer the client to determine the source of the anxiety and to alleviate it.

The counselor who fails to detect one or more of these deficiencies should delay proceeding, for either the client can secure the goal alone or the problem spurring the request for counseling has not been presented. Sometimes correct formulation of the problem will lead to termination of counseling, for the client will feel the problem has dissolved or is solvable with his current skills.

Ideally, a thorough review of the seven diagnostic elements and nine impediments occurs for every client. Time constraints, however, often force experienced counselors to make tentative judgments about particular clients, based on limited review and on their experience with other clients from the same population. Proceeding on the basis of such tentative hypotheses is legitimate, so long as a counselor continually reexamines the tentative hypotheses as data pertinent to them surface. In other words, the counselor should be very humble and open minded. The counselor asks the client whether particular conclusions are accurate rather than announcing them as fact and remains ready to expand and even to alter one's view of the client and the goal.

Screening

Screening procedures can give counselors more time for the clients likely to have problems that require career counseling. At least two alternatives are possible: to have clients complete screening tests that distinguish those needing and not needing counseling, and to enlist teachers or work supervisors in identifying counseling candidates. The former procedure now is more viable because of the many valid career development tests and checklists, especially for those in the prework phase of their careers. To implement the latter alternative, the counselor would acquaint teachers with behaviors that signal the need for referral and with the counseling strategies available for them; then counselor and teachers or supervisors together would develop a procedure for systematically observing and communicating the observations. Maurine Kukic (1973) described the implementation of such a teacher-screening system for high school students in a suburban California school district. The Security Pacific National Bank now uses such a system for its personnel management.

Stage 2: Identifying and Selecting Strategies

In Stage 2, the counselor alone or the counselor and client together do a task analysis of the goals and obstacles in order to generate alternative courses of action. They identify necessary steps for each goal, and generate a list of ways to achieve the steps. Then, they examine the requisite knowledge, skills, and resources, and the methods of acquiring them to evaluate each alternative. Client and counselor next judge the relative merit of alternatives in terms of the information from Stage 1. To accomplish Step 2, the counselor may interview, review records, test, consult, observe the client *in vivo* or simulation, and so forth. Since research on diagnosis and differential effectiveness of particular counseling exercises is just beginning, logic and common sense must guide the counselor's prescription of counseling strategies.

Excerpts from Jim's case illustrate the activities of this stage. As a consequence of his reviewing his situation and reading, Jim said his first goal would be to secure a programmer's job with potential for advancement, and his second goal would be to obtain additional training in order to advance in programming.

He and the counselor then identified the steps for the first goal. These steps included composing a résumé, presenting it to prospective employers, and then communicating competence through the interview. Jim asked his counselor to review a draft résumé and to suggest where to get it printed. The counselor wondered whether other actions would improve the résumé. Jim was not sure; but, in answer to cue questions, acknowledged that examining sample résumés and obtaining advice from an alumnus in programming might improve his résumé.

Jim also acknowledged that he was worried about interviewing and suggested he might practice on recruiters of companies in which he was not interested. The counselor noted that this practice might help Jim, but not the college's reputation, and suggested that Jim would obtain more help from reading about interviewing, viewing model recruiting interviews, then role playing some before a video camera with the center's guidance technician, identifying strengths and weaknesses, and finally practicing corrections.

When these alternatives emerged, Jim decided interview training was best. Moreover, he elected all three alternatives to improve his résumé. As the session closed, Jim said he would return to review the résumé and to report on the progress in interview training and in securing employment interviews. The counselor observed that they could contract to review the situation and to make additional plans as needed. Jim agreed.

The first and second stages of counseling overlap in operation, although not in conception. As the client considers alternative solutions, the goal as well as feelings and beliefs regarding it become clearer. By the close of Stage 2, client and counselor should agree about their respective responsibilities regarding further work on the goal.

Stage 3: Teaching and Aiding Implementation

Learning and applying strategies are the tasks of Stage 3. Client and counselor have now agreed on a goal and on a course of action that the client will execute. Traditionally, interviews and test taking and test interpretation comprised that action; but other strategies such as completing a series of job simulation exercises or reading an assertion training manual are also appropriate. Likewise, peers, family members, teachers, workers, and other resource people may be involved more directly in these activities than the counselor. The counselor's task in this stage is to support the client in learning, not only by direct teaching, but also by securing and coordinating the assistance of others.

In the case of Jim, for instance, a guidance technician directed Jim's acquisition of interviewing skills, a working programmer assisted him in composing a résumé and in deciding on suitable employer prospects, and a clerk scheduled on-campus recruitment interviews. As a consequence, the counselor felt counseling was progressing even though his contact with Jim in this stage only consisted of a brief phone call, in which Jim said that he and the technician felt he was ready to interview and that he had scheduled two campus interviews.

Application is the completion of the learning within counseling, and frequently must be done independently by the client. The counselor and others involved in the learning, of course, eagerly await the report of the results in order to help confirm their effectiveness and perhaps to know how to assist in making adjustments. When the obstacle is a situational or system restraint, which reasonably should not obstruct a person and is not easily removed by an individual, the counselor and others may also act on the client's behalf.

In the case of Jim, the counselor had to intervene with a prospective employer on Jim's behalf. Jim had committed a misdemeanor, which ordinarily would preclude employment with the firm. But the counselor's ability to present character references to the firm's vice-president, a person not accessible to employment applicants, enabled an exception to be made for Jim.

The counselor's intervention for Jim was possible because the employer recognized the counselor as a gatekeeper. Gate keeping is often a prerogative and responsibility of a counseling position. School, college, Veteran Administration, and rehabilitation counselors review a student's or client's plans and support or question his or her taking particular courses, following special schedules, and aspiring to and applying for certain schools or jobs. Sometimes counselor reactions are the main influence, but often counselors also have the power of approval or disapproval. Similarly, through years in the position, counselors establish a network of personal contacts with employers, training directors, and community service personnel, whom one can access or not access to help a client; and whom they also must warn occasionally about an unsuitable client to sustain their good will. Although the counselor's network should be an important determiner of a counselor's effectiveness, this author did not find research concerning this hypothesis. Nevertheless, counselors are urged to cultivate and to expand their networks because networks logically will help clients. Many people and institutions will assist clients in their careers if they are shown how to help and if they see the clients referred to them progressing as a result of their help. These people's resources could increase the counselor's repertoire of available helping strategies and, therefore, should allow more individualization and hence more effectiveness.

Counselors need to enlarge their networks and to keep abreast of the contributions the people in their networks can provide. Hoyt's (1965) SOS projects wherein counselors had students systematically evaluate schools and training programs and then tabulate and publish their results is a model groups of counselors might use to expand networks and to evaluate members. As director of the Office of Career Education of the United States Office of Education, Ken Hoyt has promoted the idea of networking by continually searching out community support for career education. He also has published and encouraged monographs on the kinds of contributions that particular institutions have made. Among his pertinent publications are these:

Community Resources for Career Education (1976),
Community Involvement in the Implementation of Career Education (1979),
National Alliance of Business and Career Education (1978a), and
Rotary International and Career Education (1978b), Washington, D.C.: U.S. Government Printing Office.

Stage 4: Verifying Goal Achievement

In Stage 4, counselor and client verify the application of the learning strategies and judge their effectiveness. The strategies are continued until they take effect or, if necessary, new strategies are substituted for unsuccessful ones.

This review is an important step for the client, because it clarifies how he or she solved the problem and permits timely revision. Examining the process of changing successfully can motivate the client to continue the change and can increase confidence in making future changes.

The review step also helps the counselor by providing an opportunity to make the minor adjustments needed to sustain the change; by giving the counselor evidence about the success of one's teaching; and by providing data needed by a counselor to establish accountability.

Evaluation was a crucial stage in Jim's case. He missed his first interview because of a traffic jam; and although he arranged for one off-campus two weeks later, this experience elevated his anxiety and contributed to a poor interview performance. Upon learning of this problem from the recruiter, the counselor phoned Jim, who felt ready to give up and to focus primarily on getting into graduate school. He agreed, however, to meet to review the situation.

In that review meeting, Jim began to feel better as he told of the progress he had made in defining a goal, preparing a résumé, and learning and demonstrating effective interviewing. He recognized he should have expected a setback or two. Since practice had helped before, he suggested a session of role play with the technician, and asked permission to interview the next recruiter seeking programmers.

Predictably, Jim's final meeting with the counselor several weeks later was much shorter. Jim described the programmer's job he was taking, and thanked the counselor for assisting him in "getting his head together," and in learning how to secure a job.

Crucial to evaluation are completely specified outcomes and provision for accurately assessing their achievement. Unfortunately, counseling researchers have often neglected to specify outcomes or measure them appropriately. Consequently, Chapter 6 reviews outcome evaluation and assessment difficulties and describes an approach for alleviating the difficulties.

Individualizing Well-Defined Treatments

Chapters 6 through 12 present detailed, recipe-like descriptions of successful strategies so the reader will know what career counseling has been like and will recognize the descriptive detail necessary to make a procedure repeatable. Obviously, one should not repeat the procedures thoughtlessly but should adapt the procedures to fit one's clientele. Moreover, in recognizing the limited number of strategies used in counseling, counselors will want to create new goal-achievement strategies based on how successful people in the populations they serve are learning skills that further their careers. Careful observation of the successful will surely suggest such things as how to integrate community models, reading materials, audiovisuals, directed live experiences, coaching, and self-monitoring into learning programs for clients. Unfortunately, existing counseling procedures rarely include reading, audiovisuals, or coaching.

The following steps, formulated by Sorenson and his students from fifteen years of investigation (Bates & Sorenson, 1973) should help in designing new counseling procedures and in adapting existing ones to specific client's needs.

1. Identify prospective clients.

2. Study samples from the clients' population of persons who have succeeded and those having difficulty with the goals the clients are seeking in order to establish actions leading to success and methods by which successful persons learned these actions.

3. Develop benchmarks of progress and decide upon methods of measurement.

4. Develop a tentative repeatable treatment, which is individualized for the clients.

5. Using progress measures to assess benefit, try the treatment on small numbers of prospective clients in order to learn what works and what needs modification.

6. Teach other counselors the procedure, have them apply it to a different sample of clients, and test its effectiveness with an appropriate research design.

Heuristic Principles

Guiding the counselor in every stage—from understanding the client's career concerns, through fashioning a learning program and overseeing its application, to evaluation—are the counselor's beliefs about how to get to know a person, how to create an effective career, and how a person learns the skills and knowledge required for career coping. These beliefs are called *heuristic principles*. For the professional counselor, these beliefs should be generalizations inferred from the study of social science research and personal, careful observation of human behavior. Hewer (1963) has pointed out some of the generalizations that can be inferred from career choice research.

These principles are called heuristic to distinguish them from physical science principles, such as Boyle's or Newton's Laws, which operate invariably under prescribed conditions. In contrast, heuristic principles apply to many situations, but not all. The research underlying them is frequently with limited samples and in limited contexts. Consequently, in applying heuristic principles the counselor must continually monitor the process to assure that it is working as intended.

Examples of heuristic principles include: reinforced behavior is likely to be repeated; precise statements of goals improve decision making; one is more likely to learn an operation if it is accurately modeled and if one sees the model obtaining reward for it; open-ended questions about the time, place, and people associated with a situation produce more information about the situation than true/false questions; and interacting with persons who regard one favorably increases a person's self-esteem.

Heuristic principles derive from common sense or folk wisdom and from social science research over time, as people infer principles for living from struggling with life. These principles are broad in application, but generally are not expected to be universally valid. They have guided past generations and are transmitted by sayings and proverbs, such as "strike while the iron is hot; a bird in the hand is worth two in the bush; Rome was not built in a day; and, a stitch in time saves nine." Just as our forebearers did, modern social scientists scrutinize how people live, albeit in a more systematic and vigorous manner; as a result, they provide new insights about principles of effective living. Sometimes these insights confirm and sometimes they refute principles developed by our ancestors. For example, although people have recognized the importance of rewarding behavior for many centuries, the twentieth century behaviorists have added immeasureably to the understanding of reinforcement, as reflected in the review of such work by Bandura (1976). On the other hand, the long-held belief that the realism of early adolescents' vocational choices is an important factor in career development was refuted by the work of Gribbons and Lohnes (1968), and Super and his colleagues (Super & Overstreet, 1960; Super, Kowalski, & Gotkin, 1969). Even with more vigorous discovery, however, the insights from social science, like those transmitted by proverbs, are unlikely to apply only in certain situations.

Counselors amass heuristic principles over the course of their careers; first through careful observation of their own careers and those of others, through professional preparation, and finally through systematic review of their own counseling. The quality of their counseling reflects: (a) their knowledge of principles, (b) their ability to judge which principles apply, and (c) their ability to translate these principles into effective interaction with clients and resource persons.

The concept of heuristic principles is very useful. First, discovery of principles pertinent to desired goals suggests strategies for securing them. For example, the heuristic that listing the pros and cons of a value clarifies its meaning suggests formal debate as a value clarification exercise. Second, recognition of the heuristic principles underlying a strategy makes the strategy more understandable and predictable; and pinpoints the critical components of the strategy, thereby making it easier to apply effectively. The need for accurate information, for instance, should alert the counselor using debate for clarifying values to exclude obfuscating tactics in the exercise. Third, one can judge the potential of an untried strategy for achieving a particular goal by ascertaining whether its underlying heuristic principles pertain to the goal. For example, contrasting successful with unsuccessful financial transactions is likely to clarify one's decision-making strategy, but is unlikely to teach one how to obtain accurate information. The heuristic principle, of course, is that reflecting on past decisions clarifies the process.

Often more than one heuristic applies to the same goal. For instance, giving students interesting information about occupations should increase their occupational knowledge (heuristic 1) and even their likelihood of using supplied information again (heuristic 2—interesting information is reinforcing); but providing the information may also attenuate their ability to secure information independently (heuristic 3). More importantly, it may mask their need continually to obtain information on their own (heuristic 4). The counselor who has attended to the underlying heuristic principles will realize the need for assuring a balance between giving information and stimulating clients to obtain it.

Potency

Five or six, or even ten or twelve, hours over a few weeks or months is a very short time in which to expect a person to learn to solve physics, mathematics, or chemistry problems, even though he or she has learned the relevant concepts and theorems. Yet the public expects that several hours of individualized instruction in how to relate developing knowledge and skills to career can equip one to manage a career, despite the fact that a career often embraces problems requiring information and abilities from many different disciplines.

Recognizing this public expectation, however, counselors have not forcefully contrasted the performance expected from career counseling with the resources given to it. Certainly, the typical set of individual or group interviews and testing carried on in isolation from the client's schooling and significant others can be expected to contribute only minimally to that client's career development.

Professionals should not ignore the limited potency of counseling. Following are several suggestions for improving potency. First, include in the counseling contract provision for periodic checkbacks, enabling counselors to offer different kinds of career assistance at different stages of the career, as Morrill and Forest (1970) suggested when they explored the implications of career being a developmental phenomenon. Second, establish career centers, which include career guidance courses, work simulations, self-instruction materials, and paraprofessionally administered models to complement counseling. Orient the client to the different services within the center before or during counseling. Reardon and Burck (1975) have provided a detailed description of one such center. Third, involve significant others, such as parents, spouses, siblings, coworkers, and teachers, in counseling and show them how to support the client's career development following the counseling interview. Fourth, integrate selected readings and homework assignments into counseling in order to accustom the client to relating them to career, and prescribe readings and community educational programs that will help the client follow up the career counseling. Fifth, and perhaps most important, conclude counseling by reviewing progress and how it occurred with the client, and then project the client's next steps to continue directing the career. Underscore the client's need for continued attention to career in order to manage it.

Group Career Counseling

Individualizing help does not preclude group counseling. Helpers can assemble persons with similar goals and concerns and then organize a set of group strategies that assist each individual. Often the group strategies offer the client advantages, such as multiple models and reinforcers, which are unavailable in one-to-one learning situations.

While group counseling expands the possibilities for learning by multiplying the number of trusting interpersonal relationships, it delimits the concerns that can be treated since groups focus only on the concerns members share. If a group member has problems not related to the group's purpose, it would be inappropriate to use group time to resolve them. Likewise, to obtain the benefits of group counseling, the counselor must train clients to share in reinforcing, questioning, and providing feedback to other clients. Indeed, in group counseling clients actually counsel; therefore, they influence the learning atmosphere. To ensure that the atmosphere remains conducive to personal client learning, therefore, the counselor instructs clients about appropriate ways of behaving toward each other. Counselors can tell clients how to behave; they can model the appropriate behavior; and they can point out appropriate peer models or show tapes of such models. Stewart (1969), for example, described constructing audio tapes for use in career counseling of eleventh graders, and reported these tapes helped clients in learning such things as helping each other discover ways of obtaining information. Many claim that counseling must involve face-to-face interaction, but the recent introduction of self-directed counseling manuals (Magoon, 1969); Holland, 1970) and computer counseling (Super, 1970) indicates that some counselors, including this author, believe that individualized instruction, rather than direct or repeated interpersonal exchange, is the essence of counseling. Of course, in both self-directed and computer counseling, clients should have access to counselors, not merely aides or librarians, if they wish. The accessibility of a counselor must mean a competent professional will, on request, evaluate the appropriateness of instruction, will tailor materials to make them more individualized and will assist the client in following through on the instruction. Even if rarely used, the availability of such assistance is enough to qualify the learning program as counseling.

Although not necessarily a face-to-face relationship, counseling still differs from courses designed to teach concepts or skills for their own sake. Likewise, counseling does not include self-help materials that lack provision for review and feedback. On the other hand, career counseling cannot yet be distinguished from guidance classes organized primarily for a client to apply the curriculum to personal career concerns.

This position, that counseling is not dependent on face-to-face interviews, will be disputed vigorously by some on the grounds that it leads to diffusion of research. Such diffusion, however, is welcome since those who restrict counseling research to studying benefits produced in individual or small group sessions have put the cart before the horse. Rather than focusing on goals of counseling and asking how to achieve such goals, research has concentrated almost exclusively on modification of interviews for achieving goals. Despite counseling's legacy as an educational endeavor, most researchers have excluded consideration of coun-

seling strategies other than interviewing and testing. The author hopes
that the clarification in this text of what career counseling is will
reverse that trend.

Counseling and Other Kinds of Career Helping

The growing concern of Americans for their career satisfaction (O'Toole,
1973; Terkel, 1974; Sheehy, 1976) has produced many approaches for
promoting career development. Workshops, career planning classes, do-
it-yourself counseling kits with audiovisuals, K–14 comprehensive career
educational programs, career centers, and experiential learning programs all focus on equipping persons for more productive and satisfying careers. Like counseling, the best of these instructional efforts are
based on heuristic principles derived from social science research.

Are these efforts career counseling? Unfortunately, a definite answer
cannot be given because some of these approaches include counseling
or are part of counseling, and because experimentation is now creating
new methods of career counseling.

Career Counseling and Vocational Education

Career counseling is conceptually different from vocational education
and career education, although in practice, vocational educators, career
educators, and counselors overlap in goals and in methods. Vocational
education is a school-based program intended to foster appreciation of
and competence in occupational skills such as carpentry, homemaking,
electronic repair, bookkeeping, and mechanics. Federal legislation, the
most recent of which is PL 94–482, delineates what constitutes vocational education. Needless to say, vocational education, like all other
formal education, also promotes the development of constructive work
habits such as perseverance, labeled career skills by Fine (1974).
In addition to overlapping such counseling goals, vocational teachers
often coach the students, approaching the individualization customary
in counseling. Nevertheless, vocational education retains its emphasis
on building mastery of a competence to a standard set by a governing
occupational group. These objectives stand in contrast to the counseling
objective of showing clients how to use or adapt the skills for their purpose or supporting their development of the skill to a level that is useful
for them rather than a level necessary for further study or employment.

Career Counseling and Career Education

Career education, in contrast to vocational education, is a curriculum
perspective rather than a program with its own curriculum. It seeks to
ensure that the relation of education to working remains prominent and

that every curriculum, whether elementary school, bilingual, general, college preparatory, liberal arts, or even professional, provides a learner with opportunities to explore, appreciate, and acquire career skills through schooling.

In contrast to counseling, career education focuses on the group or the cohort's development, attempting through coordination and collaboration to provide students with educational experiences which will permit mastery of career development tasks. The following broad objectives enunciated by Hoyt (1977) are generally recognized as spanning the domain of career education. According to Hoyt (1977), teachers, school boards, administrators, counselors, business/labor/government/ professional/community leaders, community organizations, parents, and coordinators all have key responsibilities for these objectives.

1. Competent in the basic academic skills required for adaptability in our rapidly changing society
2. Equipped with good work habits
3. Equipped with a personally meaningful set of work values that foster in them a desire to work
4. Equipped with career decision-making skills, job-hunting skills, and job-getting skills
5. Equipped with a degree of self-understanding and understanding of educational-vocational opportunities sufficient for making sound career decisions
6. Aware of means available to them for continuing and recurrent education
7. Either placed or actively seeking placement in a paid occupation, in further education, or in a vocation consistent with their current career decisions
8. Actively seeking to find meaning and meaningfulness through work in productive use of leisure time
9. Aware of means available to themselves for changing career options—of societal and personal constraints impinging on career alternatives

Exclusiveness in Counseling

Individualization does not require a counselor to assume exclusive responsibility for aiding a client. As no single mathematics, physics, chemistry, or engineering teacher would presume to be the only one capable of qualifying a student to be an engineer, a realistic counselor recognizes his or her limitations in helping a person to direct a career. Either directly or indirectly, the counselor encourages client exchanges with significant others. In career development, significant others are likely to be parents, spouses, employers, fellow students or coworkers, paraprofessionals, teachers, or even other members of the client's community.

Evaluation and Research in Counseling

6

To be a profession, career counseling needs a body of knowledge on which to base its practices. Counselors must have evidence that practices such as administering and interpreting interest tests stimulate students to explore occupations of interest if they are to recommend such activities for students needing occupational exploration. Similarly, there must be evidence that participating in special groups directed at imagining one's future and sharing one's hopes with group members increases the specificity of one's career goal and the motivation to achieve it, before a counselor can legitimately ask clients or public institutions to provide hundreds of dollars for such activities.

Research from the social sciences provides general direction for counseling and teaching and supplies many of the concepts and principles taught to clients in counseling. For example, the use of interest testing to stimulate career exploration is based on cognitive dissonance and reinforcement research that suggests most people find it easier to learn about occupations compatible with their ideas of what is interesting, and that such activity is likely to be more reinforcing and hence engaged in longer than learning about activities incompatible with their interests. Although there are different methods by which the compatibility can be clarified, research has not established which, if any, method increases a client's likelihood of initiating occupational exploration. Indeed, little research has been done concerning the application of social science findings to career counseling. Much more research is needed to identify and to authenticate counseling and educational practices.

Tolbert (1974) pointed out that counselors have several roles to play relative to research. Most important are those of evaluators of their own efforts and consumers of the findings of other researchers. This chapter provides tools to help counselors in both roles; it is presented early in the book so the reader can use these instruments to judge better the merits of the counseling treatments presented in subsequent chapters. The evaluator role is especially crucial since—as Tolbert (1974) and Krumboltz (1966) noted—few, if any, counseling practices have been adequately defined and studied to be sure they benefit clients. As a consequence, a counselor must continually review his or her own work to make sure it helps the client, as intended. For the same reason, the counselor must regularly study and adopt, or adapt to one's own clientele, practices that are potentially beneficial. Therefore, a counselor also must become skilled in judging the quality of the burgeoning reports of counseling practice and research.

This chapter should be especially helpful to the counselor who aspires to follow the practitioner-scientist model espoused by Division 17 of the American Psychological Association and the American Personnel and Guidance Association. As researchers such as Bergin (1971), Brayfield and Crites (1964), and Whiteley (1967) have indicated, career counseling has advanced slowly because counselors have not described their treatments in enough detail to permit others to build on what they had learned, and because of limitations in research designs applied to study counseling. Unfortunately, the "design limitations" are not resolved, but counselors surely can describe their treatments more clearly.

This chapter is not intended as a short course in research. It reviews the issues this author believes are most important to improving counseling through direct evaluation and research. The topics covered are formulating researchable questions, formative and summative evaluation, replicability in counseling, logical and empirical bases of career counseling, and implications for the counseling profession.

Formulating Researchable Questions

Research starts because a person wants to find out something. Fundamental to effective research is formulation of answerable, important questions. These questions must be specified at the start of research and must guide the research; otherwise, the effort is unlikely to succeed.

To frame answerable questions, counselors must decide what they want to know, about whom they want to know it, and why they want to know it. These specifications enable them to identify the kind of evidence necessary to answer their questions. For example, the counselor who wants to know whether it is beneficial to teach clients to redesign their jobs needs to consider at least five points. First, what is the exact question of interest and the acceptable evidence. Is the counselor interested, for example, in whether job redesign by several workers in a factory aids productivity, or in whether most workers in factory X or in occupation X who redesign their jobs will benefit? What kind of evidence will convince the researcher—pre- and postdifferences on worker and supervisor reports of satisfaction, regardless of statistical significance? This issue will, to some degree, involve questions of sample selection and size, discrimination of instruments, design, and experimental control. Second, the counselor must realize there are two questions: whether particular clients can be taught to redesign jobs, and whether they can redesign their own jobs with beneficial results. Third, one must indicate who the prospective clients are: professional managers, grocery clerks, and so forth. Fourth, the researcher must define job redesign: is it limited to a worker's rearranging the sequence of tasks and the manner of accomplishing them, or does it include interacting with management so the worker may change what is being produced and/or how the worker interacts with others in the production process? Fifth, one must determine whether the definition of benefit includes a worker spending more hours in satisfying work, experiencing less stress, or increasing productivity.

Once these preliminaries are settled, the investigator should verify that measures of the variables under scrutiny are available. For example, are there criteria for judging whether alterations in a job are job redesign, are there valid measures of worker satisfaction, and of output? Further, do such measures have sufficient categories to allow determination of worker growth?

After a question is formulated, the counselor can ask whether the question is important enough to justify the effort that answering it will involve. One therefore needs to ponder whether the answer will increase knowledge and/or benefit one's clientele. In other words, will the answer make a difference? If yes, the counselor needs to determine that the question has not already been answered. Generally, discussing the issue with colleagues or a specialist in the field, and review of the literature, will prevent "rediscovering the wheel" and often will provide insights about investigating the matter.

When convinced that the question is important and not already answered, the counselor turns to the mechanics of answering the question. This process involves deciding who will collect what kinds of data from how many subjects, and when and how the data will be analyzed to provide answers. These considerations usually are central to the design of a research or evaluation. Even if one consults a design and evaluation specialist about procedures, the counselor must recognize that one's own judgments about what are the important questions and the acceptable evidence are paramount to effective research. Specialists may help do the research more effectively, but they are unlikely to be as well versed as the researcher on what is important to learn.

Evaluation and Research: Different Purposes with Similar Operations

Research is the systematic study of a phenomena in order to create knowledge and understanding. Research is empirical when it focuses on observable phenomena, experimental when it controls and manipulates the phenomena. A researcher investigates phenomena in order to generate or to test hypotheses. One may focus on components of counseling to discover their relation to other components or to the outcome. For example, counselor empathy has been linked to positive client affective and behavioral progress and to particular modes of counselor training (Carkhuff, 1972). In examining the relationship, the researcher can study what the linkage is, why it is, whether it meets a predefined criterion, or how to change it to meet that criterion. If the latter two questions are pursued, the researcher is an evaluator. Evaluation is the research sub-area that focuses on determining whether an activity proceeds as intended.

Both evaluators and researchers of career counseling collect and analyze data about counseling in order to learn more about counseling. Their crafts require well-defined counseling activities executed according to preestablished criteria, reliable and valid measures of career development, and statistical and nonstatistical designs to enable interpretation of the data.

The fundamental distinction between evaluation and research is purpose. An evaluation tries to find out whether an activity and its outcome is proceeding as intended; research, in contrast, ranges more broadly in order to discover something about the activity and its relation to outcomes or to other activities. The evaluator's task is to verify achievement of a criterion; the researcher's objective is to discover new knowledge and to increase understanding by hypothesis generation and testing, as well as by criterion assessment. More specifically, evaluation applies a criterion to an activity or to an outcome and decides whether the criterion has been met or how it can be met. An evaluator receives or helps define criteria, and then gathers and examines data to judge whether the criteria are satisfied or could be satisfied.

On the other hand, the counseling researcher is not as concerned with whether the information has immediate use, but counsels primarily to further general understanding, and only secondarily to benefit particular subjects. Rarely has the general researcher the same accountability or commitment to the activity under study that the evaluator has. Operating on the frontiers of knowledge, the counseling researcher often lets a set of counseling components run their course in order to help establish their impact. Adjustments for the benefit of the immediate subjects are made only out of the demands of ethics, or if they do not jeopardize the research, and often data that would suggest such adjustments are not collected. The usual contract between a client treated as a subject and the researcher specifies provision of reasonable safeguards to the client during the specified treatment, whereas the typical counseling contract involves the counselor's agreeing to assist the client in pursuing a particular goal until it is achieved, deemed unattainable, or abandoned.

Of course, some counseling research other than evaluation is done *post hoc,* or as a quasi-experiment. In such research, counseling proceeds without experimental interference. After counseling, questions to further understanding of the counseling phenomenon are examined as well as possible, with procedures designed to minimize the adverse effects of limited control of the research variables.

The difference in purposes between evaluators and general researchers often leads to differences in the kinds of data they gather and analyze and in the structure of the counseling they investigate. First, evaluators direct their attention to data pertinent to their present criteria, whereas researchers often peruse a wider range of data. Second, evaluators usually examine, or at least have reference to, a complete counseling operation from initiation to conclusion; whereas researchers may focus on a small part of counseling, such as the counselor's empathy level or amount of reinforcing. Third, the researchers' desire to generalize directs their attention to concerns such as random assignment and research designs to eliminate alternative explanations of outcomes, counselor or client characteristics affecting counseling outcomes, and the like. Evaluators, on the other hand, give their primary attention to the client's starting performance on the criterion, changes in that performance following specific counseling activities, and departures of counselors or clients from the counseling program; only secondarily do they concern themselves with generalization.

Recently, the APA Standards for Providers of Psychological Services directed psychologists, including counseling psychologists and school psychologists, to evaluate their activities. Such evaluation is to include delineating a treatment reasonable for the client, monitoring that treatment to assure it is provided in accord with accepted professional practice, and judging that the intended outcome is achieved or that variable strategies, such as referral or consultation, are exhausted before concluding counseling (APA, 1977a).

Summative Evaluation

Judging whether an activity or outcome satisfied the criterion is called *summative evaluation*, regardless of whether the judgment refers to part of the activity still underway or whether the evaluation judges the outcome after the activity is concluded. Summative evaluation is the traditional type of evaluation. Increased public demand for accountability requires professionals such as counselors to verify that their activities meet minimum professional standards and to document the degree to which clients achieve their objectives. To claim that a counselor spent six hours in counseling and in consulting, or that clients were judged improved or even rated themselves improved, is not enough. More careful treatment delineation and monitoring and more specific and well-verified statements of client achievement are imperative. Since psychotherapy and counseling, including career counseling, do not have impressive success records, other professionals and the public require evidence that they benefit in order to justify continued support.

Essential to summative evaluation of outcomes is careful delineation and measurement of the client objectives. Mager (1962) and many others since, have offered clear direction for this task. In this text, each chapter on counseling methods includes a section of appropriate career development objectives and methods of assessing them. Selection of appropriate measures consistent with the counseling instruction and criteria is essential for meaningful evaluation. The recent attention to criterion-referenced tests—tests designed to assess a student's mastery according to a criterion rather than to distinguish among members of a population—underscores the fact that past counseling investigations often used outcome measures not directly or totally related to the counseling instruction and objectives. For example, grade point average often was used erroneously as an outcome measure of many different kinds of counseling, rather than only of counseling that taught the particular skills related to grade point average.

Closely related to substantiation of counseling effectiveness is verification of the counselor's professional practice. Checking professionalism is especially important since many avowed counseling goals cannot be evaluated readily at the close of counseling.

Traditionally, however, counselor training has focused on developing a broad understanding of the social sciences and eschewed teaching application of specific counseling practices. Concrete criteria of effective counseling, therefore, are not often defined. Counseling textbooks rarely delineate counseling treatments; instead they address broad topics, leaving the reader to synthesize and to formulate particular treatments. Although every counselor is expected to create counseling programs to fit client needs, model counseling programs are rarely provided in the texts.

Furthermore, even though the APGA recommends internship and practicum experience to involve practice counseling under close supervision, many school and career counselors have not had such experience. Even among those with supervision, few have applied a prescribed counseling treatment in the way a student teacher would follow a lesson plan to teach a class. Once counselors begin practice, rarely do they receive direct supervision.

Some have broadened evaluation's focus from assessing the fit of phenomena to criteria to include study of the kinds of evidence that influence decision makers who use evaluation data and the kinds of criteria to apply in order to answer policy questions (Alkin, 1969). Since evaluation increases the cost of services significantly, it is important to be clear about what the evaluation is expected to provide and the kinds of evidence that will have greatest impact. For example, career counselor evaluators not only should evaluate the counseling, but first should ask questions such as these: (1) Do high school principals and college deans regard a consultant's testimony or client gains in cognitive tests after counseling as more convincing evidence of counseling's effectiveness? (2) Is it more important to show that a group counseling procedure does not harm any student or to establish that participation in group counseling leads to substantially larger gains than individual counseling for some students? Answers to such questions, of course, will enable the counselor to decide which questions will be more meaningful.

Formative Evaluation

"What are you going to do when you grow up?" This question commands different answers at different times in history. The contemporary age is multiplying new kinds of work opportunities and new ways of acquiring the requisite skills. Fast, inexpensive transportation makes distant places imaginable as work sites, and mass communication, especially television, exposes new opportunities more quickly and more widely than in times past.

Inventions enable us to develop more skills and interests than our parents or grandparents. Developing many facets, however, requires changing more quickly than parents or grandparents could have imagined was possible or proper. Social scientists believe development will be maximally efficient and satisfying if each person sets specific goals, follows detailed plans for achieving them, and continually uses feedback about progress to modify plans. In other words, a person must be task-oriented but attentive to new or alternate opportunities; recognize that choices of direction and means can only be approximations, not the right or final selections; and welcome the chance to revise ideas because one knows revision increases the chance for success. Although change may cause momentary distress as one realizes the initial choice could have been better and experiences the uncertainty arising from leaving the familiar, one accepts with optimism the opportunity to change. A modern career enables the individual to use work to put into action multiple talents and values. This actualization, however, requires ongoing evaluation and modification of one's direction and means to achieve maximum results.

Appropriately, the profession born to help people create their careers also requires self-evaluation, for the character of its services necessarily is as experimental and evolving as are the modern careers it services. New guidelines for changing occupations are being written, but they are not yet clearly defined; likewise, new strategies for teaching problem solving are being constructed, but still need major refinement.

Modern careerists, nevertheless, must change occupations and repeatedly solve problems. They cannot wait years for precise, validated strategies; instead, they must be serviced by existing methods even as counselors improve them. Counselors, therefore, need a way to operate under these conditions. More precisely, counselors must monitor strategies as they apply them in order to identify shortcomings quickly. In this way, counselors can correct the problematic components of strategy before the client becomes discouraged.

Philosophers and educators are explicating a methodology to serve counselors in their role of practitioner/scientist (Scriven, 1967; Cronbach, 1963). The methodology is formative evaluation, which involves using feedback generated from delivering new counseling to adjust it as it is being offered and to improve future offerings. To permit distinguishing effective from ineffective aspects of the new counseling requires that the program be described as a series of components with defined objectives, that information about operation of the components be gathered as the program proceeds, and that program corrections be made on the basis of that information (Sorenson, 1971).

Formative evaluation differs from summative evaluation in its purpose and therefore in its questions, methods, design, and premises. The purpose of formative evaluation is to improve a program, not to prove the program works or accomplishes particular objectives. The evaluator: (1) examines the program elements and their interrelations before and during their operation, to determine how they can be adjusted to achieve their purpose; (2) looks at information pertaining to what these elements are producing and how they seem to be producing it; (3) considers the effect of possible adjustments to the program and its goal; and (4) observes how persons benefiting from the program are performing differently from those who are not.

Formative evaluation starts as soon as one begins formulating a program. For counseling, one establishes the objectives; relates each objective to particular counseling components, attempting to identify alternative components for each objective, if possible; and then specifies the evidence by which to judge whether the delivery of a component accomplishes its subobjectives. Formative evaluators act like systems analysts, seeking to improve operations by detecting and replacing or realigning malfunctioning or nonarticulating elements. Before new counseling is offered, formative evaluators scrutinize each component and its alignment to assure that there is synchronization with the total program and other components, that sufficient time and resources have been allocated, and that counselor and clients have been prepared to implement the component. Then, when counseling is underway, the formative evaluators monitor component operations to detect shortcomings and to generate hunches for correcting them, and they modify counseling to the degree that is feasible in order to help clients make up what they did not achieve through the faulty components. After counseling, the formative evaluators debrief counselors and clients, and they combine these data with those generated by trying counseling in order to suggest ways of improving faulty components or to pinpoint other components which can be substituted for faulty ones.

Improving an introductory career group counseling session illustrates the difference in purpose between a formative evaluator and a traditional researcher. The original purpose of the session was to have clients become acquainted with each other and to understand how the group would address their career concerns. The first approach had clients introduce themselves and state their particular concerns. At the outset, clients were urged to ask each other questions in order to be clear about one another's concerns. In listening to sessions, the formative evaluator noted some groups were sharing more about themselves and learning more about one another. In these groups the counselor had asked the lead-off clients to elaborate and had pointed out similarities and differences among clients, inviting them to react to each other. The introduction in these groups was taking much longer than in the other groups, yet questioning these clients at the end of the sessions indicated they had only limited knowledge of each other. Often, they did not even know each other's names. For a second round of interviews, therefore, a getting-acquainted exercise was added. Some counselors were also instructed to ask the first two clients to elaborate on parts of their introduction and to invite cross-talk about similarities and marked differences throughout counseling. In listening to the interviews, the evaluator heard the exercise in which a client repeated the names and concerns of preceding clients before introducing himself, providing more information and capturing more attention. Likewise, the researcher heard the interviews in which counselors were encouraging elaboration and cross-talk to produce more sharing, and at the close, persons in these groups knew more about one another. Hence, the evaluator adopted the exercise and instruction to encourage elaboration and cross-talk as part of the initial interview specifications.

The investigation method is a second major difference between formative evaluation and summative evaluation. Typically, the formative evaluator uses more informal, less precise observations, and collects a wider range of information. For instance, in creating the initial group counseling session, the evaluator did not rate how many bits of information each client shared, nor did he measure the talking time of clients and counselors. On the other hand, the researcher noted that inviting a client to comment on similarities or marked differences with another elicited elaboration on the speaker's concerns, which seemed interesting to the other clients.

A third difference is concern with design. The formative evaluator assumes the program is in its preliminary stages and therefore is not concerned with formal testing. Consequently, control of treatment time and content, method of obtaining the sample, sample size, and history are not as important to the formative evaluator as they are to the summative evaluator. In developing the initial meeting above, for example, the counseling sessions were not limited to a particular length, nor was content rigidly defined. The counselors who encouraged elaboration and cross-talk were not formally matched with those who did not, and clients were not randomly assigned to one or the other treatments. Some of these design features, of course, would help increase one's confidence in the observed differences, but arranging them would have consumed considerable energy and distracted the evaluator's attention from improving the session.

Premises are a fourth difference between formative evaluation and summative evaluation. The formative evaluator assumes that the program needs to be improved and that sensitive, systematic observation can identify possible corrections. Formative evaluation synthesizes before analyzing formally. Implicitly, the task is to fashion a potentially efficient, effective treatment. In contrast, the summative evaluator presumes the treatment is operational and focuses on establishing whether it achieves particular criteria, either in its process (operation) or its outcome (client changes). For this task, the evaluator requires defined hypotheses, precise, focused measurement, and exact statistical tests. In the formative example of developing the initial group meeting, no specific hypotheses, precision measures, or statistical tests were used.

Even when applying established procedures, a formative evaluation perspective may complement summative evaluation. The case of Henry illustrates how a formative evaluation perspective helped avert a failure. Henry was a student teacher who was losing interest in teaching and suffering declining grades. His apparently candid review of the problem made it plausible that the difficulty stemmed from an incorrect choice of field. Moreover, he clearly understood and was pleased with the agreement to embark on trait-factor career choice counseling. The ensuing information gathering indicated he understood the ideas that were presented but also showed that his initial enthusiasm about finding other possible occupations was diminishing. The counselor pointed out Henry's unusual concern that emerging options did not provide opportunity for heterosexual contacts, that professional duties could easily interfere with social relationships, and that colleagues were unlikely to provide intimate emotional support and sharing. Wondering aloud why Henry was raising these objections to options that he acknowledged as attractive to him prompted tears followed by the story of a broken romance, which was still upsetting him. At this point, the counselor and Henry revised their contract to provide for consideration of personal concerns closely related to careers. Counseling moved into identifying strategies for mending or initiating heterosexual relationships. Reading was prescribed because of the cognitive strengths Henry showed in counseling. Henry affirmed his desire to repair the broken relationship, and he outlined and then rehearsed a course of action. As his efforts rekindled the romance, he became happier with teaching, and announced at the closing counseling session that the review of his choice had confirmed teaching as his present first choice.

Training in Formative Evaluation. Counselors doing formative evaluation require a set of appropriate tools—observational skills and a knowledge of how to generate judgments from their observations. The formative evaluator gathers and then weighs evidence pertaining to the following kinds of questions in order to make a judgment about revisions in instructional strategies: Do the succeeders apply ideas or skills not manifest by the nonsucceeders or do they practice more? Why do the nonsucceeders make the types of errors they do? How far do nonsucceeders go before failing? What difficulties do the nonsucceeders report, and what suggestions do they and the succeeders make for improving the program? In what other ways might the problematic aspects of the program be taught?

Formative deliberations focus on building new program components or modifying existing ones. The kind of judgment they make is that operation X' be initiated. The main judgment is neither that X did not produce Y because Z, nor that the product of X was not Y. The formative evaluator wants to understand what is obstructing learning in order to formulate a strategy for removing the obstruction. The precise causal linking is not important, especially if it will not change the judgment about a solution. For instance, the formative evaluator does not distinguish how cueing, modeling, and reinforcing contribute differentially to sustained attention on a program task; but focuses on judging what actions a counselor can take to provide all three.

Formative evaluators are more like engineers refining a device than scientists trying to add to knowledge or consumers deciding whether to buy the device. As a consequence, formative evaluators should observe programs being refined and study how improvements have been determined and implemented. They will want to become familiar with different instructional strategies and learn ways of combining teaching operations and learning exercises in order to produce particular learning. As students, they deserve guidance and feedback about their ability to create imaginative operations for improving a learning program, as well as direction and feedback about setting up statistical designs and interpreting ensuing data.

Moreover, the formative evaluator often must be a participant observer. The data often require qualitative synthesis, rather than quantitative analysis. These counselors compile anecdotes, make ratings, and construct sociographs. They should practice these methods as they have practiced administering standardized tests. Likewise, they must not neglect qualitative methods of processing data although their professional research courses have emphasized quantitative statistics, even implying that qualitative methods are not legitimate. Instead, formative evaluators must familiarize themselves with the anthropological case study and content analysis and use constructive criticism to sharpen their skills in inducing relationships through these research methods.

Replicability

Replication of observations and experiments enable the physical sciences to achieve objectivity and to discover new information. When an experiment unearths new knowledge, another repeats its essence to substantiate the new finding. This process is called replication. In the second experiment, all the essential elements of the first are reproduced to enable the newly discovered phenomena to emerge again. The second experiment does not exactly duplicate the first; often the researcher, materials, and facilities are different. The essential elements are repeated, however. For example, scientists replicating research about the boiling temperatures of new chemical compounds would hold constant the purity and density of the liquid, the volume of the container, and the pressure in accord with Boyle's Law.

On the frontiers of knowledge, scientists do not always know what the key elements are; therefore, they provide extensive, detailed descriptions of their observations and the conditions existing as they observe. Through many, many repetitions of the experiment, in which different elements are varied, the scientists eventually learn which are the key elements.

Many counseling investigators have proposed that counseling can advance its knowledge through replication if counselors will identify precisely their actions and the circumstances surrounding them. Then one can examine the matrix of the different counseling acts, counseling circumstances, and client achievements to pinpoint the counseling actions and circumstances related to particular clients' progress.

The research of Krumboltz, Thoresen, and their colleagues (presented in Chapter 8) on reinforcement effects on career information seeking illustrates how replication has benefited counseling. First, these researchers constructed a counselor–client dialogue that would elicit client recognition of the need for, and commitment to, information seeking. Then they designated the kinds of client verbalizations that should be reinforced about information. Next, counselors trained in the dialogue administered it to clients with and without reinforcement, thereby controlling reinforcement. Subsequent examination of client achievement showed that reinforcement improved client benefit because the counseling dialogue was replicated except for the controlled variations in reinforcement.

In counseling, as in the physical sciences, the intention to achieve replicability raises the question of what to replicate. So far, work by Rogers (1967), Carkhuff (1972), and others has shown the so-called "counselor-offered conditions" of empathy and warmth affect outcome, and as reported above, Krumboltz and his colleagues have established the importance of reinforcement and, more recently, differential effects of modeling (Krumboltz & Thoresen, 1964a; 1968; Krumboltz, Varenhorst, & Thoresen (1967). In describing a counseling procedure, therefore, one should at least specify the quality of the client-counselor interaction, the pattern of reinforcement, and the nature of any modeling provided.

Other elements of counseling essential to replicate are suggested by the nature of counseling. Since counseling is a special form of teaching, the theories of learning proposed by Gagné (1970), Brunner (1966), and Ausubel (1968), for instance, indicate that one needs to replicate the ideas and actions to be taught, the process by which ideas are presented and practiced (sequence, pacing, number and frequency of practices, visual-auditory, lecture-tutorial, self-study, homework, role-play, and modeling), and the status of the teacher and conditions of teaching (counselor title, appearance and comfort of counseling facility, and privacy and freedom from interruption). The research of Krumboltz and his colleagues actually replicated these elements by keeping them constant, but their reports focused on the incremental effects of variations in reinforcement and modeling. Work following Rogers and Carkhuff, however, has attended exclusively to the counselor conditions across a range of counseling programs that taught different ideas in different ways. Such an approach assumes that variations in the range of ideas, processes, and status are distributed randomly across conditions. But this assumption is probably not valid: Truax (1966) found that Rogers's counseling included systematic reinforcement of a problem-solving approach, and Fiedler (1950) showed therapists who do well in one aspect of counseling are likely to do well in others. As a result, many studies supporting the efficacy of counselor conditions can be challenged because they did not control for the alternative explanation that clearly defined ideas and effective teaching methodology, rather than counselor empathy, accounted for client progress or satisfaction. Fortunately, a few studies have held such factors constant and thereby clearly affirm the importance of counselor conditions.

At first consideration, many counselors seem to reject the applicability of replication to counseling. They mistakenly associate replication with a rigid, standardized, robot-like interaction. But replicable counseling actually encourages the opposite, since attention to the specifics of counseling demanded by replication alerts the counselor to the ongoing client reactions, thereby enabling him continually to adjust his counseling to the emerging needs of the client. Not surprisingly, the counseling of Rogers (1951), Ellis (1979), Williamson (1939), Carkhuff (1971), and other eminent clinicians does approach replicability as evidenced by the fact that so many counselors can imitate them.

The limited research attention to replication partially accounts for the lack of clarity about what to replicate in counseling. Many counseling and psychological studies have examined elements of the therapeutic process, such as proportion of counselor-client talk, amount of interpretation, and the like, in order to isolate key ingredients; but Marsden (1971) shows that these studies have not considered the character of the total process, even though the concept of a gestalt argues the importance of a total view. Certainly the client would tend to perceive the process as a total, and is very likely to miss its subtle nuances, especially when counseling is of short duration.

This author believes that systematic replication must attend primarily to the overall scope and sequence of the counseling program and secondarily to variations within the program. The following section describes this approach to achieving replication in counseling.

Achieving Replicable Counseling

The discussion above leads to claiming that counseling is replicable to the extent that persons with comparable goals, obstacles, and resources are exposed to the same ideas under comparable conditions and within an equivalent psychological setting. Theoretically, a client's experience would be the same with different counselors. Yet two persons will never experience identical counseling, since they will not have identical goals, obstacles, or resources. Thus, counseling can never be duplicated, but it can be replicated.

Replicable counseling will not be rigid if the requirements specify classes of action rather than particular acts. With such specifications, counseling can achieve the essential individualization, yet communicate the ideas that will resolve problems encountered by several persons. For example, if the counselor praises (action) one client every time the person says that he or she will try to solve the problems, this counselor can replicate the procedure with a second client by rewarding (class of action) such statements again. With the second client, the counselor need not be restricted to verbal praise nor the same words; but only must insure use of reinforcing actions. Likewise, in a career counseling procedure with substeps in which a client evaluates self and different occupations on a set of characteristics, the person might first evaluate self and then the different occupations, or vice versa. In both instances, the counselor guides the client through the same substeps, although their sequence differs. Counseling procedures in which the counselor uses the same actions at identical points of the process are standardized as well as replicable, but replicable counseling need not be standardized.

Replicable counseling spotlights a counselor's contribution to the client's achievement. It equates counseling to providing the client with a learning program, and thereby underscores attending to (a) goals and subgoals, (b) the characteristics of the population served by the program, (c) the manner by which the program is assigned, (d) the components of the program and their execution, and (e) the benchmarks by which to judge both the counselor's performance and the client's progress.

Goals and Subgoals

Assuming that most human goals fall into a limited number of classes and that learning a particular set of concepts, principles of action, and behaviors increases the likelihood of achieving a certain class of goals leads counselors to have clients delineate their goals and identify assets for achieving them at the outset of counseling. By guiding clients to establish their goals and the priorities among them, the obstacles, and their assets, counselors not only assemble the information necessary to begin fashioning a learning program, but they also help clients to believe that counseling will be beneficial. The counselor usually follows a predictable pattern to elicit concrete specifications of client objectives and to ascertain the obstacles to these objectives. The pattern often includes perusal of records and psychological tests, open-ended questions about the client's activities, expectations, the importance of the objectives and amount of distress felt in having difficulty in realizing them, in-vivo observations, and perhaps even consultation about the client. Such a diagnostic process is described in Chapter 5.

The goals established and agreed on and the priorities set shape the ensuing learning program. Proceeding, the counselor and client identify the subgoals (understandings, behavior acquisitions, commitments of assistance) necessary to achieve the goals. Then the counselor, and the client, if able, plan a learning strategy for accomplishing the subgoals. This operation corresponds to the identification of solution strategies in Chapter 5.

To enable distinction among counseling programs, to guide delineation of the learning program, and to aid evaluation, the goals need to be as specific as possible. Broad classes, such as problem in vocational choice and lack of information suggested by Bordin (1946) and Williamson (1939), may be useful to identify the type of expertise required to assist a client, but not to designate an appropriate learning program. For the latter purpose, goal categories such as the following are necessary: resolution of conflict between two compatible occupations, knowledge and experience in seeking information about schools and training programs, and contacts for learning about vertical or horizontal occupational changes.

As counselors become familiar with components of different procedures relating to broad areas such as choice and information acquisition, a relatively small number of broad categories are likely to emerge for filing the different procedures. But, so few complete procedures are now available that it is premature to establish categories. Perhaps, to increase accountability, counselors will describe particular procedures and file them in archives such as ERIC for access by others. Indeed, such filing should become one of the criteria used by certifying boards such as ABPP for achieving status as a clinician.

Characteristics of Clients

Individual differences necessarily guide construction of a counseling program; recently, research about ability-learning interactions has underscored the importance of recognizing client differences (Cronbach & Snow, 1977). Accordingly, a replicable procedure must designate its target population and describe how to identify them.

For example, the population might be tenth graders in the college preparatory program with B or higher averages who score less than the 25th percentile on the *CMI*. Or it might be associate professors who completed their doctorates within the last four to twelve years and who, in their colleges' annual career satisfaction questionnaire, report dissatisfaction in balancing career demands against other life obligations. Since Cronbach and Snow (1977) have pointed out that differences in ability affect method and quantity of individual learning, a counselor seeking to improve information acquisition would use different language, different pacing, different resource materials, and perhaps even different models for tenth graders with low *CMI* scores and low scholastic achievement and reading than for those with high reading and achievement.

Ideally, the treatment would reflect understanding of how successful members of the client's population have learned the competence the counseling is intended to develop. Such understanding nearly always necessitates careful, direct observations of successful members of the client's population. Contrasting successful with unsuccessful people will often provide insights into how the successful have learned and how the unsuccessful might learn. The comparisons will also sharpen the counselor's ability to distinguish clients who have the problem from those who do not.

Program Assignment

Clients sometimes participate in deciding the components of counseling (Goldman, 1971), and sometimes counselors take full responsibility for their diagnosis (Williamson, 1939). In explicating the counseling process for counselors who want to replicate, it is especially important to specify the factors weighed in assigning a treatment. In our example, the counselor, without conferring with the tenth graders, their teachers or parents, juxtaposed the students' limited knowledge of career planning with their demonstrated academic competence and decided that each would receive two small-group sessions consisting of modeling and re-inforcement of information seeking, à la Krumboltz and Thoresen (1964). In contrast, the counselor working with the professors initially established with each professor his or her degree of discomfort, beliefs about how to resolve the problem, and past efforts concerning the problem. Then, for those who reported at least moderate distress, who accepted group counseling focused on redesigning one's job as a possible solution, and who had tried one or more other strategies unsuccessfully, the counselor contracted for eight two-hour small-group meetings to redesign a professorship. If alternate counseling strategies were avail-able, one should describe presentation of the alternatives and how coun-selor and client elected the one chosen. For example, if the alternatives for professors were a life planning workshop or a job redesign workshop, the counselor would report noting that life planning workshops help in identifying goals and in formulating general plans, whereas job redesign counseling involves exploring how essential job activities might be restructured to take less time or be more satisfying, and how extraneous activities might be deleted.

Combining Exercises and Counselor Responses

Task analysis of a client's goals and circumstances, appraisal of skills, attitudes and feelings, and determination of how other similar people achieve such goals suggest what has to be learned and how. For example, to process information, one requires an objective and knowledge about appropriate information sources. If one has been unsuccessful in processing information previously, one may also need special support while formulating an objective and learning about sources of informa-tion. A counseling program designed for a specific goal includes com-ponents for accomplishing each of the subgoals. Thus, a counseling procedure designed to assist a person who has failed in processing information would include components on goal setting, sources of in-formation, and reconciliation of doubts about success.

A component of counseling includes the exercises (activities such as a test interpretation or discussion of work history) and counselor responses needed to adapt the exercises so that they develop the pro-gram's subgoals. First, counselor and client consider the principles, infor-mation, or skills needed to achieve each subgoal. Then they select or develop exercises for teaching these principles, information, or skills. As the client performs the exercise, the counselor responds in a manner that maximizes the likelihood that the exercise works properly. The responses are not random; they reflect the counselor's beliefs about learning and personality theory. To construct a replicable counseling component, therefore, first describe the counseling exercise and then define the set of appropriate counselor responses. Defining appropriate responses requires categorizing client responses and enumerating the rules by which counselor responses relate to client responses. The following paragraphs discuss counselor responses, client responses, and rules for relating them.

Counselor responses support and complement the learning exercises by influencing client behavior. For example, a counseling exercise, which asks a client to discuss his or her concern, will elicit a fuller discussion if the counselor reinforces (response) the client for discussing the concerns. Counselor responses should encourage the client to act—think, feel, behave, perceive—in a way that enables the component to work. The particular client determines the specific content of a response, but the learning program prescribes the class of a response; that is, the learning program says reinforce, but the specific reinforcement depends on the client. Since counselor responses facilitate the client's use of the learning program, they can be classified in terms of their relation to the program: (a) explaining the meaning of the program's information; (b) involving the client in the program; (c) diagnosing and evaluating a client's suitability for, and progress in, the program; (d) rewarding compliance with the program; (e) clarifying the client's behavior in the interaction; and (f) problem solving. Each category is bipolar; the counselor can explain or confuse, can involve or ignore the client, and can evaluate or defer judgment. Chapter 5 provided a description of each response category.

Client reactions can be defined in terms of their relation to the subgoal of the particular counseling component. Most client responses fall into these categories: (a) using the learning program correctly; (b) seeking information in order to use it; (c) modifying the program; (d) using the program incorrectly or procrastinating in it; (e) withdrawing or remaining uninvolved in the program; (f) failing to use the instruction because of lack of skill; and (g) resisting the program. Resistance is manifested in several ways: declining to follow instructions, questioning the credibility of the counselor, attacking the credibility of the counseling process, or diverting the process to other topics.

Counseling rules can be derived once counselor responses and client reactions have been classified. These seven rules encompass many eventualities:

1. Continually evaluate your interaction with the client and the client's progress in order to guide your actions.
2. Maintain client involvement continuously.
3. Reinforce the client for using the program correctly and for attempting or intending to use it, and share your evaluation of progress.
4. Reinforce the client's modification of program and adjust pace if alteration is beneficial; clarify its shortcomings for the client if

the modification is not as effective as the original program, and explain or problem solve.

5. Clarify for the client who is proceeding incorrectly or procrastinating, and explain or problem solve as necessary.
6. Explain and/or problem solve when a client asks for guidance in using a program.
7. Clarify withdrawal from or resistance to a program, and problem solve and involve as necessary.

The simplicity of these rules should not be misconstrued as implying that counseling is a simple, mechanical exercise. Rather, counseling is complex, requiring keen sensitivity and understanding to decode client responses and a superior command of language to provide careful, precise teaching a troubled person can assimilate. For example, one must first determine whether a client's hesitation to proceed is noncompliance or a need for fuller explanation. Then, in confronting noncompliance, one must quickly make responses slightly beyond the understanding manifest in the client communication. Furthermore, one can classify client responses by their meaning within a context, rather than by relying on a predetermined set of interaction units (e.g. a counselor statement and a client statement).

Even when two counselors apply similar rules, the content of their counseling sessions may differ. First, counseling exercises exert considerable control over the material the client can introduce. For example, a counselor who is an expert in test interpretation will tend to use interpretation exercises; the client-centered counselor, however, will rarely use such an exercise (Patterson, 1964). Secondly, counselors disagree about the appropriate content of the response categories; for example, what is involving or conducive to problem solving. Some counselors will reject the notion of systematically establishing credibility to involve clients; others reject giving of direct advice to resolve a counseling problem; and not everyone will agree that direct confrontation should be used to clarify resistance.

Counseling process criteria. As one proceeds, the counselor necessarily verifies whether one is presenting counseling as intended and that the procedure is producing the expected benefits. For this verification, two kinds of indices are needed. First, one should define the counseling program in terms of a series of counselor actions and/or counselor-client interactions, which can be referenced so the counselor can verify that the counseling is accurate. Second, one should describe the client progress and outcome measures.

Figure 6–1 presents one scheme for verifying the accuracy of a session of career decision making counseling. The scheme delineates the major counselor and client actions, permitting one to rate whether the action occurred and its quality. Each action represents either the content of a learning exercise or the expected counselor or client response to that content. By way of illustration, note that in Figure 6–1 the actions "introduce G A I O P" and "define goal" refer to presenting content or informa-

Figure 6–1. Counselor Performance Rating for Career Decision Making Counseling

Counselor	Student
+ m − O	+ m − O

Learning a Vocational Decision-Making Strategy

( ) ( ) ( ) ( ) introduces G A I O P

( ) ( ) ( ) ( ) defines *Goal*

( ) ( ) ( ) ( ) gives example or uses student example   ( ) ( ) ( ) ( ) give example of *Goal*

( ) ( ) ( ) ( ) summarize or reinforce response

( ) ( ) ( ) ( ) defines *Alternative*

( ) ( ) ( ) ( ) gives example or uses student example   ( ) ( ) ( ) ( ) give example of *Alternative*

( ) ( ) ( ) ( ) summarize or reinforce response

( ) ( ) ( ) ( ) defines *Information*

( ) ( ) ( ) ( ) gives example or uses student example   ( ) ( ) ( ) ( ) give example of *Information*

( ) ( ) ( ) ( ) summarize or reinforce response

( ) ( ) ( ) ( ) defines *Outcome*

( ) ( ) ( ) ( ) gives example or uses student example   ( ) ( ) ( ) ( ) give example of *Outcome*

( ) ( ) ( ) ( ) summarize or reinforce response

( ) ( ) ( ) ( ) defines *Plan*

( ) ( ) ( ) ( ) gives example or uses student example   ( ) ( ) ( ) ( ) give example of *Plan*

( ) ( ) ( ) ( ) summarize or reinforce response

Review G A I O P

( ) ( ) ( ) ( ) asks student to review G A I O P steps   ( ) ( ) ( ) ( ) briefly explains each of five steps

( ) ( ) ( ) ( ) checks student feeling about steps   ( ) ( ) ( ) ( ) states most important or new steps

Conclusion of the Meeting

( ) ( ) ( ) ( ) reinforces student participation

( ) ( ) ( ) ( ) encourages information seeking   ( ) ( ) ( ) ( ) suggests information needed

( ) ( ) ( ) ( ) reinforce or summarize response

( ) ( ) ( ) ( ) structures next meeting

Note: The raters marked + if the counseling was excellent; m if it was adequate; − if it was attempted but not adequate; and O if it was omitted. For scoring percentage modality, the + and m were combined and the − and O combined, and the counselor received the average of the two ratings.

SOURCE: G. Snodgras. *A Comparison of student paraprofessionals and professional counselor trainees in career counseling with university students.* Unpublished Ph.D. dissertation, University of California, Los Angeles, 1978. Reprinted by permission.

tion and "summarize or reinforce response" is the expected counselor response to the "client's example of a goal." That example, in turn, is the client's response to the content. When one combines the ratings of each action unit into a single score and uses it to estimate fidelity to the counseling standard, one assumes that the action units are equally important. That assumption, of course, must be tested.

Another scheme for judging the fidelity of counseling to its standard is the matrix in Figure 8–8, which was constructed by the author to verify the accuracy of a session of Ryan's (1968) case study counseling. Following the scheme in Figure 8–8, one rates each counseling component on four aspects of counselor performance: presenting content clearly, involving clients, evaluating progress, and reinforcing appropriately. A study is now being planned to examine whether the scheme in Figure 6–1 or in Figure 8–8 is more useful for assessing the quality of counseling.

Client progress measures offer additional help in understanding what has occurred in counseling. For example, before completing the segment on goal from the G A I O P exercise, counselors must assure that the client gives an example of a goal that is specified sufficiently. By knowing the client progress measure and how it is scored, a counselor will know whether a general goal statement such as "to become a biology major" is acceptable or whether the counseling requires more detailed specification, such as "to enroll as a biology major before March and to start two intermediate biology courses in April."

A lesson plan is yet another way to remind the counselor of the essential ideas and behaviors and the sequence of their presentation (Healy, 1975). The lesson plan in Figure 6–2 describes goals and corresponding activities. At the minimum, a plan should name or describe materials and exercises used to teach particular concepts or to motivate particular actions and should delineate any response rules peculiar to these exercises. When multiple populations participate in the counseling instruction, their respective activities should be clearly associated with them.

A lesson plan will elucidate whether the organization of the concepts and skills is coherent and sequenced. The clearer the organization and defensible the sequence, it is hypothesized, the more likely it is that counseling will succeed. The visual juxtaposition of concepts and principles with skills and exercises, likewise, can clarify whether it is likely that instruction and feedback will be sufficient to enable a client to learn and carry out a solution before administering the counseling. This should increase the likelihood of success further by enabling modification beforehand. Moreover, since the lesson plan will manifest the complexity of the learning, it will enable the counselor and learner to judge the amount of effort required. Having a blueprint of the task, indeed, should make it more likely that the client will increase self-esteem through counseling. For from the outset, the client will appreciate the magnitude of the accomplishment and personal contribution. Descriptions of the counseling strategies in this book delineate sequentially and

Figure 6–2. Plan for Session 1 of Group Translation Counseling

---

Goals: 1. Clients feel they are part of group.
2. Clients indicate how procedure helps.
3. Each client identifies his work-relevant qualities.

Introduction: Outline procedure—give meeting time.

Activity 1: Members introduce themselves and share their career concerns, a brief career history, and aspirations. Successive clients summarize the highlights of preceding members' introduction before introducing themselves. Throughout the counselor prompts client interaction.

Activity 2: Each member indicates how he perceives the outlined procedure might help him. Start and finish with enthusiastic clients.

Activity 3: Each client identifies his work-relevant qualities.

a) Counselor defines work-relevant quality as attribute to be used in work or satisfied as a consequence of working. He gives examples, such as: learns math quickly, opportunity to make science discoveries, recognition from community, etc. Clients are then asked for additional examples.

b) Counselor asks clients to list the attributes which come to mind. The counselor clarifies that attributes should be activity-specific—like "meeting new people", "solving math problems", rather than general like "having satisfying work", "being challenged", etc.

c) Counselor distributes list of 100 work-relevant qualities and suggests that clients review the qualities in order to add to the list they have started. Counselor suggests that lists be kept to about 15 attributes.

d) Counselor invites clients to share with each other the 4 or 5 qualities that they feel strongly about—to examine with the group what the 4 or 5 qualities say about them and possibly to add additional attributes as consequence of that evaluation.

Summary: A client is asked to summarize and others are encouraged to help if necessary.

Evaluation: a) *Have clients identified each other?*
b) *Has each client indicated how procedure might help?*
c) *Have one or more clients paraphrased outline of procedure?*
d) *Has each client a list of work-relevant qualities?*
e) *Has each client shared and reflected on four or five work-relevant qualities?*

SOURCE: Adapted from Table 2, Plan for Session 1 of Self-Concept Group Career Counseling. In C. C. Healy, *Career Counseling For Teachers and Counselors.* Boston: Houghton Mifflin, 1975, p. 13.

concretely what the counselor does, but they are not cast in strict lesson format because most of the strategies are meant for multiple populations and thus cannot be described as precisely as a lesson.

The Psychological Environment

Counseling occurs within a given environment. From the outset, the client attributes to the counselor a certain trustworthiness and expertise and feels a certain commitment to the goals that will emerge in counseling. Social psychology suggests that the client's trust, credibility, and commitment to goals will depend on the counselor's expertise, which is evidenced by greeting, demeanor, and the counselor status as communicated by title, office location, and furnishings (Strong & Matross, 1973).

Similarly, commitment to the counseling goals and, to a degree, even the election of particular goals, will vary with the status and reputation of the counseling service within the larger institution. Sometimes referral sources and other members of the institution comment directly on counseling. Of course, peer impressions also affect the client's overall expectations about counseling.

Many counseling texts that devote considerable space to initiating the counseling reflect social psychology's findings. These presentations emphasize demeanor and the manner of greeting the client (Williamson, 1939, 1949; Sullivan, 1953b; Tyler, 1969). Almost all agree the counselor should be outreaching, calm but concerned, deliberative, unhurried, and free of interruptions in inaugurating counseling.

Some writers also address the issue of counseling facilities. They recommend comfortable, uncluttered furnishings and stimulating yet warm atmospheres, and stress the importance of privacy.

Few, if any, writers address the issue of status within the institution directly, but most advise counselors to coordinate their efforts with others in their institution, to avoid isolation from institutional goals, to keep administrators and professionals informed about achievement, and to participate in institutional goal setting. Little has been said, however, about developing a strong public image. Perhaps it is obvious that counselors advise their satisfied clients that they would welcome peers with comparable concerns. In any effort to improve image, of course, the counselor should abide by ethical considerations, such as those in the APA Code of Ethics (1977b).

Aiding Transportability

To help others replicate a counseling procedure, that is, to make it transportable; the counselor can provide a chronological narrative of a typical client proceeding through counseling. Such a narrative presents how the intended happening actually occurred. An accompanying commentary can highlight particular elements, helping the counselor to know when counseling is likely to be satisfying and exciting to the client and when the rough spots may occur.

To further communicate the character of a counseling program, one should describe the method used to train counselors. Reading a description of a procedure is not as likely to produce precise administration as applying the treatment on a pilot basis with corrective feedback after every session. Procedures administered with minimal training must depend heavily on the provided materials and/or exercises for their efficacy because a counselor without intense training is likely to communicate only the general ideas and provide only a semblance of the intended atmosphere.

Logical and Empirical Bases of Career Counseling

Very little schooling has been validated by experimental methods; yet schooling is flourishing. The probable reason for this is common sense. As a people, Americans believe that educating human beings to perform more effectively is rational. Current and earlier observations indicate that schooling has contributed to the American rise in world leadership.

Americans put great trust in science and scientific discoveries. Yet the realization that human development is complex and only beginning to be understood apparently permits following folk wisdom in continuing to support reasoned innovation in schooling, even when the empirical evidence becoming available does not show convincingly that extra expenditures and special programs improve students' development appreciably (*Federal Programs Supporting Educational Change*, 1978). Counseling flourishes for the same common-sense reason. The next section discusses establishing counseling's accountability based on logical and empirical evidence.

Logical Basis

In accord with public reliance on common sense to justify education, those who would establish the credibility, if not the validity, of an educational program must explicate its bases in common sense; that is, its rationale and the heuristic principles underlying its operations. Since counseling is special teaching, has minimal experimental support, and is unlikely to amass empirical support in the near future, the credibility of particular counseling strategies can be explained only by pinpointing their unlying heuristic principles.

Traditionally, counseling texts have used client need to justify counseling, but rarely have they shown how and why counseling is likely to address these needs. By delineating the relationship of counseling operations to heuristic principles, a counselor shows why he or she is likely to be helpful. Actually, the linkage clarifies that the counselor is operating in a manner that past (systematic and unsystematic) observations have suggested leads to the goal. (Of course, the argument requires the counselor to show that the operations are performed as claimed.) Certainly, counseling credibility increases when people recognize that its methods and guidance are based on knowledge accumulated over the ages and transmitted through heuristic principles.

Two types of learning principles are involved in counseling: Principles that the counselor follows in creating the counseling program and principles that a client must apply in order to achieve the goal. Principles undergirding the teaching of effective job interviewing, for example, include: providing clear explanations of the interview's purpose, modeling constructive interviewing, emphasizing essential behaviors, showing ways of correcting errors, and praising adequate performance. The principles that the client must apply, on the other hand, include such injunctions as: relate one's aspirations and abilities to the employer's needs in a clear and succinct manner, and communicate interest in employer concerns by attending actively to questions and demonstrating knowledge of the organization in one's statements.

This text lists the heuristic principles on which a counseling procedure is based in introducing the procedure. Many principles that the client needs to apply will become evident from reading the procedure's description and reviewing how people achieve the goals that your client is seeking. By identifying principles on which your counseling is based and the principles you teach through counseling, you enable people to judge whether the counseling has the qualities of a good instruction program. This is essential in establishing accountability.

Research in Career Counseling

Common sense and logic have definite limitations as the foundations of professional practice. They are based on what has been and are our interpretations of such events. Human knowledge is continually expanding and circumstances changing, necessitating ongoing verification of common-sense predictions as well as reexamination of the premises leading to the predictions. Even when empirical observation and hypotheses testing pose problems, they are essential operations in the production of true understanding. Indeed, the counseling profession requires an individual to contribute to knowledge expansion by empirical activities in order to be deemed a professional.

This section comments on career counseling research generally and offers suggestions for removing some obstructions to effective empirical studies. The overview is intended to alert readers to their need to evaluate studies of counseling procedures carefully and to point out typical errors. Although at first the list of shortcoming may discourage you about the viability of the profession, on reflection you will recognize that counseling has only recently become a distinctive facet of education, and that our understanding of it, as of most educational activities, is only emerging.

The counseling research studies pertinent to the counseling methods described in this text follow the description of the methods in Chapters 7 through 12. Unfortunately, as Tolbert (1974), Krumboltz (1966), and others have pointed out, the studies are few and contain serious limitations. The following paragraph enumerates the difficulties that have beset counseling research, in order that you might be sensitive to the pitfalls before evaluating the research pertinent to the career counseling methods presented in Chapters 7 through 12.

For the counseling research shortcomings, references are not made to particular studies. Counseling research is very demanding, requiring extensive preparation, coordination, measurement, analysis, writing, and rewriting, often without pay or other material reward. Perhaps even more difficult is that the counselor-researcher is in actuality trying to disprove personal beliefs; in testing a hypothesis, the researcher is risking its not being sustained. The difficulties in such research should not be extended unnecessarily by my listing the shortcomings in particular studies. Rather than be rebuked, counselor-researchers should be commended for trying what relatively few of their colleagues report trying, even though the professional model of a counselor calls for active participation in research.

The following presentation, however, will not mislead you by covering up shortcomings in particular studies. Rather, when the research is referenced later, the description will include key features of the study, such as sample size, use of control groups, and validated measures; and where control of treatment was accomplished, the description will indicate that rather than report when the treatment was not controlled.

Most counseling studies have serious flaws relating to external validity (generalizability to populations other than the subjects) and sometimes even in internal validity (the data do not justify the conclusions for the current subjects). Regularly, the following errors occur: only small samples of clients have been counseled by a few counselors, who are often only trainees in the role they are implementing; the subjects are volunteers who are meeting a course requirement and are not as anxious as clients seeking help; the researcher does not control the implementation of the counseling role, nor even specify it; objective outcome measures are not used, and clients are not studied after the close of counseling; outcomes peripheral to the counseling goal are studied; counseling studies are rarely replicated, and it is unusual for a counseling role to be refined through formative evaluation; elements or exercises within a counseling treatment are validated, but frequently the total treatment has not been examined as a whole program; often, researches of counseling are designed to examine investigator questions rather than to resolve client problems identified in an intensive intake—indeed, intensive intakes are not usually integral to the counseling treatments which are studied; Consequently, the most that can be concluded about a particular counseling role from the available empirical research is that it has been administered to some clients with favorable outcomes by some counselors.

Especially distressing is the general failure to examine or even speculate about the reasons for some clients not benefiting from particular counseling or the difference between clients who progress substantially and minimally. Since many career counseling procedures are similar in relying on interview and test interpretation, obstructions affecting one procedure would likely thwart progress in other procedures, too, and actions that enhance growth in one procedure would very likely promote growth in others. Client and counselor debriefings about the actions that thwart and bolster growth could at least generate leads about such factors, but for unknown reasons they are rarely reported.

Counseling researchers, moreover, typically have neither delineated nor examined the assumptive network of their counseling procedures. In other words, they have not identified the set of propositions that should be verified in order to judge a treatment valid. Neglecting these procedures has unfortunately reduced the yield of counseling investigations.

Fuller knowledge of a counseling procedure can certainly be obtained through examining its assumptive network. Assumptions that are applicable to many treatments include: experts agree that the components of the treatment will contribute to achieving the target goals; clients with high motivation for the target goal are more likely to benefit than are clients with limited motivation; clients with multiple problems are less likely to realize the counseling goal than are clients with minimal distractions; persons with a history of learning quickly through verbal interaction will benefit more than will other clients; clients who learn or already know and accept the concepts taught through the counseling will make more effective applications; clients who see people in their environment performing the task behaviors are more likely to succeed than are clients whose environment lacks models; and clients attending a larger percentage of regular sessions will benefit more.

In the same vein, many counseling studies have often omitted provision for testing or fully excluding the possibility of alternative explanations of their findings. This, too, reduces the information yield of counseling research. For example, in studying a variation of translation counseling, we gathered data on counselor adherence to the counseling treatment criteria as I had delineated them. We did not gather information about changes in client initiative over these counseling interactions in order to examine views about the counseling process emanating from other perspectives, as for example, the client-centered perspective. Consequently, when analysis (Snodgrass & Healy, 1979) failed to show that close adherence to the counseling treatment yielded greater client benefit, we were unable to examine whether differential client initiative to the counseling interactions related to differential benefit. Clearly, greater forethought about possible alternate explanations would have enabled us to enrich our appreciation of the procedure from this study.

The limitations of counseling studies arise partly because counseling: (a) is complex; (b) cannot be fully investigated by existing designs; (c) takes a long time; (d) has outcomes that are often subjective and rarely dramatic; and (e) is expensive.

Complex Process. Every counseling case contains multiple elements—conversation, nonverbal behavior, exercises, assignments—that express multiple ideas and feelings. Ideally, these ideas and feelings are integrated by the counselor into a purposeful, individualized teaching program. Often, it is difficult to pinpoint the element of counseling that relates to a particular idea or feeling. Elements frequently overlap and are multipurpose; often more than one element is used to communicate an idea or to induce a feeling in order to assure counseling success, even though this approach may be overteaching. Marsden (1971) has reviewed the many efforts to isolate essential elements in counseling and psychotherapy, but to date available research has only identified consistently the so-called "facilitative conditions" (Carkhuff, 1972) as crucial to outcomes.

Counseling's complexity also complicates both verifying that a particular counseling program occurred and replicating a procedure. Only careful treatment monitoring by trained personnel can establish that treatment essentials are provided. Not only is this monitoring costly, but also it may be distracting for counselors who do it themselves. Definitely, a counselor must plan to assure that treatment monitoring aids, rather than interferes with, client growth. Providing for replication requires the same detailed description of procedures plus gathering extensive background information about the client and goal. Again, forethought is necessary to assure that concern about replication does not interfere with counseling.

Design. Because counseling is complex, specifying criteria of effective process is difficult and analysis of continuous interdependent data is required. The current experimental and quasi-experimental research designs (Campbell & Stanley, 1963) employed in counseling, including the experimental case study, are not completely responsive to these data. These designs require assessing the client on concrete criteria at different points of counseling and examining whether the client changes on those criteria. In these approaches, much of the information available about counseling is ignored.

At its best, counseling helps a client in many interrelated ways. These gains often are not those the client sought or anticipated; the need for them and the possibility of achieving them often become apparent as counseling progresses. An example is Freshman Freddy, who seeks assistance in choosing a liberal arts major. Fred enters counseling, anticipating that the counselor will select a major for him. In intake, the counselor establishes that Freddy has fuzzy beliefs about how majors are selected, that he has poor information-seeking habits and skills, limited knowledge of information sources, and little notion of how to judge the accuracy and relevance of information to choices. Moreover, he has felt stymied and embarrassed for several months. He has even made three aborted efforts to get information. As counseling progresses in developing information seeking and decision making, Freddy feels strong anxiety in asking authorities such as librarians for help in locating materials. As a consequence, counseling incorporates desensitization exercises to enable Freddy to use such information sources.

Current statistical research designs for studying counseling do not fully accommodate Freddy's case. If he acquired information-seeking, processing, and decision-making skills, and as a result elected to delay his decision until sophomore year so he could use the remainder of freshman year for exploring options through introductory courses, his outcome could be judged unsatisfactory. Such misjudgment about benefit might happen if Freddy were one of several clients in an investigation using a factorial design with dependent variables, such as change in certainty of major and choice of a major consistent with his measured characteristics.

Even if Freddy's case is scrutinized by the experimental case-study method, his growth may not be verifiable, since the investigator may be focusing on readily quantifiable variables, such as number of contacts with information sources before, during, and after counseling, or change in certainty about major. With the former variable, the three productive information contacts during counseling will not appear statistically different from the three aborted ones before counseling. Obviously, certainty about major will also remain constant, since he is appropriately delaying choice until he has more information. A more observant investigator, of course, might have tested Freddy after every session to determine the number of correct beliefs Freddy had about choosing, his knowledge of information sources and processing, and his knowledge of decision making. Then, if the number of sessions was limited to six or seven sessions, typical for such counseling, the number of observations would be so small that a very powerful change on the test scores would be required to establish the growth as statistically significant.

The difficulty with the experimental and quasi-experimental designs is that they cannot accommodate nonquantifiable, changing objectives over the instructional process. To employ factorial designs, counseling researchers have had to select group objectives, hoping that they are appropriate for all the clients, or they have had to choose the objectives before counseling started, even though the relative importance of the objective to individual clients can only be estimated.

Preestablishing counseling objectives has led to many situations in which effective counseling was not substantiated, or perhaps effective counseling was not even delivered. Hal's case illustrates this problem. He reported that he was unsure of a major and randomly was assigned to Freddy's treatment. More pressing for Hal, however, were his poor study habits and limited social life. He had difficulty concentrating and learning information seeking and performed poorly from the outset. His deficiencies were similar to Freddy's, but the more pressing concerns interfered with his learning. His inability to progress obfuscated the value of the treatment. Moreover, since treatment had to focus on improved career choice making in accord with the design, the counselor did not try to treat Hal's prime needs. In her dissertation, Vivel (1975) showed the impact on a study of subjects like Hal. Vivel found that students demonstrably in need of study-habit development differed substantially in their motivation to build study skills. Not unexpectedly, their priorities related significantly to outcomes, with the result that students who accorded study skills low priority achieved minimal gains in study skills. When the total treatment group was contrasted with controls, the low priority clients' scores lowered the treatment mean to a point below significant difference.

Because of the limitations of the designs presented above, other research designs are being explored. The alternatives themselves have many shortcomings and are unlikely to replace the factorial designs as the preferred research designs in the near future. To give the reader a sample of what the alternatives can offer, the most widely publicized alternative, the adversary method, is described and illustrated below.

Levine (1974) and others have proposed that one way of augmenting experimental design is to scrutinize research and evaluation findings in a scientific hearing. In such a hearing, an advocate and adversary would argue for and against accepting a hypothesis; a hearing officer would moderate; and a jury or the hearing officer would decide whether the hypothesis should be accepted or rejected. Or, viewed differently, reasoned judgment would replace the statistical test. Such judgment, of course, might require that counseling produce more change than the statistical yardstick would require, or it might be more lenient, lacking appreciation of how much change might be due to regression or other sampling fluctuations.

The idea of nonstatistical analysis has been greeted enthusiastically by some (Goldman, 1978), but no consensus has been reached about how the adversary model should operate effectively, since only a few published studies have used it (Wolf, 1975). Disappointingly, reactions of theoretical investigators who have scrutinized the adversary method are unfavorable. Critics note that the design is very expensive (Popham & Carlson, 1977; Kourilsky, 1973); that too many issues (admissibility of evidence, numbers and types of verdicts to be delivered, and the like) have not been thought through and cannot be borrowed readily from law, since procedures regarding such matters have evolved in law over several hundred years (Popham & Carlson, 1977; Arnstein, 1975); that the acceptance or rejection of a hypothesis could depend more on the prowess of the advocate or adversary, or the competence and bias of the hearing officer and jury than on the merits of the evidence (Popham & Carlson, 1977); and that the desire to win rather than to establish truth might interfere with the operation of the model (Levine, 1973). Critics, especially Popham and Carlson (1977), propose remedies but still remain unconvinced that the adversary approach should be considered equivalent to traditional statistical designs. Among the suggested remedies are these: 1) have advocate and adversary present both the pro and con arguments; 2) do not use juries and hearing officers who are likely to be biased; 3) do not present too many hypotheses; 4) restrict verdicts to yes or no decisions.

Advantages attributed to the adversary model by Levine (1973) and others include: 1) consideration of the full range of pertinent data, many of which are often omitted in statistical treatments, either because they are not quantifiable or are not available for all cases and are presumed discounted by randomization; 2) consideration of the total context that impinges on the study and the subsequent results; 3) multiple perspective review provided by the adversarial procedure with consequent heightened awareness of alternative explanations and interpretations; 4) flexibility to evaluate hypotheses and to consider testimony and variables that emerge as important while the study is underway; and 5) full development of the data in a manner analogous to the way in which a structured interview permits development of responses that a questionnaire does not.

Clearly, definition and refinement of the adversary procedure are needed before it has the same value as the experimental and quasi-experimental designs have in uncovering knowledge. Nevertheless, even now the notion of subjecting a study to adversary scrutiny can help counselors to formulate better studies. Consequently, the following section is a projection of how an adversary proceeding might be applied to evaluate counseling.

This illustration continues with the case of Freddy. First, select an adversary, an advocate, and a hearing officer, all of whom are knowledgeable about counseling. In conference, they would decide on the hypothesis to be examined, admissible evidence, when the adversary would have access to the evidence, and how the hearing would proceed. In the case of Freddy, they might decide the hypothesis is that Freddy's career development benefited from counseling. Evidence would have to show there was growth in career development reasonably attributable to counseling rather than to other causes, such as compatibility of counselor-client personality or extraneous circumstances. The evidence need not, however, indicate that counseling was more beneficial than other services, or was incremental or cost efficient.

In regard to admissibility of evidence, the conferees might agree that the adversary could question the counselor and client about counseling after the end of counseling, and could cross-examine advocate witnesses, and that both adversary and advocate could call witnesses who were likely to contribute substantial evidence and whose appearance Freddy agreed would not violate his right to privacy. They might also concur that the adversary could examine all documentation pertaining to counseling, including counselor notes and tape records, and could ask that the counselor obtain measures or unobtrusive observations that involved reasonable effort and that could reasonably be expected to support alternative explanations.

These ground rules would optimally be established before the actual counseling. Following counseling, the advocate could describe the course of counseling, have Freddy and the counselor testify concerning the accuracy of the description, have the librarian testify about Freddy's changed approach to requesting service, and submit Freddy's notes from his information-seeking efforts before and after counseling.

In response, the adversary could proceed as follows. He could question whether Freddy received a complete diagnosis, perhaps listening to the tape of the session or even interviewing Fred; he could challenge expansion of Fred's goal (acquiring more information and subsequently developing information skills) on the basis of arguments such as "Fred was simply accepting the suggestion as a further means of delaying a difficult decision." In reply, the counselor might marshall findings from the diagnosis to support the contentions about Fred; such as, "Fred's answers to questions about majors and sources of information were often erroneous; he weighed suggestions, taking some, declining others; his mood improved on hearing that he would be helped to choose rather than be given a major."

In subsequent reviews, the adversary could challenge various inferences and question whether the pertinent evidence was complete or even being accumulated. In regard to Freddy's apparent improvement in obtaining cooperation from librarians, for instance, the adversary might wonder whether there had been enough time in desensitization to expect such a change; whether the apparent gains were not due to other factors, such as transfer of librarians, offer of help by the librarian, Fred's visiting the library with a girlfriend who assisted him, or expansion of a course's requirement for library research so that the only alternative to not asking the librarian's aid was failure in class assignments. Finally, when counseling discontinued and Freddy enrolled in exploratory courses in order to acquire "hands-on" information for deciding, the adversary could again raise the issue of whether Fred was procrastinating. He could also challenge whether Fred had a rationale for electing the classes or was simply pursuing the counselor's advice, whether Fred had corrected his misbeliefs about choosing a major, and whether his distress had abated.

If only testimony from Freddy and the counselor were available, the adversary might even ask for cognitive testing of Fred regarding choosing and exploring through classes or might even ask that Fred's acquaintances be questioned about alleged changes in Fred's mood. And, of course, the adversary would ask that the counselor show evidence that other possible explanations, such as approach of holidays, unexpected high grades, thriving romance, or athletic success, were not accounting for improved grades and that advice from home or peer, or some other help, was not accounting for apparent cognitive gains.

The inability of its designs to accommodate changing objectives has also prevented counseling research from establishing the extent of the counseling gains. In Freddy's case, for example, he not only developed information-gathering and processing skills but also learned how to interact productively with resource persons, a skill that will be useful throughout his career. This gain, however, normally would not be credited to counseling in current research designs. Counseling, therefore, needs additional research designs to accommodate the common-place phenomenon of multiple, related, personalized objectives established at different points of the counseling process.

Time. Productive counseling generally runs at least several sessions. Memory research suggests extensive forgetting occurs between sessions, especially interview sessions, and certainly multiple opportunities exist for noncounseling inputs. Controlling a whole counseling interaction is therefore difficult; and it is tempting instead to study isolated elements, although ecological research suggests that, in some cases, isolated treatment elements are not realistic approximations of the actual treatment (Bronfenbrenner, 1977).

Outcomes. Career counseling outcomes are the results of counseling; that is, they are the ways in which clients think, feel, and act and the ways in which their environment supports them after counseling that are reasonable to attribute to having been counseled. Hopefully, they are solutions, as Crites (1976) indicated, but they can be unintended and negative as well as positive and intended. Typically, an outcome is multifaceted. A client not only defines an objective more clearly and realistically as securing an entry accountant position in a CPA firm, for example, but also becomes more confident of personal success in a career, more receptive and spontaneous in talking about the future, less anxious about job seeking, more pleased with other aspects of life, surer about assets and liabilities, and better able to articulate qualifications for accounting. The client's peers and professors also take him or her more seriously.

People engage in career counseling because they are troubled and want to be relieved of their distress. They are neither as happy nor as productive at their work as they would like, or they feel that their career is encroaching on other aspects of their life. They want to produce positive results, move their career forward; but they also want to dispel the unpleasant. Sometimes their dissatisfactions and upsets are minor, and they are availing themselves of an opportunity to improve their situation before problems really arise. Career problems do not always produce ulcers or high blood pressure, but it is not unusual for a career client to be suffering such sensations as irritability, difficulty concentrating or sleeping, eating problems, or sexual dysfunction. Likewise, probing will show that many clients are doing such undesirable things as committing more errors than usual, being late or absent more than is their wont, neglecting family and friends, and fretting or just giving too much time to their career concerns. Alleviation of these unwanted sensations and behaviors is an important part of what the client wants, and counselors need to assess progress in their remediation. Yet in the past, few counselors have listed the reduction in such irritating sensations and behaviors among the career-counseling outcomes. Nevertheless, Crites (1976) said that general adjustment is one of the major classes of career counseling outcomes and reminded counselors that Super (1957) had alluded to the benefits of tension reduction from vocational counseling. One way of improving the evaluation of counseling, therefore, involves having clients, as part of clarifying their feelings, discover which unwanted sensations and behaviors are linked to their career problem and then at the conclusion of counseling having them review the status of the unwanted sensations and behaviors.

Counseling outcomes range from minor to major alterations in the manner in which a person is living. Both a person's receptivity to a change and the capacity to carry it out are doubtlessly a function of the perceived magnitude of change, and the probability of a change depends on the degree to which it requires altering the client's life style and environment.

An apparently similar outcome may require varying amounts of change by different clients. The middle-class college senior choosing to enter a Wall Street brokerage is not nearly as likely to change daily habits and types of acquaintance as is the graduate from a working class family, nor is the middle-aged man changing jobs or even occupations likely to encounter as many new changes in his daily activities and relations as his wife, who is moving from homemaking to paid employment. The outcomes of counseling have a meaning that can only be appreciated by putting them into context, viewing them from the perspective of the person realizing them. Misestimates of the amount of counseling needed and its eventual impact are likely if one simply lumps together the outcomes of heterogeneous clients.

Counseling generally is designed to bring about minor changes in clients, as Tyler (1969), for example, noted when she termed counseling "minimal change therapy." The limited degree of alteration intended by counseling is perhaps most evident in career choice and placement counseling procedures, which seek to have clients identify options that are advances but yet are consistent with who they are and have been. Few career choice counselors try to emulate Arthur Higgins in transforming Pygmalion, and few placement counselors, even Bolles and Crystal (1974), recommend discounting the present and past. Of course, counselors often encourage clients to reinterpret the present and past in an effort to facilitate growth. Great leaps are risky, and counselors are obligated to help clients appreciate the odds of such endeavors as well as to give their services for efforts with a reasonable chance of success. Most counselors, however, will help clients map out strategies whereby they can build themselves up for steep ascents. But even in such climbs, the expectations are that the client will ascend through a series of learning experiences rather than catapult or be catapulted. Counseling methods are designed to smooth transitions and to enable a person to assimilate new capacities and accommodate new operations, following Piaget (1970). Counseling facilitates a person's use of system resources; it does not challenge the legitimacy of the system or try to provide substitute resources.

Career counseling needs a scale that can gauge the personal impact of particular changes. The Holmes and Rahe Social Readjustment Rating Scale (1967) supports the feasibility of such a scale. Holmes and Rahe had people rate the stressfulness of different events, and then they rank ordered the events and assigned stress values. Subsequent research found higher stress associated with illness. For career counselors, it is noteworthy that being fired at work was rated as more distressing than retirement, which was more stressful than business readjustment and changing one's line of work, which was more stressful than changing job responsibilities, which in turn was more stressful than one's wife starting or changing work, which outranked trouble with one's boss and change in work conditions or hours in stressfulness, all of which were more distressing than change in recreation and social habits or even in eating habits.

Counseling outcomes are often hard to pinpoint and verify and difficult to attribute to counseling. Frequently, outcomes are multifaceted, emerge only as counseling proceeds or are not even anticipated, are not dramatic, and are subjective. Moreover, since clients remain in their environment, which provides assistance with career, and since other people involved in the problem may act independently of counseling, favorable client growth may be fortuitous or may be the result of other people's altering the client's situation.

Full identification and appropriate assessment of outcomes nevertheless are very important for effective and efficient counseling. The intended outcomes set the direction of counseling; and, in combination with the seven aspects of the client's individuality described in phase 1 of counseling, they determine the ingredients of the counseling program.

Early and accurate specifications enable counseling to move surely and quickly toward successful problem resolution; hazy, incomplete objectives delay and obstruct progress. The capacity to assess outcome attainment, on the other hand, enables client and counselor to monitor progress; and recognition of progress sustains the client's commitment to counseling and informs the counselor that counseling is proceeding effectively and can be continued without change.

In addition to not recognizing all the unwanted symptoms associated with a problem, clients often start counseling only vaguely aware of the new status they wish. They are not sure of the alternatives available. A new insurance claims supervisor, for example, started counseling by explaining that she felt unsuited to be a supervisor after two weeks of directing her former colleagues. She hoped something could be done, but she believed she either had to find something that fitted her personality better or return to being a claims adjuster. Only in discussing her situation with the counselor did she recognize that her recent excesses at the coffee pot and sudden sexual dysfunction were probably linked to her career problem. Then, only after she outlined the problem and reflected about what was happening and might be done, did she identify and affirm that she wanted to increase her assertiveness with subordinates.

The fact that counseling outcomes can be unintended as well as intended compounds the difficulty of prearranging measurement already created by the emerging character of outcomes. Avoiding unintended outcomes requires that counselors attend not only to the intended outcomes but also to the client's total situation. Counseling involves selected knowledge and interpretation of events and is organized in a manner that easily fosters dependence. As Bergin (1966) noted, counseling occasionally may be injurious. Clearly, the professional must insure that instruction has no harmful side effects as well as monitor whether it moves the client toward his or her objective.

Complicating outcome monitoring further is the fact that many counseling goals are often only the start of a sequence of events that must be completed before there is noticeable change in the client's situation. Career counseling leads to correcting or improving a career at a specific time. Freddy, for example, is helped over the hurdle of a choice of major, but he is then on his own to implement the choice. Likewise, the counselor will teach Hal, who was introduced in the example illustrating difficulties in research design, a study regimen and will assist him in initiating it; but then Hal, too, will be expected to sustain it without further intervention. The boost to career from counseling brings the clients to the level of normally maturing peers or perhaps even gives them a temporary edge. However, it is unrealistic to demand that the uplift or edge be sustained long after counseling in order to judge counseling beneficial, since a career is a dynamic response to changing opportunities and constraints as well as to innate potential and background.

Remembering that counseling is a learning process that has few trials, often does not achieve mastery, and rarely provides for over-

learning underscores why it is realistic to focus on circumscribed outcomes. Actions, thoughts, feelings, and plans distant in time or situation
from counseling cannot be attributed to counseling with the same confidence as can immediate events.

This is not to say that counseling does not contribute to long-term
career development and management. Effectively counseled persons who
commit themselves to following through on counseling's teachings
should be more likely to apply their special learning and should even fare
better than will comparable persons who had encountered similar obstructions but had not received effective counseling. Clients, for instance, who corrected planning deficiencies in information gathering
and processing should subsequently be more likely to gather and weigh
information than will their deficient peers. But even though their planning operations are better and their perspective more realistic and positive, their accomplishments, especially those distant from counseling,
could easily be indistinguishable. This is because many factors besides
effective planning affect career achievement and because career achievement is so important to society that the leaders designed a mechanism
to move people into positions wherein they are successful, even when
they do not plan effectively.

Who is likely to follow through effectively is predictable, although
career counseling studies have not yet become so refined as to be pursuing the issue. In addition to the number of learning trials with counseling and the closing mastery level, other learning variables such as
number and schedule of reinforcements during and after counseling,
the similarity of subsequent problem contexts, the recognition of
esteemed models applying counseling's teachings, and the client's incorporation of the teachings will affect maintenance. For instance, the
student teacher who mastered dealing with supervisory teachers through
counseling and went on to a series of teaching positions wherein he
again applied counseling's teachings is more likely to manifest effective
supervisory relations than is a student teacher who achieves comparable
mastery but took a series of sales and advertising jobs in which supervisory interaction was minimal or than is a student teacher who registered similar mastery but vows to be himself in dealing with authority
after he secures his credential.

Although clients and the public hope for enduring solutions from
counseling, although the immediate outcomes may not be as dramatic
as an advertising agency might wish, although the worth of what is
learned and applied through counseling may not be apparent unless the
client follows through successfully, and although studies such as Campbell's (1973) suggest that career counseling sometimes confers long-
term advantage, direct judgments about the consequences of counseling
can be more certain if we examine the client at the close of counseling.
If one evaluates the effectiveness of teaching in a particular subject
such as calculus, for instance, one tests differentiating skill soon after
instruction. One does not judge the effectiveness of instruction in differentiation by testing the student's capacity to integrate, even though
these are closely linked operations, and one would expect that good

instruction in differentiation would facilitate learning integration. Analogously, direct evaluation of counseling outcomes should improve by pinpointing the corrections and improvements the client has made, is making, or plans to make at the close of counseling.

Needless to say, direct, immediate outcome verification is taxing because it requires very careful, focused attention to the trend of a client's career. Counselors must sensitize themselves to nuances of developmental processes. Since these processes are not yet well delineated, moreover, counselors not only will have to search out small growth steps, but they will also have to follow up some clients in order to determine whether the processes that counseling helps to launch have high probabilities of achieving the intended benefits.

Accurate, credible outcome assessment can also be problematic when the counseling results are largely subjective. Many clients make "better" plans, feel more confident or certain in what they are doing, correct their interpretation of a situation, and feel better as a consequence of these cognitive and affective actions. Yet, the observable behavior and status of these clients remain the same, and even the degree or reality of their plans as judged, for instance, by congruence with test data may not change over counseling. Only their reports of change and the counselor's ongoing observations testify to the changes. But both of these appraisals are prone to bias, since the counselor and client have a vested interest in change's occurring because they have toiled to produce it. Moreover, the client, out of politeness and perhaps a need to meet expectations, may claim change when none occurred, manifesting the "hello-goodbye" phenomenon. Assuredly, preventing such biases requires observer training and the use of well-designed measures and careful documentation of the operation, with focus on factual events rather than on impressions.

Even the fact that counselor, client, other observers, objective measurements, residuals, and projectives may mark an outcome makes verification cumbersome. Verification is difficult because it will be unusual for two methods to give the same reading, which necessitates using multiple measurement methods and devising a systematic way of reconciling discrepancies. Indeed, since there are few measures of career development and none are yet capable of reliably marking an individual's progress toward such goals, counselors must examine multiple kinds of data about outcome attainment. These data need not be about the same facet of the outcome, although different data about a facet can increase confidence in the judgment.

In turn, inability to isolate clients from their environment in order to control learning exposure as a researcher can control the instructional input to laboratory rats and even to students in special subject classes, complicates ascribing client improvement to counseling. Other experiences and people in the environment may teach concepts and skills that lead to the career progress. For instance, career counseling at Central High blossomed when, unknown to the counselor, the local Scout units initiated occupational exploration programs. Likewise, other people in the environment who are troubled by the client's problem may move independently to correct it. For example, the supervisor who was bothered by a lab technician's persistent, nervous questioning may transfer the technician to a supervisor with whom the technician is very comfortable before the technician can improve through counseling. Or, concerned parents may offer to buy their son a car if he will enter the premed program when they see him wavering between it and a technical program that his high school performance and test scores suggest is more appropriate.

The possibility of such external influences, of course, underscores the importance of ongoing, detailed documentation of the client and his or her situation during counseling in order to be sure that counseling, rather than other fortuitous events, affects career growth. Even studies with control groups require careful monitoring, since being counseled may induce other people to provide special teaching or to intervene in the problem that prompted counseling. In the examples above, the Scout leaders, for instance, assigned occupational exploration projects only to those Scouts receiving counseling, and the parents offered the car only after learning that their son sought counseling because he could not decide his career direction.

To alleviate problems in monitoring counseling outcomes, this text recommends that the counselor develop a comprehensive profile of the client in phase 1 of counseling and gather information from different sources pertinent to the profile continuously over counseling. Williamson and Bordin (1940) reported that such a composite was necessary to take account of the individualized character of counseling. With a profile, progress can be gauged by comparing the profiles of the client at the two points of counseling to ascertain whether there is a growth trend (Crites, 1976). Figure 6–3 illustrates how a client profile on the nine sources of a problem described in Stage 1 of counseling on page 181 can be created from a counseling intake record.

Figure 6–3. Developing a Comprehensive Client Profile from Counseling Case Notes

This figure is the initial comprehensive profile of a client in terms of nine sources of career problems. The composite was constructed from the case notes of the first two counseling sessions; these notes appear after the composite.

Client Profile
1. *Unrealistic or unclear goals:* Harry has a realistic goal in terms of abilities and interests. It requires more specificity. Currently there is no plan, and no systematic action has been taken.
2. *Inadequate knowledge, ability, training, or resources:* Harry is equipped to pursue a cooking/restaurant management career, lacking only training and entree. His continued career frustration suggests that he needs help in building decision-making skills.
3. *Insufficient perseverance:* Harry has been considering a choice too long and has not yet begun implementation of an informed choice.
4. *Erroneous beliefs:* Harry recognizes the desirability of obtaining assistance in a career decision, although he may not yet accept the fact that even decisions based on expert advice entail risk.

Figure 6–3. (*Continued*)

5. *System obstructions:* GI benefits, accessibility of training programs, and the growth potential of the restaurant field support Harry's career direction.
6. *Choice anxiety:* Harry's wavering reflects choice anxiety.
7. *Inaccurate/incomplete problem formulation:* Harry appears to be on the verge of correctly identifying choice-making difficulties as his problem.
8. *Interpersonal conflict:* Harry's wife supports his choice. Although his neighborhood socializing will diminish as a result of this change; Harry is not concerned about it.
9. *Inappropriate affect:* Appropriately, Harry is troubled by his difficulty of choosing and is disappointed by past career selections. He is not overwhelmed by these problems and seems rightfully confident about his ability to alter his career direction. His belief that the problem stems from concern about career appears warranted.

Harry is displeased with the lack of stability and direction in his career. At times the problem makes him irritable and depressed, and sometimes thinking about it just makes him want to get drunk. After completing three years as an Army corpsman following high school, he had been a gas station attendant, truck driver, postal clerk, and now is a New York City transit policeman. Although each of these jobs became boring within a year or two, he kept them until he located something better. Now, after only recently completing probation as a policeman, that job is becoming very boring, and again he is wondering what might interest him.

Following more than a year of soul searching, Harry is leaning toward something in the cooking and restaurant industry, and he believes he probably will start night college in order to earn an associate of arts in cooking in order to get started in the field. He is very eager to get his career straightened out, but he is worrying more and more about whether he will make the right decision. He has obtained information about what is involved in cooking and restaurant management training and the New York schools that provide instruction. He thinks he can succeed since cooking has been a long-time hobby and he has been good at schooling, earning As and Bs in a rigorous high school college preparatory program. He knows he is entitled to GI benefits for thirty-six months of schooling, and his discussion with restaurant people and reading have convinced him that the field has good potential.

Harry is thirty, married, and has three preschool children. Even though it would be difficult, his wife is willing to work part-time to augment the GI benefits so that Harry might attend school full time for a year or two in order to enter into a career he likes. Her only condition is that Harry be sure that he really is interested and will not be bored.

Harry has not attended school since the police academy, and he is not sure how much of a strain working, school, and family will be. Although he is a regular at neighborhood softball and basketball games and at the bowling alley, he is resigned to cutting social and sporting activities drastically. He senses that working toward an interesting career will sustain him in school while he is working, even for the three or four years needed to obtain an associate degree.

As he considers it, he is not sure why he is taking so long to start. For some reason he is hesitating, unsure, even of starting part time. Whether to take a leave from the police and attend full time is an even more difficult decision. Since counseling is clarifying his situation, as he expected, he is becoming more convinced that a good decision for him requires getting all the facts and systematically thinking things through with an expert. He does not want to take any chances of making a wrong choice, since he regards past occupational choices as inadequate and believes he can guarantee success with expert advice—something he had not bothered to obtain before.

Counselors can increase the objectivity of evaluation based on the clinical profile in several ways. Neutral parties can compile client descriptions from counseling tapes and records, and/or they can keep judges naïve about whether a profile describes the client before or after counseling. Counselors also can improve clients' contributions to a profile by giving them instruction in self-observation and by furnishing them with well-defined rating scales. Clients usually have not received observation training; the limited evidence indicates that brief training and discussion of scales will increase agreement about the meanings of ratings (Sherwood, 1966). For example, the following certainty scale will enable more precise understanding of a client's certainty than will a number defined only by the extremes of uncertain (1) and certain (5).

> This rating helps you report your certainty about your career choice when you think about or are asked what your choice is. Rate 5 if you think or name your occupation or cluster of occupations immediately without qualification or reservation and with a feeling of conviction that you will enter such an occupation, based upon past calm reflection; rate 3 if you think or say your choice hesitatingly or with qualification, feeling some uneasiness about wanting or being unable to accomplish it; rate 1 if you are not yet able or are unwilling to name one occupation or cluster of occupations as the kind of work you will commit yourself to doing for an extended period of time, and rate 2 or 4 to indicate you are midway between 1 and 3 or 3 and 5 respectively.

When groups of clients are seeking similar outcomes, counselors should use scales of the new career development tests to complement ratings and reports. Appendix A describes several of these tests, which also are reviewed in the *Eight Mental Measurements Yearbook* (Buros, 1978). Scores from these tests will enable using parametric statistics in testing the effectiveness of career counseling.

Cost. Careful counseling research requires many hours of professional counselor time, ongoing cooperation of clients who are under stress, extensive data gathering and processing, and clear presentation of results. Professional counselors' time costs up to $50/hour; and research participation can consume many hours, so reliance on volunteer clients is risky. Professional associations have not yet mandated a specified number of hours per year be spent in research, a policy that would aid research. Likewise, research demands on clients are arduous and sensitive, so many clients understandably are unwilling or unable to devote the extra time and to endure the extra stress. The computer has simplified data analysis enormously, but data gathering may require several trained observers. Finally, reporting the research in the clear, interesting, nontechnical terms frequently demanded by journal editors often takes several more weeks, since the researcher is unlikely to have professional writing skills.

Unfortunately, funding for career counseling research is meagre. Although funding for career counseling practice is greater, these funds are usually part of a larger program allocation, administered by a non-counselor, who often economizes on counseling and usually spends little money to validate the counseling done. Rarely do such projects attempt to extend counseling knowledge. Examples are the funding of career counseling under the Vocational Education Acts, 1963, 1968, and 1976 amendments, and under the CETA and other employment service programs of the U.S. Department of Labor, and funding in most university student service programs, in which a dean of students or placement officer controls career counseling.

These difficulties have limited the study of counseling severely and have prevented justification of counseling on empirical bases. The *raison d'être* of counseling still rest on the realization that professionals knowledgable about career development should be able to guide the many people who need assistance in coping with everyday tasks such as those of career development.

This section has presented the rationale of identifying heuristic principles for particular counseling strategies and has noted the major shortcomings of counseling research. As part of the description of counseling procedures in subsequent chapters, therefore, supporting heuristic principles are identified and pertinent research is referenced. Following that, possible hazards associated with a procedure are noted, and suggestions for minimizing the hazards are presented.

How the Counseling Profession Can Improve Its Research

To close this chapter on research and evaluation, four steps the career counseling profession can take to upgrade research are now discussed.

First, the profession must realize that research and evaluation of career counseling are inadequate and should make upgrading its knowledge base a major priority. Counseling textbook writers should describe evidence supporting different practices fully enough for the reader to evaluate, rather than simply noting the claimed finding and reference, without even making clear that the finding is only claimed. The current practice surely overrepresents the support for counseling. Similarly, reports and convention presentations should document assumptions and findings more fully. By improving its standards of evidence now, the counseling profession can indicate its professionalism in upgrading and regulating itself, whereas inattention to evidence will leave career counseling very vulnerable when public auditors start their examinations.

A second action the profession can take is to encourage and even to support financially empirical studies of counseling. This support entails giving first priority to such studies in its journals, levying its members for such research, and coordinating multistate or multiuniversity researchers. Currently, counseling journals, eager to maintain status in the social science and educational community, seek reports of studies that are internally valid, or articles that are interesting, provocative, or at least "relevant." These policies, however, encourage "data crunchers" who inventory the introductory psychology pool, manipulate a condition, retest and then compute, and report as significant, relationships that have contributed only minimally to counseling; or they promote philosophizing and propagandizing about issues that are often peripheral to counseling. Certainly, the policies discourage investigators from risking time in case studies or field researches of counseling wherein they may have only partial control or small samples. Such studies may not be as incontestable as the better controlled research, but surely these systematic examinations of counseling would offer more valuable suggestions for counseling. The recent *Personnel and Guidance Journal* article of Richard Johnson (1978) on individual styles of decision making suggests that journal editors are becoming aware of this need to support empirically based reflection even when the study does not meet the canons of experimental design.

Perhaps, even more direct help for research could come from imposing a small levy, ($10 per professional) to support counseling research. Currently, several state counselor associations have substantial surpluses, some of which might be used to develop the knowledge base of career counseling. Surely, foundations would support such research more readily if the counseling profession underwrites at least some of its cost. To undertake such solicitation, the profession might set up committees as it now commissions administrative and legislation committees to conduct the research and evaluation of particular practices. The example of APGA's informational system and sponsorship of the national assessment effort demonstrates the feasibility of this approach. Moreover, Division 17 of APA, NVGA, and other APGA divisions are likely to impress granting institutions that they have the administrative resources, visibility, and the possibility of involving expert counseling researchers needed to tackle some of the more difficult counseling questions.

Third, the profession must involve its member more in research, perhaps even mandating that counselors allot a certain number of hours a year to participating in research studies. Certainly many studies of counseling and psychotherapy suffer because they employ trainees rather than veteran counselors (Meltzoff & Kornreich, 1970). Similarly, most counselors with doctorate degrees do little or no research after their dissertation, even though they still profess to follow the practitioner-scientist model.

Fourth, after setting its own house in order, the profession can monitor counseling funding by government agencies. Historically, federal programs and funding have exerted a powerful influence on counseling, but those policies appear contradictory. At first glance, for instance, the Veterans Administration appears to have been most benevolent to counseling, whereas funding policies of the Department of Education and the Department of Labor apparently have kept counseling subordinated to school and agency administration. These policies have limited counseling funding while allowing counseling to become the scapegoat for poor educational and manpower programs. Certainly, the profession must ask why so many of the federally funded researches on counseling are not disseminated through counseling journals but are presented only in limited edition, small circulation papers and reports. Recent APGA criticisms about CETA counseling operations show the profession is starting to accept its responsibility to be vigilant (*Guidepost*, 1978).

CAREER COUNSELING PROCEDURES THROUGH THE LIFE STAGES

part three

Over the career, a person's capabilities and challenges change. The concept of career stages proposes that people in a particular stage share common challenges and have similar career competences. Consequently, distinctive career counseling methods are likely to be appropriate for each stage. Part Three (Chapters 7–12) describes counseling methods that have helped people in different stages of career.

Each chapter enumerates concerns, challenges, and career competences that are characteristic of people at a distinctive stage and then describes appropriate counseling methods. The descriptions of counseling specify both the ideas and the operations counselors have used. Such specification enables readers to understand what particular treatments involve so they can apply the method as it is intended to be used.

The detailed specifications free practitioners to apply the methods creatively rather than strait jacket them in canned operations. Individual client and counselor differences necessitate adapting methods to fit individual learning and teaching styles. In fact, many counselors will rework a method to use it effectively; they are not obliterating the method, but putting their mark on it, in the way an artesian crafts an object from a design. A comprehensive picture of counseling methods, therefore, frees the counselor to individualize rather than having to rediscover what other counselors have already learned.

Accompanying each counseling description is a list of the heuristic principles of teaching and learning, which are the rationale for the method. These principles will help the reader to comprehend the intention of the technique, and will make it easier to identify alterations likely to be consistent with the method. More importantly, they will help counselors to justify applying a particular method because identification of the rationale shows the counseling method is based on accepted views of how learning takes place.

To aid accountability even further, each chapter in Part Three also offers a comprehensive review of the published studies of the counseling method and lists its potential hazards. The reviews identify important aspects of a study's design and treatment, such as the number and kinds of clients and counselors, length of treatment and control of delivery, and measured outcomes, so that the reader can draw individual conclusions about a study's implications regarding effectiveness and transferability of the method. The list of hazards, in turn, should remind counselors to collect information about harmful side effects in order to prevent them, and to remember that, in some instances, interventions other than counseling may be more appropriate.

Finally, to help counselors evaluate counseling programs at each stage, every chapter contains a list of objectives that are appropriate to the tasks of that stage. These lists are in tables accompanied by suggested measures, or methods of measurement when measures are not available, and by notation of studies that measured the objectives.

Growth Stage Career Counseling

7

Free associate to a five- to twelve-year-old youngster, if "employed," "unemployed," "worker," or "career" came to mind, the child is very unusual. Even Lucy's clientele in the Charlie Brown gang rarely request help in career planning or career problem solving.

In urban and suburban America, parents hope their youngsters are learning, not earning. They know the children are growing and require tender, loving care. Generally, parents delight in giving such care along with religious instruction, dancing and music lessons, scouting, camps, vacations, Little League, and all kinds of toys. They also know that children need chores and an allowance, as well as less television and more adult interaction; but parental distaste for supervision and book-keeping often makes them lax in providing for these needs.

Even though one may ask a child what he or she is going to do when grown, few parents make serious provision for a child's entering a particular occupation. Going to work is something that many youngsters want to do, and indeed by age thirteen, more than half have applied for some kind of job and nearly all have done some paid work (Mitchell, 1977). However, regular employment, even on permit, is still a few years away. Yet an understanding of people's relation to work increasingly indicates that these are important years in career. Attitudes, skills, self-concepts, and habits that influence future career progress are being created. Moreover, the democratic right to choose the nature of one's work increasingly presumes that in these years youngsters are amassing a broad appreciation of educational and occupational opportunities and their interrelation; at the same time, they should be learning and practicing the rudiments of planning and decision making. Predictably, therefore, society has moved to provide career education and guidance for elementary schoolers.

This chapter reviews the theories about career development of young-sters in the growth stage; and describes counseling roles that can help youngsters succeed in the tasks of this stage. The roles are interrelated and sometimes overlapping, but are conceptually distinct. They include career awareness counselor, consultant, needs assessor, and special project officer. Parents and teachers are the principal socializing agents besides television; and unless staffing patterns of elementary schools change drastically, teachers will remain the student's major school con-tact. Both parents and teachers are well intentioned, interested, and capable of assisting youngsters to have positive experiences in learning, exploring career options, identifying models, remedying deficits, and erecting an integrated, accurate self-concept worthy of esteem. Through consulting, counselors can collaborate with these groups by informing them about materials and programs and by joining them to establish the programs.

Regardless of how much consulting a counselor does, he or she will still need to act as a special project's officer, organizing and conducting an educational operation such as a cross-age tutoring program to aid remediation and to strengthen self-confidence; conducting group sessions on the new career options for women and minorities; or overseeing a school simulation of an economic community. Frequently, only a coun-selor has the schedule flexibility to manage the project, and only the counselor has the educational background and broad developmental perspective to carry it out.

Often, the counselor will be the one most able to manage a school's programs for assessing its students' career development and for pro-viding students with ongoing records of their career-related achieve-ments. Such functions contribute directly to pinpointing remediation needs and to helping youngsters become conscious of achievements and increasingly cognizant of their potential for creating themselves through achievements. Without such services, career development deficits may go undetected, and youngsters may not recognize that their development is a continuous process, which they can monitor and influence as they wish.

Still another role that may be an outgrowth of the counselor's schedule flexibility, responsibility for students across grades, and contact with all parents, is that of resource coordinator. The community, through its voluntary groups and businesses, often offers many resources that can be used to promote students' career development if someone can organize and coordinate their use.

Clearly, one counselor cannot perform all these roles at one time. Counselors, however, have played each of these roles in the elementary school. In this chapter, the roles of self-awareness counselor, consultant, special project officer, and assessment manager are described, along with research pertinent to them. In the next chapter, the coordinator's role is described, since that role often is more appropriate to the junior or senior high school, where strong community involvement in career development is even more essential.

Career Counseling in the Elementary School

Career counseling for elementary school youngsters, started when guidance and counseling services moved into the elementary school under the Elementary and Secondary School Act of 1965, became a major focus of elementary school guidance in the 1970s. Not surprisingly, its knowledge base is just developing, and its methods necessarily are experimental.

So far, objectives of career counseling for elementary school children have been based largely on evolving theories of career development and opinions of educators and community leaders about the competences and experiences which lead to a successful adult career. Doubtlessly, these judgments reflect multiple, informal task analyses of a career in modern society.

Needless to say, career development objectives for elementary schoolers vary widely because of their origins (Hoyt, 1973). Many states have adopted broad objectives; each of these formulations is, in some ways, different from all the others. Yet there is also a growing consensus that career development includes the broad themes of deepening appreciation of, and confidence in, self in relation to others and to work; awareness of educational and occupational opportunities and the operation of our educational-work system; ongoing, increasingly more sophisticated information acquisition and processing; planning and decision making; vocational and general skill development; positive attitudes toward working; and acceptance of responsibility to direct one's own career. Indeed, after reviewing extensive career education literature and practice, Hansen (1977) concluded that career education could best be defined as

> a continuous lifelong person-centered process of developmental experiences focused on seeking, obtaining, and processing information
> • about self (values, interests, abilities)
> • about occupational-educational alternatives
> • about life-style and role options
> • about socioeconomic and labor market trends, and
> • engaging in purposeful planning
> • in order to make reasoned decisions about work
> • and its relation to other life roles
> • with benefit to self and society.

Such broad themes imply that the career development of elementary youngsters requires opportunities to experience success in many diverse activities; to build basic academic, social, and self-management skills; to secure help with deficiencies quickly in order to keep up with accelerating challenges; to obtain information about diverse occupations and training programs; to identify and emulate positive models; to begin sorting experiences into an accurate, esteemed, evolving picture of self; and to begin recognizing ways of directing time and energy so that one increasingly controls who he or she is becoming. Comprehensive lists of objectives, such as the one produced by the American Institute of Research (Dunn et al., 1973) and state career education curriculum guides, such as those of Arizona, California, Hawaii, Michigan, New York, Texas, Wisconsin, all include these types of broad experiences.

Unquestionably, the broad career development experiences recommended here for elementary schoolers fit easily into the traditional elementary school curriculum. That curriculum has long sought to imbue basic academic, social, vocational, and citizenship skills, and to acquaint youngsters with the world around them. The major changes that formal career education and elementary school guidance and counseling have created are systematic attention to career development and deliberate coordination. For, in launching formal career education, a school or district ideally completes a needs assessment and constructs a plan that brings school and community together for coordinated delivery of career education. Such a plan includes setting objectives, training and coordinating staff and community contributors, obtaining or creating materials, measuring process outcomes, and analyzing and evaluating feedback to improve the emerging program.

Theoretical Bases of Early Career Development Counseling

Theories of childhood development support the need for the career development activities in the elementary school years. Havighurst (1953) has listed the following as tasks of middle childhood in our culture: learning physical skills necessary for ordinary games, developing wholesome attitudes toward self, getting along with agemates, acquiring fundamental skills in reading, writing and calculating, becoming aware of appropriate sex role; developing concepts necessary for everyday living, a conscience, morality and a scale of values; and forming attitudes toward social groups and institutions. Erikson (1950), in turn, termed middle childhood the period of industry vs. inferiority. He wrote:

> The child learns to win recognition of producing things. . . .
> He develops industry. . . . He can become an eager and involved unit of a production situation. His ego boundaries include his tools and skills: [he learns] the pleasure of work completion by steady attention and persevering diligence. The danger, at this stage, lies in a sense of inadequacy and inferiority.

In terms of cognitive development, Piaget (1970) has pointed out the importance during this stage of far-ranging, concrete experiences to equip the child for increasingly abstract conceptual operations.

Looking at childhood from a career perspective, but like Erikson (1963), influenced by the psychoanalytic orientation, Ginzberg, Ginsburg, Axelrod, and Herma (1951) theorized that childhood is a time of fantasy wherein youngsters engage in activities because they are intrinsically satisfying and express occupational choices without regard to their reality. By age ten to twelve, however, it is apparent that the youngster has moved from a "play orientation" to a "work orientation," such that preteens increasingly pursue activities that are socially valued. In the ensuing years, youngsters are predicted to grow in awareness and deliberation, learning to accommodate their desires to existing possible activities, which was first construed as compromising and later (Ginzberg, 1972) as optimizing (opting for a desired possibility rather than seeking a more desirable but improbable option). During these years, different self-attributes become prominent. Specifically, from age eleven to twelve, youngsters focus on likes and dislikes; from thirteen to fourteen, they emphasize abilities; from fifteen to sixteen, they attend to values; and then from seventeen to eighteen, they increase their attention to career decision-making and the consequences of their choices. After examining the research evidence for this theory, Osipow (1973) concluded that the findings offered mixed support, but that overall, the theory has heuristic value in underscoring the theme of development in career and promoting research. Summing up the findings of pertinent studies, Osipow (1973) noted that "there does seem to be evidence suggesting that boys emphasize different kinds of experience, in their vocational development at various age levels. There also appears to be reason to believe that boys must compromise their career preferences in deference to the reality of the world they observe. The evidence is mixed, however, with respect to specifically what the stages are, when they occur, and the order in which they occur" (p. 98).

Research Bases of Early Career Counseling

Minimal direct research on the career development of elementary schoolers has been done. Three longitudinal studies of eighth and ninth graders' career development by Super et al. (1957, 1960, 1969), Gribbons and Lohnes (1968), and Flanagan et al. (1964, 1966, 1971) indicate the achievements that youth has accomplished by the end of the growth stage, and recent descriptive surveys of nine- and thirteen-year-olds are relevant and offer some information about the period. The longitudinal studies are summarized in Chapter 8, and the survey results are presented here. Although these studies are only suggestive about the themes and activities that are essential if the child is to be equipped for the career tasks imposed by our system, they at least warn that some career education goals may be unrealistic. In other words, the research not only suggests aspects of career maturity to bolster, but also alerts parents and counselor to an equal responsibility to identify and remove unrealistic demands from the system.

The need to take account of children's developmental capability in deciding on career education programs was recently illuminated. After a review of quality career education program, Schager (1976) found evidence suggesting that some career education objectives for elementary schoolers might be beyond their capacity, stated the following tentative conclusions:

1. Participation in career education appears to have a positive influence on self concept and general awareness, especially in primary grades, yet the nature of the career education programs and/or the manner in which they were evaluated does not follow linking particular career education treatments with particular gains.
2. Career exploratory activities are likely to benefit middle and junior high schoolers, but not elementary schoolers. Their attitudes toward work and careers, their ability to relation occupational options to their own interests and their ability to make realistic choices seem unaffected by such activities.
3. K–12 students respond favorably to participating in career education programs. Their attitudes toward career education and school appear to improve with increased exposure to career education programs and services (129, 130).

The Career and Occupational Development Assessment of the National Assessment of Educational Progress. In 1973–74, a national sample of 28,000 nine-year-olds, 38,000 thirteen-year-olds, 34,000 seventeen-year-olds in school, and 1,000 out of school, and 2,000 adults (ages twenty-six through thirty-three) answered questions related to their career developments. Selected assessment results for nine-year-olds (Miller, 1977) and thirteen-year-olds (Aubrey, 1977) follow; results for seventeen-year-olds and adults are reported in Chapters 8 and 11, respectively.

1. In regard to career decision making, most nine- and thirteen-year-olds identified two strengths and weaknesses. Their strengths and limitations clustered in the categories of group sports, individual sports, art and music, and academic skills. At age nine, more boys than girls were able to list their strengths, but this difference disappeared by age thirteen.
2. In regard to improving abilities, about 66 percent of the nines and 75 percent of the thirteens have made efforts to improve something they wanted to do better.
3. Nine-year-olds had few methods of self-evaluation. At nine and at thirteen, girls judged themselves more often than boys by what others said about them, whereas boys relied more on comparisons with other persons or on objective criteria.
4. Knowledge of the duties of visible occupations is high by age nine and very high by thirteen. Yet thirteen-year-olds are not able to differentiate among visible occupations in terms of earning power.

5. Most thirteen-year-olds could relate at least one of their abilities and one of their school courses to work, even though the realism of the relationship is often questionable.

6. About 70 percent of the nines and 80 percent of the thirteens have had at least one out-of-school training experience.

7. More than half the thirteen-year-olds have tried to find a part-time or summer job, and nearly 90 percent have worked for pay.

8. Most nines and many thirteens do not perceive themselves as responsible for their own behavior, although thirteens take responsibility in some cases.

9. Most nines and the majority of thirteens show initiative in completing a task, and the majority of thirteens appropriately seek help in doing tasks.

10. Most nines expect other people to select their careers for them, but most thirteens accept that they will select their own life's work.

Counseling for Self-Awareness

In this role, the counselor works directly with the child to help in gathering, evaluating, accepting, and integrating information about self, especially in relation to educational and work activities. Secondarily, through this counseling, the youngster may learn about concepts such as reliability and validity of assessment, the value of obtaining different kinds of feedback, how to build abilities and interests, and environmental circumstances important to ability and interest acquisition.

Many youngsters in supportive families, schools, and communities receive much help in recognizing, accepting, and integrating the feedback from their many experiences into accurate self-pictures. They see parents and significant others integrating feedback, and often are guided informally in this process by those in their milieu. The recent school attention to affective objectives further assists these youngsters by providing them reminders and a forum for self-awareness. As a consequence, they may not need self-awareness counseling.

The new affective education may also help some less advantaged youngsters by giving them the stimulation and direction needed for integrating feedback into constructive self-concepts. Many students, however, will not have affective education, and some who do have so many needs that they will require individualized learning programs.

Accurate, comprehensive self-concepts contribute to career maturity, but inaccurate ones do not. In other words, career progress requires examining self from the perspectives of the models in Chapter 2. For example, the student who is excelling in sports because he or she devotes all extra time to them, thereby neglecting homework, should recognize several things. Clearly, one should delight in this growing athletic

prowess, but should admit one is putting interest satisfaction and team-
mate approval ahead of parental wishes, is foregoing developing other
skills and interests, and that lack of academic motivation is typical of
American highschoolers (Coleman, 1961). Moreover, one should be
aware that this academic disinterest is not something to feel guilty
about nor an adequate reason to discontinue schooling.

In deciding what aspects of self to bring into sharper focus for
career development, counselors must remember that a person has multiple attributes and that parents, community, students themselves, and
other educators should collaborate in deciding which to highlight. Likewise, the client will be well served in expanding self-awareness if it
reveals that self-learning can be many things: arduous or easy; guided,
self-directed, or fortuitous; uplifting or depressing; pragmatic or frivo-
lous; but always unending. The dynamic process of self-concept can
never be completely reducible to trait profiling, collage assembling, or
verbal description, whether in prose or poetry. How pitiful if self-
discovery should be limited to an occasional guidance exercise or counseling session. Instead, such exercises should seek to stimulate in the
person the habit of periodically reviewing one's actions and intentions
and then realigning the self-concept with whom one is becoming. The
spread of this self-review habit may not require the curriculum revolution envisioned by the Department of Education-supported Career Education curriculum development project but does surely require that
parents, and at least some teachers, promote it more frequently.

Heuristic Principles of Self-Awareness Counseling

1. Self-awareness increases when one is directed and encouraged to
   experience a range of activities and then to reflect on them.
2. Self-awareness and confidence flourish when one learns how to
   succeed and to pause to enjoy a success; that is, one learns rules
   such as those in Figure 7–1.
3. Self-awareness and confidence expand by exploring oneself in
   positive relationships, which enable initiative and include the
   expectation that one is competent.
4. Self-awareness and confidence improve by gathering and organizing information about oneself in order to teach others about oneself.
5. Self-awareness and confidence grow by obtaining and integrating
   feedback from those qualified to observe one.
6. Self-awareness and confidence expand by systematically examining oneself from the perspectives of the different models presented
   in Chapter 2. A person should reflect on the problems one has
   resolved, the plans one has implemented and is pursuing, the
   rewards and required tasks of one's different activities, one's dis-

tribution of time and energy, one's roles and institutional associations, and traits attributed to one by test scores and ratings.

7. Self-awareness increases by observing and reflecting on the significant others in one's life and one's interactions with them.

8. Self-awareness grows by gathering and reviewing one's records and other residuals in a supportive setting and deducing their implications.

Method of Self-Awareness Counseling

Self-awareness counseling as envisioned here has four conceptually, but not necessarily operationally, distinct phases. The procedure represents a synthesis of a methodology gleaned from supervising trainees working with elementary school children; from conferences with Ms. Deborah Tracey, School Psychologist, Los Angeles District; and from examination of the literature. This only partially tried synthesis is offered because the new field of elementary school guidance does not yet have a widely known, detailed procedure for helping youngsters build self-awareness in relation to career and for acquainting them with the heuristic principles for developing and appreciating self.

Phase 1. The purpose of Phase 1 is to develop relationships in which the individual clients feel secure to explore and to share themselves. The counselor invites the clients to tell about themselves, does not put them on the spot, but offers help and asks how they like to show who they are. The counselor asks open-ended questions, listens attentively, and uses other involving techniques described in Chapter 5 so the clients understand that counseling is where they will reflect about thoughts, feelings,

Figure 7–1. Principles for Increasing Likeliness of Succeeding

1. Set achievable goals that are challenging.
2. Make a plan for accomplishing your objective and follow it.
3. Recognize your assets and liabilities, then build on your strengths and make provision for circumventing or compensating for your weakness.
4. Define benchmarks of progress and obtain feedback as you act so that you can detect quickly errors to be corrected and so that your progress encourages you to persevere until the goal is attained.
5. Secure requisite materials and training, and where possible observe successful models and obtain their advice about succeeding.
6. Acknowledge your achievements, take time to feel the pleasure of their accomplishment, and tell others about them so that you develop the attitude of self confidence.
7. Allow enough time for achievement and accept the possibility of confronting obstacles and having to problem solve.
8. When frustrated in achievement, compose yourself and engage in systematic problem solving.
9. Work and interact with people who feel and are competent and who expect you to succeed and who enable you to structure the task so that you achieve.

actions, and circumstances, especially as they relate to learning and eventually to working.

Providing materials, such as a blackboard and chalk, paints, dolls, puppets, or toys, often helps the clients express themselves. The counselor either joins the children in using the materials or encourages them to talk about what they are doing. If relevant to client concerns, the counselor uses diagnostic, academic, or career development measures such as the *Assessment of Career Development* (American College Testing program, 1974) and others in Appendix A.

This initial phase of counseling elicits information from the clients regarding matters such as the scope and accuracy of self-knowledge, preferred ways of expression and learning, feelings about self, number of experiences and sources of feedback used in forming self-attributions, level of abstraction of self-attributes, the reactions of significant others to the clients and their influence as reinforcers and models, and the supports and constraints of the rest of the clients' milieus. The clients' answers indicate deficits in self-awareness; personal skills; environmental resources; and restraints that cause, and may be maintaining, the deficits. The replies also suggest actions that might overcome or compensate for deficits.

The following example of eight-year-old Phyllis illustrates the data gathered and the manner in which they are organized to suggest solutions. Phyllis acted retarded and did not feel as able as peers, yet her teacher sensed she could do much better. During several sessions with coloring, doll play, and increasing conversation, she communicated that she was being cared for by an older, retarded sister before and after school. She had minimal contact with peers because her sister was afraid to go with her to the park. Her mother could not get to school unless an emergency occurred because she was working a long day as a maid. She saw her younger daughter briefly, only in the evenings and on Sundays. Then the family usually would go to church and visit with the grandparents, where Phyllis was expected to stay in the background.

From these data and her growing rapport with Phyllis, the counselor surmised that the child would benefit from reflecting about selected class work in which she was at or above grade level, talking about hobbies as a prelude to sharing them in class, and participating in a movement group. These strategies were considered initially because Phyllis was not being helped to feel the positive feedback she was getting in school, and because she needed more experiences with motor skills, and more opportunity to interact with an attentive adult.

Phase 2. This phase furnishes a forum for reflection and integration. Dinkmeyer (1970) suggests that the younger the child the more structure is needed; he reminds counselors to assure that youngsters are actively involved in the activity by writing, drawing, pantomiming, and so forth to sustain their attention.

The objectives of Phase 2 are that clients attend to feedback about themselves, examine its meaning, learn to evaluate its accuracy and importance, and add it to their growing stock of self-attributions. The counselor guides children to react to materials such as grades, test scores, video tapes of themselves, interactions with peers or family, work simulation, role plays, a week's time usage, and favorite objects in order to acknowledge and to communicate who they are. Their reactions may be drawings, paintings, collages, or pantomimes, as well as oral or written verbalizations. Often the initial reflections emphasize the positive, with youngsters indicating the strengths they see in their performances and interactions. When negative characteristics come up, the children are encouraged to acknowledge them, to recognize the disturbances they cause, and to consider ways of overcoming or minimizing them without denying their reality. One useful technique is to identify models who have overcome the problem and whom the clients might emulate. Once a successful model is identified, plans are made for imitating the model or learning how he or she succeeded. For instance, Vaughan (1974) had high schoolers watch vignettes of common threats to self-confidence and then discuss ways of building confidence within those situations.

In their reflections, clients can learn to examine situations from different perspectives and to use several sources of data. For example, the ten-year-old judging spelling ability might not only look at several spelling tests taken during the month but might also consider workbook performances, spelling bee performance, the number of spelling errors in other writing assignments, and the evaluations of parents who helped with spelling homework. In this way, the student could discover the folly of judging on only one performance or of using only one source, such as the spelling bee or parent's estimate, or even the tests, to make a final decision.

In the case of Phyllis, she and the counselor reviewed her drawings and the reading words she did and did not know. At first, she felt she could not draw and was not good in reading because she had done poorly on a standardized test. They started with drawings, with both counselor and client identifying good points and then some errors. When these errors came up, Phyllis was shown ways of improving and given some practice, usually achieving some success. Next, the counselor obtained from the teacher the packet of words used to label items in the classroom and they composed sentences using these words. She then asked the client to read these sentences. Success was immediate. Shyly pleased, Phyllis then was ready to look at mistakes in her test. In the review, Phyllis showed she could correct some mistakes immediately, and with counselor guidance and urging, started to learn unknown words by sounding them out, noting that when her teacher had helped her in this manner, she had also succeeded.

Phase 3. This phase involves building skills, knowledge, and interests by doing. The objective is that the children experience activities and sense how they are becoming more or less interested, more or less knowledgeable, more or less able through doing. Often the reflection phase suggests the activities. In Vaughan's (1974) study, for instance, once the clients named solution strategies, they were expected to try the solutions out in real situations.

In this phase, if not developed through reflection, the clients learn heuristic principles described in Chapter 3 for building abilities and

Figure 7–2. Problem-solving Steps with a Suitable Illustration
for Children

There are definite techniques, or ways, that help people to solve problems. Here
is a plan of action for problem solving. Follow it step by step.

Step 1: Identify your problem.
Step 2: Examine all aspects of your particular situation to find out what
is preventing you from solving the problem.
Step 3: Make a list of alternative solutions to the problem. *Alternative
solutions* are different possible ways of solving a problem.
Step 4: Make another list of the probable consequences of each alterna-
tive solution.
Step 5: Select the alternative that most appeals to you and try it.
Step 6: Take a good hard look at what happens. Naturally, if step 5 works,
you've solved the problem. If it doesn't, pick another alternative.
Repeat this until you've solved the problem to your satisfaction.

How does such a problem-solving technique work in a real-life situation? Let's
look at the case of Frank Berkowitz. Frank is a shy, not very talkative person who
felt like an outsider among the seemingly confident students in shop class. Frank's
goal was to be "one of the gang," but he didn't know what to do about it. Being
one of the gang, in effect, was Frank's step 1—identifying his problem and wanting to do something about it. Examining the situation—step 2—he saw that the
other students didn't talk to him nor did he to them. So now Frank was ready for
step 3—listing alternative solutions. Here's his list:

Alternative 1:   Ask a classmate about an assignment.
Alternative 2:   Ask another classmate for help with a project.
Alternative 3:   Compliment a student on a special accomplishment.
Alternative 4:   Offer to help with another student with a project.

Frank considered all the alternatives, but his choice was easy. Frank was especially good in working with wood in shop class. He noticed that one of his classmates seemed to have difficulty in smoothing the wood. So he chose alternative 4.
It worked. The student responded favorably to Frank's interest in her work, and
soon they became friends. This friendship broke the ice, and soon Frank was talking with many classmates. His problem of feeling lonely and isolated in shop class
had been solved.

SOURCE: C. C. Healy. *Discovering you.* Copyright 1976, McGraw-Hill Book Company. Reproduced with permission.

interests. They receive reinforcement for persevering and for obtaining
and evaluating their own or other's feedback about their performance.
When problems arise, they can be guided through the problem solving
steps outlined in Figure 7–2. Marcon (1976), for instance, taught fourth
graders to apply problem solving beneficially to everyday concerns.

Phase 4. This phase involves integrating the increasing self-
perceptions into coherent concepts and configurations; recognizing and
enjoying the process of change in self due to growth, aspirations, altered
contexts, new role demands and opportunities; and learning to value
keeping track of who one has become and projecting who one would become. The counselor invites the clients to capture new self-understanding
in autobiographies (prose or poetry), drawings, paintings, collages, or
pantomimes. The instruction and medium selected provide varying degrees of structure. The effort is focused on aspects of self developed in

the counseling: the clients are primed to discover how their efforts and external circumstances (the counselor, available resources, cooperativeness of others, and so forth) contributed to growth. If old enough, they can be helped to formulate key heuristic principles. With guidance, if necessary, they summarize the course of counseling, contrasting who they have become with who they were at the start of counseling. They then project who they might be and what they might do to become it.

Counseling success warrants celebration, and the clients are encouraged to delight in their accomplishment. The counselor can join in proclaiming how expanding self-awareness led to such pleasure. Completing self-ratings, tests, and evaluations of counseling will not only further knowledge of counseling and aid accountability, but will also let the clients appreciate the growth that has occurred and perhaps pinpoint new goals. As such posttesting is a key part of counseling, the clients should understand the relevance of each measure they complete. If feasible, they might also collaborate in selecting outcome measures.

During the school year in which Phyllis worked with the counselor, she periodically drew pictures of herself with family members, updated the counselor about her skill improvements in the movement group, talked about her improving reading ability, became more at ease in expressing her pleasure about growth, acknowledged compliments about her dress, and started to be able to tell the goals she hoped to achieve. At the close of the term, Phyllis was able to look forward to a happy summer school session and the prospect of being able to acquire new skills, even though she would not see the counselor until the fall.

Consultant Role

Counselors consult on career development so that other adults can contribute more effectively to children's career development. They seek to provide a direct service function to adults, teachers, parents, administration, community (Dinkmeyer & Carlson, 1973). Their goal is to join with the consultees in designing and implementing career education programs. Consultants come with ideas to share, with suggestions, and with knowledge and information of exemplary programs and resources; but they also come to observe what the consultees are doing, to hear what the consultees believe is needed and expect to do. These counselors recognize that the consultees have a vital stake in their students' or children's development, that they are already contributing to career development, and that they have firsthand knowledge of the target youngsters. Consultants anticipate that the programs and solutions erected will be tailored to the individual needs of the consultees, although they may be adaptations of standardized programs and solutions. The consultants recognize that they will be both teacher and learner, are ready to receive correction, and are prepared to give it. The consultants exemplify openness in communicating with consultees and expect the same from them. Whether teaching or learning, evaluating or being assessed, the consultants regard the consultees as colleagues and expect similar treatment. The relationship is collegial; neither is the other's patient. Teachers, parents, and other school personnel will assume major responsibility for implementing programs and solutions, while the consultants will service rather than direct or implement them.

Consulting, as sharing expertise, is as much generating the right questions as giving correct answers. The consultants must learn about the consultees—what they know about and wish for a student, what they can do and believe they should do, and what they are doing. Consultants must also be up-to-date about the state of the art of career development to help consultees recognize student needs related to career development and to accept their responsibility for addressing those needs. But the consultee must also recognize the problem and accept some responsibility for solving it. Often school administrators, teachers, and parents first become acquainted with children's deficits by helping a consultant carry out a needs assessment. The evaluation findings not only answer the consultant's questions, but often also are the stimuli that urges the other involved adults to launch a career development effort.

Before counselors can consult, the institutional authority, e.g., the system superintendent or school principal must sanction the consulting. Moreover, a study of high school teachers' career education follow-through suggests that a viable consulting program requires allocation of working time for consultant and consultees to confer with one another (Bloss, 1975). Similarly, the expectations of teams of consultants for implementing career education programs with teachers were related more to perceived administrative support and number of training days allocated for such training than to knowledge of the instructional concepts or to satisfaction with preparation for such training (Healy & Quinn, 1977).

Career consultants for elementary school children work exclusively through the schools. School counselors are generally internal consultants, operating either as faculty within one large elementary school or as district staff serving several schools. Occasionally, a school or district may also hire an external consultant or secure services from a state or county consultant. The primary difference between the internal and external career consultant is ongoing availability and role in program implementation. The internal consultant is available continually to the program, and frequently accepts a sustaining role, such as that of coordinator, resource reviewer, internal evaluator, inservice trainer, or trouble shooter. On the other hand, external consultants are used primarily to launch operations or to trouble shoot. Ordinarily, they leave when a program is underway.

Counselors can consult in several ways. They can share their expertise on subjects such as career education, measurement, community referral resources, and group dynamics with parents, teachers, and administrators formally or informally; they can join teachers or parents to make educational conditions more consistent with desired development; they can appraise and classify a child, and suggest individual programs; they can examine the interactions among school personnel, and the distribution of responsibility, power, and actual production in order to identify problems and to offer solutions. This section will focus only on the first two kinds of consultation. In terms of sharing expertise, the presentation will treat career development issues exclusively.

Heuristic Principles Underlying Consulting

Consulting operates on the heuristic principles that:

1. By sharing expert knowledge about career development and guidance with significant adults in the student's school and family, consulting enables those adults to alter the student's life space to better support career development.
2. By scrutinizing a career development program or problem in a collaborative, problem solving-planning context, consulting increases the probability of the program or problem solving being effective.
3. By enabling a child's own natural life space to accommodate career development needs, consulting increases the likelihood that a student can obtain continued assistance in career development.

Information-Giving Consulting

Even when they have created successful careers for themselves, parents and teachers typically have not studied either career development or methods of assisting youngsters to increase their likelihood of having successful, satisfying careers. As a consequence, many may not know what a youngster should be doing to increase the likelihood of career success; may not be aware of how to learn about or contribute to children's career development; and may be uninformed about what the school is doing, or might do, and how they themselves should contribute.

These adults will welcome and use information about children's career development recommended by a counselor. Their concern, competences, and resources will enable them to use the knowledge to change the child's life space to better support career development. Typical parent alterations may include increased family field trips to work sites and discussion of what is seen; joint reading about educational and work experiences; less pressure for a realistic occupational choice or high occupational aspiration.

In discharging the information-giving function, the consultant considers the goal and the nature of the target audience. Goals often have more than one facet. For example, the consultant who introduces parents to career education not only will want them to know its rationale and methods, but also will want them to be enthusiastic and ready to join in a career education program. As a consequence, the consultant will ascertain what kinds of presentations have excited this or similar groups before—simulations, movies, prominent speakers, observing their children demonstrating career education, small group discussions with the consultant—and then will organize such a presentation.

Consultants organize their presentations carefully. They arrange for appropriate space and equipment and for notification of the target audience, often soliciting suggestions for appropriate time and place from members of the audience. They rehearse their deliveries; brief and, if possible, rehearse speakers; preview films and other instructional materials; and verify the condition of the audio-visual equipment. They show consideration of the consultee's time and comfort. And, most importantly, the consultant attends as much to presentation as to content, remembering that the audience's eventual enthusiasm for the topic will reflect how ably the consultant presented the message.

Of course, the content of career guidance information may involve many things: sharing the growing understanding of career development; explaining results of testing and needs assessment; demonstrating how to use materials; introducing career development programs, activities and readings; acquainting parents and teachers with what other schools and parents are doing; and alerting them to local educational and occupational opportunities and trends, projected costs of schooling, and financial aid possibilities. Sometimes information dissemination requires several meetings, other times the best or most efficient communication is through written materials, newsletter, or completion of a programmed exercise.

Whatever the information and the dissemination methods, the consultant always evaluates the effort to identify where follow-up is needed. Consultants do not usually test consultees on their learning, but often will ask them to rate how well they understood particular components. At other times, the consultant gathers data more subtly: for instance, having consultees periodically summarize, answer questions, give examples, or form subgroups to reflect on certain points.

Problem-Solving Consulting

One widely advocated approach to consulting is the problem-solving method. Essentially, consultant and consultee develop rapport, examine the consultee's problem, establish a contract about goals and respective roles, generate alternate solutions, scrutinize those appearing feasible, select and try out solutions, and evaluate the arrangement. The four major phases of this dynamic, not always sequential, process are detailed below.

Phase 1: Set the contract. The object of this first phase is for consultant and consultee to establish a working relationship; to frame the problem so the factors that the consultant and the consultee consider pertinent are accounted for; to establish the character of the consulting relationship and the respective roles anticipated; and to settle on one objective or group of objectives, which will give direction to the consulting activity, and which, if achieved, will advance the goal of the consultee.

The working relationship develops when the consultant respects the consultee's or consultees' capability and concern with the problem. The consultant's approach is friendly, yet indicates their relationship concerns a professional objective, which requires that each bring different expertise. The consultant interacts collaboratively, rather than as a counselor guiding a client. The consultant presents information and confronts more directly than in counseling, anticipates a give-and-take dialogue between adults, and expects emotion to be less relevant.

If feasible, they confer in relaxed surroundings as colleagues, perhaps over a cup of coffee. One is not being treated by the other, and the consultee is not made to feel inadequate by partaking in consulting. Effort is made to be matter-of-fact and "up front," rather than therapeutic or manipulative. Especially when the consultant is appointed by the consultee's superiors, consultant and consultee quickly clarify the kind of reporting to occur.

The consultant has the consultee describe the problem, including what he or she and others have done, hope for, believe is appropriate, feel about it; what has been done with similar problems in the past; and who the involved parties are. Since part of the consultant's expertise is in framing problems, the consultant asks for information about factors that experience and knowledge of such problems suggest are important. For instance, in conferring with junior high school science faculty about the prevocational curriculum students' apathy to the occupational awareness program, the consultant probes the teachers' overview of a spectrum of occupations and clarifies their intentions about occupations below the professional level. Having learned that the science faculty prefer to target teaching for the college-bound science courses, the consultant helps them reflect about the likely reaction of students who envisage more practical work for themselves. As in counseling, one anticipates that many problems presented by the consultee will not be solvable unless problem framing introduces factors and perspectives not considered by the consultee in the initial synopsis. Problem definition often is restricted to consultant-consultee conferring but can extend to reviewing records and other accumulated data; to gathering additional data by both parties, including *in vivo* observation; and to adding other parties to the deliberation.

In the course of the dialogue, consultant and consultee spell out what each expects of the other, and the part each expects to play in carrying out the solution(s) they agree to attempt. The consultant avoids promising more than one is able, or intends, to deliver. The consultant is sure to ascertain how much energy and time the consultee has for resolving the problem and to recognize that overcoming the difficulty may not be a major priority in the consultee's work. Likewise, the consultant is honest about one's own commitment and priorities. To communicate respect for the consultees' and one's own time commitments, the consultant is punctual in opening and closing the meeting and later in making and answering requests for information gathering, reading, coordinating, reporting, and so forth. Together, consultant and consultee project the time commitment and cost, and, where appropriate, communicate them to the school authority involved.

When the problem crystalizes and the mutual capabilities for addressing it become manifest, consultant and consultee define goals and subgoals. When more than one goal, or set of goals, emerges as important, they establish priorities. In group consultation, the delphi procedure (Dalkey, 1975) is sometimes used to set priorities among goals. Sklare used this method for a school faculty selecting career education goals (Splete & Sklare, 1977). When different goals emerge as satisfactory resolutions of the problem, consultee and consultant deliberate, obtain additional counsel if appropriate, and decide on one.

Phase 2: Identify and delineate acceptable strategies. The object of this second phase is to pinpoint one or more feasible, clearly specified actions that both parties are willing to attempt for achieving the objectives. The parties first generate alternatives and examine the requirements and likely outcomes of each strategy. Since consultant and consultee both are offering suggestions, alternatives often should not be evaluated until all are generated. The desire for many alternatives often will lead one party to build on another's suggestion and then both will feel more ownership for the suggestions. To generate lists, consultants use task analysis, experience, and familiarity with other programs. In getting ideas for alternatives such as career education programs, either or both parties may wish to visit programs, to confer with teachers or parents who have used programs, or even to review the professional literature.

Once the alternative strategies are identified, both parties delineate what each involves. If too many alternatives are given, consultant and consultee can reduce the list on the basis of feasibility and expected results. Then they scrutinize each strategy alternative, projecting the time required, needed personnel and resources, and likelihood of different outcomes. To increase the accuracy of their projections, they may acquire additional information.

Phase 3: Implementation. The objective of Phase 3 is that the consultee select and implement actions, which have been planned, rehearsed, and coordinated and which will provide information to allow evaluation of their success. The consultant may participate in the implementation.

The parties first pick a strategy that is both feasible and likely to achieve the goal. Often this strategy is not the most likely to succeed nor the most feasible. Frequently, the most likely to succeed are very costly. They must also consider feasibility, based on considerations such as time required to learn and to implement the strategy, and cost of needed resources. If only unfeasible strategies are likely to succeed, the parties consider how to secure more resources for achieving the objective rather than pursue a "long shot." Most certainly they inform the institutional authority of the problem.

Once a strategy is selected, the parties project what is needed; make necessary arrangements, especially for other participants; inform superiors; and coordinate. If possible, they rehearse key elements and specify the responsibilities of each in the action, including maintaining communication. In a prolonged strategy, consultants will often trouble shoot and periodically be updated to ensure the strategy is working and to provide positive feedback to the consultee. When the consultee is the one who requires training or assistance in training collaborators, the consultant often aids in the training; frequently, the consultant assumes responsibility for gathering evaluation data.

When planning is complete, the consultee launches the action and moves forward confidently, knowing that careful preparation has heightened the chances of succeeding. Yet the consultee observes progress carefully; and evaluates, perhaps with the consultant's assistance, the accumulating feedback, to determine the need to make correction or even change the strategy.

Phase 4: Evaluation. The objective of evaluating the strategy is to verify its implementation and ascertain whether it achieved the desired goal. Evaluation should not come after implementation, but should be ongoing with it, so problems can be pinpointed and corrective action taken quickly. Indeed, in specifying the strategy, the parties should agree on the data to be gathered and the criteria to use in judging success. Recent attention to formative evaluation has underscored the importance of gathering, in the evaluation process, information to suggest improvements as well as information to judge the effectiveness of components.

In evaluation, both parties judge what the data indicate about their success. When successful, this review affirms the value of their systematic work and enables them to feel deserved satisfaction. If the data are negative, they know they must recycle, but at least they have valuable information to help them succeed when they try again.

Assessor Role

Traditionally, pupil personnel services professionals (counselors, school nurses, school psychologists, and social workers) have orchestrated a system to provide an individual information file for the placement and guidance of each student (Shertzer & Stone, 1976). The information comprising this cumulative record includes grades, classroom deportment ratings, attendance data, personal history and health data, ability and aptitude scores, academic and extracurricular history, and occasionally teacher anecdotes. The student's general characteristics and trends reflected in these records are part of the information the pupil personnel professional brings to recommendations about the school curriculum. All, or parts, of these records are used in parent and student conferences and in making special placements. Although such usage is generally not systematic over time, one text, *Strategy for Guidance* (Roeber, Walz, & Smith, 1969) has described how the cumulative record could be used in a longitudinal counseling relationship with a student and parents.

The rationale of the assessor role is straightforward: Students are developing individuals. By tracking their growth and identifying their individual differences, the school can provide a more responsive education. Insofar as career development is part of general development, student assessment should include attention to individual differences and to growth rates that are career relevant.

The assessor role essentially involves ongoing needs assessment; that is, select student objectives; define, and locate or develop appropriate indices of the objectives; administer the indices; tabulate and analyze results; interpret and report these data; and make decisions about revising or continuing the program. To be useful, needs assessment must provide information about both the cohort's and individual youngster's career progress that can be used to verify adequate growth or to pinpoint deficiencies. Since the demands of career and the mix of students are changing constantly, a viable needs assessment system continually revises objectives and involves new participants.

Heuristic Principles of Needs Assessment

1. Regular collection and analysis of feedback about learners' progress enables prescription of curriculum more likely to meet learner needs.
2. Ongoing needs assessment ensures constant review of an education unit's priorities and underscores the importance of teaching to those priorities.
3. Continued needs assessment increases the likelihood of identifying students with difficulties before their deficiencies compound, and program problems before they become exacerbated.

The Process of Needs Assessment

This process is taught in various courses, and its mechanics are described in many sources. Here, therefore, is a brief overview.

Step 1: Deciding on student objectives. Since the findings of the needs assessment produce suggestions about what parents, teachers, the community, and students themselves should do to improve student career development, one should involve representatives of these groups when deciding about the objectives. Make the representatives into a committee. Help them share in the decision about objectives by informing them about the "state of the art" of career development through films, recommended reading, and if possible, through having them visit career development programs. Bringing these groups in "on the ground floor" should increase the likelihood of their acting on the needs assessment results.

Step 2: Selecting evaluation measures. These measures are the indices to establish whether an objective has been attained. One may use standard or homemade measures. In this step, the consultant helps the task force make decisions on issues, such as whether "aware of occupations of interest" means ability to answer multiple choice questions about occupations in the Career Development Inventory (Super et al., 1979), or whether it means being able to summarize an occupation's description from the *Occupational Outlook Handbook* (U.S. Department of Labor, 1978b). When asked, the consultant may help construct rating forms, interview formats, or contract for measurement services. One should help consultees anticipate the data processing that different measures and sample sizes will require and permit without overspending time and resources and make sure the data will answer the intended questions. If part of a large district, one can verify the feasibility of the assessment plan with the district research specialist.

Step 3: Gathering and processing the data. Depending on the data, the committee and consultant may take full responsibility for gathering and processing or may delegate the task; for example, have teachers complete referral ratings and have the results punched into the computer to obtain a printout ready for interpretation. The data gatherers must be trained and must perform conscientiously. Before the teachers complete referral ratings, for instance, the consultant should instruct them in the purpose and use of the ratings and the benefits to expect from them. One must administer tests according to the standardized instructions and must carry out other measures, such as interviews, teacher ratings, and peer nominations, under specified conditions. Many measurement texts (Super & Crites, 1962; Thorndike & Hagen, 1969) offer specific guidance on data gathering.

Processing of data includes data analyses. Therefore, if the data includes complex questions, ask a research specialist or computer programmer for guidance about statistical methods and programs before, not after, gathering the data.

Step 4: Interpreting and reporting the results. The tabulations and statistical formula will yield facts such as percentages, statistical significances, magnitude of correlations; but one must judge the meaning of such results and communicate their meaning so the intended users will understand them. For example, the results may document that sixth graders made slightly higher career maturity scores than fifth graders; scores of the sixth graders, but not those of fifth graders, were significantly above a national mean for the grade. On consideration, one will interpret these findings as indicating that both grades are progressing adequately and that the sixth grade may be somewhat ahead of sixth graders nationally.

Once the results are understood, the consultant and the other decision makers judge whether to continue gathering data and whether to make alterations in the questions being asked or the manner in which data is being gathered. Clearly this expensive process should continue only as long as its information is contributing directly or indirectly to children's growth. Unless the nature of contribution is evident, a needs assessment should be discontinued.

Appendix A describes several new career development measures that appear useful to career development needs assessments. Clearly, one will want to use only those measures that assess objectives of interest to the consultant and an assessment committee.

Special Projects Officer

Counselors sponsor or conduct many projects in elementary and junior high schools to assist youngsters in their career growth. These projects include cross-aged and senior citizen tutoring; nontraditional occupational awareness programs, which are termed programs for countering career stereotypes; school or grade level minisociety simulations (Shirts, 1966; Kourilsky, 1974); and school or grade level personnel and placement simulations (Leonard & Stephens, 1967). This section examines tutoring and nontraditional occupational awareness programs.

Tutoring

A tutoring project requires identifying clients and tutors; pinpointing the level of client competence and the obstacles to progress; training the tutors; coordinating with tutees, tutors, teachers, and perhaps parents; and monitoring and evaluating the tutoring. The needs assessment for tutoring is similar to the one described above under the assessor role; coordination is described in the next chapter; and evaluation has been considered in Chapter 6. This section describes the tutoring sequence and considerations in training tutors.

Paraprofessional tutoring programs can offer many benefits. Such programs enable students to have individualized instruction, to have more models, and to recognize that their community or peers regard learning as important. Tutoring frees teachers to move the class more rapidly through subject matter, assured that students in need of remedial help are receiving it. Tutoring projects can involve community persons or older students meaningfully in education. When older students tutor, they can increase their mastery of the subject and their confidence in themselves when their tutoring succeeds. For instance, Bloom (1976) reviewed peer programs that measured tutor gains, and found 80 percent showed tutor gains in academic achievement, and 55 percent in self-confidence or attitude toward school.

Heuristic Principles

Some of the principles supporting tutoring include the following:

1. Individual instruction in learning processes such as attending, organizing, and reviewing illuminate the tasks more than group instruction does. Tutors can "show learners the ropes," to help them acquire good habits more efficiently. For instance, after observing that successful readers were operating differently than

unsuccessful ones, McLaurin (1974) had tutors teach the unsuccessful students to look at context, cues, sound out words and think before speaking just as the succeeders were doing; she showed that the treatment bolstered reading. Moreover, if a learner identifies with a tutor and believes the tutor obtained rewards for learning, then modeling principles complement role clarification in improving student learning.

2. Individual instruction and guided exercise can promote learning more surely and more efficiently than a classroom teacher because a tutor can identify suitable tasks, pace more in accord with the student's tempo, and reward more directly and immediately than the teacher.

3. Individual attention to the learner enables more timely feedback on performance and immediate, direct diagnosis of learning obstruction, enabling more efficient frustration reduction, and thereby increasing the student's willingness to engage in learning.

4. A cooperative, ongoing relationship with a confident tutor reduces the student's anxiety about learning and frees energy for mastering the challenge.

Method

Tutoring is individualized instruction in a subject or skill, generally for a student who has difficulty mastering the subject through typical group or self-instruction. Often the tutee's anxiety because of past failure impairs learning capacity and motivation. Thus tutoring is like counseling, since the tutor tries to understand and to reduce anxiety in order to enable learning to proceed.

One can conceptualize tutoring as proceeding through the same phases as counseling. In Phase 1, the tutor and tutee identify goals and obstacles. Typically, a tutor observes how the tutee approaches learning the particular subject. Tutor asks about what the tutee believes is the obstruction, and how upset he or she feels, what has been tried, how much progress has been made, how he or she learns well, and how the tutee thinks learning should proceed. The purpose of the inquiry is to pinpoint obstacles and to suggest possible solutions. In this diagnostic phase, tutor and tutee take particular notice of such things as attentiveness; understanding of, and response to, instructions; pacing; preparation and organization; practice; and so forth.

An important part of tutoring and counseling is establishing mutual respect and rapport. The tutor needs to show an interest in helping the tutee to master learning and does not condemn the student for failing. On the contrary, the tutor is patient in repeating strategies and graciously tries an alternate strategy when one does not succeed. The tutor recognizes the frustration the tutee encounters in failing, and responds in a way that will lessen rather than elevate the student's anxiety.

When persistent problems exist in basic skills, the tutor recognizes the possibility of a physical or developmental deficit requiring special observation. When problems occur suddenly for learners in areas in which they had been succeeding, or when performance is sporadic, or difficulties are restricted to one or two subjects or areas, the tutor explores the possibility of psychological causes.

In establishing learning difficulties and identifying methods of rectifying them, tutors can obtain valuable advice from subject teachers. Their experience has enabled them to witness many of the problems, and their professionalism keeps them aware of the latest aids and approaches for surmounting the difficulties. The tutor, therefore, should interview the classroom instructor to secure leads to diagnostic and instructional resources; to corroborate the tutor's emerging understanding of the problem; and also to enlist the teacher's help in providing the student with extra feedback, encouragement, and so forth.

The objective of Phase 2 is that tutor and tutee agree about their mutual roles. This agreement not only includes deciding on the solution strategies but more importantly the contract refers to the roles they will play vis-à-vis one another. The contract may be set before they reconnoiter the problem or after they identify strategies for correcting the situation. Typically, the contract provides that the tutor will review concepts and exercises with the tutee, will work examples and answer questions, will select materials and give assignments, will test the tutee's understanding and provide feedback, and perhaps will consult with the tutee's instructor and/or parents. Generally it is implicit that the tutor will assist the tutee to feel confident in approaching the learning task. In return, the tutee agrees to follow the tutor's direction, to complete assignments diligently, and to inform the tutor about confusing points and other difficulties.

Phase 3 of tutoring encompasses execution of the learning program. Tutor and tutee follow the regimen that their review of the problem and the tutee's learning resources have suggested. The tutor generally assumes more responsibility for selecting the strategy than does a counselor in counseling. All forms of teaching strategies and aides may be used. On an ongoing basis, the tutor tests the tutee's skills to assure that the strategy is appropriate. Thus, Phase 4 (evaluation) is interwoven with the treatment phase of tutoring.

Effective practices during tutoring execution include activities such as identifying and then starting the tutee at a point commensurate with his or her development, organizing learning into manageable units, and showing the tutee how to form manageable units, modeling or demonstrating the desired performance in other ways, providing immediate feedback about correct and incorrect performance, encouraging the tutee to attribute improvement to individual effort and ability, and rewarding and showing the student how to reward oneself for progress. Depending on the subject matter, the tutor applies principles relating to massed and distributed practice and to overlearning (Hilgard, Atkinson, & Atkinson, 1976).

Frequently the tutoring treatment consists primarily in providing exercise, encouragement, and feedback to the tutee. In many cases, the student's grasp of prerequisite skills or concepts is not on par with classmates. Hence, the tutee assimilates new instruction more slowly than do classmates. As one progresses through tutoring and catches up with classmates, the tutee typically begins to find he or she can proceed without special tutoring. Or, in other cases, as the tutee experiences the organized, disciplined structure for study given by tutoring, the student finds he or she has incorporated the required habits sufficiently to function successfully without the tutor.

Either kind of development, of course, is a sign of the success of tutoring. Once achieved, tutor and tutee can review the reason for these achievements and end the tutoring.

Tutor Preparation

How to prepare teachers, how to teach, and who can teach whom successfully remain controversial questions. Since tutoring is special teaching, different views abound about the merits of different kinds of tutor preparation, tutoring, and tutors themselves. Following are this author's suggestions about tutor preparation. Research on tutoring is presented under validity evidence toward the close of this chapter.

Most importantly, tutoring projects require sound organization and ongoing supervision. The supervisor must recruit, train, monitor, and debrief tutors; and also must establish procedures for accepting assigning, and evaluating tutees. One must allot and schedule space. Indeed, Bloom (1976) after an extensive review of tutoring studies, judged that "lack of adequate provision for space and time-dimensions" led to failure of many tutoring programs. Since tutoring involves sharing in a teacher's function, cooperation and ongoing communication between teachers and tutors must be established. Often teachers are the referral source; and they necessarily observe the effectiveness, or lack of effectiveness, of tutoring.

Essentially, tutors must learn or recall major elements of teaching, such as subject organization, clear explanation, pacing, practice, feedback, and encouragement. Generally, tutors have mastered the material to be learned by the tutee and are from the same population as the student. Often, but not always, their learning strategy will be appropriate for the tutee, since they share the tutee's background and cultural resources.

Logically, the tutor should join a professional in joint needs assessment of target clients in order to pinpoint needed competences and approaches to building them. According to the researches of tutoring, tutors frequently are not involved in this phase, although including them at this point would give them more ownership of tutoring. Recognizing the importance of diagnosis, Bloom (1976) believes that a professional should prescribe the learning tasks to overcome the learning deficit. Before or during the needs assessment, tutors can learn various observation and recording techniques. They also can review and rehearse methods of relating to tutees. Next, they can learn to apply to construction of a tutoring strategy teaching concepts, such as sequencing, successive approximation, positive reinforcement, modeling, reducing anxiety, rehearsal, spaced practice, self-guiding rules, attribution of internal locus of control, distraction reduction, supportive setting, and so forth. In training peer tutors in elementary school, Bloom (1976) has found that they need: a) clear directions about what they are to do and how to do it; b) a specific learning task and specific material for the task; c) a model of appropriate tutoring behaviors for the task; d) an opportunity to role play or to practice with feedback and correction, and possibly a second opportunity to review the model and to practice further; and e) some opportunity to make a choice of either creating or reinterpreting learning materials.

Once the tutoring program is formulated and underway, the counselor-sponsor can periodically review the tutoring progress with the tutor in order to reinforce correct actions, point out and help correct errors, and assist in trouble shooting obstacles. This ongoing review also can become the evaluation.

Countering Career Stereotypes

Chapter 3 indicated that women and minorities have had, and are having, their career options unfairly restricted. White males, too, are denied some options because certain careers are nontraditional for men, and hence unacceptable. Although laws now proscribe such restriction, and customs are changing to support equal career opportunities for all people, existing distributions of workers and extensive informational and literary descriptions of working support past stereotypes. Consequently, systematic prevention of possible misinterpretations of the career opportunity structure is needed. Especially important is the need to communicate information about the following:

1. Stereotypes and acceptance of them. For example, girls often characterize engineering as a male competence, although in Russia there are more female than male engineers.
2. The limited knowledge of nontraditional career possibilities and the reluctance to consider them. American, unlike European boys, for instance, quickly dismiss secretary or nursing careers, and are not as aware of the variety of specializations in these occupations.
3. Educational and experiential prerequisites for high-level careers and information about assistance available for pursuing such careers. In a recent report on the California guidance system, for example, Olsen (1979) pointed out that black and Hispanic students still are frequently not informed about academic prerequisites for professional and science careers in high school because teachers and counselors do not believe they would be interested.

4. Models and potential sponsors in nontraditional careers, especially for minorities.

5. Projections about the place of career in the lives of men and women from different social classes and various ethnic and racial groups in the 1980s and 1990s.

One relatively popular remedy to obstructive career stereotyping has been a short-term small group or class unit on nontraditional careers. Often, counselors initiate such projects and/or announce their availability to help teachers conduct them. Following are heuristics underlying such exercises, and two representative programs.

Heuristic Principles Concerning Programs to Counter Career Stereotypes

1. Alerting youngsters to the existence of stereotypes and their potential for falsely obstructing pursuit of a desirable career direction reduces the effect of the stereotype. Just as a tutor can help a youngster "learn the ropes" of the student role, youngsters need to learn the realities of occupational roles.

2. Distinguishing those aspects of occupational stereotypes based on the nature of the work from aspects extraneous to the work encourages students at least to consider pursuing occupations from which members of their race or sex have been unfairly and illegally barred in the past. Since many restrictive aspects of stereotypes are subtle and long seated in our culture, special attention to debunking stereotypes is needed.

3. Personal interaction with workers who are not members of the traditional stereotyped race or sex of an occupation, or even interaction with nontraditional filmed, audio, or print models, increases the number of "nontraditional" occupations a youngster considers.

4. Enabling youngsters to enjoy role play, or in other ways imagine themselves performing duties of nontraditional occupations, increases their willingness to consider pursuing such nontraditional careers.

Representative Methods

The projects promoting nontraditional careers almost always involve small group discussion and values clarification exercises. Frequently they incorporate films, appropriate female or minority models on panels, and reading material about nontraditional occupations, which is free of stereotypes. These programs tend to be conducted as classes in accordance with a daily lesson plan that specifies goals, introduction-motivation, the activity, and summary. Following are exercises Rabin and Scott (1971) and Birk and Tanney (1973) reported:

The Los Angeles YWCA Vocational Readiness Package was designed to help adolescent girls to become aware that working outside the home will be more important in their lives than it was in their mothers' lives. Groups of ten girls are subdivided into pairs. Each pair creates and then describes an ideal life for a fictitious woman of 75 years with a given number of years of schooling and work completed. They give the woman a name, interests, abilities, a family, and a work industry. After sharing their creations, each pair draws "chance cards," and the group discusses the modifications in the career plans required by the "chance cards." One "chance card," for example, states that the woman will be widowed at age 34 and will be required to care for her three small children. As part of the exercise, the girls are told about such predictions as: "One of ten women will not marry," and "The average woman can expect to work for 25 years." (Rabin & Scott, 1971)

In the next exercise, each pair of girls selects a person who was their age twelve years ago. The pairs plan twelve years for this person and see how close their plan approximates what happened to the actual woman. They are told about her interests, abilities, personality characteristics, and aspirations. At various points during their planning, each pair spins a "wheel of fortune" to determine whether their girl can pursue their plan for her. For example, if the girl is to obtain a particular job, the spin might indicate "hired if you have experience," "hired regardless," "not hired," "hired if you can type forty-five words per minute," "hired if your high school average is better than B," "yes, if this is a typical female job," and so forth. At the end of planning, the girls examine their creation and then role play the way they would expect her to answer questions about herself on a television panel show. The program requires one hour a day for five days.

Birk and Tanney (1973) tried similar consciousness-raising techniques with mixed results. First, their tenth-grade girls played "What to," a game in which students first identify their occupational preferences from a list of traditional and nontraditional female jobs, and then discuss the reasons for their selections with girls who made the same choices. Next, the girls observe the frequency with which different occupations were chosen, and join with the counselor in examining the implications of such choices. Then the students receive an "opinionnaire," which lists clichés about working women. Each student judges whether the cliché is myth or reality; the counselor tabulates their judgments about each cliché and they discuss their beliefs; and finally, students receive a list with only true statements about working women. After this exercise, the girls divide into triads and share their perceptions of each other as members of occupations in which few women are employed. Finally, two role-play situations are enacted and discussed. In the first role play, a female lawyer and her male secretary discuss a possible raise for him; in the second, a girl wishing to take Industrial Arts discusses her plan with her parents, her boyfriend, and her counselor.

Outcome Measurement

Since career counseling for the growth stage is a relatively new service, Table 7–1 lists objectives and measurement methods that have been used in published counseling studies and suggests others as well. The following paragraphs examine each part of the Table separately.

Table 7–1. Some Goals of Growth-stage Career Counseling, Consulting and Special Projects

Goal	Measure	Study
Self-Awareness Counseling		
1. Increase in self-esteem or self-confidence	*Tennessee Self-Concept Scale*	Vaughan (1974) Hansen & Putnam (1976)
2. Fuller self-description and greater justification of descriptors	*Readiness for Vocational Planning Interview*	Jessee & Heimann (1965) Andersen & Heimann (1967)
3. Increase in self-disclosure	Interview, teacher rating Essay rating	None
4. Expansion of number of positive relationships	Self-report, sociogram, peer nomination, teacher rating	None
5. More and wider successful self-exploratory activities	*Career Oriented Activities Checklist of New Mexico Career Education Test Series*	None
6. Greater ability to interpret and process information about self	Locally constructed Self-confidence test *Readiness for Vocational Planning Interview*	Vaughan (1974) Jessee & Heimann (1965) Andersen & Heimann (1967)
7. More frequent use of problem solving to resolve difficulties and greater ability to describe how to be successful	Self-report, Observation	Marcon (1976)
	Simulated scheduling	Quatrano & Bergland (1974)
Consulting		
1. Teachers/parents more aware of resources to use in developing child's career	Locally constructed test of career development resources	None
2. Teachers/parents more willing to increase their attention to career development of children	Self-report	None
3. Teachers/parents more aware of their children's career development progress as it is reflected in assessment file by tests, grades, experiences	Teacher/parent estimates of career development scores contrasted with test scores	None

Table 7–1. (*Continued*)

Goal	Measure	Study
4. Teachers/parents increase opportunities available for their children	Checklist of activities	None
Stereotype Debunking		
1. Improved attitude toward working women/minority workers	Self-report Attitude rating by teacher/parent	None
2. Greater understanding of stereotypes in work and education	Local test	Cramer, Wise & Colburn (1977) Harris (1974)
3. Increased exploration of educational and occupational options, especially in nontraditional fields	Self-report Unobtrusive observation	None
4. Increased willingness to entertain nontraditional career	Self-report	Cramer, Wise, & Colburn (1977) Harris (1974)
5. Expanded appreciation of place of career in lives of men and women, minorities, and members of different classes	Local test	None
Tutoring		
1. Improved tutee academic skills, perseverance, carefulness in work, social skills	Locally constructed mathematics test	De Vivo (1978) Sparta (1978)
	Standardized reading tests	Ellson, Harris & Barber (1968); McCleary (1971)
	Criterion reading tests	Niedermeyer & Ellis (1971) McLaurin (1974)
	Teacher/grades/ratings	McCleary (1971)
2. Increased tutee self-confidence in subject and higher aspiration	Self-report Parent/teacher rating	None
3. Improved tutor academic and/or interpersonal skills	Standardized achievement test	Cloward (1967) Hassinger & Via (1969)
4. Increased tutor self-confidence	Self-report Teacher/parent rating	None

The objectives of published self-awareness studies focus on feelings about self, ability to interpret and process information about self and environment and on problem-solving skills. Because youngsters need to try many activities and learn to improve in them during the growth period, the observer should note the range of self-exploratory activities and accomplishments, scrutinize the extent to which adult (parent, teacher, coach, neighbor) and peer relations support trial and improvement.

The self-development counseling outcomes have been assessed by many methods, including direct self-reports, inventory, intensive interview, simulation test, and counselor observation. Since parent and teacher feedback is likely to be especially influential on youngsters during the growth years, and since these observers can often describe their youngster quite accurately, using the ratings of these observers to chart self-development is logical. Indeed, counseling should use their input whenever possible, for commentary by Miller (1977) and Aubrey (1977) about the kinds of evidence nine- and thirteen-year-olds cite in establishing that they have skills suggests that they do not reference parent or teacher feedback frequently. Other social science research, however, indicates that parents and teacher feedback has major impact on self-concept before adolescence.

Discussing the child's perceptions of what parent and teacher feedback means could clarify for the youngster the positive regard and pride such feedback is likely to convey. These reviews may be necessary since Flanders's (1964) observations of student-teacher interactions and Becker's (1975) study of parent-child interactions suggest that these interactions have many negative and corrective elements. As a consequence, it should help to remind childen that teachers and parents may correct and rebuke several times during an activity and only praise occasionally, yet still be very pleased with performance. Although the adults perceive nuances in the quality of their own comments, the child, who is more concrete and literal, may only tally criticisms and overlook the adults' overall satisfaction. This author, for instance, recently noted a soccer coach correcting a twelve-year-old's actions continually throughout a game. When the coach cheerfully extolled the girl's play at the close of the game, he was surprised by her tearful rebuff.

The direct objectives of consulting are better informed parents and teachers who are more willing and able to help their children have experiences to bolster their careers. As these adults learn how they can expand and enrich children's experiences for building skills and interests and learning about opportunities, the youngsters should profit. When counselors communicate the nature and purpose of consulting, parents and teachers should be willing to furnish feedback about its impact on their actions and understanding, in order to decide how to proceed. Therefore, consulting ratings, recording number of activities or exercises tried, and even testing parents' and teachers' understanding of concepts should be acceptable, but having parents report about teachers or vice versa, or having children report is less tolerable.

According to Table 7-1, published counseling efforts to increase freedom of choice have tried to educate clients about barriers to free occupational choice and to encourage them to expand their occupational options. Future counseling is likely to seek more immediate behavioral outcomes, such as increased enrollment in nontraditional courses and nontraditional activities. Counselors will help more black and Mexican American youngsters, for example, to enroll in and to complete college preparatory and professional study programs; more girls to accept the challenge of mechanics and engineering training; and more males the advantages of nursing and secretarial studies. Similarly, more girls will join team sports, soap box derby contests, and model airplaning and rocketing clubs, and boys will increase the ranks of candy stripers and baby sitters.

When assessing, counselors will be able to use unobtrusive measures more frequently than in the past. Enrollments in classes, clubs, and sports teams by sex and cultural group can indicate the degree to which students are trying out nontraditional activities; and reviewing student career growth folders, increasingly being adopted through career education, should enable pinpointing individual reaction to stereotype debunking counseling. Also, parents will be enlisted to help their children expand their range of choices by rating their own child's range of activities and openness to nontraditional opportunities. In addition, evaluators are likely to test all children's ability to identify nontraditional workers' contributions in particular traditional fields and to scrutinize student attitudes about persons who work in occupations not traditional for their sex, racial or ethnic group.

For tutoring objectives of academic skill, there are many commercial tests, and ratings can be used for self-confidence and the other personality attributes. Since effective learning will be essential throughout a career, academic skills, self-confidence, and the other attributes should be a central career development objective during the growth stage.

Comprehensive Self-Awareness Counseling

Activities representing different phases of comprehensive self-awareness counseling for children are summarized below. In combination, the following research and the heuristic principles underlying the activities, persuasively show the benefit of self-awareness counseling for youngsters.

Blaker and Sano (1973) described the Object Game, which might easily be used in Phase 1 of comprehensive self-awareness counseling in a group. In the game, each group member obtains an object that portrays his or her feelings at the moment and puts it in the middle of the circle. Then each explains the significance of the object. The group members help clarify the presenter's feelings in a supportive way. Following the sharing, every member writes positive statements about all the members, including oneself and the counselor. These statements are collected and shuffled. Then each member draws one statement and reads it to the group. Finally, the students discuss how hard it is to say positive things. Although they did not study the game experimentally, the authors reported that the children using it reduced their inhibitions about discussing themselves and improved their regard for one another.

A similar technique is the "stolen birthday present" by Gazda (1970). Here puppets dramatize the problem of a special birthday present, which has been stolen at school. The puppets ask questions about valuable possessions, how people should obtain goods and services, how they feel when they lose them, how the thief is likely to feel, and so forth. Although aimed at reducing thefts, the procedure might be structured to have youngsters talk about the skills and interests they are using and will use in their careers to earn goods and about the benefits they feel from exercising their talents. Of course, research is needed to verify that such dramatizations stimulate and facilitate sharing oneself.

Over the past ten years, teachers have devised and tried many exercises for initiating self-exploration and sharing. One fine published source is *One Hundred Ways to Enhance Self-Concept in the Classroom* by Jack Canfield and Harold Wells (1976). Unfortunately, these authors are not aware of research validating the techniques, although their content suggests they will arouse public self-reflection and exploration.

Studying a form of career self-awareness counseling, Jessee and Heimann (1965) had thirty eighth-grade boys counseled individually, thirty-six counseled in two large groups, and thirty designated controls. In three sessions of counseling, with two doctoral students, the boys reviewed their hobbies and interests, received interpretations of their *Differential Aptitude Test* scores and other achievement data, and then summed up their understanding of the findings in a self-portrait. In three subsequent sessions, the boys studied the *Occupational Outlook Handbook,* prepared worksheets for four occupations, and then discussed working with the counselor. Postcounseling contrasts after the intervening summer vacation revealed that the individually counseled subjects had higher career maturity. (Career maturity was measured by structured interviews based on the work of Super et al. (1961) and Gribbons and Lohnes (1968).)

Testing a similar form of self-awareness counseling, Andersen and Heimann (1967) contrasted the career maturity and occupational knowledge of thirty eighth-grade girls counseled individually by two counselors with the maturity and knowledge of thirty other girls. More specifically, the counselors had guided each girl through three thirty-five-minute sessions in which she considered her interests in making career choices, her assets and barriers to realizing particular choices, and her perceptions about what to consider in making vocational choices. Then, for another three sessions, the girls completed informational sheets on an occupation of interest and considered the degree to which the occupation might be satisfying and accessible to them. The contrasts showed that the counseled girls excelled in career maturity measured by interview, but not on overall occupational information.

Phase 3 of comprehensive counseling often involves problem solving. Following a true experimental posttest design, Marcon (1976) showed that fourth graders altered their problem-solving behavior and knowledge of problem solving following either of two, four-session treatments. Twenty-five inner city nine-year-olds in four groups learned a problem-solving sequence through a series of four well-defined lessons built around school difficulties, such as missing a bus home, not having access to a game, and so forth. Instruction took the youngsters through the steps of problem definition, subgoal identification, brainstorming alternatives, finding a solution consistent with goals, need for additional information, choice, and evaluation of outcome. Following each lesson the children completed a five-minute quiz in which they gave examples of the concepts. A second treatment had twenty-four students in four groups, led by the same two counseling students, engage in thirty minutes of free play in which only two toys were available. Initially, the youngsters were told they were to solve problems themselves. In the last five minutes of the play session, each youngster listed individual play activities, problems encountered, and means of resolving them. Students from both groups made significantly higher scores after counseling than did twenty-four students who served as controls, on teacher ratings of problem solving in classroom situations, the *Purdue Elementary Problem Solving Inventory* (Feldhusen et al., 1972), and on a test of problem solving constructed by Marcon.

Perhaps starting a desirable trend, Otte and Sharpe (1979) coupled group counseling embodying many elements of Phase 3 self-awareness counseling with work experiences in school and in business establishments. They found the program improved the occupational knowledge, self-esteem, and achievement motivation of twenty-five disadvantaged seventh graders. In the small groups, which met twice a week over a semester, Sharpe facilitated discussion and role play of topics such as "sharing personal reactions to career exploration experiences, reporting information about work settings, discussing group members' growth in relating to others, and working through problems of common interest, even if they were unrelated to work." At the beginning of second semester, comparisons of the twelve students receiving the treatment in the first semester with the thirteen who received it in the second semester program showed that the experimentals surpassed the wait-controls on all three measures. In addition, the pre-post comparisons for the two groups separately showed both made after-program gains on the *Self-Esteem Inventory*, an author-devised test of achievement motivation, and a one-hundred-item career information test.

Theoretically, accurate self-awareness and true self-confidence assume that a person sets achievable goals and appreciates reasonable achievement. Focusing on goal setting based on past achievements and reasonable future prospects is included in Phase 3 of the comprehensive self-awareness counseling. In one approach to assisting youngsters with this aspect of self-awareness, Warner, Niland and Maynard (1971) found that six sessions of a model-reinforcement, group counseling treatment assisted fifth and sixth graders from rural, suburban, and urban schools to reduce unrealistic grade expectations more than did six open-ended discussions. In the treatment groups, three children with discrepant achievement (C or B) and aspiration (B or A) were grouped with three nondiscrepant students for six sessions. The counselor led discussion of topics related to goal setting and reinforced statements favoring realistic goal setting. The models were included in the hope that they would support realistic aspirations, but they were neither coached nor treated differently.

Sense of responsibility for actions and planning, as well as other facets of self-awareness, received attention in Phase 3 of comprehensive self-awareness counseling. Focusing on teaching planning in order to expand one's sense of self-control, Quatrano and Bergland (1974) assigned seventy-three elementary school boys to one of three four-hour treatments. One counselor administered all treatments. In each experimental treatment, the boys worked on a simulation scheduling problem, discussed correct answers, and received different amounts of candy depending on their performance. Other boys did the simulation and received the differential rewards, but did not have the directed discussion. A third group of boys heard a lecture about the scheduling tactics covered in the simulations. Analysis of the data indicated that the simulation-discussion group improved in planning more than the other groups but that sense of self-control, attitude toward school, and school behavior did not change.

Whether or not self-awareness counseling complements affective education programs has not yet been researched. Even the empirical evidence for widely used programs, such as *Developing Understanding in Self and Others* (Dinkmeyer, 1970, 1973), is remarkably limited.

Case study counseling for career choice is described in Chapter 10. However, the principles underlying case study counseling suggest that it can benefit clients at various stages of development with different concerns, especially self-awareness and esteem. Two researchers have already demonstrated this.

In a relatively large study, Hansen and Putnam (1976) found that 123 randomly assigned high school and junior high school students, who participated in modified case study counseling, made higher self-esteem scores and more mature career attitude scores on the *Tennessee Self Concept Test* and the *Attitude Scale of the Career Maturity Inventory* respectively than did 123 controls. Fourteen experienced counselors led the fourteen groups of eight to ten youngsters through six fifty-minute sessions. They used the case studies "to initiate discussion and to illustrate the relation of self-esteem and vocation development." The authors did not report the guidelines students followed in constructing their cases, nor did they identify the evidence students used to develop their cases; but they did note that the students "were encouraged to focus on their individual values, interests, aspirations, capacities, and abilities"; that particular points about school curriculum were introduced; and that counselors acquainted clients with occupational information. In addition, the discussions treated reasons for course selection, information necessary for selection, options opened and closed by particular selections, and the role of parents and teachers in planning and decision making. Moreover, counselors made sure that students considered concerns about the personal self and gave some time to the physical, ethical, family and social self.

Consulting

Aside from the logic of its heuristic principles, the validity of career consulting relies primarily on a limited number of studies promoting general youth development. Such studies affirm the efficacy of the principles underlying consulting. Several are described below.

Many studies have shown that consultation enables parents and teachers to apply behavior modification techniques effectively. In one study, Fineman (1972) which was followed up a year later (Young, 1972), had counselors teach parents to observe and to record their children's behavior and then deliberately to reinforce or to ignore behavior to induce desirable behavior in a variety of home situations. At the close of treatment, Fineman (1972) found that the children's behavior had improved significantly, as rated by parent and independent observer. In a followup, Young (1972) found that the majority of parents whom he could contact reported that the improvements were maintained.

Studies under the author's supervision have shown that the consulting procedure described in this text helps teachers improve classroom management. Specifically, Horowitz (1972) had nineteen elementary teachers meet in groups with either of two graduate students in counseling. In six one-hour sessions they reviewed a problem-solving approach for reducing target children's disruptive behavior and completed directed reading and homework exercises from a series of manuals for teaching application of problem solving (Bank, Culver, McCann, Rasmussen, & Ruble, 1972). Using a posttest design with a delay control, Horowitz found that consulting increased teachers' reinforcement and confidence in their ability to solve classroom management problems, and improved student attention in their respective classrooms. Adapting the Horowitz (1972) treatment for individual consultation and using the revised problem solving manuals (Bank, et al., 1972), Zinar (1975) found that consultation with two teachers led to demonstrably more effective classroom management. Extending the procedure by teaching and practicing positive expectations and reward, but deleting the manuals, Morrison (1973) showed that consultation altered the long-term classroom management strategies of a veteran elementary school teacher. The consultation included the teacher altering strategies, returning to former strategies, and then reinstating the new strategy. The empirical case data showed the teacher then continued the new strategy successfully.

Consultation and counseling with students may well be the best procedure. Testing such an arrangement on classroom adjustment, Palmo and Kuzinar (1972) had groups of children with adjustment problems from eight first through fourth grade classes randomly assigned to group counseling, group counseling and consultation, consultation, and control. The counseling followed the Dreikurs model (1968): for twelve one-hour sessions two counselors helped youngsters to realize the behavioral purposes and goals and to alter their behavior to be more consistent with their aims. The consultant, in turn, met individually twice a week with the teachers and every other week with the parents of the target children. In these meetings, the two counselors gathered information to aid their understanding of the children, explained particular behaviors of the child, suggested strategies to correct the child's behavior, and involved the parents and teachers in the guidance program. By the close of treatment, all treated groups exceeded the controls on teacher and independent observer evaluations of classroom behavior. The consultant-only students were significantly higher than the others, with the combination of group counseling and consultation higher than group counseling alone on the independent rater's evaluation. Why the combination of group counseling and consulting was not better than consulting alone is not clear. Perhaps teachers and parents felt less responsibility for altering behavior when the child was in counseling, or perhaps these youngsters were somewhat confused about their own behavior responsibility, since they partook in a group of peers with similar, but probably different, nonadjustive behavior. In any event, the study demonstrated the efficacy of coordinated parent/teacher consultation.

In a study combining counseling and consultation with teachers and parents following the Dreikurs model (1968), Platt (1971) found that the ten sessions and twenty hours of consultation produced desired improvements in school adjustment. He found that the eighteen treated third graders surpassed the six control and six placebo control students in school adjustment, as rated by parents and teachers.

In a contrast of teacher consultation with a combination of counseling and consultation, Anderson (1969) found support for the effectiveness of both types of treatment in bolstering self-esteem (not fully described). Her study involved 327 students from the fourth, fifth, and sixth grades, 12 teachers, and 2 counselors. Her data also indicated that fourth graders benefited more from the combined treatment, whereas sixth graders profited more from teacher consultation. All groups except the controls gained from the treatments, which unfortunately were only described minimally. In still another study contrasting teacher consultation with a combination of consultation and counseling, and with Dreikurs (1968) type counseling, Marchant (1972) found all treatments more effective than a control condition in improving classroom adjustment for 37 treated fourth and fifth graders.

Whether consulting should substitute for, or complement, counseling to improve student self-control in classrooms is not clear from these studies. Their limited evidence suggests that either treatment will produce benefit, but that extra benefits will not accrue from combined treatments. Clearly, future research should examine whether some types of children will profit more from one treatment than another and whether some types may even gain more from the combination.

Examining teacher receptivity to consulting, Splete (1971) found that 103 teachers and 23 counselors asked to report on effective and ineffective consulting behavior listed considerably more effective incidents. Moreover, teachers described significantly more incidents in which consultants helped them in understanding their students than themselves. Although teachers did not object to focusing consultation on helping them discover themselves, consultation, which emphasizes teacher self-understanding, is unlikely to succeed. Clearly, the premise that consultation is a relationship to help a third party presumes that the emphasis be on the milieu and concerns of that party, not on the consultee.

Assessor Role

Usually a counselor will combine the assessor role with either self-awareness counseling, consulting, or special projects officer, to assure a context for presenting students, parents, or teachers with the assessment data. To this author's knowledge, research has not yet examined whether particular assessment programs themselves have raised the career maturity of elementary-aged children. A few researches, notably those of Jessee and Heimann (1965) and Andersen and Heimann (1967), have incorporated assessment in successful counseling activities, as have several of the studies examining consulting. However, these studies were not large or controlled enough to ascertain the contribution of assessment to the children's career growth. Therefore, the arguments for using assessment to improve children's career maturity still depend almost wholly on the logic of the underlying heuristic principles.

Stereotype Debunking

Despite widespread concern about stereotype debunking, few research studies have been published on the topic. Cramer, Wise and Colburn (1977) demonstrated impressively the effectiveness of stereotype debunking. Thirty eighth-grade girls met in two separate groups of fifteen with a male or female counselor for eleven fifty-minute sessions. These sessions involved discussions; films; exercises; and homework on stereotypes, alternate options, information about women at work, and future trends; and speakers from nontraditional careers. Posttreatment comparisons with thirty controls showed the stereotype-debunking program gave the participants a better appreciation of the negative aspects of stereotypes and a better appreciation of woman's work potential. One of the two counseled groups also chose significantly more nontraditional occupations.

In another important study, Vincenzi (1977) met with a total of fifty-nine sixth grade boys and girls in two classrooms biweekly in half-hour sessions for ten-weeks. The boys and girls reviewed newspaper stories about men and women in nontraditional occupations, examined and discussed the issue of stereotypes, and listened to seven thirty-minute presentations by women in nontraditional occupations. In the presentations, each woman gave a brief demonstration of her work, explained her job, and told why she chose it. Pre-post treatment comparisons with two control groups of fifty-nine students each showed the treated sixth graders reduced the number of occupations they felt were sex-typed. Student statements suggested that the guest speakers were especially influential, particularly on girls.

In one small study of a program to combat sex stereotype, Harris's (1974) evidence suggested that a six-session, small group program could increase the range of girls' occupational choices. She led five girls through activities focused on pursuing interests through work. She found these five girls reported more occupational choices after the program than thirteen controls, and tended to make less sex-stereotyped choices, although the result did not achieve statistical significance.

Tutoring

The following is an overview of tutoring research followed by descriptions of several representative tutoring studies. Research indicates long-term tutoring in reading and mathematics benefits some elementary students and some peer tutors if their tutoring succeeds. Research, such as Ellson, Harris and Barber's (1968), McCleary's (1971) and Hassinger and Via's (1969), suggest that initial peer and paraprofessional efforts are more effective if the tutor follows a highly structured program. The following research studies and the heuristic principles underlying tutoring indicate that well-managed, peer or paraprofessional tutoring programs can make a valuable contribution to students' career development.

Overview. Tutoring research has focused primarily on establishing that tutoring with particular strategies or materials increases academic achievement. Many published studies report success for a range of strategies and materials (Bloom, 1976). Fewer studies have examined whether tutoring improves a student's self-confidence or attitude toward learning, but several have shown such gains (Bloom, 1976). Rare are investigations about whether tutoring enables students to acquire the study skills or the motivation to progress adequately in group instruction without tutoring. Generally, research has not investigated whether the benefits of tutoring are maintained over time.

Most of the published research on tutoring has concerned elementary school children learning reading and arithmetic. The tutors are frequently older children or adults from the local community, who are not trained in teaching. Ordinarily, the tutors receive preservice training in using the program's structured materials and processes. During the project, they customarily have weekly supervision sessions. No mention is usually made about their tutoring proficiency. Frequently, the child tutors service only one client. Research has not examined whether peer or cross-aged tutoring improves with practice and feedback.

Researchers have viewed tutoring primarily as supplementary instruction to provide extra practice in an academic subject. Most studies describe the initial achievement and aptitude level of tutees. Recent studies, such as McLaurin's (1974) and DeVivo's (1978), have even pinpointed learning deficiencies and aimed tutoring exercises and materials at them.

Few tutoring studies have mentioned the level of the students' motivation or study skills and habits, although Sparta's (1978) efforts to increase chronically failing students' sense of control over learning may represent more attention to these factors. Tutees in the studies usually accept invitations to participate, rather than seek tutoring. Almost never do they or their parents pay for the tutoring.

Parental and peer support are important factors in academic achievement (Sewell et al., 1970), but tutoring studies have not yet examined these contextual variables. Instead, they have tried to study tutoring as an isolated phenomenon, in the same manner as counseling research has studied counseling. Even when the performances of tutored students are contrasted with the performances of untutored students in the regular program, no mention is made of the value placed on tutoring and academic success by the school faculty and students. Nor do research reports usually mention tutor interaction or collaboration with teachers. Also, there is generally no explicit role in the tutoring process for the student's parents or other family members. Hopefully, DeVivo's (1978) findings that suggest even minimal parental involvement spurs completion of homework will bring about more tutoring programs with explicit parental roles.

Study Skills Counseling. Research has not yet examined the effects of combining tutoring and study skills counseling; nor have studies usually compared them, although the two programs have similar and complementary objectives. Certainly, knowledge gained from study skills counseling should be useful in tutoring. So, here is a brief overview of study skills counseling.

Most study skills programs have been of two kinds. One type focuses on concrete ways to improve skills such as concentration, note taking, recall of lectures or reading, composing essays, and so forth. Typically, these programs use workbooks, such as Robinson's (1946) *Studying Effectively.* The second type emphasizes increasing motivation and organizing oneself to study and to succeed despite distraction or anxiety. In some treatments, a counselor guides a client in developing insight about obstacles to achievement or self-acceptance as an achiever. In other instances, counselors teach clients self-reinforcing or anxiety management techniques so that they can better regulate their studying.

Research of study skills counseling suffers from many of the deficiencies that characterize career counseling studies, especially small samples and lack of treatment specification. As a consequence, no clearly validated procedures exist for study skill counseling. Bednar and Weinberg (1970) and Mitchell and Piatkowska (1974) investigations of college study skills counseling reviewed and agreed counseling was more likely to succeed if it lasted at least several sessions and if the students came voluntarily. The two studies, however, found different evidence about the benefits of structured or unstructured counseling.

Bednar and Weinberg (1970) included twenty-three studies from 1927 to 1968 in their review. Of these, 57 percent claimed significant gains in grade point averages (gpa) for counselees. The Mitchell and Piatkowska study included thirty-three studies, only eleven of which were in the Bednar and Weinberg sample. Twenty-six percent of the thirty-three studies showed statistically significant gpa gains for clients. Since many of the published studies have not shown gpa improvement, and since published studies are more likely to show significant gains, one must conclude that improving gpa through counseling is difficult.

Tutoring Research. Ellson, Harris, and Barber (1968) reported a study of long-term tutoring that compared programmed methods with traditional methods. Their programmed materials covered sight reading, comprehension, and word analysis; it used successive approximation and other reinforcement principles. Operation manuals ensured precise program implementation by tutors, who were community people. The traditional approach also focused on sight vocabulary and word attack skills.

The authors tested the merits of two variations of each approach by comparing forty-three first graders receiving each treatment with forty-three youngsters receiving only the regular reading instruction. The statistical analysis showed that students receiving two fifteen-minute sessions of programmed tutoring each day throughout the school year surpassed control group students on most of the reading-readiness, outcome measures. Surprisingly, neither the students receiving a single session each day of programmed tutoring nor those receiving one or two sessions of traditional tutoring, surpassed their control groups. Evidently, reading readiness is not easily accelerated, requiring in this case half an hour of tutoring each day for nearly 200 days.

A similar study by McCleary (1971), with different programmed procedures, confirmed the effectiveness of long-term, structured tutoring for improving reading readiness. The programmed tutoring followed manuals, which prescribed each teaching act. It emphasized sight reading, comprehension and work analysis; and included comprehension and word analysis books to supplement the regular readers. In the study, McCleary found the 141 students receiving the daily fifteen-minute, programmed tutoring from adults trained to deliver the program had higher reading scores than the 130 students who were not tutored. Moreover, significantly fewer of the tutees were retained in first grade, so tutoring apparently had increased their overall readiness for schooling.

Attending especially to replication of tutoring, McLaurin (1974) showed that trained lay tutors could effectively deliver a structured tutoring program. She had two counselors tutor thirteen randomly assigned first graders and thirteen third graders for two half-hour sessions a week for six weeks. In each session the tutors followed these steps, as verified by independent observers:

1. The tutor and tutee record administrative details identifying the session and assignments.
2. The tutor reviews and verifies client understanding of the four reading rules: "Look for context cues." "Wait to hear all directions before starting." "Use time for thinking before answering." "Sound out words." Whenever a student makes an error, the tutor asks the child to identify the rule violated. If the child cannot answer, the tutor points out the rule.
3. The tutor starts new sessions with direction to the last frame in the *Sullivan Programmed Reader* completed in the previous session.
4. The client responds.
5. The client uncovers the correct answer. Then the student either receives praise and proceeds, or receives the correction described above.

6. The tutor logs each client response, noting the type of error and the practice needed to correct it.

7. At the close, tutor and child complete the administrative data sheet.

Throughout the session, the tutor speaks in a friendly voice, exercises patience, reinforces effort and correct responses, enables the client to work at his or her own pace, smiles, permits free response, and so forth. The rationale and content of the treatment derived from McLaurin's observations of the children and conferences with their teachers.

Following tutoring, the thirteen tutored first graders made higher scores on the *Sullivan Placement Test* than the twelve controls, but the difference between third grade tutees and controls did not achieve significance.

Examining the impact of reinforcement on mathematics tutoring, Zack, Horner, and Kaufman (1969) had graduate students tutor thirty inner-city fourth graders. All students received thirty-minute sessions twice a week for six months. Half the students received scheduled reinforcements (tokens, which could be converted to candy) for correct performances. The other fifteen received periodic verbal reinforcement. At the close of the project, both tutored groups exceeded thirty controls on their understanding of arithmetic concepts, but not on their computational skills.

In studying the impact of mathematics tutoring on the achievement of fifty-four carefully screened, "helpless" fifth and sixth graders, Sparta (1978) contrasted an "attribution treatment," a "self-management treatment without attribution elements" (Meichenbaum, 1975), and a control condition in which the students practiced problems and were verbally praised for correct solutions. Sparta prepared mathematics problems commensurate with each child's achievement. The attribution subjects learned to attribute success to effort, and failure to external difficulty; the self-management group learned to verbalize the steps of problem solving as they attacked a problem in calculation. After ten group sessions with different tutors over a two-week period, the "attribution" students had become more careful in problem solving than had the management or control students. However, both self-management and "attribution" tutees persisted more than did controls. In spite of these gains, at the close of treatment controls and tutees showed equal willingness to attempt problems. Apparently, the treatments led to better performance, but did not make calculating more enjoyable.

DeVivo (1978) examined the impact of programmed tutoring, with and without parental home follow-up, on the mathematics achievement of seventh graders. DeVivo, a former mathematics teacher, constructed the tutoring program based on her examination of mathematic's problems encountered by seventh graders at her junior high school. She had three groups of seven or eight students meet twice a week for four weeks with one of two community college students. To complement the meetings the parents of these students met once with the tutors to learn how to help with the mathematics homework and to verify its completion.

Three other groups of students also met with a tutor, but their parents were not contacted. Another twenty-three students' parents received letters describing how to help their children with mathematics homework and requesting that they review their child's homework. Finally twenty-three other students served as controls. Posttutoring comparisons of homework turned in and achievement on a teacher-made mathematics test showed that parental involvement and tutoring produced more completed assignments, and that either tutoring alone or combined with parent involvement produced higher achievement.

Cross-aged tutoring may be an effective method of coping with learning deficiency as more parents are working full-time and as education budgets drop. Cloward (1967) reported an extensive project featuring 97 tenth and eleventh graders from the inner city tutoring 356 fourth and fifth graders. The tutors received eight hours of preservice training and two hours of inservice throughout their twenty-six weeks of tutoring. They provided 100 tutees with four hours of tutoring a week, and 256 with two hours per week. By the close of the project, the tutors had substantially increased their reading scores in comparison to a control group of fifty-seven high school students who did not tutor. Less dramatic, but nonetheless significant, gains in reading were registered by the students receiving four hours per week of tutoring. Over the five month period, they averaged six months of growth in reading compared to five months for students who had had two hours of tutoring, and three and one-half months of growth for 157 students without tutoring. Perhaps using programmed material would have produced more tutee benefits. Certainly, the control elementary students' slow reading progress without tutoring underscores the need for some special assistance beyond what is typically provided.

In another study of the impact of cross-age tutoring on tutor and tutee, Hassinger and Via (1969) trained one hundred low socioeconomic, poor readers of high school age to assist elementary students. The tutors learned to follow a tutoring outline in their tutoring, although adherence to it was not verified. By the close of the six-week program, the tutors had increased their reading test scores significantly. As in the Cloward (1967) study, the tutees' scores also improved, but not as substantially.

Niedermeyer and Ellis (1971), likewise, found cross-aged tutoring effective in improving reading readiness. Special reading materials developed by the *Southwest Regional Laboratory* were used by kindergarteners. The materials contained criterion-referenced unit tests that prescribed make-up exercises for failed items. Seventy-five fifth and sixth graders were trained to guide low-achieving kindergarteners through the make-up exercises for four weeks. Training taught tutors to engage their charges in friendly conversation, to let the student know when he or she was correct, and to tell or show the current response after an error and then to elicit the current response from the learner without prompting. The tutoring was provided to children after they failed items on the criterion test, which was given at the culmination of their regular classroom instruction. Consequently, tutees had a varying number of tutoring sessions, depending on the number of their errors.

After four units, the researchers contrasted the performance of fifty-seven tutees with twenty-nine control subjects. The tutees outperformed the controls on a reading readiness test. Moreover, the tutors outperformed another group of fifth and sixth graders, who were nominated to be tutors but had no training, on the tutoring behaviors learned and practiced in the project.

Snapp, Oakland, and Williams (1972) found that lower scioeconomic fifth and sixth graders can help younger children to acquire reading skill. Snapp trained forty tutors to conduct twenty-minute sessions in which they introduced new words by writing, spelling, and saying each, and then they guided the tutee in oral reading. Half the tutors reinforced correct responses systematically and ignored errors, while half did not emphasize positive reinforcement. All tutors were observed in their tutoring weekly and had weekly supervision to correct errors. After eight weeks of daily tutoring, the forty tutees recognized significantly more words on a local *Word Recognition Test* than controls. Systematic reinforcement tutoring did not produce results different from tutoring lacking that feature.

In one of the few studies contrasting methods of training cross-aged tutors, Frager (1969) did not find a difference between the effectiveness of giving fifth and sixth graders a structured format to follow and teaching them to apply problem solving to resolve difficulties arising in the tutoring. He had forty-eight tutors either take five hours of problem solving instruction or five hours of instruction in using a structured format. The twenty-four tutors in each group raised reading readiness of their kindergarten charges, compared with nontutored students, and had equally positive attitudes about their experience.

Allen (1978), has suggested a new dimension to peer tutoring—tutoring while being tutored. She contrasted the growth of twenty-four students tutored by college students with the growth of twenty-four other students who were taught by the college students how to tutor, then tutored a peer, and in turn were tutored by the peer. All the students met in pairs for fifty minutes, twice a week for twelve weeks. Following treatment, the students who learned how to tutor, tutored, and were tutored increased their reading scores more than those who had only been tutored. Allen did not mention whether the students in the two treatments differed in their understanding of the tutoring process or in their involvement in it. It would be interesting, for example, to examine whether the prospect of having to tutor a peer increased attentiveness to the college student's tutoring or even led the tutees to do extra preparation for their tutoring.

Hazards of Career Counseling

Each growth stage career counseling procedure has hazards, which counselors should monitor. Several are described below. Since research in counseling has rarely attended to negative outcomes, evidence is not available about the actual risk of the following hazards.

Self-awareness counseling may oversensitize a child to oneself, leading one hastily to evaluate interests, talents, and values, without sufficient experience to make conclusions. More than twenty years ago, Tiedeman and O'Hara (1959) showed that adolescents typically did not perceive their interests, abilities, and values clearly until high school. Longitudinal studies by Super and his colleagues (1961, 1969) and by Gribbons and Lohnes (1968) have also suggested that eighth and ninth graders' self-awareness is still developing, and that early attributions might be premature. Similarly, the Project Talent findings have indicated that predictions of future occupation were considerably better for twelfth than for ninth grade performance on ability tests and interest inventories.

Closely linked to premature characteristic attribution is the child's overestimating personal power to direct development. Elementary schoolers still depend heavily on the permission of parents and teachers. These adults control, to a large extent, the children's activities and milieu, with its models and resources. Children's powers to change what is available to them, and hence what they will become, are limited. Therefore, in reviewing goal achievement, the youngsters should not be totally blamed for their shortcomings or held totally responsible for correcting their problems. Although controversial, the counseling of Warner, Niland, and Maynard (1971), which helped youngsters to reduce academic aspirations, might well be expanded to help youngsters to become more realistic and self-accepting of nonacademic career skills, such as leadership, sociability, sports skills, and so forth.

A useful counseling treatment to develop a child's power would be skill in negotiating with adults—teachers and parents—to change demands and to get help to meet demands. Certainly many high school and college teachers have found themselves negotiating assignments at the initiation of talented students. Often the ensuing arrangements have involved extra instructional time from the teachers. Executive recruiters, too, claim that persons who take initiative in reorganizing their work are more desirable job candidates.

Consulting introduces still other problems, not the least of which is taking counselor time away from direct contact with students. Managing, consulting, and delegating are functions rewarded more highly in our society than teaching, counseling, and tutoring. The former activities are considered more complex and more efficient. Yet, clearly, care is needed continually to decide whether denying individuals needed services is justifiable because consulting commitments will offer different benefits to more clients. The dilemma is whether it would be better to afford a future Einstein or Shakespeare supportive career counseling or to assist parents so many youngsters can become engineers and have communication careers. The 1980s promise to be a time of limits, so that choices about resource allocation are required.

Consulting about careers can also exacerbate the pressure for children's achievement, which is already high. Assurance of a quality job requires increasingly higher academic and social achievements. Many parents and children still equate quality work with at least technical-level jobs. As women rightfully achieve a fairer share of such jobs and stay in the labor market longer, competition will remain keen for high-level jobs. Although consultation may address the issue of realistic expectations, many parents and teachers will still go away affirming that vocational education is for someone else's children. Hopefully, career education's coming of age will lead to upgrading the quality and dignity of existing occupations. Perhaps social science's increasing understanding of how political power allots status and rewards to work activities will reveal that jobs using clerical and maintenance skills are as demanding and contribute as much to society as do selling, managing, constructing, healing, and researching. Hopefully, career education will lead the typical worker to appreciate more accurately how job duties become defined, and how pay and prestige are assigned to work. Indeed, recent litigation by the U.S. Equal Employment Opportunity Commission questioning low clerical salaries on the basis of salaries paid to nonclerical personnel suggests that equal rights will stimulate review of what makes occupations valuable.

The assessor role also has its risks, since children's performance measures have limited reliability. So findings must be used cautiously in individual guidance and even in educational programming. Furthermore, counselors and others are still discovering what is important in career. Critics have pointed out that many current school programs are atavistic, preparing persons for the subordination of the industrial revolution rather than for the self-direction of the postindustrial age. As a consequence, student insubordination and other apparent failures may not indicate defective career development but instead may show some youngsters are perceiving their needs to question and to challenge the status quo. Needless to say, assessors must keep abreast of the latest understanding of career development as they gather data to define and to evaluate programs.

Even the projects officer organizing a tutoring program or offering a class in debunking stereotypes can harm while trying to help. Poor tutoring can be another failure experience, telling the youngster that he or she is incompetent again, even when extra help has been given. Identifying and remediating learning disorders are talents school psychologists develop through several years of intensive training and practice. Although experience shows that tutors can often help remedy learning problems, the tutor program organizer needs to monitor client progress carefully to assure that the tutors are not working beyond their limits, which would be debilitating both to themselves and to their intended beneficiaries. In several tutoring studies that showed the effectiveness of paraprofessional tutoring programs, researchers prediagnosed the clients.

Stereotype debunking, too, has its pitfalls. Two come to mind: first, the youngsters may be jaundiced about the work system from focusing on its biases and heavy reliance on personal contracts; second, continual attention to occupations may communicate that work is a more important part of living than it is, just at a time when the percentage of an adult's time in work is decreasing.

Exploratory Stage Career Counseling

8

After putting the tasks confronting junior and senior high school students into context, this chapter presents a range of counseling methods that counselors are employing to help adolescents with their career tasks. These tasks generally are those of the exploration stage. The career counseling methods are designed to stimulate and guide exploration of educational and work opportunities, to initiate conceptualizing about working and career management, and to introduce the rudiments of planning and decision making.

The 1957 Sputnik alarm brought the American public's attention to the importance of career development during adolescence. Suddenly, Congress recognized the importance of the secondary school years for careers, and the importance of adolescent career decisions for national survival. In addition to bolstering science and engineering, the ensuing *National Defense Education Act* encouraged thousands of teachers to become guidance counselors to expand and upgrade career guidance services for secondary school students. That professional training program and the subsequent *Elementary and Secondary Education Act* helped to increase the number of secondary school counselors fourfold from 1958 through 1978.

Now that there are enough counselors to help students with different problems in the exploratory stage of career, more of the methods described in this chapter are becoming routine offerings of a junior or senior high school guidance program. Of course, these counseling methods should complement rather than substitute for other guidance services such as career centers, field trips, work study programs, and career guidance classes. Indeed, to underscore the importance of a comprehensive program and coordination of services, the chapter outlines coordination activities before describing more traditional counseling methods.

The exploratory stage methods generally were designed for and applied to child and adolescent populations. More people will now be repeating tasks of the career exploration stage. Therefore, counselors may ask whether the methods described in this chapter should be different for initial and repeat or recycling explorers, since the repeat explorer is likely to be an adult, whereas the initial explorer is an adolescent. Knowles (1978), among others, has suggested that adults learn better with more collegial teaching strategies, and common sense suggests that the repeat explorer will be able to start exploration at a more advanced level and will be able to do more of the counseling program on his or her own. Unfortunately, research has not yet considered such practical concerns; clearly, studies contrasting novice and repeat explorers would be helpful.

Counselors working with teenagers beginning exploration, of course, should remember that this stage begins while a youngster is still developing and refining skills, interests, and values. As a consequence, the activities of novice explorers not only enable them to examine particular opportunity structures, but also the kinds of exploration determine the skill, interest, and value foundations that they lay. In other words, committing energy to examining areas such as manual crafts and science opportunities equips youngsters with general skills and values that later can be refined into job skills and also gives them the opportunity to consider related work. Omitting exploration of a particular area in turn, may preclude development of the skills requisite for later entry into the field. Examples of stunted development abound. For instance, after ten or eleven years of age people cannot learn to make phoneme sounds outside of their language, and persons who fail to master mathematic concepts as youngsters rarely can learn them as adults.

Clearly, counselors will want to reinforce advice to try many things before specializing. The focused exploration envisaged by career education programs is likely to generate energy and enthusiasm for general exploration, rather than curtail it. Logically, extra time in specialized exploration will reduce activities such as television viewing and "rapping," rather than other exploratory activities.

Adolescence

Adolescence is a turbulent period because a teenager's body, powers and roles undergo radical change. It is not unusual for a youth's stature and weight to increase by from 20 to 25 percent in a one- or two-year period. Voice and figure change almost as drastically, and the growing body produces new moods and urges, which often bewilder the child-becoming-adult.

The new weight and stature equip the adolescent to perform the physical tasks of an adult. Sexually, the teenager can produce or bear children. Intellectually, concrete thinking becomes abstract thinking and reasoning, and these powers progress as the teenager accumulates new knowledge and realizes potentials by applying them to challenging problems.

The teenagers' social roles differ dramatically from children's roles. The family still provides major support for development, influencing the child's opportunities and status (Blau & Duncan, 1967; Coleman, 1961). Yet family direction of adolescent activities diminishes, and expectations become fuzzy. Parents reduce their commitment to organized sports (Little League, American Youth Soccer Organization), clubs (Boy and Girl Scouts, Campfire Girls), lessons (dance, music), and even parent-teacher meetings, as the American child moves into adolescence, leaving the teenagers in control of their recreation and schooling. Within the household, adult initiative and cooperation on family matters are expected of the person who now looks and talks like an adult, even though these expectations have rarely been told directly to the teenager. At other times, however, society demands the docility and submissiveness of the child, since teenage activity still depends on parental authority and subsidy and teenagers are still forming their value systems and lack the experience base on which to make many decisions, at least as far as parents are concerned.

Social interactions also change. Suddenly, heterosexual relations and group acceptance assume critical importance. Perhaps in response to the covert societal message to keep out from underfoot, teenagers spend many hours together, apart from parents and other adults. Their apartheid has led to the development of the so-called "teenage culture," which at the extreme challenges adults norms of dress, speech, entertainment, use of drugs and liquor, sex, crime, and even physical violence. Indeed, over the last twenty years the steep rise in teenage use of drugs and liquor, in the incidence of venereal disease and extramarital pregnancies, suicide, and commission of crimes—especially violent ones—has alarmed the public and its officials.

Age thirteen or fourteen not only initiates adolescence but the American youth also generally starts their junior high school career. Children leave neighborhood schools, in which they related to one teacher and twenty-five to thirty peers in a self-contained classroom, for the regional school, where they confront five or six teachers and up to two hundred peers daily, as they move from class to class.

The switch to departmental instruction means more advanced challenging study and provides or imposes more independence, since junior high school teachers cannot know and guide student efforts as readily as did elementary teachers. Junior high usually requires more homework and self-regulated reading and research. Often, the increased time span of assignments gives teenagers more control over when and how to do their work. Because high school students are often moving to the limits of their parents' education, for knowledge has expanded and specializations such as economics, psychology, botany, zoology, and data processing were not available in high school twenty years ago, parents are less able to help their children and are less comfortable in monitoring their efforts. Moreover, the high incidence of working mothers diminishes parental time available for supervising the teenager's learning.

Paradoxically, society does not make it easy for adolescents to accommodate their new powers and roles. Most startling, perhaps, is the exclusion of teenagers from adult activities. School attendance laws and labor laws prevent youngsters from working at most occupations until they are sixteen or eighteen, or from entering apprenticeships until eighteen, and "primary labor force" jobs traditionally have been restricted to people over twenty-one. Voting laws prevent adolescents from voting before they are eighteen. Although teens are the clients of schools and current students of government, they cannot be on school boards or directly influence government policy, about which they often know more than do adult voters. Furthermore, now that many opportunities are inaccessible without an automobile, auto vehicle regulations essentially prevent driving before seventeen or eighteen, and auto insurance underwriting procedures penalize young drivers in some states, not because they have committed a legal infraction or had an accident.

Learning by doing and by imitating are major means of expanding knowledge and skills; yet excluding adolescents from work, political, and often social activities (where liquor is served), denies them these means of learning adult behavior. Even nuclear families and extensive geographical mobility limit teenagers' opportunities to try or closely observe different adult interactions.

Instead, teenagers rely extensively on the media to provide models of adult behavior, despite the fact that the movies, television, and radio portrayals of living are grossly distorted in order to "entertain." Leading educators even estimate that by high school graduation, the typical teenager has logged more television hours than school hours (Hurlock, 1973). Consequently, although the contemporary American high school graduate may know much about the science and governmental structure that undergird the system, he or she is often seriously confused about how adults act in making the system work. Indeed, recent assessments of adult development and of career development suggest this confusion is common. (Aubrey, 1977; Mitchell, 1977.)

Adolescent Priorities

Clearly, adolescents have several major concerns to resolve; implicitly, the spiraling increase in their crime and violence suggests that they are not resolving these difficulties and feel that the society is not assisting them. Certainly, focusing on only one concern—social, familial, or school-career—and ignoring the others is counter-productive. Likewise, educators would be naïve to move alone to assist adolescents, since, as noted above, teenagers are denied access to the primary ways of learning about the major life roles. Obviously, then, the adolescents' counselor first will want to inform the community about its apartheid system in order to assist and encourage correction of the system.

Since this text focuses on counseling for career development, it only presents procedures appropriate for career development. Yet the author cautions the fervent career educator working with adolescents to recognize *all* their developmental concerns and to avoid overemphasizing the career aspect of their development.

Career Development Concerns

Our education-work system is organized so that adolescent career choices, or neglected choices, affect the career a person will have. By taking algebra instead of business mathematics, and a foreign language instead of typing or shop in ninth grade, a person increases one's chance to enter an academic high school program; and by taking an academic program in high school, one considerably influences one's chance to enter and graduate from college. Similarly, one increases one's employability after graduation by taking a high school vocational or business education program, rather than a general track. In the realm of particular occupational options, many observers, such as Cooley and Lohnes (1968), have pointed out that failure to take proper mathematics and science courses in high school almost preclude a career in science and medicine; and that lack of mathematics is considered a major stumbling block to those entering accounting and economics majors.

Such observations about the system's structure and constructive responses to it have led to the formulation of general career tasks for adolescents such as these:

1. Maintain and expand linkages to parents and other adults in the work world, and learn how to interact in an adult manner;
2. Learn about the spectrum of occupations and work settings, and how to gain access to work and training;
3. Acquire knowledge of educational and vocational resources;
4. Develop competence in, and sense of responsibility for, career decision making, planning, and problem solving;
5. Try out multiple activities to develop and become aware of abilities, interests, and values;
6. Build self-confidence and a sense of agency;
7. Strengthen constructive work habits, such as systematic study and time management;
8. Develop a desire to participate in work.

Figure 8–1 presents a more detailed behavioral list.

Jordaan's (1963, p. 59) description of vocational exploratory behavior sums up the career development tasks of the adolescent age. He writes: "Vocational exploratory behavior refers to activities, mental and physical, undertaken with the more or less conscious purpose or hope of eliciting information about oneself or one's environment, or at verifying

Figure 8–1. Career Development Tasks of Adolescents

The tasks are defined for the areas of knowledge, information seeking, planning, attitudes, and skills.

Knowledge

1. Knows the high school programs which are available.
2. Knows the salaries in occupation of interest.
3. Knows the supply/demand situation for occupations of interest.
4. Knows the costs in time and money of training programs for occupations of interest.
5. Knows how far in school people with similar tests scores and grades usually go.
6. Knows the job satisfactions of workers in occupations of interest.
7. Knows about the available college, junior college, and technical school program.
8. Knows how people advance in occupations of interest.
9. Knows the principal duties of the occupations of interest to him/her.
10. Knows the education and experience requirements of occupations of interest.
11. Knows which occupations use the abilities which he or she has.
12. Knows the occupations which satisfy his or her values.
13. Knows the subjects that are required for his or her high school program.
14. Knows the personal characteristics which are important in career planning.
15. Knows the progress he or she is making in his or her career development.
16. Has an accurate understanding of own interests and abilities.
17. Knows how to obtain a job in the occupations of interest.
18. Knows how to locate local job openings.

Information Seeking

1. Reads books and pamphlets to find out about occupations.
2. Reads catalogues from colleges, business schools or other vocational schools to learn about them.
3. Discusses career choices with either parents, teachers, or counselors.
4. Discusses financing post-high-school training with either parents, teachers, or counselors.
5. Talks to people in those post-high-school training or work programs of interest about their experiences.
6. Takes particular course or work study or volunteer/paid jobs in order to find out own ability and interest.

Attitudes

1. Believes he/she must make his/her own decisions, but can get advice.
2. Believes in systematic approach to planning and problem solving.
3. Accepts responsibility for obtaining information about career.
4. Believes in trying out various activities to learn abilities and interests.
5. Believes in discussing plans with adults but retaining responsibility for making them.
6. Believes that solving school and work problems is his or her responsibility, although he or she may seek advice.

Figure 8–1. (*Continued*)

Planning and Decision-Making

(Sound reasoning assumed for all)
1. Has considered several different occupational alternatives and chosen one.
2. Has decided how many more years of schooling to complete.
3. Has decided what to do after high school graduation.
4. Has chosen courses that will clarify his or her interests and abilities.
5. Has decided whether to work in the community or to work outside of it.
6. Has considered the advantages of different life styles and has chosen one.

Career Skills

1. Can utilize informational resources such as the *Occupational Outlook Handbook*.
2. Can determine appropriateness of information resource for particular information needs.
3. Can describe a decision making process.
4. Can progress in academic and non-academic skill acquisition.
5. Can use self-instructional materials and heuristics in improving skills.
6. Can manage time effectively.
7. Can comment upon validity of data about himself in terms of validity across situations.
8. Can demonstrate effective work habits: punctuality, cooperativeness, etc.

or arriving at a basis for a conclusion or hypothesis which will aid one in choosing, preparing for, entertaining, adjusting to or progressing in an occupation."

The importance of such adolescent tasks is affirmed in many standard texts, such as Super's (1957) classical *Phychology of Careers,* Herr and Cramer's (1972) *Vocational Guidance and Career Development in the Schools,* and Bailey and Stadt's (1973) *Career Education,* and these undertakings appear in most states curriculum guides, including those of Minnesota (Tennyson, Klaurens & Hansen, 1970) and Hawaii (Kudo, Lee & Ryan, 1974). Moreover, several new tests that measure career development in adolescence also concentrate on such tasks.

Research on Adolescent Career Development

Three longitudinal studies and several cross sectional studies have tested aspects of adolescent career development and have found support for the notion of career development. Findings of these studies are summarized below.

Career Pattern Study (CPS). In 1950, Super and his colleagues and students launched a longitudinal study of 342 eighth- and ninth-grade boys from Middletown, New York, a typical American small city. The youngsters were tested in their eighth or ninth and twelfth grades, mailed questionnaires two years after high school, and when possible, intensively interviewed and tested at age twenty-five and age thirty-five. In addition, their parents and teachers were interviewed at the outset, and their school records were made available.

Early analysis of the study data indicated that eighth- and ninth-grade boys' occupational information, planning, and interest maturity related to characteristics of the boys eleven years later when they were twenty-five, such as self-reported career satisfaction and success, college grades, and quality of job changes. Morever, occupational information and planning were moderately stable from ninth to twelfth grade; the twelfth-grade scores were even more predictive of career maturity at twenty-five. Not surprisingly, ninth- and twelfth-grade parental levels of occupation, intelligence, and grades also related to the boys' career maturity at age twenty-five. By twelfth grade, the students' after-school employment, avocational pursuits, and participation in school activities also correlated positively with career maturity (Jordaan & Super, 1974).

Perhaps even more important than these positive relationships were the findings that consistency of occupational preference before and during high school and agreement of occupational preferences with measured potential did not reflect career maturity in ninth grade. Clearly, these findings warn against pressing students to choose early and to be "realistic" in such early choices. Even in regard to those indices that related to adult maturity, one must be cautious, for Super (1969) noted that these indices are at best only moderately stable. Indeed Jordaan's (1976) comment about the career maturity of ninth- and twelfth-grade CPS boys in the early 1950s bears repeating: "While the great majority of boys in ninth and twelfth grade accepted or expected to accept responsibility for their vocational choices, their use of appropriate resources, their knowledge of the world of work, and their plans for achieving their goals were unimpressive if not seriously deficient" (Jordaan, 1976, p. 5).

Table 8–1 presents a summary of the findings about the CPS boys' adolescent career aspirations and maturity. Again, their limited progress in career maturity by ninth and twelfth grades warns against setting career development goals that are too ambitious for children and adolescents, even when they have the advantage of quality career education. Certainly, before defining with confidence the performance criteria for career education, one needs a fuller appreciation of career development during the growth stage.

Career Development Study. Starting in 1958, Gribbons and Lohnes (1968) traced the career development of fifty-seven boys and fifty-four girls from Boston suburbs from eighth grade until they were two years out of high school. Using structured interviews, they examined these students in eighth grade just before participation in an experimental guidance program built around *You: Today and Tomorrow* (Katz, 1958),

Table 8–1. The Aspirations and Vocational Maturity of Boys at Ninth and Twelfth Grade as Found by the Career Pattern Study

Aspirations and Background

1. The 103 subjects at this phase of our longitudinal study, like the larger group at the 9th grade, are of average ability and live in a typical small American city.
2. In the 12th grade, 15 percent of the boys had fathers who were in high-level occupations, about one-half (54 percent) had fathers in middle-level occupations, and nearly one-third (31 percent) had fathers in low-level occupations.
3. As 9th- and also as 12th-graders about a third of the boys aspired to high level occupations; nearly two-thirds to middle-level occupations; and only 1 or 2 percent to low-level occupations.

Vocational Maturity

1. In nearly two-thirds of the cases, the subjects' 12th-grade vocational preferences bore little or no resemblance to their 9th-grade preferences.
2. In the 12th as well as the 9th grade, most boys had several occupations and several fields of work under consideration. In both the 9th and the 12th grades, about one-half were considering occupations that were in different fields or at different levels.
3. About 40 percent of the boys at both grade levels thought they knew the field they wanted to enter but not the level, or vice versa. Only one out of every ten at the 9th grade and only one out of every five as 12th-graders had settled on an occupation or a specialty within an occupation.
4. Eight out of every ten boys as 9th-graders and two out of every three as 12th-graders had very little confidence in or commitment to their expressed vocational goal.
5. At both grade levels a majority of the boys (67 percent at the 9th grade and 75 percent at the 12th grade) had a primary interest pattern in at least one occupational group on the Strong Vocational Interest Blank when this is defined as a median rating of B+ or higher.
6. Five out of ten boys as 9th-graders and four out of ten as 12th-graders entertained occupational goals that were not in keeping with their measured interests.
7. At least half of all the boys as both 9th-graders and 12th-graders contemplated goals that were not in line with their socioeconomic resources or their level of ability. The vocational preferences of 12th-grade boys do not seem any more realistic than those they held as 9th-graders.
8. About half of the boys in the 9th grade and considerably more than half in the 12th grade (83 percent) had held two or more part-time jobs or one or more full-time jobs during their high school careers.
9. As a 9th-grader the average boy was aware of 13 important features of occupations out of a possible 51; as a 12th-grader he was aware of 17. However, most boys at both grade levels knew relatively little about the occupation that they hoped to enter. The aspects they were most knowledgeable about were those pertaining to the requirements of the occupation.
10. The subjects' sources of information were also inadequate in both grades, especially in the 12th when career decisions must be made.
11. At both time periods, the great majority of boys accepted or expected

Table 8–1. (*Continued*)

to accept responsibility for their vocational choices. In addition, somewhat less than one-half as 9th-graders and somewhat more than one-half as 12th-graders said they had made or intended to make their own decisions about securing needed schooling, training, or work experience.

12. Approximately one-fourth as 9th-graders and about one-half as 12th-graders seemed to have well-thought-out plans of a general nature, particularly with respect to preparing for their prospective occupations. On the other hand, very few (5 percent or less) had well-thought-out plans for actually getting the needed training, education, or beginning job, or for entering the occupation once they had completed their training.

13. As a group the CPS boys showed little awareness, in either the 9th or 12th grade, that circumstances might compel them to change their vocational goals or their plans.

14. In both grades, most boys could point to a number of vocational decisions or choices they might make, could make, or were considering.

15. Two out of every three 12th-grade boys appeared to have done little or nothing to implement or to realize their vocational preferences.

SOURCE: Reprinted by permission of the publisher from Jean Pierre Jordaan and Martha Bennett Heyde, *Vocational Maturity During the High School Years* (New York: Teachers College Press, Copyright © 1979 by Teachers College, Columbia University. All rights reserved.

then again in tenth grade, in twelfth grade, and two years after high school graduation.

The interviews were coded to provide seven subscores. The subscores correlated only moderately and had low test-retest reliability over the two-and-one-half years between the eighth- and tenth-grade interviews. The seven subscales were the following:

1. Curriculum choice factors, including knowing the relation of attributes to different curricula and courses in different curricula
2. Occupational choice factors, including knowing relevance of abilities and the amount of information about preferred occupations
3. Ability to describe strengths and weaknesses
4. Accuracy in estimating abilities and achievements
5. Adequacy of evidence for self attributes
6. Awareness of interests
7. Awareness of values.

Gribbons and Lohnes (1968) found that the *Readiness for Vocational Planning (RVP)* scores derived from the subscales increased from grade eight to grade ten, and that their canonical correlation suggested that scores at the two points shared moderate common variance. The scores related to student IQ and curriculum in the predicted manner; that is, higher scorers had higher IQ's and were in the academic rather than business, industrial arts, or general curriculum. The *RVP* did not correlate significantly with socioeconomic status in eighth or ten grade, although such status related to career maturity at age twenty. These findings support the view that the composite *RVP* score reflects career maturity.

The eighth-grade *RVP* scores correlated positively, but low, with both the age twenty criteria of level of aspiration, occupational level achieved, and career adjustment, and with the twelfth grade criteria of realism of occupational preference, evidence of occupational planning, and constancy of occupational field preference. The tenth grade *RVP* did not correlate with the age twenty criteria, nor with as many twelfth-grade criteria. This fact suggested either that the *RVP* does not assess career maturity sensitively, or that, contrary to theory, career maturity is not developing continuously. Supporting the former is the low test-retest reliability of *RVP* itself and its subscales. The guidance experience after eighth-grade testing might also account for the inconsistent relations of tenth-grade scores to twelfth-grade and age twenty criteria. That guidance tried to improve the career maturity of every student, especially those lagging in this attribute.

In addition to verifying the limited relation between eighth-grade career knowledge and skills and career behavior at age twenty, the inclusion of a self-knowledge component in the *RVP* and the *RVP's* relation to career maturity suggests that self-knowledge becomes a factor in career maturity earlier than had been detected by the *CPS*. Noteworthy, too, is that despite finding positive relations between the eighth- and tenth-grade *RVP* and subsequent career behavior, the authors caution against interpreting the data as indicating that eighth and tenth graders have adequate self- or career knowledge for planning. As they note, such knowledge varies widely among pupils and across time.

Other findings of the study reaffirm that, collectively, high school youngsters reduced the level of their educational and occupational aspirations as they grew older, especially those students with lower IQ and lower socioeconomic class. Certainly the guidance treatment provided in eighth grade would have tried to counter this tendency, but unless assistance were provided at subsequent points of the student's education, the only effect of this intervention may have been unattainable aspirations.

Project Talent. Flanagan and his colleagues (1964, 1966, 1971) launched Project Talent in March 1960 in order to provide, among other things, an inventory of the talents of youth, information about how occupations are selected, and data about the effect of education on occupational preparation. More than 400,000 students in grades nine through twelve from more than one thousand high schools completed two days of testing, including forty aptitude, ability, and information tests, a demographic questionnaire, an interest inventory, an activities inventory, two open-ended essays on their view of an ideal occupation, and questions about school and guidance service. The examinees were followed up one, five, and ten years after their high school graduation and may be followed up twenty years after. Data from the testing and follow up are stored by the American Institute of Research.

To date, major findings include:

1. Ninth graders' career plans are very unrealistic but improve somewhat by twelfth grade (cross-sectional comparison).
2. A substantial majority of high schoolers do not make an appropriate career choice in high school.
3. Eleventh graders in 1970 were making more realistic career
   choices than eleventh graders in 1960.
4. Girls were choosing a wider range of occupations in 1970 than
   in 1960, although these choices are often not realistic in terms
   of their tested abilities.
5. Approximately half the students change their occupational goals
   radically within a year of leaving high school.
6. High school interest, ability, aptitude and information test scores
   relate somewhat to occupation pursued five and eleven years after
   high school. This finding led Flanagan (1973) to recommend that
   students complete the same measures (*The Planning Career
   Goals Program,* American Institute of Research, 1976) in order
   to "obtain a clear picture of their interest in various vocational
   areas, the amount of information they have about these fields,
   and the extent to which they have developed abilities that Project
   Talent students have found are necessary to do well in these
   fields."

Other research. Cross-sectional studies or shorter-term longitudinal
studies also confirm that major growth occurs naturally in high school
and warn against over-emphasizing detailed knowledge and early career
choices. Several studies show significant increases in occupational
knowledge about duties, worker attributes, required training, and in use
of planning and decision making without special intervention (Herr &
Enderlein, 1976; Noeth & Prediger, 1978; Westbrook & Parry-Hall, 1973).
Moreover, Jepsen (1975) found indications that the basis of career
choices becomes more sound from ninth to twelfth grade. Clearly, these
studies support the view that the elementary years should be a time for
try out and growth, free from pressure to amass detailed education or
occupational information or to select one occupational direction and
rule out others.

Counselor Roles

Among the counselor roles designed to meet the adolescent career development needs are these: coordinator, facilitator, teacher, and inventory
interpreter. Consultant continues to be an important role, but since the
preceding chapter has described this function, this one will treat it
minimally.

In the facilitator role, counselors have employed structured simulation methods to alert students to upcoming career decisions and to sustain their attention to career development tasks, especially information
seeking. Also, they have increasingly engaged adolescents more in value-

clarifying activities. As teachers, counselors have guided clients individually, and in groups, through structured exercises designed to promote information seeking or career problem-solving; to orient them to the world of work or education; and to build career skills such as time management, assertiveness, and decision making. They also have had students complete career development tests and then taught them their errors and how to correct them in order to increase career maturity. Counselors have interpreted inventories, and have indicated—individually or in groups, by computer, or by self-guided manuals—the areas of a student's interests or the occupational or educational groups likely to have interests similar to the student's.

Surprisingly, little use has been made of students' autobiographies, which would appear to be useful vehicles for alerting teenagers to their growing autonomy. Likewise, no research has documented a counselor's providing periodic career development check-ups for clients. Hence such a role will be described even though there is no research on it.

Coordination

Not every counselor will want or be able to fill the coordinator role, which involves bringing together people and resources so they can assist students, rather than helping students directly. A coordinator may see the beneficiaries only occasionally. He or she locates and secures resources and sustains their operation, and keeps communications channels open among resource providers and among users' and providers' representatives. The coordinator encourages participants to express their differences to one another directly and to resolve them on their own or with mediation, rather than becoming an advocate of particular parties.

The coordinator's professional relationships are generally collegial rather than counselor-client. The immediate objectives are an articulated operating program with open communication among participants, with feedback about the services, and with regular consideration of program changes based on operating feedback or new knowledge of career development.

The coordinator's skills are not the traditional client-appraisal, counseling skills of the professional counselor. Instead, coordinators employ entrepreneural, organizational, and managerial skills. They persuade administrators, teachers, parents and community leaders of the merits of a career development program; they bring them together and orchestrate their efforts into a program; they employ techniques such as the roundtable discussion and delphi to keep communication open; they delegate responsibilities, help identify and secure needed resources, and assure that communication channels remain open and are used. They are enthusiastic about the project, yet assure that its participants feel a sense of ownership for it.

Few counselors have had academic training or experience in sales, organization, or management that develop these skills directly. Their teaching assignments generally have not required such skills or offered them opportunities to see these skills exercised. Often, their current duties do not afford time seriously to attempt coordination, or their organizational table does not call for, or perhaps even allow, their involving others in their career development programs. Clearly, many educators will balk at counselors' assuming that they are to be coordinators. In a meeting of teachers' college faculty, counselor educators endorsed counselors' becoming coordinators of career education, but most other educators questioned counselors' competence for the position (Briggs & Green, 1975). Furthermore, states that have created coordinator positions, such as California, Michigan, and Wisconsin, have not made counseling credentials a qualification. Thus, although Hansen (1970) has described exemplary programs coordinated by counselors, most counselors will find it difficult to win credibility as the natural coordinator.

Heuristics Underlying Coordination

Underlying coordination are the following heuristic principles:

1. Career development is a multifaceted process, which benefits from systematic, articulated exposure to career concepts and models in multiple contexts and from multiple perspectives.
2. A coordinated career development program is likely to be more enduring and more powerful because participants sustain one another's enthusiasm, derive benefit from group participation, can access more resources, command more attention, and have more impact.
3. Many educators, parents, and community people will assist in career development programs if they are informed of the need and how they can contribute.

Method

Effective coordination involves the six broad activities presented below.

1. Visualize the overall project by creating a concrete but flexible image of what elements will be involved, what their orchestration will be like, and what will be produced. These images should continue to guide coordination efforts throughout the project. They will indicate the needed resources and how these will interface. Frequently, one's view of the project will alter, but this change should reflect new understanding or resource availability, not simply change for its own sake. Inspecting and reading about similar programs is helpful. Needless to say, one should be enthusiastic about the enterprise one is coordinating.

2. Identify prospective contributors; brief them about the goals and their potential contributions; persuade them to join the program, but do not mislead them about their commitment; listen carefully to their suggestions and comments. Figure 8–2 presents an outline of how to induct prospective employers in a work experience program.

Figure 8–2. Securing Employer Entry to a Work Experience Program

Employer Entry refers to outreach and recruitment of potential employers, selection and enrollment of suitable employers, and assessment of the identified jobs of suitable employers.

The activities in Employer Entry are essential to reach those employers who may not be aware of the program; to select systematically those suitable employers who can provide meaningful work experiences; and to assess adequately and accurately each identified job.

Successful performance of Employer Entry activities can be expected to:

- Ensure that those employers who agree to participate in the program are the most suitable ones.
- Establish individual job descriptions that document the requirements and responsibilities of the job, and the services to be provided and responsibilities of the employer (work supervisor).

Employer Outreach and Recruitment

Employer Outreach and Recruitment refers to all efforts to identify, inform and attract potential employers to the program.

Direct staff effort is necessary to seek out employers who are not familiar with the program, and to explain the program to them.

A policy decision is necessary to determine the types of employers to be used in the program. This decision must be made prior to program implementation.

First, Identify Potential Employers

- Establish a list (name, address, phone number, etc.) of employers in the area. Similar programs have used the following sources for information on public and private non-profit employers: United Fund directors; local or regional catalogs of human service organizations; telephone directories; individuals in such organizations as the welfare office, local employment service, service clubs, and community and neighborhood associations.
- Sources for private employers might include: local employment service offices; local chambers of commerce; city directories; telephone books, area development authorities; the National Alliance of Businessmen; and local service clubs.

Second, Make Initial Contact

- Using the list of potential employers, contact each one to arrange a meeting. Be sure to explain: the purpose of the meeting; objectives and services of the program; who will be representing the program; and anticipated outcomes of the meeting.

Some Tips

- Similar programs have first determined the major occupations presently in demand and those occupations which will be in future demand to ensure relevant work experience in the service area.
- Identify and contact as many employers as possible. A surplus and variety of employers will permit a choice of meaningful jobs.
- The advertising used to reach and recruit enrollees will also help inform potential employers.
- Program directors may arrange to speak before community organizations and service clubs to spark employer interest. Occasionally, former or veteran enrollees participate in such a presentation.

Figure 8–2. (*Continued*)

- Initial contact with and commitment from the chief executive of an organization will ensure better cooperation.
- Programs may include employer representation on advisory groups and special committees to enhance communication and increase outreach and recruitment efforts.
- Include unions in initial contact work if appropriate.

    If you are having Outreach and Recruitment problems:
- First, don't get discouraged. Good working relationships with employers take time to develop.

Reluctant Employers

- Some programs have arranged meetings to bring reluctant employers and cooperative employers together to discuss the program, identify problems and suggest resolutions.
- Other programs develop a list of cooperative or veteran employers to help convince hesitant employers that they should participate.
- Trial periods may be arranged to enable prospective employers to evaluate the program on a short-term basis.
- Some programs have arranged group meetings for similar types of employers to explain the program and secure their cooperation.
- Some have used former and veteran enrollees to assist program staff in outreach and recruitment.
- Cooperative or veteran employers are asked to assist in identifying and contacting prospective employers.

Negative Past Experience

- Approach the problem directly and honestly. Discuss the negative experience with the employer and, by using examples of other employers, assure him that the program staff will work to provide a positive experience.
- Perhaps the employer needs assurance that he will be involved in all decision-making affecting him.
- Former enrollees may explain their past experiences to employers.
- Other suggested selling points include the fact that enrollees need work experience with reputable employers and the joint efforts of the program and the employer will assure the program's success.

Contacting and Informing Employers

Meetings with potential employers are necessary to explain the objectives and services of the program; to describe the roles and responsibilities of participating employers; to gather background information on the employer, and to secure an agreement to cooperate with the program.

Suggested Points to Cover in Such a Meeting

- Program Introduction—to the goals and objectives, and the services provided.
- Roles and responsibilities—of the enrollee, the employer, work supervisor and the program staff.
- Employer background—as to type; major service(s) provided or product(s) produced; general occupations in the organization; experience with other programs and younger workers; work environment; facility, caliber of work supervisors, and other work-site conditions.

Figure 8–2. (*Continued*)

A Few Reminders

- Types of jobs enrollees could perform.
- Employer's agreement to participate.
- Obtain some background information on potential employers prior to the meeting if possible. Some programs have used this information to prepare a list of suggested jobs enrollees could perform.
- Remember that this meeting literally is to "sell" the program. Similar programs have suggested the following themes: enrollees are in school and need an opportunity to succeed; enrollees need work experiences with reputable employers; the program and employers have civic responsibility to insure that all young people become productive members of the community.
- Encourage the employers to participate actively in the meeting by means of questions and answers.
- Remember to explain the job rotation process to employers, if appropriate.
- Explain that the agreement of intent to cooperate does not necessarily mean that the employer will be selected to participate in the program.
- Obtain thorough background information on each employer who agrees to participate and categorize this information for future reference.
- Some programs distribute brochures, pamphlets and other written materials to the employers.
- Other programs explain the job specification forms which will be used during employer assessment to describe each identified job.

Employer Selection and Enrollment

Employer Selection and Enrollment refers to those activities necessary to 1) determine the eligibility of employers, 2) identify potential job assignments offered by each eligible employer, 3) determine the suitability of each eligible employer and 4) secure the formal intent of all suitable employers to participate in the program.

Successful Employer Outreach and Recruitment should generate many formal employer agreements to cooperate. By using a formal set of selection criteria, the program staff members can more systematically select from eligible employers those most suited to participation, i.e. they will provide a variety of meaningful work experiences. It is important to remember to select a surplus of suitable employers to ensure that enrollees will have a choice of jobs.

First, determine the eligibility of all employers agreeing to cooperate.

- The criteria to determine eligibility should be resolved as a policy decision prior to program implementation.
- Use the information collected on each employer during outreach and recruitment to determine the eligibility of employers.
- Notify in writing those employers who do not meet the eligibility requirements.

Selecting Suitable Employers

The purpose of selection is to determine the most suitable employers to **participate** in the program. Suitable employers will be **utilized** only if a successful job match is made during Matching and Alignment.

SOURCE: Systems Search Incorporated. *In-school youth manpower: A guide to local strategies and methods.* Washington, D.C.. U.S. Department of Labor, Contract No. 42–26–72–09, 1973.

The coordinator should be aware of the program's needs, and should ascertain the strengths, limitations, and priorities of the contributors. Obtain information about the contributors' current responsibilities, and how well each assisted in previous programs to anticipate how the planned roles fit their capabilities and current priorities. Solicit and listen carefully to their input since they have needed expertise and the coordinator's posture toward them will influence their cooperation. In coordinating a career education project, for instance, the author and his associate secured recommendations from state career education officers about possible site organizers, ascertained each nominee's occupational responsibility and professional reputation, and then briefed each and listened carefully for enthusiasm and understanding of the role. Finally, the author and his associate solicited recommendations about times, sites, prospective participants, and then basically concurred with these recommendations. By following this procedure Healy and Quinn (1977) secured enthusiastic, hardworking site managers.

3. Once contributors commit themselves to the project, the coordinator periodically assembles them so that they get to know one another as teammates, identify how their separate contributions are integrated into a total program, ascertain with whom and when they are to interface, and have opportunity collectively to overview the program and suggest improvements. Clearly, this group should meet periodically to review and report feedback on the program's progress and come to a consensus about how to sustain and improve the program. The group's social character can be developed in order to support the program goals, without overshadowing the original purpose. If major changes are suggested, the coordinator must promote full examination of the implications of the change and then enable the program leader—whether it is the coordinator, a principal or superintendent, or the whole group—to make a decision.

4. Assure that individual contributors participate in learning the target population's need for their service and that contributors are aware of, and share responsibility for, deciding how they should participate. For example, the librarian in a school's career development team should be part of the group that assesses student informational needs and source usage and should also be assured that his or her knowledge about informational materials and delivery would be a major determinant of how the project's library component operates. At the same time, the coordinator must help contributors get needed assistance. For instance, if the librarian needs a piece of equipment or a part-time aide to accomplish a priority program objective, the coordinator should inform the principal about the library's contribution to the program and should join the librarian in, or even take responsibility for, requesting the extra resources. Especially when contributors are not school employees, the coordinator should assure their sense of ownership over their contributions. For instance, if a utility public relations specialist is the liaison for the field trips to that utility, the coordinator should assure that he or she can work out visit procedures and prerequisites with teachers and will participate in setting learning goals to be accomplished by the visits.

At the minimum, the coordinator must brief him or her about the visit's purpose and get suggestions about feasibility and procedures and then arrange a previsit meeting with teachers, so that together they can arrive at realistic goals and activities for the visit. Following the visits, of course, feedback should be exchanged by the teachers and the public relations specialist.

5. Establish time schedules and time lines, set up meetings, verify that necessary communication and cooperation among contributors are occurring, and verify that resources are secured or ready for scheduled events. These mechanical tasks are essential to effective organization. Attention to these details shows contributors that one regards their time as valuable. A coordinator should verify that what is supposed to occur is happening.

6. Assure that feedback by which to evaluate the program is being collected, analyzed, and translated into understandable language for project contributors. The contributors may be collecting, analyzing, and interpreting data, or helping in these functions, but the coordinator must ensure that evaluation is operational and that timely reports are fed back to contributors. Sometimes a coordinator can rely on a consultant or resident evaluator, but must retain responsibility for the operation although not necessarily the efficacy of the technical operations.

Instructional Counseling

Following are four structured instructional procedures that rely on the counselor's identifying skill deficits, defining expectations, pointing out models, reinforcing desirable performance, and pacing learning of the skill. The procedures often include homework, and their focus on client action enables both client and counselor to monitor progress easily. The reinforcement-modeling paradigm popularized by Krumboltz and Thoresen (1964) has been studied extensively. A relatively simple procedure, it is designed primarily to promote information gathering. The vocational exploration group (VEG) is more complex, intending that clients learn the concepts of categorizing occupations and of projecting their affinity for occupations, as well as gain facts about particular occupations. It has been examined in both employment programs and schools. More ambitious still are skill training programs to equip clients with skills such as ability to interact in small groups, time management, and career assertiveness. These increasingly popular efforts teach clients the behavior and exercise them in its use and may teach the rules for attacking a problem rather than merely providing a new habit or new understanding. The last procedure, the experimental teach-the-test method, under study by Crites (1974c), contains the teaching operations characterizing the other procedures, but differs because client activity focuses on developing career maturity through learning correct responses to a test rather than through completing information-gathering and decision-making exercises.

Heuristic Principles

The following heuristic principles underlay instructional counseling procedures:

1. Clients will perform tasks, such as acquiring information, considering alternatives, and interacting in small groups, more effectively if the expected performance is made clear by detailed description, by the modeling of attractive figures who win reward, and by use of multiple media.

2. Clients will improve their performance of career development tasks more readily when they understand pertinent concepts underlying the task and its performance, and have a plan for completing the task. Pertinent concepts might include modeling, reinforcement, pacing, and so forth.

3. Clients will achieve developmental tasks more readily after they recognize the need for such accomplishment.

4. Clients will learn tasks more quickly and thoroughly when they believe peers expect such performance, when they have made commitments to do the tasks, and when they help peers in such accomplishment.

5. Clients will learn more effectively if they receive feedback on their efforts so that they practice effectively, are reinforced for progress, and monitor their programs.

6. Clients gain confidence in managing their career by tracing gains in their own career development, especially those due to their deliberate efforts, and by telling peers how they achieved such progress.

Instructional counseling recipients need environmental support for the tasks they are mastering. Appropriate, novel, and attractive informational materials, and cordial information givers will increase exploration; the family or immediate community should include people who exemplify the desired behavior; and the family, school, and community should be operating so that career-mature behavior will be rewarded or at least not thwarted. Clearly, many inner-city communities, troubled families, and penal institutions lack some or all of these prerequisites. Therefore, to increase the potential success of people from such environs, the counselor should alert parents and community and school leaders to the obstructions, and concomitantly may want to join with these people in reengineering the situation, as Shoben (1962) suggested.

Reinforcement-Modeling Counseling

Reinforcement-modeling counseling has several purposes: to have clients identify career development tasks, such as information seeking or deliberating about choices related to career progress; to reward them for intending to do the task and for its accomplishment; and to clarify their ideas about what constitutes successful performance, through discussion specifying these expected actions and/or through observations of models. A counseling procedure consisting of one modeling session and two discussion sessions serves to accomplish these purposes.

Modeling can come first or between discussion sessions. The procedure has been successful individually and in groups.

In the *modeling session*, the client views or listens to segments of two counseling sessions. In the first, a peer in discussion with a counselor pinpoints occupational information wanted and promises to secure it; in the second, the peer tells the counselor of personal experience gathering the information, and they discuss the relevance of the information for the peer's career. Throughout, the counselor rewards the peer verbally for intending to seek information and for deliberating about it.

In the first counseling interview the client presents personal career thoughts to a counselor, who is structuring the interview so that the client recognizes informational needs. When a need is established the counselor guides the client to identify precisely what must be learned and how to learn it. If the client has limited experience in information gathering, the counselor can help discover the merits and limitations of different sources. For example, in the case in Figure 8–3, the counselor had Mike recall that a cartoonist's notion of the expected supply of 1985 job openings would ordinarily not be as accurate as the projection available from the U.S. Department of Labor. On the other hand, Mike realized that shadowing the cartoonist for a half day in his studios would offer a much more concrete idea of what cartooning entailed than would a description in the *Occupational Outlook Handbook*, or even a film.

Once the need has been established in specific terms, such as "I want to find out the percentage of applicants who will be admitted to the AA art program at 'Y' community college in two years and the qualifications expected," the counselor guides the client in specifying how to secure the information. In the case of Mike, he recognized that in regard to future openings at a particular institution, the most to expect would be estimates, and that probably he would have to secure them personally from a representative of the school. Thus, following counselor cues, he said that on Wednesday he would visit the art department to schedule an appointment with its department chairman. He would go an hour early to the appointment in order to have time to read their informational material in preparation for the meeting. Throughout this session, the counselor cues clients to acknowledge information needs and to consider the advantages of different information sources and then to reinforce the client for this thinking and for commitments to secure the information.

At the close of the first interview, counselor and client schedule a second meeting to review the information that the client promises to gather between sessions and to review the client's thoughts about it. In this review, the counselor again uses cueing tactics and reinforcement to

Figure 8–3. A Reinforcement-modeling Counseling Illustration

Mike visited the Career Center on Tuesday and told the aide that he was interested in discussing art careers. The aide invited Mike to listen to a tape of a kind of counseling that might help him after signing up for an appointment with a counselor.

On Wednesday Mike met the counselor. In reply to her invitation to tell his reasons for coming, he indicated that he believed he wanted the counseling he had heard on tape to help him start planning for a career as a cartoonist. Elaborating in response to her "Go on please," Mike told how he had liked drawing cartoons and working with clay and molds since he was in kindergarten. Now that he was ending eleventh grade, he was thinking that he might study art and become some type of commercial artist. Continuing, he said he had already read several books on cartooning and now was doing the editorial cartoons for the school paper. Pausing, he wondered had she noticed his caricature of the governor's debate.

Following on her reflection that he was interested enough to read and even try himself out, Mike told how he had visited a cartoonist friend of his mother and discussed career possibilities. The experience was pleasant. He liked the studio and the way she worked, but he wondered was it really as hard as she said to break in? And how about his talent, would he be good enough?

Noting that Mike had at least two important questions, the counselor guided him in considering how he could answer each. With prompting, Mike recognized the importance of identifying several commercial art activities he would enjoy and arrived at the need to look at government projections to know how competitive cartooning was nationally, and then to interview people who placed and hired commercial artists in order to obtain their view about the local employment opportunities. Turning to judging his talents, Mike was encouraged that the counselor supported his idea of establishing a portfolio of work and obtaining criticism and feedback from art teachers. Turning to skill development, Mike said that he had thought he would go to the local community college. In discussing this, he was surprised that there might be special requirements or perhaps even better programs. He then resolved to visit the college and find out before the second meeting.

In their second meeting, Mike told how helpful the librarian had been in locating the employment projections. And while the junior college placement officer had confirmed that cartooning work was scarce locally, he was encouraging by pointing out the opportunities in advertising. At the junior college, Mike had learned that he could take an advanced placement course in twelfth grade to sample the art department. Moreover, good performance in that course and his high grades would qualify him for one of the twenty yearly slots. Heeding the counselor cues, he would investigate where that particular AA degree would lead.

Continuing, the counselor reinforced Mike's plans to investigate other art programs and to confer with his parents. The counselor agreed with Mike that finding out about his talent and choosing a direction in art would require judging the feedback he would get over the next year or two. In closing, Mike thanked the counselor for helping him to get all the different kinds of information and promised to tell her which program he and his parents would choose.

---

encourage the client to consider all facets of the information, to note additional information needs, and to acquire more information. For example, when Mike returned with the information that he could qualify for the junior college by doing well in an advanced placement course and by keeping up his grades, and that the program prepared people primarily for transfer to one particular state college, the counselor wondered aloud whether that state college emphasized Mike's interests in cartooning and costume design. This question prompted Mike to resolve to find out.

Vocational Exploration Group (VEG)

Daane (1971; 1972) developed VEG as a two-session review of factors for disadvantaged Employment Service clients to consider in relating to work. Delivery time ranges from two to five hours. The following description is based on a component outline published by Bergland and Lundquist (1975), on Cochran and Hoffman's (1975) description that elaborated on parts of the outline, and on this author's clinical experience with similar procedures. This author provided titles for the four phases, which were suggested by Cochran and Hoffman. To date, no published research indicates close monitoring or verification of counselor implementation of the VEG procedure.

Introduction. The leader describes the VEG program and its purposes briefly, invites participants to introduce themselves, and tells them to consider how they would spend one million dollars and then to share this with the group. Once the fantasies are shared and everyone knows each other's names and feels comfortable talking, the leader introduces a two-dimensional job classification, involving function (people, ideas, and things) and training required (high school, AA degree, apprenticeship, and so forth). The classification helps guide the group naming a wide range of occupations. Each participant is encouraged to contribute entries, with focus on filling all the cells of the matrix. The leader is careful not to reject occupational titles named by a client. This can be handled without confusing clients, either by noting that the title adds to understanding its particular cell but is not the cell suggested, or by allowing that the occupation might be considered in the cell (when true), but is often considered to be in another cell. Indeed, the latter case can remind clients that many occupations can be entered by more than one route, and that many jobs within an occupation permit variations in the "typical" mix of functions.

Cochran and Hoffman (1975) call these exercises the inception phase, underscoring the fact that their purpose is to build group cohesion. Throughout counseling, but especially in this phase, the leader responds enthusiastically to client input, encourages clients to recognize similarities and differences with their peers, and invites and rewards clients for dialoguing with one another.

Job Preferences. In this segment, each client tells the group his or her most and least preferred occupation and hears what each peer considers suitable and unsuitable occupations for them. The counselor prompts and cues the clients to elaborate on their preferences by sharing their reasons for choosing and their beliefs about what the occupation entails and what is required to enter it. As facilitator, the counselor points out similarities and then reinforces clients for noting similarities with one another, for asking questions eliciting elaboration, for reinforcing one another, and for deliberating about and sharing reactions to suggestions. To encourage such participation, the counselor can point out the advantage of the open-ended versus closed question in eliciting peer views and can urge clients to pose open-ended questions to one another.

Once all participants have heard their peers' occupational recommendations for them, they write down occupations they are entertaining and their thoughts about these. For instance, next to lawyer a student noted "Class believes I can do it," while next to police officer appeared the entry "If I become more assertive."

Proceeding, each client then establishes the place of these occupations on the function x training matrix, with the counselor's providing individual assistance as needed. To further help envision these occupations, the group members examine pictures of workers doing different functions and name the occupations that might be pictured in such work. The pictures should allow the work to be construed as representing several occupations. For instance, two people dialoguing in a business office can be construed as a supervisory session, a sales session, a counseling session, a legal consultation, an employment interview, and the like. For more clarification of occupations, the counselor encourages clients to read informational booklets about the occupations they are considering.

Occupational components and preferences. At the start of the second session, clients review, discuss, and start to identify their preferred occupational satisfiers and demands, and they identify occupations that fit their satisfier-demand preferences. The leader explains that satisfiers are nonmonetary work benefits, such as prestige, good working conditions, and opportunity for travel; the leader encourages the clients to name and talk about satisfiers that appeal to themselves or that they feel would appeal to a particular peer. Time permitting, brainstorming can produce a list of satisfiers. Proceeding, the counselor guides clients in noting occupational differences in terms of satisfiers.

Next, the counselor notes that work also makes demands for skills, abilities, and even interests, and again directs clients to reflect and to interact about the appealing abilities and interests. Continuing, the clients discuss the occupational differences regarding abilities and interests.

This phase of counseling closes by relating client insights to training requirements. The counselor directs them to think of four categories of occupations: those they like and for which they have training, those they like but for which they lack training, and those they dislike and for which they have training, and those they dislike and for which they lack the requisite training. Each client lists three or more occupations in each category.

When the client's preferred occupations differ from the list of preferred occupations in session 1, he or she is encouraged to discuss the reasons, since, as Cochran and Hoffman (1975) have noted, the purpose of the program is to bolster career choice skills such as deliberating and planning, rather than to result in a final choice.

Alternatives and next steps. The final phase of the program involves clients' expanding their lists of potential occupations by reviewing occupations on the function x training matrix and adding them to their appropriate preference list. Again, occupational briefs are available to help them judge occupations, and a counselor could also guide clients in using their expanded knowledge of one another to suggest additions to their two preferred categories.

After adding alternatives, each client reflects on current career goals (occupational objectives) and necessary steps, pondering and tentatively answering the questions: "What do I need to enter occupation x, how do I prepare? When do I obtain the necessary experience and skills? The session closes with each client sharing these answers and obtaining group feedback about them. When necessary, a client can confer individually with the counselor to round out planning, reconcile reactions, or review feelings and ideas generated in the sessions.

Rule-learning Counseling

Phelps (1978) designed this structured procedure, and building on the work of McGovern (1970), she had counselors teach college students the following rules for improving their classroom and small group interaction skills.

1. To start a conversation, *act* by telling the person something about what you are doing, thinking or feeling, and then to sustain the conversation, *react*, by sharing your thoughts or feelings about the other's communication.

2. To improve an interaction, *attend* to what the other person is telling you rather than worrying about what you will say next, and try, by using devices such as paraphrase and perception checks, to *understand* what he or she is communicating to the point of being able to empathize.

3. To sustain a conversation, *relate to*, and *elaborate on*, the speaker's topic by talking about yourself in relation to it. If this would be tiring, then smoothly change topics by building a bridge or *associating* what is being discussed to a fresh topic.

4. To improve a conversation, *answer* the question about yourself before *asking* it of your partner, since this does not force him to disclose more than you.

5. To sustain your involvement in group interaction in spite of fear, control your interfering feelings by telling yourself to "*Stop,*" perhaps taking a deep breath and exhaling slowly in order to break the fear buildup, *and then think* about the reality of the situation, pinpointing especially the limited risks, so you can start or continue to make your input.

6. *Inquire* when you are curious, by looking the teacher straight in the eye and asking a clarifying, probing or diverging question

in a confident, strong voice, then *respond* verbally or nonverbally to indicate that you understand or support the answer, or to review your understanding.

7. To enter a discussion, either *inform* the members by orienting, clarifying, elaborating, repeating or relating, or *interpret* the meaning or implications and share your feelings about it.

8. To enter discussion toward the close of the group interaction, either *summarize* what has been discussed and/or verify consensus or *suggest* next steps or implications.

9. To participate effectively in groups, listen critically, *evaluate*, and take a risk by *expressing* your views about the ideas and values under discussion.

10. To express disagreement without inducing defensiveness, preface your *critique*, with *support;* that is, before critiquing a person's view, summarize your understanding of the other person's view, state something positive about the person, or share the experience that led you to a contrary position.

11. To decrease distance between you and another person, *identify* your feelings about yourself and *express* verbally and nonverbally your feelings openly and honestly, even though you may not have the precise word or the most appropriate situation.

12. To decrease distance between you and others, *focus on your feelings* toward and perceptions about the other person in order to experience them and *respond* so that the other person has feedback.

These rules were taught in ten one-and-one-half hour meetings of five or six students and a female counselor. Before the actual treatment the subjects attended two sessions in which they got acquainted and were apprised of the counseling and its administration; completed self-report measures about their interpersonal skills; listened to an explanation of the interpersonal skills diary they would maintain throughout counseling; received feedback on their self-ratings; and discussed special needs, concerns, or goals they had for counseling.

After these two initiation and screening sessions, the next ten sessions followed a uniform format below. Figure 8–4 then presents the guidelines for session 6 to illustrate format implementation.

1. The leader outlines the session.

2. The group reviews last session's rule(s).

3. The group reviews homework.

4. The leader collects diary and homework.

5. The leader presents rule and appropriate background about its importance and situations where it applies.

6. The counselor models application of the rule and plays a recording wherein actors model the target skill. The counselor underscores essentials through discovery questions.

7. Students ask questions in order to become more concrete about how they are to act in employing the rule.
8. Students role play applying the rule in scenarios provided by the counselor, and they observe and rate peers' roleplaying.
9. The clients review their own performance and the counselor and peer feedback, and they comment on their peers' performances.
10. The group members summarize the rule's application.
11. The leader presents predetermined homework and engages the group in troubleshooting past or potential difficulties in carrying out the assignment.

Figure 8–4. Plan for Session 6: Initiating, Entering, or Concluding a Verbal Problem-solving Sequence in a Group Discussion

GOALS: 1. Students can accurately identify the rules being applied during the sample conversation and by other students during the Guided Practice step (i.e., rules #1–#8).
2. Students demonstrate their recall of rules learned during previous sessions and can give examples during the Review and Guided Practice steps.
3. Students demonstrate an understanding of the rules for this session, "Inform-Interpret" and "Summarize-Suggest", and can apply them accurately during Guided Practice.

STEP 1: REVIEW OF PREVIOUS SESSION
_____ A. *Brief Review of Skills Learned in Previous Sessions*
_____ B. *Review of Homework Assignment:*
   a) *Students Report on Experiences*
   b) *Collection of Homework Sheets*
   c) *Feedback on Step 4 Worksheets*
_____ C. *Collect Diary & Record Student Progress*

STEP 2: STRUCTURING OF CURRENT SESSION
_____ A. *Presentation of Content for This Session:* "Today we are going to look at two more communication rules, each of which deal with participation in a small group discussion in class. From our observations and interviews with students such as yourselves, we have learned that many students avoid entering into or initiating class discussion because they do not know *how or where to begin.* Students with such a problem are (1) often unable *to gain* or hold the *attention* of others in a group while speaking; (2) they are *usually followers* rather than leaders in a group discussion; (3) they *avoid standing by themselves* and saying what they think; and (4) they *may be unprepared* for class discussion."

Such students have said the following: (1) "I am reluctant to talk freely because of what others might think . . . or . . . because I'm afraid the group won't follow." (2) "There just wasn't anything new generating inside of my mind that was worthwhile saying or else I didn't have a good enough grasp of the material." (3) ". . . maybe they had a better understanding of the course than I did . . . I just wanted someone else to give me their opinion." (4) "I'm a follower; I'd rather not take the responsibility."

"On the other hand, students report that when they *do* participate in class discussion it results in greater learning for themselves. It causes them to organize their thinking and it reinforces what has just been taught or learned."

Figure 8–4. (*Continued*)

_____ B. *Discovery Questions for Current Session:* In presenting the following discovery questions to the students, the counselor should keep in mind an objective for this session that each student understand the wide range of means or techniques for entering or initiating a discussion.

      a) "How might you attempt *to gain* the *attention* of a small group of people or a class?" (Possible responses include the following: voice projection, eye contact, posture, gestures, facial expression, body position relative to group, leaning in toward group.)

      b) "   (name)   , do you feel that what *you* have to say in class is worthwhile? Why or why not?"
      (Counselor should repeat this question with each student.)

      c) "How might you verbally initiate or enter a discussion? Where would you begin?"

_____ C. *Display Card with "Inform-Interpret" Rule:* "The best way to initiate or enter a discussion group is by providing some *input* to the group. Provide *information* (orientation, clarification, elaboration, repetition) for the group. *Tell* about your past experience (or lack of it) relative to the task or topic of discussion. *Restate* the assigned task or problem-solving situation."

"An alternative way to enter the discussion is for you to give your *interpretation* (ideas, opinions, feelings, evaluation, analysis) of the task at hand. What are *your* ideas about it? What do you think the group should be doing?"

"Are there any questions about that?"

_____ D. *Display Card with "Summarize-Suggest Rule:* "Even if you have not participated initially or during the body of a discussion, you can *still* enter the group discussion towards the end by assuming the role of summarizing or suggesting. For instance, you might take some notes (be an informal recorder for the group) and then provide the group with a summary of their comments toward the end. Often the person who assumes this *summarizing role* can appear as the leader of the group! After presenting your summary, you might tentatively (using 'perception check') state, 'Do we all then agree that . . . ?' Such a summary might identify essential elements of the problem discussed, it might refer to the major conclusions which the group seemed to agree upon, and/or it might evaluate the completeness of the discussion."

"A second way of concluding a discussion is by making a *suggestion*. This might include *setting a goal* for the group (e.g., 'I think we should all be in agreement before we proceed with our group project.'), *giving alternatives* (e.g., 'It seems that we have several options to choose from—these are . . .'), *directing action* (e.g., 'Sally, will you be in charge of gathering information on . . . for the group?'), or *stating implications* (e.g., 'What we have been saying seems to mean that students *do* want to be responsible for their own learning.')"

"Are there any questions about that?"

_____ E. *Modeling and Sample Dialogue:* "Let's listen to a sample conversation in which three students are discussing a task assigned by their teacher. The task is that the students are to decide, as a group, how they would like to be evaluated in a course. Let's listen for applications of these two rules as well as the other rules which we have already learned."

Counselor plays "Sample Conversation #7" while students follow on their transcript copy.

Following the tape the counselor says, "Let's go back through the transcript and note the rules being applied." The counselor then briefly goes

Figure 8–4. (*Continued*)

through the dialogue pointing out examples of how the communication rules learned thus far are being applied.

_____ F. *Student Questions and Clarification of Rules:* "Before we begin our practice for today are there any questions about these two rules?"

STEP 3: GUIDED PRACTICE

_____ A. *Practice Triad Dialogues:* For the practice dialogues the counselor should suggest several possible problem situations or tasks which the students may be familiar with and which might have some interest for them. The hypothetical tasks should approximate what might actually occur in a classroom situation. For example: students deciding on a course's content or requirements; students who are doing a group project for a class assignment and who must agree upon a topic of interest to all members; a student committee responsible for selecting campus activities for the term; students who are to make recommendations to the housing committee on dormitory regulations; etc.

Counselor proceeds with guiding the practice in the same manner as previous sessions.

_____ B. *Feedback on Performance and Reinforcement:* Counselor should note examples of how rules are being applied by the students and reinforce all accurate applications. Also note and reinforce the non-verbal behaviors (eye contact, facial expression, clarity and volume of speech, posture, gestures).

_____ C. *Continue Triad Practice Dialogues*

STEP 4: SUMMARY

_____ A. *Review:* "Let me summarize what we have done today. First we reviewed the use of the rules which we have already studied and then we looked at two new communication rules which relate directly to small group discussion or problem-solving situations. We discussed a number of ways in which a person might enter such a discussion whether *or not* they have specific ideas or knowledge about the topic or task in question."

_____ B. *Opportunity for Student Questions:* "Before I give you the new homework assignment, are there any questions about what we have done today?"

STEP 5: HOMEWORK ASSIGNMENT

_____ A. *Distribute Step Six Worksheet:* Counselor should call to their attention that the homework this week focuses only on the first of the two rules taught at today's session, namely, "Inform-Interpret". They will focus on the other rule in their homework next week.

_____ B. *Reminder of Maintaining the Diary and Importance of Practice*

SOURCE: A. T. Phelps. *Development and evaluation of an instructional counseling program for the treatment of reticence.* Unpublished Ph.D. dissertation, University of California, Los Angeles, 1978. Used with permission.

During every session, the group used instructional aids: set of rule cards that visually present essential aspects of the new rule, a set of gummed labels for the students to apply to their rule sheets, and a list of sample phrases illustrating the rule taught.

The counseling program sought to change behavior in small progressive steps. Every step included both concepts relevant to the content being taught (i.e., effective interpersonal communication rules), and coping skills for applying the cognitive content (i.e., appropriate self-talk). For example, one might say, "This is an important question for me to ask if I am going to succeed on the next test." Also taught are cognitive control devices, such as "I'm tense . . . stop for a moment . . . deep breath . . . sit back . . . calm . . . relax, that's better, speaking up won't kill me." Throughout, counselors emphasized that effective communication and participation are habits acquired through repeated practice over an extended period of time. The guided practice and performance criterion increased in complexity over successive counseling sessions.

During each session, the counselor structured practice so that all subjects had the opportunity to participate in at least one behavioral rehearsal of the new communication rule. Every guided practice was followed by self-evaluation, feedback from peers and the counselor, reinforcement for effective behaviors, and consideration of alternative responses. To aid observation, to insure peer feedback, and to help the counselor determine attainment of each session's behavioral goals, clients rated the extent to which different peers applied each of the twelve rules. During the session, a client practiced until his or her behavior approximated the criterion for that session's skill.

In addition to behavioral rehearsal during counseling, the clients were assigned homework to apply the new skill. During the initial and concluding portions of a session, subjects discussed past and current homework assignments in order to identify and provide opportunity for reinforcing successful interpersonal contacts and to troubleshoot difficulties. Particular emphasis was placed on the value of between-session practice in real-life situations. These assignments were coordinated with the cognitive and behavioral content of each session, and involved progressively more challenging extra counseling communications. Figure 8–4 includes the homework assignment for session 6.

Other concepts and heuristic principles also might be taught to teenagers. The author's manual, *Discovering You* (Healy, 1976), for instance, teaches many of the concepts and principles that derive from the different models. Some suggested by the scientific person model for building self-confidence include: acknowledge achievements and announce them to others; occasionally pause to feel and savor the happiness that achievement gives; place yourself in supportive, constructive groups where you are expected to succeed and are given responsibility; recognize that decision making is a process, so that as you are moving through a decision, you use the feedback becoming available to ensure that your decision fits your intentions and capabilities, and thus is likely to be successful.

The sociological model, in turn, suggests: maintain and expand communication with parents and other adults in order to receive assistance in acquiring skills and in obtaining access to opportunities; and engage in ongoing interaction with adults through activities and groups, such as volunteering, work study, the "Y" Eagle Scouts, and your church, in order to become fully aware of adult behaviors and expectations. The economic model suggests: follow a balance-sheet approach to judge what you are gaining and losing by your time allocation. On the other hand, the behavioral model emphasizes the value of learning task analysis and systematic planning for building specific academic, social, athletic, or other skills.

To further observe how these principles might be taught, consider the behavioral model for the high school junior who wants to become the senior starting guard on the football teams. He can be taught task analysis as he is assisted in defining the competences needed in that position: ability to move laterally, to start quickly from a sprint-like stance, and to block and tackle vigorously. Next, he can learn systematic planning as he works out a regimen for building up the requisite competences: repeated pulling drills, instruction and feedback in springing, repeated short sprints, and a regular weight lifting regimen to build shoulder and leg strength. Concurrently, he can learn to use reinforcement to sustain his commitment to the plan: keeping a record of gains in sprint-times and weight lifted, rewarding himself with a day off, and/or lifting weights to enjoyable music.

Although principle and concept learning have only recently been emphasized in counseling, many studies have shown that study skills counseling has helped some students to improve school performance. Since these programs often involved teaching the concepts and principles of task analysis and studying, one can argue that learning the concepts and principles contributed to growth. Indeed, three studies (Bates, 1971; Vivell, 1972, 1975) of time management, a component of study skills, tend to support this assertion. They are noteworthy because they controlled the counseling treatment more than most other studies and had the subject-clients complete paper-pencil exercises as part of counseling, to show they understood and were able to apply the concepts and principles learned in the group counseling to their own situations. These studies will be described and discussed later in the chapter, along with other rule-learning studies.

Teach the Test

Renewed interest in competence-based instruction and performance or criterion-referenced testing suggests another didactic career counseling procedure: teach the career development test. With the introduction of cognitive career development tests, such as *the Assessment of Career Development* (1974), *the Career Development Inventory* (Super, et al., 1971), *The Career Maturity Inventory* (Crites, 1973), *The New Mexico Career Education Test Series* (Healy & Klein, 1973), and the *Career Skills Assessment Program* (Educational Testing Service, 1977), sets of career development problems in different content domains are available for such use. Indeed, Crites (1974c) has experimented with this counseling procedure and even has provided a video tape illustrating its operation.

There are at least two approaches to this procedure. First, one can review the concepts to be assessed by a test; test the client on the reviewed material; score the test; discuss the incorrect answers to teach the pertinent rationale; and, on the basis of this teaching, decide whether additional instruction is necessary. Alternately, one might have a client complete a test spanning the spectrum of career development competences as part of the career development appraisal; review incorrect responses to teach missed concepts and principles; and then decide whether other kinds of assistance, such as systematic study of decision making, is warranted.

The former approach should reduce client errors, thereby lessening anxiety associated with career development learning; whereas the latter would use the test to identify systematically clients who need counseling and would provide a clear rationale for the content covered in their counseling. Crites (1974c) suggested and described the latter approach. The former approach is illustrated here briefly for the case of a Jorge, who was a member of a group distinguishing among sources of career information.

To acquaint the students with the data available from different sources of information, the counselor first used discovery questions to generate a list of sources and then reviewed the kinds of data each source was likely to produce. The group named these sources:

1. Written information
2. Teachers
3. Parents
4. Friends
5. Watch people working
6. Movies of work

Next, the counselor had Jorge and the others recall that the government produced written information, such as that in the *Occupational Outlook Handbook,* which described the duties, the requirements, number of workers, likely number of openings, average salary, and where to secure more information. On the other hand, parents could tell their experiences, which jobs they could help him get, how much training they could support, and what they thought was important about him in regard to working and learning. On the basis of his performance in their classes, teachers, too, could give him information about whether occupations related to their specializations were right for him, and they could tell him about college training and occupations they had performed.

Following this review, the students answered ten questions, such as the five in Figure 8–5. After finishing the questions, they scored them on a key that provided a rationale for each answer. Jorge checked those questions he missed and those that followed a different rationale than the one he applied, so he and the counselor could discuss them during the individual conference time. The key appears in Figure 8–6.

Jorge missed questions 1 and 4 in Figure 8–5. He had marked B for both questions. When he handed the counselor the scored test, she noted that he had answered eight of the ten questions correctly, thereby showing a good understanding of information sources. Then she asked Jorge

Figure 8–5. Questions on Sources of Career Information

1. After talking with the crew of the jet plane on which she returned from vacation, Martha wanted to get some specific facts about transportation jobs. She wanted to know about skill and training requirements, duties, rates of pay, and the unions and professional groups from which to obtain further information. Which of the following will be most helpful to her?
   a. *Occupational Outlook Handbook*
   b. A formal interview with each of the air crew members
   c. Discussion with peers
   d. A film about the transportation industry
2. Terry is graduating from high school and wants to be self supporting within a year. There are several one-year training programs open to Terry, and she feels she could enjoy and be successful at the occupations which each teaches. However, she wants to know which occupation is most likely to be in demand in the community when she graduates. What would you recommend for her?
   a. Ask the directors of the programs about their local placement rates
   b. Ask students in each program about their job prospects in the community
   c. Try to line up a job now for the future
   d. Read the *Occupational Outlook Handbook* to find out about job outlooks
3. Frank is interested in sketching, painting, and sculpting and wants to find out about different occupations which might use these talents so that he could learn more about them. What would be his best course of action?
   a. Confer the *Dictionary of Occupational Titles*
   b. Ask the art teacher
   c. Take an interest inventory
   d. Read magazines on art and sculpting
4. Miguel is finishing his freshman year and thinks he wants to be a physician like his uncle, but he is wondering whether he has enough talent. Since medical schools are very selective, he wants to be sure he has a chance to enter one before committing himself to major in biology. Which of the following is most likely to give him the most accurate information about whether he has appropriate talent?
   a. Friends who are already in the premedical program
   b. His uncle who is a doctor
   c. His mathematics and biology teacher
   d. The college counselor
5. Gregg's parents want him to finish at least two years of college but cannot afford any tuition or even to support him fully for the two years. They told him to find out about scholarships and financial aid. Where do you recommend he go to get the information?
   a. His friends in college
   b. The career section of the library
   c. His bank's loan department
   d. The school counselor

why he chose B for question 1. When he told her that he had thought a worker could give a first-hand account of jobs in transportation, the counselor agreed that many workers would be able to give accurate, concrete descriptions of their own jobs and of some of the jobs around them, but often they would not be able to give such information about many other jobs in their industry. Moreover, they frequently do not keep

Figure 8–6. Rationales for Answers to Career Information Problems Missed by Jorge

---

A. *Occupational Outlook Handbook* is the best answer because it presents the facts, which Martha seeks, about more than eight hundred occupations. These facts are based on careful examination of occupations and the probable state of the economy in the future. A worker in the transportation industry is unlikely to have as up-to-date data as the *Handbook,* and a film will focus more on being interesting and is likely to omit facts, such as pay, which change regularly, since films cannot be revised as often as printed material. A discussion with peers, of course, will depend on their knowledge and may not teach about pay or supply and demand.

C. Ask his mathematics and biology teachers if he has the requisite talent for biology is the best answer because they have had many opportunities to observe Miguel's performance of tasks basic to biology. Teachers are expert in their fields and have learned to judge people's ability to learn their subjects. Therefore, they probably can make objective assessments. A counselor, in contrast, would not have first-hand knowledge about Miguel's math and science performance. Occasionally, a counselor would have contingency table data or tests that could help Miguel judge the probability of a person with his grades or test scores succeeding in a particular biology program, or some counselors could administer and interpret a test that provided estimates of Miguel's abilities relative to others his age. However, a counselor might not use these resources for Miguel unless he asked for more than just his qualifications for medicine. An uncle, even a physician, probably would not have observed Miguel's work first-hand or be trained to judge his potential for medicine objectively. Likewise, older friends would not be likely to have first-hand knowledge of Miguel's performance and ordinarily would not be able to give as accurate information about what constitutes potential for studying biology as could teachers, although they have the qualificaitons themselves.

---

abreast of the projected supply and demand of workers, although such information would be valuable in their own career planning. Proceeding, the counselor asked Jorge to recall what the *Occupational Outlook* contained and how its information was assembled. Having listed its elements, Jorge agreed it was the correct answer.

Next, the counselor asked about item 4. Jorge said he was hoping his uncle would take him into practice after graduation. The counselor replied that it was important to have a sponsor in some trades, but was not essential in a profession such as medicine. Moreover, since Jorge was wondering about his abilities, it would be wiser for him to confer with a teacher who had often observed him perform tasks related to medical studies. Because the teacher would not be a relative, would have had many observations, and would be knowledgeable about mathematics and biology learning skills, he or she would probably be more objective than his uncle.

Jorge half-heartedly agreed, but then asked whether the counselor would know more about medicine, and could she not give him a test to predict his performance. The counselor replied there were tests that could give pertinent information about Jorge's ability that would be different from the teacher's information, and that in some cases the test information would be more accurate. Continuing, she added that if Jorge were able to take such tests and to get accurate interpretation, she hoped he would put both kinds of data together in judging his qualifications. Then Jorge noted that the A answer did not mention testing, and so he agreed that B was the better response. The counselor nodded, and pointed out that Jorge's thinking about the question had clarified that there are several ways to determine ability.

Jorge's discussion of his errors, coupled with his 80 percent performance, indicated no further instruction in the areas was needed currently. Had the discussion, however, indicated confusion or minimal acquaintance with information sources, the counselor would have prescribed activities to develop the deficiencies indicated.

Career Checkup Role

Another approach that could build on "the teach-the-test" method is a career checkup method. This technique involves conferring periodically with a student throughout school to update understanding of his or her career development. This role has not been researched or delineated in the literature, although it seems to be the role envisioned when counselors assume responsibility for student programming.

The role could be practiced in the following manner. At annual or semiannual meetings, the student would bring the counselor up to date about career plans and aspirations, school courses, extra-curricular activities, and other pursuits that might be career-relevant. The counselor's objectives would be to encourage a student to reflect on what discoveries the student is making about self in regard to career, especially ensuring that the student has sufficient evidence for self-attributions, and to verify that the student's career progress was positive. The youngster might prepare for the session by completing self-review exercises, such as those in *Discovering You* (Healy, 1976) or by composing an autobiography to ensure that the spectrum of data pertinent to career development is fresh in mind. The counselor might even teach the student to use alternate frameworks for construing career (see Chapter 2) in order to recognize the multiple factors that career can involve. But essentially the meeting's purpose would be hygienic, verifying the growth of the career and alerting the student to developmental tasks and remedial needs. Even apparently excelling careerists periodically would experience the checkup.

The heuristics supporting such a role include:

1. A person will increase the effectiveness of career development efforts if he or she expects periodically to review progress and to receive feedback from an expert in career.
2. Since careers are developmental, early identification and remediation of potential problems are likely to be easier and more effective than are corrections after failure.

Simulation Case Study Counseling

Simulation as a counseling tool is increasing in importance. Krumboltz and his colleagues (1967) designed a set of exercises that simulate different occupational tasks and assist youngsters in exploring occupations. Classrooms have become small economies or businesses to teach career skills (Shirts, 1966; Kourilsky, 1974), and schools have even simulated businesses in an effort to develop career awareness (Leonard & Stephens, 1967). In terms of the elements to consider in adolescent planning, Boocock (1967) designed a game that informs teenagers about adolescent development tasks as they play; and Ryan (1968) has designed group counseling programs around simulation.

Simulation is a potentially valuable adjunct to counseling because it enables creation of scenarios that cover the spectrum of career developmental tasks. Furthermore, simulation permits preassembly of pertinent problem-solving resources to assure their access and subsequent satisfying use by clients and confronts clients with anxiety-arousing situations in a nonthreatening context. Myers (1978) has pointed out that advancements in computer technology are likely to add to the realism of exploration simulations, and has noted that the availability of such simulations can increase the fun in career exploration, one of the important, albeit frequently missing, elements in programs designed to stimulate exploration.

Of course, simulations, like all instructional methods, are likely to be engaging when they are adapted to the learner's capability and needs. When these tasks are defined clearly and necessary equipment is available, and when the teacher is knowledgeable and enthusiastic about the activity and acts to involve students in it, more learning is likely to occur. Below is outlined one simulation that has been described in detail and studied in an exacting field research by Ryan (1968). The procedure is one of the most thoroughly described in the literature because not only does it present the simulation materials, but it also carefully delineates the facilitator's role and provides a counseling typescript to illustrate how the role is implemented.

Heuristic Principles

1. Clients will become aware of their career development tasks if they engage in simulated career management activities.
2. Clients will more likely attempt career development tasks when they have indicated how a simulated character would do the task, or after they do the task for him.
3. Clients will more likely become aware of developmental tasks and perform them when they have been rewarded for identifying and managing career tasks in a simulation.

The goal of the Ryan (1968) simulation is for clients to learn about decision making and the career decisions facing them, and to apply career decision-making skills in managing the career tasks of a peer. In the simulation, a group of clients produce immediate and future plans for students like themselves. As a byproduct, clients should recognize their need for: a) identifying their own aspirations and characteristics, b) considering and using methods for learning about occupations and training programs, c) setting immediate training goals, and d) pondering future possibilities. Ryan used the procedure to complement a vocational guidance class that included personal and vocational testing and group interpretation and lectures about the world of work.

Throughout simulation counseling, clients are encouraged to provide information and to ask questions of each other and of the counselor. At the first lesson, clients introduce themselves and then learn about the counseling process and how they should participate. Ryan suggested an introduction such as the following:

> You will be helping to plan the life of an individual for the four years after high school. You will get to know him, his likes and dislikes, his background, and his abilities. As you plan his life, you will begin to consider alternatives which occur each time a decision is made. You will discuss the consequences of his decision. (Ryan, 1968)

Figure 8–7 presents a sample case used by Ryan's counselors. At the opening of each session, the counselor reminds the clients that their purpose is to develop planning skills and informs them that they may ask for information about the consequences of different courses of action for the fictitious student, and then distributes a case study and points out its essential elements.

During the main part of the session, the counselor is responsible for providing requested information, giving verbal cues to elicit responses related to decision making, and reinforcing decision-making responses. Verbal cues include such leading questions as, "Where do you think _____ (name) _____ might find information about job openings in this area?" Throughout the session the counselor is warm and attentive and encourages the group members to act in the same way. When closing, the counselor interrupts the session by saying something such as, "OK, I see the time is up for today. I am looking forward to seeing you next week. We had a good session. Some of the things we discussed today will be helpful to you in planning, and I hope that you will think about them." In other words, the counselor ends on a positive note, while setting the stage for subsequent meetings. The original counseling ran for ten fifty-minute sessions, and one case study was reviewed for every two sessions. Forty minutes of each session were devoted to the case, and the remaining ten minutes were used to open and to close counseling.

Once the session is underway, the students examine the case carefully. The counselor asks cue questions to enable the clients to examine pertinent aspects of the fictitious person's situation. Ryan's (1968) description of the counselor's procedure implies that the following aspects are examined:

1. The kind of person he or she is—goals and problems.
2. Personal factors important in career choice—interests, aptitudes, experience, physical characteristics.
3. Occupational characteristics important in career choice—options, travel requirements, on-going training.
4. Occupational alternatives—the ability of alternatives to meet needs and utilize his talents.
5. Educational and vocational programs available—their relation to his past experience, their requirements and cost, and the potential for meeting the client's goals.
6. The impact on the client of his choice—the expected life styles the job demands, and the probable rewards.

Several information updates on the client are inserted to move the case along. In addition, such unplanned events as loss of a part-time job or parents' divorce are introduced to provide practice in dealing with chance.

In supervising counselor trainees applying the procedure, this author found that counselors should specify beforehand the points to be discovered and rehearse alternate questions to involve clients in discussion.

Following is a typescript of portions of a session in which students are guided to plan the career of Uria, whose profile appears in Figure 8–7. Accompanying each excerpt is commentary to illustrate major elements of the counselor role.

Counselor: All right, now you have Uria's background. Remember he is just finishing the summer's work on the farm. He finished high school last June. His first decision is what is he going to do this fall. Will he go on to school? What do you think?

Rick: I think he should go to work on the farm. I mean that's it. He . . .

Counselor: What information do you think he will want to consider to help him decide about going to school this fall, Elaine?

Elaine: He seems to like mathematics. He should look at that. He has B in high school math.

Counselor: Yes, his high school record is important to consider in thinking about whether to go to school or not. What else?

Randy: Well, on this he scored high in clerical. And on this he was high in clerical too.

Counselor: Good points to notice. What might this information mean to Uria in thinking about whether to go on to school or not?

Elaine: He probably would enjoy working in some kind of clerking. He didn't like change. Clerking is just a lot of the same thing. Maybe he would like to be a clerk.

Figure 8–7. Profile of Student Used in Simulation Counseling

E-13 Uria Fox

Uria Fox is eighteen years old. He is 5 ft. 11 in. tall and weighs 195 lbs. He is in excellent physical condition. Uria graduated from high school in June and has been working at home during the summer with his step-father. He lives with his parents and half-sister about ten miles out of town on a small farm, and his half-sister is in the first grade. Uria's mother was born on an Indian reservation. His father died when he was eight years old, and his mother remarried when he was ten. He and his mother then went to live on his step-father's farm. Uria's mother never has worked outside the home.

Uria's hobbies are sports, bulldogging and horses. He was on the football team in high school and made name for himself. He doesn't know what he wants to do now.

Name: URIA FOX

Kuder Vocational
Percentile

40	Outdoor
5	Mechanical
33	Computational
85	Scientific
76	Persuasive
22	Artistic
15	Literary
30	Musical
68	Social Service
63	Clerical

General Aptitude Test Battery
Percentile

48	General Learning Ability
46	Verbal Aptitude
39	Numerical Aptitude
78	Spatial Aptitude
68	Form Perception
70	Clerical Perception
84	Motor Coordination
28	Finger Dexterity
88	Manual Dexterity

American College Test
Percentile

2	English Usage
14	Mathematics Usage
10	Social Science Reading
9	Natural Science Reading
4	Composite

My Vocational Choice

1. College
2. . . . .
3. . . . .
4. . . . .
5. . . . .

Kuder Personal
Percentile

86	Group Activity
66	Stable Situations
15	Dealing with Ideas
13	Avoiding Conflict
79	Directing Others

Edwards Preference Schedule
Percentile

20	Achievement
18	Deference
65	Order
95	Exhibition
12	Autonomy
76	Affiliation
27	Intraception
60	Succorance
70	Dominance
40	Abasement
22	Nurturance
10	Change
58	Endurance
79	Heterosexuality
68	Aggression

Otis Quick Scoring Mental Ability
104

Average High School Grades

D	English, 4 yrs.		For. Lang.
C	History, 2 yrs.	C	Auto. Mech.,
B	Mathematics,		½ yr.
	1 yr.	A	P.E., 4 yrs.
C	Science, 2 yrs.	B	Agric., 2 yrs.
D	Typing	C	Health Occ.,
	Bookkeeping		1 yr.
	Shorthand		Home Ec.
C	Music, Art		Dis. Ed./
	½ yr.		Div. Occ.
B	Wood, Metal		
B	Plastics, 3 yrs.		

SOURCE: T. A. Ryan. *Effect of an integrated instructional counseling program to improve vocational decision making.* Washington, D.C.: Department of Health, Education, and Welfare, Project No. HRD 413-655-0154, 1968.

Counselor: These are good observations and very important considerations. Does it seem then that clerical work might be one possibility for Uria? Are there other points he should consider? How does this relate to his problem about deciding whether or not to go to school this fall?

Steve: Well, he is just average in intelligence. Look at his high school grades and his IQ. I don't care what he wants to do. He's got to think about how smart he is.

Counselor: Yes. These are good points to think about. How will these factors—his mental ability, his school records, his achievement in school so far—affect his decisions? What about his thinking of clerical work as a possible job choice? How would this affect his going on to school?

Steve: I don't know that it will keep him from doing clerking. That doesn't take too high an IQ. That speaker yesterday said that much. He should stay away from college though—from any kind of that 'cause he's just not that good. Even though he says he likes school O.K., he's no hot-shot student and probably he'd flunk out at U. of O. I know a guy like him and he did flunk out. Now he's a mess.

Rick: Ya, but he said he wanted to go to college. Look, the only thing he wrote for choice was college. He still wants to go to college, and . . .

Clara: Yes, this is what he wrote, but he wasn't thinking about all that might happen. He probably wrote that last year when we filled out all that stuff. Remember?

Counselor: Yes. This information is from the forms completed while he was in high school last year. Now, the question is what does he decide, now that it is getting to the end of the summer, taking into account the information he has about himself and what he knows about different kinds of work. Will he want to go on to school this fall? Art?

Art: Well, he has worked out on the farm a lot; and he knows about that, but he likes people, and he's high on social service . . .

Rick: Why doesn't he just stay on the farm. He should stay on the farm. That's just it.

Counselor: The facts that he enjoys working with people and is high on social service are important points to consider Are there other things—other information to take into account?

Art: Well he likes sports—football, bulldogging, horses.

Rick: He should think about farming.

Counselor: So, does it seem that thinking about farming—something related to farming—might be a possibility to consider, along with other possibilities?

Art: Ya.

Counselor:	Of course, he might come up with other possibilities later, don't you think; even though right now he might want to make his decision about whether or not to go to school this fall, taking these two possibilities, clerical and farming, into consideration. What do you think?
Steve:	Well, he could decide whether to go to school or not. He hasn't got all day. If it's already the end of summer.
Counselor:	This is an important point. He really does need to make some kind of decision right away about school, doesn't he? What do you think?
Randy:	One thing, farming is something he knows. He's had work on the farm, and he knows it.
Counselor:	Good point to consider—his experience on the farm, so he has information about the kinds of work involved and can use this information as he considers alternatives.
Rick:	It's a normal thing to do to go on with the farm. I know a lot of guys around here who just naturally take over when their dad gets old. They just stay. Don't even go to school.
Counselor:	What other information might he consider in thinking of farming. Are there different kinds of agriculture—related jobs that he might want to investigate? Clara?
Clara:	His outdoor score was not high.
Counselor:	This is something to be considered, isn't . . .
Al:	Yes, but he likes sports though, and baseball and football. He likes horses and bulldogging and that sure as hell is outdoors. I don't think you can go altogether on what these tests say. Sometimes they are all off.
Counselor:	Good point. You think it takes more than just looking at test scores to make decisions? Are you suggesting that Uria might want to look at all the test information and also think about other things he knows about himself—things he enjoys doing; things he does well; the kinds of situations he enjoys? In looking at all these things, what does it seem Uria might want to do this fall?
Al:	Well, he likes sports and baseball. He likes horses and bulldogging. He might like the farm O.K.
Counselor:	Are you suggesting that one possibility for Uria would be agriculture-related work?
Al:	Ya, that's one thing for sure.
Counselor:	Would you say then, that at this point Uria might want to consider agriculture-related jobs and clerical work as two possibilities?
All:	Ya. Yes.

This excerpt illustrates how the counselor encouraged the clients to articulate the evidence they were considering in answering the question, "Will Uria go to school?" Note that Rick's hasty answer was ignored.

The counselor's intent is that clients identify necessary information for making the decision in a nonpunishing context, if possible. Observe that the counselor used several questions to help the group focus on Uria's decision and seemed to have determined that a number of factors will be discovered before proceeding to the next issue.

A second excerpt illustrates how the counselor encouraged the group to weigh alternatives for a decision. As they deliberate, the leader supplied a case update to help them rethink their options for Uria. Observe how the counselor sustained group focus on the alternative choices until they explored several facets of each. In this excerpt, the counselor summarized the consequence of staying out of school for a quarter, and then solicited client views about other possible consequences.

Similarly, the counselor was flexible, moving from the outcome of one alternative to generating another alternative in order to keep the group involved.

Counselor: What do you think would be the consequences for Uria if he should go into either of these kinds of work?

Al: I agree with what Art said. Farming is something he knows more about. He likes working the horses and bulldogging. He's not sure about clerking—what it really means. He might not like it. And with farming he's got a good idea and with clerking it's anybodys' guess.

Counselor: These seem important considerations. What do you think he might want to decide now. Remember, it is almost time for fall term, so if he is going to go on to school he will need to make some immediate decisions. What do you think?

Steve: Looks like the thing to decide now is to do something with farming. He can find out more about these other jobs too. He might want to work at something for a company or the government, and then when his dad gets old he'd take over.

All: Ya. Yes.

Art: But I say he wants to go to college and two years of college won't hurt him. He can get a better idea of what he wants to do.

Counselor: Steve, what information will Uria need to consider in thinking about whether to go on for more schooling this fall?

Steve: Well, he's got to figure out if he needs to go to school, to college, to get into the kind of work he wants. He could . . .

Counselor: All right. Good point. Then, if he has tentatively decided on clerical work—some kind of job in this field— or farming—some kind of agriculture-related work— the question is does he need to go to school this fall?

Randy: If he goes to school for two years before he starts full time work, maybe he can even learn enough to do something with it, the farm, make more out of it. His old man never made money. Maybe he can make something there.

All: Sure. Yes.

Counselor: Taking these factors into consideration, do you say that Uria will want to enroll in school for this fall—go to school for two years?

All: Yes. Ya.

Counselor: Then, where will he go to school? Which school will he go to?

Steve: We already talked about that. He can't make it at U. of O. He'll flunk out. Be a mess. We decided he would go to a community college. Like here. He doesn't need a degree to be a farmer or a clerk, and like I said you can find out a lot more about other jobs here too.

Counselor: That's fine. It looks as if Uria has considered consequences of taking a four-year college as opposed to community college, and in terms of his background in school and his decision to look into the general occupational areas including agriculture-related and clerical—he has decided to go to community college. Fine. Now, I have some information about Uria that you will want to take into account. Just before the term begins, an unexpected event happened. Uria's father is in an accident and has to go to the hospital. He will be there for several weeks. How will this influence Uria's decision about going to school this fall?

Al: Maybe he could stay out of school fall term. This would give him time to work on the farm. This way he could get the feel of running it. See if he likes it.

Counselor: Sounds like a possibility. What about this?

Rick: Probably with the added responsibility of taking over the running of the thing like his father did, he probably would . . . well it'd be different from just working like he is now. He could see if he likes it.

Counselor: You think having responsibility of running the farm would give him more of a chance to see if he likes it?

Al: Hey. This would be a good deal. He could use his math too. He'll have a lot of figuring to do. My old man always is.

Counselor: So one consequence of his planning to stay out of college and to take over at the ranch this fall would be that it would give him a chance to see how he likes the managing part of farming. Right? And it would give him a chance to see how he could use his math background, too? Any other consequences?

Art: Ya, I think this is going to louse things up. If he stays out of school fall term, it would be easier to stay out

	another term and another and maybe never go to school.
Counselor:	You mean one consequence of staying out would be he might never get started to school? Clara?
Clara:	Well, it might come to be a habit and he'd never get started.
Counselor:	Very possible. So this is one possible consequence of his staying out of school this fall and just taking over on the farm while his father is sick. What else might he do?
Al:	There's something else about his staying out, the draft will get him. I think he should go to school.
All:	Ya.
Steve:	He can go to school and fix his schedule to get home early. That way he can still get some hours work in on the farm. He'll have to plan his schedule.
Counselor:	So this is another possibility—going to school but getting a schedule to get home early. What would be the consequences of this action?
Randy:	Well, it would be O.K. He could get in the courses and still keep the farm going.
Counselor:	All right. Then, does it seem that after thinking of the consequences of staying out of school as compared to going to school this fall, that Uria will decide on going with a light schedule? Is this right, Rick?
Rick:	Yes, but he has to schedule his courses so he can get home early to work on the farm.
Art:	He is going here instead of U. of O. and that will make it easier for . . .
Steve:	Ya. This is what he does.
Counselor:	All right. Now, then, what about the courses?

In a final excerpt, the counselor updated again and guided the students to review methods of obtaining information. Note that cue questions elicited several ways, but the counselor did not try to "fill in" methods missed at the close of the session. This author's observation of UCLA counselor trainees delivering the procedure showed that giving clients time to discover information-gathering methods sustained their participation, even though they did not discover all methods. Note also in this excerpt how a homework assignment evolved and how the counselor directed clients to relate the session's discussion to themselves.

Counselor:	All right, now. I have some information about Uria for you to consider. The fall quarter gets underway. Uria takes the courses related to agricultural technology and keeps the farm going while his father is sick. In November his father is ready to take over again. What will this mean to Uria? What about winter term?

Randy: Well, that will depend on his grades. What grades did he get?

Counselor: Good point to consider. According to information on Uria, his grades for fall term are all C's.

Steve: Well. He only had twelve hours and nothing that he couldn't understand.

Art: Yes. That's right.

Randy: Then why not just go ahead and take the next terms courses like they are here in the book. He could take the full course this time 'cause he won't be working.

Counselor: That sounds like a possibility. What do you think? Steve, you mentioned that Uria might get information about other jobs. What about this?

Steve: Well, he could find out about different kinds of jobs . . . like something that might let him be with people. . . .

Art: Say, what about this police course? Look at this. He likes people and he's big enough, and this might be a possibility, and . . .

All: Ya. Yah.

Counselor: Yes, this sounds like a good idea. Now, do you have any idea where he might get that kind of information—in addition to what he will learn from his classes and the catalog that you have here?

Steve: Well, I know Mr. Heyer said there were books in his office that had information about different kinds of jobs, and we could use them anytime, and I think there is a book in the library on this.

Counselor: These sound like good sources for getting added information about occupations. Do you think it might also be a good idea to talk to . . .

Steve: Yah, my high school teacher. He'd know a lot about this.

Counselor: Good. I hate to break in here, but I see our time is up for today. It looks as if Uria is off to a good start, despite a couple of problems that came up for him. The next time you can plan Uria's life for the next couple of years. Before we stop today, how about summarizing what happened in our session today? Rick?

Rick: Well, the main things that happened. We decided to start out with farming. We thought about being a clerk, but it didn't seem too good for him. Farming was more like what he knew, let him be out-of-doors, and he could find out about different kinds of jobs that have to do with farming, and business and clerical and police work . . . those others that were in the catalog, and he can look into these. I got the idea myself of having to think about all that might happen to a guy in deciding on something. I never thought about coming here before or you know not coming. I just came but I didn't really know what I was here for, I guess. I never thought about all this.

Counselor: Good observation, Rick. I agree, it is important to think of consequences of different actions in making plans for work and schooling. Anything else to add? Elaine?

Elaine: Well, he decided against a university. He didn't need it . . . He

Art: He . . .

Steve: He didn't need university . . . being a farmer or a policeman . . . he didn't need it. So that's why he went here. I got the idea that you know you got to think about all this stuff, like how smart you are and what you're going to do and that stuff, and not just say "college" like he did on that test.

Randy: Yes, and I got an idea on taking courses. Like he decided at first on the ag tech course. It was closest to farming, and he could get more ideas on other jobs that he might want to do. That's a lot like me. I'm going to look up that stuff in the books we talked about, for me.

Counselor: Very good. Al, anything to add?

Al: Well, he thought about it, and he looked at the college catalog. He thought about it because he wanted to take something to do with farming, I guess, and didn't know what to take, but . . .

Steve: That's right. He talked about it and decided on taking something that had to do with farming at first, and looking at the college catalog that gave me an idea about using the catalogs.

Counselor: Good. Anything else?

Rick: You got to think what happens if you do things like if he stayed out completely he never would go back.

Counselor: That's fine. A good point to mention. You've done a good job of summarizing our session today, and you've done a fine job of pointing up the importance of using information to decide on alternatives. You've pointed to the need to think of consequences before taking steps, too. Very good. Next time we will complete Uria's plans to the time he goes into work full time. In the meantime, you might want to be looking up some of the information you mentioned he will be needing to make up his mind about his future educational plans and work decisions.

And, how about during the coming week, looking up information on law enforcement for Uria, and seeing if you can do some of the same things for yourselves that you have done for Uria today—look at your own interests and aptitudes and see what kinds of work might be possibilities for you to consider . . . look in the references in the occupational library to see what kinds of jobs are listed that might be possibilities for you . . . talk to people about different kinds of jobs . . . O.K.? Bye, now. See you next week.

Facilitating Clarification of Career Values Through Literature

Throughout the ages, poetry and lyrics have moved and informed people. Recognizing this, Markert (1980) reasoned that poetry and lyrics might be employed by a counselor-facilitator in promoting career development in a similar manner to simulation. Thus, he has created the structured, four-session, small-group procedure below to stimulate students to experience and reflect on potential values expressed in work.

The heuristics are these:

1. Listening and reflecting on poetic and lyrical portrayals of values expressed by workers increases appreciation of work's impact on values.
2. Discussing work values and feelings about them with peers and a facilitator heightens appreciation of work's impact on values and awareness of society's expectations about work values.

The objectives of session 1 are that clients understand the purpose of the counseling, recall methods of learning about self, and practice methods of self-discovery. First, the counselor tells clients that they will "reflect on their lives, listen to poetry and rock music about working, discuss these, and complete special assignments in order to identify personal qualities and relate them to career decision making." The clients then read a statement about career development and values and share their reactions.

Proceeding, the counselor states that knowing ourselves is an important step in preparing for satisfying work and invites clients to enumerate what they think would be important to learn.

Next, clients listen to an audiotape of the poem "Who Am I?" (Solomon, undated) and share their reactions. The facilitator prompts consideration of what is being said, the speaker's feelings, things important to the counselor, and clients' identifications with the feelings expressed. They then hear "On the Road to Find Out" (Stephens, 1970) and note the important elements in this poem and its similarities to "Who Am I?"

The session then becomes more didactic. The facilitator guides clients to discover that they can learn about themselves by such methods as trying out new activities; thinking about their qualities and experiences; noting how others respond to them; observing their records, residuals, possessions, and time usage; completing tests and inventories; and teaching others about themselves. Through discovery questioning and other involving techniques, the counselor encourages the clients to share their experiences, especially positive ones, in using particular techniques and to tell one another about various methods.

This experience culminates in a homework assignment from *Discovering You* (Healy, 1976). Each client is to list strengths significant others see in them, the activities they like, and the reasons that they enjoy the activities. Then each is to compose a short poem about self in relation to work, using a format such as "I would like to be . . . , But I would not like . . . ," if he or she prefers.

The objectives of session 2 are that clients both recognize (feel as well as know) the values they are expressing in their activities and those others express in work and contemplate the effect of performing work that is not consistent with one's values.

The session starts with clients discussing their homework. As they share their productions, the counselor guides them to recognize how their short poems express particular work values; and the counselor reflects their feelings and encourages clients to sense their feelings as they share their homework accomplishment.

Next, clients close their eyes, relax, and visualize themselves walking alone in a forest. The facilitator immerses them in this with imagery, and then announces that the trail forks so that they must elect one direction. After several minutes, students then tell how they felt when confronting a fork in the trail and how they proceeded. In the sharing, the counselor and other clients point out values implicit in their actions at the fork.

Next, the counselor reads "The Road Not Taken" (Frost, 1977a), and the group members imagine what following a discarded option in their own lives would have been like. Then they discuss the similarities in their fantasies. Proceeding to develop the implications of this poem, the counselor, if time permits, points out or has clients recall that decisions are made in different ways, such as by default, impulse, or systematic consideration of options. In addition, they review that systematic decision making involves knowing self, recognizing desires to change, appreciating environmental and self-limitations, acquiring information about options, their likelihood, their requirements, and the like.

Turning more directly to value expressions, students listen to "But I Might Die Tonight" (Stephens, 1970) and name the values that the speaker and other characters hold. Proceeding, they listen to "A Bill of Sale" (Dennis, 1978), identify the speaker's work and attitudes, and speculate about the kind of person he is. Continuing, the group listens to the "Millworker" (Taylor, 1978), and the counselor elicits student thoughts about the worker's feelings and means of coping, inviting them to tell about similar feelings they have had. Moving on, the facilitator reads "Quota" (Brodine, 1977a), asking about feelings and values not being met and examining the notion of different personalities fitting different environments. Then the group hears *Factory* (Springsteen,

1978) and reflects about what work gives to and takes from people. Following the closing song, "Blue Collar Man" (Shaw, 1978), students consider how its values compare to those in "Factory."

The session closes with clients receiving the homework assignment to write a paper that compares and contrasts "Maggie's Farm" (Dylan, 1971) and "Two Tramps in Mud Time" (Frost, 1977b). After the assignment is clear, the counselor invites clients to summarize the session.

The third session's objectives are that clients examine the concept of work values and identify work values important to them.

First, the homework assignment is reviewed and the values felt and recognized are acknowledged. Next, the group listens to "The Mason" (Kelly, 1978), and members tell their reactions about the mason's feelings for his work. They also share feelings they have had that are similar to the mason's, in order to identify work values they have developed.

During the discussion of "The Mason," the counselor intersperses a definition of work values as "preferred ideas and beliefs stemming from what we personally define as important to us about work," and makes points such as: "values act as guideposts," "we feel good when in accord with our values," and "changes in values occur with living." This exposition is conducted so that the students share personal or vicarious experiences related to the point so the counselor can verify their understanding.

Next, clients hear *The Pretender* (Browne, 1976) and identify its tone, the speaker's values, and the changes that not achieving his values has made in him. Then they reflect about and share similar experiences of their own and others they know. In eliciting these contributions, the counselor emphasizes how being congruent with one's values is satisfying; whereas, acting inconsistently is frustrating.

As a change of pace, each client next indicates whether he or she, the mason, or the farmworker endorses fourteen work values (leadership, recognition and success, helping others, and so forth). Volunteers share their answers, and the group speculates about occupations that are more likely to satisfy particular values. When sharing is over, clients are assigned to ask parents or other working adults about values satisfied in their jobs and to compose a "values poem" about one important work value. The session then closes when one or more students define work values and give examples.

The objectives of session 4 are to consider sources of worker dissatisfaction in jobs, and to recognize the need for compromise, but the dangers of overconforming.

First, clients share their homework poems and feelings about them. Then they listen to "Five O'Clock World" (The Vogues, 1965) in order to identify the values the poet feels are missing from work, and they tell similar experiences of their own. Moving on, the students listen to "The Receptionist is By Definition" (Brodine, 1977) and consider how well she is coping with conflicts about lying and other values. Proceeding, they hear "The Harlem Dancer" (McKay, 1976) and are encouraged to consider the implication of the final line, which indicates how, by a false smile, the dancer tells that she does not want to be there. In developing client reactions, the counselor reflects that different cultures, different generations, and different groups have both different and similar values.

Proceeding, the counselor plays "For Free" (Mitchell, 1969) and has clients consider the place of materialism in their lives. Finally, the counselor reads "Mr. Guder" (Carpenter, 1968), and has the group discuss what is happening to Mr. Guder, the feelings they have had or have seen others have about work value conflicts, and how these can be resolved.

The session closes with volunteers identifying values conflicts in work and potential means of reducing them.

Interest Inventorying

Traditionally, students have completed interest inventories and received interpretations to help them identify activities and occupations of likely interest, to determine whether their expressed occupational and interest preferences matched their inventoried preferences, and to motivate them to explore potentially interesting activities and occupations. Many researches have shown that interpretation of interest inventories using varying formats and under different conditions (group vs. individual) has increased client knowledge and retention of scores (Myers, 1971). Research, however, has not established that interest inventorying and interpretation per se either increases the number of activities a person considers interesting or spurs exploration of interesting occupations or activities. Indeed, recent studies of the latter objective by Zenner and Schnuelle (1972) and by Zytowski (1977) failed to detect such an outcome.

Underlying interest inventorying are the assumptions that the clients understand the inventory activities and even have experienced most under favorable circumstances, that their preferences will be relatively stable, and that they have accepted the belief that one's occupation should employ some of one's measured interests. (This belief may not always be held by women and lower-class people.)

Heuristic Principles

The heuristic principles supporting interest inventorying include:

1. Systematic consideration of a wide range of activities, subjects, and occupations at one time helps to pinpoint interests and assures that one does not omit possible interests.
2. One is more likely to be interested in an activity, subject, or occupation if one is interested in related activities, subjects, or occupations, than if one is not interested in related options.
3. One is more likely to be more motivated to explore activities and occupations if one recognizes that they fit one's interests than if one lacks information about fit.

Method

The direct contribution of interest inventorying and interpretation to career development has been relatively unexplored. Only recently has Holland (1970) proposed that his interest inventory, the *Self-Directed Search*, might be used exclusive of counseling.

Most interest inventories are to be used within counseling, and the review of career choice counseling studies in Chapter 10 will show that several counseling procedures incorporating interest inventories have benefited clients. Nevertheless, Goldman (1972) noted that interest inventorying and interpretation have not been integrated effectively into counseling. This failure probably results from the dearth of research to show how test interpretations complement other counseling activities in boosting career-development as measured by criteria different from the congruence of expressed and inventoried interests. Clearly, there is need to tackle such a question rather than to focus exclusively on the ability of an inventory to differentiate occupational and curricular groups and to contribute to regression formulae for predicting performance, as most studies of inventories now do. Otherwise, counselors will not be able to justify their use of inventories.

Although it is beyond the scope of this text to review the major interest inventories now in use, the *SDS* is examined because it has been used exclusive of counseling and research of such use has been reported. It must be noted, however, that its author indicated that its use within counseling will yield more information (Holland, 1976c). Moreover his recent manual implies that only clients wishing to identify occupations for further exploration and those whose preferences are consistent across subparts of the *SDS* can use the *SDS* without counselor assistance.

Rationale

Holland theorizes that there are the six basic personality types: realistic, investigative, artistic, social, enterprising, and conventional (see Chapter 3), and that most people are more like one or two types than like the other four or five. Similarly, he posits that jobs and occupations form a constellation of parallel environments (described in Chapter 4) and that people gravitate toward work environments compatible with their personality. By way of illustration, he hypothesizes that artistic occupations are pursued by persons with artistic personalities, that artistic people are more likely to seek entry to artistic environments than into other environments, and that their proclivity for such an environment will be higher than that of people of another personality type. When a person's personality is incompatible with a work environment, that person will be dissatisfied and tend to change to a more compatible one. The tasks of career counseling become assisting clients to identify their personality type and to direct them to occupations in the corresponding work environments.

The *Self-Directed Search Program (SDS)* is comprised of the *Occupations Finder,* the *SDS* inventory booklet, and more recently the *Understanding Yourself and Your Career Booklet.* The *Occupations Finder* presents summary occupational codes, which are an occupations classification in terms of Holland's six work environments, for 500 common occupations; it presents the education level required by each of these occupations; and it lists the occupation's *D.O.T.* code. For example, the summary code of architectural drafting is listed as R I A, since occupational analysis indicated that realistic, investigative, and artistic activities were most salient in drafting (Holland, Vernstein, Kuo, Karweit, & Blum, 1972). Although empirical study summarized later in this chapter tends to confirm that workers in an occupation such as drafting are more likely to score higher on the first personality type of the summary code than on one of the other five types, empirical contrasts have not generally been made of differentiations by the second or third letter of the code, and when they have been, have not been as supportive (Doty & Betz, 1979).

Clients start the *SDS* booklet with an *Occupational Daydreams* section, wherein they list up to eight occupations that they have considered and even dreamed about, and then locate and list the occupational codes for these occupations from the *Occupations Finder.*

Clients next complete a detailed self-review of experiences, preferences, and self-evaluations, which research pioneered or stimulated by Holland has shown relates to the pursuit of particular occupations. More specifically, clients check whether they like or dislike sixty-six activities (such as repairing appliances or attending basketball games), judge their competence in sixty-six parallel activities, review their preferences for each of eighty-four occupations, and conclude the self-rating by estimating their level of skill on seven-point scales in two sets of skill areas. The activities, competences, occupations, and self-estimate sections include equal numbers of items from the six occupational types.

The computation step, especially in the 1977 revised *SDS* booklet, is relatively simple, although researchers have found that even some college students made errors in it. Clients are guided to count the number of activities, competences, and occupations that they checked within each Holland occupational type and to transfer those counts and the fourteen self-estimates to a profile sheet. Then, the clients sum the five subpart counts to obtain a total raw score for each type. Next, they list the first letter of the three higher types from first to third highest in order to obtain their summary code. As an illustration, Pamela had the total raw scores of R = 40, I = 32, A = 28, S = 20, E = 5 and C = 21. Therefore, her summary code was *R I A.*

After the code is compiled, the *SDS* booklet again directs clients to the *Occupations Finder,* in order to identify and list some occupations with identical codes and some with codes that are permutations of the client's three highest types. (For Pamela, the permutations of *R I A* are *R A I, I R A, I A R, A R I,* and *A I R.*) Space is provided in the *SDS* booklet for twelve identical coded occupations and twelve derived from codes that are permutations of the original code, but the clients need not limit themselves to twenty-four occupations.

After clients compile their lists of occupations, the *SDS* booklet directs them to check whether the occupations from the Daydreams section appear on the lists. If they do, the clients proceed to obtain more information and even try out occupations through part-time jobs. If their present and past occupational aspirations do not appear in their lists, the booklet advises conferring with a counselor. Further direction for following up scores is offered in another companion booklet, *Understanding Yourself and Your Career* (Holland, 1977). Here, Holland enumerates the traits associated with each of his six personality types and explains how occupations tend to arrange themselves in terms of the types. He closes his brief presentation by offering five suggestions for increasing the quality of career decisions: 1) inspecting the fit of a potential occupation on factors such as ability training and life style; 2) reviewing one's ratings with significant others to check their realism; 3) seeking professional consultation if desired; 4) searching for other occupations that resemble one's code; and 5) conferring with workers in a potential occupation.

Counselor Interpretation of SDS

For the counselor interpreting an *SDS*, Holland (1979) provides more information about *SDS* scores, some of which will probably appear in the self-interpretation materials after more research. Some of the more salient nontechnical points and their implications are:

1. Differences of 6 or 7 between raw type scores may occur by chance; therefore, one should equate scores different by less than 8 in compiling summary codes. For some clients, this practice will expand the number of occupations to be explored.

2. Most occupations contain people with a range of occupational codes, and research on the codes indicates that occupations differ in terms of their intra occupational variability. In time, it is hoped that the *SDS* manual will indicate which occupations vary substantially and which do not and what codes are typical in an occupation. Currently, the presence of intra occupational variability argues against foreclosing exploration of an occupation because one does not have its code and perhaps even a code similar to its code, if there are other good reasons for pursuing it. As a consequence, this also suggests exploring a broad range of occupations, not just those corresponding to codes of one's first and second highest personality types.

3. Sufficient data on the *SDS* has been gathered and census data analyzed to enable estimates of the popularity of different codes and the availability of jobs corresponding to the codes. In 1970, the large majority of men worked in realistic and enterprising

occupations (75.5 percent), with only 1.8 percent and 6.9 percent working in artistic and conventional jobs respectively. Yet only 46.7 percent of a sample of high school boys had realistic or enterprising codes, whereas there were at least three times as many boys with investigative and artistic codes as there were corresponding jobs. Likewise, the majority of women worked in conventional, social, and realistic jobs (41.5 percent, 23.1 percent, and 17.9 percent respectively). And only 2 percent had investigative employment and 1.3 percent artistic work. However, fewer than 12 percent of high school girls had conventional codes and fewer than 2 percent realistic codes, whereas 12.7 percent had artistic codes and 7.9 percent investigative codes. For counseling, such discrepancies between available and predicted employment suggest that clients with codes for occupational clusters employing few people be alerted to the likelihood of keen competition for such jobs and be informed of occupational clusters with relatively large numbers of jobs that are at least not contraindicated by their scores.

4. The consistency or lack of consistency across subparts of the *SDS* and between the *SDS* codes and Daydream codes have implicacations for prediction and prescription. High consistency across profiles relates weakly to decision-making ability and to maintaining a choice within a code. Low consistency has related to satisfaction with counseling. Exploration of discrepancies should pinpoint needs for self-improvement and re-evaluation of preferences.

Validity

This section presents the logical and empirical evidence for the procedures described in this chapter and discusses outcome assessment. Collectively, the evidence justifies professional application of these or very similar interventions on an experimental basis.

Coordination

Common sense indicates that coordination is necessary for different people and elements to coalesce into a single delivery program. Elements must interact to complement one another rather than to obstruct or distract from one another's purposes. Such interaction requires communication, organization, and cooperation that can be effected only by someone taking responsibility for coordination.

Coordination is a management function (Bishop, 1976) that is essential to effective programs. The general view is that coordination activities, like other leadership activities, vary with the program and its participants. To this author's knowledge, research has not contrasted effective and ineffective coordination practices in career development programs or projects. Rather, project and program directors move to improve or alter coordination when it appears that elements are not synchronized. Judgments about such needs typically are based on informal analysis of the operation but can be based on a formal systems analysis.

A systems analysis of a program will pinpoint its coordination problems but will not necessarily indicate how to resolve them. The total operational view provided by the systems analysis will show where communication and interaction break down but will not identify why linkages are not functioning or how they might be established. The latter coordination competence reflects the art of the activity; that is, it involves knowing the operations that are out of sync and understanding the personalities of the operators. For example, in a program wherein academic departments have agreed to give ten hours a semester to preparing students for job seeking, the social studies department and the English department may both be teaching form completion and employment interviewing but with somewhat different and contradictory foci. To correct the situation, the coordinator would first have to determine why each department elected to pursue a particular focus and how it fits with that department's members' educational philosophy. Then the counselor would have to know how to approach each department leader about changing or collaborating, without alienating either.

These coordination skills can be estimated by task analysis, but they have not been isolated in empirical studies of career development programs. Since several publications present brief descriptions of successful career development programs, the coordinator should review them to see what elements have been brought together in particular projects. In addition, the coordinator should locate persons currently coordinating educational programs and secure permission to shadow them to observe different styles of coordinating. Hansen (1970) and McLaughlin (1976) both refer to successful programs.

Simulation Case Counseling

Logically, simulation case study counseling following Ryan's (1968) approach is valid because it consists of studying a series of cases that embody the tasks and solution strategies with which clients are expected to cope. The cases allow the counselor to make requisite career development concepts and principles more concrete, and they enable the clients to explore the consequences of possible solutions to career problems without punishment. The case method has been employed widely in management training to alert trainees to potential management problems and to give them exercise in constructing solution strategies. Moreover, the method embodies the three heuristic principles on page 322.

Two empirical studies have investigated this type of counseling. Ryan contrasted the effects of simulation counseling and reinforcement counseling on 300 junior college students from Oregon. These students either had scholastic aptitude scores below the 50th percentile or had vocational goals inconsistent with their measured abilities or interests. Contrasting postcounseling performance of clients in the two treatments with one another and with control subjects, Ryan found that simulation case counseling increased occupational information knowledge more than did the control condition and increased deliberation about career decision-making more than did the control and the reinforcement counseling situations. In another study, this author contrasted the effects of an adaptation of the Ryan case simulation with the effects of an adaptation of the translation procedure on inner-city tenth and eleventh graders. Four groups totaling twenty-six clients completed nine forty-five-minute sessions of each procedure along with administration and interpretation of the *Differential Aptitude Test* (1947) and Kuder's *Preference Inventory* (Kuder, 1948). Students in both treatments rated themselves very satisfied with the program, but neither group manifested growth on the problem solving scale of the *Career Maturity Inventory* (Crites, 1973). This failure to show progress on the objective criterion was attributed to three factors: tape transcripts indicated weak performance of the novice counselors, although they generally adhered to the counseling guidelines in Figure 8–8; observation of the client efforts to secure information indicated that they often were hampered by lack of accessible information and models; and many subjects had difficulty reading the *CMI*. To date, no other studies of the Ryan (1968) procedure have been published.

Unfortunately, studies of other short-term simulation exercises for promoting career development of adolescents do not lend much support to the heuristics underlying Ryan's method for this age group. Swails and Herr (1976) had three counselors each lead groups of eight students through one of four eight-hour treatments: a "relationship" career counseling experience, a modeling-reinforcement experience, the *Life Career Game* (Boocock, 1967) simulation, and a control situation. Pre-post testing on the attitude and competence scales of the earlier form of the *Career Maturity Inventory* (Crites, 1973) did not show that the twenty-four students in any treatment outperformed student controls, leading the authors to hypothesize that career development at this age is complex and not easily bolstered by short-term treatments. In an even smaller study of the *Life Career Game*, Johnson and Euler (1972) reported that two counselor trainees did not find teaching career information through the game to twenty ninth graders to have more effect on retention or interest than conventional instruction. In another small study, Varenhorst (1968) had groups of ten and eighteen high school students use the *Life Career Game*, and she judged that the games were successful "because they provided motivation and involvement, illustrated future factual realities, and led to discussion; . . . thus meeting some needs which were lacking in group guidance sessions."

Others who have reported using simulation contend that it is a useful approach. Two kinds of simulation were incorporated into a larger career guidance project by Meyer (1971). First, twenty cases illustrating problem situations about people and employment were created to teach decision making. Second, each class group formed a "company" and

Figure 8–8. Form for Rating Simulation Counseling

	Explana-tion	Clients Involved	Client progress manifest	Appro-priate reinforce-ment	Not modal
Present case or summarize case to date					
Courses available for student					
Sources of information about courses					
Relevant characteristics of student					
Ways of learning more about student					
Systematic decision making/planning					
Career consequences of choices					
Relevance to members					
Activities for case student					
Relevant characteristics of student					
Ways of finding out/ verifying self- and activities information					
Systematic decision					
Career consequences relevant to members					
Summary by members					

Note: Rate each segment of counseling on the left in terms of whether it was explained clearly, clients participated, their participation enabled judgment of their progress, reinforcement was for appropriate action, and the content was accurate. Put ratings in the respective columns. Rate 2 if element was excellent, 1 if adequate, and 0 if inadequate. After close of session, fill in all blanks with 0.

simulated its personnel and other decisions. Reports from the University of Houston Center for Human Resources, apparently based on clinical observation and staff debriefings, indicated that the simulation experiences contributed substantially to increased knowledge about work, to increased job-seeking behavior, and to favorable attitude about guidance. Rabin and Scott (1971) created the YWCA game outlined above and delivered this program to students in more than thirty Los Angeles area high schools, to the apparent satisfaction of the students and teachers.

Studying the vicarious work-value clarification provided by poetry and lyrics, Markert (1980) pilot-tested his procedure with a group of six clients and then had six counselors apply it to other groups. On a pre-post basis, the pilot high schoolers named more values in their reasons for occupational aspirations. In the formal study using a true experimental posttest design, two counselors led forty-four high school students, in groups of ten to fourteen through the four hours of values clarification; two other counselors led forty students through four hours of career guidance films focused on work values; and two other coun-selors led thirty-eight students in a placebo control condition to discuss the literary qualities of the values poems and lyrics. Contrasts of ability to relate values to career goals in essays showed that the poetry-lyric groups and the film groups exceeded the controls. There was no differ-ence in attitude toward work, however, among the three treatments, as measured by *the New Mexico Career Education Test Series scale.* (NMCETS) (Healy & Klein, 1973). This lack of attitude difference re-flects the fact that the mean of all these students was in the upper 5 percentile of the *NMCETS* scale. The very positive work values of all the students may reflect a change of attitude toward work among high school students from 1973, when the *NMCETS* was normed, to 1979, when Dr. Markert conducted the study.

Model Reinforcement Counseling

Model reinforcement counseling is built on heuristic principles 1, 2, and 3. By offering this counseling in groups and providing related materials, as Thoresen and Hamilton (1972) did, one can undergird it with heuris-tics 4 and 7. Identifying and commiting oneself to acquire information and to implement particular decisional steps under the approval of a counselor with whom one contracts to discuss outcomes at a subsequent meeting logically should help one succeed. The merits of this logical ar-gument are confirmed by the empirical studies described below.

In the pioneering study, Krumboltz and Schroeder (1965) had 9 counselors guide 18 volunteer eleventh-grade boys and girls through two sessions of reinforcement counseling with a 15-minute modeling tape and 18 students without modeling. Comparison of the clients' re-ported information seeking in the three weeks following counseling with the information seeking of 18 controls showed that the males, but not the females, exposed to modeling reinforcement sought more informa-tion than did the controls; and the males, but not females, sought more after modeling reinforcement than after reinforcement counseling with-out modeling. In contrast, the females, but not the males, exposed to reinforcement alone sought more information than did the female con-trols. The authors speculated that the use of a male model diminished the effects of modeling on the girls. Of interest, too, were the significant correlations of the intention to seek information in counseling with extra counseling information seeking. These correlations support the conten-tion that eliciting commitment to such information seeking and reinforc-ing it within counseling influenced extra counseling behavior.

In a subsequent study of model reinforcement counseling employing 192 subject, Krumboltz and Thoresen (1964) compared the informa-tion seeking of 80 boys, who had two sessions of individual or group model reinforcement counseling or reinforcement counseling without modeling with 112 boys who watched career planning films or served as inactive control. They found that both kinds of counseling produced more information seeking and a wider range of information seeking than did the control treatment.

Operating independently with college students, Wachowiak (1972) found that twenty college students who received a two-session version of model reinforcement counseling increased their certainty and satisfaction with their major and increased their *Vocational Decision-Making Checklist* (Harren, 1966; 1972) scores more than did twenty clients who received two sessions of traditional career counseling and more than did twenty controls. The twenty traditionally counseled clients also improved more than did the twenty controls.

As a part of a forty-minute career information center program designed to acquaint users with career decision making, fourteen college students viewed a client's being counseled about using information material and rewarded for information seeking, à la Krumboltz and Schroeder (1965). Fisher, Reardon, and Burck (1976) found that these students increased the kinds and amount of information they sought more than did fourteen students who completed the program without viewing the modeling and fourteen controls who used the center without the programs.

In yet another small study, Bergland, Quatrano, and Lundquist (1975) examined whether five thirty-minute sessions of small group counseling involving reinforcement and modeling affected the career information-seeking and decision-making skills of eleventh graders. Twenty students received five sessions of well-described counseling that involved directed information seeking and decision making from two counselors; twenty viewed twenty to thirty-minute videotapes of sessions staged to represent excellent counseling and received a five-minute overview of the session from either of the two counselors; twenty viewed the counseling and then completed the counseling under direction of either of the two counselors; and twenty served as controls. Surprisingly, compared with the controls or on a pre-post basis, none of the counseled groups registered significant gain in attitude about information seeking, in knowing how to use and process information, in amount of information seeking, or in vocational planning simulation.

In an effort to pinpoint critical aspects of modeling, Krumboltz, Varenhorst, and Thoresen (1967) had fourteen eleventh-grade girls view a coed receiving information-seeking encouragement in a fifteen-minute counseling session from a high-prestige, attentive counselor; fourteen from a high prestige, unattentive counselor; fourteen from a low-prestige attentive counselor; fourteen from a low-prestige, unattentive counselor; and had fifty-six hear about the tape from a counselor, receive advice to seek information, and be invited to return to discuss their findings; and fifty-six as inactive controls. Two weeks after the modeling observation, the fifty-six girls who viewed the counseling film had acquired more information than had the active and inactive control girls. There were no differences in information seeking attributable to the prestige or attentiveness of the counselor in the model tape, although the girls identified the inattentive counselor as less attentive.

In another study of the nature of the modeling, Thoresen and Krumboltz (1968) examined the effects of different audiotape models combined with reinforcement counseling on career information seeking. They found that twelve high school boys, who heard a prestigious athletic peer resolve to acquire information, sought more information and more varied information than did comparable students, who listened to students with middle or low athletic prestige or who had received an adult's advice. The eighteen who heard "high-status" academic peers, however, were no different in amount or variety of information seeking from the fifty-four who heard an average and a low-status academic peer or an adult's advice.

In terms of model similarity, the students responded more favorably to the high-prestige than to the middle- and low-prestige athlete, regardless of their self-rated athletic prestige; but there was no difference among the academic models or adult adviser in effectiveness, regardless of a student's self-rating. Students who rated themselves high academically sought more information, regardless of the model to which they were exposed.

This well designated, internally valid study again showed the effectiveness of model reinforcement counseling, but suggested that only special models would be more effective than no modeling. Moreover, the study also suggested that the academically able student would be more responsive. The small number in the different conditions, of course, limits generalizability.

An earlier study of group counseling, which included video modeling but not control of reinforcement, provides more limited support for incorporating modeling into career counseling. Catron (1966) had thirteen pairs of counselors lead groups of five to twelve high school students through fourteen 90-minute sessions. Counseling for the seventy-eight students included: viewing a counseling session that featured test interpretation, vocational testing and interpretation, discussion of career aspirations and issues, and exploration of a wide range of adolescent concerns. Postcounseling contrasts of forty-six of the fifty-six finishing clients with forty-six matched controls showed that the clients produced more positive self "Q" sorts, but that their self-ideal congruence was not higher, contrary to expectation.

In another effort to identify clients most likely to profit from model reinforcement counseling, Wachowiak (1973) found limited support for the proposition that improvement in counseling correlated with selected personality factors. For the twenty Southern Illinois students who completed model-reinforcement vocational counseling described above (Wachowiak, 1972), he found that increases in the *Vocational Decision Making Checklist (VDMC)* (Harren, 1972) correlated positively with high defensiveness, heterosexuality, and affiliation, and low counseling readiness as measured by the *Adjective Checklist* (Gough & Heilbrun, 1965). These instruments were administered at the start of counseling. For these twenty clients, none of the *Adjective Checklist* scales correlated with changes in certainty or satisfaction with career choice. For the twenty clients who completed traditional counseling, growth in the *VDMC* was related positively to aggression and self-confidence and negatively to abasement. For this group, growth in certainty and satisfaction was related to dominance, and growth in certainty was related to abasement. The small sample sizes and multiple relations, of course, require that these hunches be verified in additional research.

More direct and more comprehensive forms of model reinforcement counseling also have been studied (Ryan, 1968; Thoresen & Hamilton, 1972; Evans & Cody, 1969; and Johnson & Myrick, 1972). One can, for example, teach directly the steps for solving a problem, making a decision, or constructing a plan, and then help the clients in applying those steps to their careers. Texts, such as *Deciding* (Gelatt, Varenhorst, & Carey, 1972), *Decisions and Outcomes* (Gelatt, Varenhorst, Carey, & Miller, 1973), and *Discovering You* (Healy, 1976), assist in this teaching; or one can construct one's own written materials, as Thoresen and Hamilton (1972) have.

As emphasis in such counseling moves from solving a problem or making a decision to learning the steps so that the client can apply them to a wide range of situations, the procedure adopts a more cognitive tone and becomes a form of rule-learning counseling. On the other hand, when the client is guided to apply the procedure in finalizing decisions about options with long-term consequences, such as choice of major or occupation, the procedure becomes career choice counseling, as exemplified in studies by Fogel (1973) and Snodgrass (1978) reported in Chatper 10.

In their study, Evans and Cody (1969) found that five individual counseling sessions involving systematically teaching, practicing, and rewarding application of a problem-solving technique had increased the problem solving of twenty eighth graders, whereas forty controls did not register similar improvement with the passage of time or from five hours of nonguided practice. Their investigation included five counselors.

In a study of a more elaborate model reinforcement procedure, employing four thirty-minute group sessions designed around materials to teach career planning, plus four fifteen-minute video tapes illustrating a peer group pursuing the procedure successfully, Thoresen and Hamilton (1972) found the procedure more successful than no counseling. Yet, it was not statistically more powerful than four thirty-minute sessions of working through the materials or four thirty-minute sessions of viewing peers in the process. More specifically, the sixteen eleventh-grade boys receiving the full treatment scored higher on a test of career knowledge and on a simulated career problem, but not on frequency of information seeking, than did eight active and eight inactive controls. These boys who received the full treatment, however, did not exceed the sixteen boys viewing only the modeling tapes or the sixteen using the materials without the modeling film. Further, the sixteen boys using the materials only outperformed the controls on the simulation test. The results led the authors to suggest that modeling enhances structured materials.

Truncated reinforcement counseling may not be effective. Young (1979) contrasted brief reinforcement counseling with a "values confrontation counseling" in which clients were shown that their immature career behavior was not consistent with their professed values, and with no treatment. In one forty-minute session, either of two counselors interpreted the *Career Development Inventory* (Super et al., 1979) to thirty adolescents who had scored in the lowest 25 percentile. Then, in an ensuing discussion, the counselor reinforced "vocationally mature" responses. The students did not expect a follow-up interview. As predicted, internal adolescents (Rotter, 1966) receiving the value confrontation treatment sought more vocational information than did the adolescents in other treatments. The reinforced, external adolescents, who were also expected to excel, however, did not. The reinforced students did not even differ from the control. Possibly, absence of a follow-up interview diminished the impact of the reinforcement treatment by not affording the students opportunity to gain counselor reinforcement for their actual information-seeking behavior.

Thus, the findings of different studies do not agree. Even the efficacy of reinforcement, reinforcement in combination with modeling, or modeling alone is not always manifest. Nevertheless, the weight of evidence supports the contentions that reinforcement, reinforcement combined with audio-visual modeling of counseling, and audio-visual modeling of counseling by itself or within counseling do promote career mature behavior. To a lesser degree, the evidence suggests that same-sexed, prestigious client models are more inspirational than are other types of models. Moreover, the aggregate findings of the studies show that audio-visual modeling and reinforcement sometimes complement one another and other activities, but the findings do not indicate the counseling activities that modeling or counseling are likely to enhance or the conditions under which one can expect incremental gains. Logically, of course, repeat presentations of key concepts and principles through audio-visual modeling provides more learning opportunity and should enhance many different kinds of exercises.

On the other hand, sufficient evidence has not yet been amassed to indicate whether particular types of client are more responsive to modeling and reinforcement than others. Nonetheless, the immediate practicality of model and client type differences makes it important to continue searching for differences. Although the issue has already been explored, further contrasts of internal and external types are warranted. Moreover, examination of Holland's (1973) hypotheses about differential responsivity of his types to particular learning environments seems especially appropriate. One can deduce, for example, that an artistic person will receive more inspiration from modeling through a quality portrayal than will a social or conventional person, that social and enterprising types will respond to modeling and social reinforcement more than will realistic and investigative types, and that reinforcement through challenging tasks will have more impact on investigative and enterprising types than on realistic types.

Many other research questions can extend knowledge of how reinforcement and modeling work in counseling. Especially needed is clarification about their operation with disadvantaged students. Questions that should receive high priority include: 1) How aware must clients be that their counselor is reinforcing them for promising to seek information and expects them to seek information on their own? 2) How much material and attitudinal support for information seeking and systematic planning must a student's school offer for information seeking to follow modeling and reinforcement? 3) Must students have the prospect of choosing a major, electives, or training program in the near future? 4) What minimum experience and competence in independent information gathering and decision making, if any, must a student have in order to benefit from a reinforcement and/or a modeling intervention? 5) What minimum of understanding of the disadvantaged student's situation, if any, must a counselor convey during reinforcement and/or modeling counseling for the intervention to stimulate constructive client behavior? 6) What permanence in a school or organization, if any, must counselors have for their praise to be deemed rewarding by disadvantaged students? Concerned primarily about internal validity, the studies discussed above reveal nothing about factors such as the accuracy of client perceptions about counselor expectations, the responsiveness of students in the subject's school to educators' requests for information, the population's customary follow through on commitments to academic assignments, the quality and availability of information resources, and the school's and community's attitude toward proactive planning. Many students in schools peopled by immigrant groups and/or the disadvantaged are not likely to be as supportive of information seeking nor to regard counselor wishes for such behavior with the same urgency as are students in schools that are linked closely to universities such as Stanford.

Vocational Exploration Groups

Underlying VEG procedures are heuristic principles 4 and 5. Through adaptations, such as previewing a tape of counseling and a discovery exercise about what to consider in a career choice, principles 1 and 2 could also be brought to bear. The efficacy of these principles plus the logic of the proposition that self-review in terms of components that research suggests are important in career choice should promote career development are major reasons for considering VEG an effective procedure.

The published research on *VEG* is limited. Bergland and Lundquist (1975) led twenty Mexican-American ninth graders in four groups of five each through *VEG*, twenty in groups without peer interaction, and employed twenty as wait controls. They found no after-treatment differences in student ability to differentiate occupations in terms of skills, interests, functions performed, or job satisfiers. But the forty *VEG* clients said they would recommend the program to others and felt that they had gained in the tested areas.

Hay, Rohen, and Murray (1976) contrasted twenty-four clients completing *VEG* with twenty-four controls and twenty-four receiving group interpretation of the *Strong Vocational Interest Blank* (Strong, 1927), Edward's Personal Preference Schedule (Edwards, 1959), and Kuder's Occupational Interest Scale (Kuder, 1948). They did not find differences among the groups on self-reported career information seeking or satisfaction, but they did find that the test interpretation group was more satisfied with counseling. Certainly, the lack of support for *VEG* in the study is tempered by the facts that the authors relied exclusively on self-report measures and failed to establish that counselors delivered *VEG* as intended.

Neely and Kosier (1977) reported that *VEG* had been applied by 24 counselors to a total of 640 students in 1974 and by 32 counselors to 401 students in 1975. In evaluating the *VEG's* effect, they contrasted changes in self-rating by 54 physically impaired students with changes by 89 normal high school students in terms of change in whether they were "strong, average, or weak" on a set of work satisfiers and on a set of work potentials (abilities). They found no difference between the groups in relative changing and did not explain why they would expect differential change. Apparently, clinical impressions led them to conclude that *VEG* is especially helpful to handicapped students in knowing and identifying with jobs.

A recent relatively large study of *VEG* with eleventh and twelfth graders is more promising. Torrez, Lundquist, and Bergland (1979) found that the sixty-four boys and girls who completed three to four hours of treatment outperformed fifty untreated controls in their abilities to identify interests and skills needed for selected jobs and to classify jobs in terms of their functions. Yet *VEG* did not produce more information seeking or a more favorable attitude toward gathering career information. One small study by Yates, Johnson, and Johnson (1979) however, suggests that *VEG* can produce broad cognitive, as well as affective, gains in career maturity. One counselor guided six groups of five eighth- and ninth-grade rural school youngers through five, one-hour *VEG* sessions over a five-week period. Pre-post testing showed that thirty randomly assigned *VEG* clients improved their scores on the *Career Maturity Inventory* scales of attitudes, knowing yourself, knowing about jobs, choosing a job, and looking ahead more than thirty controls. A six-month follow-up revealed that the gains on attitudes and knowing about jobs were maintained (Johnson, Johnson, & Yates, 1981).

Working with junior high school students, Johnson and Myrick (1972) found that a six-session reinforcement counseling procedure, which they termed *MOLD* and which resembles the *VEG* procedure, increased the career information of eighteen clients more than eighteen matched controls. Their procedure involved leading classroom-size groups through six steps: 1) describing one's abilities and interests on a profile sheet; 2) sharing and discussing occupational aspirations and expectations; 3) exploring career fields and making tentative choices; 4) writing a plan for next year's education, home life, jobs, and leisure; 5) receiving feedback based upon probability data; and 6) evaluating the experience.

Rule Learning Counseling

Logically the heuristic principles underlying rule learning counseling on page 306 and the manner in which a rule learning program is developed support its efficacy. To build a treatment, counselors do a form of task analysis; that is, they scrutinize persons with a particular problem and those who have overcome it, in order to determine rules for solving the problem; they review the literature to increase their understanding of the problem and to discover past or possible treatments; and then they fashion a treatment and revise it through formative evaluation.

Moreover, Gagné's (1970) extensive research and theorizing has shown the merits of arranging exercises sequentially to teach concepts and rules. Cognitive psychologists have shown the importance of rules in competence acquisition (Bruner, 1966; Weiner, 1972), and White (1966) has argued convincingly that competence acquisition is a powerful motivator. The motivating power of competence acquisition implies that when clients recognize the linkage of competence and rule, they will seek to learn rules.

Empirically, several researchers have examined classroom and interpersonal communication skills. In her study, Phelps (1978) employed a quasi-experimental design to test her procedure with students from two suburban Southern California private colleges. She analyzed the data from each school separately. Coeds from one school who volunteered after learning of the treatment were assigned to a group; they each identified a friend like them who would serve as control. In the second college, volunteers for psychology course "bonus points" who agreed to participate after learning about the treatment were assigned randomly to treatment or control status, and then the experimentals were assigned to one of three treatment groups based on schedule compatibility. Pre-post and three-month follow-up comparisons were made. Phelps (1978) found the clients' self-reports of attitudes about communication, their ability to communicate, their understanding of communication, and their communication frequency in groups changed significantly over counseling and compared with control subjects. Self-reported academic performance, level of communication anxiety, and professors' ratings of classroom participation revealed no significant changes. A three-month follow-up revealed that the significant gains between the experimental and controls in attitudes about communication, self-reported communication skills, and communication understanding persisted.

Focusing on communication skills important in dating, McGovern, Arkowitz, and Gilmore (1975) randomly assigned thirty-four male volunteers to a control condition, or to one of three versions of a rule-learning procedure, and contrasted their postcounseling performances on heterosexual interactions, social anxiousness, social avoidance, fear of negative evaluation, and self-rated social skill. The rule-learning procedures consisted of six 105-minute weekly meetings, which focused on readings from a specially prepared manual, discussion, or role play with a peer and a surrogate about getting-acquainted situations, and general discussion of the concerns that the discussions or role play revealed. Clients in the three groups improved significantly more than did the control on most of the outcomes, but neither group was superior to the others, perhaps because the small N in each group did not permit detecting the fine differences that would be expected from role play versus discussion embedded in the larger treatment.

In a related study, Pendleton, Shelton, and Wilson (1976) designed and studied a related social skills training program. The procedure involved systematic relaxation, modeling, and rehearsal of particular social interactions, training in thought control, and the homework of practicing with people in their natural environment. The six female and five male college students who participated in the eight weekly, two-hour sessions significantly reduced their anxiety about social contacts and negative evaluation, as measured by pre-post contrasts.

In a study of another well-delineated, rule-learning, counseling procedure that focused on time management, Bates (1971) compared thirty-eight disadvantaged veterans in a special college preparatory program who received counseling with thirty-eight matched, no-treatment controls. She found the thirty-eight counseled veterans reduced their unproductive use of time, tried more assignments, and felt better able to manage time than did the thirty-eight controls. They did not significantly increase their self-confidence, however, as measured by the Ghiselli (1971) self-esteem scale. In her first replicaton, Vivell (1972) found that the Bates's procedure helped thirty-two black twelfth graders increase their study skills and grades. Unfortunately, her design did not include a control group. Her second replication was a shortened treatment focused on assignment planning, distributive study, coping skills, and self-reinforcement. In this study, eighteen students from the same population referred for counseling by teachers were contrasted with thirty other students similarly referred. Vivell (1975) did not find gains in the time management skills of the clients. Post hoc analysis of covariance suggested that clients who attended regularly benefitted as expected, whereas irregular attendees did not.

Teaching the Test

Paper-pencil career development problems stimulate a person to articulate how to resolve career problems and thereby enable a counselor to pinpoint deficits in the respondent's approach to career problems. Direct counseling to correcting those deficits employs heuristics 1, 3, and 5 on page 306 and can incorporate heuristic 4 if the counseling is conducted in small groups. Moreover, since the clients can see that most of counseling is focused on helping them correct erroneous responses, this counseling should have high credibility if the career problems are appropriate.

But, little research has examined the merits of such a procedure. Indeed, Flake, Roach, and Stenning (1975) have published the only report of such a method. Examining a combination of trait-factor counseling and abbreviated teach-the-test counseling, they showed that the combination counseling enabled seventeen tenth-graders, who had scored below the career maturity mean for their grade, to improve their *Career Maturity Inventory* (Crites, 1973) score more than nineteen controls. Since the treatment consisted primarily of a day of testing and interpretation and only one session of teaching the *CMI*, attributing the gain to teaching the test is questionable.

Inventorying and Interpretation

One can examine the validity of an inventorying and interpretation procedure by considering the reliability of the procedure, the validity of the information produced, and the procedure's impact on career development criteria. This brief review of the validity of the *SDS* treats these three points:

First, several studies have shown that the *SDS* codes are as reliable as other interest inventory scores, thereby indicating that the outcome of *SDS* is relatively replicable. In their study of 1,092 high school students, Zenner and Schnuelle found that the rank order of the six Holland scales had a median test-retest reliability of .82. In another study, O'Connell and Sedlacek (1971) found a median test-retest correlation of $r = .75$ and a Spearman Rho of .92 for 4,000 University of Maryland freshmen.

Second, the fidelity of the *SDS* to the rationale of Holland's vocational choice hypotheses and constructs can be examined by determining whether the *SDS* summary codes correspond to summary codes produced by other inventories; whether the operations by which the codes are produced fit the theory; whether the six work environments postulated by Holland attract students and workers with distinctive activities, competences, perceptions and values; and whether these environments relate to one another in a manner such that adjacent environments draw persons similar to one another and provide similar experiences and rewards, whereas environments opposite one another draw different kinds of people and offer different experiences.

Regarding similarity of codes from different inventories, Zytowski and Harmon (1980) found that summary codes for fifty-two women from the *SDS*, *SCII*, and *KOIS* were related but clearly not identical. Often a summary code from one inventory omitted a personality type in a code produced by another inventory. Although this finding is not surprising in view of Osipow's (1973) conclusions that correlations among interest and value scales of the same name have generally been low to moderate, it should caution *SDS* users against foreclosing exploration of particular occupations only because they do not have a code resembling their *SDS* summary code.

Considering the fidelity of the *SDS* operation with the rationale of type and environment matching, Crites (1978) correctly observed that discrepancies in matches across the five subparts of the *SDS* have different implications and therefore implicitly require careful scrutiny. Current *SDS* materials do not alert the user to the need for such scrutiny, especially regarding discrepancies in competence, but overseeing counselors could certainly do so. Holland does not advocate disregarding competence in judging the desirability of occupational options, and his booklet, *Understanding Yourself and Your Career* admonishes verifying appropriate competence. This position seems especially important when SDS is used to narrow choices and to promote commitment. Yet, when the SDS is intended to expand options under consideration, there is less need for concern about competence. This lessened need is especially true when occupational entry is years away and a client has the possibility of building requisite skills.

On the other hand, it has not been demonstrated that the SDS samples the range of qualities that contribute to a person's type proportionately or that type and occupational environment compatibility is accurately gauged by a simple summation across interests and competences. In researching a similar process for helping people to begin to identify compatible work, termed *translation counseling* and described in Chapter 10, this author judged that compiling incorporation scores was helpful to most clients, whereas the scores themselves were not valid for as many clients. As a consequence, this author recommends that research examine whether the SDS or the new VEIK can be enhanced by providing opportunity for such activities as in-depth profile analysis, consideration of the availability of jobs in occupations with one's summary code, and the meaning of having a popular or rare primary code, within a complementary counseling procedure.

In terms of the distinction among occupations, there have been many studies of Holland's hypotheses. As such, it should come as no surprise that the findings are mixed in support of the SDS's validity as a classification and predictive device. In support of SDS are the many studies of different populations that have shown that persons in a particular major or occupation tend to achieve SDS scores whose first letter code is consistent with their affiliation (Apostal, 1970; Bates, Parker, & McCoy, 1970; Fabry, 1975, 1976; Harvey & Whinfield, 1973; Lacey, 1971; Mount & Muchinsky, 1978; Salomone & Slaney, 1978; Walsh, Horton & Gaffey, 1977). Similarly, numerous studies showing that different environmental groups arrange themselves so that incumbents of adjacent environments are more similar than are those in opposite environment on type scores derived from the *Vocational Preference Inventory*, the *Self-Directed Search*, or the *Strong-Campbell Interest Inventory* support the construct validity of the SDS (Bates, Parker, & McCoy, 1970; Bingham & Walsh, 1978; Horton & Walsh, 1976, Hughes, 1972; Mathews & Walsh, 1978; Morrison & Arnold, 1974; O'Brien & Walsh, 1976 Shudt & Stahmann, 1971). Not as supportive are studies of the compatability and satisfaction hypotheses. Although some studies have shown that persons in a congruent field are more satisfied (Nafziger, Holland & Gottfredson, 1975; Wiggins, 1976), others have failed to find a relationship between congruence and job performance, tenure, or satisfaction (Bates, Parker & McCoy, 1970; Hughes, 1972; Kerlin, 1976). Even more difficult to explain are recent findings by Rounds, Shubsachs, Dawis, and Lofquist (1978) that the Holland hexagon does not correspond to the manner in which work environments order themselves on reinforcers, based on occupational analysis, as opposed to analysis of the personality of the workers in the occupation. As a consequence, they suggested that "occupational reinforcers and behavioral requirements describe aspects of the environment different from those reflected on vocational interests." By implication, at least some of differentiation among environments provided by SDS is not directly attributable to differences in the work environments.

A related controversy concerning the SDS types is how they are calculated. Holland (1976b; Holland et al., 1975) has maintained that raw score computation is the preferred method, whereas Prediger and Hanson (1976) argued that standardized scores from machine scoring are preferable and even ethically essential. Their argument is based on the fact that the SDS raw scores show how close the individual's responses are to the inferred responses of people now in particular occupations. But some of those very responses are linked more to the fact that currently the occupational incumbents are male or are from the majority culture rather than to their compatibility with the job tasks. For instance, being on an organized sports team may register positive on the entrepreneural scale, but few women may check it because in the past there have been few sports teams for women. As a consequence, the raw scores tend to perpetuate the status quo, discouraging women, men, and minorities from pursuing nontraditional occupations. For the counselor, the best resolution, at least until research shows the contrary, seems to be to have clients consider both raw and norm-referenced scores. Certainly individuals whose norm referenced scores suggest exploring an occupation, but whose raw scores do not, will want to be alerted to the fact that they may be different from people who are now in the occupation, even though they are likely to find it more interesting and compatible than are agemates of the same sex.

Third, to warrant the claim that it is an effective self-administered counseling program requires evidence that completing SDS pinpoints occupations worthy of a client's exploration, and thereby stimulates increased information seeking, clarity about career direction, and satisfaction with that new direction. Again, the evidence is mixed, but the fact that several studies have shown SDS to generate positive, although expectedly modest gains (Holland, 1979), is promising.

In the first direct study of SDS's effectiveness as a form of counseling, with 1,092 high school students, Zenner and Schnuelle (1972, 1976) found that completion of SDS, in contrast to no counseling, increased the number of occupations that a client was considering, increased certainty and satisfaction with personal preferences, and increased the probability that occupational preference was consistent with inventoried interests and competencies. Surprisingly, completion of SDS decreased requests for vocational counseling and did not increase requests for specific occupational information.

In a second, smaller study, Redmond (1972) found that completion of the SDS by 120 high schoolers increased their information seeking as much as did completion of SDS and a contingency contract by another

120 students, and that these 240 students gathered more information than did 120 control subjects. In a related study of SDS's influence on information seeking, Nolan (1974) found that 45 veterans completing a GATB and SDS without counseling did not seek as much career information as did 45 veterans receiving two sessions of trait factor counseling. Nolan (1974) did not use a control, which would have enabled determination of whether the SDS veterans had increased their information seeking and whether both groups apparent equality on the criterion of the reality of plan represented a gain from counseling.

Still another contrast of the SDS with traditional counseling showed that both produced change, perhaps because it included a control, provided clients and controls with a list of information resources, and alerted them that they would be followed up. Krivatsy and Magoon (1976) randomly assigned 103 college student volunteers to complete the SDS, a supervised version of the SDS, traditional individual vocational counseling, or a control. Pre-post comparisons seven weeks apart indicated that students in each of the three treatments increased their information seeking and thinking and satisfaction with career and decreased their desire to see a counselor and need for information. Most of the students, including the controls, reduced the number of jobs they were considering and the need for information about occupations in general over the seven weeks. Inter-treatment comparisons, in turn, showed that the SDS, the supervised SDS, and the traditional counseling students surpassed the control students on selected criteria involving information seeking, understanding, and decreased desire for special information.

Examining the experience of other high school students with SDS, McGowan (1977) found additional support for SDS. Specifically, more of the 63 undecided seniors who took the SDS and were encouraged to use accessible career information announced an occupational choice after the experience than the 63 undecided seniors randomly assigned to a control status.

Contrasting the effect of three self-administering procedures on coeds volunteering for testing and interpretation, Atanasoff and Slaney (1980) found minimal differences among the procedures and only slight impact for any of them. Specifically, the thirty-five women taking an SDS, a card sort, or an SCII and receiving the National Computer Center interpretive format distinguished themselves from thirty-five controls on only one of seventeen ratings and did not differ on the number of occupations being considered or on satisfaction with choice. Moreover, fewer than 20 percent of the coeds changed choices over counseling. As predicted, the treatment groups increased their ability to relate themselves to occupations more than did the control, and unexpectedly, the SCII surpassed the other treatment groups. Somewhat puzzling, the SCII and control groups reported increases in their need to learn more about one or two particular occupations and increased discussions with peers about themselves and careers, whereas SDS and card-sort groups decreased their need for such information and also reduced the number of peer conversations related to careers. Moreover, like Krivatsy and Magoon (1976), Atanasoff and Slaney found a possible reactive affect to rating career issues, such that both counseled and control coeds reported significantly lower confusion about choosing an occupation and less need for self or general career information three weeks after the pretest. Appropriately, the authors urged that future studies include a control group without a pretest in order to determine whether simply being asked about career does not prompt college students to upgrade their planning.

In an effort to determine the impact of the SDS directions, the *Occupations Finder*, and *Understanding Yourself and Your Career* on client change, Holland, Takai, Gottfredson, Hanau (1978) had 100 high school girls complete various forms of the SDS and several pre- and post-outcome measures. The multivariate analysis was not statistically significant, but 7 of 42 univariate Fs were. The interpretable univariate Fs suggested that the directed self-scoring of the SDS leads to considering more occupational options, but that providing the *Occupations Finder* leads to *doing* more types of information seeking and to considering a greater number of options.

To clarify further the contribution of SDS components, Talbot and Birk (1979) examined whether groups of college women receiving the SDS alone, a card sort alone, or the *Vocational Exploration and Insight Kit* (VEIK) (Holland, 1979), which combines SDS, the card sort, and a planning exercise, would differ. They randomly assigned these college volunteers to the three treatments and to a control condition. One month after the counseling, they solicited feedback about the career options that the women were considering, the amount of their career exploration, and their satisfaction with treatments. As predicted, the SDS and VEIK women were considering more options overall, although not more nontraditional occupations. On the other hand, the groups did not differ in the amount of their information seeking. Nevertheless, in spite of the minimal advantage manifested for the SDS and VEIK groups, there was a tendency for the VEIK clients to be more satisfied than were the card sorters, evidenced by statistically significant differences on three of ten contrasts.

To ascertain the stimulus value of interest testing without interpretation, O'Neil, Price, and Tracey (1979) compared the effects of using only the SDS, only the SCII, and both the SDS and SCII on college students accepting an invitation to be tested. Multivariate analyses of variance and contrasts indicated that, immediately after testing, the group of thirty-three college men and women completing only the SDS reported more stimulation about career planning, and the group of twenty-nine who took only the SCII reported clearer directions than the SDS group or than a group of thirty-four students taking both inventories. There were no differences in certainty about career planning or personal relevance. One month later, apparently before the SCII was interpreted, the groups did not differ on satisfaction with career planning, clarity about planning, and time spent in planning. The findings support the stimulus value of SDS; but even though the authors do not mention it and one cannot accept a null hypothesis, the failure of students completing the SDS, which includes making personal interpretation, to be more satisfied and certain with career planning than those taking the SCII without an interpretation raises doubts about the efficacy of SDS as a self-counseling program.

In examining the preceding studies of SDS, you may have asked why expanding occupational options is deemed beneficial in one study, whereas narrowing career options is judged beneficial in another, or how one can applaud increasing satisfaction and certainty about one's choices and career plans without knowing the starting point and objectives of the clients. Clearly, future studies of the SDS should attend to the issue of opposite outcomes. To judge the SDS or any other procedure beneficial because it changes certainty, satisfaction, or range of options without knowing the nature of the client population is unwarranted.

A recent study by Prediger and Noeth (1979) with another inventory illustrates the difficulty of evaluating the meaning of client change. They found that their sample of ninth-grade girls increased the agreement between their occupational choices and inventoried interests after a mini small-group counseling program featuring inventory interpretation. They contended that this change was beneficial even though they also found that the counseling did not affect information seeking appreciably. Their judgment about benefit, however, overlooks the fact that fitting occupational choices to inventoried interests without activity tryout may not aid the vocational maturity of youngsters. The students' interests are changeable, and simply bringing occupational choices into agreement with unstable interests is not necessarily beneficial. One might even argue that the youngsters are being harmed, since they are being told that they can increase the quality of their career planning without extensive tryout and deliberation.

The nature of the SDS has required examining its reliability and content, construct, and predictive validity in order to establish its merits. Overall, the evidence suggests that this first generation procedure can help a person's career development if understood and used as directed in the booklet. Unquestionably, the SDS oversimplifies the process of choosing an occupational direction; but it is not intended to be the sole activity in the decision process. Similarly, it should not be faulted because people can abuse it by faking their ratings or by declining to follow through on the information seeking it advises. Clearly, more research on the kinds of instruction or structure that will promote or decrease such activities and decisions as information seeking and expansion of career options will make later generations of the procedure more valuable. Until further research and refinements are completed, however, this author believes that the SDS should be given to the public only under the aegis of a counselor. Counselors need not offer counseling along with the SDS, but they should clearly be accessible in case clients have questions.

Outcome Assessment

The evaluations of career counseling for people in the exploration stage have focused on four classes of tasks: self-awareness, career awareness, decision making and planning, and career skills—"adaptive" skills, as Fine (1974) termed them. Table 8–2 lists many of the objectives that have or might be used to appraise growth on these tasks and notes the methods by which counselors have assessed them. In addition, Table 8–2 lists several objectives not yet studied but which nevertheless merit attention.

Table 8–2. Some Objections Appropriate for Exploration-Stage Career Counseling

Objective	Study	Measure
1. Develop those abilities that improve general career functioning	Phelps (1978) Bates (1971)	Self-rating Written tests and home-work assignments
2. Expand knowledge of rules relating to skill acquisition and problem solving	Vaughan (1974)	Self-confidence test
3. Increase awareness of characteristics; that is, self-estimated characteristics correspond with estimates from other sources	Zytowski (1977)	Self rating vs. *Kuder Occupational Interest Survey*
4. Increase knowledge of occupations and/or educational programs in general	Hamdani (1977) Johnson & Myrick (1972) Bergland & Lundquist (1975) Swails & Herr (1976)	*Career Development Inventory*, Project test Project test *Career Maturity Inventory*
5. Increase knowledge of career options of particular interest	None	*Career Development Inventory*
6. Increase knowledge about informational resources	Ryan (1968)	Project test
7. Use more information resources and do more information seeking during and after counseling than before counseling	Hamdani (1977) Healy (1973, 1974b) Krumboltz & Thoresen (1964)	*Career Development Inventory* Self-report
8. Improve knowledge of planning and problem solving through counseling	Evans & Cody (1969)	Project cognitive measure
9. Feel more confident in one's capability to perform career development tasks	None	Self or another's rating
10. Alter career attitudes so they more closely resemble the attitudes of working adults	Hamdani (1977)	*Career Maturity Inventory*
11. Take more responsibility for career decision making and planning	None	Self or another's rating
12. Increase satisfaction with career progress and/or certainty about it	Healy (1973, 1974b) Fogel (1973)	Self-rating

Of course, many other objectives might be examined in scrutinizing career progress during the exploratory stage. In one review of objectives, for instance, Westbrook (1975) located fifty-four different objectives identifiable in the career maturity tests described in Appendix A. Unfortunately, there is only limited empirical evidence linking most of the objectives identified by Westbrook to adult career maturity. Indeed, only the recent work by Kohen et al. (1977) has linked adolescents' general occupational information to adult career maturity. The work of Super (1969) and his colleagues Jordaan and Heyde (1979) and Gribbons and Lohnes (1968) related adult maturity to information about preferred occupations.

Because many potential objectives have not yet been linked empirically to adult career maturity, counselors will need to explicate the rationale of their objectives fully. Moreover, they will want to verify that their procedures move the clients toward the goals that they and their clients agree to pursue. Many potential criteria should facilitate identifying proper goals, but they also increase the need for deliberation in choosing an objective.

In addition to the career development objective, many studies have asked clients to rate their satisfaction with the counseling experience. This evaluation seems especially appropriate because all career counseling at the exploratory stage should help clients to appreciate the contribution of planning and deliberation to career. Satisfaction with the process allows such appreciation; dissatisfaction does not, and probably makes one less likely to seek counseling in the future.

Surprisingly, researchers have relied heavily on tests, inventories, and self-reports to assess clients' growth. They have not asked those immediately affected by improved student career development, namely teachers and parents, to report changes. But, even though secondary school teachers and parents have less contact with these students than do those dealing with children in the growth stage, they should be involved in student appraisal. Not only is their testimony likely to be very reliable since they observe the student often, but their involvement also seems very important from a program perspective, for their teaching can support or interfere with career development goals. Indeed, counselors would do well to gauge faculty, parent, and administration satisfaction with career counseling in addition to monitoring student approval, since these adults' negative response to counseling, regardless of whether the counseling actually is constructive, may obstruct client growth, whereas their satisfaction is likely to strengthen and supplement the counseling effects.

Before moving to the hazards of career counseling at this stage, a perusal of Table 8–1 will recall the kinds of career development objectives that have or should be sought at this stage. Clearly, the objectives span the domains of self and career awareness, self-confidence, decision making, planning skill and intention, and attitudes about working. Equally clear is that one can and should progress on all objectives throughout life. Insofar as the targets of career counseling at this stage are points on a continuum, it is appropriate to judge particular counseling, not only in terms of whether it moves the person to a particular level of maturity, but also in terms of whether it alerts the person to the need to continue to advance and increases the determination to advance. In other words, a sense of achievement in career development along with determination to continue to develop are as important outcomes as are gains in any of the particular objectives enumerated in Table 8–1.

The open-endedness and relativeness of the objectives should also remind us that the short-term counseling interventions described and critiqued in this book can only be stimuli or correctives to the career. For lasting effect, they most probably should be parts of larger career education programs or at least be periodically repeated or used with one another. Immediate and perhaps intermediate assessment of the counseling interventions should detect their effects; but we must not expect long-term effects unless there is an ongoing effort to advance the career systematically.

Hazards

Every counseling method involves hazards, which should be monitored as the method is being used. Some of the dangers associated with the methods described in this chapter are discussed in this section.

Often one erects programs because one finds individuals having difficulties. Once in place, however, such programs require articulating and following procedures, which can easily lead to ignoring or rejecting individuals who do not fit the program. Since counselors are supposed to be advocates of the individual, they must be especially attentive to individual needs when they assume a coordinator posture or use procedures with extensive standardization, such as simulation, model reinforcement, and VEG.

A coordination danger arises from the pressure to secure cooperation and to maintain harmony among the contributors. At the outset, the counselor who convenes community, faculty, parent and students for a joint career development effort must recognize that each group is not going to view student career development needs and their respective responsibilities in the same way. Dialogue, joint workshops, and formal procedures, such as the delphi procedure, may bring them closer together (Healy & Quinn, 1977; Valdry, 1977), but on some issues they will not achieve concensus. In spite of this, the coordinator should orchestrate contributors so that meaningful programs result. Often this may mean that some parties' priorities are not taken into account, or that even some activities occur that are opposed by contributors. For example, a union official may balk at in-depth student examination of craft jurisdiction, or management may object to students asking about job redesign possibilities, or parents may feel that field trips should be a school-borne cost. At such times, the coordinator will need tactfully to show the contributors that the disagreeable element does not offset the total program benefit they support. Most important, the coordinator must be able to sustain criticism to ensure that the integrity of the career education effort is not compromised because of controversy.

The simplicity and limited duration of the career counseling procedures for the exploration stage may lead clients and the public to conclude erroneously that career development is a simple process that can be attended to when convenient. To counter this notion, counselors can point out that the plans discussed, information obtained, or routines established are only appropriate for the moment's concerns. They definitely should be reviewed in terms of changing demands and aspirations.

Clearly the limited objectives obtained by the career counseling procedures—extra information seeking or deliberation—and their difficulty in effecting more general gains, such as increased career maturity test scores, should show counselors, parents, and students that these treatments may not substitute for more comprehensive programs. Several writers have noted this possibility. Moreover, findings, such as those of Hamdani (1977), that inner-city high schoolers improved only modestly on career maturity after an extensive, long-term program, also suggests the difficulty in strengthening career maturity at this age for inner-city children. Hamdani's study concerned the impact of a semester-long, one-hundred-hour, career guidance program directed at increasing the career development of inner-city youth. Pre-post testing of the students in the program, which involved special curricular materials, modeling, field trips, simulations, job analysis and videotaping, indicated cognitive, behavioral and attitudinal gains for the forty-two boys and thirty-five girls who participated, and a three-month follow up indicated these gains were maintained.

Counseling procedures often operate apart from the client's environment and significant others, perhaps unintentionally leading the client to discount the community's ongoing responsibility and concern for career development. Perhaps encouraging clients to inform others of their efforts in the program, to acquire information and advice from the community, and, if possible, to have others participate in counseling would be helpful in reducing possible isolation. For example, the second reinforcement-modeling session might be conducted jointly with parents, who had been alerted to reinforce information seeking and deliberating.

Another hazard, especially in *VEG* counseling and in inventorying-interpretation is heavy reliance on broad client experience, self-understanding, and knowledge of occupations and occupational information gathering. Research has shown that such knowledge is developing during adolescence, but contains many inaccuracies (De Nisi & Shaw, 1977; Tiedeman & O'Hara, 1959; Super et al., 1969; Gribbons & Lohnes, 1968; Mitchell, 1977; Aubrey, 1977). As a consequence, one must not mislead adolescents into believing that they know themselves or occupations when they do not. The counselor must recognize that many teenagers have not considered the relative value of different kinds of information, and judging from the slow growth of test scores during adolescence on the *CMI* (Crites, 1973), many are still learning to draw valid conclusions from self and career data through eighteen years of age. To avoid misleading teenagers about their knowledge and deductive skills in regard to careers, self-instructional materials or paraprofessionally supervised modules for reviewing and upgrading client self and career knowledge should be made available. Following *VEG*, for instance, a client might be directed to compare personal estimates of the satisfiers and demands of the preferred occupations with a master list of satisfiers and demands. Such lists could be prepared by paraprofessionals working from the *Dictionary of Occupational Title* and the *Career Development Inventory* (Super et al., 1979). Likewise, as part of the inventories, a teenager might compose a list of activities and subjects that he or she did not recognize and then be guided to explore these.

Counselors may become bored and mechanical in administering the structural exploration procedures, especially because of the precision and focused character of these and several other procedures described in this text. Clearly, there will be a sameness over clients. To avoid tedium, therefore, a counselor will want to focus on the uniqueness of each client. This individual focus may occur through adapting the procedure for the client's benefit. Noteworthy is one counselor's comment that repeatable counseling is like a well played Dodgers' baseball game. Seeing one provides an idea about their play, yet every new one can show something new and exciting.

Another hazard for procedures such as simulation, teach-the-test, and model reinforcement counseling is that performance on the indicator of the competence (increased scores on paper-pencil tests, reported increased information seeking) may be confused with actual change in how the career is being managed. Life is full of examples where people seem to know how and what they are supposed to do, but still do not do it. Especially when clients receive instructional treatment for objectives that are not pressing, counselors will have to help them create links to their current living and build resolve to apply the learnings they acquire in counseling at that future point when the competence is needed. But first a counselor must realize these needs in order to reduce this hazard.

Yet another hazard, especially for procedures such as simulation, teach-the-test, and rule learning counseling, is for the counselor to assume that the counseling content coincides completely with the problems the client is encountering or will encounter or that the rationale of the counseling solution will always apply in the real world. Again, the best safeguard against this hazard appears to be modesty, with the counselor and client acknowledging that counseling is practice. Like all practices, the counseling may have to be repeated and changed as the game changes, and even the best players and teams can expect some losses.

The counseling experience, especially simulation or rule learning, implies that key concepts, principles, information sources, and the like, can be learned or contacted easily, or that when the linkup is made, the expected solution will follow. Actually, careers unfold in a competitive environment, wherein one's own anxiety often interferes with learning, or environmental constraints and human limitations lead resource people to perform in other than expected ways. Solutions emerge over time, not instantly. Rarely are decisions completed as soon as all information has been carefully gathered and systematically weighed. Indeed, the work of Tiedeman and Miller-Tiedeman (1975) suggests that when this sequence occurs, the decision may have already been made, and this deliberation is simply reassuring oneself of the reasonableness of the choice. In addition, applying new rules is likely to be inconsistent at first. Even when one is consistent, other people will take time, often considerable time, to respond as one now intends them to respond.

Concluding Note

This chapter has focused on career counseling procedures that are suitable for helping persons engaged in career exploration. Many of these procedures have been aimed at and studied with adolescents, but they also appear adaptable to adults who may be repeating this stage. In many guidance programs, such as Meyer (1971) and Hamdani (1977), counselors are combining several of these procedures to increase the power of career guidance. Since each procedure is limited in scope, such combination is reasonable, if not mandatory.

Transition from Exploration to Establishment

9

Eighteen is a momentous birthday. Upon reaching this age a person may, for the first time, do many things on his or her own volition—vote, marry, stop school, join the Armed Forces, enter apprenticeships, or work in industry. The two or three years before and immediately after this birthday are very significant in a career. Society expects the mature adolescent to have become independent and to begin partaking in its work. Not surprisingly, one popular idea of career education is that every student leaving school will possess a "salable" skill (Marland, 1974).

During this stage, the mature adolescent should hone in on a career direction, refine work skills, enter appropriate training or work (Super, 1957), and begin the process of commitment (Perry, 1968; Dudley & Tiedeman, 1977). Awareness of opportunities is broader and deeper (Super et al., 1969; Gribbons & Lohnes, 1968), and decision making is exercised more consciously and more frequently (Crites, 1973; Healy & Klein, 1973; Super et al., 1969). Identity is becoming more certain and more accurate, and by now, contains an appreciable career component (Erikson, 1963; Havighurst, 1964). The prerogatives of adulthood have blended with the idealism and vitality of youth.

These multiple tasks are interrelated but can be distinguished conceptually as transiting from school to work and identifying and accepting a series of component career positions. This chapter focuses on transition from school to work, and Chapter 10 covers career choices. First, Chapter 9 summarizes recent survey findings of youth in transition to illuminate what is typical of careers during these years. Next, it reviews some of the difficulties peculiar to the school-to-work transition and suggests possible educational alterations to alleviate this stormy passage. The author then proceeds to describe and to critique three counseling procedures that aid transition: work experience counseling, placement counseling, and anxiety reduction counseling. Since these procedures differ substantially from one another, pertinent research and possible hazards follow the description of each procedure.

Characteristics of Youth Moving from Work to School

Mitchell's (1977) survey of data about 34,000 in-school and 2,000 out-of-school seventeen-year-olds provides some sense of what is currently happening to youth who are about to disembark from school. Among her findings were these:

1. Nearly 90 percent of seventeen-year-olds expect to choose their occupation themselves, and most have talked to someone about their career. Many (33 percent), however, do not feel that those with whom they conferred were aware of the student's abilities.

2. Counselors and teachers are not the primary source of career advice. Only 35 percent of the students had talked to school counselors or advisors, and even fewer talked to teachers (14 percent). These 14 percent may or may not be part of the 35 percent who conferred with counselors.

3. Most seventeen-year-olds have systematically sought to improve some ability, with 50 percent using verification from live sources and 15 percent using formal lessons or courses.

4. Seventeen-year-olds justify their skill claims by noting testimonials and outcomes of their skills, such as prizes and team memberships (43 percent); by testimony of others (17 percent); by personal comparison (12 percent); and by grades or tests (9 percent).

5. In terms of occupational information and relating self-attributes to career, most seventeen-year-olds (98 percent) could answer five of nine multiple choice questions about occupations. Most seventeen-year-olds (64 percent) could also list a hobby, sport, game, or other activity that might relate to work. Boys listed team sports five times more often than did girls, and girls listed music and art more often. When asked for one school subject useful to working, 91 percent identified a subject they had taken. The subjects listed fell into these categories: business education (27 percent), mathematics (17 percent), vocational education (11 percent), science (9 percent), English (7 percent), and industrial arts (6 percent).

6. Reasons given by seventen-year-olds for taking or not taking a promotion to supervisor suggested more seventeen-year-olds held extrinsic than intrinsic-oriented work values. The most frequent reasons for accepting a job were prestige/status, work conditions

and benefits, advancement opportunity, and challenge. The most common reasons for declining were too much responsibility, dislike of the job duties, dislike of working conditions, inadequate interpersonal relations, and lack of capability.

7. Answers to an assignment to write a response to a want ad suggested that seventeen-year-olds would write incomplete letters, even though most had held and had applied for part-time work. Most letters contained a greeting, closing, a signature, described qualifications and job duties, and listed the applicant's traits related to the job. Most did not list the applicant's educational achievements, seek an interview or other employer contact, give a return address, mention references, ask for information about the job, indicate reasons for wanting a job, or point out how the applicant met all the job's requirements.

8. Many seventeen-year-olds prefer, and have considered entering, high-status professional and managerial jobs, but considerably fewer consider lower-level occupations, although the distribution of jobs suggests that most will be employed in such work.

Selected data from a four-year follow-up study of more than twenty thousand high school graduates shed additional light on making the school-to-work transition in our society (Eckland & Wisenbaker, 1979). Relevant issues that are illuminated include: the 1976 educational attainment compared to 1972 expectations, the primary activities by sex, memberships in voluntary organizations, and feelings about high school.

In terms of educational attainment versus expectation, the data suggest that only one third of those anticipating college and one-fifth of those aspiring to graduate school had realized their ambitions four-and-one-half years later. More than half of each group had some college, but had not completed a degree. No doubt, some of the latter eventually will attain their goals. Indeed, the authors found that 9 percent of current undergraduates are in five-year programs, and another 22 percent are former dropouts returning to complete their degrees. Nevertheless, the data again affirm that many high school graduates with high education aspirations reduce their educational, and probably their occupational, aspirations after leaving high school. Graduates who had either aspired to no college training, or to only some college, or to vocational-technical training were much more likely not to have reduced their objectives. Possibly, they had already reduced their aspirations so that their achievements were more in line with accomplishments. Unfortunately, the data analysis to date does not answer the question of whether the graduates felt it was better to aim high even if they did not succeed or to acknowledge one's probable achievement level and not strive for more. In any event, less than 1 percent of those not aspiring to a degree or graduate school had achieved a degree within four and a half years.

The following primary activities reported in 1976 suggest that most twenty-three-year-olds are into the work phase of their careers and that surprisingly few are still in formal education. The facts are: a) more than three-quarters of these men and two-thirds of these women are working full or part time; b) fewer than one-fifth of the men or women are enrolled in college; c) only one-twentieth of the 1972 class is in graduate studies; d) even less of them are taking vocational or technical courses; e) less than one-tenth of the men and one one-hundredth of the women are in the Armed Forces; f) well over one-third of the women and only one one-hundredth of the men are engaged in homemaking; g) about one-tenth of the men and women are out of work, but are either waiting to enter or trying to find a job. By 1976, 53 percent of the graduates combined had one or more children. Ten percent of those who had married were divorced or separated.

Hispanics and whites generally are similar. The black youth differ in that nearly twice as many black men as other groups are in the Armed Forces. As a result, proportionately fewer black men are working in the civilian labor force. Moreover, about 25 percent fewer black than white and Hispanic women are homemaking.

The organizational memberships of the group are somewhat surprising. Instead of reflecting the concern of establishing one's occupational place, they reflect more interest in religion, socializing, and recreation. The percentages reporting 1976 memberships are as follows: church or related activities, exclusive of worship—33 percent; sports teams—31 percent; social or hobby club—24 percent; worker organization—21 percent; cultural or study group—12 percent; civil affairs—10 percent; political clubs—9 percent; youth organizations—10 percent; volunteer groups—7 percent; community service organizations—5 percent; education organization (PTA or academic group)—7 percent; campus leadership or paper—5 percent. Erikson (1963), among others, has noted that there are several life tasks besides career at this age. Apparently these youth are using their organizational memberships to accomplish such tasks.

Underscoring the need for career education in high school, the feelings of the 1972 graduates about the adequacy of their apparently noncareer-oriented high school programs became more negative over the four and a half years. In 1976, 51 percent believed that schooling should have emphasized basic skills more; 64 percent thought there should have been more attention to vocational-technical programs; 65 percent felt their schools did not have enough practical work experience opportunities. Four-and-one-half years after high school, only 39 percent said their educational counseling in high school had been adequate, although 57 percent had rated it sufficient at graduation. Barely 23 percent rated their employment counseling sufficient, even though 32 percent had judged it adequate at graduation.

Additional data illuminating the nature of transition can be gleaned from the national longitudinal studies of fourteen to twenty-four year olds by Herbert S. Parnes at the Center for Human Resource Research of the Ohio State University for the Department of Labor (Parnes et al., 1976; Kohen et al., 1977). Some of the early, pertinent findings from these studies are reported in Chapter 11.

Transition from School to Work

Work has become separated from home and school. In the 1970s, few people worked at home or on farms as they did in the 1890s. People now leave home and commute to the workplace. Their work increasingly is specialized and complicated, involving equipment and processes not normally duplicated in our otherwise well-equipped households. Few people outside education, executive suites, medicine, and law can take their work "home"; they must instead stay late at the office to finish necessary tasks. Perhaps fuel shortages and new computers and communication will prompt more working at home, but the separation of work from home limits youth's information about work.

In the same vein, schooling has become preparation for advanced schooling more than preparation for work or citizenship. Its relationships, activities, and products are increasingly different from modern work. More specifically, on jobs, workers often function as members of teams rather than as individuals competing with one another. They perform a limited set of tasks repeatedly instead of continually advancing in different tasks. Rarely have these tasks a pronounced academic character, and almost never are they changed periodically, certainly not every forty or fifty minutes. Workers produce parts of products or services for others, not for their own development, and their outputs are coordinated with and dependent on the output of other workers. Moreover, these outputs must meet strict specifications and be produced on time.

Until the career education movement, society and its schools had given little direct attention to teaching about occupations. Clearly, however, such knowledge is essential for a person to exercise a full range of career options. Few people regard their occupations as recreation and consequently do not invite others to observe their work. Furthermore, workers hesitate to discuss the details of their jobs with nonworkers lest they bore them, and persons outside an occupation are reluctant to ask about job details because their questions may suggest they are ignorant or perhaps prying. Since there have been few systematic, sustained efforts to induce people to learn about occupations and since such learning is not usually considered recreation, occupations are mysteries to almost everyone but their incumbents.

Isolation of work from home and school leads to misunderstanding about preparing for working. Assessments of a broad sample of high school students shows inflated expectations about the benefits of working with deflated estimates of the requirements and disadvantages (Prediger, Roth, & Noeth, 1973; Mitchell, 1977). In the past decade, many students who had completed fourteen, sixteen, and even eighteen years of school in order to enter challenging, prestigious occupations have been disappointed. In part, the disappointment reflected their failure to find out how they were going to relate their studies to work or how many opportunities of the kind they desired were available. Unfortunately, they heeded the advice of education propagandists that additional education invariably leads to more and better career options. Today, of course, reputable educational institutions are modifying, if not dropping, such claims. Yet, it is predicted that more than 15,000 college graduates each year will be unable to locate suitable work.

The disadvantaged groups, ironically, especially are affected by the isolation of work from schooling. Informal contacts that allow others some access and insight into the world of work are closed to them. Their peers and neighbors often are unemployed or hold marginal positions; consequently, they are inadequate models and information sources. Many of the disadvantaged attend schools where graduation or promotion does not require completion of assignments, punctuality, or even regular attendance and cooperation. In these schools, assignments are made but never collected or corrected; class starting times are posted, but tardiness and absence are expected; and lack of cooperation and insolence are tolerated. As Oetting and Miller (1977) point out on the basis of years of counseling the disadvantaged, many of these youth have not acquired the habits and attitudes fundamental for modern employment.

Even persons from advantaged circumstances have observed relatively few occupations and probably have not reflected on the significance of what they observed (Mitchell, 1977). As a consequence, their understanding of what a worker is supposed to know when hired and what is to be learned on the job is limited. They often are naïve and frustrated about working. College placement offices, for instance, have found that many new graduates take jobs primarily on the basis of salary, only to find within a year or two that they had neglected to consider several other satisfactions they now wish to secure by changing jobs or even occupations.

The consequences of the widespread lack of understanding about working are tragic. The victims are often rejected by employers who mistakenly attribute their lack of habits, attitudes, or general understanding to malfeasance rather than to lack of appropriate preparation (Oetting & Miller, 1977). On the other hand, others become dissatisfied in their jobs, not because the jobs are unworkable, but because they do not conform to fantasies about what work ought to be.

Major assistance is needed to help youth move from school to work. Here, the author describes and critiques three kinds of counseling: work study counseling, placement counseling, and test anxiety counseling. Other kinds of counseling, such as financial aid counseling, are also provided, but they have not been described in detail nor evaluated.

Before turning to the counseling methods, however, first consider the sources of high youth unemployment and possible system alterations that might alleviate them. In the role of evaluator, the counselor has an obligation to bring such data to the attention of appropriate officials and to the general public. Here are some youth unemployment problems, their causes, and possible solutions.

1. Once a year, within a thirty-day period, hundreds of new graduates seek employment. Although their graduation is predictable and some large corporations and government agencies are pre-

pared to accommodate a large influx of employees in July, many employers are not. Consequently, many graduates have to wait several months for an available position. Of course, this problem might be alleviated by enabling students to complete graduation at different times, depending on the availability of work. For example, schools might conduct weekend and evening programs or correspondence courses as alternative ways for the graduating senior to complete the last semester. Likewise, employers might assist by hiring "near" graduates initially for twenty or twenty-five hours per week to enable them to complete their degree requirements while beginning work.

2. New graduates and dropouts leave school where their primary objective was to develop themselves. They then take employment in a job whose primary objective is to produce for someone else. The workplace is intolerant of many of the sophomoric habits of students—tardiness, sloppiness, desire for variety, questioning authority, uncooperativeness, and so forth; several studies have shown that the majority of job terminations for young workers are based on such faults. Stemming from different institutional tolerances, this problem could be reduced by requiring the student to engage in real work, possibly community projects as suggested by Coleman (1975), in the final months of schooling. The primary intention would be to benefit the customer or public, but the student would also gain by experiencing a work environment and by receiving guidance in how to cope. Many students now undergo some work experience as part of high school, yet this experience may be counterproductive in fostering work habits if it is over-adjusted for student idiosyncracies. Certainly proponents of work experience should study the relative success of students with work experience in retaining their subsequent job. For, as Silberman (1974) found, not all work experience is beneficial.

3. Even when students have satisfactory work habits, they often lack a work history, which seems to make veteran workers more employable. Yet, they must receive the same scale or minimum wage as older, experienced workers. CETA's experience in securing enduring jobs for the unemployed, however, suggests this initial disadvantage may be reduced by the government's underwriting a portion of a new worker's salary for the first six months of employment, perhaps making the stipend reimburseable to the employer after the employee completes a year of service.

4. Many new graduates finish studies in geographic locations far removed from areas where employment is expanding, and they often lack the resources and contacts to move to those jobs. In the past, this age group eventually became very geographically mobile in search of work. Government relocation subsidizes and interstate cooperation of the U.S. Employment Service should facilitate relocation to areas with jobs, enabling job seekers to avoid the frustrating months of unemployment or underemployment.

Schools, colleges, and civic organizations might abet students in relocating for jobs by sponsoring "junior or senior years exchange" programs wherein the student could complete some studies in areas with many employment opportunities.

5. Most students graduate with a broad range of skills. Generally, however, they lack the particular skills the marketplace wants, and their schools and college often lack porgrams to develop such high-demand skills quickly. If graduates had such skills, employers would be in line at the graduation ceremony with job offers. Since high-demand skills can be developed quickly with properly focused training, schools and colleges could smooth students' transition into work by contracting to have high-demand skills training programs available as electives for their students in the final year or months of their formal education. California has done this through Regional Occupational Centers. Certainly, the increasing mobility of workers among occupations and the occupational mobility of vocational education students should dispel fears that such training will permanently lock a worker into a job simply because the slot was open. Rather, educators should recognize that it is easier to obtain a desirable job when one is employed than when not working. Counselors and career educators can help students accept the value of preparing for available jobs, not only for their preferred occupations, by informing them and their parents about the nature of modern careers. Critical points about a modern career include these: workers will perform several occupations; every occupation enables a person to acquire general career as well as occupation-specific skills; moving from employer to employer early in one's career tends to benefit a worker, at least in terms of improved salary; and it is easier to obtain a job when employed than when out of work.

Work Experience Counseling

Work experience counseling complements work experience or cooperative education programs and is usually mandated as part of those programs, especially school programs. Many different activities are labeled work experience counseling. They range from scheduling programs, verifying attendance, and providing orientations, to offering individualized, instruction in basic academic skills to help a client function in the work experience. Although the former administrative tasks are important in a quality work experience program, counseling is most likely to add to the effectiveness of a work experience program when it furnishes each individual with insights into the work setting or into oneself. More specifically, work experience counseling succeeds when it helps the individual to recognize and to identify with effective models; to start with appropriate assignments and to progress in a manner that maintains challenge; to identify, to understand, and to resolve on-the-job-difficulties; or to recognize the work values and issues connected with the practiced occupations.

Work experience coordinators and counselors often are not trained in counseling and sometimes have not even taken a formal counseling course. Most often they are business education and vocational education teachers who have become, or are becoming, administrators. Their orientation is often administrative, and they regard the coordinator position as a lower rung of the school or civil service administration ladder. This accounts for the fact that little systematic effort has been given to improving the counseling component of the work experience coordinatorship in school-based programs and in federal manpower programs.

Heuristic Principles of Work Experience Counseling

Underlying the provision of work experience, and especially work experience counseling, are the following assumptions about moving from school to work:

1. One can facilitate the necessary learning by providing many models and showing the learner what the models are doing that should be imitated. Working among regular employees enables students to observe several different models. This then enables a counselor to highlight the models' behaviors that are effective and necessary for the job. Silberman (1974), for example, in contrasting job satisfaction of 1,016 work experience students with that of 696 students working outside a job experience program, found that availability of adult models was an important factor in the greater satisfaction of the work experience program participants.

2. Appropriate work skills, habits, and values develop if they are practiced, critiqued, and rewarded in work settings. Real production in real businesses affords students opportunities for performing various job functions and receiving corrective feedback and praise for work well done. By facilitating communication between the student and the supervisors and workers, the counselor can assure that the student samples a range of job tasks and receives and appreciates feedback. Silberman (1974) found that availability of feedback was an important component of students' satisfaction with work experience.

3. Students will learn effective work behavior more quickly and surely if they begin with tasks that fit their competence and graduate to more demanding tasks at a pace that keeps them challenged. Super and Hall (1978) concluded that industrial studies suggest that the challenge that college graduates experienced in their initial jobs is an important factor in their overall career progress. O'Toole (1977) similarly argued that opportunity to continue learning is an important element in job satisfaction

among workers. Research on instruction indicates that beginning
the learner well below or above competence level blunts learning
(Gagné, 1970). Therefore, counselors must be versed in psycho-
educational assessment to assist work supervisors in assigning
students duties and in pacing rotation among tasks (Norris et al.,
1979, Herr & Cramer, 1972). In the previously noted study of Silberman (1974), work experience satisfaction correlated positively
with having meaningful work assignments.

4. Application of problem-solving strategies to on-the-job difficulties
increases a student's capacity to cope with obstacles to job performance both in the present and in the future. Inevitably, functioning in the workplace creates problems for the worker. Guiding
students in employing problem-solving strategies to reconcile such
difficulties shows them how to apply problem solving effectively
and habituates them to such an approach in career-related
problems.

5. Students acquire productive work values and practices more
quickly when they recognize such characteristics in people like
themselves and when they can examine issues about work practices openly and honestly. Counseling can provide a forum in
which a student examines personal similarity to workers in particular occupations regarding values of concern. Raths, Harmin,
and Simon, (1978) indicate that such talks require openness and
honesty. Of course, such discussions occasionally, and perhaps
even regularly, unearth dysfunctional work practices and contradictions between work practice and worker values. Students of
work, such as O'Toole (1977), argue that it is better to acknowledge such difficulties in a context of deliberation and problem
solving than to deny their existence and to suffer the psychological or physical stress in the belief that they are an inevitable part
of working. O'Toole (1977) and others imply, however, that many
managers and administrators are reluctant to encourage such
honest deliberation because they fear the work routine changes
that may result from an aroused work force. Certainly, coordinators will have to choose worksites for work experience carefully
in order to assure student access to productive, self-directed workers. Indeed, they will have to be stalwart in defending open
scrutiny of work practices. Their success in the latter surely will
correlate with the notice they will attract from school boards and
administrators, who may be harried by bosses disgruntled by the
agitation of new perspectives on the work practices within their
firms.

Work Experience Counseling Methods

No single work experience counseling procedure is likely to embody all
five principles listed above and rarely does a procedure contain only one.
Therefore, isolating and relating particular practices to the principles is

difficult. Moreover, the dependence of work experience counseling on the work experience itself confounds the issue of what a particular counseling action or exercise produces. An advantageous placement is likely to benefit clients regardless of counseling, while an otherwise effective counseling practice may not be powerful enough to overcome the obstacles to student development encountered in a poor placement. Although isolating counseling practices in operation is difficult, separating them conceptually aids their identification and study.

Focusing on models and exemplary work behavior. Guided observation and discussion of model workers' and trainees' on-the-job actions, role playing desirable and undesirable behavior, and role reversal can assure that the work experience trainee identifies constructive work behavior and recognizes that such behavior is rewarded. Hoffnung and Mills (1970) found that application of such methods over fourteen weeks in a "client-centered," one-hour counseling session helped disadvantaged, adolescent work-experience trainees. Present at each session were the group leader, the trainees, an observer, and the job trainers. The trainer facilitated discussion of topics such as job responsibilities, pay scales, criteria for advancement, and trainee behavior. Trainees were encouraged to express their feelings about the work experience and to problem solve related difficulties. In the last five minutes of the session, the observer summarized the meeting. Hoffnung and Mills (1970) reported that the seventeen trainees who met twice a week had significantly better work attitudes and peer relationships and were rated more likely to succeed on regular jobs than were the fifteen clients who had only one hour a week of counseling, or the thirty-two clients who served as controls.

Field internships offer many opportunities to direct learners to exemplary work behavior. In supervising school counseling internships, a form of work experience counseling, the author has found it useful for counselor trainees first to observe systematically, but unobtrusively, what the individual counselors in the school are doing; how the counseling and guidance program is integrated into the total school program; how particular counselors interact with other school staff in securing resources and cooperation; and what the administrator, faculty, students, and community expect of counselors. An initial lecture describes observation techniques. Then, analysis of the observations pinpoints what to imitate and how to get resources for specific projects. In addition to this directed observation of the system, trainees keep a diary and tape record some of the activities. The three kinds of data are reviewed in supervision to help the student counselor to identify the deficiencies and to plan corrective action.

Correction often entails directed reading, rehearsal of techniques, role reversal exercises, and so forth. When the learner encounters obstacles to development in the work location, the supervisor will confer with the site liaison to iron out the problem. Occasionally, the student counselor, supervisor, and site counselor confer jointly about the difficulty, and generate possible solutions. The author's experience with these methods has been positive. But the following kinds of problems have surfaced from time to time: student-site counselor incompatibility, lack of consensus between supervisor and site counselor about student counselor duties, limited referral sources, limited space for the student counselor, and student counselor feelings of being overburdened by clerical work.

Practice, Critique and Reward Appropriate Skills. One reported skill-building program involved Alabama prison inmates. After it became evident that ability to manage interpersonal relations, money, and leisure time contributed substantially to postprison adjustment, Smith administered two variations of a twenty-hour *Rational Behavior Therapy (RBT)* program to inmates in an Alabama work release program in order to build these skills (Smith, Jenkins, Petko, & Warner, 1979). The variations consisted in contacting or not contacting relatives.

In the initial hours of treatment, Smith lectured about the rudiments of *RBT*, the method of problem solving using *RBT*, and the importance of the abilities to manage interpersonal relations, money, and leisure time. Volunteer group members then used the *RBT* format in Figure 9–1 to outline their personal problems and to generate solutions. Subsequently, passouts about the three target skills further explicated desirable behaviors, provided illustrations to help the inmates recognize their own problems in the three areas, and assigned homework exercises. During the rest of the group meetings, the inmates analyzed one another's problems. Again they used the *RBT* format and also supported one another in vowing to carry through solutions. Among the money management topics covered were credit counseling, checking and savings accounts, purchasing essentials, and the preparation of a budget by each inmate in accordance with handout guidelines. Specific leisure activity and interpersonal activity topics were not mentioned in the research report.

For half the groups, Smith mailed information about the program to the members' families. Then he conferred with them in their homes about the program. He reported that the visits were strictly informational, not therapeutic.

Using a pre-post, true experiment design, Smith, Jenkins, Petko, and Warner (1979) tested whether the thirteen inmates completing the *RBT* treatment and the seventeen inmates completing the treatment supplemented by family contacts differed from one another or from the eighteen controls. The criteria were twenty ratings derived from official records and behavioral interviews. The analyses showed that the treated inmates scored higher than the controls on all three skills, even though the controls improved somewhat over the five to six weeks of treatment. Informing family members about the program did not produce significant differences, but there were numerical differences, which suggested that it might be a useful supplement, worth testing again.

Another study of a skill-building program to promote work adjustment of a special group was reported by Roessler, Cook, and Lillard (1977). They tested the effectiveness of a program for general rehabilitation clients aimed at improving communication, problem solving, and self-control skills. One counselor led twenty clients in groups of five to

Figure 9–1. Flowchart Showing How to Rethink Irritating Experiences Constructively

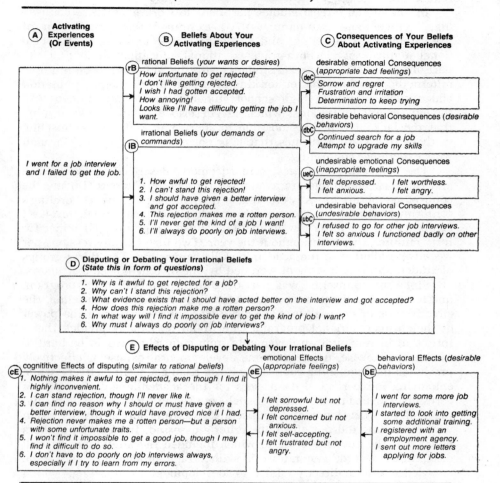

SOURCE: Rational Self-Help Form. Used with permission of Albert Ellis and The Institute for Rational–Emotive Therapy.

eight through fifty hours of training over a five-week period, using structured exercises and workbook assignments. The leader guided the groups through self-exploration, self-understanding, and constructive action as recommended by Carkhuff (1969). They did these activities so that each client could make a public commitment to a goal and an appropriate behavioral plan. Once this was achieved, all members made periodic progress reports to the group and received feedback and support. Post-counseling contrasts on self-ratings of the twenty clients with twenty controls showed that the clients felt that they were making more progress. Both groups had rated themselves on vocational maturity, vocational functioning, interpersonal maturity, and movement toward their rehabilitation goals.

In one of the largest studies pertinent to work experience counseling, Prediger and Baumann (1970) examined the contribution of "developmental counseling" and academic skill counseling to the vocational maturity of eleventh-grade vocational education students. Comparisons of the 205 counseled students with the 211 controls on multiple criteria did not show that either kind of counseling or their combination added substantially to high school students' career development. Although several limitations, which are described below, allow arguing that the lack of benefit is not due to shortcomings in the counseling methods, the study indicates that it is not easy to help youth through work experience counseling.

The counseling activities were succinctly described in the article, and fuller specifications are available in a technical report. During the counseling, observations were made to demonstrate the counseling's conformity with the guidelines. Essentially, one experienced, MA-level counselor led the thirty developmental counseling groups. They met for forty minutes a week throughout the year. Two forty-minute sessions per week were allotted to the academic skills counseling. The thirty groups of students in this treatment were led by one of four novice instructors.

Since the counseling was part of a larger comprehensive program, and because the clients interacted extensively outside of counseling, the effectiveness of counseling necessarily was interwoven with the power of the entire vocational program. One would reasonably predict, therefore, that incremental improvements from counseling would be hard to establish. Likewise, using only one developmental counselor effectively precluded distinguishing counselor effects from counseling effects, while employing inexperienced counselors for the academic skills counseling certainly lessened the potential of such counseling. However, the unusual focus of the "developmental counseling" was probably a major reason why counseling did not affect the criteria assessed. Indeed, the authors noted that the outcome criteria, which included the attendance record, disciplinary record, general work skills, trade proficiency, and trade knowledge, only indirectly related to "developmental counseling," which in their interpretation emphasized creating a forum for open expression in order to learn about one's impact on peers. Consequently, the counselor envisaged his role as facilitating interaction on issues brought up by the students for three quarters of the sessions. In the remaining meetings, the counselor served as a "participant observer" as the students dealt with topics such as employee-employer-customer relations and job interviewing. Much of the open discussion, as one knowledgeable about adolescence would expect, focused upon boy-girl relations.

More on target with the assessed outcomes, educational skills counseling featured "remedial, developmental, and enrichment activities in reading, writing, oral communication, and mathematics." Where feasible, the leader assisted students in relating their instruction to their trade coursework.

Commentary on Work Experience Counseling Research

Insofar as work experience counseling depends on the work experience that the clients are undergoing, studies of such counseling should describe the work experience program, the support for work experience within the sponsoring institution, and the work experience staff's views about the counseling. Proper replications require a similar contextual climate, since these variables are likely to affect counseling outcomes. Prediger and Baumann (1970), for example, conjectured about the impact of the vocational program in which their counseling was embedded. Yet, most work experience studies have only hinted at such contextual variables, by allusions to details, such as whether work experience staff joined counseling meetings or whether counseling had to be rescheduled to accommodate higher institutional priorities.

Limited research on practice. There is a general dearth of research about work experience counseling. The studies reviewed here, and the several studies of using guided inquiry method with student teachers reviewed in Chapter 11, are the only ones known to this author. Clearly, work experience counseling needs more research, especially since many educators now seek alternatives to traditional classroom schooling. This author was especially disappointed that the Experienced-Based Career Education Programs have not reported about the systematic counseling done within their operations. The benefits of such counseling cannot be assumed to be self-evident!

Reviewers of manpower programs, indeed, have concluded that work-experience counseling has not contributed to the success of these programs. Walther (1976), for instance, noted that the evidence from manpower programs about the counseling contribution was disappointing. He stated:

> No studies were located which demonstrated a positive relationship between amount or type of counseling and achievement of program goals. A number of successful programs, on the other hand, have deemphasized counseling after gaining experience with the relative contributions of various program components. . . . In a Longitudinal Study of Neighborhood Youth Corps' programs, a negative association was found between hours of counseling and employment outcomes. Although it seems reasonable to attribute the negative correlation to counselors spending more time with the troubled participants, the study certainly provides no evidence of the beneficial effects of counseling.

In spite of these criticisms, Walther proceeded to recommend that counseling focus on the following activities:

1. Providing vocational information;
2. Arranging vocational exploration;
3. Teaching job seeking skills;

4. Teaching job application skills;
5. Helping youth to understand their own behavior;
6. Helping youth identify and understand career advancement skills;
7. Helping youth resolve work problems in order to improve work performance;
8. Helping youth to schedule employment experience at levels appropriate to their ability and motivation.

Like Walther, this author believes that counselors can provide services that will increase the benefit of work experience. To contribute, however, counselors must first do task analyses of the criteria as Smith, Jenkins, Petko, and Warner (1979) did; and they also must refine their treatments through formative evaluation.

Placement Counseling

Placement counseling typically is part of an overall school or college placement service. The service usually includes: a) part-time and volunteer opportunities; b) full-time local job listings; c) on-site recruiter interviews; d) an occupational and job library; e) assistance in résumé preparation and job search; f) counseling; and g) classes in goal identification and job search. Indeed, a recent College Placement Council survey of 1,400 four-year colleges and universities found the following percentages of the 860 respondents reporting that they offered the services listed below (Beaumont et al., 1977):

Campus interview	96%
Full-time placement	93%
Career counseling	89%
Alumni placement	87%
Résumé service	81%
Part-time and summer job	79%
Credential service	37%
Career planning or employment readiness courses	37%
Vocational testing	31%

Placement services, including counseling, aim to help each client to specify suitable employments and to convince an employer to offer that client an acceptable job. New graduates, students leaving school, and occasionally alumni seek placement services in order to contact prospective employers. Placement officers generally are commissioned by their institutions to assist these fledgling workers in securing proper employment. Many have not sought full-time professional or technical-level work before, and consequently are not knowledgable about using résumés and interviews to persuade employers of their qualifications. In pursuing their studies, moreover, they may have become separated from the job market and may not have discovered organizations likely to have openings attractive to persons with their qualifications.

Free placement services theoretically are available to all. Each state maintains an employment service underwritten by the U.S. Department of Labor. This agency especially assists underemployed and unemployed workers in entering the labor force but will offer services to all citizens, if requested. Its services include aptitude testing, counseling, referral to Department of Labor manpower programs, such as the Work Incentive Program, and job referral. Emphasis of the United States Employment Service is usually on special groups, such as Vietnam veterans, welfare recipients, the chronically unemployed, and so forth. Its immediate goal is a worker's entry or reentry into the labor force. In 1976, the Employment Service reported nearly 7.68 million job listings and 3.36 million placements. The bulk of these listings were for unskilled and semiskilled workers, with only 6.1 percent for professional and 4.2 percent for sales positions (*Employment and Training Report of the President*, 1977). Indeed, the Department of Labor recently concluded that jobs listed with the employment service already had undergone a "picking off" and filtering process through other formal and informal channels preferred by employers. As a whole, the USES listings and newspaper want ads represent a last resort employer recruitment method (U.S. Dept. of Labor, 1978c). The local state employment office can be located under the state's name in a telephone directory.

A third agency providing placement services is the private employment agency. Such agencies are profit-making businesses that help employers hire appropriate workers and help aid workers locate receptive employers. These agencies accumulate information on job openings and provide it to job seekers, and as well as screeing prospective employees for employers. They also provide assistance in résumé and interview presentation and occasionally advise on selecting occupational goals. Some agencies specialize in certain occupations, such as engineering, management, clerical, or temporaries; others are general. The yellow pages of the local telephone book lists local agencies, and the Better Business Bureau can provide information about the reputability of particular agencies.

The success of a school and college placement service is certainly a function of the quality of its candidates and the prestige of the institution. Harvard graduates predictably will outperform Nowhere State graduates in securing management trainee positions. Placement, however, is not designed to develop job skills in its candidates; consequently, its contribution to eventual client employment necessarily is limited. Of course, job seekers who use placement services have an advantage over those who do not.

The effectiveness of placement counseling also depends on other placement services. If the placement officer has located receptive employers who need workers with the client's qualifications, or if accurate occupational information is available to clients, placement counseling will be more productive. This interdependence of counseling services and the limitations of its contribution make it difficult to attribute gains to particular placement services such as counseling. This text necessarily limits itself to explication of placement counseling. Detailed description of and instruction in other placement services are available in these sources:

> A. G. Beaumont, A. C. Cooper and R. H. Stockard. *A Model Career Counseling and Placement Program* (Bethlehem, Pa.: Collegement Placement Services, 1977).
> J. Fielding and M. Fielding. *Conducting Job Development Programs* (Palo Alto, Ca.: American Institute of Research, 1978).
> J. Fielding and M. Fielding. *Conducting Job Placement Programs* (Palo Alto, Ca.: American Institute of Research, 1978).

Heuristics of Placement

Placement counseling operates on the basis of several beliefs about why workers are hired, how one should approach an employer, and how people learn about job acquisition.

Several generalizations about why a person gets hired. First, employers prefer people known to them or recommended directly by a trusted colleague or employee. Many people, not surprisingly, still obtain their jobs through personal contacts. Therefore, work experience and internship programs are very effective tools for students in securing jobs. Similarly, this fact is the reason that job placement clients universally are enjoined to let all their friends, relatives, and teachers know they are seeking work. Some schools are even setting up short-term externships or shadowing experiences to build visibility for placement clients.

Although fewer than 20 percent of the unemployed use personal contacts in job search (*Education and Training Report of the President,* 1979), evidence supports developing and using such contacts, but cautions against relying upon them exclusively. McKersie and Ullman (1966) and Granovetter (1974) found that jobs secured through personal contacts yielded higher starting salaries than did jobs obtained through placement services. They had studied college graduates, business school graduates, and technical/professional workers. In contrast, Allen and Keaveny (1980), who examined graduates of two-year programs in business and engineering, found formal placement services, not personal contacts, related to securing more responsible positions with greater training opportunities. Neither job search strategy produced advantage over the other in salaries.

Second, employers are more likely to offer employment to persons who can relate their skills and aspirations to the employer's needs. Even though most placement counselors urge clients to find out as much as possible about the prospective employer and to be able to relate their skills to the firm's needs, applicants' inability to do so is a major reason given by college recruiters for rejection.

Third, employers prefer workers with demonstrated commitment to their occupation. Quick turnover is an employer's loss. In addition, many believe that people committed to their work, as evidenced by reporting high satisfaction, are more professional and more productive, even though studies of work satisfaction do not show a clear relationship between satisfaction and productivity (Crites, 1969).

Fourth, employers hire people who have succeeded before they hire those who have not. Want ads often include experience required or preferred. The adage that the past predicts the future supports this practice, especially when past activities are similar to the employer's needs. In response to the desirability of experience, many placement counselors, following Bolles (1974), guide clients through an in-depth consideration of their past experiences in order to help them identify and articulate past achievements relative to prospective jobs.

Fifth, employers prefer to hire persons with whom they feel comfortable, and for whom minimal accommodation will be necessary. This preference, unfortunately, has been an excuse to discriminate unjustly against women, senior workers, and minorities; but when not based on sex, race, age, religion, social class, or handicap, it is understandable since organizational work requires compatible relations and accommodation problems reduce profits. Unfortunately, the recruiter or the firm's personnel officer often use the questionable evidence of one or two interviews to establish compatibility. Not surprisingly, recruiters reject a significant percentage of applicants for lack of interview presence or motivation, which often reflects only the interpersonal incompatibility of the two parties. Other indices also used to predict compatibility include hobbies, number of job or educational changes, attendance records, and grades. The strong concern about compatibility has led placement people to stress the importance of interviewing skills and to seek out and correct potential weaknesses in résumés.

In obtaining access to employers, several principles apply. First, the likelihood of access to an employer increases when one has a plan that includes identifying desirable employers and avenues of access to them. The *College Placement Annual,* placement office job files, civil service announcements, and newspaper and professional journal ads indicate employers who hire for particular occupations. Research suggests that an applicant should apply not only to those employers actively seeking workers in his occupation, but also to all employers who employ such workers (Sheppard & Belitsky, 1965; *Manpower Report to President,* 1975). Once a client specifies an occupational choice, the placement counselor can assist in using these sources to identify how one applies for particular jobs.

Second, favorable access to an employer is more likely if one is referred by someone known to the employer. As noted, placement officers urge applicants to let everyone know they are looking for employment. They also maintain a recruiting schedule, which in actuality is an institutional introduction of the candidate. Recently, more and more schools have been calling on their alumni to assist in introducing new graduates to the work community. Some employers even require prospective employees to be screened by private employment agencies.

A third access strategy is to introduce one's talents in an attractive manner. Employers have limited time for hiring, and therefore they may be impressed by applicants who can persuade them of their value in a striking, clear, and quick fashion. If it cannot be striking, the introduction should at least be clear and brief. College graduate and management applicants write concise, individualized letters to replace or to introduce the traditional résumé, which of course must be executed carefully. Creative workers, such as writers, cartoonists, and so forth, keep portfolios of selected work for presentation.

The fourth axiom admonishes persistence. An acceptable job offer is often the consequence of contacts with numerous prospective employers. Contacts not resulting in an offer should be reviewed to suggest corrections in approach and then should be forgotten.

Learning job acquisition. In regard to learning career transiting skills, placement counselors are far ahead of other counselors in using brochures, books, speakers, paraprofessionals, and audio-visuals to inform clients about the process of seeking work. In the last decade, many schools and colleges have added classes, some for credit, in job acquisition. These efforts are based on the first heuristic principle for teaching job getting skills: that people will learn about job seeking if they are given direct, clear information when they begin looking for work.

The second principle states that job search techniques will be learned more readily if one provides enough time and support of their acquisition. Counselors are enlisting candidates in the process earlier and often make learning a "club" activity, as in Azrin's (1978) job clubs, or a full-time job, as in the Job Factory (Shapiro, 1978). Preparing a candidate for obtaining a job can take weeks and sometimes even months. Candidates must decide on their objectives, learn to relate their talents to those objectives orally and in writing, and learn where opportunities are. Then, most importantly, they must initiate multiple contacts and continue to search in spite of initial rejection.

The third adage is that feedback for the client on job-seeking efforts will help the client improve. Therefore, counselors debrief campus interviewers about the strengths and weaknesses of their clients, and they offer job interview and résumé preparation workshops for strengthening these aspects of job search. Clearly, they apply the principle that one can improve job seeking by correcting errors detected during rehearsal or in initial efforts.

Individual and Small-Group Placement Counseling Methods

In addition to the placement brochures, speakers, audio-visuals, and classes, most placement offices still provide nearly every applicant with individual or small-group counseling. Traditionally, this counseling consisted of two meetings. However, as competition for professional openings increased and as specialized qualifications were expected more often for entry-level professional positions, several subroutines have been added to traditional placement counseling.

The traditional interview is outlined first, followed by a description of the new subroutines. In the first placement counseling session, which is diagnostic and information giving, the counselor reviews the client's job search expectations. Preferably, the client completes a draft résumé before the interview and receives instruction on how to utilize the first interview. This author, for example, developed a thirty-minute audiotape to guide clients in completing a draft résumé and to prime them for the concerns to raise during the counseling interview. Informal reports by four counselors indicated that the procedure improved their placement interviews by enabling clients to discuss more personal concerns and to receive more information. Ten years after the author's departure, this innovation was still being used in the placement office.

In the interview, the counselor may follow a résumé format, asking the client to state goals and to relate education, abilities, experiences, interests, and aspirations to those goals. As the interview proceeds, the counselor judges whether the client has well-defined objectives and is persuasive in presenting qualifications relative to the objectives. Some clients will demonstrate their competence on both criteria, but many will reveal weaknesses in clarifying objectives, in selecting work objectives, in interviewing, and in feeling confident about achieving their objectives. Occasionally, the counselor will confront a seriously disoriented student who is troubled at the prospect of leaving school and finding or taking a job. Most placement counselors will assist clients with the first four problems and will refer the confused student. Before such assistance is described in subroutines below, the basic procedures for a focused client are presented, since eventually every client experiences them.

Once the client is judged ready in terms of persuasiveness and focus, the counselor informs him or her of firms of probable interest on the recruiting schedule, tells the client how to schedule interviews, alerts him or her to other prospective employers not interviewing on campus but who are likely to have openings, and advises about the job board and library of materials on prospective employers. Ordinarily, the counselor will also have the client answer some typical recruiter questions, such as these: "Tell me what made you seek work with us?" "Where would you like to be in five years?" "Tell me honestly, what are your strengths and your weaknesses?" Some counselors also remind clients of points, such as these: 1) employers are interested in learning how one will contribute to their firm rather than hearing how much one needs them; 2) employers expect one to show that one has researched their firm and are interested enough to ask questions about particular duties, training, and advancement. At this point, books by Figler (1975), Loughary & Ripley (1976), and Bolles (1974) and excerpts from the *College Placement Annual* are often suggested. Throughout the interview, of course, the client is encouraged to ask questions and to share personal comments. Finally, the interview closes with the counselor's scheduling a second interview to review feedback from the client's initial interviews with campus recruiters.

The second interview consists of discussing the initial recruiter interviews. Formally or informally, the counselor secures recruiter reactions to the client regarding general appearance, knowledge of employer and position being sought, nonverbal communication skills (eye contact, posture, social responsiveness, facial expression, voice modulation, gestures, level of anxiety), and ability to do things such as explain skills, solve problems, ask for pertinent information about the employer, and praise or criticize self. The client, too, has impressions about these interviews and is eager to compare them with the feedback from the interviewer.

When the client has succeeded in securing invitations to follow up with employers, counselor and client discuss what to expect in the rest of the hiring process. Very likely, they review content of a follow-up interview, how to practice for employment tests, and the conventions about thank-you notes, follow-up letters, acceptances, and salary negotiation. At this point, many counselors suggest readings from the *College Placement Annual* or local manuals.

This interview often concludes placement counseling, although a third session may be held to help the client choose among options or to assist a client who is having difficulty obtaining a job offer. For the former purpose, the counselor acts as a reflector and sounding board, helping the client to recognize that this is one of many job choices one is likely to make. When the client is not succeeding with campus recruiters, the counselor and client discuss the difficulties pointed out by the recruiters and the client. Then both consider possible strategies for correcting the difficulties. Often this discussion results in adding one or more of the subroutines below.

Sometimes, however, solutions can be worked out immediately. For instance, the client who had not researched the employer fully can agree to fill out a research sheet on firms before the next interview. Or, the client with difficulty in explaining a low grade in a course of particular interest to the recruiter can be helped to clarify the reasons and to formulate an acceptable explanation. The explanation must, of course, be honest and may include completion of make-up work by the client. Regardless of the correction, a third session is necessary to review feedback from subsequent recruitment interviews. Only after it is clear that the client can succeed in the initial recruiting interview should the counselor discuss what to expect in the remainder of the hiring process.

Specifying objectives. Clients who are sure of the talents they wish to use and the rewards they seek from working often require guidance specifying a suitable job or preferably jobs. An accounting major, for instance, may not have decided whether he or she wants to launch a career with a certified public accounting firm, the Internal Revenue Service, the Federal Bureau of Investigation, or a corporation. Or the social science major bent on helping others may be aware only of jobs as case worker and social worker and may feel stymied by the paucity of job openings for either occupation.

Clarification often involves the client's first reading descriptions of likely jobs. Many placement offices, such as UCLA's, for example, maintain a library of job descriptions of entry positions secured by past clients to complement commercial and government occupational information, which Ginzberg (1975) has described as inadequate. Following the reading, counselor and client discuss the appropriateness of the different jobs, especially the career ladder associated with each. Recently, more placement officers are enlisting the assistance of alumni in this process, primarily as sources of first-hand information (Kaufman, 1976), but also as providers of work/discussion experiences (externships) in a particular job (Forney & Adams, 1976). Since the lack of specificity in client objectives often stems from limited information about jobs and their career ladders, such activities frequently are very critical.

Specifying goals and relating one's background to them is the essence of résumé development. A concise, well organized résumé helps to focus job seeking. Clearly, a job seeker will profit from reviewing their work-related history and pinpointing goals. Identifying the key elements of past experience that highlight one's talents will probably enhance self-esteem and certainly suggest whether particular new challenges are commensurate with the foundation one has built.

But excessive attention to résumé production is unwarranted. Some placement counselors urge clients to individualize résumés for each occupation for which they hope to interview, and even to compose a new résumé for each prospective employer. They argue that résumés either open the door to further consideration by an employer or result in rejection, and some even recommend costly printing of résumés.

However, research does not show that excessive time or cost should be expended for the résumé format, certainly not for the new job seeker. Stephens, Watt & Hobbs (1979), for instance, found that fifty-nine of the hundred corporate personnel officers who rated different aspects of résumés did not attribute differential power to short or long résumés, to printed or photocopied ones, to standard or specially spaced ones. Rather, the executives differentiated on factors such as correct spelling, prominently displaying education and work, and specifics about education and work experiences.

Deciding career direction. Some clients are not just unclear or non-specific about their objectives; they have not decided what they want to do. For instance, the biology major may not know whether to enter pharmaceutical sales, laboratory technician work, an MBA management program, or an assistant buyer position in a local department store. Similarly, the liberal arts major may be unsure of whether to pursue a law degree, become a publisher's representative, enter the civil service, or sell insurance. Often, these clients arrive at the placement office just before graduation, hoping that the counselor can get them the proper job. Frequently they are very anxious, feel they must do something immediately, and are irritated or angry if the placement counselor does not tell them about a suitable opening. In spite of their agitation and perceived need for an immediate job, their first requirement is choosing a direction. Before placement counseling can continue, therefore, they must undergo career choice counseling (described in Chapter 10) either on a referral basis or through formal contract with the placement counselor. Formalizing the contract is necessary to ensure that the client accepts responsibility for participating in the appraisal process and acknowledges that the process will be time consuming.

Interview training. Employers emphasize the interview as a major tool in deciding whether to hire persons for technical and professional positions, even though its validity as a selection device is questionable.

For other jobs, too, the impression made at the interview is important. Consequently, the fledgling job seeker often can profit from interviewing training. Barbee and Keil (1973; Keil & Barbee, 1973) have outlined an effective procedure using videotaping to improve interview behavior for disadvantaged persons. This procedure consists of the client's role-playing the interview while being videotaped, reviewing the videotape to pinpoint strengths and weaknesses, practicing corrections in another role play, and then reviewing again to see the improvement.

Employment interview training often will include training in areas other than attending and conversational skills. Based on a review of employment interview literature, Clowers and Fraser (1977) had six interviewing recommendations. Below, four particularly appropriate ones are amplified.

1. Review and rehearse the client in communication and appearance factors important for the particular type of job. These factors might include social and academic balance, interview responsiveness (attending, eye contact, positive conversational feedback), discussing one's own shortcomings constructively and how one overcame obstacles in the past (telling how one worked hard and persistently in advancing one's career), showing a relaxed and pleasant conversational manner, and being prepared and punctual for the interview.
2. Inform the client about the interview process. Include instruction on screening interviews with recruiters and hiring interviews with potential supervisors. Point out that the likely duration is fifteen to thirty-five minutes. Distinguish between structured and unstructured interview formats. Point out the importance of creating a favorable impression early in unstructured interviews and of closing a structured interview by highlighting positive characteristics related to the job.
3. Coach the client in points such as mentioning positive job-related assets early in the interview; emphasizing these characteristics periodically during the interview; and acknowledging shortcomings, such as incomplete courses, but instead of dwelling on them, telling how he or she resolved them constructively. For example, a student might point out how a low grade in calculus prompted obtaining a tutor to ensure improvement in integral and differential calculus, and then move to another point.
4. Encourage the client to establish before the interview and within its early stages the context of the target job so that one can relate one's assets to its particular demands.

Feeling confident. Class ranking and tests, such as the Graduate Record Exam, place 50 percent of graduates in the lower half and 10 percent in the bottom decile by design. This labeling does not mean these students have not profited from school nor achieved the expected competences, for the fact of their graduation shows that they have achieved the expected skill. What the labeling means, of course, is that these persons are behind fellow students on certain academic criteria. Their rank on the criteria has only limited relevance to their academic performance in graduate school (GRE morning scores average about .20 correlation with graduate school grades), but only has minimal, if any, relevance to work performance (Ghiselli, 1966; Thorndike & Hagen, 1959). Many employers, however, consider grades and test scores as one important factor, though not the only factor, in hiring young workers (Benson & Chasin, 1976).

Students, too, often consider less than excellent grades as indicating that they are somewhat incapable. Indeed, schools, in spurring excellence through competition, create many achievers who feel unsure of their abilities. Such feelings are incongruent with the person's accomplishments, but are real and painful, nonetheless. These feelings are more than symptoms of inadequate interviewing skills, for not only must people with such feelings identify and practice effective interview behavior, but they also must correct their feelings about themselves.

Lack of confidence suggests at least two causes that, in turn, suggest two possible solutions. First, one's repeated low ranking may have conditioned the person to feel insecure in discussing past achievements, or misinterpretation of the meaning of low ranking may have persuaded the client to feel inadequate. If the former explanation is true, then a desensitization procedure, such as that outlined below, for test anxiety should be helpful; if the latter is true, the cognitive self-awareness procedure in Chapter 12 should assist.

Even bolstering the client's esteem may not be enough, however. Employers are likely to react negatively to low grades. Consequently, counselors should confront the employers directly with the limited relevance of grades and perhaps as a profession should stimulate corporations to study their own experiences with personnel who had achieved various grades. Neal (1977) had additional suggestions for helping graduates with low grades. She advises: a) determining whether the graduates have special interest to compensate for low ability; b) calling employers specially to introduce such promising prospects; and c) dealing with one's own fears that such a student may disgrace the school.

Validity of Placement Counseling

Clearly the separation of educational and work institutions argues for placement counseling to allay students' anxiety as they confront a new set of expectations and demands. Because few educational programs equip or direct their graduates to a particular set of jobs, and because the new job seeker sometimes must look beyond the local community to find work, a service is needed that will inform the person about how to begin locating suitable jobs and how to negotiate with employers to secure them. What is most surprising is that school and employment services often have failed to meet such needs for graduates or school dropouts. Reubens (1977), for instance, noted that the United States trails other industrial countries in the percentages of youth who report obtaining their first employment through school or public employment service assistance.

Goals. Placement counseling should address several objectives, including the following:

1. The client can identify the advantages and disadvantages of different jobs for his or her career.
2. The client can state the current do's and don't's of seeking work in his or her field.
3. The client secures interviews for suitable jobs.
4. The client creates a favorable impression in job interviews.
5. The client obtains offers of suitable jobs.

These objectives, of course, can be measured by cognitive tests, ratings of the quality of proffered jobs, and obtaining interviewer feedback on client interview performance.

Research. Recently, many studies have examined the effectiveness of placement counseling in enabling disadvantaged and handicapped clients to secure jobs commensurate with their talents and aspirations. Fewer studies have been done of college placement services. Nevertheless, 55 percent of the 860 colleges and universities that responded to the College Placement Council inquiry indicated that they conducted follow up of their graduates, 95 percent of the respondents provided full-time placement service employing 16 to 60 percent of professional staff time, and 89 percent of the respondents indicated they offered career counseling that used 1 to 45 percent of professional staff time. These replies suggest that informal impressions about college placement counseling's success are accumulating and that they are being interpreted as favorable (Beaumont, Cooper & Stockard, 1977). Of course, substantial investment in college placement counseling also argues for formal study of this area and dissemination of the findings.

Interview skills development has received considerable research attention. In two of the more illuminating studies, Barbee and Kiel (1973); Kiel & Barbee (1973) have evaluated job interview training using video feedback of role-played job interviews. Working with small numbers of disadvantaged youth, they showed that the combination of viewing a video tape of a simulation job interview and identifying and being reinforced for correcting inappropriate interview behavior increased the favorability ratings of these youth on subsequent simulated interviews. Successful use of the video feedback included counselor's cueing clients to inappropriate behaviors and even pointing out errors directly, client rehearsal of a correct alternative for an error, and reinforcement of correct responses by the counselor. The Barbee and Kiel studies, coupled with the numerous reports showing the effectiveness of similar microcounseling techniques in improving interview performance (Ivey, 1971), indicate that interview training can help many clients. Moreover, the recent work by McGovern and his colleagues (1978, 1979), showing considerable consensus among recruiters and college students and between the two groups on the nature of effective interviewing, suggests such interview training has value.

Other studies of employment interview training suggest that alternate methods may be effective but that a counselor should evaluate the training since it will not invariably work well. In an early study of video feedback job interview training with hospitalized neuropsychiatric patients, Logue, Zenner, and Gohman (1968) contrasted the impact of typical counseling, programmed material, and programmed material plus video feedback on a role-played job interview. Their outcome criteria were ability to complete an application and performance in a mock job interview with the hospital personnel officer. There were no differences among the twenty-five patients undergoing the treatment. The authors speculated that this might have occurred because the feedback from video taping elevated anxiety, which eradicated the benefit of having had errors pinpointed. An alternate explanation suggested by the Barbee and Kiel (1973) study might be that the clients needed an opportunity to practice correcting their errors in a rewarding context before the benefit of videotape practice became apparent.

In a more recent study of interview training, Hollandsworth, Dressel, and Stevens (1977) contrasted the performance of fifteen college students randomly assigned to a treatment resembling Barbee and Kiel's with fifteen in a class on job search, and fifteen in a control group. Subject's pre-post changes in a simulated employment interview indicated that the behavioral treatment increased the percentage of eye contact more than discussion or control treatment did. The class group, in turn, produced more speaking and more ability to explain skills than did the behavioral or control condition, and more expression of feelings and personal opinions than did the control condition.

In an effort to pinpoint the effective components of interview training, Speas (1979) assigned fifty-six soon-to-be-released male inmates to one of five treatments rendered by one of two counselors. Thirteen prisoners received nine hours of training with modeling, role playing, and video feedback; eleven had nine hours of modeling and role playing; eleven took five hours of only modeling; and eleven acted as controls. The analysis of their performances on simulated post-test employment interviews indicated that the inmates receiving full training and those receiving the combination of role play and modeling outperformed controls on all aspects of the interview. (Inmates were judged on ability to explain skills and to answer problem questions, on mannerisms and appearance, on opening and closing interview, and on enthusiasm.) Role-playing inmates surpassed controls on enthusiasm, but the modeling-only group did not differ from controls. In a follow-up interview with a personnel worker from the community, the group receiving all training elements again surpassed the controls on half the particular interview scores and on the "probability of being hired" rating. Surprisingly, the model-only group also scored higher than did the controls on the "probability of being hired" rating. Overall, the findings suggest that all training components add to the effectiveness of the training.

Comprehensive placement programs for the disabled and disadvantaged now have been studied a number of times in different places. Such programs typically feature several days of small-group instruction in skills such as identifying and informing prospective employers about work-related assets; answering questions about limitations from a disability, especially how such limitations are minimized; discussing the job enthusiastically; suppressing annoying mannerisms; and dressing appropriately. In an early study, Anderson (1968) found that 90 percent of the disadvantaged clients exposed to the program secured jobs within two weeks and required less counselor help than typical. McClure (1972) provided further support for such training when he contrasted clients who received the instruction with an untreated control group. Fifty percent of the trained clients obtained work within thirty days, whereas only 24 percent of the controls did. Moreover, the trained clients required less counselor time, exclusive of the job-seeking training. Investigating a more extensive program, which also included tours of work sites, Pumo, Sehl, and Cogan (1966) found that 73 percent of their handicapped trainees were able to secure appropriate work.

Less comprehensive job-search programs have also helped handicapped workers. Mooney (1966), for example, reported that 49 percent of the clients who received job-seeking instruction after failing to find work during three months of searching had jobs two years later. In contrast, 50 percent of the clients who obtained leads to jobs either by counselor solicitation or by reviewing want ads with the counselor and 24 percent of the clients who received no special attention had jobs at the end of two years.

Apparently, self-directed job search materials can also help handicapped workers without direct counselor contact. Keith, Engelkes, and Winborn (1977) contrasted the growth of nineteen rehabilitation clients who used their materials with two groups of twenty and twenty-five clients each, who did not have access to such materials. They found that the clients with the job search materials secured more job leads, more job interviews, and more actual jobs than did the others.

Building on the power of group dynamics, Azrin, Flores, and Kaplan (1975) have launched and tested "job seeking clubs." After screening for motivation, job seekers enroll in clubs whose purpose is to have members obtain suitable jobs. Meetings lead members through systematic job-search techniques and enable them to practice and to discuss techniques with one another in pairs. While actively looking for work, members must attend club meetings daily for encouragement and review of their efforts. Counselors offer direct assistance with matters such as informing a client's family about the client's activities and how to be helpful to the client, giving job leads, critiquing the client's interviewing skills and résumé, and providing the impetus through aids such as checklists for a daily review of the job search activities. The first two training sessions last three hours each, with subsequent ones running up to two hours.

In a contrast of sixty college club participants with sixty matched controls seeking membership, Azrin et al. (1975) found that the median time a member took to find work was fourteen days, compared to fifty-three days for nonmembers. Furthermore, members obtained significantly higher starting salaries for their jobs. A second, more extensive project involving almost 1,000 *Work Incentive Program* (WIN) clients from Harlem, New Brunswick, Tacoma, Wichita, and Milwaukee provided additional support for the "job club" program (Azrin, 1978). In the WIN project, 62 percent of the club clients found jobs, in contrast to 33 percent of the controls. Comparing the 337 club members and 302 controls who remained in the WIN program throughout the project, 80 percent of the club members (compared with 46 percent of the controls) secured jobs. In contrast to the college group, however, WIN job club members did not obtain jobs with higher salaries or more prestige. But fewer club members took CETA-subsidized jobs than did controls (16 percent compared with 25 percent).

Wegman (1979), in a fine review of recent job-search articles, described similar programs that apparently have lessened the time it takes disadvantaged persons to acquire jobs. One impressive program is the Job Factory devised by Joseph Fisher and Albert Cullen for the Cambridge, Massachusetts, CETA program. The Job Factory requires considering job search a real job. It requires seeking work from 8:30 A.M. to 4:30 P.M. while receiving a CETA subsidy. First, the client clarifies personal work history, obtains help in résumé preparation, and receives guidance and practice in interviewing and in making phone inquiries. The client then arranges interviews by telephone, contacts prospective employers, and reports back daily to review the efforts. Of the 159 CETA-eligible workers serviced from 1976–78, Fisher reported that 66 percent found employment.

Although many different people have been pleased with interview training provided by many different trainers (Hollandsworth & Sandifer, 1979), the power of interview training must not be overestimated. As yet research has not established directly how much effective interviewing contributes to acquisition of different kinds of jobs. Such knowledge requires estimating, perhaps via regression equations, the relation of several variables such as interview performance, grades, and experience, to the criterion of hire or not-hire.

Likewise, interview training may not be able to effect all factors weighed in evaluating a candidate's interview. Hollandsworth, Dressel, and Stevens (1977), for instance, have noted both verbal and nonverbal elements are likely to affect the evaluations. Nonverbal factors, such as a firm handshake and attentiveness, may be bolstered readily. It is more difficult, however, to improve general self-expression, such as that involved in relating skills and experiences to particular aspects of a job or in explaining how one dealt constructively with past problems. Certainly, Grinnell and Lieberman's (1977) finding that six interview training sessions improved the eye contact and body posture but not other conversation skills of eighteen mentally retarded workers suggests this limitation is true for people with learning handicaps.

On the other hand, a higher level or better quality job than a worker could obtain independently is not the objective of job search. Wegman (1979) has pointed out that job search programs for the disadvantaged raise clients' confidence, at least temporarily, and provide a knowledgeable support system for those lacking one. These seem to be useful aids for expediting job acquisition, but not necessarily for improving the quality of job offers. Zadney and James (1977), in their fine review of recent studies of placement services for the handicapped, also suggested that job-search activities elevate self-esteem. Moreover, they pointed out that the confidence gained from landing the job may help a handicapped worker to become confident enough to keep it. Expediting employment for those job seekers and increasing their confidence obviously are important accomplishments.

Hazards

In an effort to equip the client for the job search, a placement counselor can err in two ways. First, the counselor can overvalue teaching the client interviewing skills and superficial means of pleasing an employer, and undervalue enabling the client to appreciate personal assets and the parameters of the jobs that he or she might pursue. Employment interview training should be a part of placement counseling, for first impressions are important. But self-promotion needs to be put into perspective. The client is negotiating a contract for serving the employer. The client's integrity demands that he or she present assets and expectations honestly and completely. The client's welfare requires the employer to act in similar good faith. Clearly, winning a contract is important. Equally important, however, is the process of contracting and understanding the types of opportunities available to a person with the client's experience and talent. No doubt preparing a candidate to impress an interviewer is easier than helping the client appreciate the bargaining position for the type of work being sought. Yet, unless one believes that any job the candidate can get will suffice, the candidate must understand how a particular job can enhance his or her career and appreciate his or her competitiveness for a position in order to bargain effectively.

In a rare look at the process of searching for work, Ullman and Gutteridge (1973) followed 251 Masters of Science of Industrial Administration graduates over the 1968–69 year. Although generalization can only be speculative, several of their findings merit consideration. Among these are the following: graduates with detailed knowledge of many firms made better career progress, had longer tenure, and experienced more satisfaction in job search; visiting work sites was instrumental in accepting or rejecting job offers and in knowing the nature of the firm; the better informed students were less likely to accept the job with highest initial salary; within three years, those who had not taken the highest salary job had caught up in salary with those taking the highest salary offer; most of these students had not thought of working for the firm that eventually employed them before initiating the job search; and many students changed their job objective during the search process because it provided more information for them; and fully 40 percent had no specific job preference at the start of the process. Clearly, these findings should alert counselors of new graduates against forcing premature specification and demanding intensive employer exploration before the job search starts.

Second, placement counseling can suggest falsely that job acquisition is totally an individual's or the family's responsibility. When placement counselors are school or government employees, however, clients should recognize that the public is helping with an inherently difficult task. By right, their counselors should help them to locate and to obtain suitable jobs. Such assistance should include coordinating with educators and employers to identify or develop jobs that use the client's skills, as well as training in job search methods. Placement counselors must remember to inform prospective employers and the community of the number and qualifications of graduates. They should alert school and community of the difficulties graduates and dropouts are having in securing suitable jobs. Moreover, this activity should include alerting educators to aspects of their curriculum that become outdated in contributing to student employment.

To the extent that position changes are predictable and a characteristic of career, each person has a responsibility to prepare for and to exert energy in accomplishing the transition. But when the transition is difficult because the institutions of school and work are not synchronized, the candidate should understand that he or she is a victim of the system's shortcomings. Certainly one ought not to blame oneself. Indeed, the job candidate is entitled to some redress, even though resolving the problem oneself will enhance one. Currently, the Department of Labor is experimenting with providing new workers subsidies for geographical relocation to secure work. (*Employment and Training Report of the President*, 1978). Should that or other services become available, the client should recognize that using them does not reflect ineptitude but instead overcomes a shortcoming of the work-education system.

Third, school placement counseling that promotes campus interviewing can advantage large employers unfairly. In encouraging students to contact firms that can afford to visit campuses, the counselor is ensuring that these firms have an opportunity to select from a range of candidates. Since smaller firms generally are not encouraged to interview on campus, they are disadvantaged. The disadvantage will be magnified unnecessarily if the counselor does not arrange for information to be available about the nature and advantages of jobs in smaller firms as well. Descriptions of jobs that past graduates have obtained with small firms and commentary about these jobs' impacts on their careers would help to provide balanced information for candidates.

Fourth, current placement emphasis on job interviewing and résumé preparation may be slighting clients who seek work with small firms.

Currently, about 16 percent of the 100 million jobs in America are in federal, state, or local government and 30 percent in companies employing 100 or more workers. About 8 percent of American workers are self-employed, leaving 46 percent of the workforce in small firms (*Employment and Training Report of the President*, 1978).

Although research has not examined whether job search strategies are differentially effective with small and large employers, analyses of the employer requirements and resources suggest they would be. Small firms, for instance, are unlikely to have resources for sophisticated candidate screening, are likely to desire workers who can be flexible about hours and job duties, and unlikely to keep files of job applications. They are likely to weigh personal recommendation and referrals highly, and to favor applicants appearing at the time of their need. Persons seeking to work in small firms, therefore, might be aided in placement counseling by focusing on establishing referral networks, communicating their flexibility about job duties, demonstrating through a more personable approach than that often taught in interviewing their likelihood of relating effectively with prospective colleagues and customers, and learning how to determine the small firms that are expanding or the season when openings develop.

Test Anxiety Counseling

With ever higher credentials required to be employed (Squires, 1979), test anxiety is sure to obstruct more careers. Test-anxious students have consistently made lower aptitude and ability test scores and earned lower grade point averages (Alpert & Haber, 1960; Paul & Eriksen, 1964; Sarason, 1961). Although research has not examined the issue, it is probable that many people have foresaken their aspirations because of the fear of testing and that many others failed tests and subsequently did not realize otherwise attainable goals because of test anxiety.

Test anxiety appears to be a combination of uncomfortable feelings and worry induced by the prospect of being evaluated (Liebert & Morris, 1967). Low anxious people appear to be cued by the uncomfortable feelings to attend to a test's content and to expect to cope and succeed. In contrast, high anxious people seem to become much more sensitive to their physiological discomfort, attending to these and other irrelevant distractions in the testing situation and wondering about their competence instead of focusing on the test content.

For many years, counselors have helped test-anxious clients by counter-conditioning relaxation for the anxiety that arises at the prospect of taking an exam and during the exam. The underlying rationale of counter-conditioning, the most famous example of which is Wolpe's (1969) desensitization, is that test anxiety overwhelms the person, obstructing coping behaviors. Alleviating the anxiety is supposed to unfetter the client's natural coping behavior.

More recently, investigators have hypothesized further that anxiety is both facilitative and debilitative and that reducing test anxiety may eliminate its facilitative properties as well as its debilitative ones. As a consequence, investigators are studying modifications of desensitization that enable the client to understand how he or she is controlling personal counter-conditioning and to have more control over it, and some investigators are even combining instruction in attentional strategies and positive thinking during testing with these self-control procedures.

The alterations in traditional desensitization that appear necessary for clients to have greater control over it are ones that enable them to condition relaxation to internal stimuli such as tension rather than to external stimuli such as a testing room. Goldfried (1971) recommended the following modifications in traditional desensitization to achieve this relaxation, and many of the new procedures incorporate his recommendations.

1. Telling clients that the rationale of the treatment is to enable learning the skill of relaxation in order to "relax away" anxiety.
2. Using tension as a cue to "relaxing away" tension rather than only distinguishing tension from relaxation.
3. Creating one general hierarchy of increasing anxiety and helping a client to learn to build up capacity to react to the internal cues the stimuli of that hierarchy arouse.
4. Instead of having a client stop visualization of an anxiety producing scene, teaching the client to relax until the scene can no longer evoke anxiety.
5. Assigning clients to practice in real life identifying internal tensions and instructing themselves to "relax them away."

Among the new test anxiety counseling procedures are: cue controlled relaxation (Russell, Wise, & Stratoudakis, 1976); applied relaxation training (Denny, 1974); relaxation as self-control (Deffenbacher, Mathis, & Michaels, 1978); self-control desensitization (Goldfried, 1971); anxiety management training (Suinn, 1976); and cognitive modification (Meichenbaum, 1972).

Denny (1980) pointed out that these self-control treatments order themselves on a continuum of decreasing cognitive emphasis and that the more cognitive tend to include the less cognitive. He concluded that most treatments, starting with the basic cue-controlled relaxation and applied relaxation procedures, start with a self-control rationale and feature training in inducing relaxation and applying that training in stressful situations. More complex treatments such as relaxation as self-control, anxiety management, and self-control desensitization add on the opportunity for guided rehearsal, wherein a counselor teaches clients to discriminate the cues of tension and anxiety and oversees their practice of their new anxiety control. Finally, a treatment such as cognitive modification also shows clients how some of their beliefs increase their anxiety and how to reformulate the beliefs so that the reformulated beliefs help test performance instead of interfering with it. In order to acquaint the reader with these test-anxiety counseling procedures, this section includes Paul's (1965) description of the long-used desensitization treatment and Meichenbaum's (1972) description of cognitive modification.

So far, most research has involved application of test anxiety counseling to clients identified by inventory as anxious and willing to accept such treatment. Counselors would be remiss in offering such help to the self-referred unless they first ascertained that the stress did not stem from such factors as inadequate test preparation, difficulty understanding the subject matter, or inept or unfair evaluation. Moreover, since test-anxious students are often deficient in study skills—and several studies have shown that a combination of study skills training and test anxiety treatment improve academic performance (Anton, 1976)—a counselor may also have to judge whether a client deficient in study skills needs both test anxiety counseling and study skills training or only study skills training.

Test Anxiety Desensitization Counseling

The heuristic principles underlying desensitization include:

1. Imagining or experiencing a feared situation (taking a test) successfully while relaxed reduces the anxiety produced by the threatening situation. In other words, being relaxed breaks the association between anxiety and the situation (deconditioning) and substitutes the association of relaxation with the situation (counterconditioning).
2. Since anxiety generalizes in a gradient, it is easier to desensitize a fear-provoking situation by enabling a client to relax when imagining or experiencing a situation low on the fear gradient and then proceeding up the gradient as the client becomes able to relax in the presence of the preceding situations.
3. Counterconditioning of relaxation to a formerly anxiety-producing situation is more efficient when the client understands the operation of systematic relaxation and agrees with its intent.

Treatment[1]

This treatment is basically the Systematic Desensitization Therapy of Wolpe, with several modifications directed toward reducing the number of sessions required for anxiety reduction. There are five major procedures involved in the use of this technique: (1) exploration of history and current status of symptoms; (2) explanation of rationale; (3) construction of anxiety hierarchy; (4) training in progressive relaxtion; and

[1] *Source:* Reprinted from INSIGHT VS. DESENSITIZATION IN PSYCHO-THERAPY by Gordon L. Paul, with the permission of the publishers, Stanford University Press. © 1966 by the Board of Trustees of the Leland Stanford Junior University.

(5) desensitization proper—working through the hierarchy under relaxation.

Although flexibility is normally the rule with this approach, the goals of research require that all therapists follow the outlined procedures as closely as feasible. Unlike the interpretation given by several writers in the area, this procedure is *not* to be carried out as a cold, manipulative operation; instead the therapist should be as warm, interested, and helpful as he would be in any helping relationship. The main differences between this approach and more traditional methods is that the therapist *openly* guides and directs the course and content of treatment, with a minimum of time and effort spent on introspection, and little or none spent on the client's searching for etiological factors. All happenings and incidences will be interpreted within this system if questioned, and dynamics left uninterpreted unless questioned. If questioned, interpret in a *general* manner—only superficially. In any case, it is most important that the therapist remain *confident* and stay with this specific treatment. Since the "target behavior" (speech anxiety) will have been determined prior to the therapist's contact with the client, focus on retraining will begin with the first session, with desensitization proper beginning in the second session.

The following time schedule should handle most clients.

First session:

1. Exploration of history and current status of symptoms (5–10 minutes).
2. Explanation of rationale and course of treatment (5–10 minutes).
3. Construction of anxiety hierarchy (10–15 minutes).
4. Training in progressive relaxation (20–35 minutes). Test imagery if time available.

Second to fifth sessions:

1. Check on success with relaxation and correct any problems arising (2–10 minutes).
2. Induce relaxation—present visualizations.
3. Check on images and anxiety both in treatment and outside.

Specific Procedures

1. *Exploration of history and current status of symptoms.* For the research project, this phase will be relatively short, serving primarily as an "icebreaker" and as a period in which to establish rapport. To help describe subjects and to further therapist understanding, determine (a) *how long* the subject has experienced performance anxiety, (b) to what *degree* performance anxiety *interferes* with functioning, and (c) whether other social or evaluative situations also arouse anxiety. This should be completed in no more than 10 minutes of the first session.

2. *Explanation of rationale and course of treatment.* It is important that each subject understand and accept the treatment process. Both the theory and course of treatment should be briefly explained and repeated if questions arise. It should be made clear that the anxiety is a result of learning, and that the treatment is a learning process. If any subject seems to have trouble understanding, rephrase your explanation in language he can understand. Be sure to allay any doubts the more sophisticated subjects may have, *e.g.*, "this does *not* produce inhibitions that might lead to symptom substitution, but is desensitizing—removing the problem." The following brief explanation usually suffices for introductory purposes.

"The emotional reactions that you experience are a result of your previous experiences with people and situations; these reactions oftentimes lead to feelings of anxiety or tenseness which are really inappropriate. Since perceptions or situations occur within ourselves, it is possible to work with your reactions right here in the office by having you image or visualize those situations.

"The specific technique we will be using is one called desensitization. This technique utilizes two main procedures—relaxation and counterconditioning—to reduce your anxiety. The relaxation procedure is based upon years of work that was started in the 1930's by Dr. Jacobsen. Dr. Jacobsen developed a method of inducing relaxation that can be learned very quickly, and which will allow you to become more deeply relaxed than ever before. Of course, the real advantage of relaxation is that the muscle system in your body cannot be both tense and relaxed at the same time; therefore, once you have learned the relaxation technique, it can be used to counter anxiety, tenseness, and feelings like those you experience in the speech situation.

"Relaxation alone can be used to reduce anxiety and tension, and I'll be asking you to practice relaxation between our meetings. Often, however, relaxation is inconvenient to use, and really doesn't permanently overcome anxiety. Therefore, we combine the relaxation technique with the psychological principle of counterconditioning to actually desensitize situations so that anxiety no longer occurs.

"The way in which we will do this is to determine the situations in which you become progressively more anxious, building a hierarchy from the least to the most anxious situations with regard to giving a speech. Then I will teach you the technique of progressive relaxation, and have you practice this. You will see how this operates in a few minutes when we actually start training. After you are more relaxed than ever before, we will then start counterconditioning. This will be done by having you repeatedly image the specific situations from the anxiety hierarchy while under relaxation. By having you visualize very briefly, while you are deeply relaxed, the situations that normally arouse anxiety, those situations gradually become desensitized, so that they no longer make you anxious. We start with those situations that bother you the least, and gradually work up to the speech itself. Since each visualization will lower your anxiety to the next, a full-fledged anxiety reaction never occurs.

"We've used these procedures on many different types of clinical problems, including several students with performance anxiety, with excellent results. Most of these procedures will become clearer after we get into them. Do you have any questions before we continue?"

3. *Construction of the anxiety hierarchy.* The anxiety hierarchy is one of the most important aspects of this treatment. The object is to determine situations related to speech presentation which run from very slight, controllable amounts of anxiety to the most extreme anxiety attendant upon the actual speech presentation. It is not necessary to determine every instance, since generalization from one instance to another will bridge the gap. It is necessary to determine situations close enough together to allow generalization to occur.

Figure 9–2 illustrates a test anxiety hierarchy suitable for use in desensitization. Osterhouse (1976) integrated this hierarchy, which Mc-Millan (1973) had developed, in group desensitization work.

This hierarchy is to serve only as a guide; each subject should have his own. The procedure is as follows. First explain that you wish to determine specific situations from the least to the most anxiety producing. Ask the subject *when* he first notices feelings of tenseness and anxiety; then work through each of the 16 items to determine if some items should be excluded or others included. *Write down* the specifics associated with each item, so that you may better control the imagery of the subject, *i.e.*, exactly where the subject studies, cues in the room, times, etc. You should have enough understanding so that, if necessary, you may "fill in" another item during desensitization without help from the subject. Most hierarchies will not be shorter than 8 items, or longer than 20 items.

4. *Training in progressive relaxation.* This is a most important procedure, and one that should be mastered. It should be explained to the subject that this technique will take some time (20–35 minutes) at first, but as he learns, the time for inducing deep relaxation will be shortened. Training begins by having the subject systematically tense his gross-muscle systems, holding them tense until you say "relax," at which time the subject lets go immediately. If the muscles are first tensed, they will relax more deeply when they are released. Also explain that you want the subject to focus all his attention on each muscle system as you work through the various groups, so that after practice he will not have to tense the muscles first in order to achieve deep relaxation.

4a. *The Method.* Seat the subject in an overstuffed chair, with the therapist sitting slightly to one side. Legs should be extended, head resting on the back of the chair, and arms resting on the arms of the chair. No part of the body should require the use of muscles for support. Have the subject close his eyes to minimize external stimulation. The room should be quiet and lights dimmed if possible.

1. Instruct the subject to "make a fist with your dominant hand [usually right]. Make a fist and tense the muscles of your [right] hand and forearm; tense until it trembles. Feel the muscles pull across your fingers and the lower part of your forearm." Have

Figure 9–2. Test Anxiety Hierarchy

_____You are sitting in your class and the instructor announces that you will have an examination during the next class session. You wonder if you can prepare in time. There is so much material to be covered.

_____It is the day before an important examination. You talk to some of your classmates who tell you how much preparation they have done for this examination. You have spent far less time on the readings.

_____You are studying for an important examination to be given the next day. Your grade in this course will probably depend upon your performance on this examination. You are wondering how you will remember the information on the test.

_____It is late evening before an important examination. You are tired and having trouble concentrating, but you do not feel really prepared.

_____You are in bed the night before an important examination which will determine your final grade. Your mind flashes to the examination.

_____You wake up and realize that you have an examination today which will determine your final grade. The test is scheduled for later that same day.

_____You have an hour of study time left before you will take a very important examination. As you look over your notes, you realize that you have become confused. You wonder whether you should continue reviewing your notes or just put them aside.

_____You are walking to an important examination which will probably determine your final grade.

_____As you enter your classroom on the day of an examination, you hear several students discussing possible questions. You realize that you probably could not answer these questions if they were asked on the test.

_____You are sitting in class, waiting for your examination to be passed out.

_____You receive your examination. You look at the first question and cannot recall the answer.

_____As you read over your examination, you realize that many of the items are very difficult. You look up from your test, wondering where to start, and notice the students around you writing furiously.

_____Many questions on this examination request information that is hazy to you. You realize that you must have skipped over some important facts in your study.

_____On this extremely important examination, you find that you have spent too much time on the first portion of the test and must hurry up a bit in order to finish on time.

_____With five minutes left on this examination which will probably determine your final grade, you see that you have left a number of items blank.

SOURCE: From COUNSELING METHODS edited by John D. Krumboltz and Carl E. Thoresen. Copyright © 1976 by Holt, Rinehart and Winston. Reprinted by permission of Holt, Rinehart and Winston.

the subject hold this position for 5 to 7 seconds, then say "relax," instructing him to just let his hand go; "Pay attention to the muscles of your [right] hand and forearm as they relax. Note how those muscles feel as relaxation flows through them" (20–30 seconds.)

"Again, tense the muscles of your [right] hand and forearm. Pay attention to the muscles involved" (5–7 seconds). "O.K., relax; attend only to those muscles, and note how they feel as the relaxation takes place, becoming more and more relaxed, more relaxed than ever before. Each time we do this you'll relax even more until your arm and hand are completely relaxed with no tension at all, warm and relaxed."

Continue until subject reports his [right] hand and forearm are completely relaxed with no tension (usually 2–4 times is sufficient).

2. Instruct the subject to tense his [right] biceps, leaving his hand and forearm on the chair. Proceed in the same manner as above, in a "hypnotic monotone," using the [right] hand as a reference point, that is, move on when the subject reports his biceps feels as completely relaxed as his hand and forearm.

Proceed to other gross-muscle groups (listed below) in the same manner, with the same verbalization. For example: "Note how these muscles feel as they relax; feel the relaxation and warmth flow through these muscles; pay attention to these muscles so that later you can relax them again." Always use the preceding group as a reference for moving on.

3. Nondominant [left] hand and forearm—feel muscles over knuckles and on lower part of arm.

4. Nondominant [left] biceps.

5. Frown hard, tensing muscles of forehead and top of head (these muscles often "tingle" as they relax).

6. Wrinkle nose, feeling muscles across top of cheeks and upper lip.

7. Draw corners of mouth back, feeling jaw muscles and cheeks.

8. Tighten chin and throat muscles, feeling two muscles in front of throat.

9. Tighten chest muscles and muscles across back—feel muscles pull below shoulder blades.

10. Tighten abdominal muscles—make abdomen hard.

11. Tighten muscles of right upper leg—feel one muscle on top and two on the bottom of the upper leg.

12. Tighten right calf—feel muscles on bottom of right calf.

13. Push down with toes and arch right foot—feel pressure as if someone were pushing up under the arch.

14. Left upper leg.

15. Left calf.

16. Left foot.

For most muscle groups, two presentations will suffice. Ask the subject if he feels any tension anywhere in his body. If he does, go back and repeat the tension-release cycle for that muscle group. It is often helpful to instruct the subject to take a deep breath and hold it while tensing muscles, and to let it go while releasing. Should any muscle group not respond after four trials, move on and return to it later. *Caution:* some subjects may develop muscle cramps or spasms from prolonged tension of muscles. If this occurs, shorten the tension interval a few seconds, and instruct the subject not to tense his muscles quite so hard.

Although the word "hypnosis" is not to be used, progressive relaxation, properly executed, does seem to resemble a light hypnotic-trance state, with the subject more susceptible to suggestion. Relaxation may be further deepened by repetition of suggestions of warmth, relaxation, etc. Some subjects may actually report sensations of disassociation from their bodies. This is complete relaxation and is to be expected. Subjects should be instructed to speak as little as possible while under relaxation.

In bringing subjects back to "normal," the numerical method of trance termination should be used: "I'm going to count from one to four. On the count of one, start moving your legs; two, your fingers and hands; three, your head; and four, open your eyes and sit up. One— move your legs; two—now your fingers and hands; three—move your head around; four—open your eyes and sit up." Always check to see that the subject feels well, alert, etc., before leaving.

The subject should be instructed to practice relaxation twice a day between sessions. He should not work at it more than 15 minutes at a time, and should not practice twice within any three-hour period. He should also practice alone. Relaxation may be used to get to sleep if practiced while horizontal; if the subject does not wish to sleep, he should practice sitting up. Properly timed, relaxation can be used for a "second wind" during study.

By the third session, if the subject has been practicing well, relaxation may be induced by merely focusing attention on the muscle groups, and instructing the subject to "concentrate on muscles becoming relaxed, "warm," etc. However, if any subject has difficulty following straight suggestions, return to the use of tension-release.

5. *Desensitization proper*—working through the hierarchy under relaxation. Preparatory to desensitization proper, usually at the end of the first session, the subject's imagery should be tested. This may be done by asking him to visualize item (0): "Now visualize yourself lying in bed in your room just before going to sleep. Describe what you see. Do you see it clearly? Do you see color? Do you feel as if you were there? All right, now stop visualizing that and go on relaxing." Some subjects may report clear, distinct images, as if they were watching a movie; this is fine, but not necessary. The minimum requirement is that their visualization be as clear as a very vivid memory. Describing these visualizations as a dream is often helpful. With more practice, images will usually become clearer. It is also important that the subject can start and stop an image on request, and this should be determined. If difficulties arise in any of these areas, present a few more common, nonanxious

images, describing for the subject just what he should experience; for example, entering the office. It is important that the subject visualize situations as if he were there—*not* watching himself!

Before inducing relaxation in the second session, explain exactly what you'll be asking the subject to do, since his verbalizations are to be kept at a minimum. Tell him that if *anytime* during the session he feels any tension or nervousness whatever, to signal by raising his [right] index finger. This is important, and should be made clear from the beginning.

After relaxation is induced, presentation of images begins with item (1). "Now I want you to visualize yourself sitting alone in your room two weeks before a speech, reading about speeches" (10 seconds). "Stop visualizing that, and go on relaxing." Ask if the subject felt any tension and if he was able to start and stop the image on request. Then repeat item (1) again. "One more time, visualize yourself, two weeks before a speech, sitting alone in your room, reading about giving a speech" (10 seconds). "Stop visualizing that, and go on relaxing—completely relaxed, no tension anywhere in your body, warm and relaxed."

Follow the above paradigm throughout the hierarchy *if the subject does not become anxious: i.e.*, present each item in the hierarchy, specifying all major aspects of the image. Allow 10 seconds to elapse after each presentation, then instruct the subject to "stop visualizing that, and go on relaxing." Continue suggestions of warmth, relaxation, lack of tension, heaviness, etc. for 30 to 45 seconds, and again present the image. Present each item in the hierarchy at least twice. If the subject does not signal anxiety, and the therapist does not detect anxiety during two 10-second presentations of an item, move on to the next item in the hierarchy.

If, on the other hand, the subject signals anxiety or the therapist detects anxiety in the subject, immediately instruct the subject to "stop visualizing that, and go on relaxing." Then continue with suggestions of relaxation (at least one minute) until the subject reports as deep a relaxation as before. Then inform him that you will shorten the presentation so that anxiety will not occur. Then, present the same item again for a period of only 3 to 5 seconds. If anxiety is still aroused, drop back to a 10-second presentation of the previous item in the hierarchy. If, however, the 3- to 5-second presentation does not arouse anxiety, give 30 to 45 seconds of relaxation suggestions, and present the same item again for 5 seconds, then 10 seconds, then 20 seconds. If the item can be presented for 20 seconds, move on to the next item in the hierarchy.

It is precisely at these points that clinical sensitivity must guide the presentations; one must know when to go back, when to construct new items, and when to move on up the hierarchy. However, the above guides should handle most situations. Some items may require as many as 8 to 12 presentations of differing time intervals, with lower level items interspersed. Most items will be handled successfully in 2 to 4 presentations.

Never end a session with a presentation that arouses anxiety. Approximately 5 to 10 minutes before the end of a session, either stop with a successful item, or go back to the previous item in the hierarchy. "Awaken" the subject, and discuss the session with him, reassuring him about any difficulties that may have come up. If by some quirk any of the presentations are nullified, or they do not carry over into real life, rapidly repeat those items in the next session. Normally, each session will begin with a single presentation of the last successfully completed item.

All subjects should easily complete the hierarchy in the five sessions. However, if any subject does not complete the hierarchy, take note of the number of items still to be covered, so this fact may be taken in account in evaluation. As many as six of the easier items may be covered in the second session, and only one or two items in later sessions; however, be sure to keep a record for each subject so that the proper items are covered.

Only minor modifications are necessary to adapt this procedure for group counseling. Paul modified desensitization for group counseling in these four ways: (1) Counselors fostered cohesion during discussion by techniques such as "emphasizing similarity between member problems, experiences, and emotions and referring questions to the group"; (2) Clients constructed hierarchies that included elements common to them all, but amplified particular elements by writing in unique aspects when appropriate; (3) Clients used hand signals to report their discomfort during relaxation lest they disturb others; and (4) Desensitization sessions began with presentation of the last session's items to enable clients who had been absent to catch up with the group. Regarding a single anxiety hierarchy as useful for all group members, Osterhouse (1976) noted that having the group rank predetermined situations from a set such as McMillan's (1973) above has been as effective as having a group generate its own list. Likewise, Osterhouse (1976) reported that one can overcome the problem of one or two clients slowing a group down because their anxiety for a situation does not extinguish as quickly by preestablishing a maximum number of trials for every situation and moving to the next situation when they have been provided.

Cognitive Test Anxiety Counseling

One cognitive approach to test anxiety incorporating desensitization is Meichenbaum's (1972). He described its purpose as follow: "To make test anxious Ss aware of the anxiety-engendering thoughts and self-statements they emitted both prior to and in test taking situations and to train them explicitly to emit incompatible self-statements that would facilitate task attending and incompatible relaxation behaviors."

Heuristic principles. The heuristic principles underlying cognitive treatments include:

1. Imagining and rehearsing coping responses to a feared situation while relaxed substitutes coping for the disruptive responses formerly associated with the behavior.

2. Delineating the behaviors that succeed and disrupt, recognizing what triggers these behaviors, and developing habits of controlling them through self-instruction increase the probability of a person's producing coping behavior in a formerly frightening situation. More specifically, distinguishing the signs of tension from the anxiety reaction in a response to a stressful stimulus enables a person to condition a coping behavior such as focused attention to the tension as a replacement for distracting behavior. Then practicing the new habit of associating focused attention with tension will increase the likelihood of focused attention in stressful situations,

Treatment. Meichenbaum (1972) described modification counseling as follows[1]: "The cognitive modification treatment procedures were designed (a) to make the test anxious Ss aware of the anxiety-engendering thoughts and self-statements they emitted both prior to and in test-taking situations and (b) to train them explicitly to emit incompatible self-statements that would facilitate task-attending and incompatible relaxation behaviors. The first aspect of therapy consisted of an "insight" treatment approach which emphasized that test anxiety is the result of thoughts and verbalizations which are emitted both prior to and during the test situation. The Ss were informed that one of the goals of therapy was for each S to become aware of (gain insight into) the self-verbalizations and self-instructions which he emitted in evaluative situations and second to produce both incompatible self-instructions and incompatible behaviors. Over the course of the eight sessions, this group discussed the following points: (a) the specific self-verbalizations group members had emitted in the pretreatment test situation; (b) the range and communality of evaluative situations in which they made the same or comparable self-verbalizations; (c) the often irrational, self-defeating, and self-fulfilling aspects of such statements; and most important (d) the behavioral and affective effects of the emission of such thoughts. Thus, the first aspect of treatment was designed to train Ss in a general awareness of both the internal and external eliciting cues in the test situation which lead to task-irrelevant thoughts and inferior test performance.

The second aspect of the cognitive modification treatment was designed to train Ss explicitly to emit task-relevant self-statements and to perform behaviors such as relaxation to facilitate test performance.

In order to train the high test anxious Ss on a set of incompatible responses which they could use to inhibit both the cognitive and arousal components of anxiety, the basic desensitization treatment procedure was followed except for two modifications. During the basic relaxation-training procedure and also during the remaining desensitization, the

[1] SOURCE: D. H. Meichenbaum, "Cognitive modification of test anxious college students," *Journal of Consulting and Clinical Psychology, 39,* 373–374. Copyright 1979 by the American Psychological Association. Reprinted by permission.

use of slow deep breathing was emphasized, with slow inhalation and exhalation highlighted. Research by Wescott and Huttenlocher (1961) Wood and Obrist (1964), and Deane (1964) has indicated that amplitude and frequency of respiration have a directive effect on heart rate and accompanying experiences of anxiety. Following the relaxation-training procedure, group hierarchy and imagery training were conducted as in the systematic desensitization group. The second modification came in the desensitization procedure during which Ss were asked to imagine both coping and mastery behaviors. The Ss were asked to visualize themselves as clearly as possible performing the specified behaviors (e.g., studying the night before an exam; taking an exam); and if they became anxious, to visualize themselves coping with this anxiety by means of slow deep breaths and self-instructions to relax and to be task relevant. The Ss were encouraged to use any personally generated self-statements which would facilitate their attending to the task and inhibit task-irrelevant thoughts. If the incompatible behavior techniques did not reduce their anxiety, then they should signal the therapist by raising a finger, terminating the image, and subsequently relaxing. Thus, Ss in the cognitive modification group cognitively rehearsed ways of handling anxiety by means of imagery procedures. The assumption underlying the use of such coping imagery is that the closer imagery comes to represent "real" experiences of the most complete sort, the greater the likelihood of generalization. There is a high probability that test anxious Ss, even though desensitized, will experience anxiety following treatment. The proposed modifications of the desensitization procedure were designed to have Ss develop a cognitive discrimination set in order to be able to cope with experienced anxiety and combat irrevelant thoughts such as worry.

Validity

This section summarizes the major findings of many studies, which have been ably reviewed by different authors. In order to acquaint the reader with current trends in test-anxiety counseling research, the section then examines several recent studies of the new self-control test anxiety treatments. It concludes with brief descriptions of some of the more frequently used test anxiety measures.

Reviewers' Conclusions. Desensitization has been applied by many different counselors and therapists to many different anxieties in multiple contexts (Wolpe, 1969). Reviewers of test anxiety treatments such as Allen, Elias, and Zlotlow (1980); Anton (1976); Paul (1969); Rimm and Masters (1974); and Tryon (1980) have concluded that the trends in numerous studies affirm that desensitization helps test-anxious students become more comfortable in evaluation situations. However, they also concluded that desensitization is unlikely to influence test outcomes unless it is combined with study skills training. They reached these conclusions even though they found that most studies of test-anxiety counseling suffer deficiencies common to counseling research such as: a small number of clients and only one or two counselors, lack of a credible placebo control, failure to verify the fidelity with which counseling was delivered, and dependence on a single measure or on only self-report measures to gauge the outcome of counseling.

Recent research has focused on variations of desensitization involving greater client awareness and control of the process and on using desensitization as the standard against which to compare other treatments. Reviewers who have scrutinized the range of alterations in test-anxiety counseling are especially optimistic about the self-control and cognitive variations (Allen, Elias, Zlotlow, 1980; Denny, 1980; Tryon, 1980). Indeed, all three reviews concluded that the new treatments offer as much potential of improving client comfort as desensitization, while promising greater likelihood of improving test performance without extra study skills instruction.

Selected Test-Anxiety Counseling Studies. In the experiment introducing his procedure, Meichenbaum (1972) had one counselor guide eight test-anxious students through the eight sessions of cognitive modification treatment, eight through the desensitization only treatment, and had five remain on the waiting list. Three of each treatment group had individual counseling and five had group counseling, but no significant difference appeared between the group and individual treatments. Comparisons of the treatment and control groups after counseling showed that the cognitive modification clients increased their grade point averages (gpas) more than did the other students, the desensitization increased gpas more than did the control, and both cognitive modification and desensitization clients outperformed the controls on the digit symbol tests but not on an abstract reasoning test. Pre-post comparison further showed that the cognitive modification clients lowered their anxiety more than did the other clients, as measured by an adjective checklist. Moreover, cognitive modification clients registered increases in facilitating anxiety and decreases in debilitating anxiety after treatment and in a one month follow up, whereas the desensitization clients only decreased their debilitative anxiety.

Denny and Rupert (1977) followed Goldfried's (1971) recommendations and created an active self-control desensitization treatment that they contrasted with the traditional one. Fourteen college students (ten women, and four men) were enrolled in one group of each treatment or in a placebo, and twenty-eight others were designated an inactive control. Pre-post measures of test anxiety and general anxiety feeling were analyzed. The performance of the student on the *Wonderlic Anagrams Test,* which consists of 18 anagram substitutes for 18 of *Wonderlic Personnel Test* items, was also examined. In all treatments, each student completed an individual eighteen-item fear hierarchy. They found that clients in the self-control took fewer sessions (M = 7.9 to M = 10.2) and fewer scene exposures (M = 34.7 to M = 10.2), than did students in the standard desensitization treatment. All treatments including the placebo were effective in reducing debilitative anxiety, but only the self-control treatment modification was demonstrably effective in enhancing facilitative anxiety and actual test performance. Although the single group and single counselor preclude generalization and signal caution in concluding that treatment rather than counselor effects account for differential gain, the results at least suggest that increasing client control over treatment will lead to cognitive as well as affective improvement.

In an earlier comparison of an eight-hour self-controlled desensitization with a standard desensitization, Spiegler, Cooley, Marshall, Prince, and Puckett (1976) found that the fourteen undergraduates in the self-controlled desensitization reported less test anxiety than did fifteen untreated controls. However, the fifteen students in the standard desensitization were not statistically different from the controls nor from the self-control group on test anxiety after counseling.

In that same year, Chang-Liang and Denney (1976) examined whether teaching students to apply relaxation to anxiety situations would be as effective as desensitization or learning to relax in reducing general and test anxiety. They found that the twenty highly anxious students who received the three 45-minute, directed relaxation treatments reduced their test anxiety more than did twenty control students and were able to improve their *Wonderlic Personnel Test* scores more than were the twenty controls, the twenty-one relaxation students, and the twenty-three desensitization students. On the general anxiety measure, the directed relaxation was also more effective than was the control or relaxation-only treatment, whereas the desensitization group did not exceed these groups.

Contrasting systematic desensitization, cue-controlled relaxation, and no treatment, Russell, Wise, and Stratoudakis (1976) found both treatments effective in reducing self-reported test anxiety but not helpful in improving test performance. The limited duration of treatment (five 45-minute desensitization sessions) and the small number of clients ($N = 21$) made it unlikely that the study would detect differential effects between subjects or small increments on test performance, especially as one would expect only small test performance gains.

Contrasting five sessions of desensitization with anxiety management training, Deffenbacher and Shelton (1978) found that Shelton's rendition of both treatments produced comparable, immediate relief from test anxiety. Six weeks later, the anxiety management treatment's gains still registered effective on two measures whereas the desensitization's effect registered effective on only one measure. Of course, the limited number of clients ($N = 43$), the limited duration of treatment (five 45-minute group sessions), and the use of one counselor preclude concluding that either treatment is superior.

Comparing the effects of an attentional treatment, desensitization treatment, a combination procedure, a placebo treatment, and a control treatment, Holroyd (1976) found that the ten test-anxious clients receiving group cognitive treatment from one of two counselors improved more on a digit symbol test at post-test and follow up and on grade point average in the following semester. On both occasions, they also decreased general anxiety more than did the clients in the other groups. The nine clients in the combination counseling, in turn, did better in the digit symbol tests than did the remaining clients, and they and the twelve clients in desensitization showed more gains in gpa than did the placebo and a waiting list control group. The clients in the three treatment groups were indistinguishable from the ten students in the placebo group at post test and follow up on debilitating and facilitating anxiety. However, the wait-list control did not show gains of any kind during the counseling period and grade point averages tended to decline. All of the findings support cognitive counseling and suggest that any systematic, calmly conducted approach to relieving test anxiety may help clients feel better.

To ascertain whether different treatments affect the worry and emotionality components of test anxiety hypothesized by Liebert and Morris (1967), Finger and Galassi (1977) divided forty-eight text-anxious volunteers among three treatments and a wait control. The clients in the three treatments did not report differential gains in worry or emotionality after their eight 45-minute sessions, contrary to Liebert and Morris's hypothesis. However, the thirty-six treated clients showed less worry and emotionality than did the control, and all tended to have less debilitating anxiety. The clients in the three treatment groups and in the control condition did not differ on facilitating anxiety nor in their performance on a vocabulary and digit symbol test. Collectively, the findings suggest that worry and emotionality are interrelated, as the authors concluded.

Supporting the findings of Wine (1971) that the cognitive aspects of modified desensitization are the source of its benefit are the findings of Kaplan, McCordick, and Twitchell (1979). They had five test-anxious college student volunteers complete ten hours of the cognitive portion of Meichenbaum's treatment, seven complete ten hours of the desensitization portion, six ten hours of the full treatment, and six serve as wait controls. For each treatment, there were two groups of two to four members led by one of two doctoral clinical psychology students. Comparisons across treatments indicated that the cognitive only group decreased worry and emotionality significantly more than did the other groups and that the groups ordered themselves in terms of benefit from treatment on these two dimensions in the predicted manner; that is, cognitive only, full treatment, and desensitization. Although the study demonstrates the power of a relatively long term treatment to register significant gains for a small number of clients, arguing for a sufficiently long treatment period, the small number of subjects and counselors precludes generalizing about the relative effectiveness of the three treatments beyond the experiment.

Contrasting students in self-control relaxation, in self-control desensitization, and students awaiting counseling, Deffenbacher, Mathis, and Michaels (1979) found the two 7-hour treatments equally effective. Thirty-two treated students reduced their test and general anxiety more, than did thirty-five in control groups. Moreover, the students sustained their increased comfort with testing over seven weeks and even achieved higher semester grades in their psychology course. Follow up one year later showed that students in both groups maintained decreases in debilitating and nontargeted anxiety, but not their gains in facilitating anxiety (Deffenbacher & Michaels, 1980).

In yet another study, Deffenbacher, A. Michaels, T. Michaels, and Daley (1980) examined whether self-control desensitization and test anxiety management differed. Ann Michaels guided fifteen students (four male) through six weekly 50-minute sessions of self-control desensitization and sixteen clients (four male) through six sessions of anxiety management training. Sixteen other randomly assigned clients served as wait-list control and fifteen were put in a no expectancy of treatment control pool. No differences on inventories or self-reported anxiety, analogue testing, or grades appeared among the small number of clients in both treatments. The authors, however, found that the subjects in both treatments exceeded control on debilitating anxiety and facilitating anxiety improvement and made significantly higher grades in the psychology courses from which they were drawn, although they did not perform better in the analogue testing task.

Exploring whether clients with different anxieties could be treated in the same group, Deffenbacher, Michaels, Daley, & Michaels (1980) compared the effectiveness of anxiety management training groups conducted by one of three counselors with test anxious, public speaking anxious, and combined anxiety groups of college students. The thirty-one test-anxious and twenty-five speech-anxious clients who completed six weekly 50-minute sessions had less debilitating anxiety and less emotionality and state anxiety but they did not worry less nor perform better on an analogue test than did the fifteen test-anxious and sixteen speech-anxious control clients. Homogeneous groups were superior to heterogeneous groups on nontargeted anxiety, but speech-anxious students from heterogeneous groups reported more confidence in speaking than did subjects in the homogeneous speech-anxiety group. The findings suggest that group anxiety management training is effective for test and speech anxiety and suggests that clients with different fears can be counseled in the same group.

Test anxiety measures. Several experimental inventories and ratings have been used in multiple anxiety counseling studies. Five of the more frequently used are described here.

The *Achievement Anxiety Test* (Alpert & Haber, 1960) consists of ten likert ratings of test interferences associated with anxiety and nine ratings of instances wherein anxiety aids test performance.

The *Test Anxiety Scale* (S. Sarason, 1978) has thirty-seven true-false items about anxiety in evaluation situations, such as: "I am nauseous in an exam," and purports to predict poor performance under the stress of evaluation.

The *Suinn Test Anxiety Behavior Scale* (Suinn, 1971) requires clients to visualize each of 50 test situations similar to one's that might be produced in an anxiety hierarchy and to rate the amount of anxiety experienced on a five-point scale, ranging from not at all to very much. Endler (1978) noted that the rationale for the inventory items has yet to be produced, but extensive use suggests that it may be self-evident.

The *Worry Emotionality Scale* (Liebert & Morris, 1967) consists of ten likert-type items, which yield a total score and two subpart scores—worry purporting to tap concern about test taking and competence—and emotionality tapping, self-perceived physiological arousal.

The *State-Trait Anxiety Inventory* (Speilberger, Gorush & Lushene, 1970) has two scales. The *A trait scale* has twenty items such as: "I worry about trivia" to which the client reports how he generally feels by checking almost never, sometimes, always, almost always. The items are designed to assess proneness to anxiety. The *A state scale* taps a client's current anxiousness. It has 20 items about immediate feelings, such as: "I feel tingly," to which the client reports his present feelings by checking: not at all, somewhat, moderately, and very much so. The state and trait scales have items with comparable internal consistency, while the trait scale has considerably higher test-retest reliability as predictable. Dreger (1978) has noted that the trait scale is likely to tap some state anxiety and notes evidence is not available to confirm that the trait scale measures a single factor.

Career Choice Counseling

10

Identity is an ongoing effect of development, but society expects the adolescent-becoming adult to decide the career identity that will characterize him or her and then to commit oneself accordingly. Suddenly, the person leaving the exploration stage and entering establishment has an occupation. One's status and lifestyle depend on this occupation. Supposedly the person has decided, and is aware of, how to carry out the decision to achieve satisfying work. Yet, research indicates that many people do not deliberately choose their occupations (Renwick & Lawler, 1978). Even by age twenty-five, at least 20 percent or more of workers will be without clear direction or occupational allegiance, "floundering" as Super et al. (1969) have termed this state.

Decision making is not easy as one moves from exploration to establishment. More than half of all college students change majors, and more than that change occupational goals from the beginning to end of their college years (Davis, 1965). The Bureau of Labor Statistics suggests that youth who enter work make many career changes; in 1977, sixteen- and seventeen-year-olds had a yearly occupational mobility rate of 27 percent; eighteen and nineteen-year-olds a rate of 41 percent; twenty- to twenty-four-year-olds at rate of 27 percent; and twenty-five- to thirty-year-olds a rate of 16 percent (U.S. Department of Labor, 1980).

Tiedeman's observations that career decisions are collaborative, developmental processes explains some of this job changing. Since the decider not only must choose but must also be chosen, simply wanting or striving to enter a major or occupation does not guarantee acceptance into it. The engineering major and medical professions, for instance, are notorious in being the initial college objective of three and four times,

414

respectively, as many candidates as ultimately are accepted. Likewise, despite the fact that employers would rather not label a job dismissal as such, a study of youth unemployment by Cook & Lanham (1966) indicates that many job changes by novice workers are involuntary. On the other hand, the developmental character of the career process suggests that, as one makes more decisions in the expanded freedom of college, working, and independent status, awareness of each of the steps in the process, as well as the process itself, grows; thereby providing more points at which to change, alter, or refine a decision and greater willingness to make more changes (Tiedeman & Miller-Tiedeman, 1975).

Tiedeman's observation that choice is only the third step of a seven-step career-decision process spotlights the fact that decisions are not purely cognitive phenomena. Instead, once the decider chooses, he or she often experiences multiple, mixed feelings about the choice, even while trying out the chosen path, gauging the reception, and then gradually implementing the choice more intensely as a result of this approval, until the decision is reality and one has been changed. This insight (that choice is a part of, rather than equal to, decision) is especially important to counseling, because it clarifies the fact that the career-choice counseling procedures described in this chapter generally do not support clients through a full decision. Although before World War II, the follow-up of trait factor counseling may have been extended several months after a choice was established, current renditions of that and the other counseling methods do not allow enough time for many clients to clarify and then to try out, win acceptance, and achieve integration of their choice. Even when the decision involves an academic major or program, counseling typically is terminated before the decision is finalized. Certainly, this early termination partially explains why career-choice changes occur after counseling and probably is a reason that many people take initial jobs not directly related to their postsecondary training (Solmon, 1977; Wilms, 1975).

Commitment is a process that "involves living with balanced tensions which we have achieved and which help to define us as individuals; it involves doubting, narrowing, choosing, assuming responsibility, caring for the choices we have made, and risking an investment of self in the face of the unknown. As the process arises through interactions with the environment, so it reaches fulfillment in some kind of engagement with the external world" (Kroll, Dinklage, Lee, Morley, & Wilson, 1971, p. 91).

Commitment is intertwined with decision making, reflecting a person's accepting responsibility for a decision and intending to be what the choice entails. Although ability to commit can be construed as an index of career maturity, current career counseling procedures are not aimed at increasing commitment *per se*. Yet, there are systematic ways to increase commitment, and several heuristic principles underlying them are suggested below. These principles are already embedded in the career choice counseling procedures or can be incorporated in them. This author hopes that some future counseling procedures will be designed specifically for increasing commitment.

To help meet the recurring challenge of deciding and committing, the original and still most common career counseling role evolved. This is the role of facilitating career choices. It was formalized at the turn of the century by Parsons (1909) and refined to integrate test interpretation by Paterson, Schneidler, and Williamson (1938), Darley (1941), and Williamson (1939, 1949). This chapter describes different methods that counselors have used in implementing this role.

Career Decision Counseling Heuristics and Assumptions

Essentially, facilitating career decisions involves guiding a client through the steps of considering and formulating career goals, recalling or discovering assets, learning about opportunities consistent with the assets and goals, and reviewing problem solving and planning. Counselors regard career decision or choice counseling as "traditional" or "typical" vocational counseling, and laymen often consider it the only kind of career counseling. Most career development courses contain significant elements of this role. Not surprisingly, most research of career counseling has concerned decision counseling or elements of it.

Career decision counseling presumes certain client skills and expectations. First, clients are supposed to have experienced and refined different aspects of themselves, including abilities, interests, and values, and presumably can become accurately aware of these attributes relatively quickly through testing or self-inventory. Two or three sessions are all that is usually spent in recalling the attributes. Second, clients are expected to be seeking a framework to help them integrate their self and occupational knowledge. The objective is immediate decisions about educational or occupational options; long-term exploration is not anticipated. Third, counselors presume that clients are familiar with the world of work and with locating and interpreting career information. When an occupation or training program is indicated for in-depth exploration by the client, a counselor occasionally may assist by interpreting some informational points, but even then the counselor assumes that the client understands the world of work well enough to understand the points. Surprisingly, few counselors recommend background reading, such as Darcy and Powell (1972), *Manpower and Economic Education: Opportunities in American Economic Life,* for clients to understand the increasingly complex world of work. Fourth, counselors expect clients to implement their plans without intervening with the educational or employment establishment. They direct their energies to helping clients learn to plan or to gather and synthesize information in order to generate courses of action and estimates of their acceptability. Today, many counselors do not cultivate a network of contacts that might facilitate their client's launching or sustaining a plan produced in counseling, even though in the past many counselors had such networks and occasionally interceded for clients. Fifth, counselors presume that clients recognize that career planning is an ongoing process of defining, reviewing, and redefining or refining career goals based on ever-increasing knowledge of self and of opportunities. The counselor assumes that clients need and want to learn how to plan and to choose, as well as to make a particular choice or plan. Understanding the process is as important as the resulting decision. Neither counselors nor test data usurp the clients' rights and responsibility for planning and choosing.

Heuristic Principles

The heuristic principles pertinent to career choice counseling are those related to planning and decision making, individual differences, and commitment. Those related to planning and decision making include the following:

1. Decision making and planning improve when a person is aware of the need and is permitted to plan or decide.
2. Planning and decision making improve when a systematic approach is taken.
3. Plans and decisions get better when one corrects strategy based on feedback from past efforts.
4. Plans and decisions are more successful if the accuracy of relevant information is verified.
5. Planning and decision making improve when a person follows the strategies of others who have succeeded with similar goals and decisions.
6. Planning and decision making improve when one recognizes that this process can be divided into a sequence of decisions to be managed more easily and to be corrected while in progress, as feedback about initial steps becomes available.
7. Planning and decision-making skills become keener by assisting others like oneself to plan and to decide.
8. Planning and decision making improve by receiving didactic instruction on the planning process and/or expert advice about one's plans.
9. Planning and deciding ability increase by teaching others about one's own plans and decisions.

Heuristic principles relating to individual differences include:

1. Every person can be classified reliably in terms of rank in a particular objective characteristic such as an ability, interest, value, and the like.
2. Each occupation requires its incumbents to abide by a specifiable set of tolerances; the occupation can be described as involving a limited range of particular objective characteristics.

3. People can enter occupations compatible with their characteristics and succeed in them more easily and more certainly than they can occupations that are incompatible.

Several heuristics relate directly to commitment to an occupational or educational group, for example:

1. Commitment to a group increases when a person can see that personal goals, abilities, interests, and values are shared with the group.
2. Commitment increases as the person recognizes his or her acceptability to group members and capability of entering and succeeding in the occupation.
3. Commitment grows when the person or significant others feel positively toward the occupation and membership in it.
4. Commitment to an occupation expands when the person is rewarded by performing the occupational duties.
5. Commitment to an occupation deepens when one acknowledges and accepts its strengths and weaknesses.

Similarly, commitment to a course of action increases when one:

1. Publicly affirms his or her intention of pursuing it,
2. Delineates its concrete actions and specific benefits,
3. Refutes arguments against its pursuit,
4. Assures that rewards periodically are forthcoming from its pursuit.

Counseling Strategies

Many strategies have been used in career decision counseling. Here are three of the better defined strategies, representing the spectrum of approaches. In addition, the chapter describes a test interpretation program, which can be considered an offshoot of trait-factor counseling.

Trait-Factor Counseling

Unquestionably, Williamson (1939; 1949) was the leading proponent of trait-factor career counseling, but other outstanding contributors include Paterson et al. (1938), Froelich and Hoyt (1959), Hahn and McLean (1950), and Tyler (1969). The objective of trait-factor counseling is to pinpoint suitable educational and occupational opportunities by analyzing reliable estimates of personal characteristics, especially abilities, and estimates of the demands and potentials of available opportunities. Today, this analysis may be done by computer, as in the *Career Planning Program* (American College Testing, 1972).

In trying to identify suitable opportunities, the client is guided to survey personal and environmental factors relating to career choice systematically and then to consider how the traits relate to career opportunities. Under Williamson, a client participated in the survey, the development of an explanation about the relevance of traits to options, and a review of possible courses of action to the extent of personal ability and interest. Today, counselors using the trait-factor approach stress the need for the client's active involvement and understanding of all phases of the counseling process. The six phases of trait-factor counseling are inception, reconnaissance, hypothesis development, hypothesis dissemination, planning, and follow-up. Williamson termed the phases "analysis, synthesis, diagnosis, prognosis, counseling, and follow-up." The phases are described below. Although counseling tends to move sequentially from phase to phase, overlap is normal, and sometimes counseling moves back and forth from reconnaissance to hypothesis development, from hypothesis dissemination to hypothesis development, or even from planning to hypothesis development.

Inception

In inception, the counselor greets the client, invites him or her to be comfortable, and initiates discussion about the client's vocational indecision. The counselor models a calm, attentive, and deliberate posture that sets the stage for planning. He or she elicits the client's expectations about counseling and helps to correct any misunderstandings about the process. The counselor insures that the client realizes that choosing an occupation is a "logical process of collecting, reviewing, evaluating, accepting, and rejecting the evidence of experience, school, grades, psychological tests, and other data" (Williamson, 1939). Inception is successful when the client indicates understanding of the processes of counseling and choosing an occupation and desires to engage in them. Krumboltz (1966) developed this stage more fully with the concept of contracting; that is, client and counselor explicitly agree what each will do in advancing the client toward goals. With increased availability of audio-visual devices, particularly recorders, counselors might have prospective clients preview a career counseling case in order to facilitate entry into counseling. Stewart (1969) showed that exposure to such modeling improved counseling for eleventh graders.

Reconnaissance[1]

The objective of the reconnaissance phase is to collect data relevant to the client's decision. According to Williamson, the counselor oversees the information to be gathered, how to gather it, and when to stop gathering it. Even before counseling starts, and between sessions, the coun-

[1] The term *reconnaissance* was chosen because this aspect of Williamson's counseling is very similar to the reconnaissance explicated in detail by H. S. Sullivan in the *Psychiatric Interview* (1953b).

selor reviews anecdotal records, autobiographies, questionnaires, psychological tests, and inventories to begin developing a picture of the client.
The review of materials, in light of clinical experience and the client's
expressed concerns, suggests the probing needed during the interview
and any psychological tests to be prescribed. Williamson recommended
gathering a broad range of data, including information about abilities,
achievements, family background, response to counseling, time usage,
health, recreational pursuits, hobbies, work experiences, interests, and
expectations of significant others. Open-ended questions, reflection of
feeling, paraphrasing, and expectant silence are especially useful in this
type of probing.

The following questions pertaining to this phase come from Ryan's
(1968) adaptation of trait-factor counseling for junior college students.

1. Looking at the present:

    What kind of person are you?
    What kind of person do you want to be?
    Why did you come to a community college?
    What do you think of yourself at this time?
    What problems do you have?
    What are your long-term goals?
    How do you decide on goals (personal factors/occupational
        information)?

2. Looking at yourself—Personal factors to consider in choosing a
    vocation:

    How do personal interests influence choice?
    How do personality characteristics influence choice?
    What about intelligence?
    What about health, physical characteristics?
    What about special aptitudes?

3. Finding out about oneself—Sources of information:

    Where to find out about yourself?
    Test data: What do they mean?
    School records: What do they suggest?
    Self-evaluation: What do you think of yourself?
    Professional evaluation: What do others think?

4. Looking into the future.

    What kind of person are you?
    What kind of person do you want to be?
    Do you belong in a big organization or a small one?
    Do you belong in a pressure-job?

Do you belong in a job demanding careful, detailed work?
Do you want to take risks and chances?
How can you keep your career options open?

Hypothesis Development

As data accrue, hypotheses are developed through content analysis. The counselor induces a tentative hypothetical picture of the person from the information and relates this emerging model to available opportunities, thereby deducing hypotheses about the appropriateness of particular choices. Hence, the counselor must have multiple models of options. For example, a coed who enjoyed cooking, had liked waitressing and candy striping, but not babysitting or tutoring, excelled in chemistry, and had nearly as much scholastic potential as her college peers and other home economics majors could be pictured as a person with interest and potential for culinary arts, either as a contact person or technician, with possible capability as a researcher, but less potential as an instructor. Therefore, occupations such as dietician and home economist technician would likely be feasible and attractive, whereas those such as home economics, or elementary school teacher, or social worker would be less appropriate. Such content analyses can be systematized by using the format in Figure 10–1, devised by Magoon for his self-guided, trait-factor counseling procedure.

Williamson and early writers on hypothesis generation, such as Hahn and McLean (1950) and Froelich and Hoyt (1959), provided little detail about the process, and merely discussed its intentions. More recently, Goldman (1971) described and diagrammed the process (see Figure 10–2).

The model is built through a series of steps, beginning with *inductive inferences* from individual data, then comparing inferences with each other, retaining the compatible ones and rejecting or modifying others as contradictions appear, testing each inference against new data, and thus moving on to the next step of stating *hypotheses* which pull together several inferences into a broader pattern. The hypotheses are themselves tested for consistency with other hypotheses about the person and tested also against new data to see whether the hypotheses will accept them. At this point, there is one of the greatest challenges to the counselor's capability for flexibility, for he must be able to give up or at least to modify an hypothesis in the face of contradictory data. This is, as emphasized by the Pepinskys (1954), one of the occasions in which the counselor functions both as counselor and as scientist. That is, while trying to be helpful to his client, he tries also to maintain the scientific attitude, which here is exemplified in a high degree of readiness to give up a belief or an hypothesis that does not hold up in the face of empirical data.

Figure 10–1. Summary and Evaluation Sheet for Vocational Planning

Note: Pulling together all of the information for planning is a hard job, but this sheet will be of considerable assistance to you in doing so.

CODE FOR COLUMN 3:

(1) Graduate or Professional school degree beyond college.
(2) College degree.
(3) Two year college (academic or vocational program).
(4) Technical, business, or specialized school.
(5) Military services schooling.
(6) Apprenticeship or on-the-job training.
(7) No particular educational requirements.
(8) Other (explain).

COLUMN 4

RELEVANT INFORMATION

How do you evaluate yourself regarding each of these kinds of information you have gathered for each of the occupations listed?

Use these ratings:
+ supports this plan
0 neutral or indeterminant
– contradicts this plan
? need for information

COLUMN 1 OCCUPATIONAL GROUPS (Refer to Groups on Your Interest Sheets)	COLUMN 2 OCCUPATIONS WITHIN EACH GROUP (Be Specific Enough to Evaluate Each)	COLUMN 3 REQUIRED EDUCATION OR TRAINING (Use the Codes from Upper Left Corner of This Sheet)	Study Time	Study Efficiency	Achievement, High School	Achievement, College	Work Experience	Leisure Experience	Other's Opinions	Measured Interests	Expressed Interests	Occupational & Educ. Facts	Other

SOURCE: T. Magoon. Developing skills for educational and vocational counseling. In J. D. Krumboltz and C. E. Thoresen (eds.). *Behavior counseling: Cases and techniques.* New York: Holt, Rinehart and Winston, 1969.

Figure 10–2. Schematic Representation of a Clinical Process of Interpretation

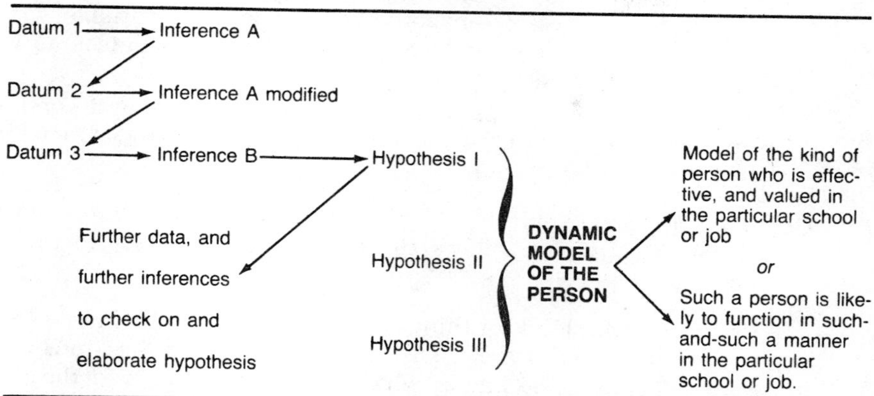

SOURCE: From USING TESTS IN COUNSELING (2nd ed.) by L. Goldman (p. 196). Copyright © 1971 by Goodyear Publishing Co. Reprinted by permission.

> There is at this point some *deductive* thinking: If this hypothesis is true, then it should follow that such-and-such would be found in further study of the case. Failing to find such-and-such, and finding instead its converse, we are forced to question the hypothesis as it now stands.[2]

Relating people to options in hypothesis development ranges from actuarial to clinical. Actuarial extrapolations are based primarily on statistically established relationships of the test scores with selected criteria. For example, if discriminant analysis had indicated that engineering students in a college differed from other students on scales of the *SVIB*, one actuarial datum for a client who had taken the *SVIB* would be the likelihood of being in the engineering or nonengineering student group. Or, if there were a regression equation predicting engineering grades in the school from *GATB* scores, the client who completed the *GATB* could receive estimates of making different grades.

In contrast, clinical extrapolations result from counselor judgments about the fit of his or her model of a client to his or her models of the criterion to be predicted. Since several options are usually under consideration, the counselor will need to build several criterion models. Goldman (1971) noted that the criterion model should be constructed as carefully as the model of the person. He identified four approaches to building a criterion model:

1. The analytic model—construct a model person to represent the criterion by closely scrutinizing people adjudged high on the criterion and tease out their common qualities.

[2] From USING TESTS IN COUNSELING (2nd Ed.) by L. Goldman (pp. 196–197). Copyright © 1971 by Goodyear Publishing Co. Reprinted by permission.

2. The empirical or concurrent approach—identify high and low groups on the criterion and find out what differentiates them.

3. The synthetic approach—hypothesize an important variable, construct a measure of it, and try it on appropriate samples as in the empirical approach.

4. The configurational approach—use discriminant analysis or inverse factor analysis to locate patterns of traits associated with being high on the criterion.[3]

Goldman further noted that clinical interpretation will be most effective when a counselor follows the eleven guidelines set forth by Horst (1956):

(1) He knows what kinds of things are to be done. (2) He knows what kinds of behaviors are regarded as desirable in what kinds of activities. That is, he knows what constitutes success in the various activities. (3) He has a way of indicating how desirable the various kinds of behaviors are even though these ways may be very crude. He has some way of making discriminations among behaviors. (4) The methods he has for discriminating among behaviors are reasonably consistent. He does not roll the dice or spin a roulette wheel in order to get numbers to characterize the performance of the client. (5) Whatever method the counselor uses, no matter how vague or crude, in evaluating behaviors in life activities, he does arrive at evaluations with which other persons including the client will tend to agree. (6) He has some system—certain items of information—in terms of which he describes people, no matter how simple or complex. (7) He has ways of indicating to what degree these various things about people can exist. These may be very crude or they may take on any degree of refinement which he chooses. They may be all or none, more or less, yes or no, maybe yes—maybe no. (8) He has ways of knowing to what degree each of these things about people are true about a particular client. (9) He is somewhat consistent in evaluating the client with respect to each of his descriptive categories. He does not describe the same behavior as withdrawn one minute and extroverted the next. (10) He has a system for discriminating the variables, or quantifying them, such that there can be at least some measure of agreement with other observers. (11) Finally, he has a method, or system of methods, whereby he can combine or synthesize information about people in such a way that the synthesized information will indicate to what extent the client will exhibit desirable behaviors in the various activities available to him. (p. 167)[4]

---

[3] Leo Goldman. *Using Tests in Counseling* (2nd Ed.). Los Angeles: Goodyear, 1971, pp. 196–197.

[4] P. Horst. Educational and Vocational Counseling from the Actuarial Point of View. *Personnel and Guidance Journal,* 1956, 35, p. 167.

Figure 10–3. Presentation of Appraisal Results in Accord with
Canons of Trait-factor Counseling

As far as I can tell from this evidence of aptitude, your chances of getting into
the medical school are poor, but your possibilities of business seem to be much
more promising. These are the reasons for my conclusions: You have done consistently failing work in zoology and chemistry. You do not have the pattern of
interests characteristic of successful doctors which probably indicates you would
not find the practice of medicine congenial. On the other hand, you do have an
excellent grasp of mathematics, good general ability, and the interests of an accountant. These facts seem to me to argue for your selection of accountancy as
an occupation. Suppose you think about these facts and my suggestion, talk to
your father about my suggestion, see Professor Blank who teaches accounting,
and return next Tuesday at 10 o'clock to tell me what conclusions you have reached.
I urge that you weigh the evidence pro and con for your choice.

SOURCE: E. G. Williamson. *Counseling adolescents.* New York: McGraw-Hill, 1949.

Figure 10–3 presents a clinical interpretation from Williamson.
Observe that Williamson's model of doctor is one who must do well in
zoology and chemistry, in addition to having good general academic
ability. In generating hypotheses, according to Williamson, the counselor
judged the representativeness of each datum and told the client reasons
for differential weighing. Test and inventory data were weighted more
because Williamson believed they had higher reliability.

More and more, however, counselors are realizing that clients need
to join in gathering and analyzing data, and that they can be taught to
provide more reliable testimony. As a consequence, counselors often
furnish detailed instruction on the meaning of test scores to enable the
client to work with such scores in hypothesis generation (Goldman,
1971). One might also have clients practice on other cases and receive
feedback. Moreover, tests are now available to judge client competence
in weighing case information and generating hypotheses. For instance,
the *CMI* and *NMCET* problem-solving tests require identifying relationships between personal attributes and career options.

Since client involvement in hypothesis generation is considered important, clients must acquire considerable occupational information in
order to build models of different career options. Hoppock (1976) suggested that most of the following particulars should be considered in
studying occupations: employment prospects, nature of work, work environment, required preparation, entrance methods, advancement opportunities, earnings, qualifications, union affiliations, discrimination, number and distribution of workers, and advantages and disadvantages of
the work.

Ryan[5] (1968), in her adaptation of trait-factor counseling, encouraged clients to answer the following questions about career prospects:

[5] T. Antoinette Ryan. *Effect of an Integrated Instructional Counseling Program
to Improve Vocational Decision Making.* Final Report for U. S. Department
of Health, Education and Welfare Project. Washington, D. C.: U. S. Government Printing Office, 1968, pp. 81–82. (ERIC No. E D 021 132).

1. Looking at the world of work—Occupational information to consider in choosing a vocation or looking at occupations:

   What vocational-technical opportunities are likely in this area?
   What are requirements for career entry in different jobs?
   What are chances of getting work in various jobs?
   What training or education is required for different jobs?
   What are the rewards: advancement, financial, security, transfer possibility, personal satisfaction?

2. Finding out about the world of work and leisure—Sources of information

   Where to find out about the world of work and leisure?
   Library references
   Local resources
   Occupational files
   Employment office

3. Considering occupational areas—Deliberating about alternatives:

   How to relate personal information and occupational information
   How to consider consequences of different alternatives

4. Considering educational and training programs for possible vocational choices:

   Looking at personal characteristics:
   What learning problems do you have?
   What special aptitudes, personality characteristics, and interests do you have?
   Looking at educational and training programs:
   What are entrance requirements?
   What is the cost?
   What is availability of program?

One well-described method for involving the client in hypothesis generation and in clarifying the motives underlying personal occupational preferences is the *Tyler Vocational Card Sort* (Tyler, 1961). First, the client is given a list of occupations suitable for his or her educational aspirations (such as those indicated on the *Strong Campbell Interest Blank*) and sorts them into three piles—those one "might choose," those one "would not choose," and those about which one "has questions." Second, one is given the "would not choose" set to be further subdivided on the basis of why they were rejected. The client picks the categories and tells the counselor what they are. For example, the client might use subcategories, such as no advancement possible, mechanical work, and poor pay. Third, the same procedure is repeated for the "might choose" group. Following these sortings, the client ranks the "might choose" occupations in terms of preference for them, proceeds to rank a set of work values, and then examines the record of the subdivisions and the comments made while sorting and ranking so that clients and the counselor can reflect on the implications of the exercises.

For college students, the occupational sorts correlate with *Strong Vocational Interest Test* scores (Dolliver, 1966). Dolliver and Will (1977) found that the *TVCS* preference coincided with the occupations of 69 percent of 47 college freshmen ten years later. Recently, Dewey (1974) suggested a list of 76 occupations and a slight procedural modification to ensure its being nonsexist. Moreover, Cooper (1976), studying 120 undecided women, found that the *TVCS* was more effective than was reading a computer printout of one's *Strong Campbell Interest Inventory* scores in broadening career options and in increasing occupational exploration.

Dissemination

In the dissemination phase, the counselor reports the findings from the reconnaissance and hypothesis generation nontechnical language. The presentation is deliberate and paced so the counselor can weigh client reaction in order to judge where and when to elaborate. When clients share in hypothesis generation, as now generally happens, dissemination becomes part of hypothesis generation.

Williams opposed use of charts and other visual aids in dissemination lest the counselor be distracted from the client's reaction to the hypotheses. Today, however, standardized formats, such as the one in Figure 10–4, can expedite systematic review of the counselor's conclusions and reduce confusion about them.

According to Williamson, client acceptance of counselor inferences is the purpose of dissemination, since the client who rejects the counselor's opinion is less likely to act on them. Consequently, the counselor creates an atmosphere favoring acceptance, omitting extraneous data and mustering supportive arguments for his or her opinions. If Williamson were confident about directions for the client, he presented them persuasively. When there were competing alternatives, pertinent evidence for each was provided and, where possible, alternatives were ranked in order of appropriateness. In regard to options such as training programs or schools, contingency tables have been developed. These tables provide probability estimates of incumbency or achievement in different options.

Tyler (1969) noted that information dissemination is often difficult, especially if the information contradicts a client's beliefs or wishes. Her discussion suggests the following procedures for helping clients accept information:

1. Plan the presentation carefully to accord with the information and decision needs and the learning style of the client.

Figure 10–4. An Innovative Way of Displaying Test and Inventory Results

PETERSON CHARLES P	392-11-0971	DATE SCORED	02/77
323 APPLE LANE	MALE	EDUCATIONAL LEVEL	SENIOR
WHEAT RIDGE CO 80023	08/23/59	RACIAL ETHNIC BACKGROUND	CAUCASIAN/WHITE

CAREER CLUSTERS

ACT CAREER PLANNING PROGRAM

STUDENT REPORT

1. BUSINESS SALES & MANAGEMENT
SAMPLE EDUCATIONAL PROGRAMS

Agriculture Business
Business Administration
Finance & Credit
Hotel/ Restaurant Management
Sales & Retailing

BUSINESS CONTACT INTERESTS	HIGH
BUS CONTACT EXPERIENCES	SOME
SOME IMPORTANT ABILITIES*	
LANGUAGE USAGE	MED
NUMERICAL SKILLS	HIGH
CLERICAL SKILLS	MED

2. BUSINESS OPERATIONS
SAMPLE EDUCATIONAL PROGRAMS

Accounting
Data Processing
Office Machine Operation
Office Management
Secretarial Science

BUSINESS DETAIL INTERESTS	HIGH
BUS DETAIL EXPERIENCES	SOME
SOME IMPORTANT ABILITIES*	
NUMERICAL SKILLS	HIGH
CLERICAL SKILLS	MED
LANGUAGE USAGE	MED

8. SOCIAL & PERSONAL SERVICES
SAMPLE EDUCATIONAL PROGRAMS

Child Care
Home Economics
Physical Education & Recreation
Police Science
Teaching

SOCIAL SERVICE INTERESTS	MED
SOCIAL SERVICE EXPERIENCES	FEW
SOME IMPORTANT ABILITIES*	
LANGUAGE USAGE	MED
NUMERICAL SKILLS	HIGH

3. TRADES, CRAFTS, & INDUSTRIES
SAMPLE EDUCATIONAL PROGRAMS

Appliance Auto Other Repair
Carpentry
Farming
Food Service
Welding

TRADES INTERESTS	LOW
TRADES EXPERIENCES	SOME
SOME IMPORTANT ABILITIES*	
MECHANICAL REASONING	LOW
NUMERICAL SKILLS	HIGH
SPACE RELATIONS	LOW

9. YOUR CAREER PLANS

YOUR EDUCATIONAL PROGRAM PREFERENCES		CAREER CLUSTER NUMBER
1st	ACCOUNTING	2
2nd	CIVIL ENGINEERING TECH	4
YOUR LONG-TERM CAREER GOAL	BUSINESS ADMINISTRATION	1

SOME CAREER SUGGESTIONS

YOUR INTERESTS SUGGEST YOU MAY LIKE TO WORK MOSTLY WITH DATA & PERHAPS PEOPLE. JOBS IN REGION 03 (SEE WORLD-OF-WORK MAP ON BACK) OFTEN INVOLVE THESE KINDS OF WORK ACTIVITIES.

7. CREATIVE & APPLIED ARTS
SAMPLE EDUCATIONAL PROGRAMS

Architecture
Art & Photography
English & Literature
Interior Decorating
Journalism

CREATIVE ARTS INTERESTS	LOW
CREATIVE ARTS EXPERIENCES	NONE
SOME IMPORTANT ABILITIES*	

Consider your ability to express thoughts or feelings in clear or inventive ways and your specific skills in fields such as art music writing etc

4. TECHNOLOGIES
SAMPLE EDUCATIONAL PROGRAMS

Computer Programming
Engineering (Civil Elec Mech etc)
Engineering Technical (2 years)
Mechanical Drawing
Pilot Training

TECHNOLOGY INTERESTS	LOW
TECHNOLOGY EXPERIENCES	FEW
SOME IMPORTANT ABILITIES*	
MECHANICAL REASONING	LOW
NUMERICAL SKILLS	HIGH
SPACE RELATIONS	LOW

6. HEALTH SERVICES/SCIENCES
SAMPLE EDUCATIONAL PROGRAMS

Dental Assistant
Medical Technology (Lab Work)
Nursing
Physical/Occupational Therapy
X Ray Technology

HEALTH INTERESTS	MED
HEALTH EXPERIENCES	NOT ASSESSED
SOME IMPORTANT ABILITIES*	
NUMERICAL SKILLS	HIGH
MECHANICAL REASONING	LOW

5. NATURAL & SOCIAL SCIENCES
SAMPLE EDUCATIONAL PROGRAMS

Biological Sciences
Law School
Math
Physical Sci (Chem . Physics etc)
Social Sci (Soc Work Psych Econ)

SCIENCE INTERESTS	LOW
SCIENCE EXPERIENCES	FEW
SOME IMPORTANT ABILITIES*	
NUMERICAL SKILLS	HIGH
LANGUAGE USAGE	MED
MECHANICAL REASONING	LOW

*NOTE: Reading is an important ability in each Career Cluster

Figure 10–4. An Innovative Way of Displaying Test and Inventory Results (*Continued*)

ED. PLANS & BACKGROUND	PLANNED ENTRANCE DATE	FULL TIME STUDENT?	DAY OR EVENING?	WORK PLANS hours week	HIGH SCHOOL ATTENDED		
	SFPT 1977	YES	DAY	16-20	WHEAT RIDGE HS WHEAT RIDGE CO 80023		364-892

	LONG RANGE EDUCATIONAL PLANS	STUDENT ASKED FOR HELP WITH							HIGH SCHOOL GRADES				
		FINAN CIAL AID	EMPLOY MENT	HOUS ING	CHILD CARE	HEALTH PROB	TRANS POR TATION	CHOOS ING A MAJOR	ENGLISH	MATH	SOCIAL STUDIES	NATURAL SCIENCE	BUSINESS VOCATIONAL
	2 YEAR DEGREE	*	*			**		*	B	A	B	C	B

ABOUT YOUR INTERESTS, EXPERIENCES, & ABILITIES

Your interests, experiences, and abilities can help you discover which parts of the world of work you may want to explore further. As you explore, be sure to consider all the things you know about yourself, in addition to your test results.

- INTERESTS & EXPERIENCES—Your interest scores summarize your *likes* and *dislikes* for a variety of work-related activities. Your experiences in each area are summarized by the words NONE, FEW, SOME, and MANY. Your interest and experience scores are compared to those of other students of your sex.

  Look at your interest and experience scores in each Career Cluster. Your interests may change as a result of your experiences. Have you tried some work-related activities in areas where your interests are high? Remember: high interests do not always mean you have the abilities needed to be successful in that area.

- ABILITIES—Your scores give you an estimate of your abilities as compared to those of a nationwide group of beginning students (men and women) in technical and community colleges.

  Look at each Career Cluster to see how you stand on the abilities that are often important for success in jobs in that cluster. Do you have the abilities needed for jobs in the clusters you are considering? Abilities can sometimes be improved with the right kind of study or practice. Talk with your counselor about this.

Your *Planning* booklet can help you explore jobs that interest you. It also includes a more complete description of the interests, experiences, and abilities measured by the CPP.

EXPERIENCES RELATED TO INTERESTS	INTERESTS	NAT'L STA NINE (1 9)	LOWER QUARTER 5 10 25	MIDDLE HALF 40 60 75	UPPER QUARTER 90 95
SOME	BUSINESS CONTACT	7			-XX-
SOME	BUSINESS DETAIL	8			-XX-
SOME	TRADES	2	-XX-		
FEW	TECHNOLOGY	3	-XX-		
FEW	SCIENCE	3	-XX-		
NOT ASSESSED	HEALTH	4		-XX-	
NONE	CREATIVE ARTS	1	XX-		
FEW	SOCIAL SERVICE	5		-XX-	

Score Bands—The —XX— on the charts show how your scores compare to those of the nationwide group. Bands are used because tests are not exact measures. When two bands do not overlap, chances are good that one score is higher than the other

N—An N means you did not answer enough questions

Placement Information—If your English or math composite is 3 or less, ask your counselor about how you can improve these skills

ACT Composite Range—This estimates what your score would be if you took the ACT Assessment. The average score for students thinking about attending college is 17 to 21

ADDITIONAL NORMS STANINES	ABILITIES	NAT'L STA NINE	LOWER QUARTER 5 10 25	MIDDLE HALF 40 60 75	UPPER QUARTER 90 95
2	MECHANICAL REASONING	3	-XX-		
6	NUMERICAL SKILLS	7		-XX-	
3	SPACE RELATIONS	3	-XX-		
4	READING SKILLS	4	-XX-		
6	LANGUAGE USAGE	5	-XX-		
6	CLERICAL SKILLS	6		-XX-	

PLACEMENT INFORMATION		
BASIC SKILLS	ASKED HELP?	STANINE ON
STUDY SKILLS	**	LOCAL NORMS
READING SKILLS		
ENGLISH COMPOSITE	*	6
MATH COMPOSITE		7
ESTIMATED ACT COMPOSITE RANGE:		15-19

PERCENTILE RANK: A percentile rank of 40 means that 40% of students had scores below this point

ADDITIONAL NORMS FOR	SEE BELOW	5 10 25 40 60 75 90 95
INSTITUTIONAL CHOICE		1 2 3 4 5 6 7 8 9
ARAPAHOE CMTY COL LITTLETON CO		STANINES: Stanines are a special type of scale which is divided into 9 equal parts Stanine bands are numbered 1 (low) through 9 (high), with 5 being the average score for a norm group

2. Encourage client feedback by waiting for responses before proceeding from one datum to another, and verify that client attributes the same meaning to words as the counselor does.

3. Point out the range of choices available, emphasizing options of which the client was initially unaware, the length of time that changing is likely to require, and the kinds of feelings that can be expected as one changes goals.

Test interpretation is a subject worthy of several volumes, and full treatment is beyond the scope of this book. Here are some considérations that this author regards as major to integrate testing into counseling. Helpful textbooks about interpreting educational and psychological tests have been written by Anastasi (1976), Cronbach (1970), Goldman (1971), and Super and Crites (1962).

Most test and inventory results are reported as percentiles, standard scores, and/or raw scores. The percentiles and standard scores indicate the client's standing in terms of the norm group. Raw scores, however, are also designed to clarify the person's standing. Ordinarily, they do not indicate the percent of the competence, ability, or trait the person has, since the items are not selected to sample the criterion proportionally, but rather to create a (normal) distribution on the criterion. Consequently, the person with a relatively low raw score, and even a low percentile score, may have enough of the ability or personality trait for a particular occupation because the score is not measuring proficiency, only relative proficiency, interest, or personality. Figure 10–5 indicates the relation of different norm-referenced scores to one another.

Percentiles and standard scores are point estimates of the person's standing. They are the best estimates; but the actual standing is likely to differ from them, at least somewhat. Thus, most writers on test interpretation suggest presenting the client with a percentile range or band rather than a percentile score. To speed communication and to avoid confusion over the meaning of percentiles, some manuals recommend using only descriptions such as very high, high, average, low, and very low. The effects of these descriptions of performance on clients have not been tested. Of course, these are also norm-referenced rather than criterion-referenced scores and clearly must be presented as such.

Some scores from inventories, such as the *SCII*, indicate potential membership or nonmembership in particular occupations or academic majors. Often, manuals advise interpreting scores in terms of what they indicate about potential memberships. In presenting such information, the counselor must clarify for clients whether their affinity for a career group is based on their possessing attributes that distinguish members of that group from people in general, or whether the affinity is based on possessing attributes that predict career performance in the group. The former is likely for scores based on discriminant analyses, the latter for scores based on regression analysis. This information also should be in the test manual. The difference between the two analyses can be very important, for Goldman (1971) noted that many of the qualities that distinguish career groups may be related minimally to performance,

Figure 10–5. The Relation of Different Scores to the Normal Distribution

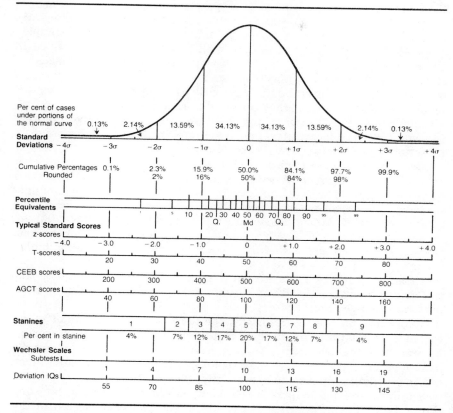

Note: This chart cannot be used to equate scores on one test to scores on another test. For example, both 600 on the CEEB and 120 on the AGCT are one standard deviation above their respective means, but they do not represent "equal" standings because the scores were obtained from different groups.

SOURCE: Test service Bulletin No. 48, *Methods of expressing test scores.* New York: Psychological Corporation, 1955.

whereas the qualities related to performance may not distinguish groups. For instance, success in medicine, law, and science will require high scholastic ability, sustained energy, capacity to delay gratification, and the like; but there is likely to be little difference in the amount of these qualities among professionals in these three areas.

Furthermore, the relations between attributes and occupation are based on studies of people currently in the career groups rather than on direct analysis of the occupational or curricular requirements. Therefore, the distinguishing characteristics may not be those most essential to working in the career but may be the attributes that most readily distinguish workers in the field from those outside it. Failure to recognize

432 Career Counseling Procedures Through the Life Stages

this fact has resulted in many tests being sex- and race-biased. They support the status quo by adding the characteristics of white males to those thought to be relevant to work performance in certain fields.

Two facts explain this source of test error and bias. First, the statistical analysis is done on a particular sample so some of that sample's qualities, actually unrelated to career affiliation, will appear related in the analysis. Second, items in the test or inventory are not selected to represent proportionately the requirements of the occupation or major but are chosen to differentiate among fields. Important group requirements will be excluded if they do not differentiate.

Before using and interpreting tests, one should recall the following concepts: norm-referenced vs. criterion-referenced test, descriptive vs. prescriptive test, and sign vs. sample test.

Most current instruments are *norm referenced*, not *criterion referenced*. Their items are designed to maximize examinee differences rather than to indicate how much of a domain the examinees know or might master. Half the college graduates, for instance, score below the 50 percentile on the Graduate Record Exams, an indicator of potential for graduate study; all may be able to master graduate studies, but the high scoring students have a slightly higher probability of earning higher grades.

Most tests indicate the examinee's present status (*descriptive*) on the quality measured, without providing data on how to empower the person to change (*prescriptive*).

Most instruments test *signs* rather than *samples* of a quality. For instance, standardized math tests require a testtaker to pick the correct answer to a problem rather than to solve it directly, and inventories have clients check their preference for a set of activities rather than examine whether, given the opportunity, they do choose those activities over others. Probably, a person who can pick the right answer can solve the problem, but how surely is unknown. The test exercise is called a sign, however, because it is not a direct measure of the problem solving.

Because most tests are norm referenced, descriptive, and signs, they rarely indicate how much of the ability, interest, or personality trait one possesses; how he or she might acquire more of the quality; whether such growth is possible; or how the person implements or manifests the ability, interest, or personality trait. Similarly, the test and inventory scores do not reveal the client's feelings and aspirations about the qualities assessed, his or her own and significant others' expectations regarding the client's achievement in the quality, or personal experience regarding the quality and feelings about them.

Obviously, these data are important to the person choosing and planning because they clarify how much personal energy will be required to implement a particular quality, how much support the client's reference groups will provide, and how satisfying implementation is likely to be.

Unlike the client and counselor, the Armed Forces, the Employment Service, business and industry, and college and school administrations— who have supported development of most standardized instruments— seek primarily to classify people in terms of the efficiency with which they can achieve particular competencies. The personal consequence of acquiring or not acquiring training are of secondary concern to these institutions; consequently, they rarely include such data in the appraisal of an individual. Not surprisingly, the one major longitudinal study, Project Talent (Flanagan et al., 1973), designed to furnish information for personal guidance, and the new test batteries designed for guidance rather than selection, differ from previous manpower research primarily by including indices of some self reports about feelings and aspirations.

Choice and Planning

After one's options are clear, the client chooses. When an alternative is at least tentatively selected, counseling turns to planning the actions necessary to carry out the choice.

Williamson advocated active counselor participation in planning, assuming that the counselor was familiar with the various routes by which clients would implement their choices. Today, with more options possible, most counselors cannot know alternate routes in detail. Nevertheless, the counselor can at least ensure that client plans are logical, comprehensive, and consistent with ability and other resource data considered in the reconnaissance.

Fogel (1973), and Snodgrass and Healy (1979), following the lead of Krumboltz and Baker (1973), taught clients a simplified planning paradigm as part of the planning stage of their modified trait-factor counseling. The paradigm consists of (a) specifying the occupational and training goals elected by the client, underscoring the need for concrete objectives; (b) generating alternative means of training for, and entering, the chosen position by examining occupational information, interviewing present incumbents, brainstorming, and reviewing training catalogues; (c) obtaining information about the nature of each alternative and the steps involved in pursuing it; (d) projecting the outcomes of each alternative for the client by using objective data, such as the fact that graduates of a part-time or night law program rarely obtain positions in prestigious law firms, and by using subjective estimates, such as the person's belief that he or she completes academic work more effectively if he or she is working while attending school; and (e) selecting the alternative and adopting a plan that specifies when to complete each step and how to obtain the needed resources.

A very important part of the plan is having the client identify benchmarks to determine how satisfactory the progress is. Since choices may take a long time to implement, the client will want to review progress periodically to assure that the choice and means of achieving it remain satisfactory in view of personal implementation experience.

Follow-up

Follow-up, rather than the client's accepting an implementation plan, is the proper close of counseling, according to Williamson (1949). Although rarely done, follow-up can be especially beneficial, for it shows the client the counselor's genuine concern and affords an opportunity to re-open counseling in order to resolve difficulties that have arisen during implementation. For the counselor, follow-up provides the invaluable opportunity to evaluate the accuracy of previous hypotheses and to become aware of forces affecting implementation of career plans. In addition, follow-up often can be professionally gratifying for counselors, since it often indicates the counselor's contribution to the client's career.

When and how to follow up are procedural issues in counseling, that have received little research attention, although the new consciousness about accountability makes follow-up mandatory for more counselors.

Tests and Computer Scoring in Trait-factor Counseling

Consistent with trait-factor counseling, several career testing/planning computer scoring programs now offer the benefits of psychological testing and actuarial predictions concerning suitability of particular options. The Career Planning Program of the American College Testing Program (1972) for twelfth graders and higher is critiqued below. The American College Testing Program also has one for grades eight through eleven. Other programs include the Psychological Corporation's *Differential Aptitude Test* and *Career Planning Program* and McGraw-Hill's program relating performance to Project Talent Norms.

The *Career Planning Program* requires a student to complete three and a half hours of tests and inventories in order to receive predictions about the suitability of different posthigh school training programs. The major output is via a student report, such as that in Figure 10–4.

The report in Figure 10–4 tells the student: (a) whether inventoried interests in each of the clusters are high, medium, or low; (b) whether the number of reported competencies in each cluster are many, some, few, or none; (c) whether tested abilities in a cluster are high, medium, or low; (d) whether chances for making a grade of C or higher are high, medium, or low in up to twenty-five training programs at two institutions of his choice and a composite school; and (e) whether students in the different composite programs have interests and preferences similar to the test subject. A broad scope of information is furnished by the one-page report. Equally impressive is how the data are economically organized and clearly communicated.

The reference group for the comparisons are 10,000 male and 6,000 female students entering posthigh school vocational-technical programs. Additional norms are provided in the *Handbook* for special groups, such as part-time students and Afro-Americans. User institutions can also arrange for *ACT* to develop local norms.

The basis of the *CPP* report is the student's performance on its ability tests, interest inventory, and self-rating form. The prediction's validity depends on the quality of these measures. They are examined below.

Ability test. The eight abilities measured in CPP are important for a wide range of occupations. The tests were constructed to be short, relevant to performance in training programs, and minimally verbal. The measures, number of items, and testing times are listed below:

Ability	Items	Time (Minutes)
Reading skill	40	20
Numerical computation	30	6
Math usage	20	15
Nonverbal reasoning	35	10
Mechanical reasoning	42	15
Clerical ability	35	6
Space relations	40	6
Language usage	40	6

Limited data about the measures' reliability are provided. They suggest moderate reliability. KR 20 reliability estimates, ranging from .82 to .88, based on a sample of 92 students, are presented for five scales. Test-retest reliabilities based on a sample of 314 students are presented for the other three scales; they range from .65 to .79. Since KR 20 measures internal consistency, and the aptitude tests of the CPP are speeded, additional test-retest evidence of reliability is needed.

Several types of validity data are given: content, concurrent, and predictive. Pertinent to content validity are the percentage of examinees completing different portions of the tests, the percentage who pass items in different portions of the ability tests, and the correlation of items with scale scores. These data indicate that the tests were well constructed and are internally consistent. Concurrent correlations of CPP ability scales with *General Aptitude Test Battery* (1958) range from .35 to .72, and generally support the validity of the CPP scales. In addition, correlations of the CPP scales with the *GATB Verbal and General* scores indicate that ACT achieved its goal of creating scales that are minimally influenced by verbal ability. With the exception of the *Reading* scale ($r = .61$) the *GATB Verbal* score correlated minimally with the CPP scales (range $= .27$ to $.43$), and the *GATB General* score correlated moderately with CPP scales (range $= .41$ to $.64$).

For predictive validity, multiple correlations (mean $R = .48$) of CPP scales with grades in nineteen training programs are presented. The Reading score and the Numerical Computation score are important in most of these correlations and in the regression equations. The regression equations are the basis for predicting a student's chances of making grades of C or higher. The multiple R's compare favorably with historical efforts to predict performance in occupational and academic training.

The Vocational Interest Profile (VIP). This Profile assesses interests for the eight clusters. The student rates the degree of personal preference for 100 activities, such as sketching or sorting mail. The student's ratings of activities in each cluster are compared with those of the norm group and reported as a standard score, which in turn is interpreted as indicating high, medium, or low interest.

The publishers present minimal evidence to support the reliability and independence of the *VIP* scales. Alpha coefficients indicate that the scales are internally consistent, but test-retest correlations based on 119 males and females indicate only moderate reliability. The retest r's of the male Trades and Technical scales are below .70. The correlations among scales suggest that six scales are relatively independent, but the Technical and Science scales are highly correlated, especially in view of their retest reliabilities.

The validity of the *VIP* scales depends on their ability to differentiate students enrolled in occupational training programs and on their relation to scales measuring similar interest constructs. *VIP* scales generally distribute the normative group in the manner suggested by the Roe (1956) and Holland (1959) clusters, which is impressive because differentiating nonprofessional groups on the basis of interest has been difficult (Super & Crites, 1962). Data concerning the relation of the scales to other standardized interest measures, such as the *Kuder Preference Record* or the *Strong Vocational Interest Blank* are not provided, nor is information about the interest scores' relation to grades or to other achievement indices. Such information is needed to evaluate the meaning of the scales.

Self-report. One-item scales assess the student's self-reported characteristics, values, and work condition preferences. There are ten characteristics, six values, and four preferences. For the competency scales, the student reports the frequency with which he or she does things such as fix televisions and design clothes. Scale scores are based on a comparison of the frequency of client-reported activities with the frequencies reported by the general norm group.

The individual Self-Report scales generally differentiate the training groups. Group differentiation by discriminant analysis of the *VIP* scales and the Self-Report scales is sufficient to permit statements about a student's similarity to those in various programs. (Discriminant analysis determines the combinations of variables that provide greatest differentiation among groups.)

Minimal study has been done concerning the effect of the *CPP* or similar programs on career choice accuracy or increase in self or career awareness. Nor has anyone determined whether a particular type of counseling will complement the program, although the manuals of these programs support complementary face-to-face counseling.

Translation Counseling

This author and his students developed translation counseling so that each client could learn career planning and problem-solving skills and apply those skills in forming career plans. In achieving these goals, each client identifies personal goals and assets, considers the fit of different occupations with these goals and assets, recalls and uses methods of learning about occupations and self, selects a tentative occupational direction, identifies entryways to occupations of interest, and considers strategies for overcoming obstacles to career plans.

This procedure, which has been used with groups of three to seven clients and with individuals, consists of five sessions, each of which has specific objectives. Although individuals have completed the procedure in five fifty-minute sessions, the typical session is one hundred minutes long.

Session 1

The objectives of the first session are to develop a group that will encourage its members to explore their career potential and to make plans, give the members an overview of the counseling activities and goals, and allow each client to select at least ten to fifteen work-relevant qualities. To accomplish the first objective, the counselor tells the group that he or she expects help and learning among members. This means they must understand one other. The group members introduce themselves in a manner that encourages interactions about career concerns. Each identifies personal concerns and then identifies by name and concern every client who preceded. The counselor encourages clarifying crosstalk about similarities and differences among group members and reminds them that such help is expected.

To accomplish the second objective of this initial session, the counselor describes the counseling procedure and asks different clients to comment on its relevance to their concerns. Questions about the procedure are welcomed. Next, the counselor guides the clients in the selection of work-relevant qualities. These qualities include both the attributes a client can bring to a job to perform it and the benefits wanted from working. In introducing the task of choosing work-related qualities, the counselor gives example of traits that can be brought to a job and those that can be acquired from working. In order to insure that the task is understood, clients are asked for examples of qualities after generating their own list of traits for five to ten minutes, and clients receive a list of qualities to insure that a wide range is considered (see Figure 10-6).

Clients who are unsure about what they can do or what they want from working are encouraged to generate principles such as: "skills developed in a school major and in previous jobs will help in one's occupation," and "at work it is pleasant to do what one has enjoyed doing previously." Clients are also encouraged to be specific about qualities, e.g., to list "working with advanced math" rather than "working with numbers."

After every client has a list of qualities, the counselor explains that those qualities a person considers important can offer some insight into the person. Accordingly, the clients share with the group the four or five qualities personally most important to them, and everyone discusses the implications of these qualities for different work roles.

Figure 10–6. Work-relevant Qualities

Good under pressure	Enjoys mental challenges	Friendly
Careful and neat	Has a sense of humor	Quick reflexes
Stick-to-itiveness	Likes to keep busy	Good spatial relations
Unconventional	A problem solver	A leader
Honest	Enjoys routine tasks	Religious
Enjoys being with people	Learns quickly from reading	Likes cultural/civic activities
Needs variety in work	Has a large vocabulary	Enjoys business
Enjoys taking risks	Strong	Likes outdoors
Examines own motives regularly	Up-to-date on current events	Interested in flying
Likes clerical tasks	Carefree	Patriotic
Enjoys math	Thinks before acting	Needs to be famous
Helpful to the needy	Works well alone	Tall
Interested in science	Sociable	Musical
Good at math	Not prejudiced	Physically attractive
Good in English	Good memory	Considers money very important
Imaginative	Fine with children	Persuasive
Good at clerical job	Writes effectively	

Session 2

The objectives for the second session are that the clients understand that a wide range of occupations can be examined by looking closely at a selected few. They examine six such occupations in terms of the qualities selected during the first session, recall different sources of occupational information, and share occupational information.

In order to spur involvement, the session starts with a volunteer identifying the other clients and their concerns. Everyone is encouraged to participate. Next, the clients report their experiences with the tasks they had chosen for themselves in session one, and they recall the first session and their understanding of the total procedure. The counselor then explains the significance of session two.

For the first objective, the counselor explains how occupations can be grouped in several ways and helps the clients to recall ways, such as nature of work and level of skill. The counselor notes that if the occupations are grouped and if a representative occupation from each group is examined, then a wide range of occupations can be surveyed by examining only a few. Discussion is elicited in order to evaluate client comprehension.

Objective two is accomplished when each client rates a personal concept of the typical person in at least six occupations on the qualities chosen in session one. The counselor asks the clients to list occupations

Figure 10–7. Occupations and Workers in Holland Clusters

Conventional (20,020,000)	Artistic (500,000)	Enterprising (12,740,000)
accountant	actor/actress	administrative assistant
business machine operator	artist	airline stewardess
bookkeeper	architect	banker
cashier	drama coach	buyer
legal stenographer	editor	economist
credit manager	entertainer	truck dispatcher
airline ticket clerk	advertising man	sales engineer
telephone operator	designer	contractor
bank teller	interpreter	government official
secretary	interior decorator	production manager
business teacher	journalist	supermarket manager
keypunch operator	fashion model	attorney
civil service clerk	writer	radio announcer
sales clerk		salesman
		real estate salesman
		bank executive

Social (14,005,000)	Realistic (36,400,000)	Investigative (7,280,000)
recreation administrator	appliance repair person	airplane pilot
athlete	baker	anthropologist
bartender	shoemaker	biologist
social worker	bookbinder	chemist
cosmetologist	bricklayer	physician
counselor	carpenter	dentist
insurance correspondent	typesetter	engineer aide
dental hygienist	cook	mathematician
dietician	civil engineer	research analyst
librarian	draftsman	TV repairman
historian	fireman	psychologist
home economist	game warden	oceanographer
interviewer	forester	X-ray technician
nurse	machinist	laboratory technician
physical therapist	sailor	tool and dye maker
politician	plumber	computer programmer
retail saleswoman	auto mechanic	electronic engineer
school principal	custodian	mechanical engineer
waiter/waitress	assembler	
	truck driver	
	factory supervisor	

Note: Numbers of employees in parentheses are approximations by Charles Healy based on extrapolations from data in the 1979 *Occupational Outlook Handbook* for principal occupations within field. Workers at all levels, from unskilled to professional, are included.

they might consider entering. The counselor then distributes a sheet (Figure 10–7) with occupations grouped into Holland's (1959) six clusters, and helps the clients to discover the basis of each cluster. Each client proceeds by identifying the clusters to which the occupations listed belong. Clients with more than one occupation from a cluster are asked to rate only one or two occupations from that cluster. Next, the counselor explains the use of a seven- or five- or three-point rating scale and illustrates its use by leading the group in rating two occupations on

Figure 10–8. Instructions for Occupational Rating

Please rate the six occupations on the work-relevant qualities you wrote down by lining up your list of qualities with the rating sheet so that line #1 on the rating sheet corresponds with line #1 on your list. To rate an occupation, think about the typical successful person in the occupation and rate what you believe he or she is like on the 7-point scale described below. Even though each member of a given occupation is unique, the duties of the occupation tend to make people in it similar to each other and these duties attract people with similar interests. Consequently, we can think of and therefore describe by rating, a typical basketball player, pharmacist, machinist, etc.
Use your rating to mean the following:

1. A person in the occupation is very low in the quality. About 95% of adults are higher.
2. A person in the occupation is low in the quality. About 75% of adults are higher.
3.–4.–5. A person in the occupation is about average in the quality.
6. A person in the occupation is high in the quality. He is higher than 75% or more of adults in general.
7. A person in the occupation is very high in the quality. He is higher than 95% of adults.

As an example: *basketball player* is rated below.

Traits	Basketball player rating
tall	7
mathematical	3
uses language well	4
agile	6
learns quickly	4

some of the qualities individual members have chosen. Following this activity, the clients rate the six occupations on their work-relevant traits (Figure 10–8).

To meet objective three, guide group members into: (a) asking one another for help; (b) analyzing their experience in order to make a specific rating; and (c) noting information they lack, but can obtain. When clients disagree about a rating or lack information, the counselor encourages them to recall ways of securing occupational information, such as reading, observing workers, or asking employers. After the occupational ratings are finished, the counselor asks for reactions and feelings about the ratings, and when someone lacks information of interest, the counselor elicits a commitment to obtain the information and to share the experiences in gathering it at session three.

Session 3

The objectives of the third session are that each client accurately rate oneself on the qualities chosen in session one, recall and use appraisal methods, and compute the differences between the self and occupational ratings. The clients first report their extracounseling tasks and summarize sessions one and two. The counselor explains the function of self-rating and elicits the clients' reactions. Clients usually question the subjectivity of self-ratings and of the whole procedure. If the clients do not raise the issue of subjectivity, the counselor should. In ensuing discussion, the counselor emphasizes that the procedure depends on every client's having and reporting ideas about occupations and self, which are realistic and not inflated by social desirability. The counselor helps clients recognize that expending the effort to obtain such knowledge and to recall ways of knowing themselves is in their interest. For example, clients enumerate ways of knowing self accurately, such as: deliberating about one's experiences, taking tests and receiving interpretations of them. After rating themselves on the work-relevant qualities, the clients share their reactions, but not their ratings, especially concerning those qualities about which they would like more knowledge. The counselor helps them decide how to obtain such knowledge.

To accomplish objective three, each client computes the sum of absolute differences between the self and each occupational rating and subtracts that sum from 100 ($100 - \sum_{1}^{n}$ self-rating–occupation rating) (see Figure 10–9). The self-rating is aligned with each occupational rating, and the differences are added. After inspecting ones difference scores in order to determine similarity to each occupation, the client shares initial reactions and the group briefly discusses them.

In applying and researching the procedure and in teaching counselors how to use it, this author found that the computation of difference scores is sometimes difficult or distracting, and perhaps misleading. Although difference scores have correlated moderately with *SVIB* scores (Healy, 1968), their function is not predictive: The objective of their

Figure 10–9. Computation of Difference Scores

To compute the difference between your rating of yourself and the ratings of each of the representative occupations:

1. Put your self-rating next to a representative occupational rating;
2. Subtract one rating from the other and disregard the + or − sign;
3. Write the number in the space to the right of the dotted line; and
4. Add the column of differences in order to determine your perceived similarity to the occupation.

For example, the computations below were done for John Doe and the occupations of basketball player and school teacher.

Traits	John Doe Self	Basketball player		John Doe Self	Teacher	
tall	2	7	=5	2	3	=1
mathematical	5	3	=2	5	5	=0
uses language well	4	4	=0	4	5	=1
agile	4	6	=2	4	4	=0
learns quickly	5	4	=1	5	4	=1
			10			3

computation is to stimulate a client to weigh a particular occupation's appropriateness on a series of characteristics simultaneously. Indeed, the scores themselves are not likely to measure the fit of a particular occupation accurately because each characteristic is weighted equally, whereas they are likely to be weighted differentially by the translator, and because the self and occupational ratings have had only limited verification. In fact, the author's own research has failed to find correlations between fit for an occupation measured by the difference scores computed within counseling, and certainty or satisfaction with career plans following counseling, or gain in certainty or in satisfaction (Healy, 1974b).

As a consequence, the author is studying the following alternative to computing a difference score. The client, after rating the occupations, pictures each occupation separately and estimates whether the occupation fits on each characteristic, writing *yes* or *no* beside the rating for the quality. After considering all occupations, the client tallies the suitability estimates and considers whether those occupations with the most yeses offer the best opportunity for expression. Then, the client shares personal reasons for accepting one or more occupations as potentially suitable and reacts to feedback about the choice and rationale.

Session 4

The objectives of session four are that each client examine the implications of difference scores in the group and formulate a plan of action consistent with these scores. After the report of between-session tasks and a client summary of preceding sessions, clients share their difference scores and their feelings to them. The client who is satisfied with the difference scores then considers entering an occupation, such as those in the Holland cluster, to which he or she is similar. Group members discuss steps of entering the specific occupation, clarify the need for additional information, and share their reactions to the client's identification with that occupation. Positiveness is encouraged.

During the interaction, the counselor relates the plans of at least one client to formal planning by labeling the components of the client's plan. (The planning labels are these: set goals, specify and weigh alternatives, select one alternative, carry out plan, and evaluate the plan.) If the labels of the planning paradigm indicate the client's plan is incomplete, the group helps to complete the plan. Subsequent clients are encouraged to use the labels in formulating their plans.

Clients who are dissatisfied with their difference scores seek the source of their dissatisfaction and plan corrective action. Those who dislike their identification with specific occupational groups, but feel a similarity is real, consider methods by which to change themselves and/or to examine the implications of accepting the similarity. Those whose difference scores are not differentiated, review the accuracy of their self and occupational ratings. One major reason for lack of differentiation is hasty rating. Such clients either re-rate the self and the occupations, or they re-examine their ratings to determine those qualities in which they are especially interested and then compute difference scores for only those qualities. If there still is no differentiation, clients are encouraged to name how the occupations differ and to identify what their preferences are regarding the differences.

Session 5

The objectives of session five are that the clients report their efforts in implementing their plans and consider problem-solving strategies for overcoming obstacles to their plans. Clients first report their extra-counseling tasks and summarize the previous sessions. The clients who re-rated and recomputed their difference scores share their results and feelings and speculate about how to enter the occupations suggested.

Clients who had made plans in session four are asked to discuss their first implementation efforts and to specify the concrete actions they can take next. As plans become more concrete, the counselor, in accord with the second objective, asks the group to name obstacles that might prevent individual clients from executing their plans. The individual client and group brainstorm methods for coping with such obstacles. The counselor relates the coping methods to the problem-solving steps by labeling the components of the solutions and by encouraging the clients to use the labels when discussing the obstacles and the solutions of subsequent plans. The problem-solving components are these: specify goals, define obstacles, determine alternative solutions, weigh alternatives, select and try alternatives, and evaluate outcome. The counselor concludes by summarizing the five sessions and by congratulating the clients on having completed the procedure.

To illustrate key elements, Figure 10–10 presents excerpts of group translation counseling with junior college students.

Figure 10–10. Excerpts from Translation Counseling

Session 1: Obtaining Commitment After Explanation of Procedure

Counselor: Tell us Barbara, in what way will you be helped by attending these meetings?

Barbara: Well, you said we would consider what we want to do and find out what jobs allow that. I need to do that because I am not sure about what I want to do, and I'd like to see how the others do it. Did you say we would take tests?

Counselor: Like Fran, you feel a need to think through what you want to get from working and see what jobs might have those things. Good! We'll be doing that. And testing, we won't give you tests here, but you can see Mr. C in the Counseling Center for testing if you feel testing will provide needed information. Does counseling seem like it will help you Barbara?

Barbara: Yeah, it sounds O.K.

SOURCE: C. C. Healy. *Career counseling in the community college.* Springfield, Ill.: Thomas, 1974.

Figure 10–10. (*Continued*)

Session 1: Sharing Qualities

Paul: Some of the qualities important to me are high salary, entertaining, big business, be my own boss, and having recognition.

Counselor: What do you say about Paul?

Fran: Well, executives could have them all.

Doris: They require a lot of education and aggressiveness.

Paul: Yeah, entertainment is aggressive, sort of. Not mean aggressive, just willing to get out and hustle and do your best.

Mary: And step on people to get on top.

Paul: No, I wouldn't hurt anyone; I am not competitive in a mean way, but fair.

Counselor: So having these qualities is pointing out that you are competitive.

Fran: I can tell that already.

Paul: I know that, but it is not too important.

Counselor: Should you have it on your list of work-relevant traits as something about a job that you would want to consider?

Paul: I guess so. I like to compete some, and the job would not interest me if there weren't some challenges in it. At least a little competition.

Session 2: Sharing Occupations

Steve: My occupations are a credit manager, advertising manager, production manager, principal, engineer, and physician.

Counselor: Do they say anything about you Steve?

Steve: I don't think so, nothing in particular.

Fran: They are all on top. I feel that you want to get to the top.

Paul: Yeah. In all of them you tell others what to do. You're kind of a boss.

Counselor: Does that sound like something important in a job—managing people?

Steve: I like to. I like directing things and people. They usually go along. I'm not bad at it.

Counselor: Great! That sounds like something that you really want to keep in mind.

Session 3: Deciding on Needed Occupational Information

Doris: I don't know how much schooling hospital administrators need.

Paul: Oh, they need a master's.

Counselor: Asking people is a good information source, and it was good of you to volunteer that information Paul. Are there other ways Doris could find out about schooling required?

Doris: I could look it up in that occupational book or ask someone.

Paul: Yeah! Go down to the hospital and ask the administrators. They have to know.

Counselor: Will you do that for next time?

Doris: Well, I'll try, and if I can I'll find out more about the job because I only have a general idea about it.

Counselor: Sounds like something worth doing. We'll expect you to tell us about your findings next time. O.K.?

Figure 10–10. (*Continued*)

Session 4: Reactions to Difference Scores

Counselor:	O.K. Barbara, suppose you tell us about your difference scores.
Barbara:	Well, they sound the most like dental hygienist, but I don't know.
Counselor:	You are not sure dental hygienist fits you?
Barbara:	No. I'd like dental hygienist, but I don't know if I could do it. I'm O.K. in biology, but I don't know.
Doris:	But you gotta try. If you put your mind to it, you could do it.
Steve:	When I try something it usually works out. You just gotta try.
Barbara:	Well, there is a lot of responsibility, and well, secretary is also close and I wouldn't mind working in an office. I would be with people.
Paul:	That would be less responsible.
Doris:	Or maybe you could take a less responsible dental job.
Barbara:	I don't know, secretary is all right, or maybe a receptionist.
Paul:	Receptionist is easy, but it doesn't pay much. All you need is some typing. How well do you type?
Barbara:	I'm doing O.K. in typing and steno.
Counselor:	But getting back to dental hygienist, are you saying you wouldn't consider it because you don't feel confident?
Barbara:	Well, it is a lot of responsibility. I don't know.
Fran:	Yeah! Not feeling confident seems to fit you. You weren't confident in waitressing or in YWCA receptionist. Perhaps you could take a job helping people at a lower level, requiring less skill.
Doris:	But you did O.K. in school and won't low confidence stop you in secretarial?
Fran:	Yeah! That's right.
Barbara:	O.K., O.K., you like helping people and you know you can do it, but even though I want to, I don't know I can. Like babysitting, I love kids but I lose patience when they scream. Kids are great but I don't want to traumatize them.
Doris:	But you can learn patience. You can play games or read. Kids will behave.
Barbara:	But I don't want to let anybody down. You know. Medical work is serious; you can't make mistakes.
Doris:	You could change.
Barbara:	I don't know. People don't change. I know lots of people who try to change and they don't.
Counselor:	Doris and Fran are pointing out that your low esteem is preventing you from doing something you want to do. Maybe you could do something . . .
Barbara:	(low voice) I know.
Doris:	Yeah! Maybe you could go in at a lower level, and build up your confidence. Working with adults doesn't require that much patience. Even two or three would be enough.
Fran:	You have to try. You just can't give up.
Paul:	Yeah! That's important in business. Never give up.
Counselor:	Barbara?
Barbara:	Well . . . I'll try to find out more about the qualifications and think about it more. Maybe I could start lower and get confidence.
Doris:	I think you can do it.
Counselor:	Where will you get more information?

Figure 10–10. (*Continued*)

Barbara:	In that Occupational Outlook Book that Fran used.
Steve:	And you can talk to Mrs. Y. She teaches dental hygiene.
Counselor:	O.K. Suppose we talk about your thinking next time, Barbara, and see where you are. O.K.?
Barbara:	O.K.

Session 5: Problem Solving

Counselor:	Last week Barbara was hesitating about dental hygienist because she lacked confidence. Lack of confidence was an obstacle to her goal. What are some alternatives for getting around that obstacle?
Barbara:	Well, I read more about it and talked to Mrs. Y. It didn't sound as hard as I thought, but I'm going Tuesday to watch a dental hygienist work. I think I will try it, though.
Counselor:	O.K. Barbara is using one alternative to tackling the obstacle. What is she doing?
Paul:	She is not worrying, and she is asking questions instead.
Counselor:	Good! She is getting more information to see whether she should be worried. Are there other ways she should attack the obstacle of low confidence?
Doris:	She could study and practice hard in training so she would be good, so she could build up her confidence.
Paul:	Yeah! She could start lower and work up to it like we said last time, or she could just relax and forget about it. You have to try things and not worry about how well you do. Before I do a show I'm scared, but I just do it and it works. You can't worry.
Counselor:	Good! You have given some alternate ways of handling confidence—to learn more about what is asked of you, to practice so you can improve, to start at a level you can handle, and to try your best without worrying.
Fran:	You could use them all. Yeah! They make sense.
Counselor:	Barbara, do you think that you will be able to use them?
Barbara:	I am going to try it out as a major. I do O.K. in school and I will work hard. I don't know if I can just stop worrying. I am not as worried—but everybody worries. It's helped thinking about what I'm going to do and getting more information. I think it will be O.K.
Steve & Doris:	You're right to try.

Vocational Choice Case Study Counseling

Counselors at the University of Minnesota and at California State University at Hayward adapted the case study to help clients make an occupational choice by analyzing case study data about themselves and fellow clients. Each client presents his or her own case, and he or she and the group examine the data as if they were staffing a case. All clients organize their cases, which consist of data from testing and other sources relative to interests, aptitudes, achievement, and values. They present their case to the group for staffing and react to questions and suggestions about characteristics, experiences, relationships among them, and their implications for career options.

Hewer (1959; 1968) assisted by Volsky at the University of Minnesota, and Sprague and Strong (1971), at California State University at Hayward, successfully used the case study procedure with college underclassmen. Their procedures include the following steps: orientation, information acquisition, interpretation of test results, explanation of other data to be discussed in the case studies, presentation by each client of individual appraisal data in a case study format, and periodic progress reports by clients. The sequence of case study counseling is described below. Figure 10–11 illustrates the picture that case study counseling produces for a client.

Orientation

The first session launches the program by teaching the clients about the process and by giving them a chance to get acquainted. The counselor starts by explaining what clients will do and how they will interact with one another during the case presentations. The counselor clarifies that the purpose of the process is to help them consider alternate career goals, weigh pertinent factors, discover needed information, learn how to integrate self and career information to establish a goal, and begin building and implementing a plan for their career.

Following the overview, the counselor helps clients get acquainted. Using modeling, explanation, and reinforcement, the counselor structures the introduction process so that clients realize they are expected to broaden their understanding of one another's career aspirations and problems, feelings about their careers, and their history as it relates to career.

Next, the counselor introduces the tests and inventories to be used, shows clients how to induce a hypothetical model of themselves, reviews ways to obtain occupational information in order to construct models of different occupational options against which to compare the self-models, and illustrates how to compile and present a case.

In introducing the tests, the counselor provides clear, nontechnical descriptions of what different scores mean and how they can be related to possible occupational options. For example, the author has introduced SCII occupational scores in the following manner:

> The SCII occupational score tells how similar your SCII responses are to people in the particular occupations. They don't indicate whether you can qualify for the occupation. You have to examine the duties, entry requirements, and competition in order to judge whether you will be able to get in. A score of 45 or higher indicates that many people in the occupation answered the SCII in a way comparable to you. In contrast, a score of 30 or lower indicates few if any of them share your interests. Chances are that

Figure 10–11. An Illustration of Case Study Counseling

Henrietta is a twenty-eight-year-old married woman who is pursuing a Ph.D. in the social sciences but has not decided which occupation to enter. She is the eldest child in a high achieving, upwardly mobile Southern California family. From her earliest memory, she has been competing athletically and academically with talented brothers. Her desire to win and to lead has been intense, and she has persisted in competition in spite of being chided for her lack of femininity by some of her teachers. Neither has she received encouragement from her mother, who prefers a homemaking role for herself.

Henrietta has mixed feelings about her competitiveness. She has enjoyed the activities and rewards striving produced, but at times she feels her competitiveness has resulted in her being isolated and rejected. In college she was active in several social organizations and earned high grades; but, nevertheless, she was unable to choose a particular occupation.

She was optimistic at graduation, hoping to conquer the world of work as she had mastered academia. The recession of the early 1970s was in full swing, however, and Henrietta had to take a series of unskilled and semiskilled jobs. After trying to market herself with only a B.A. in anthropology, as some male peers were doing, Henrietta accepted that she needed an "entry skill." Enlightened, but undaunted, she completed a six-month secretarial program and landed a job as a secretary in a midwestern college admission's office. Her organizational and communication skills impressed the dean, and when an assistant dean's position opened, Henrietta obtained the job. After securing the position, Henrietta entered a M.A. counseling program to augment her skills for the deanship and to explore more fully the counseling program. Coincidentally, she met and renewed her relationship with a college beau and soon married.

After securing her master's degree, Henrietta and her husband relocated, and Henrietta secured another assistant deanship. The challenge of this job diminished after a year, although she was performing well.

She therefore engaged in case-study counseling to learn more about the procedure and to consider options—especially the possibility of earning a doctorate in counseling, administration, or clinical psychology.

Test Results

Henrietta's SCII and OPI profile appear in Figures 10–12 and 10–13, respectively. Her GRE verbal score was 730 and her quantitative score was 640, placing her in the upper 5 percentile of college graduates in scholastic potential. In college and in her M.A. program, Henrietta earned As and A-s. These achievements also indicated strong potential for further graduate study. In college, Henrietta preferred challenging courses and worked hardest in statistical and computational courses because they were difficult and in anthropology courses because she enjoyed them.

On the SCII Henrietta compiled a moderately high S theme, an average A theme, and low R, I, E and C themes. Her Holland code was SAE or SAC. Her high basic interest scales were teaching, social service, domestic arts, and public speaking. Her low scales were adventure, military, science, math, medical service, sales, business management, and office. Her high f-referenced occupations were English teacher, YWCA staff, guidance counselor, recreation leader, elementary school teacher, and home economics teacher. Her high m-referenced occupational scales were speech pathologist, interior decorator, advertising executive, reporter, English teacher, public administrator, guidance counselor, social science teacher, personnel director, and lawyer.

On the OPI, Henrietta portrayed herself as moderately intellectual compared to college students, although preferring the concrete more than most. She has higher need for autonomy and for helping others and felt relatively more positively about her overall mental health.

In regard to occupational similarity, Henrietta indicated that her five highest occupations (English teacher, reporter, advertising executive, YWCA staff, ele-

Figure 10–11. (Continued)

mentary teacher) did not surprise her, since she felt the activities of these occupations would be very compatible with her interests. She was somewhat perplexed when a peer pointed out that she was high only on male advertising executive and reporter, perhaps because her typically feminine art and literary interests made her more like males in these occupations than like men in general; but since many women had these interests, they did not make her more like the women in the occupations than like women in general. Wondering aloud, Henrietta noted that she had been assertive, competitive, creative, and more inquiring than many of her peers in the past, and as a consequence she had felt advertising executive, reporter and lawyer might be possible occupations. Even her public speaking interest supported these fields. In reaction, another peer wondered, hesitatingly, whether she might be more domestically oriented, like her mother, than she was admitting and wondered whether she was not in conflict about pursuing further graduate work.

Unperturbed, Henrietta said that domestic arts were very much an enjoyed hobby. She sews her own clothes, bakes bread, and keeps a vegetable garden. She was not denying her interest, but instead she was surprised that her leadership experiences had not emerged more clearly, for she definitely saw herself as helping, but also as willing to speak out and take charge of helping activities.

Implications of Test Scores

Turning to the implications of the SCII for a Ph.D., Henrietta said that a person with her profile typically would not be pursuing such a degree. Her AOR score was very low and her scores in investigative pursuits and occupations were low. Nevertheless, her grades and GRE scores clearly indicated that she could handle Ph.D. work. A reconciliation of these contradictory data could be found, she felt, in the view that she preferred the concrete and practical rather than the esoteric, and therefore a doctorate in an applied field such as counseling or administration would not be incompatible. Indeed, her academic experience has taught her that she enjoys challenge, such as a Ph.D. thesis. Summarizing, Henrietta felt that the overall picture emerging was that she felt no constraint to follow a "typical feminine career path," although she had some traditional female interests. She further noted that tolerance for different ideas and preference for minimal social controls, which characterized autonomous, fit her wishes for herself, and high altruistic, clearly described her. Proceeding, she explained that her high personal integration seemed accurate since she is a confident person, in charge of herself and her environment. The low anxiety level, indeed, indicated her comfort with herself.

Responding, a peer noted that Henrietta was explaining the scores well, but he wondered whether anything new emerged from her completion of the inventory and its interpretation. For instance, he was surprised that the highs and lows were not more pronounced. After a moment's consideration, Henrietta said she had not considered that question, especially, but would think about it. The OPI had not produced any surprises, but she felt reinforced that her mental health was high relative to students. Sometimes, she added, she did feel some conflict when pondering about a Ph.D. helping her to enter a challenging, helping position, on the one hand; and thinking about her family roles, on the other. The SCII, in contrast, was somewhat surprising, especially her low psychologist score and lower-than-anticipated E theme and occupation scores. As a result of these scores, she did not consider clinical psychology or administration as much a possibility, although she would explore them further.

Reporting back several weeks later, Henrietta told how she had found out more about counseling and was thinking about counselor education as a possible goal. Her assurance and writing interests, she noted, could help her do practical rather than scholarly activities. Moreover, limited counseling practice in preparation for the field would be very informative in helping her ultimately decide.

Figure 10-12. Henrietta's Omnibus Personality Inventory Profile

Scales	Raw Score	Std. Score[a]	Standard Scores

a. SCORES ABOVE 80 ARE PLOTTED AS 80; SCORES BELOW 20 ARE PLOTTED AS 20.

Intellectual Disposition Category: _____ 5 _____ (See manual for explanation.)

Scales	Raw Score	Std. Score[a]
Thinking Introversion (TI)	31	57
Theoretical Orientation (TO)	19	49
Estheticism (Es)	14	53
Complexity (Co)	9	39
Autonomy (Au)	37	66
Religious Orientation (RO)	12	50
Social Extroversion (SE)	22	48
Impulse Expression (IE)	29	54
Personal Integration (PI)	48	67
Anxiety Level (AL)	17	60
Altruism (Am)	28	63
Practical Outlook (PO)	10	42
Masculinity—Femininity (MF)	23	42
Response Bias (RB)	16	56

you are more likely to enjoy working in an occupation on which you have a high score than in one in which you have a low score. If you are looking for occupations which are likely to be interesting for you, it is logical to start by examining those for which you have high scores. If you are already considering particular occupations, you can regard a high score as providing one more bit of evidence that the occupation would be attractive and a low score as indicating that you should investigate whether the people doing that kind of work are obtaining the satisfactions you seek. If they are not, you will need to ask yourself what can be special about you that will enable you to be different in the occupation.

The information about tests and guidelines for examining occupations is likely to be extensive and could be made into a workbook to be used in conjunction with counseling. Having to present one's own case will motivate most clients to pore over these materials.

Once clients understand what counseling involves and the standardized instruments available to them, they can help determine other kinds of data to be included in the cases. One question (such as "Should your grades and your parents' social class be part of the case since they affect many people's careers?") can assure that all relevant information is included. In addition, one might brainstorm possibilities and then let each client choose the kinds of information to be added. This approach should increase clients' ownership of counseling, thereby increasing their openness about themselves and assuring that the elements that they believe are relevant to career are included in the case. Occasionally, this activity also will raise questions such as whether to mention a past psychological disturbance, a criminal record, or the like.

By the close of orientation, counselor and client should have agreed on the data that will be in the case study, even though they may add other kinds of information as the cases develop.

Testing and Information Acquisition

Several different inventories and tests, including the *Strong Vocational Interest Blank (SVIB)*, the *Strong-Campbell Interest Inventory (SCII)*, the *Kuder Occupational Interest Survey (KOIS)* (1966), the *General Aptitude Test Battery (GATB)* (1958), and the *Career Planning Program (CPP)* (1972), are appropriate for use in case study counseling. In addition to the standardized inventories, this author recommends that clients consider sampling work simulations such as the Krumboltz kits (1972) and complete an in-depth autobiography or perhaps an "experiography," which, according to Barkhaus and Bolgard (1976), is a collection of significant experiences such as working or interacting with significant others. The counselor should also help clients secure prescriptive testing of abilities of particular concern to them, and if time permits, encourage

Figure 10–13. Henrietta's Strong-Campbell Interest Inventory Profile

SVIB-SCII PROFILE

F 812 1341 1

DATE SCORED	01/30/78
TOTAL RESPONSES	325

STRONG-CAMPBELL INTEREST INVENTORY OF THE STRONG VOCATIONAL INTEREST BLANK

PROFILE FOR USE WITH BOOKLET T325 STANFORD UNIV. PRESS

OCCUPATIONAL SCALES

CODE	SCALE	NORM	STD SCORE
RIA	OCCUP. THERAP.	f	43
RIE	A.F. OFFICER	m	6
RIC	ARMY OFFICER	m	23
RIC	CARTOGRAPHER	m	13
RI	VETERINARIAN	m	9
RI	NURSE, REGIST.	m	25
RI	NAVY OFFICER	m	18
RI	MERCH. MAR. OFF.	m	21
RI	RAD. TECH. (X-RAY)	f	15
RI	FORESTER	m	27
R	SKILLED CRAFTS	m	8
RS	PHYS. ED. TEACH.	f	34
RE	ARMY OFFICER	f	23
RSE	HWY. PAT. OFF.	m	5
RES	POLICE OFF.	m	19
REC	DIETITIAN	m	38
RCE	VOC. AG. TCHR.	m	9
RC	INSTR. ASSEMBL.	f	17
RC	FARMER	m	6
CRE	BEAUTICIAN	f	35
CRI	NURSE, L. P.	f	19
CR	DENTAL ASSIST.	f	22
C	SECRETARY	f	31
C	ACCOUNTANT	f	12
CSE	EXEC. HOUSEKPR.	f	25
CES	BUS. ED. TCHR.	m	26
CE	BUS. ED. TCHR.	f	24
CE	DEPT. STORE SLS.	f	17
CE	CREDIT MGR.	f	22
CE	BANKER	m	36
CE	BANKER	f	25
CE	ACCOUNTANT	f	7
ESR	CHIROPRACTOR	m	19
ERC	PURCH. AGENT	m	15
ERC	AGRIBUS. MGR.	m	7
ECR	REALTOR	m	25
ECS	FUNERAL DIR.	m	26
ECS	CREDIT MGR.	m	25
ECS	BUYER	m	27
EC	BUYER	f	23
EIC	PHARMACIST	m	9
EI	INV. FUND MGR.	m	43
EI	COMPUT. SALES	m	16
E	LAWYER	m	47
E	LAWYER	f	30
E	LIFE INS. AGENT	f	30
ES	LIFE INS. AGENT	m	27
ES	SALES MGR.	m	25
ES	CH.OF COMM.EXEC.	m	38
ESA	FLIGHT ATTEND.	f	37
ESC	HOME ECON.TCHR.	f	48
ESC	DEPT. STR. MGR.	m	31
SEC	PER. DIR.	m	45
SEC	SOC. SCI. TCHR.	m	47
SEC	SOC. SCI. TCHR.	f	44
SEC	GUID. COUNS.	f	45
SEC	RECREATION LDR.	m	38
SER	RECREATION LDR.	f	51
SCE	GUID. COUNS.	m	47
SCE	PUBLIC ADMIN.	f	46
SCE	SCHL. SUPT.	m	42
SC	ELEM. TEACHER	f	39

(Score ranges: 15, 25, 45, 55 — VERY DISSIMILAR, DISSIMILAR, AVE, SIMILAR, VERY SIMILAR)

SOURCE: *Strong-Campbell Interest Inventory Profile*. Minneapolis, Minn.: Interpretative Scoring Systems. Reprinted by permission.

Figure 10–13. (Continued)

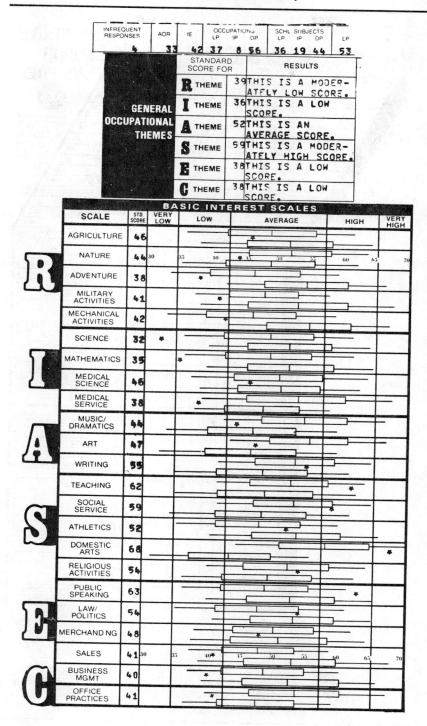

INFREQUENT RESPONSES	AOR	IE	OCCUPATIONS LP	IP	DP	SCHL SUBJECTS LP	IP	DP	LP
4	33	42	37	8	56	36	19	44	53

GENERAL OCCUPATIONAL THEMES	STANDARD SCORE FOR	RESULTS
	R THEME	39 THIS IS A MODER-ATELY LOW SCORE.
	I THEME	36 THIS IS A LOW SCORE.
	A THEME	52 THIS IS AN AVERAGE SCORE.
	S THEME	59 THIS IS A MODER-ATELY HIGH SCORE.
	E THEME	38 THIS IS A LOW SCORE.
	C THEME	38 THIS IS A LOW SCORE.

BASIC INTEREST SCALES

SCALE	STD. SCORE	VERY LOW	LOW	AVERAGE	HIGH	VERY HIGH
AGRICULTURE	46					
NATURE	44					
ADVENTURE	38					
MILITARY ACTIVITIES	41					
MECHANICAL ACTIVITIES	42					
SCIENCE	32					
MATHEMATICS	35					
MEDICAL SCIENCE	46					
MEDICAL SERVICE	38					
MUSIC/ DRAMATICS	44					
ART	47					
WRITING	55					
TEACHING	62					
SOCIAL SERVICE	59					
ATHLETICS	52					
DOMESTIC ARTS	68					
RELIGIOUS ACTIVITIES	54					
PUBLIC SPEAKING	63					
LAW/ POLITICS	54					
MERCHANDING	48					
SALES	41					
BUSINESS MGMT	40					
OFFICE PRACTICES	41					

Figure 10–13. (*Continued*)

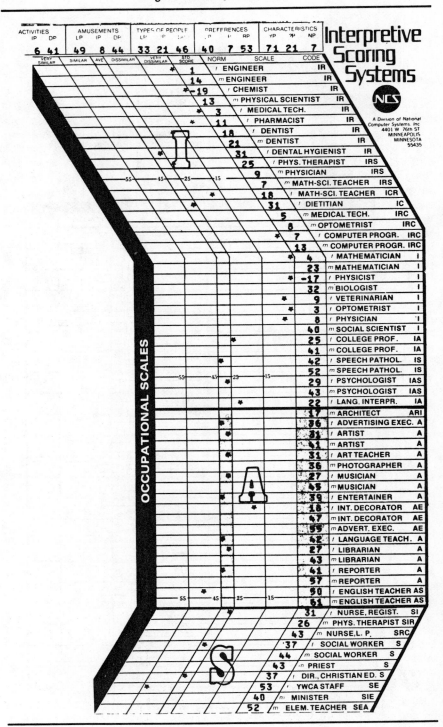

them to study particular career situations by shadowing cooperative workers or advanced students.

Interpretation

As data are accumulated, clients can organize them in an orderly manner and interpret them systematically by using forms, such as Magoon's (1969) in Figure 10-1. Interpretation can proceed either by constructing a hypothetical person from the accumulating data or by tallying the data as supporting or questioning potential choices. In the former, for instance, one would interpret high mechanical and scientific interest, in addition to high spatial ability and moderate numerical ability, as indicating a person who enjoys discovering and working with gadgets and machinery, is very competent in picturing objects from their blueprints, and moderately effective in numerical work. In the later method, interpretation would relate to particular options; for example, engineering school, business school, and social science. Mechanical interest, therefore, would lead to a plus for engineering, but be nonrelevant for business and social science; scientific would register plus for engineering and social science, but not relevant for business; spatial would be plus for engineering and neutral for business and social science; and numerical would be plus for all three.

Although Hewer and Volsky (1959) and Sprague and Strong (1970) do not state explicitly whether clients used psychological test manuals without assistance, clients should have a written or oral guide for using a manual and should review their test interpretations with a paraprofessional or counselor before integrating them into the case study. The detailed computer explanations of test results furnished by companies such as Roche and Minicorp might be an acceptable substitute, but data are not available to evaluate their use.

If there is no individual session or printout, the counselor should at least walk the group through one interpretation of each test, underscoring the major contributions of each instrument.

Client Presentation of Data

Teaching others often clarifies a subject for the instructor. Organizing and presenting one's own case to a supportive group should help the individual clarify personal career potential. The supportive atmosphere will make it easy to identify new alternatives, potential problems, and inconsistencies, and to accept suggestions for change and follow-up.

In this phase of counseling, the counselor can act as moderator/recorder—encouraging interchange, assuring that staffers present and react to major issues, underscoring comments, and generating public commitment to follow-through. The counselor should confer with the client after the presentation to review major comments and to guide the reintegration. In following through, the counselor can also correct errors in the case without embarrassing the client.

In overseeing a presentation, a counselor should maximize client control while assuring that essential factors in career development are covered. Although not essential, a uniform method of reporting one's case would facilitate asking the standardized questions. Some questions to guide a client in considering his or her case are these: "What kinds of people are in occupations for which I have primary or secondary interest patterns?" Or, if no primary or secondary interest patterns, "What kinds of people are in occupations in which I have As, and in what kinds of activities do they engage?" "How do these activities compare to mine?" "How could I obtain more information about the occupation?" "What abilities and training are required of persons in occupations that interest me?" "How do my achievements and plans compare with those requirements?" "What specific courses and experiences are needed to enter such occupations?" "What additional thinking and planning do I need to do?" "How will friends and family react to my membership in the occupation of interest, how will training and occupational duties influence my life style, and what will I be like five years after entry into the occupation?"

Progress Report

The final phase of counseling involves reporting progress in implementation efforts. Staffers will be interested in knowing whether their interpretations and recommendations are working out, and each client will feel an incentive to begin carrying out a plan if he or she knows that peers expect to find out what is happening. To set the proper tone, counselors should initiate progress reports with clients who are following through effectively.

Frequently, an early presenter will glean many new insights from later presentations, and a client's ongoing participation in the group can illuminate strengths and needs. In preparing progress reports, therefore, counselors might ask clients to reflect on aspects of peers' cases that are pertinent to them and what their group contribution suggests about their career. For example, the counselor can help the client whose enthusiasm for career planning has increased by being a member of this career advancement group to recognize that support-group membership was a significant factor and to consider how to secure another group's support for career efforts when the case study group terminates.

Validity

The validity of career-decision counseling is based primarily on rationale and secondarily on empirical evidence. The heuristic principles underlying each procedure are identified below, followed by an overview of the empirical support for each of the procedures. The empirical studies support the thesis that some counselors have administered career-choice counseling with some benefit to some clients. The studies are summarized to acquaint the reader with the scope of formal evaluation research.

Table 10–1. Goals of Career Decision-making Counseling

Goal	Measure	Study
1. Client will have a career goal which is satisfying and of which he is certain	self-rating	Healy (1973b, 1974b); Fogel (1973); Ogilvie (1977); Snodgras (1978); Forgy & Black (1954); Hoyt (1955)
	self-report	Barahal, Brammer, & Shostrom (1950)
2. Client will have a career plan which is congruent with his assets and the state of economy	expert rating from records	Hanson & Sander (1973)
3. Client can describe a process for resolving career problems which at least includes: specifying goal, generating alternatives, evaluating alternatives, implementing favorable alternatives, evaluating implementation	expert rating cognitive test	Snodgras (1978)
4. Client can describe a process for selecting a goal, including identifying factors to consider, how to become informed, how to hierarchize objectives	expert rating cognitive test	none
5. Client will increase capacity to solve career problems and to pick appropriate career options	CMI NMCETS	Fogel (1973); Snodgras (1978)
6. Client will increase understanding of career choice process, including its continuity, the benefits of changing based upon feedback, etc.	Harren Vocational Decision Checklist self-rating	Smith & Evans (1973) Wachowiak (1972) Graff, Danish & Austin (1972)
7. Client will increase accuracy of self-estimates and improve ability to infer self-attributes from data	CMI NMCETS	Flake, Roach, & Stenning (1975)
8. Client will increase deliberation about career and increase information seeking	CDI self-report	Healy (1973b, 1974b); Mirov (1974) Krivatsy & Magoon (1978); Nolan (1973); Graff & Maclean (1970)
9. Client will perform more effectively in career as evidenced by higher grades or reduced absenteeism, higher productivity	grade check rating by experts	Williamson & Bordin (1940) Williamson & Bordin (1940); Campbell (1963)

Following the research summaries, Table 10–1 lists outcome objectives and measurement methods appropriate for evaluating career-choice counseling and notes the studies in which the objectives and measures appeared.

Trait-factor Counseling

Trait-factor counseling, unlike other career-choice counseling, stresses the importance of accurately characterizing people and career options and of objectively fitting people with options. Williamson (1939, 1949) assumed that a professional expertise rendered a counselor more capable than the client to identify personal characteristics pertinent to career, to decide how to estimate them, and to interpret their implications for the suitability of particular options. Although today's counselor is more modest, the trait-factor counselor still retains responsibility for designating pertinent characteristics and advising clients how to estimate them, and for informing clients about the likely fit of particular options. Although the counselor cannot know the particulars of every occupation, he or she is expert in how to obtain occupational information. Almost always, trait-factor counseling includes objective testing and use of actuarial prediction.

Logically accurate information is an essential ingredient of effective decision making. Systematic collection and review of self and occupational information with an objective, trained observer should increase the accuracy of such information. Similarly, expert direction should assure a more objective fitting of self to available options. Neither postulate has been tested directly. But contrasts of the actuarial and clinical models repeatedly have shown that assessing characteristics by test, inventory, or rating, and weighting the scores in accord with discriminant or regression equations are more effective in predicting performance on a particular criterion for groups of people than is having a clinician identify, assess, and weight; assess and weight without identifying; or only weight the same characteristics (Kelly & Fiske, 1951).

In regard to specific heuristics, trait-factor counseling uses planning principles 1, 2, 4, and 8 on page 417, individual difference principles 1, 2, and 3 on pages 417–418, commitment to occupation group principles 1 and 5 on page 418, and commitment to action principles 1, 2, and 3 on page 418. Homework assignments could increase the power of these principles, however, and might bring other principles to bear. For example, in the reconnaissance phase, an exercise such as contrasting good and poor financial decisions in order to identify actions associated with successful personal decision making could deepen the person's self-awareness.

Early validation. In one of the most definitive studies of counseling effectiveness, Williamson and Bordin (1940) contrasted 384 Minnesota students who had received educational/vocational counseling at the Minnesota Counseling Bureau before November of their freshman year, with 384 students who had not and who were matched on college entrance test score, high school rank, size and type of high school, age, sex, and college class. The postcounseling adjustment of these students was assessed by interview in their sophomore year. Data analysis indicated that the counseled students had adjusted better and achieved higher GPAs by that time. Subsequent analysis by Campbell (1963, 1965) indicated that the 62 controls, who subsequently sought counseling, were comparable to the remaining controls before seeking counseling, but the 62 were more like the originally counseled students on GPA and successful graduation after counseling. Direct interview and test follow-up of the students 25 years later further indicated that the counseled students had more impressive achievements. Clearly, they excelled academically, with a larger percentage graduating, receiving honors, and obtaining more advanced degrees, and there was a statistically significant difference on a "contribution to society" rating based on interview analysis favoring 244 counseled students over 244 noncounseled students. (These 488 students comprised all of the original 384 matched pairs in which noncounseled students did not seek counseling subsequently and for which interview data could be obtained.)

Although the degree to which counseling followed the canons of the trait-factor model faithfully was not documented, one can assume that the counseling done under Williamson's aegis represented the best of the "state of the art" at the time; one therefore can consider that the results support the merits of trait-factor counseling for college clients who complete it.

In another early and carefully controlled study, Barahal, Brammer, and Shostrom (1950) offered vocational counseling to one hundred Stanford freshmen who volunteered for vocational counseling. Half of the students received a directive version of trait-factor counseling, and half a more nondirective version in which they participated in test selection and received guides to facilitate extracounseling information seeking, review of test results, and postcounseling planning. In interviews immediately following counseling, the clients who had received the nondirective counseling reported more satisfaction with the process, although both groups were satisfied. On a follow-up of 87 percent of the traceable and cooperative original students three years later, Forgy and Black (1954) found that most clients were still satisfied with the counseling, but the nondirective form was no longer regarded more favorably. Furthermore, extended analyses of their data showed that the counselors were differentially effective with the forms of counseling; one counselor produced more satisfaction using the directive format, but two were more effective with the nondirective format.

Still another early study by Miller (1952) supports the value of trait-factor counseling with high school youngsters and is impressive because it employs multiple outcome criteria. He investigated the effectiveness of the brief trait-factor counseling that the Northwestern Guidance Laboratory had given 381 high school students from 1946 to 1949. A special feature of this counseling was the counselor's opportunity to discuss the implications of a client's testing and background data with colleagues before interpreting for the client. Miller found that clients generally reported improved self-understanding, knowledge, problem-solving skill, and self-confidence, but that they did not believe their interpersonal relations were effected. Moreover, they suggested that counseling could improve by providing them with more specific occupational information and clearer, more detailed information about the meanings of their test scores.

Abbreviated trait-factor counseling. Williams (1962) has led the way in demonstrating the value of abbreviated trait-factor counseling for college students. He compared forty-five Wake Forest students who received counseling immediately with forty-six wait controls and thirty students in a psychology class on the changes in their self-ideal and self-ordinary person congruence and adjustment scores elicited by pre-post counseling "2" sorts. The immediately counseled and eventually counseled students increased their congruence and adjustment scores, but not until completing counseling. Moreover, he found that the improved adjustment brought the client to a level with the thirty student controls, which was maintained for a four-month follow-up. The thirty student controls were assumed to be well adjusted since they had not sought counseling.

Williams achieved this growth through a two-session procedure. In the first counseling meeting, he clarified the client's educational or vocational choice concerns and background in order to identify tests and inventories that could help give the clients direction. Emotional problem areas were not usually examined. In the second, and usually final, meeting after testing, Williams (1962) and his client reviewed the test results and discussed their implications in a general way "for various possible courses of action." Williams (1962) emphasized "areas of college study and vocational fields." In addition to their testing, an unspecified number of the forty-five clients examined educational and vocational literature in the two-to-four-week interval between sessions.

In a follow-up study, Williams and Hills (1962) showed that Hills's similar counseling produced comparable growth for nineteen other Wake Forest students. Furthermore, by delaying the initial self and ordinary person "Q" sorts for thirty-five other clients counseled by either of them until just before the second interview, they were able to show that the interpretation session, not the initial probing interview and testing, produced the changes in congruence and adjustment.

To probe the source of benefit further, Hills and Williams (1965) tested whether knowledge of test results produced the benefit. They composed individualized written explanations of the test results around these headings—abilities and aptitudes, interests and preferences, and summary—and had clients read the test interpretations before their second interview. They had forty-five clients complete their second "Q" sorts before their second interview, while another forty clients waited until after their second interview to complete their second "Q" sorts. Pre-post comparisons indicated that the second interview was necessary to bring about the increased congruence and adjustment.

In another study of two-session-plus-testing, trait-factor vocational counseling, Matulef, Warman, and Brock (1964) showed that such counseling increased ability to think in future terms, at least temporarily. Specifically, they found that about fifty Iowa State College students who received vocational counseling from one of five professional counselors wrote longer stories in response to a lead requiring a future perspective than did fifty students waiting for counseling. In addition, analysis of the concepts in these stories suggested that counseled clients were using more future-oriented concepts.

Group studies. By 1955, group procedures were being examined. In that year, D. P. Hoyt (1955) reported examining whether a group of fifteen University of Minnesota freshmen receiving individual trait-factor counseling and a group of thirty receiving group trait-factor counseling differed from one another or from a group of fifteen controls in terms of gains in the certainty, satisfaction, and realism of their career choices over the counseling period. He found that the counseled students gained significantly more on each of the three variables than the controls but that individual and group counseled students' gains were not significantly different from one another.

Ryan's (1968) study of the differential effects of four methods of group career counseling on three hundred junior college students was reported under simulation counseling. Her data showed that modified trait-factor counseling increased knowledge of career information sources and deliberation about career decisions more than a placebo or inactive control treatment. A study employing a similarly modified group trait-factor method with randomly assigned subjects and careful control of counselor cueing and reinforcing indicated that cueing a client about responsibilities regarding information seeking and participation in counseling is important. In that study, Anderson (1970) found that trait-factor counseling with cues about the information to seek between counseling sessions, whether accompanied by verbal reinforcement or not, increased thirty-six Vietnam veterans' reported career information seeking more than no treatment for six veterans and treatment with reinforcement without cues for twelve veterans.

Programmed learning. By the late 1960s, computers and programmed materials were being introduced into counseling. Magoon (1969) constructed a series of written materials, *The Effective Problem Solving Materials*, to enable the client to be self-guided through appraisal counseling with minimal interaction with a counselor. Of the ninety-two college students completing *EPS* in 1966–68, only 1 percent felt it was no help, 79 percent thought it to be quite or very helpful, and 20 percent of some help. Of the forty-one who had previous counseling, 98 percent felt *EPS* was more helpful than other forms. (The *EPS* materials are described in detail in Krumboltz and Thoresen (1969).)

EPS has been used in several researches. Graff, Danish, and Austin (1972), using the adapted *EPS* materials of Danish, Graff, & Gensler (1969), contrasted students who used the materials with those who obtained traditional (not described) individual or group counseling about help received in learning about career opportunities, in making decisions, in setting goals, and in discussing personal-social factors affecting choice. Analysis of the self-reports of the 208 participating students indicated that the *EPS* adaptation was more effective in teaching about opportunities, decision making, and goal setting, and as effective in facilitating discussion of factors affecting career choice.

Krivatsy and Magoon (1978) reported that twenty-two Maryland college students receiving two sessions of traditional vocational counseling improved their career development as much as did forty-nine clients using self-guided methods and more than did twenty-three controls. Improved career development was inferred from the client's reading occupational information, sending for career material, and understanding of jobs suited to personality. The traditional counseling procedure was not defined, the method of monitoring its appropriate delivery was not recorded, and the number of sessions was minimal. Therefore, one might argue that the "traditional counseling" was a marginal rendition of trait-factor counseling, but even in such a case it resulted in some measurable client improvement.

In 1972, Nolan (1974) tested whether another self-directed program, the SDS, was as effective as an abbreviated form of group trait-factor counseling in increasing reality of vocational choice and career information seeking. He found that the forty-five veterans randomly assigned to the four-to-seven-member groups in ninety-minute sessions consisting of SVIB and GATB test interpretation and vocational exploration discussion, increased their information seeking more than the forty-five who completed a GATB and SDS without additional counseling; but there were no differences between the groups in the rated realism of their vocational choices.

Sytematic integration of social learning variables. As the 1970s arrived, the possibility of systematically manipulating reinforcement, modeling, and simulation in trait-factor counseling was realized. Clearly the work of Krumboltz and his colleagues, especially a case presentation (Krumboltz & Baker, 1973) illustrating in detail how social learning research pertained to trait-factor counseling, stimulated several researchers to investigate, within a trait-factor treatment, the effects of particular social learning phenomena such as simulation, direct instruction in decision making, cueing, and reinforcement.

Smith and Evans (1973) investigated the effects of modified trait-factor group counseling with systematic reinforcement on maturity growth in choosing a major and an occupation by contrasting this counseling regimen with individual counseling, and with no treatment. The criteria were measured by the *Vocational Decision Checklist* (Harren, 1972). Four counselors led twenty-two clients through a five-week, two-hour "guidance" program that combined large group meetings, interest testing, video modeling, directed assignments, directed reinforcement, and small group sessions in support of each meeting's theme. Twenty-two other clients followed the same sequence in individual counseling without the meetings, videotapes, and assignments, and twenty-two clients served as "wait controls." Pre-post comparisons suggested that growth was greater for those in group guidance than for individually counseled students, and that the individually counseled student matured more than did the "wait controls."

Fogel (1973) combined elements of translation counseling with trait-factor counseling and incorporated the Krumboltz and Baker (1973) planning paradigm with the mnemonic GAIOP to strengthen the planning phase of counseling. She had three counselors apply the four-session, eight-hour procedure to four groups of West Los Angeles students. Her counseling procedure was refined in detail, and ratings of counselor faithfulness to the procedure assured adherence to its guidelines. The twenty-two students who completed counseling increased their certainty about career goals, felt counseling was worthwhile, and were more able than were twelve untreated controls to list sources of career information and to resolve career choice and planning problems from the *CMI* (Crites, 1973).

Snodgrass and Healy (1979) had ten counselor trainees and eight paraprofessionals provide modified, individual trait-factor counseling, which emphasized the learning of decision making, for thirty UCLA underclassmen. Following six hours of individual counseling, the students increased their knowledge of informational sources and the decision-making model, as well as the certainty and satisfaction about their career choices. Snodgrass and Healy (1979) monitored the counselors' performance to confirm that they adhered moderately to counseling procedure (two-thirds of the rated sessions were judged to have provided 60 percent or more of the required counseling elements), and all eighteen were able to apply the method with at least some benefit to a client.

General counseling evaluation. General evaluations also provide limited support for trait-factor counseling. In 1970, Graff and Maclean (1970) followed up 297 clients who had received individual vocational or academic counseling from 9 doctoral level counselors, 6 advanced trainees, and 13 beginning practicum students. Although counseling did not follow specific guidelines and direct measures of counseling were unavailable, ratings by the 207 responding clients suggested that the doctoral counselors and advanced trainees had delivered elements of trait-factor counseling effectively to the benefit of clients. In contrast, the practicum students were rated as significantly less effective. Clients of the veteran counselor reported more often that in counseling they had made a comprehensive appraisal of themselves, selected a major, set goals consistent with interests and abilities, improved study habits, interpreted career-relevant characteristics, received advice, and discussed their philosophies and concerns. Although most directly pertinent to counselor preparation, these results also provide limited support for the efficacy of trait-factor counseling.

Flake, Roach, and Stenning (1975) found that modified trait-factor counseling improved tenth graders' scores on the *CMI*, as reflected by significant gains of counseled over control students. Seventeen of thirty-six tenth graders who had scored below the mean on the *CMI* individually discussed career plans completed the *GATB* and *Gordon Occupational Checklist* in group testing, reviewed the results in terms of possible career plans with one of two counselors and then discussed the testing/interpretation experience and their precounseling immature *CMI* responses. In the discussion, the counselor avoided indicating that the client had responded immaturely.

Conclusions and Unanswered Questions

The trait-factor studies summarized above warrant at least these three conclusions:

1. Trait-factor counseling, even if brief, can contribute to the career and life adjustment of clients of various socioeconomic and educational backgrounds. This counseling has helped people to select and enter suitable training programs, college majors, occupations, and jobs, to become more aware of their assets and liabilities, and to translate their knowledge into effective career plans.
2. Trait-factor counseling procedures relying upon different psychological tests generally benefit its clients more than no treatment.
3. Whether administered individually or in groups, trait-factor counseling generally has contributed to the career development of its clients, most of whom regarded the treatment as satisfying.

Two types of issues, however, deserve research: those concerned with delineating the parameters of the process, and those concerned with attribute treatment interactions. Illustrative of the former are questions such as these:

1. Does the amount of self and occupational information gathered and discussed in counseling influence the amount of extracounseling information seeking, the expansion of self-awareness, and the accuracy of self- and occupational awareness?
2. Do scope, depth, and accuracy of self-information improve the realism of the client's choices and the client's likelihood of pursuing the choice?
3. Does focusing on interests rather than on demonstrated and tested abilities and aptitudes reduce choice realism and increase the likelihood of abandoning one's goal?
4. What proficiency in test interpretation and communication must a counselor achieve to administer trait-factor counseling effectively?
5. What concepts, such as ability, interest, percentile, must a client be able to recognize or define in order to profit from trait-factor counseling?
6. Will use of multiple assessment methods rather than reliance on paper-pencil tests and inventories increase client-counselor agreement about assessment results?

In terms of client attribute treatment interaction, important questions include: (1) Will clients who have average or lower scholastic aptitude increase their chances for benefit from counseling by emphasizing assessment data derived from reflecting on experiences and de-emphasizing data from paper-pencil tests, by focusing on a narrower range of assessment data, and by receiving simple predictions about attainablility of particular objectives; for example, being told that they have high, moderate, or low probability of success in a particular major? (2) Will established workers changing occupations, who can be termed recyclers, adults in general, or adolescents with strong field independence or internal orientation benefit more if they are provided resources such as test manuals and practice exercises in synthesizing data in order to enable them to participate in counseling than if they receive a more counselor-controlled treatment? (3) Will clients who have strong allegiance to peer groups or have tended to accept traditional stereotypes, such as the notion of male-female occupations, benefit more from group or individual counseling? (4) Must clients be experiencing the need to make a decision, such as the choice of major, occupation, or job within the near future, to benefit?

Translation Counseling

Translation counseling, a first-generation effort to test Super's (1969) hypothesis that occupational choices that are implementations of the self-concept will be more satisfying, is based on the work of Starishevsky and Matlin (1963). Research shows that professionals are in, or are entering, occupations that they feel fit them better than do other occupations (Englander, 1960; Stephens, 1961; Morrison, 1962; Healy, 1968; Hunt, 1967; Healy 1973a); that professionals remaining in an occupation produce an interest profile more like the composite of their profession than is produced by professionals who change their occupation (Campbell, 1971); and that teachers becoming counselors report themselves as more like counselors than teachers (Bingham, 1966; Shiner, 1963). These studies support Super's hypothesis and, indirectly, the counseling procedure. Healy hoped that the simple framework for relating self to work in the procedure would help clients consider multiple factors in their career planning. Likewise, the transparency of the translation process should increase the client's accepting responsibility for the resulting choice. The group examination of the rationale of the choice should increase the likelihood that the choice is realistic.

These heuristics underlie translation counseling: planning 1, 2, 3, 4, and 7 on page 417; individual differences 1, 2, and 3; commitment to occupational group 1 on page 418; and commitment to action 1, 2, and 3 on page 418. Additional principles for improving planning could be included by teaching the clients that a plan's implementation is a process that can be performed in parts and corrected as information about the sections becomes available. For example, a goal of becoming a chef/restaurateur is divided into securing training, a suitable position, and capital. If, during full-time training the client is offered a position that enables him to practice a not-fully-acquired skill with hope of becoming part-owner, he can continue schooling on a part-time basis and accept the position. This job enables him to expedite his total goal achievement, although delaying completion of its schooling aspect. Also, it will provide experience in the role of restaurateur without the necessity of becoming an accredited chef. Thus, it may lead to his reexamining whether to continue pursuit of chef's training.

Five studies of translation counseling have been reported at junior colleges in Southern California, and two have examined its impact on disadvantaged students in a Southern California high school.

College use of translation counseling. In the first study of thirty-five students, twenty-two of the twenty-five who returned follow-up questionnaires felt they had benefited from translation counseling, and the twenty-five subjects' mean certainty about their work goals and choices of occupation and major increased significantly after counseling. The counselors felt that twenty-seven of the thirty-five clients progressed; five regressed or made no progress; and three dropped out. Clients reported benefits that included motivation to obtain information and to choose and to enter a major (Healy, 1973b).

The second study used a delayed-control design. Three groups of students started three weeks before the other three groups. Students starting at different times did not differ in certainty about major or occupational goals. After the first groups finished counseling, however, their certainty was significantly higher than those just starting. In addition, the twenty-six of thirty-four clients who completed counseling increased their certainty about occupational choice, major and goals significantly from the beginning to the end of counseling (Healy, 1974b).

In a third study (Healy, 1974b), twenty-two of twenty-four clients meeting in four groups of five to seven completed the five-session, ten-hour program with almost unanimous satisfaction. Rating of tapes indicated that the counselors administered at least 80 percent of the counseling elements. Pre-post assessment on the *CDI* subscales of career deliberation and self-reported knowledge of chosen occupation (Super et al., 1971) showed that the clients increased their scores significantly over counseling, while similar comparisons of client use of informational resources showed no change. In a follow-up eight months later, eleven of the original twenty-four clients interviewed by telephone were still satisfied with the counseling experience, were generally pursuing the same goal, and felt that the peer sharing was the most valuable part of the counseling (Sparta, 1975).

The procedure has also been used with one group of junior college women. In the women's group, the counselor felt much more attention was given to formulating goals appropriate for women than had occurred in the mixed-sex groups. During planning, concerns of women, such as expected size of family, resentment of moving to accommodate a husband's career, and so forth, were raised; they might not have been raised in a mixed group (Szabo, 1974).

In a second, all-female application, Ogilvie (1975) modified the translation model by (1) incorporating a team-building activity to stimulate clients to generate work-relevant traits and to identify career obstacles, (2) adding a group interpretation of the *Strong Vocational Interest Blank* (Women's Form), and (3) shortening the time spent on career planning and problem solving. Five female counselors, working individually, led three groups of all coeds and other groups of all homemakers through the procedure. Monitoring showed the counselors provided more than 88 percent of the counseling elements. Outcomes were disappointing, however. Compared to twelve controls, the sixteen coeds improved their clarity and certainty about goals over counseling, but not their knowledge of career obstacles, sources of career information, or career alternatives. More disappointing, the home-maker's outcome measures reflected no change over counseling. Ogilvie attributed the difference in homemaker vs. coed outcomes to the fact that coeds had more time to plan and clarify, whereas many of the homemakers sought immediate occupational entry. Perusal of client ratings and observation of the procedure itself suggested that insufficient time in developing concepts, irrelevance of the team-building exercise, and lack of integration of the *SVIB* interpretation within translation procedure reduced the efficacy of the experience for all clients.

Use in an inner-city high school. In 1974, translation counseling and Ryan simulation counseling procedures were simplified for black inner-city youngsters (Healy, 1974). Fifty-six youngsters in seven groups of seven to ten students, under the direction of pairs of UCLA counselor trainees, participated in up to nine forty-five-minute counseling sessions and received three hours of testing on the *DAT* (forms) Verbal, Numerical, Mechanical, and Clerical subtests and one hour of group interpretation. Tape ratings indicated that the counselors delivered the essential elements of counseling. The test interpretation emphasized developing interests and bolstering ability scores rather than viewing low ability as an obstacle to pursuing an occupation.

Pre-post counseling evaluation failed to show improvement in career planning and problem-solving ability measured by Problem Solving Scale of the *CMI* (Crites, 1973) for thirty-two students in translation counseling or for the twenty-four students in simulation counseling. Student reactions to counseling were largely positive; in weekly ratings, the counselors reported that the clients improved in self-awareness, career planning skills, and self-confidence, and that they remained relatively involved in the counseling interaction.

Debriefing of counselors, interviews with the students, and observations of the counseling confirmed clients enthusiasm but suggested factors that should be improved for proper counseling. Among the factors were these: (1) the clients were barely literate (also confirmed by low *DAT* Verbal score), and thus they often were unable to understand the *CMI* test; (2) the clients were increasingly reluctant to concentrate on cognitive tests; (3) the clients lacked access in school or in their community to quality career information resources, either reading or audio-visual material, or people; (4) the clients had limited experiences by which to evaluate themselves and tended to overgeneralize; (5) the fourteen counselors needed more training in order to provide high-quality counseling, even though all had completed a course in vocational guidance, had received twelve hours of intensive training in the procedure used, and received three hours of individualized corrective feedback during counseling; and (6) the attendance of some clients was poor, with nine missing four or more sessions.

In a previous exploratory adaptation of translation counseling with inner-city youngsters, Mirov (1974) guided two groups of five and six academically talented, black twelfth graders from an inner-city high school through elements of the first four sessions. Analysis of the tapes of the counseling and their self-reports indicated that they found the counseling stimulating and productive. Compared to eleven matched controls, the counseled students did not increase their occupational certainty or satisfaction over counseling. The eleven clients did increase significantly, however, their career deliberation and occupational information, as measured by the *Career Development Inventory* (Super et al., 1971).

Conclusions and Unanswered Questions

Overall, the limited evidence supports the following two conclusions: (1) group translation counseling helps college students identify major and/or an occupation, which they enter or at least prepare themselves to enter; (2) most high school and college students who experience translation counseling think that it helps them decide on majors or occupations.

Many questions about the procedure and its clientele, of course, remain to be investigated. In terms of the treatment itself, unanswered questions include these: (1) Does rating three or four occupations from each Holland area, instead of one, increase the accuracy of the person's Holland-type identification, the client's appreciation of the sampling concept, and the likelihood of one's entering an occupation or major consistent with the Holland type? (2) Does use of work-relevant qualities from a source such as the *D.O.T.* that would allow objective ratings of occupations increase the realism of choices produced by the translation procedure and bolster the client's confidence in the appropriateness of the choices? (3) Does requiring a client to list supporting evidence for each self-rating increase both the agreement of those ratings with other estimates and the realism of the eventual incorporation scores?

Future research on attribute treatment interaction is needed to learn: (1) Will clients whose self-ratings disagree with other estimates of them or who are externally oriented and field dependent profit more from translation counseling that requires the client to list evidence in support of individual self-ratings than from translation counseling which does not require such a list? (2) Will adult recyclers profit more from selecting their own attributes after thinking about what has become work relevant for them, and students benefit more from being directed to attributes that research has linked to success in entry-level-work? (3) Will clients seeking immediate employment benefit more if the occupations they rate include only those with openings in the community and students deciding on training programs or majors benefit more by considering a wider range of occupations?

Case-study Counseling

Logically, case-study counseling offers several benefits. It provides a client with objective assessment data, stimulates an individual to understand and integrate the data, furnishes professional and peer feedback about the data and the clients integration of them, establishes a peer group for supporting implementation, and enables a person both to imitate and assist peers in career planning and problem solving. Principles of human learning and development suggest that these characteristics of case-study counseling will increase the probability of its helping a person to choose a suitable career direction and to implement it, but there has been no direct research on the contribution of any one element.

These heuristics operate in case-study counseling: planning 1, 2, 6, 7, and 9 on page 417; individual differences 1, 2, and 3 on page 417; commitment to occupation group 1 and 5 on page 418; and commitment to action 1, 2, and 3 on page 418. Planning principles 4, 5, and 8 on page 417, can be brought to bear by challenging clients to verify their informational sources within and outside group meetings, by encouraging clients to confer with those who have already made similar decisions, and by assigning reading in manuals such as *Decisions and Outcomes* (Gelatt et al., 1973).

Limited empirical evidence on the effectiveness of the vocational choice case-study method is available. Sprague and Strong (1970) reported that twenty-five of thirty-five clients answering follow-up questionnaires responded favorably to participation in such counseling. Hewer, in a personal communication, has indicated that students responded favorably to case-study counseling at the University of Minnesota.

In a more recent report, Hanson and Sander (1973) studied whether group case-study counseling or individual case-study counseling would assist eleventh and twelfth graders to adopt more realistic goals. They found the ten students with higher goals than appropriate for their characteristics who received group case-study counseling, and the ten with lower goals, who received individual counseling, increased the reality of their goals in contrast to ten untreated controls, whereas the ten overshooters in individual counseling and ten undershooters in the group did not change.

In another small study, Westbrook (1974) examined one counselor's use of case-study counseling and his use of two approximations of trait-factor counseling. He reported that ten clients from eight-week case-study groups indicated at the end of counseling, and fifteen weeks later, that they had achieved more of the career goals they sought through counseling than other possible goals not related to counseling, whereas thirteen control clients and ten clients in one of the two trait-factor approximation groups did not achieve more of their career goals than of other goals not related to counseling.

The principles underlying case study counseling suggest that it can benefit clients at different stages of development with different concerns, especially self-awareness and esteem. Two researchers have already demonstrated this.

In a relatively large study, Hansen and Putnam (1976) found that 123 randomly assigned high school and junior high school students who participated in modified case-study counseling made higher self-esteem scores and more mature career attitude scores on the *Tennessee Self Concept Test* and the *Attitude Scale of the Career Maturity Inventory* respectively than did 123 controls. Fourteen experienced counselors led the fourteen groups of eight to ten students through six 50-minute sessions. They used the case studies "to initiate discussion and to illustrate the relation of self-esteem and vocation development." The authors did not report the guidelines that students followed in constructing their cases, nor did they identify the evidence used by students in developing their cases; but they did note that the students "were encouraged to focus on their individual values, interests, aspirations, capacities, and abilities," that particular points about school curriculum were introduced, and that counselors acquainted clients with occupational information. In addition, the discussions treated reasons for course selection, information necessary for selection, options opened and closed by particular selections, and the role of parents and teachers in planning and decision making. Moreover, counselors assured that students considered concerns about the personal self and gave some time to the physical, ethical, family, and social self.

Outcome Assessment

Studies of career-decision counseling have examined a range of immediate outcomes using a variety of methods. Table 10–1 shows that evaluators have probed client attitudes about career choices and plans, self and career information, career decision maturity and accuracy of self-appraisal, productivity in school and in work, and overall adjustment. Moreover, evaluators have used cognitive tests, expert ratings, and inventories as well as self and counselor ratings to measure these objectives. This range of objectives and variety of measurement methods offers useful examples for readers who would study career decision counseling.

The literature is unexpectedly silent about measurement of comprehensive plans, however. Since three counseling methods focus on creating a career plan, one would expect evaluators to verify that a client produces an evidence-supported, realistic plan by the close of counseling. Yet no research reviewed here verified such an achievement.

Unfortunately the task cannot be resolved simply by agreeing that counselors can accurately verify the quality of a plan, as Williamson's (1939–1949) work implied. Especially disconcerting are Hewer's (1959, 1966) observations that counselors were unable to predict whether college clients of case-study groups would implement their plans. She further found that the predictions of the clients themselves were accurate, suggesting that the clients had insight about how they would proceed, which the counselors lacked. Logic and social science research suggest that factors such as time span of a plan; concreteness and comprehensiveness; verified possession of requisite skills, interests, financial resources, and social networks; sense of ownership; public commitment to plan; and the relative accessibility of the objective would relate to likelihood of implementation. But research in career development has yet to demonstrate a relation of these plan characteristics to career progress. Although clients probably will have better plans after completing counseling, research silence about the ingredients of a plan that's likely to succeed—not just the plan goals—makes verification of a plan's quality problematic.

Identifying which components of a plan relate to implementation should be a major research priority because the plan's components that are emphasized influence the content of counseling. Logically, key components will vary with the kind of goal sought. For example, a plan to acquire a degree in a demanding course-oriented program with a high attrition rate would seem to require verification that the planner has at least the minimum talents for the selected major, anticipates extensive study, will develop a support system to encourage perseverance in the face of occasional setbacks, and anticipates the likelihood of requiring occasional tutoring. On the other hand, a plan for completing a major emphasizing independent study and completion of a thesis is likely to require verifying possession of sufficiently strong interest in the subject matter to sustain autonomous, continued study and either the capacity or the resolve to learn how to manage intense, long-term, collegial interactions with a small number of peers and advisers. In other words, the setting addressed in the plan dictates the components and their nature. For example, the setting will determine whether a goal should be general or specific, firm or tentative, and whether the planner needs to attend to his or her affect and cognition, material assets or social network in considering resources.

Therefore, this author hypothesizes that plans focused on the particular demands of the target environment will be more viable than those that address a standard set of elements. Although a standard plan may cover all the points necessary for implementation in the particular situation, it undoubtedly will divert the planner's attention to irrelevant issues, thereby limiting attention to the key issues. Since pre-establishing a set of components necessary for a comprehensive plan will produce many elements, the time on irrelevant ones can be substantial. While creating a plan, reviewing the standard plan components to pick pertinent ones may be helpful. But, including all the standard components in a plan is likely to be distracting and even counterproductive.

Granting that the most helpful plans reflect the demands of particular contexts has definite implications for the role of counselor and for judging the quality of a plan. In terms of role, helping clients create such a plan would require guiding a client in discovering the particular demands. Logically, by personally inspecting the target environment and acquainting oneself with the patterns typical of people in that milieu, a counselor will be better able to guide a client's discovery. At the minimum, a counselor will need access to a network of people with first-hand knowledge of the situations with whom to confer and/or arrange for a client to consult. Regarding plan evaluation, evaluators should have direct knowledge of the target environment in order to evaluate plans for operating within it. Hewer (1966) found that counselors' evaluations did not distinguish between plans eventually realized and those not realized and that they considerably underestimated the rate of plan implementation, whereas 90 percent of the clients realized their plans. Therefore, one may speculate that these results reflect the facts that the clients had a better grasp than their counselors of the environments they would enter, and that their plans considered the existing nuances. The counselors, however, probably judged the plans in terms of a standard set of components and were unaware of particular nuances. More appropriate plan evaluators, one might hypothesize, would have been educators or employers in the occupations and industries to which the clients aspired.

Another important research priority in outcome assessment of career decision counseling is establishing the relationship between the immediate outcomes in Table 10–1 and more intermediate outcomes. Among desirable intermediate outcomes are (a) greater use of concepts, such as ability and interest to construe people, perhaps as gauged by the Kelly (1955) *Role Repertory Test*; (b) using more assessment modes and observations before coming to a conclusion about oneself and others; (c) feeling well oriented to the selected career path; and (d) persevering in the decision. Regressing immediate outcomes on intermediate outcomes will identify the immediate outcomes whose manipulation is likely to influence the intermediate outcome. Then, one can create a manipulation and examine whether it alters the intermediate outcome. Such actions should help improve counseling procedures.

Whether the three procedures differ in their likelihoods of helping clients to achieve selected outcomes is another question worth exploring. Their distinctive rationales and components suggest that each procedure would favor different outcomes and different populations. As yet, however, contrasts have not been reported, even though recent reviewers of career counseling have called for such efforts (Fretz, 1981; Super & Hall, 1978). Counselors who would accept such a challenge will want, of course, to insure that both treatments are rendered with comparable fidelity. When they cannot directly verify the quality of counseling, they will assign counselors of equal competence and commitment to the respective treatments. They also will be careful to avoid measuring outcomes by an instrument or method that may favor one treatment because of its content or operational similarity to that counseling procedure. An example of subtle measure bias would be comparing the impact of trait-factor and translation counseling on an ability to synthesize personal data into an appropriate occupational choice by having the clients make choices for a series of fictitious persons who were described primarily in terms of test and inventory percentile scores. Since trait-factor, but not translation-counseling had involved directly working with such data, the trait-factor client would be expected to have some advantage.

Possible Negative Effects

Possible negative effects of career decision counseling generally have not been considered, although practitioners in this age of accountability and malpractice are very concerned about them. In career decision counseling, there are three general dangers: (1) increased client dependency on the counselor; (2) overreliance on, or misinterpretation of, one form of evidence; and (3) false confidence in or overcommitment to, the resulting choice.

Concerning the first problem, a client may act passively in counseling and delay all decisions until they are made by the counselor or may attribute every decision to the counselor even when making it. When this happens, the counselor can confront the client's denial of responsibility for choosing and can structure counseling so that it progresses only as the client chooses and/or acknowledges choosing. Structuring activities can include reviewing the decision-making process, changing the amount of counselor input, and asking the client to summarize more frequently.

In terms of information, clients can disregard their experience and acknowledge only test scores or other's ratings of them, claiming that these data are more "objective." At the other extreme, clients may reject tests or ratings as biased and rely exclusively on their own interpretations of their experiences. Either extreme usually produces inaccurate information. To thwart this difficulty, the counselor must challenge the client to expand the basis of self-estimates. For instance, in translation counseling, where testing and external observer input are not mandated, the counselor should verify that clients are reminded and even challenged to justify their self-ratings. Similarly, in case-presentations counseling, the clients must be reminded to integrate experiential and test data in making decisions.

One additional comment about test interpretation is necessary in view of the recent controversies about racial, sexual, and socioeconomic biases in tests and inventories and because of the questionable competence of most counselors in using tests (Goldman, 1972). Tests clearly favor the group to which the test maker belongs, because he or she generates test material from personal experiences before norming the test. Similarly, inventories such as the *Self-Directed Search*, which offer career direction by comparing the client to people in different educational/occupational positions, tend to be biased because some elements linked to characteristics of incumbents unrelated to the work are not eliminated in weighing one's similarity to particular occupational groups.

In regard to competence, Goldman (1972), Prediger (1972), and others have noted that counseling's use of tests is questionable because most tests and inventories do not provide information that can be translated accurately by a counselor. Minimally, according to Goldman (1972), a counselor must (1) understand basic concepts of measurement statistics, (2) understand the rationale of different types of tests, (3) know well the tests being used, (4) use up-to-date information on the tests, and (5) develop and use local norms. Logically, training for test use should involve supervised organization and interpretation of tests for many clients' but, unfortunately, few counselors receive such training. Therefore, Goldman (1972) proposed a counselor specialization in appraisal. Another alternative suggested by Prediger (1972), who believes that it is unrealistic to expect counselors to understand fully the technicalities of test scores, is that test producers turn test results into information relevant to counseling and counselors transform that data into exploratory activities and self-evaluated experiences. Hanson and Cole (1972) noted that American College Testing has provided this service for its *Career Planning Program*.

On the other hand, as Wesman (1972) noted and Goldman (1972) implicitly agreed, tests provide information that often is otherwise unavailable and is usually more reliable and more objective than assessments by anecdotes, ratings, and the like. Moreover, having reviewed studies of modes of interpreting tests, Oliver (1977) concluded that some test interpretation has been found to be superior to no interpretation. Clearly, tests cannot be abandoned, but surely they must be understood more fully and used more carefully.

Finally, every client must recognize that choices involve risks. He or she must guard against overconfidence in the likelihood of realizing one's choice. One works hard to create a rational formulation of career, and therefore, reasonably expects to benefit. But, any formulation of the choice situation is only an approximation that necessarily contains errors and may easily produce incorrect predictions and untenable choices. Unfortunately, many choice situations are too complex to determine how much error may be involved; due to the dynamic nature of the situations, the amount of error probably is always changing. Of course, since a choice is a process, one can increase potential effectiveness by reviewing it periodically in light of new data.

Indeed, the client needs to be able to alter or even to relinquish a choice for new ones that time shows are more appropriate. But although reviews will reduce risk, they will not eliminate it. Excessive review, of course, is likely to be unproductive and doubly frustrating by suggesting a false security.

Counseling for Career Establishment

11

The young adult is freed of the restraints of compulsory schooling and given options about structuring his or her life. This young adult is challenged to establish oneself within an occupation and to balance working with other life pursuits. Studenthood, with its clear benchmarks, regular feedback and promotion, guaranteed sanctuary, intellectual stimulation, and stress on individual performance is traded for employment with its "liberating" paycheck; adult prerogatives, responsibilities, and expectations; task and coworker regularity; variable feedback, challenges, and risks; competition for establishment and promotion; and team, rather than individual, performance.

The new worker is supposed to be finalizing decisions about an occupation, rounding out skills, acquiring necessary licenses and certifications, learning the avenues to stabilization and advancement within the occupation, and laying the groundwork for years of satisfying production in an occupation. The individual should be making pertinent contacts; projecting energy, eagerness, and commitment to a firm; getting the "right" assignments; and acquiring prerequisites for further personal growth. At the same time, the fledgling worker is supposed to be ordering life commitments—family, social, civic/service, religious, and work—in a manner that leads to being a productive, self-starting, self-directed, happy person.

The particular achievements that announce an adult has achieved establishment status are likely to vary because each occupation takes its incumbents in a somewhat different direction. Super (1957, 1977) noted this fact and proposed that career maturity in establishment and maintenance is manifest by career-general and occupation-specific achievements. In terms of general career, task analysis suggests indices such as employed in satisfying work; making job changes that increase, or at least maintain, one's benefit from working; holding jobs for sustained periods; changing jobs because of one's own volition, rather than involuntarily; progress in salary schedule, especially when increases are not automatic; increase in work efficiency; acquisition of requisite credentials, licenses, training, and degree. Occupation-specific achievement might include professional or employer recognition for achievement, such as outstanding teacher award, American Board Professional Examiner's Psychology certification, ABCorporation sales representative of month or year award; salary; participation in professional or union concerns as committeeman, delegate, officer, editor of newsletter or professional journals; establishment of constructive linkage with coworkers, colleagues, superordinates, and subordinates; broadening knowledge and capability of performing one's own and related jobs; expansion of job duties; and increased specialization within the job.

Early adulthood not only is a busy stage of life but also is the period in which a person's powers peak. Society expects much of the young adult. Ideally, the individual has integrated personal life experiences into a set of personal goals and priorities and is well along in refining skills and performing appropriate roles. The young adult's decisions and plans are entrusted entirely to the individual, although society is deeply effected by their quality. Society presumes that this adult will: act maturely; be skilled in anticipating life's and work's viscissitudes; be competent in identifying career options and prerequisites; persevere in spite of obstacles, change, and even occasional setbacks and frustrations; be accomplished in problem detecting and solving; be self-confident and optimistic.

No one claims that young adulthood is easy, but current American mythology implies that its tasks be managed independently. Career counselors leave young adults almost entirely on their own after helping them to identify a suitable occupation and to find a job. Even though workers average several changes of employers in their first few years of work, counseling to help young adults establish themselves in this work phase is still relatively rare. Although this chapter presents promising procedures to help with some establishment tasks, other needs have no counseling treatments yet, and research concerning the existing procedures is still scarce.

Counseling for this stage focuses on bolstering establishment skills, on helping the person use them, and on pinpointing what peers are experiencing at this stage. This chapter describes and reviews three procedures: guided inquiry counseling, discovery counseling, and personnel review and planning counseling. Guided inquiry counseling teaches the client how to resolve the inevitable problems that arise on the road to career establishment; discovery counseling helps one take stock and balance commitments through structured peer interaction and guided fantasy; personnel review and planning counseling is a computer program being developed by the United States Army to help junior officers organize their military careers in terms of the Army's opportunity structure (Myers, 1978). The counseling procedures defined for the maintenance stage may also be appropriate for helping clients at this stage, since research has not clearly distinguished between the tasks and competence of establishment and of maintenance.

To help readers recognize the relevance of these procedures and to acquaint them with some characteristics of persons in this stage that are suggested by theory and by survey research, the chapter first reviews ideas and findings about people in the establishment stage.

Establishment in Terms of Developmental Theory

Theorists have said surprisingly little about establishment in terms of developmental tasks. Blocher (1973) synthesized theoretical views from Erikson (1950, 1963) and Havighurst (1964) into the following developmental tasks for the age span twenty to thirty and thirty to fifty, respectively: "learning to commit self to goals, career, partner and to children and to give unilaterally," and "learning to be inner directed, interdependent, handle cognitive dissonance, or be flexible and effective emotionally, develop creative thought processes, develop effective problem solving techniques." More recently working from a psychodynamic perspective, Levinson (1978), who was joined by colleagues Darow, Klein, Levinson, and McKee and Gould (1978) have proposed that adults develop accommodations (life structures) and periodically alter or transform them, experiencing a series of transitions. Based on study of the careers of forty men between the ages thirty-five and forty-five, who were seen six to ten times during a two-to-three-month period with a follow-up interview two or three months later, Levinson and his colleagues proposed general age-appropriate activities. The following excerpts from the treatise are organized in the manner of developmental tasks.

Age 17–22:   "To start moving out of the pre-adult world: to question the nature of the world and one's place in it; to modify or terminate existing relationships with important persons, groups, and institutions; to reappraise and modify the self that formed in it" and "to explore possibilities of adult world, to imagine oneself as a participant in it, to consolidate an initial adult identity; to make and test some preliminary choices for adult living."

Age 22–28:   "To fashion a provisional structure that provides a workable link between the valued self and adult society." In doing this, the adult must both "keep his options open" and "create a stable life structure."

Age 28–33:   "To work on the flaws of the first adult life structure and to create a basis for more satisfactory structure."

Age 34–40:   1. "to establish a niche in society. . . . To anchor his life more firmly, develop competence

in a chosen craft, become a valued member in
a valued world."

2. "to work at making it: striving to advance,
to progress on a time table" and

3. "to become one's own man . . . to accomplish
the goals of the Settling Down enterprise, to
become a senior member of one's world, to
speak more strongly with one's own voice, and
to have a greater measure of authority."

Age 40–45:   "To question the way one has lived and wants
to live, to reappraise, test, explore in preparation for erecting a new life style."[1]

Addressing career development tasks directly, Jordaan (1974)
summed up Super's view of establishment as involving "the tasks of
settling down, securing a chosen place in the chosen occupation and of
consolidation and advancement" after having acquired necessary skills,
training, or work experience in the last phase of exploration. Exemplifying entrants to the establishment stage are the boys who have become
men that Jordaan (1974) described in the Career Pattern Study.

Status at Age Twenty-Five. A brief discussion of the subjects'
status at age twenty-five will help to place the foregoing and following material in context. By age twenty-five four-fifths of the
subjects were in possession of a high school diploma or its
equivalent, one-fourth had completed two years of post-high
school education, and approximately one-fifth had earned a
bachelor's degree. The average subject had changed positions
six times in seven years and not always for the better. Only
about half of the subjects could be said to have engaged in pre-
dominantly stabilizing behavior since leaving school. About one-
third appeared to be floundering and one-sixth showed equal
proportions of floundering and stabilizing behavior. By age
twenty-five, however, about four-fifths appeared to be stabilizing or getting established. Five percent were in professional and
management positions and 25 percent in semiprofessional and
lower level managerial positions. About 30 percent were in
skilled occupations, another 30 percent in semiskilled occupations, and 10 percent in unskilled occupations. Since leaving
high school, less than half (about 40 percent) had actually entered any of the occupations they had specified as students. The
great majority of the subjects (90 percent) felt they were doing as well as, or better than, other people of their age in their
occupation. While most (about 80 percent) said they were satisfied with their job, many of them also indicated that they were
not sure whether they wanted to or would continue in the occupation.

[1] SOURCE: From Daniel J. Levinson, THE SEASONS OF A MAN'S LIFE,
copyright 1978, by Alfred A. Knopf, Inc. Reprinted by permission.

Empirical Studies

Little research has been conducted to verify empirically the achievements that lead to career maturity in the establishment stage. In the only longitudinal study directly examining the career progress of youth into this stage, Super (1979) related multiple variables to five career success indices. The relation of student characteristics in twelfth grade to age twenty-five criteria were examined by step-wise regression analysis, the outcomes of which appear in Table 11–1. Clearly, twelfth-grade characteristics such as grades, parental occupation level, independence of work experience, occupational information, and vocational aspiration level related in the manner expected, yielding R's ranging from .54 to .80. These correlations confirm the importance of school and other achievements, although not discounting the advantages conferred by social class. They also support the proposition that career maturity is developmental.

Data from Terman's Gifted Child study also clarify the nature of career maturity in early adulthood. Oden (1968) contrasted the one hundred highest and one hundred lowest career-achieving men when they averaged fifty years of age. He found that twenty years previously, the high achievers had more self-confidence, perseverance, and integration, of their goals; had achieved more scholastically; had considered schooling, friends, and leadership more important in their school years; and had done more career planning. By inference, career maturity at thirty is manifest by such personality characteristics as self-confidence, goal integration, and persevering, and actions such as scholastic achievement and career planning.

In a more recent longitudinal study of 274 American Telephone and Telegraph adult male managers during their establishment stage, Bray, Campbell, and Grant (1974) found that occupational advancement was achieved by emphasizing the work role, while deemphasizing, but not necessarily neglecting, the family and recreation roles. Surprisingly, eight years of managerial experience did not increase managerial skills; yet the authors speculated that the managers were more valuable because they had knowledge about AT&T and its operation. Correlations of advancement with quality of work environment in the study, as well as in studies summarized by Korman (1977) on work motivation, suggest that positive work environments promote advancement. By inference, therefore, career development criteria of an effective management trainee are incumbency in a favorable environment in which constructive supervision is provided and personal emphasis on the career over other life roles.

Several recent longitudinal surveys of adults over parts of their careers, sponsored by the U.S. Department of Labor and by the U.S. Office of Education, shed additional light on what constitutes career maturity during the establishment stage. In 1968, the Bureau of the Census interviewed a nationally representative cross section of 5,159 women ages 14 to 24, a group of 5,083 women ages 30 to 44, and a group of 5,225 men ages 14 to 24. These subjects were reinterviewed each year

Table 11-1. Variables Forming Five Criterion Factors of Career Maturity at Age 25 for Subjects of the Career Pattern Study

Criterion Variable N = 103

	Criterion Factors with Loadings				
	I Career Satis-faction	II Job Satis-faction	III Attained Status	IV Career Progress	V Occupa-tional Advance-ment
Educational Level	-06	-05	83*	-02	-14
Occupational Level	03	08	59*	02	19
Attainment: School-Leaving Occupational Goal	-20	28*	-06	45*	-25
Career Establishment, Self-Estimated	91*	-09	-06	01	-05
Occupational Success, Self-Estimated	30	-05	06	20	06
Career Success, Self-Estimated	30	07	09	38*	01
Career Satisfaction, Self-Estimated	81*	03	00	-01	01
Occupational Satisfaction, Self-Estimated	05	69*	00	07	-06
Position Satisfaction, Self-Estimated	-02	68*	-26	04	00
Utilization of Assets	68*	11	05	-12	04
Opportunity for Self Expression	06	80*	07	-04	02
Number of Moves	-36*	41	12	-49*	08
Average Progress: Change in Equity	-24	-03	-18	70*	26*
Average Progress: Realism of Reasons for Moves	-02	10	26	54*	-12
Final Status Judgment: External Psychological	38*	37*	02	-04	12
Improvement Over Own Initial Occupational Level	-08	06	-11	05	65*
Improvement Over Father's Occupational Level	08	-19	16	-01	49*

N.B. Signs reversed where necessary to facilitate interpretation.
* $p \le .05$.

SOURCE: Donald E. Super, Adolescent predictors of success and satisfaction in young adulthood. Paper presented at the American Education Research Association Convention, San Francisco, 1979. Reprinted by permission.

through 1973. Follow-up telephone interviews were completed in 1975 and 1977, and an intensive interview was planned for 1978. The nature of the data permit following these persons, job by job, through the 1968–1973 period or looking at the group collectively. Here are selected findings:

For the fourteen to twenty-four-year-old women, the following results relate to establishment activity of young women:

1. Disruption of marriage forces women back to school or work and puts them at an economic disadvantage.
2. The number of workers satisfied with working increases dramatically over the five-year period of working.
3. There is an increasing trend for women to delay marriage and family for career pursuits. Fifty-seven percent of the twenty to twenty-four year-old white women had not married in 1968, but 67 percent had not married in 1973.
4. Social class, especially as reflected by parental income, is a powerful determinant of the likelihood of college attendance and the quality of the college. This relation increases during recession periods. Intelligence is also related to these outcomes.
5. More women stay in the labor force until well after they are pregnant and may return to work more quickly than they did in the past. This tendency is especially true of black women. Increasingly more women follow the continuous work pattern typical of men.
6. The overwhelming majority of women in 1968 and in 1973 expected to pursue traditional female occupations.

Parnes, Jusenius, Blau, Nestel, Shortledge, and Sandell (1976) reported these findings from the 5,083 women between ages thirty and forty-four, who had been followed from 1967 to 1972 and had provided information about their earlier work history in 1967. Their findings provide useful clues about how women are faring in establishment.

1. These women increased their participation in the labor force and improved their positions over the five years. They seem to react to the same economic forces as men.
2. Only a small minority of the women had worked at the same or a related occupation for as much as 75 percent of the years for which they were out of school. As many as half the unmarried women, and as many as one quarter of the childless married women, had such work histories, but only 7 percent of married, or formerly married, women with children reported such employment histories. The continuous careerists fared better in upward career mobility than those changing occupations.
3. Marrieds do not complete as much education, nor do they advance as much in pay and occupational status, as never-married women when other variables are held constant.

4. Black women were neither able to achieve comparable status positions in their first jobs nor to advance equally with the white women, even when other variables were held constant.

5. Career success measured by status and salary are related most to a woman's educational attainment. Her education influences her first job, which affects subsequent achievement. Her number of years of schooling, in turn, is correlated with the educational and occupational attainment of her father and the educational attainment of her mother. As a consequence, the authors noted that women's career advancement reflects similar factors as men's career advancement. Improvement in career also relates to receiving training outside formal school, good health, and a history of working in related occupations.

6. In regard to who will work, the authors found that women with more education, especially university, professional schooling, who obtained licenses, were more likely to work. Also, women from rural areas and small cities, and women with mothers who had worked when the present women were adolescents, were more likely to work. Finally, women who felt that their husbands viewed their working positively and who themselves had a favorable attitude toward work were more likely to work.

Kohen, Grasso, Myers, and Shields (1977) examined a set of issues pertinent to starting work for the group of 3,987 young men who remained in the sample over the five-year period. Their major findings and inferences are reported here, in order to illuminate the nature of the school-to-work transition and the initial years of working.

1. Many of the men who were working full time in 1966 had changed their occupational aspirations downward, especially if they had aspired to professional or technical-level work (70 percent of the white professional aspirants did so). Likewise, high schoolers reduced their aspirations substantially (50 percent of the white professional aspirants did so). Over the period, the percentage of men uncertain about their goals also decreased (from 15 percent to 12 percent for the working males, and 19 percent to 14 percent for the males who had been in school in 1966).

2. Many of the youth experienced involuntary unemployment during the period. Of those in the work force for five years, half the white, and two-thirds of the black workers suffered unemployment. In any one year, 16 percent of the white and 27 percent of the black workers with at least four years in the labor force, had one or more weeks of unemployment.

3. Over the five-year period, the fourteen to twenty-four-year-olds upgraded their occupational level substantially. From 33 percent to 60 percent increased their occupational level.

4. Level of occupational and educational aspiration and attainment related to IQ, amount of educational and occupation information, and encouragement from family and school. The authors recommended focusing on these concomitants of social class, which may be upgraded, rather than on social class itself.

5. Many of the 1966 high school students (40 percent) had occupational goals inconsistent with the number of years of schooling they envisaged for themselves, and many (more than 50 percent) of the high school graduates were aspiring to technical/professional jobs. At least 20 percent or more held very unrealistic goals judged by discrepancy between aspirations and ability and background. Not unexpectedly, about 25 percent were pessimistic about realizing their goals.

6. Youth with more accurate career information were more likely to earn more, occupy prestigious jobs, make realistic choices, and have congruent educational and occupational aspirations. The high school youth with considerable work experience were likely to possess more information and have congruent educational and occupational aspirations.

7. Two-thirds of the young men made changes from occupations in one field to occupations in another. The average time these young men were working was six years, with some working as little as one year and others as much as fifteen years.

8. Youth entering work in the 1960s were more likely to start at a higher occupational level than their fathers had started. The young men who did not complete college were more likely to advance occupationally if they left their first employer than if they stayed. Promotion by one's current employer depends more on demonstrated ability, job information, and health; whereas elevation by changing employers depends more on educational credentials.

9. Married, better educated, and longer-tenured youth are more likely to have new jobs lined up before they resign and are less likely to lose their jobs because of layoffs or firing, than are unmarried and less-educated young men. However, when unemployed, they do not suffer shorter unemployment

10. Veterans of the Armed Forces were more likely to be in the group with average educational and mental ability. The white veterans have not achieved wages or occupational status comparable to their peers, unless they have upgraded their education through their GI Benefits. Education after military service appears to reduce their early disadvantage in working. Clearly, military training during the Vietnam era did not give white youth employment advantages, as often claimed, although it may have aided black youth somewhat.

11. Overall, schooling, formal training, and on-the-job training and learning are important and complementary contributors to

young men's early work advancement. This is less true for blacks than for whites, however. Contrary to widespread proclamations, a college degree gave new workers in the study period as much advantage as it had previously. However, wages and status for all new workers were down in the period, requiring many college graduates to settle for positions below their expectations. There appears to be a "bumping down" effect, rather than a diminution in the relative advantage conferred by a bachelor's degree.

12. Black youth did not move ahead to the same degree that white youth of comparable education and experience progressed, and they suffered disproportionately higher unemployment. Unquestionably, they are still victims of discrimination.

From Westbrook's (1977) summary of the survey data on the one thousand adults from the National Assessment of Career and Occupations Development, the following conclusions are pertinent to career development:

1. Adults, just as nine, thirteen, and seventeen-year-olds, were more interested in developing leisure than work skills.

2. Adults have a high knowledge of the characteristics and training requirements for a variety of occupations.

3. Most adults consider working conditions, personal goals and satisfactions, prestige, and advancement opportunities to be important considerations in the choice of a job. However, less than half consider job qualifications, personal abilities, constraints, present and future job availability, job responsibility, and job challenge as factors to think about in choosing a job.

4. In contrast, the same adults judge their work satisfaction by whether the job allows them to do the best they can and provides them with likeable coworkers. Only 10 percent based satisfaction on pay. These data suggest that adults are using criteria for selecting a job that are different from the standards by which they judge their satisfaction. Perhaps the apparent contradiction occurred because of the way in which the questions were posed or because these adults believe that their own salary and working conditions are adequate. If not, adults' satisfaction would improve if they would consider more seriously the job's potential for engaging their skills and permitting them to interact with likeable people before taking a job. Moreover, since knowledge of educational supply and demand relate to job and career satisfaction, these adults might make better career decisions by giving more attention to such information.

5. Nearly 40 percent of the adults had never taken a test for career direction, and of those who had, less than one-third had reviewed the test with a counselor.

6. Only slightly more than half of the adults had formal continuing education experience, including correspondence courses and on-the-job courses.

7. Few adults were able to compose comprehensive job application letters, which may reflect the fact that only clerical and professional/managerial jobs in large corporations and government require such applications.

Newsmagazines are also contributing to our understanding of adult career development. One recent survey, based on two thousand three hundred respondents, acknowledged to overrepresent young, higher-level workers, provided insights about the basis of adult occupational choices, adult views toward job change, amount and kind of perceptions of adult job satisfaction, and amount of discrimination (Renwick & Lawler, 1978).

Surprisingly, 40 percent of the sample felt they had "happened into" their current job; only 23 percent had selected them; and 16 percent had "settled for" their occupations, preferring something else. Equally surprising, more than half the respondents at all occupational levels saw at least some likelihood of their changing occupations within the next five years. Not unexpectedly, lower-level workers anticipated change more often, with only 16 percent of the semiskilled not anticipating some chance of change; and 42 percent of the manager-executives and 43 percent of the professional groups did not anticipate a change. In regard to work satisfaction, the Renwick and Lawler (1978) findings parallel Westbrook's (1977) findings. Both studies found workers most satisfied with coworkers but feeling that self-growth satisfiers were most important. For the men and women of the Renwick and Lawler (1978) study, the most common reasons for continuing working were job enjoyment, sense of identity, and avoiding boredom. Nevertheless, when pressed about changing a job, only 41 percent of the respondents would take a pay cut to obtain a more interesting job, but 46 percent were clear they would not. Another surprising finding was that 43 percent of the respondents felt they had been victims of [sex or racial] discrimination. Major complaints included more work in comparable positions, lower pay, and lack of access to informal sponsorship and training.

Another perspective on adult careers and guidance service needs was recently provided by a study of adults making or anticipating a career change. Arbeiter, Aslanion, Schmerbeck, and Brickell (1978) analyzed telephone interviews with 998 randomly selected adults, 400 of whom reported they were changing or expecting to change their career. These adults were termed "in transition" and estimated to be 36 percent of the population aged 16 to 65. Their median age was just over 30, with 65 percent between 25 and 45 years of age.

The interviews confirmed Renwick's and Lawler's (1978) findings that persons across the socioeconomic spectrum have recently experienced or anticipate career change. The majority (63 percent) of those in transition were leaving or planned to leave a job; 33 percent were reentering the workforce, generally from homemaking or unemployment; and only 4 percent were going to work for the first time. The major reason for career change was a desire for more money (50 percent); other reasons mentioned included greater professional advancement (18 percent), more interesting job (15 percent), and pursuit of an interest (10 percent).

In terms of objectives, most job changers (70 percent) listed a specific career goal, and 88 percent of them claimed familiarity with their goal. Their extent of knowledge was not examined. Interestingly, more of these adults had learned about their goal through work experience than from any other source. Among the other frequently named sources were schools, families and friends, and hobbies and interests. Reading and professional guidance had had minimal influence. The majority of changers experienced or anticipated problems; lack of experience or credentials (17 percent), unavailability of jobs, and child care/ family responsibility (10 percent).

More than half those in transition aspired to skilled/professional employment, and those with more education aspired higher. Of particular importance, 62 percent of these adults anticipated more schooling, with the majority expecting to acquire professional or vocational/trade education, while a small portion looked forward to liberal arts education to facilitate their career transition.

In terms of counseling needs, the interview survey examined desire for particular kinds of assistance and the acceptability of various strategies. Expectedly, the adults wanted a wide array of services, and most were willing to pay modest fees for such assistance. Table 11–2 shows the percentage of adults interested in particular services. Noteworthy in Table 11–2, as the authors pointed out, is considerably more frequent desire for information (1, 2, 4, 7, 10) than for counseling (3, 6, 9,

Table 11–2. Comparison of Interest in Career Services of In-Transition and Not-in-Transition Adults

Services	Percent of Adults with High Interest		Percent of Adults with High or Medium Interest	
	In Transition	Not in Transition	In Transition	Not in Transition
1. List of available jobs	62%	26%	83%	45%
2. Facts on occupational fields	52	24	82	52
3. Examination of career possibilities and most rapid path for advancement in your field	50	25	78	46
4. List of educational or train- programs	49	25	79	48
5. Job skills training	47	27	78	47
6. Discussion of ways that your abilities/strengths can be used in various jobs	44	23	79	49
7. List of financial aid sources	44	24	69	45

Table 11–2. (*Continued*)

Services	Percent of Adults with High Interest		Percent of Adults with High or Medium Interest	
	In Transition	Not in Transition	In Transition	Not in Transition
8. Explanation of educational programs in a given field that are offered at different schools	41	26	73	50
9. Discussion of which schools could best meet your personal needs	41	18	69	41
10. Facts on how personal abilities relate to educational success	38	20	72	45
11. Advice on eligibility for specific types of financial aid	37	23	73	47
12. Occupational ability testing	35	18	71	47
13. Advice on ways to resolve personal problems such as child care and family commitments	34	22	59	38
14. Training in self-analysis and decision-making techniques	31	15	64	40
15. Discussion of your family's attitude toward your career	30	17	55	35
16. Training in writing career resumes and being interviewed	28	12	59	31
17. Advice on ways to deal with problems which block career progress	27	17	58	39
18. Training in using classified ads, employment agencies, and other ways to locate jobs	27	15	58	33
19. Discussion with someone about problems you are having with your employer	25	15	51	30
20. Training in locating and using directories and other occupational information	23	12	56	34

SOURCE: Reprinted with permission from *Forty Million Americans in Career Transition* by Solomon Arbeiter, Carol B. Aslanian, Frances A. Schmerbeck, and Henry M. Brickell. Copyright © 1978 by College Entrance Examination Board, New York.

15, 19), guidance (8, 11, 12, 13, 17), or training (5, 14, 16, 18, 20) services. Perhaps these information requests reflect the adults' acceptance of responsibility for their own career management.

In terms of preference for strategy, most adults rated work experience programs, formal courses, individual contact, and observation of work as very acceptable, whereas fewer than 30 percent deemed role play, mass media, computers, or telephone as very acceptable. Printed materials and group contact were endorsed by somewhat more than one-third and less than one-half, respectively. As the authors observed, these adults seemed to want help through direct human interaction, perhaps because they have not been as immersed in group interaction and computer technology as their children and younger siblings. But, a follow-up evaluation of satisfaction with "telephone counseling" by these same authors suggests that these attitudes would not prevent their using indirect assistance strategies, such as the telephone, effectively.

Variations Among Fields in the Challenge of Establishment

Studies of selected fields, such as Solmon's (1977), suggest that establishment is likely to be more difficult in some fields than others because of factors such as supply-demand for workers and salaries. This fact is true even for college graduates. In 1974, Solmon asked a large sample of 1965 college graduates about their satisfaction with their jobs and with their college preparation. For this group who had not gone beyond the baccalaureate, he found considerable differences in annual salary by major, with education majors averaging $10,300; English, humanities, $12,253; economics, social science majors, $15,754; natural science, math and engineerings students, $16,865, and business majors, $19,353. In answer to questions about overall job satisfaction, business and education majors, described themselves as very satisfied most often, 59 percent and 60 percent respectively. In contrast, only 46 percent of the English and arts and humanities majors were very satisfied. Perhaps more revealing were the respondents' willingness to recommend their college major to others. Eighty-four percent of the business majors, 80 percent of the engineering majors, 64 percent of natural science majors, 58 percent of the mathematics majors, 68 percent of the education majors, 54 percent of the English, 53 percent of the arts and humanities, 45 percent of the economics, and 53 percent of the social science majors would recommend their fields. Particular attitudes towards work by graduates of different majors are reported in Table 11–3. Those who achieved professional status were satisfied more often than those who had not. Office workers, allied health workers, and social workers tended to be less satisfied than accountants, engineers, administrators, sales workers, and educators.

One other finding of Solmon (1977) concerning establishment success is the relation between career choice of college seniors and their actual occupations nine years later, in 1971. Some majors expect change more, as Table 11–4 shows. Predictably, persons selecting natural and social sciences and college teaching, who do not take advanced degrees, change occupational choices more frequently. Many of them move into business. Also, in most majors, women change their choices considerably more often than men.

Table 11–3. Attitude of Workers Toward Job, by Occupation (in percentages)*

Attitude	Accountant	Office Worker	Administrator	Sales	Mathematics Science	Allied Health	Engineer	Educator	Social Worker	Nonprofessional	Professional
I would like to remain with my current employer for the foreseeable future	77	64	71	81	68	55	71	66	54	52	74
I have sufficient status or prestige on my job	70	45	80	69	62	67	64	61	64	54	80
I am satisfied with my career progress to date	64	44	77	60	59	64	60	64	52	43	74
I am satisfied with the quality of interaction with my supervisor	63	65	55	67	63	52	62	61	54	41	63
My job fits my long-range goals	57	31	66	58	45	44	53	51	38	42	63
I am well paid for my work compared with:											
—persons in general with the same amount of education	52	25	61	53	51	43	56	14	21	25	49
—persons at the same job level in other work settings	49	37	49	49	48	45	41	18	28	31	45
—persons of the same job level in my place of employment	54	35	43	52	47	43	38	30	27	27	40

* Percentage responding in the affirmative.

SOURCE: Lewis C. Solmon. Rethinking the relationship between education and work. UCLA EDUCATOR (Vol. 19, No. 3, Spring, 1977). Reprinted by permission.

Table 11–4. Changes in Occupational Choice by Occupation:
1971 Occupation Related to 1965 Career Choice
(in percentages)

Occupation	Career Choice*											
	1	2	3	4	5	6	7	8	9	10	11	12
						Men–1961 Cohort						
1 Business related	69	7	17	8	15	18	22	26	14	16	15	32
Professions and Sciences												
2 Allied health	3	79	0	*	*	3	*	0	*	*	0	1
3 Engineer	*	0	71	*	*	12	*	5	1	4	44	3
4 Health (M.D., D.D.S., D.V.M.)	1	1	0	74	0	1	*	0	*	*	0	1
5 Lawyer	*	*	*	*	60	0	0	*	*	1	0	3
6 Natural scientist	1	2	1	2	0	34	2	0	2	13	0	3
7 Social scientist	*	1	*	1	0	0	15	3	*	1	12	*
8 Other (artist, clergy)	0	0	0	0	2	0	20	35	2	2	0	1
Teaching												
9 Elementary, secondary	4	5	2	3	4	9	13	7	61	12	0	7
10 College	2	1	2	1	2	5	5	5	6	37	0	6
11 Trades	1	1	1	*	1	1	2	1	1	1	10	2
12 Other (military, farmer)	18	3	6	11	16	18	21	19	12	13	19	41

Women—1961 Cohort

	1	2	3	4	5	6	7	8	9	10	11	12
1 Business related	41	13	72	*	3	49	20	11	10	22	48	22
Professions and Sciences												
2 Allied health	1	56	0	17	0	15	0	*	2	3	0	5
3 Engineer	3	1	9	0	0	3	3	1	1	2	0	1
4 Health (M.D., D.D.S., D.V.M.)	0	6	0	43	0	*	*	*	1	1	0	1
5 Lawyer	*	2	0	1	45	0	1	3	1	1	0	1
6 Natural scientist	1	*	0	15	*	9	0	1	*	7	0	1
7 Social scientist	*	0	0	0	0	*	19	1	*	5	0	4
8 Other (artist, clergy)	2	2	0	4	1	*	27	41	3	4	11	18
Teaching												
9 Elementary, secondary	21	5	5	12	36	2	12	9	67	21	0	15
10 College	*	9	14	1	0	9	6	5	5	26	0	7
11 Trades	1	1	0	1	0	4	0	*	*	0	0	*
12 Other	31	6	0	7	15	9	13	27	9	7	41	25

* Numbers refer to same categories as those under Occupation.

Note: Read vertically to determine percentage of graduates who realized their choice. For example, 69% of the business graduates were in business and 79% of the allied health grads were in allied health occupations in 1971.

SOURCE: Lewis C. Solmon. Rethinking the relationship between education and work. UCLA EDUCATOR (Vol. 19, No. 3, Spring, 1977). Reprinted by permission.

491

Adult Career Maturity Measures

Currently, no commercial tests of adult career maturity are available. But, in 1973, Super, Thompson, and Zelkowitz added a scale to the experimental *CDI* in order to tap factors contributing to adult career maturity, and in 1977 Super cited the findings from several dissertations in support of its construct validity. The scale asks adults to indicate the amount of consideration they have given to a wide range of issues, such as making a place in their company, planning a retirement budget, qualifying in a specialty, and obtaining experience needed for promotion.

In a recent study of 111 secondary school educators from 4 metropolitan areas, this author found that the adult maturity scale scores based on 20 items from the *CDI* Experimental Adult Scale (Super, Thompson, & Zelkowitz, 1973) correlated with occupational level and with a cognitive test of career education concepts, but not with salary, years as educator, or number of leadership roles in school and community (Healy, 1980). Although supporting the construct validity of the *CDI*, these findings suggest that some logical indices of career maturity may not reflect career maturity. One may argue that the higher an educator's salary, the longer the tenure, and the more leadership positions held in the community, the more maturity he or she has manifested; but one also can point out that salary is determined primarily by district policy rather than individual merit, that educational tenure policies have guaranteed seniority to poor as well as good quality educators, and that community achievements may compensate for limited teaching achievements, rather than complement them.

In an independent effort to establish factors in career maturity, Sheppard (1971) constructed a pool of items similar to ones used in the *Attitude Scale of the Career Maturity Inventory* (Crites, 1965, 1973). From the pool he selected items which distinguished fifty graduate students from fifty vocational trainees, and the fifty trainees from one hundred unemployed men. He called the scale the *Adult Vocational Maturity Inventory (AVMI)*. Next he cross-validated the distinguishing items by showing that they differentiated a comparable group of graduate students, vocational trainees, and unemployed men. To date, he has not published additional studies, nor has this author nor his students been able to secure a copy of the scale.

Two researchers subsequently have studied the construct validity of the *AVMI*, although Sheppard's limited work makes one doubt that he intends to develop it further. In the two studies, Wallis and Gulkus (1974a, b) correlated the *AVMI* with reported preferences for work reinforcers. As expected, they found the measure repeatedly related to desire for two work reinforcers—"getting a feeling of accomplishment" and "doing work without feeling it is morally wrong" for samples of vocational rehabilitation clients and students. In the one study of job aspirations, expectations, and the discrepancy between them, Wallis and Gulkus also found that *AVMI* related significantly to career aspiration and expectations, and negatively to the degree of difference between the two.

Guided-Inquiry Counseling

Guided-inquiry counseling is being developed by Sorenson (1967) and his students at UCLA to enable adolescents and adults to resolve everyday problems of living. This approach assumes that one can remove obstacles to personal goals if one understands the forces that produced and are sustaining these barriers. Furthermore, the guided-inquiry counselor postulates that careful, objective, common sense observation and review of the situation will elucidate the problem's causes and suggest corrective action.

One can administer guided-inquiry counseling individually or in groups. In either case, the counselor paces counseling based on feedback about client learning. Emphasis is on the client's problems in operating within individual lifespace, with minimal attention to the dynamics of interaction between counselor and client or group members except as they provide information about the client's extracounseling situation. The procedure is designed for all types of problems but has been found especially helpful in career problems such as difficulties with one's supervisor or peers, difficulty in learning job skills, and confusion about a career decision.

Persons undergoing guided-inquiry counseling are presumed able to (1) accept ownership of their problem, (2) gather information relatively independently, (3) learn and understand behavioral psychological principles, and (4) tolerate their distress while planning to correct the situation.

Heuristic Principles

These common sense principles underly guided inquiry counseling:

1. An objective, comprehensive appraisal of a problem will illuminate the causes of the problem.
2. Understanding the heuristic principles that cause or maintain a problem will suggest solutions.
3. Reviewing a problem and planning its resolution in a calm, deliberative fashion increases the likelihood of its successful solution.
4. Rehearsing and then following a systematic problem-solving strategy increases the likelihood of resolving problems.

Method

Each client is guided through the same phases of problem solving (Table 11–5), but their content depends on the client's problem and understanding of behavioral science principles. Counselors model a calm, deliberative problem-solving approach and use a uniform repertoire of responses. Each client eventually specifies goals, obstacles, and strategies in terms of behaviors at definite times and places. However,

Table 11–5. Four Phases of Guided-Inquiry Counseling

Phase 1	Develop picture of person Explain how counseling will help Specify goal Specify obstacles Summarize
Phase 2	Relate obstacles to behavioral science concepts Identify solution strategies Delineate consequences of each strategy Summarize
Phase 3	Choose one strategy for implementation Plan implementation Rehearse Establish review/report time
Phase 4	Report on strategy trial Continue with, or modify, strategy or recycle to Phase 1 Summarize entire procedure to aid transfer

each client has individual goals, obstacles, and strategies, and clients may use different behavioral science principles to accomplish similar goals.

For example, two technicians, Harry and Louise, may be concerned about their inability to get along with their laboratory supervisor and their consequent inability to profit from his supervision. The counselor helps each to define his or her goal as performing lab procedures effectively and broadening skills. Harry discovers that his many questions make the supervisor anxious. Louise, on the other hand, realizes that she is encouraging the supervisor to tell her only about the negative aspects of her laboratory efforts in their conferences, resulting in her becoming dejected and angry. Harry needs to recall or discover that making another person anxious reduces his ability to relate; Louise must recognize that by establishing the supervisor as a punitive figure, she is insuring that she will not relate well to him. Table 11–5, outlines the phases of the guided inquiry procedure. They are described below.

Phase 1. In Phase 1, the counselor helps the client with three objectives: (1) to feel that the counselor is interested in the client and concerned about his or her needs; (2) to describe accurately the problem and its place in the client's life; and (3) to state the problem in terms of specific situations and obstacles. The counselor accomplishes the first two objectives by listening attentively and nonjudgmentally, in guiding the client to describe what the client believes are personal concerns, how he or she feels about them, what is believed to cause them, what he or she believes should be done about them, and what he or she has already tried to do.

Open-ended questions, paraphrasing, reflection of feeling, and expectant silence are used to help the client describe himself or herself and the impact of the problem. For example, Harry might be asked questions such as these: "What happens between you and Mr. X? Am I correct that you are feeling frustration in trying to resolve it? What impact is this having on your other studies and social life? What might explain why you are not getting along with him? Oh, you have hunches about resolving the problem! And what happened when you tried that?"

To accomplish the third objective, the counselor attempts to help the client, through open-ended and cueing questions, to identify what the client wants to occur, what is preventing it from happening, and what goals should be sought first. For example, Harry would clarify points such as these: "What would a good working relationship be? What occurs before you feel you cannot relate to him? What does he do? What do you do? What appears to be constant when you are not relating well?"

The counselor gathers details about the actors, their actions, the time, place, and context carefully because clinical experience suggests that not all pertinent facts are included until the scenario presents data that the client had not considered before counseling. In deciding when to accept a cause as probable, and consequently when to proceed to consider alternate solution strategies, the counselor relies on personal understanding of the problem area. This understanding comes from study of such problems and from experience. To sharpen counselors' skills in this crucial diagnostic effort, Sorenson (source: personal communication) is experimenting with a set of case studies that provide practice in using information to diagnose. Once the client identifies the specific goal and its obstacles, the counselor guides the client to summarize an understanding of what they will be after in treatment. Counseling then moves to the second phase.

Frequently during Phase 1 and even during subsequent phases of guided inquiry counseling (for example, Farmer, 1972; Horowitz, 1972; and Zinar, 1975), the client will be asked to make observations about his or her situation, as homework. To prepare the client for this assignment, the counselor may teach observational techniques, prescribe readings, and/or provide forms on which to record observations. Occasionally, the guided-inquiry counselor will visit the client at the worksite (Farmer, 1972) or create a simulation in order to observe the client directly in the problem.

Phase 2. The objectives of Phase 2 are to help the client generate alternative strategies for overcoming the obstacles specified and to review the probable consequences of each strategy. Generation and portrayal will be more germane to the problem if the client understands the concepts and heuristic principles pertaining to the difficulty. For example, Harry needs to learn about concepts such as anxiety (a state of threat interfering with communication) and positive reinforcement (something that sustains action). Also, he needs to understand principles relating to the concept of anxiety, such as (1) a barrage of problems elevates anxiety in most people, (2) an anxious questioner elevates anxiety in the respondent, (3) people seek to avoid anxiety, (4) actions followed by positive reinforcement are repeated, and (5) a person can sustain desired behavior by arranging positive reinforcers for it.

To enable the client to learn the pertinent concepts and principles, the counselor can employ either discovery learning or didactic teaching.

Discovery is preferred because it appears to give the client more ownership of the concepts. Regardless of how understanding is transmitted,
however, Sorenson (1967, 1978) insists that client comprehension be
verified by eliciting from the client an example of the concept. Harry,
for instance, reported that he understood the concept of anxiety because
he would get it before a test and now even before speaking to the supervisor. And he agreed that he was less able to talk or listen when anxious.

After the client isolates a probable cause and establishes the heuristic principle that appears to support it (Supervisor X is made anxious
and therefore acts negatively), the counselor helps the client identify
strategies for removing, preventing, circumventing, or even tolerating
each obstacle. The counselor tries to elicit any strategy that the client
may have used successfully in other similar situations, any ideas he or
she has about the "logical," "common sense," or "scientific" solution for
this type of problem, and any hunches he or she can formulate from
recalling how others resolved difficulties with similar causes.

After noting that the supervisor was anxious after a barrage of questions, Harry was asked: "Might you rehearse your questions before conferring with him in order to avoid arousing his anxiety? How can you
use the principle that people become anxious when they are asked too
many questions at once?"

After the client specifies several strategies, the counselor has him
or her consider what each strategy involves and the probable consequences of each. The preview includes the client's actions and feelings
and the likely duration, as well as other participants' actions and feelings. Especially important in the preview are the information, skills,
and cooperation required, as well as the amount of time and energy
that implementation can be expected to take. For an extended strategy,
the client also needs to consider how to sustain the commitment when
distracted. Often one must alert family and friends in order to secure
their cooperation and to assure support.

When Harry proposed an alternative of asking one question at a
time and writing them down to test their coherence before asking them,
the counselor helped him picture the action and anticipate the consequences. The counselor asked questions, such as: "How will you get an
opportunity to write down your question? What will you do so that you
are composed as you ask? Why do you believe this strategy will work?
What could go wrong?"

Each viable alternative must be examined. For instance, for Harry,
other viable alternatives included securing a position in a research laboratory, which rewarded continual questioning; applying a procedure
such as successive approximation to increase the supervisor's tolerance
for questions; psychotherapy to develop insight into and correction of
the apparent insecurity suggested by the questioning; and ignoring the
supervisor's anxiety and hoping that the supervisor would acclimate.

Phase 3. In Phase 3, the client selects a feasible strategy, delineates
it, rehearses it as necessary, specifies the criteria to use for its continuous evaluation, and agrees on times for review and progress reports.

First, the counselor invites the client to identify the strategy to be used and to review the reasons for choosing it.

Selecting an alternative is a complex, subjective process. The client values the goal, which is the target of the alternatives, relative to the worth placed on other goals. That relative value usually influences how strongly and faithfully the client will pursue the goal. The alternatives generally differ in terms of the time, energy, and money they require; typically they also differ in their likelihood of producing the goal. After recognizing the cost of various alternatives and the comparative chances of achieving the goal through them, people sometimes select a lesser goal; that is, they compromise. A client, for instance, changed from pursuing law to become a probation officer when he learned that law school required three years of graduate study.

One scheme for reviewing the merits of particular alternatives involves estimating the costs and probabilities of succeeding with each. This procedure can make concrete the factors entering a decision. Table 11–6 presents estimates of Harry's alternatives. These estimates, like many, are subjective. Table 11–6 also shows how long the alternative is likely to take before correcting the problem, how many hours have to be devoted to the alternative, its direct cost (the estimate here is based on $35/hour counseling charges), the effort required (none, little, moderate, much, mental or physical), and the probability that the alternative will succeed (minimal, moderate, high, very high). In this case, for instance, asking fewer questions will probably take at least

Table 11–6. Weighting Harry's Alternatives for Improving His Relationship with His Supervisor

Alternative	Time of Completion	Cost in Hours	Cost in Money	Cost in Energy	Success Probability
Ask fewer questions when supervisor and oneself are calm	6 weeks	90	$ 210.00[a]	Moderate	High
Secure a position where questioning valued	6 weeks	120	$1010.00[b]	Moderate	Fair
Recondition supervisor to appreciate questioning	8 weeks	80	$ 280.00[a]	Heavy	Minimal
Undergo psychotherapy	26 weeks	52	$ 810.00[a]	Heavy	High
Wait and see	8 weeks	0	$ 35.00[a]	0	Minimal

[a] Cost in money is based upon a charge of $35/hour for therapy, career counseling, or placement services. The client estimates one visit per week until completion. For example, since asking fewer questions requires six weeks, the client estimates six sessions with a counselor, costing $210.
[b] Securing a new position requires a placement fee of one month's salary of $900 and $110 for three hours of placement service and registration.

six weeks before showing results; will require about fifteen hours per week of planning, review, and vigilance; six more counseling sessions will be needed to review progress, make corrections, provide support, and enable summarizing counseling; the energy required will be moderate; and the likelihood of this alternative's succeeding is high.

Regardless of the schema used to depict selecting an alternative, every client can recognize that choosing an alternative is a type of wager. A person commits energy, hoping to attain a goal, but without absolute certainty of success. The importance of the stakes and past experience influence the wager. For example, Harry may wish to relate more constructively with people generally and to feel better about himself, and therefore may choose psychotherapy. Or he may need to commit all his time and money to the care of an ill parent, and therefore opt for the wait-and-see strategy, since it offers at least some hope. In another case, a student wished to earn an A on an examination, so she estimated the effectiveness of different study approaches. The study of the text and review of notes, she calculated, offered a one in four probability of producing an A and would take six hours; formulating and answering questions for an additional four hours would increase the probability to one in two; whereas adding another four hours of review would bring the probability of A to two in three. There is no simple choice for Harry or the student because the costs and the hours of potential study must be balanced against the value of the other activities that will be forgone. Considering one's actions in such circumstances should, however, clarify one's personal values and one's risk-taking proclivity in different circumstances, one's feeling about the appropriateness of "sure" and "long-shot" bets, and how one would like to operate in particular situations.

Clearly a client needs to identify how he or she makes choices and which choice-making styles are personally effective. Krumboltz and Baker (1973) recommended exercises, such as success bombardment, or homework assignments, such as simulation games, to help clients identify their choice styles. Similarly, many clients would profit from studying high school texts such as *Decisions and Outcomes* and *Deciding*, which present comprehensive treatments of decision making.

Several authors have classified choice approaches or styles. In their text, Gelatt, Varenhorst, and Carey (1972) identified nine approaches or styles: impulsive, fatalistic, compliant, delaying, agonizing, intuitive, planning, and paralysis. Recently, Johnson (1978) established these choice types: spontaneous-internal, spontaneous-external, systematic-internal, and systematic-external. In formative research, he has found counselors and trainees at the University of Southern Illinois (Carbondale) counseling center able to categorize clients reliably and to use the categories successfully to predict behavior. Currently, however, so much is still unclear about decision making that a counselor must be cautious in guiding a client through it, insuring that the client retains the power of deciding. Nevertheless, in addition to providing a decision schema, the counselor can assist a client at this phase of counseling by actions such as the following: remind the client that selecting an alternative is gambling, but that one can increase the chances of winning by being willing to try more than one alternative; teach the client that selecting an alternative is actually a process, which can be reviewed continually and modified on the basis of feedback from implementation; point out how the client appears to be approaching choices and what self-presentation in counseling suggests are important factors to weigh in a choice; stimulate one to recall the decision-making styles that have worked in the past; point out weaknesses in this decision strategy—such as mis-estimating probabilities of alternatives succeeding, being unsystematic, or using unverified information—and recommend means of correcting these problems; and recall the dangers of extremes in deliberation by using proverbs, such as "Strike while the iron is hot!" "Fools rush in where wise men fear to tread."

After the client selects a strategy, client and counselor detail its steps, noting essential considerations such as information, skills, timing, and cooperation. For reducing the supervisor's anxiety, for instance, Harry was asked to imagine a past situation and how he would redo it. The following questions illustrate the detail to seek in the plan: (1) How do the questions arise? (2) What will you do to stop yourself from going directly to the supervisor as the questions arise? (3) Do you need anyone's cooperation, or a prop? (4) Where and on what will you write out the questions? (5) How long will you wait before reviewing the questions for coherence? (6) Should you try them on a coworker? (7) When and how will you approach the supervisor? (8) Who will be there? (9) How hectic a situation is it? (10) How will you compose yourself? (11) What reaction do you expect? (12) How will you respond to the expected? (13) What if the supervisor responds in an unanticipated manner?

If need for instruction or reference materials arises in the rehearsal, the counselor provides them or indicates how and where the client can secure them. The counselor's instructional repertoire is not limited to discovery; one can teach skills such as relaxation or give information didactically; one can prescribe self-instructional materials, reading, or refer to a paraprofessional, aide, educational specialist, or community resource person. Any applicable technology may be used.

Often walking through or role playing the strategy is required to ensure that the client understands it. Routinely, athletes and other performers rehearse new performances, often repeatedly; and rarely will a successful student attempt a test without practice. Certainly, this author's own experience with teaching demonstrations, employment interviews, and doctoral orals confirms the value of rehearsal.

Rehearsal may involve the client's performing the strategy, or perhaps switching roles and playing its target. Sometimes, by experiencing a protagonist's perspective or another person's portrayal of him or her, a client can understand the situation better or discover where the performance needs to be changed. The following guidelines can enhance both role play and role reversal:

1. Specify the concepts, principles, and skills to be acquired beforehand to ensure that the scenario has elements related to the target skills and concepts.
2. Provide descriptions of the scenario and the roles in sufficient time for clients to study materials and to obtain clarification, but do not use scripts. If some members of a counseling group are to be an audience, describe their function.
3. Have the simulated scenario approximate the real situation as much as possible.
4. As soon as the role playing is completed, let the client share individual reaction about what happened, receive reinforcement feedback about the positive aspects of the performance, and discuss methods for improving the performance. Make sure each important element of the situation is discussed.
5. Give the client the opportunity to repeat the performance after planning corrections in order to receive reinforcement for improvement, especially if role playing occurs in groups.
6. Role play continuously unless the scenario specifically calls for interruptions. The realism of the role-playing situation and consequently its learning impact can be lost if a player steps in and out of the role. This fact is especially true in role reversal.

The counselor next asks the client about the criteria by which he or she will evaluate success. Harry would list signs that indicated that the supervisor's anxiety was diminishing during their conferences, and that he was following the strategy. In addition, the counselor reminded Harry to distinguish reduced anxiety from receiving constructive feedback, since it was only his hypothesis that anxiety was preventing the supervisor from giving feedback.

After the client chooses a strategy and defines the steps and indices by which to determine its success, the counselor asks him or her to review what he or she will be doing. The counselor closes the session by establishing with the client the support the counselor can provide as the client implements the strategy and the points at which they should meet.

Phase 4. The objectives of Phase 4 are to have the client report the results of individual actions and modify the strategy, continue it, or select a new one; and to outline the counseling course in order to increase the likelihood of being able to apply it to other problem situations. If a new strategy is required, the counselor recycles Phases 1, 2, and 3, adding the data the client has acquired from having tried a strategy. If the client has been unable to apply the strategy, he or she and the counselor determine the reason and then add corrective measures to the strategy steps. Harry's efforts with his supervisor, for example, produced sporadic results, which seemed to stem from an occasional departure from the strategy. This problem was identified and corrective action planned.

When the client is successful, the counselor encourages him or her to describe the success and personal feelings about it and asks the client to review how he or she can proceed to ensure future success. The counselor and the client then decide whether to continue counseling to resolve other problems or to terminate counseling with this session.

Providing support is often difficult. At the first sign of success, many clients feel the problem is resolved and wonder why they need to review how closely they are following their strategies and how to maintain them. Moreover, they may feel it is superfluous to verify that their successes are as complete as intended. Yet, frequently the initial success is only a prefiguration of what will occur if the client maintains the new strategy. Consequently, overlearning the strategy and discovering its nuances through its review will not harm, but probably will aid, the client, even if the strategy is succeeding. Research suggests that overlearning contributes to acquiring complex behavior (Hilgard, Atkinson, & Atkinson, 1976). Certainly recounting and re-experiencing success in learning to solve a problem can also be helpful, for most people tend to dote on educational failures, but rarely take time to bask in their successes.

Sustaining a client in a strategy that is not showing results may be even harder. It is painful, but necessary, to review in detail what the client is doing, and to agree on specific alterations and on persevering. To accomplish these tasks, the counselor guides the client to recall that estimates of when the strategy would work were only educated guesses, and that delay in succeeding does not mean the strategy is failing, but merely that client and counselor underestimated its gestation period. For example, Harry took ten instead of six weeks to alter his approach to the supervisor.

When the review uncovers a knowledge or skill deficit, providing support may be easier because the client can act to acquire the knowledge or skill. In our instant, speed-oriented society, however, waiting and persevering are frequently discounted as attributes of winners. A counselor may, therefore, have to help the client recognize the advantages of persevering.

Empirical Validity

Since 1967, guided-inquiry counseling has been developed under the leadership of Garth Sorenson via formative evaluation in at least ten counseling dissertations at UCLA. Most of the dissertations examined counseling for particular populations directed toward predetermined goals; that is, clients from a group, such as UCLA student teachers, agreed beforehand to focus on solving problems within the area of teaching or on relating to their supervisor rather than to establish the priority of their concerns at the initiation of counseling. Observation had shown that the problem concerned many people in the population, and the dissertation candidate typically established that prospective clients had the problem. Several studies involved clients enrolled in special teacher preparation classes who earned credit by improving their teaching skills and/or capacity to interact constructively with supervisors. As a consequence of the predetermined focus, many of these studies necessarily eliminated parts of Phase 1, wherein a client established priorities among life concerns.

In accordance with the formative evaluation thrust, the guided inquiry treatments underwent multiple changes to refine the method of control. Earlier studies involved short periods of counseling, which only briefly overviewed the notions of heuristic principles and systematic problem solving, and relied almost exclusively upon interview. Their control of treatment was based on response classifications then in use, such as reflection, leading, structuring, and summarizing, although these categories were only minimally related to the procedure's cognitive structure.

The guided-inquiry counseling that evolved in later studies contained more instructional time, introduction of teaching aids such as recording forms, self-directed exercises, assigned readings, and systematic use of reinforcement and modeling, extensive training of counselors for the protracted treatment, and closer treatment control. Studies in the early 1970s (J. Bates, 1971; Duff, 1972; Vivell, 1975) had counselors work *verbatim* from scripts, whereas later studies (Farmer, 1972; Horowitz, 1972; Vivell, 1976; Phelps, 1978) prescribed topics or ideas and principles to be covered and categories of counselor responses to be made for categories of client responses. For instance, the counseling protocol for a client like Harry would specify that he be guided to identify the concept of anxiety; learn or review the principles of anxiety relating to his interaction with his supervisor; illustrate understanding by providing examples; and be reinforced for identification, participating in the learning, and providing correct examples of the concept and related principles. The counseling rater could then observe or listen to a recording of counseling to ascertain whether the counselor focused on the concept of anxiety and principles relating to it, gave examples, elicited examples from Harry, and reinforced the client at pertinent points of the process.

Most studies employed counselor trainees as the counselors; therefore, even though some later studies included intensive counselor training, including a pilot or an equally closely supervised trial with real clients (Farmer, 1972; Zinar, 1975), many counselors characteristically manifested an awkward rigidity in guiding clients, and had a limited number of heuristics on which to draw. Due to this fact and to the evolutionary character of the procedure, the full potential of the method has not yet been explored.

Following are summaries of UCLA dissertations using guided inquiry counseling or a minimally structured variation of it. Studies using its essential assumptions, but a very structured format for specific objectives, by Bates (1971), Vivell 1972, 1975), and Phelps (1978) have been described in Chapter 8.

In a post-test only experiment with new student teaching candidates who volunteered for the study, Quinn (1970) contrasted the effects of group guided inquiry and group sensitivity counseling on self-reported learning, satisfaction, peer influence, peer popularity, and stress in student teaching. All four groups were led by the same pair of counselors, but the treatments were carefully monitored and proved distinguishable. There were no outcome differences between the eighteen students randomly assigned to guided inquiry and the twenty-one assigned to sensitivity training. Reported satisfaction ranged between some and much. Interestingly, especially for its implications for prescription, students who were classified task-oriented were more satisfied in the guided inquiry, whereas those dubbed person-oriented were more satisfied with the sensitivity counseling.

O'Reilly (1968) examined whether four sessions of guided inquiry counseling, "advisory" counseling, or "affective" counseling would help student teachers reduce either their reported stress in student teaching, their problems with pupils in their teaching assignments, or their conflicts with training teachers. Moreover, she asked whether any or all treatments would increase learning of teaching concepts. Her sample included sixty-four students identified as having either high conflict with pupils or training teachers. They were assigned randomly so that fifteen were in two guided-inquiry groups, sixteen in advisory groups, seventeen in affective groups, and sixteen in control. Although no counseled subjects improved more than did the control students, O'Reilly observed that students receiving affective counseling reduced their pupil problems more than did those receiving guided-inquiry counseling. The meaning of this finding is unclear, since it was the only one of several post hoc contrasts that was significant and one would expect some significant findings when several contrasts are examined at the .05 level.

Broadbent (1970) had four counselors administer a discovery and directive form of guided-inquiry counseling, consisting of four half-hour sessions, to thirty-two student teachers to help them overcome problems in student teaching. Her results suggested that externally oriented student teachers were more satisfied with counseling and that students preferred the advisory form of counseling to the inquiry form.

Lin (1970) had three counselors lead eight student teachers through individual guided inquiry counseling of five half-hour sessions, and eight through group counseling, to help them resolve problems in student teaching. The forty-eight clients collectively did not differ from eighteen controls at the close of treatment on student teaching problems. The sixteen clients of the counselor who was highest in self-confidence and democratic attitudes, however, reported significantly decreased student teaching problems compared with the clients of the low-confident, low-democratic counselor and with the eighteen controls. Although all three counselors were rated as delivering counseling according to the guidelines, Lin (1970) judged that differences among counselors was a significant factor in guided inquiry's failure to produce impact for two groups.

Ogle (1972) contrasted fourteen randomly assigned female student teachers receiving an early form of structured guided-inquiry counseling over twelve two-hour sessions, from one of three counselors, with fourteen females engaged in sharing and clarifying feelings with three other counselors. She found that the guided inquiry clients reported trying out more problem-solving strategies, and, regardless of treatment, internally oriented subjects produced more problem-solving plans. Moreover, internal subjects in guided inquiry reduced their anxiety considerably more than did other subjects.

Horowitz (1972) adopted guided inquiry counseling by employing directed reading (Bank, Culver, McCann, Rasmussen, & Ruble, 1972) for teachers agreeing to participate in an in-service workshop for improving classroom management skills. Horowitz (1972) contrasted performance of two treatment groups totaling nine teachers with two delayed groups totaling ten, and both with a nonequivalent control group of six teachers, Her carefully controlled treatment was delivered by two female counselors in six one-hour sessions. It significantly improved teachers' independently observed use of positive reinforcement, their tested understanding of problem solving, their reported success in solving problems, and the independently observed classroom behavior of the children who were the targets of the teachers' problem solving.

Extending the guided-inquiry adaptation of Horowitz (1972) through more refined programmed reading materials but decreased time (five sessions) and more detailed delineation of counseling, Zinar (1975) showed via two intensive case studies that the two teacher clients increased their knowledge of problem solving, and their observed classroom teaching and interactional skill.

Farmer (1972) had seven counselors apply discovery or directed guided-inquiry counseling to seventeen student teachers identified as likely to have difficulty in a student-teaching assignment. Her seven counselors' training had involved their using the guided inquiry with an actual client under Farmer's supervision before the start of the experiment. Over counseling, the student teachers' performance improved, as measured by classroom observation of them. Likewise, their attitude about teaching became increasingly positive and they felt better about themselves, as evidenced by the positive slope of the curve connecting self-ratings on these variables.

Outcome Assessment

Application of problem-solving strategies or plans is the foremost objective of guided-inquiry counseling. UCLA evaluators have examined its application and participants' satisfaction with it. Table 11–7 displays the primary objectives and measurement methods and notes the studies in which they have appeared. Although client reports and ratings are the dominant assessment method, three studies included observation of clients using strategies developed in counseling, and Farmer's (1972) study tested client understanding of relevant concepts and principles.

Other assessment techniques might also be used to judge growth on the criteria in Table 11–7. An evaluator, for instance, might rate clients'

Table 11–7. Outcomes and Corresponding Measurement Method
for Guided Inquiry Counseling

Outcome	Measurement	Study
1. The client presents a clear, comprehensive description of his or her problem with which the counselor agrees.	Discrepancy between the client-counselor description of the problem	None
2. The client specifies the heuristic principles pertaining to overcoming the problem.	a) List of heuristics pertinent to the problem	None
	b) Criterion-referenced test of principles	Farmer, 1972
3. The client increases confidence in his or her ability to resolve the problem or reduce stress or anxiety in engaging in the problem situation.	Forced-choice self-rating (Ghiselli, 1971)	Bates, 1971
	Self-rating	O'Reilly, 1968 Quinn, 1970
4. The client tries out or names more alternatives by which to resolve the difficulty.	Self-report of solutions for resolving problem tried	Ogle, 1972 Horowitz, 1972
	Lists solutions for a problem	None
5. The client rehearses a systematic problem-solving strategy.	Rating by self or another	None
6. The client resolves a problem by systematic problem solving.	a) Observation of situation by researcher	Farmer, 1972 Horowitz, 1971 Zinar, 1975
	b) Self-report of outcome	Broadbent, 1970 Lin, 1972 Bates, 1971 Vivell, 1972
	c) Significant other rating	None
7. The client delineates a systematic problem-solving strategy, which he or she has applied successfully.	Self-reported strategy	None

statements during counseling to gauge their understanding of heuristic principles involved or a change in knowledge about alternative strategies. Likewise, a work supervisor or teacher could rate change in client school or job performance.

Although the rationale and operation of guided inquiry lead one to expect that clients will become more sensitive observers of their environments and more deliberative problem solvers, no research has investigated such outcomes. To judge such changes, a counselor might scrutinize a client's portrayal of a subsequent problem to detect whether the client observed more carefully, reflected about the observations and their relevance to past experiences, or searched for and identified concepts and principles for resolving the problem. More immediately, at the close of counseling the counselor might examine the client's explanations of success, attending particularly to personal understanding of deliberative problem solving and identification of pertinent concepts and principles. In still another approach, the counselor might test the comprehensiveness of client descriptions of different role interactions to ascertain whether the client had become a more sensitive observer; one could also examine the client's approach to problem simulations to gauge whether the client had become more systematic and reflective.

Risks in Guided-Inquiry Counseling

Guided-inquiry counseling requires time, concentration, and patience. These qualities can be advantages in a hurried world, but they also can create risks for the client. A person, for example, in a crisis demanding quick or immediate action may not communicate the immediacy of the problem, nor may the counselor indicate the protracted character of counseling. Consequently, the counselor may be engrossed in clarifying and teaching, when the problem has grown or produced the feared consequences. The counselor can reduce this danger by informing the client about the required time commitment, by evaluating the client's level of distress and sense of urgency, and by considering data in addition to the client's self-report.

A second, related danger is embarking on the lengthy procedure for a concern that is minimally bothersome or will resolve itself. For example, the expert mechanic may have made a poor impression in an employment interview and therefore may temporarily believe she needs to upgrade her approach to employers and fellow employees. Guided inquiry may help, but if an interview with another employer is very likely to produce a desired job, the counselor may wish to advise such an interview. Then, after the mechanic has her job, she can determine whether she needs to work on her communication skills.

A third danger arises from applying the procedure to a person whose problem-solving approach is radically different. An incompatible type appears to be the spontaneous-extrinsic described by Johnson (1978), who selects options and commits oneself to them quickly, and is very sensitive to pressures from significant others and the immediate circumstances to change. This sensitivity could easily lead one to try to please the counselor, but the penchant for acting quickly would interfere with full data gathering and deliberation, leading him or her to accept the counselor's solution in the guise of personal solutions. Indeed, this might be the dependent client who has long plagued counselors.

Discovery Groups

Career discovery groups have become popular throughout the country. They help people put careers into perspective, balance them with other roles, identify new directions, increase motivation, and develop capacity for new initiatives. Group meetings promote career exploration and career planning by dispelling the loneliness and impersonalization that can be part of an adult career.

The groups operate like seminars, usually including a predetermined number of sessions, a variety of self-appraisal and guided fantasy exercises, with frequent sharing and homework assignments to gather information and to try out ideas on family or friends. Some also incorporate speakers, field trips, autobiographies, psychological testing, bibliographies (which are sometimes annotated), and workbooks, which outline the workshops and provide exercises for completion during and after the group experience.

The dynamics of the groups are directed at promoting sharing, positive interaction, mutual support, and involvement in the exercises. Positive thinking reminiscent of Dale Carnegie is stressed, and revivalistic enthusiasm is generated for the group. Occasionally, group leaders point to selected member interactions within the group in order to illustrate a client's characteristics, but the groups rarely dwell on their own dynamics as sensitivity groups or psychotherapy groups do. People normally leave the sessions happy with themselves and one another and eager to act.

Underlying discovery groups are several assumptions about the participants: (1) they are emotionally stable and can deliberate and fantasize about various life changes (divorce, loss of structure) without undue trauma or impulsive actions; (2) they can self-disclose moderately to elicit constructive feedback while protecting their privacy; (3) they appreciate a range of educational and working experiences, which enable them to picture job/training positions accurately; (4) they can recall and recognize their talents, work interests, and values through introspection; (5) they are competent in obtaining and evaluating career information; (6) they possess implementation skills, such as capacity to judge when and when not to be assertive and how to persuade others; and (7) they expect and recognize that life and career changes require follow-through and persistence, but can be less disruptive if supported by discovery-group peers.

Usually clients contract, generally implicitly, to participate fully in the exercises, to perform the extracounseling assignments, to commit themselves to action, to accept responsibility for judging its appropriateness, and to build the skills necessary for such action.

The counselor's responsibilities include screening clients, organizing the activities, being enthusiastic and personal, stimulating involvement and interaction, and providing resource referrals. Although not researched, logic suggests that group leaders knowledgeable about how people from the client's population integrate careers and living and how they advance their careers would be most effective in eliciting specific aspirations and realistic plans of action. Similarly, an individual who reviewed his or her career with a knowledgeable professional before and after a discovery-group experience probably would assure that resulting plans were feasible.

Published research suggests that the members of career discovery groups tend initially to be strangers or acquaintances and only occasionally or accidentally friends, work colleagues, lovers, or spouses. Since more couples are trying to integrate two careers into their marriage, it is surprising that the impact of such counseling on couples has not been examined. Similarly, although several discovery-group exercises originated in industry, reported research has not examined the dynamics and effects of grouping together people from the same work milieu.

Heuristic Principles

The heuristic principles underlying discovery groups include these:

1. Membership in a group committed to career development legitimizes considering career change, adopting an assertive approach, and pursuing aggressive, systematic advancement strategies.
2. Imagining exercises generate desired goals, some of which are likely to be feasible.
3. Engaging multiple sensory modalities (smell, touch, sight, hearing) enriches fantasy.
4. Presenting (teaching) one's aspirations and plans for realizing them to relative strangers helps one specify a career goal, identify methods of achieving it, and increase commitment to it.
5. Examining the aspirations and concerns of relative strangers in order to help them identify career directions and develop motivation improves one's own ability to direct a career.
6. Recalling and analyzing one's successes to identify one's skills increases confidence.
7. Identifying others' strengths and interacting with others, who are primed to be positive, increases self-confidence.
8. Incorporating positive and negative information about self is easier in a supportive group.

Workshops and Exercises

The professional literature contains descriptions and research reports on two complete discovery workshops—the life planning workshop and the human potential workshop. Both seek to help the client formulate short-term career goals and to gain the motivation and confidence needed to pursue them. The life planning workshops are sequenced around these questions "Who am I? What am I? What do I want to be? How can I get there? (Johnson, 1977). They include exercises 1, 2, 3, 4, 5, 6, 7, 8, and 16 below (Birney, Thomas, & Hinkle, 1970) or exercises 1, 2, 3, 4, 5, 6, 8, and 16 (Johnson, 1977).

The human potential seminars differ from life planning ones not only in particular exercises, but also in that class size groups complete the exercises together under the direction of one leader rather than in four to five person subgroups under a facilitator. In addition, human potential meetings are scheduled throughout an academic semester or quarter, whereas life planning workshops are often delivered in a marathon fashion over a day or a weekend. Moreover, human potential groups introduce planning and goal setting concepts at the outset and members report on plan implementation at the start of each meeting. The exercises that have been reported for human potential counseling, which is an adaptation of Herbert Otto's (1968) work, include 16, 13, 14, and 15 below and occur in that order.

Below are described some exercises from discovery workshops. These exercises typically follow a general orientation and get-acquainted session.

1. *Life line* uses a line to delineate the scope and sequence of career, attending especially to its changes and perhaps projecting into the future. For example, clients might describe skills and aspirations of five years ago and of today, and then project skills and aspirations for future years. The purpose is to identify trends and forces underlying this change, and to initiate thinking about the future, rather than to dwell on what has happened.

Clients can list or portray significant incidents or describe key transitions on a line, or they can use a continuous curve to express the vicissitudes of their careers. Kaye (1982), for instance, has clients shape telephone wires in order to express the movement of their careers. After rendering the spectrum of their careers, clients share their portrayals, answer inquiries, and receive reactions. Generally, they record corrections and amplifications for later reflection.

2. and 3. *Identification and stripping of roles* help clients recognize the influence of specific roles on their lives and on their future plans. This activity enables them to "experience the remainder of the exercises free of the influence of their role."[1] The client lists significant roles: spouse, student, and so forth, in the order of their importance. He or she then "strips the roles one at a time, pausing to imagine life without that role, and then discussing feelings about giving up each. After relinquishing all roles, the client fantasizes about himself or herself without the roles and shares the findings. Through role divesture, individuals are expected to learn how certain roles are in conflict with their plans. This author's experience indicates that the client must use roles, not simply characteristics such as angry or outgoing, because using qualities reduces the concreteness of fantasies and few clients have attributes as pronounced as their roles. Allport's (1937) extensive observations of personality demonstrated the latter point especially. This author's experience further suggests that role stripping will have more impact if the client publicly dramatizes giving up the role by discarding real symbols of the

---

[1] The authors warn users to insure that clients are psychologically able to engage in this exercise before allowing them to participate.

role, such as keys to an office or a picture of children. At the minimum, the client should put aside an index card that lists the role.

4. *The Typical or Special Day of the Future* requires a client to fantasize about a typical or a special day in the future. A relaxing atmosphere, which may be induced by relaxation exercies, and cue questions elicit clients' projections about what is important in living. Typical cue questions are "Where do you awake and who is there? What are you doing in the morning? Concentrate! What are the sounds and colors surrounding your activity? Now it's lunch time—who is there, what are you having, and what are you thinking about? What does your afternoon feel like and what are you doing that produces such feelings? It's evening; how are you spending it?"

After ten or fifteen minutes of imagining, the client tells the fantasy. Fellow clients ask about the goals and desires reflected in the presentation, ensuring that presenters distinguish the ideal from the real, and yet being careful not to dampen their creativity. For example, a client who concluded her day casting pottery in her workshop overlooking San Francisco Bay was asked how she would afford such a location on a teacher's salary. Reflecting a moment, she indicated that a pottery kiln and workshop were very important to her, but that she could wait until she had enough income for such beautiful surroundings.

The objectives of these exercises are abstract in order to permit a range of concrete results that accommodate individual needs and competences. The intent is to provide a framework for the client to organize thoughts rather than to achieve a structured, focused result (Morgan & Skovholt, 1977). A news release, which a client would compose to announce the achievement of the fantasy, for example, need not contain particular elements, but should depict intended achievements vividly.

Often the particular, concrete objectives are hard to anticipate, but considering likely outcomes helps the exercise to proceed as intended. In thinking about beneficial outcomes, however, a counselor must resist letting second guessing dominate the exercise; for as Morgan and Skovholt (1977) noted in recommending fantasy exercises, the objective is "the maximum amount of individual expression." They should, therefore, insist on spontaneity, as shown in the following example.

First, the counselor instructs all clients to spend ten minutes concentrating on the activities of their preferred typical day so that they feel the pleasure of doing them. Then, following the counselor's direction, they outline their day's activities, including their changing feelings. Sharing starts with Jesse, who is a client reconsidering his decision to become an educational administrator. He describes his day for the group, expecting his fellow clients to ask about the scenario to help him portray it more concretely. He also expects them to tell their feelings about the person he has painted.

Jesse tells of walking to his downtown office, sharing coffee and light conversation with colleagues. This conversation turns into a discussion of the implications of the report he was doing. After they go through two cups of coffee and weigh several implications, Jesse retires to his office to organize the data, draft a final report, and then examine the guidelines for securing more funding.

As Jesse speaks, a member noted that teamwork is important and wonders whether his excitement in telling about the project's deadline suggested he preferred working under pressure. Apparently enlightened, Jesse says that he values collaborating with able people and that deadlines and competition help him to perform. He needs to work with people, not just around them. Then after a moment's thought about the counselor's question on what he was researching, Jesse replies that activity and collaboration are more important than the subject of study. Psychology, sociology, economics, anthropology all interest him, but how programs get organized and operate fascinate him. Problems such as those that state departments of education, the U.S. Department of Labor, or the U.S. Department of Health, Education and Welfare tackle really excite him, although he would prefer to work in a private firm. He continues, noting that contacts and reputation are important to obtain such positions, but his current program excels in developing contacts.

Jesse proceeds to describe his preferred lifestyle, his apparently heavy involvement in civic and cultural affairs—fitting theatre and a town meeting into a single evening. This leads one member to ask about marriage and family and where he will live. Without hesitation, he tells that he prefers an energetic, intelligent woman who might share his civic and cultural pursuits, who would have her own career, and perhaps would take time out for one or two children. He continues with a vivid description of his centrally located neighborhood, to which a member replies, "I could probably draw a map of it." As Jesse closes, the counselor reflects that Jesse's day was "packed full" and wonders whether he is exhausted. Spontaneously, Jesse says he has forgotten to mention his thirty to forty-five minutes of daily exercise to ensure good health and energy, and notes that this activity may also be social. Deliberating further, he acknowledges that time could be a problem but notes his civic pursuits would probably tie into his work and that living in a well-located neighborhood will put him close to the people and activities he wants. Even though that will save time, he does feel he should think more about how to include all his desired activities.

Jesse's passage through the exercise touched on aspirations, roles, and their interrelation; but, more importantly, its semistructured format enabled the group members and counselor to help Jesse recognize the importance of collaborative, trouble-shooting work, to recognize his need to accommodate other roles, such as exerciser, and to think more about time allocation. But, evaluating roles by rank ordering them or attempting to assign aspirations to them seems premature. Sufficient for evaluation is the counselor and client agreement that the exercise produced, examined, and reflected on vivid aspirations within the context of the roles that might occupy a particular day in one's future.

5. *The Life Inventory Exercise* requires the client to specify, in answer to a series of stimuli, what he or she would like to do differently and what he or she does well.

Stimuli may include:

a. your greatest experience
b. things you do poorly or would like to stop doing
c. skills
d. skills you would like to acquire or improve
e. what you would like to do most regardless of costs or other requirements.

Ensuing discussion should identify the values associated with the new or revitalized goals that are emerging and should pinpoint skills needed for realizing them.

6. *The School Reunion Exercise* is designed to elicit what the client hopes to be in twenty to twenty-five years and how he or she hopes to achieve the role. Clients imagine themselves returning to their high school or college, meeting old friends, and bragging about how they achieved success. They are encouraged to amalgamate their notions about new goals, new skills, and new prominence and to present them to their fellow group members for approval and suggestions.

The benefit comes from feeling "it's okay" to be the winners they are portraying, from practicing reporting positively about themselves, and from the suggested alternatives for reaching their goals.

7. *The News Release Exercise* requires the person to forecast one's major roles, accomplishments, and pleasures at some future time in the form of a news release for a hometown paper. Group discussion examines whether and how the individual is moving toward these goals. The benefit is similar to that of the school reunion exercise.

8. In the *Reassume Roles Exercise*, each client either reassumes old roles or substitutes more desirable roles and announces the reason as he or she takes on each role. The client may substitute roles or may rearrange the priority of old roles. Johnson (1977) noted that clients are allowed to substitute a new role for an old one only if "they see themselves as capable of making such changes in their own lives." This exercise is intended to accentuate the changes one is planning to make, and to provide a sense of control in making decisions about one's future.

9. *The Favorite Childhood Fantasy* requires the client to recall a story, fairy tale, movie, or radio serial, that was shared with a parent in early childhood and that was so enjoyable that the child wanted it repeated regularly. In order to generate insights, the client describes the fiction to a fellow participant for several minutes and tells the associations he or she has with the major characters.

The participant listens carefully, asks for clarification, reflects what the client is communicating and reacts after the client concludes. For example, one participant related how at age five or six she was an avid fan of "The Lone Ranger" radio serial and listened regularly to it. She summarized the story of a Texas ranger surviving an outlaw massacre, being nursed to health by an Indian named Tonto, adopting a mask to fool the ambushers, and then together with Tonto pursuing a career of bringing law and order to the West. With the reactor's assistance, the narrator gleaned the *modus operandi* of the hero that was similar, at times, to the client's approach to people—giving assistance and "riding off into the sunset" without revealing herself or expecting reward, even though she enjoyed personal interaction. Apparently this fantasy exercise draws on the concept of life script from transactional analysis.

10. *The Award Ceremony Fantasy* involves a client imagining him or herself at a testimonial banquet receiving a public award for special competence. The client concentrates on visualizing who is there and the form of the award; on hearing the elements of the testimonial, especially the points that elicit applause; on experiencing the congratulatory embraces; and on feeling the glow of being the center of attention among the festive sounds of a party. The exercise elicits public goals and the skills a person feels can enable him or her to achieve these goals and it tries to increase motivation for pursuing them. Moreover, the exercise legitimizes and provides practice for the client's viewing himself or herself as a "winner."

11. *The Mid-career Change Fantasy* engages the person in anticipating tasks, feelings, and reactions involved in the process of changing occupations. A facilitator helps each client to imagine oneself in scenarios, such as securing a new occupation or entering training; experiencing the new tasks, new environments, new people; interacting with family, friends, former employees, and colleagues at the start, during, and after the transition; and adjusting time schedules, budgets, commitments, and general lifestyle. Upon completion of the exercise, the participant should realize more fully the personal impact that such change will make and should have an increased awareness of how to make the transition smoother.

12. *The Peak Work Experience* is a self-explorative exercise, reminiscent of Flanagan's (1954) critical incident technique, designed to elicit characteristics, especially skills, that contribute to success. The person concentrates on one major work episode and tries to "live it again," sensing the feelings, activities, and interactions, and then sharing them (including movements and expressions) with the subgroup as if the episode were actually happening. After the experience is presented, the group helps the client to select the factors that make it important, and one group member records these.

13. *The Strength Bombardment Exercise* enables a person to experience positively the realization and the use of personal strengths. Each client, in turn, becomes the center of attention. For several minutes, he or she describes strengths, such as "mechanical," "strong," or "good talker," and

then asks the group to relate his or her attributes. Usually, the group also adds strengths the client has not mentioned (Otto, 1968). Then, the client asks the group to tell what they feel is preventing him or her from using the strengths to better advantage—to describe weaknesses. During interaction with the client, group members may ask for information related to the client's strengths and weaknesses, but avoid having the individual enumerate weaknesses. Instead, constructive suggestions or acceptance of some weaknesses is encouraged.

The intent of the exercise is to bombard the client with the positive, rather than to recall weaknesses. In order to prevent the client from feeling that an unreal person is being discussed, however, weaknesses he or she regards as major must not be ignored. Accordingly, the counselor asks a client whether there are additional weaknesses whenever the group appears to omit one. After the client's characteristics are identified, the counselor asks the group to relate their dream about what the client would be like in five or ten years if using all his or her strengths. After hearing these predictions, the client shares personal feelings about the strength bombardment. Sometimes the clients are so overjoyed that they hug and caress one another, tearfully expressing their warm feelings.

14. *The Success Bombardment* helps a client become aware of a personal success pattern, the differences between the success and nonsuccess experiences, and the areas in which he or she has not investigated potential. The client tells the group about three most successful experiences, such as "winning a sporting event," "earning a grade," and so forth. Then he or she describes three recent unsuccessful experiences. The group questions the client to determine whether he or she was doing something when successful that was not done when unsuccessful. For example, the group might help the client to discover that success in a track meet came after long, hard practice; whereas failure in an English test occurred because of minimal preparation.

15. *The Discussion of Values* enables the client to clarify and to acknowledge values and to gain peer acceptance. Clients are helped to feel that they can want to help people, be financially comfortable, be good students, and so forth, and still be accepted. To begin the exercise, each client tells the group his or her three most important values. (Quirck [1971] found displaying cards with the names of different positive values helped participants.) The group reinforces these values by asking him or her to clarify the meanings. By relating values to strengths and goals, a client may realize how they fit together.

16. *Goal Setting* is a closing exercise in many workshops. Each client lists specific behaviors he or she can perform immediately, or in the near future, to direct him or her toward personal goals. To guide the client, review pointers such as these: (1) Start with the abstract formulation of your goal (e.g., better relations at work) and make it more

concrete (e.g., enjoy lunches with Bill or Joan), to identify what you are doing, with whom and when, when accomplishing the goals; (2) pinpoint where you are now in relation to your goal and list the criteria (Joan is eager to hear about your hobby) you may consult to judge whether you are succeeding or failing as you proceed (talking about hobby at lunch would be a success); (3) assure that you project a realistic goal and allow sufficient time for achieving it (suggesting a luncheon x days in advance—and attending to Joan's conversation before embarking on hobby discussion). Sometimes a form helps guide the client in formulating goals. Of course, after outlining the goals, a client tells them to the group and listens for their comments about the goals' consistency with the desires and skills noted during the workshop.

Validity

Logically, discovery counseling offers at least three important aids for career development: membership in a support group that legitimizes devoting time to career development; exercises for identifying career goals, teaching advancement strategies, and for increasing motivation; and opportunity for learning from peers and other resources. Aside from a few local fraternal or business associations, discovery groups are the only identifiable groups whose primary rationale is the members' individual career development. In a society in which many people suffer from loneliness and from lack of information about adult careers, such a group should offer substantial benefit. Whether the group needs to continue beyond the typical fifteen-week semester or weekend marathon, of course, should be examined. Perhaps incorporation within an alumni or professional association would enhance and sustain its viability and effectiveness.

At present, discovery experiences for stimulating goal setting, planning, and career strategizing have only limited direct empirical substantiation, although they build on several heuristic principles. Psychological research, for example, suggests that one can increase goal pursuit by specifying the goal concretely; making public commitment to pursue it; experiencing positive feelings about it; observing models with whom one can identify pursuing it; and anticipating obstacles and formulating solutions for them. Implicitly, discovery exercises bring such principles to bear. Similarly, research on the predictive validity of the career aspirations of college students (Whitney, 1970; Holland, 1977) suggests that projecting oneself into the future, at least for those able to enter college, is potentially constructive. Supporting the value of fantasy are data from Holland's National Merit Scholars Study (1963; 1964) showing that fantasies have predictive valdity for career attainment. More recently, Touchton and Magoon (1977) found that the most recent vocational daydream reported at college matriculation predicted choice of major and occupation for 68 percent and 61 percent, respectively, of the 152 coeds studied. Moreover, careful observation by theorists, such as Ginzberg et al. (1951; Ginzberg, 1972), suggests that fantasy is an important, natural part of career development. Consequently, imagining and examining one's fantasies may help to pinpoint desired goals and to motivate their pursuit. Of course, research indicating that the prestige level of fantasy aspirations declines with age and social class, and that the probability of realizing one's childhood aspirations is related to social class suggests that fantasy exercises will be more productive for persons with the resources to pursue their aspirations.

Empirical Evidence

Ideally, the merits of discovery counseling should be judged by evaluating an entire program and the impact of individual exercises. Currently, only limited research has focused on either issue. The following paragraphs summarize the published research.

Researchers at Colorado State University have examined life planning workshops in several studies. Birney, Thomas, and Hinkle (1970) found that forty clients increased their self-regard and self-understanding, reduced their anxiety, and felt other people were more meaningful after participating in life-planning workshops. In another study, Thomas (1972) reported that students completing life-planning workshops significantly increased their internal locus of control, as measured by pre-post counseling change on the I–E scale (Rotter, 1966).

In presenting life-planning workshops to counselors and in arguing their merits, Johnson (1977) mentioned that he and Becker studied the impact of life-planning workshops on 350 students at Brigham Young University and found similar increases in internal locus of control. In discussing the workshop, Johnson (1977) also reported that in his research he substituted the audio-visual presentation or written guidelines for a group leader without effecting the procedure.

In a study of a slightly different workshop, Tichenor (1977) reported that seventy-six participants in the life-work planning workshop led by its originators, Arthur and Marie Kirn, increased their scores on the inner direction, time competence, existentiality, self-regard, and self-acceptance scales of the *Personal Orientation Inventory* (Shostrom, 1962) more than sixty wait-controls. These gains, moreover, held over a five-month follow up. The workshop, according to Tichenor, has two phases and lasts thirty hours, which can be subdivided in different ways over various timeframes. Phase 1 consists of a series of structured self-exploration and guided fantasy exercises carried out in groups of four or five with postexercise sharing. Among the exercises are drawing a lifeline, compiling self-characteristics, writing a diary of a current and future work day, composing an obituary or epitaph, and a peak work experience. Phase 2 assists in further goal clarification by having clients, individually or in small groups, choose a goal and the means of pursuing it. The exercises cover objective setting, trend analysis, force field analysis, creative problem solving, priority setting, decision making, planning, and getting ahead of problems. Following the exercises, clients share their results.

In their study of human potential counseling Trueblood and Mc-Holland (undated) reported that thirty-three educationally disadvantaged college freshmen who received this counseling increased their self-regard and became more self-directing on the *Personal Orientation Inventory* (Shostrom, 1962) than did sixty-six similar students without counseling. On the basis of clinical observation and client self-report (source: personal communication), an Ulster County Community College counselor reported that human potential counseling, in combination with remedial study, improved students' academic motivation, willingness to speak in groups and to share concerns, and clarity of goals.

Comparing eighteen hours of human potential counseling with no treatment, Paritzky and Magoon (1979) found that human potential counseling increased self-affirmation, self-determination, self-motivation, and regard for other people as measured by both the *Personality Orientation Inventory* and by self-rated goal achievement. The nineteen volunteers who completed counseling with one of two pairs of counselors exceeded volunteers awaiting counseling in eighteen of nineteen comparisons. Although the authors did not directly verify counselor fidelity to human potential standards, the four counselors had been certified to render the treatment. Moreover, the authors pointed out that the two counseling groups were not distinguishable on any one of the outcome criteria, yet both groups differed from the controls on those criteria, indicating replication of results and supporting their contention of replication of treatment.

In a study of another complete discovery workshop, Manis and Mochizuki (1972) reported favorably about a discovery program targeted at adult women at the Western University of Michigan. It included "moonlanding" (Pfeiffer and Jones, 1972) and "trust walk," panels, testing, and sharing. Its five goals were learning to work in groups, improving communications skills, improving self-understanding and confidence, learning to make decisions, and learning about career opportunities. The authors reported that questionnaire feedback from 110 clients indicated they had improved on goal setting, group support, decreasing isolation, and taking the first steps in their plans. The questionnaire items were not presented, nor were the statistics on which the interpretations were based.

Setne (1977) administered still another modified discovery procedure involving extensive interest testing and interpretation to a group of thirty-three women in six two-hour sessions. She reported that the clients evaluated the program favorably, saying that it met a community need. Their suggestions to increase facilitator contact time, supply written examples of an inventory interpretation, and deemphasize inventories in career exploration suggest that the guided peer interaction, rather than objective information, pleased these clients.

In regard to particular exercises, the literature is minimal. Otto (1968) claimed that his strength bombardment, if administered after clients were acquainted with each other, helped them identify several strengths they had not reported previously. On the basis of clinical observation, he thought the procedure enhanced participant self-confidence.

Nicholson (1975) contrasted the impact of his administering thirty-five-minute guided fantasy with effects of two alternatives—completing the *Self Directed Search* and having a thirty-five-minute career orientation, and no treatment—on self-information seeking and satisfaction with the experience. The fifteen prison inmates completing guided fantasy sought more information and were more satisfied than were the fifteen controls, and the fifteen *SDS* inmates were also more satisfied than were the untreated ones. The guided fantasy and *SDS* groups did not differ, however.

Skovholt and Hoenninger (1974) indicated that career counseling groups of University of Missouri students typically included guided fantasy exercises. Those authors said the exercises were useful and elicited lifestyle elements (place of residence, leisure activities, family members, personal needs) more often and more clearly than did other career counseling methods. They provided no statistical data to support these clinical observations.

Researchable Outcomes

Table 11–8 portrays the outcomes that discovery counseling studies have assessed. Motivation, acting in accord with values, undertaking plans, and self-confidence are immediate outcomes clearly intended by discovery counseling. Researchers rightfully have focused on their attainment. To gauge growth, they have used client and counselor progress

Table 11–8. Some Discovery-group Counseling Objectives

Objective	Measure	Study
Client will adopt career goal, that is motivating or will increase motivation for existing goal.	Counselor rating Self-report	Quirck (personal communication) Manis and Mochizuki (1972)
Client will feel more able to control the direction of own career and its place in his or her lifespace.	*Personality Orientation Inventory* *Rotter Internal-External Scale*	Trueblood and McHolland (undated) Tichenor (1977) Thomas L. (1972)
Client will increase general self-confidence.	Self-report Counselor rating	Birney, Thomas, & Hinkle (1970) Otto (1968)
Client's time and energy allocation will parallel life objectives.	*Personality Orientation Inventory*	Tichenor (1977)
Client will complete initial steps of implementing goal.	Self-report	Manis and Mochizuki (1972)

ratings and computed changes in personality inventories. They might also have had significant others, such as spouses or supervisors, rate client changes, and for some criteria, such as self-confidence and motivation, they might have had clients "Q"-sort current and ideal self and goal statements, expecting greater congruence over counseling.

Other immediate outcomes expected from discovery groups are formulation of concrete, realistic plans; increased maturity of career choice and commitment, as measured by Harren's (1966) checklist; knowledge of more strategies for boosting one's career; and more awareness of personal skills, interests, values, and limitations. These outcomes can, of course, be rated by client, counselor, and significant others, and the two knowledge goals might also be assessed by tests. For example, if clients and controls were asked to list strategies for overcoming particular career problems or to predict their aptitude, ability, and interest scores and the ways others would rate them, one would expect clients to outperform controls on the range and the quality of solution strategies and in the accuracy of prediction.

Although evaluation of discovery groups has not yet examined outcomes in the months after completing counseling, this research logically would scrutinize criteria such as satisfaction with daily activities, using a rating such as Flanagan's (1978b); the ratio of completed to attempted projects; and the time expended in nonconstructive activities, such as television watching. Assessments of these outcomes would have to rely heavily on self-report; but for some groups, records of school and work attendance and performance would be pertinent. For others, residuals such as outlays for self-help or hobby projects or expenditures for cigarettes, alcohol, or tranquilizers would be informative.

Risks in Discovery Counseling

Positive thinking is a powerful force, doubtlessly a contributor to achievement; although academics may not have validated Dale Carnegie-type workshops, thousands of satisfied customers testify to their efficacy. But discovery groups not only rely heavily on positive thinking techniques reminiscent of revivals, they also go far beyond them; therein lie their risks.

A moment's reflection will suggest the following dangers: rash, impulsive actions, such as quitting a job, relocating, and disrupting family and community ties based on inappropriate, group-supported goals and plans; public commitment to a goal that is inappropriate in terms of abilities, existing realities, or life priorities because enthusiasm has dimmed judgment or beclouded lack of information; excessive revelations of weaknesses to fellow discoverers, with ensuing abuse or breech of confidence; miscalculation of the new goal requirements, resulting in initial setback, disappointment, and abandonment of a potentially satisfying goal because of poor preparation; disillusionment with the "outside world" because it does not provide the "warm glow" of the ersatz group; and overreliance on grouping, fantasizing, and mediating, while neglecting actual experience and information gathering in setting goals and selecting means to achieve them.

In our promotional, competitive world one feels the need to claim a product or service is better than it actually is in order to get the public's attention. Yet, honest presentation of what discovery groups are—what most people gain, not what happens to the exceptions; how ideas and plans are generated on limited information; how participation is intended to produce a "warm glow" that will launch, but not sustain change; and how groups tend to be an ersatz rather than a significant reference group—is essential.

Likewise, counselor sensitivity to clients' inappropriate behavior or distress during counseling, follow-up after counseling, and availability for periodic review are also necessary to reduce the dangers inherent in these groups. Manis and Mochizuki (1972) for instance, mandated an individual follow-up interview two weeks after the counseling. Peers teaching one another their views of career management, with limited facilitator input or control, is often the most popular and perhaps the most influential aspect of discovery counseling. Unfortunately no study has verified the realism of what clients learn. A debriefing interview or postcounseling essay on effective career management seems necessary to reduce the risk of erroneous learning. Clearly, Campbell's (reported in Goldman, 1978) suggestion that psychotherapists offer clients a free six-month to one-year follow-up visit to verify and reinforce therapy benefits also has application for discovery counseling.

Personnel Review and Planning Counseling

More large corporations, government agencies, educational, health care, and other nonprofit institutions are offering employees increased opportunities for job movement within the organization. These employers realize that the knowledge gained from being in the organization contributes to productivity even when the employee performs different jobs. Therefore, they hope to retain the employee by offering other attractive jobs within the organization. For example, the Los Angeles County Sheriff's Department has recognized the advantage of attracting officers, who are about to resign because they no longer like prison guard and street patrol duties, into other nonenforcement positions.

For many years, personnel management has involved coordinating and assisting supervisors to appraise subordinates' performance and plan their careers. In the Armed Forces, perhaps because of its dependence on volunteers for nonentry jobs and perhaps because of its well-defined organization, these appraisal and planning functions are well established. Indeed, the Armed Forces have written manuals to help specialists implement career evaluation and planning.

Below are outlined the elements of a personnel review and planning program being developed for the Army by Professor Rogers Myers

(1978) and his colleagues. Although this author has not found detailed descriptions of other personnel review and planning counseling programs, this chapter will review the purposes, assumptions, and functions underlying other types of personnel counseling before presenting Myers's (1978) outline of the Army's experimental procedure. Several authors have discussed such efforts (Bowen & Hall, 1977; Cotton & Fraser, 1978).

Personnel review and planning counseling seek to enable the employee to understand how one's career achievements, aspirations, and the organizational support systems can contribute to one's career development within the employer's opportunity structure. They encourage ambition by showing how the organization helps make the desirable feasible. Moreover, this review and counseling give feedback about current performance, and the positions that fit the client now informs about future alternatives and facilitates preparation for some of those possibilities. The personnel counselor helps a client understand the probable consequences of different actions on an organizational career so the client can perform in a manner likely to produce desirable outcomes. The counselor facilitates and supports some directions for the client but may close out others.

This personnel counseling is anchored in information—information about the organization's structure, about the career histories of people passing through the structure, and about the employee's performance. Typically, estimates of the organization's future are also made available, and the client will be alerted to projected developments. Sometimes the counselor will enable the client to imagine different scenarios arising from alternate future events, as in the procedure for the Army outlined by Myers (1978) below.

These past and present facts and future projections are furnished to a client under the assumption that they will enable the employee to comprehend more fully how one has worked and can continue to work successfully within the organization. The major purposes of this type of personnel counseling are cognitive, affective, and behavioral. The counselor wants the employee to grasp the opportunities offered by the organization, the paths to them, their requirements and benefits, one's progress relative to different paths, and the resources available for pursuing various options. The counselor also desires the client to commit oneself to undertake horizontal or vertical career development and to act on such commitment.

In informing the employee about the organizational structure, counseling intends to show that advancing vertically or horizontally within the organization will enhance overall development. Without doubt, this counseling promotes accommodating to the organization's objectives and needs in order to realize one's own objectives.

Personnel counseling often has the dual responsibility of gatekeeping. Developmental assignments, special training, and the like, are coordinated and frequently regulated through the personnel office. An employee, therefore, may gain access to such opportunities through personnel counseling or may even have to undergo counseling in order to be eligible for such career-enhancing opportunities.

In showing a client where one fits or might fit into the organization and in determining eligibility for different developmental assignments, the personnel counselor draws from biodata, test data, and limited achievement data accumulated during the client's selection and performance ratings within the organization. Generally, counseling will also touch on personal data about interest, values, aptitudes, extra work roles, resources, and life style, that a client furnishes.

In using test and other performance data to grant assignments or to allocate resources, the personnel counselor will tend to emphasize courses of action supported by actuarial predictions more than a career choice counselor might. The personnel counselor seeks to assist client career development, but within parameters feasible for the organization. For example, the technician with low academic achievement, who aspires to an engineering degree, is likely to be treated differently by the personnel and career choice counselor from another such aspirant with excellent grades. Recognizing the limited actuarial probability of this technician's achieving an engineering degree, the personnel counselor will point out the advantage of other kinds of career action, especially those supported by data. Moreover, the counselor will be reluctant to assist the client in acquiring organization resources for such a risky endeavor. Thus, the technician might well be encouraged to take supervisory courses, and even offered some released time for them, but not be given assistance to acquire an engineering degree. In contrast, a career choice counselor would be more likely to explore with the technician how one might achieve an engineering degree. Such a counselor would not ignore nor minimize the risks; but once the client had acknowledged them and the counselor judged that the goal might be attainable, the counselor would join the client in searching for feasible strategies. Certainly, a career choice counselor would support alternatives involving job change as fully as alternatives involving retaining the technician position or pursuing other advancement within the organization. On the other hand, the personnel counselor would be unlikely to give equal time to extraorganizational alternatives. In part, this counselor's information does not extend beyond the organization's alternatives; furthermore, this counselor's commitment is both to the worker and to the organization.

Heuristic Principles

Several heuristic principles support personnel review and career planning counseling. Among these are the following:

1. Employee morale and organizational commitment grow when the employee believes that the organization is attempting to accommodate personal goals and talents and to offer opportunity for development.

2. Persons are more likely to build career skills if they recognize that attractive, accessible positions require these skills and if they are shown how to build them.

3. Employee career motivation and organizational commitment increase when the employee recognizes alternate career ladders accessible within the organization.

4. Employee career' motivation increases when the employee periodically reviews progress and projects for improvement with a trusted expert.

Personnel review and planning counseling require employer and employee preparation. In discussing preparation for appraising potential, Kellogg (1975) indicates that an employer needs to do things such as review both the performance of the employee to pinpoint skills, trends, education, and his or her background, which would suggest areas of development; ascertain the kinds of work toward which the employee might grow and for which there may be future demand; think through knowledge and skills the worker should acquire for possible vertical or horizontal advancements; and specify points to be established, such as these:

1. Agreement of employee and employer evaluation of the employee
2. Employee career goals and dedication to them
3. Employee realism about his or her career future, including probable rate of advancement and kinds of upgrading required
4. Consistency of employee goals with the organization's intended development
5. Opportunities for employee development within present position, and
6. Help from organization desired by employee.

The employee should prepare by reviewing his or her career and noting successes and shortcomings; pinpointing work situations that have and have not contributed to growth; obtaining third-party feedback on personal attributes to improve self-knowledge, including vocational ability and interest testing; considering the impacts of trends likely to affect his or her career; identifying skills and experiences needed for desired positions; and establishing specific points with the employer, such as these:

1. The employer's views about performance level,
2. The implications of vocational testing results,
3. The realism of career aspirations,
4. The prerequisites of target jobs, and
5. The possibilities within the current position for skill development.

Method

Phillips, Cairo, and Myers (1980) graciously provided the following preliminary description of the Officer Career Information and Planning System and also furnished the tentative illustrations of its modules, which appear in Appendices B through G.

The Officer Career Information and Planning System (OCIPS)

OCIPS is being developed in response to a need seen by the Army for a cost-effective career planning system which (a) would place computerized data at the disposal of both the career development manager and the officer and (b) would facilitate the implementation of the Army policy of officer professional development and utilization as expressed in DA Pamphlet 600–3. Prior to the initiation of the project, several legitimate complaints on the part of officers had been recognized. These included, specifically, the lack of readily available, consistent, complete, and current information regarding the officer career progression system. There was also evidence to suggest that better use of officer interests and abilities was possible and that inefficient officer career decisions were being made (Macpherson, 1978; Macpherson, Eastman, & Yates, 1977).

Drawing on theory and research in counseling psychology and technologies in computer science, OCIPS is envisioned as a computer-aided career information and planning system for Army officers (Cairo, 1977; Cory, Medland, & Uhlaner, 1977; Cory, Medland, Hicks, Castelnovo, Weldon, Hoffer, & Myers, 1976; Van Nostrand, 1979). It is hoped that this system will provide a number of benefits to the Army officer and to Army management, including:

> greater ability of an officer to take responsibility for his or her own career decision making;
>
> greater officer satisfaction and increased knowledge of the career-enhancing potentialities of various assignments;
>
> better fit of officer-to-job based on the consideration of aptitudes, values, interests, education, training, and experiences; and
>
> greater equity and efficiency in the career management system.

In order to begin to accomplish these goals, the initial phase of the system's development, described in this report, called for a long-range career planning dialogue unit that would enable Army officers to explore planning strategies and decision-making techniques and to develop and apply career goals and values to their own long-term career planning. It was decided that the system would need to conform to a number of specifications. First, the dialogue units should allow the officer to explore career-related values and strategies for implementing those values. The units should advocate flexibility in career planning and be applicable to Army careers. Second, the dialogue should appear as a natural conversation between an officer and a human counselor, using explicit, concise language tailored to Army officer background and interests. Finally, the dialogues should be designed to increase the officer's awareness of the notion of a career as a time-ordered sequence of positions, mediated partly by his or her own choices.

System Description

The current system consists of interactive, or conversational, dialogue units. The user's path through the units is determined by his or her responses to questions or by selection from among alternatives posed at several choice points within each unit. (Examples are provided in Appendices B through E.) Each module is self-contained and connects with the other modules via an executive monitoring system. At present, SIGNON, FORESIGHT, OVERVIEW, and ALTERNATE SPECIALTY have been programmed and are usable in demonstration form. The remaining modules—CAPTAIN'S INTRODUCTION, SELF-ASSESSMENT, and CAREER STRATEGIES—are in script form but have not yet been programmed. The various modules are described below.

SIGNON. This introductory module introduces the officer to the system, instructs the officer as to how to use the terminal, and asks for a variety of identifying data such as military specialty, type and level of civilian education, and current military status.

FORESIGHT. This module is designed to introduce the user to long-term career planning. It begins with consideration of the belief that individuals can influence their career progress if (a) they know what they want, and (b) they know how the system works. The basic career concepts described earlier are assigned code names: "Must"—choice is inevitable; "Value"—you have to know what you want; "Surprise"—unexpected events happen even if you plan; "Tension"—simultaneously firm and tentative planning; and "Stage"—predictable life changes. The user may elect to look through any or all of the five- or six-frame interactive explanatory illustrations for each concept. The conclusion of the module integrates the concepts in a sample career path that shows an officer making choices and confronting situational changes at different stages in his career. The ability to convey to the user the most current available knowledge about career planning and career development in an understandable and thought-provoking manner is the most outstanding quality of the FORESIGHT module. (See Appendix B for an excerpt from FORESIGHT.)

OVERVIEW. This informational module includes the Army's overall plan for the progression of an officer's career and attempts to make the user aware of those factors which can influence the ways in which an officer's career develops. These include:

> changes in needs, goals, and objectives of the Army
> military and technological changes
> timing of career decisions
> Officer Evaluation Reports
> military education
> alternate specialty assignment
> civilian education and training

It dissects the patterns and determinants of Army careers with the use of a series of off-line charts and offers the user answers to a series of typically-asked questions. It reinforces the concepts introduced in FORESIGHT and adds some Army-specific concepts such as officer responsibility and dimensions of utilization and training. OVERVIEW facilitates the officer's comprehension of "how the system works"—a necessary ingredient in career decision making—and does so in a manner that enables officers to incorporate the understanding of the complex officer career progression system into their planning. (See Appendix C for an excerpt from OVERVIEW.)

CAPTAIN'S INTRODUCTION. Experience with the system has shown that, while younger officers (lieutenants) profit from FORE-SIGHT and OVERVIEW, officers who have achieved the rank of captain or above have already acquired much of the information contained in the modules. Therefore a substitute introductory module was designed for users already familiar with the Army Career Progression system. This module, called CAPTAIN'S INTRODUCTION, includes the information in FORESIGHT and OVERVIEW in a more abbreviated form (See Appendix D).

ALTERNATE SPECIALTY. One of the system's long-range objectives is to provide the user with access to data relevant to important choice points in an Army officer's career. The submodule of OVERVIEW and CAREER STRATEGIES, called *ALTERNATE SPECIALTY*, is an example of how this can be done. Due to the implementation of dual occupational specialties for Army officers, expressing a preference for an alternate specialty is a critical choice point in an officer's career. A rich data file relating officer characteristics and preferences to alternate specialty designation affords the user a unique opportunity to engage in meaningful career exploration. The ALTERNATE SPECIALTY submodule was developed to make use of this data file and includes information about the alternate specialties that are available, how they are designated, and how career plans can influence them. In making the data available to the user and in offering suggestions about useful ways to interpret them, the submodule provides the officer with the opportunity to explore and compare his or her characteristics with those of officers for whom any given specialty was designated during the previous year and to integrate this information into an effective career strategy (See Appendix E).

SELF-ASSESSMENT. Other modules (OVERVIEW and ALTER-NATE SPECIALTY) have addressed the issue of "how the system works." The SELF-ASSESSMENT module is designed to help users clarify "what they want"—a necessary component of satisfactory career planning. The officer uses a representative list of skills and values to create an invidualized profile based on preference and performance (skills), and subjective importance (values). The list of skills was derived from an analysis of Army officer job performance dimensions (Oliver, 1978) and available inventories of relevant career skills (Haldane, 1974; Katz, Chapman & Godwin, 1972). Similarly, the values list represents a combination of work value inventories (Super, 1968; Katz, Chapman & Godwin, 1972), lists of values used in industrial personnel development programs, and values derived from Army Research Institute surveys. Once the officer has created a profile, suggestions are offered about integrating self-assessment into planning and the user is asked to evaluate previous and anticipated assignments in light of this profile. (See Appendix F for an excerpt from SELF-ASSESSMENT.)

CAREER STRATEGIES. This module is designed to help officers implement their career aspirations through exercises in setting long-term goals and in translating goals into action plans for immediate objectives. The introduction conveys to the officer:

> that goals provide the basis for long-term planning;
> that goals are arrived at by assessing the structure of Army career opportunities and by assessing one's own characteristics;
> that long-term goals can only be obtained by achieving intermediate objectives; and
> that concrete plans of achieving intermediate objectives provide the link between career planning and intelligent action.

The process of creating a career strategy is introduced by the use of a career planning game which incorporates the major aspects of an officer's career: military specialties, education and training, skills, job performance, rank, contribution, assignments, family, and values. The game uses the computer to present "moves" at decision points and uses an off-line playing board, called the Career Planning Wheel, for charting hypothetical career progression. The player starts the game as a second lieutenant, selects preprogrammed goals, seeks to move forward toward those goals in a series of computer managed decisions, and arrives at an end point that signifies goal achievement. The decision points require the player to deal with four career issues: the inevitability of Surprise, the necessity of Choice, the awareness of Opportunities, and knowledge of Requirements. (The game is called SCOR.) The user creates long-term goals for each of the career aspects and is guided to examine the congruence and conflicts among the several goals. This activity requires that computer-based career data be assessed.

After the game has led to the creation of career goals, these goals are examined with a series of eight criteria for effective career planning goals and revised until they satisfy the criteria. The revised goals are then translated into action plans for intermediate objectives. For example, users are guided to convert goals to actions by choosing a specific standard for gauging success, identifying resources and barriers, setting checkpoints and deadlines, and so on.

The results of this module include clarified career goals, contibutory intermediate objectives, and action plans which have been tested for their adequacy. (See Appendix G for an excerpt for CAREER STRATE-GIES.)

Hazards

Personnel counseling presumes that the employee recognizes that he or she is dealing with the employer's representative. The relationship is not an adversary one, but unless identified as otherwise, the counselor expects to be the worker's confidant only to the degree that it does not injure the organization. Consequently, the client must be wary of providing self-information to which the employer is not entitled, and which if made available, may adversely affect the employee. For example, a woman may not wish to reveal that her husband recently obtained tenure in his position lest the counselor conclude that her organizational development should no longer include expanding her current duties to assistant supervisor, which might equip her for a supervisory position in another geographic location.

A second hazard involves giving too much credence to the organization's opportunity structure and insufficient attention to alternatives. Because the organization reaches out to one, flatters the employee with its concern, and makes it easy to understand its opportunities, an employee may be lulled into focusing on the organization, neglecting to obtain equally extensive information about options outside the organization. Achieving a balanced understanding of prospective opportunities, of course, is an ideal that few workers now realize. Unfortunately, many now have limited information about possibilities, within or outside their firm or agency, so that the danger of imbalance generally should be outweighed by the value of the new information.

Maintenance Stage
Career Counseling

12

After equipping themselves for work, finding, and then sucessfully pursuing an occupation for several years, people may expect years of
untroubled productivity and satisfaction. They have arrived, they are
considered part of the "establishment," have mastered the many nuances of their occupations, and are entitled to pride in their accomplishments. Working should not be as stressful or uncertain for these veterans as for newcomers; their entry to middle age and the stage, which
Super (1957) termed *maintenance*, certifies that they have identified
and secured worthwhile positions and have redesigned their jobs to
make them acceptable. But not everyone enters the maintenance state
successfully. Unfortunately, some people at this age lack a secure job,
suffer downgrading and financial setbacks, and toil at tasks with associates who are not congenial (Super, 1957). The middle-aged worker
is entitled to a sense of accomplishment, but, unfortunately, some only
reap discouragement from their work.

This chapter first will summarize views about career development
during the maintenance stage of career and point out the counseling
objectives that such views suggest. Then it will describe and critique
three counseling procedures. The first is a comprehensive career counseling workshop that brings adults of different ages together to examine
where they are, have been, and might go, in order to renew their enthusiasm for career management and to recognize their accomplishments. The second procedure combines rational-emotive and client-
centered techniques into a vehicle to help the adult rediscover who he
or she has become as a consequence of the career, and to project and
plan who he or she might yet be. The third procedure is outplacement
counseling that helps workers to reestablish a career after a sudden,
unwanted interruption, usually from job termination or elimination.

The Maintenance Stage in
Career Development

People enter this stage around the age of forty to fifty, often at the zenith of their careers. They leave this stage at retirement, around age sixty to seventy. The entry and exit ages vary with type of career pattern and sex; conventional careerists tend to enter around forty-five and leave at sixty-five; stable careerists may enter later and stay later; unstable and multitrial careerists, if they enter the maintenance stage at all, will enter later and stay for a shorter period. Homemakers or mothers, in contrast, are likely to enter this stage later and to stay later, especially if they achieve professional-level employment.

Developmental theorists have been relatively silent about this period of adulthood, and empirical research is even scarcer. Blocher (1973) calls the period the stabilization stage and summarized its tasks identified by Havighurst (1964) and Erikson (1950): "learning to be aware of change, having attitude of tentativeness, developing broad intellectual curiosity, developing realistic idealism, and developing a time perspective. Recently, Levinson (1978) and Gould (1978) have extended psychodynamic theorizing about this age, particularly developing the theme that adulthood requires a series of transformations for full human realization to occur. Levinson (1978) speculated that, after moving into the period, one faces a crisis because new accommodations are required. The extent of the crisis depends on how fully the person has resolved earlier career difficulties. The years from fifty-five to sixty, following the resolution of the crisis, can be happy for those who have rejuvenated themselves. The period of age sixty to sixty-five, in turn, are years of preparing for retirement, a stage about which Gould (1978) appears even more optimistic. In words reminiscent of Erikson's (1963) notion of generativity, he notes, "People live with a sense of having completed something, a sense that we are whoever we are going to be— and we accept that, not with resignation . . . but with a more positive acceptance."

More specific to career, Super, in Jordaan (1974), points out the need to preserve achieved status and gain. As Jordaan explains, "The individual is less concerned with registering new gains than with maintaining present status in the face of competition from younger, more enterprising coworkers who are in the advancement stage (substage of establishment)." Jordaan goes on to point out that this is not a period free of stress, noting that ". . . the individual may have to run hard just to stay where he is. . . ." Super (1957) had commented: "The choices at this stage are not merely choices between competing for new gains and holding one's own. It is not as simple as that, for there are misgivings about ability to hold one's own unless one actively breaks new ground."

In general, there is consensus that maintenance is not a static state, but a time of consolidation, and eventually of winding down. If maintenance is successful, slowing down is acceptable. At its start, some workers may still be adding to their achievements and directing their careers to take advantage of the varied accomplishments their careers have produced. For example, the journeyman carpenter, who has developed a skill in finish carpentry and has built a reputation among contractors for reliability and quality, secures a contractor's license and opens his own subcontracting finish carpentry business to gain more control over his work.

The knowledge explosion and technological advances require that workers in many occupations, such as engineer, scientist, nurse, secretary, accountant, and auto mechanic, continually acquire new knowledge and adapt their skills. Organizational alterations and consolidations, in turn, force managers and sales people to keep abreast of changes and to build new linkages and expertise that enable them to avoid becoming obsolete.

Veteran workers often operate as if they were remodeling a home. They adapt to new challenges and opportunities, adding on or combining, realigning, altering, refurbishing, and abandoning some things without eradicating the beauty, steadfastness, and character of the building. The essential foundation and structure were put in place during establishment, but the maintenance stage involves more than cleaning and making repairs. One can polish and bring out the highlights of one's personhood, which successful establishment has put in place for mellowing. Maintenance can be a joyful time. The veteran worker has mastered his or her work and is now producing ably, recognized as one who has "made it." Status and esteem are a self-made reality; they are not intangibles given by parents or being pursued, perhaps never to be acquired. Many things come to fruition during these years. Typically, one's career is stable; he or she has produced and has gained recognition and acceptance as a worker. Salary is at or near its apex, and one is a valued employee, not easily replaced.

During this time, many things testify to the person's value, not only at work, but also at home and in the community. This veteran is called on to teach and to sponsor others at work. On the job, he or she is respected, and the community beckons him or her to responsibilities that accord with a successful career. He or she takes leadership roles in civic, social, charitable, and political activities and sponsors or coaches youth activity. For the few workers who move out of their occupational areas at this stage, the change is often to a supervisory or managerial position (Gottfredson, 1977). This advancement to direct others in one's occupation further affirms societal esteem. Moreover, during the maintenance stage, society expects the worker to act as mentor to younger, less-advanced workers, either as a supervisor or senior colleague. Although researchers are only beginning to clarify mentoring behavior, many high-level workers, consider mentors as important contributors to their careers. But, before one can be a mentor, one must have established one's own career (Phillips, 1977).

On the other hand, maintenance is also a time of great challenge. Family and society require these workers to sustain and even to increase their productivity, to socialize new workers to work, and to recognize and then support alternatives in working. People in this stage must lead and support the "establishment," must prepare others to lead, and must gradually relinquish leadership and prepare to leave work. Many challenges for maintenance-stage workers do not stem directly from particular jobs but doubtlessly do affect their careers. Requirements for prolonged, increasingly expensive education for one's children, and an ever-rising consumption lifestyle for one's family pressure the worker continually to strive for higher earnings and more security.

Today's world makes midlife difficult for many workers. While the society asks for increased allegiance and renewed commitment to production, many find it harder than ever to maintain faith in the system. Inflation, the spectre of unemployment, disillusionment about Vietnam, Watergate, pollution, energy, and daily exposés are prompting people to question the system. Promotion of leisure, the younger generation's questioning of a work-dominated lifestyle, and publicity about the "workaholic" syndrome are stirring middle-aged workers to reflect on the place of career in life.

The so-called "mid-career" crisis underscores the challenge of the maintenance stage. Walz (1979) claims that between ages forty and fifty as many as 35 percent of men experience dissatisfaction, confusion, and disruption in careers. Diminishing satisfaction with working, apathy about one's career, and uncertainty about one's identity are the primary symptoms. The causes and solutions appear to be multiple (Brim, 1977). But even though the varied symptoms and causes suggest that "mid-career crisis" is not one, specific sociological, psychological, or physiological malady, the wideranging experience of difficulties among workers in mid-life indicates that the maintenance stage is not the pacific course one hoped it would be. Clearly, further study of those experiencing and resolving its various crises will be helpful.

For the many men entering this stage who unexpectedly find their wives preparing to resume careers, often because their earnings are not considered adequate, additional adjustments become necessary. Perhaps most important, these men have to sustain their esteem while recognizing the logic of their wives' working to enrich their standard of living. Then, too, they must adjust to more shared chores and more attention to one another's time demands within the family. In addition, they have to cope with children becoming teenagers who will soon depart, requiring another change in family living. During these changes, their wives often will be seeking the kind of support in becoming "established" in career preparation and work that they had formerly given their husbands. In many cases, however, husband and wife will not concur on the importance of the wife's working, as they did on the necessity of the husband's career at the start of their marriage.

Middle-aged women, too, face special challenges; and like men, they find these challenges arise while their self-esteem is being called into question. Those women who have devoted their main energies to homemaking and parenting now hear that such achievements have become less important and that true fulfillment requires success in paid employment, especially in traditionally nonfemale fields. Their own age and societal mores reduce the importance of raising children, supporting a husband's career, and volunteering within the community, thus robbing many who have succeeded in these activities of the self-esteem they deserve for their accomplishments. Small wonder that most say that they would not do it over again. Fortunately, task forces, new legislation, and special programs for displaced homemakers are helping women to secure their fair, equal place in the work system.

Logic and our legal structure affirm the merits, if not the necessity, of equal work opportunity for men and women. Little is known, however, about how women can achieve equality or the psychological costs involved in doing so. Certainly, the task will not be easy, for the American work system favors those people over twenty-one and under forty who have secured membership in the primary "labor market." Clearly, the work world foils qualified workers' free access to paid employment opportunities by means of excessive licensing and credential requirements, by demanding perhaps unnecessary past experience, and through the gatekeeping of ingroup networks such as unions, professional association "old boy" networks, "headhunter" recruitment firms, and so forth.

Of course, parenting and homemaking develop myriad planning, budgeting, purchasing, communicating, supporting, teaching, coordinating, repairing and maintaining skills (Bolles, 1974). Logic and, to some degree, justice dictate that it should not be any more difficult for a woman completing twenty years of parenting-homemaking to start a "second career" than it is for a man completing twenty years of military service or police or fire fighting work. However, both the gatekeeping mentioned above and the differential value placed on paid and unpaid work balance the scale against women.

Up to now, marriage and parenting have been more important factors in American women's careers than in those of American men. Marriage does not generally appear to have benefited women's careers, although there are many individual exceptions. In contrast, stable marriage has related positively to the career success of Terman's "gifted men" (Oden, 1968; Sears, 1977). The Department of Labor Study found that marriage has been associated with less career stability and less work and educational achievement for women in mid-career (Parnes et al., 1976). Moreover, married women changing the geographic locations of their jobs tend to lose salary, whereas unmarried women making such changes have gained.

In terms of renewing a career after years of homemaking, husband and family support are important. Astin (1977), for instance, in an interview study of three hundred carefully selected women found that spouse support was related to success in continuing education. Similarly, Phillips (1977) found that successful career women thought spouse support was an important factor in their work success.

How homemaking and parenting experiences can be turned into career assets for women has not been seriously explored. Logically, these experiences broaden the person's repertoire of skills and confidence, and society would benefit if the workplace tapped those talents. Likewise, if society values nurtured children and stable families, it should reward, rather than punish, successful parenting and homemaking.

The maintenance period can be anticlimatic. A person has achieved many career summits: graduation, first mainline job, big promotion, major recognition, and high salary. Many of life's other satisfactions have been long ago realized: independence, first car and apartment, marriage, first home, dream home, children, country club memberships, and community leadership positions. For this maturing person, the climb up has been exhilarating, but most, if not all, peaks have been experienced. Future successes are likely to be more of the same. At this stage, therefore, one begins to feel that the zenith has been reached and decline is inevitable. The slope may be very gentle, but ultimately the person realizes the route is downward, nevertheless.

Even as the stage starts, physiology, in our appearance-conscious society, reminds the person that he or she is getting old. As people turn forty, they feel the tiring effects of exercise more quickly and notice that weight is harder to take off. Vitality diminishes; muscle tone is harder to maintain; and visual and auditory acuity wanes. Many people will have forty, perhaps even fifty good years left, especially if they followed a good health regimen; but few are likely to achieve any new physical triumphs. Gordie Howe, George Blanda, Satchel Paige, and Archie Moore are legends because they proved able to perform athletically into their late forties. None claimed, however, that their achievements at fifty matched those of their prime.

As the fifties become sixties, the decline in physical prowess accelerates and most soon-to-be senior citizens diminish arduous physical activity. Along with moderating their physical pace, these workers generally are expected to be directing their attention to retirement, which some have characterized as the first insult of aging. Companies and agencies are sponsoring increasing numbers of retirement planning workshops to enable seniors to equip themselves for leaving working.

Because of society's great concern with appearance, physical decline, doubtlessly, is often assumed to signal general deterioration among workers in the maintenance stage. Sinick (1977), in discussing career counseling of older adults, suggests that counselors help senior clients debunk such views by informing them of evidence that:

1. From biological maturity until age 60, physical strength seems to be maintained at its maximum; 2. Maximum intellectual functioning appears to occur between the ages 45 and 80; 3. There is little change in the ability to learn new skills and acquire new information between 20 and 65; 4. Morale drops low in the 20s but rises to new highs in the late 50s.

Arguing further against too ready acceptance of a general decline, Sinick (1977) referenced a U.S. Department of Labor (1956) survey wherein employers attributed these traits to older workers: stability, dependability, responsibility and loyalty, seriousness about work, and capability of functioning with less supervision than younger workers. Moreover, Sinick (1977) reminded counselors that the U.S. Department of Labor's (1971) publication, *Myths and facts regarding older workers* points out the fallacy of stereotypes, such as "older workers are too slow, can't meet physical demands of work, are often absent, and are not adaptable."

Career Counseling Objectives

From reviewing the limited research and extensive speculation on adult career development, one can generate a set of career counseling needs such as those below. The scope and extent of adult career needs, however, is not well established. Reports such as O'Toole's (1973) *Work in America* suggest that career difficulties are widespread and produce considerable distress; but no one has yet estimated systematically the percentage of psychiatric, medical, familial, and societal disturbances attributable to career difficulties. Certainly, the fact that psychiatrists such as Gould (1978) are writing about patients' career problems suggests that they are treating many whose problems are aggravated, if not initiated, by career concerns. Likewise, the findings of Bachman, O'Malley and Johnston (1978) that unemployed youth engage in considerably more than average illicit activity, and Morley's (1971) description of the deterioration that beset some workers when they were laid off and could not find other suitable work, points to serious societal disruption from personal career difficulties. Nevertheless, the paucity of information about the frequency of adult career problems and the concomitant lack of data about how these difficulties are resolved necessitates careful diagnosis and goal setting with the client, as well as ongoing vigilance about how persons actually are resolving their concerns.

In this time of accelerating change, the major need of people in the maintenance stage of their careers may well become changing their career direction. Certainly today, as perhaps never before, changing one's occupation or how one plays one's work role is possible. Supporting such flexibility is the proliferation of community colleges and business and proprietary schools, as well as the willingness of four-year colleges and universities to give credit toward degrees for life experiences. Moreover, the aging of the population, diminishing age discrimination, and the introduction of portable pensions are also facilitating more career changing.

To the degree that different occupations allow expression of different facets of a human being, changing career directions several times during one's life may enable fuller self-expression. Clearly, the U.S. Bureau of Labor Statistics forecasters believe that such adaptiveness will be needed, and some corporations and government agencies are promoting it. Certainly, if American industry begins guaranteeing employment security throughout a career, as Japanese industry has, employee career flexibility will be necessary for the corporation to sustain its competitiveness through innovation.

Currently, there is little evidence about the equity of job and occupational change at the maintenance stage. Observers of job changers in management, such as Jameson (1978) have claimed that nearly 90 percent involve salary reductions; in education, for example, recall most districts will award teachers and counselors only 50 percent or 60 percent credit on their years of teaching in other places. Research, unfortunately, is silent about other aspects of career changes, such as alterations in level of tension or balance among life roles. Those contemplating a career change, however, should assess the consequences carefully.

Career counseling appropriately might help clients in the maintenance stage to seek the following objectives:

1. To renew and sustain motivation for career achievement and to obtain familial and collegial support for career improvement efforts;
2. To acquire information about how to improve or sustain one's career;
3. To rehearse, and perhaps refurbish, skills important in directing a career such as job searching, decision making, and so forth;
4. To reestablish an accurate self-concept, feasible goals, and realistic beliefs about work;
5. To feel pleased with past and current achievements and hopeful about future prospects;
6. To act effectively in righting one's career in the face of a crisis;
7. To negotiate with employers to obtain greater satisfaction from one's job;
8. To change the direction of one's career by moving from one occupation to another, from one firm or enterprise to another, or by changing the way in which one discharges a position.

In the 1970s, more employers provided "career counseling workshops" to assist employees in (1) renewing motivation, (2) acquiring information, and (3) refurbishing skills. This chapter describes one workshop and the limited research that has been reported on such efforts. Skills-building counseling procedures from earlier stages should also be relevant to these objectives.

In terms of revising goals and enjoying career achievements, objectives (4) and (5), a combination of client-centered and rational emotive counseling seems feasible. Both kinds of counseling have been directed at helping adults with career problems (Thoroman, 1968; Ellis, 1979). Their combination is logically appropriate for the mature worker who has expanded one's conceptualization of self, options, and how work should be; yet who has not had the opportunity to verify the revised self-concept with an expert in career development.

Object (6), dealing effectively with crises, is now being addressed by outplacement counseling, described below. Objective (7), negotiating with employers, flows especially from the ombudsman function; but this author has not located a succinct operational description of how to render that role, and knows of no direct research on it. For objective (8), changing career direction, workshops such as the one described below and/or one of the career choice counseling procedures in Chapter 10 seem appropriate. But no evidence of their validity for this age group has been reported.

Other counseling formats might be developed to teach or to remind maintenance-stage workers how to redesign their jobs and to teach and support such workers in mentoring. While the job development function is often a facet of the rehabilitation counselor's role, and job developer is often a specific job title in CETA programs, this author has located neither detailed descriptions of the activities nor empirical research verifying their efficacy.

The objectives above are not meant to be exhaustive, and clearly the methods to be described are not the only ones to use in addressing these needs. Certainly, guided inquiry and discovery counseling, for instance, would also appear appropriate. Moreover, additional interventions clearly are needed. The author hopes publication of these procedures will stimulate practitioners to describe other methods in detail.

A useful adjunct to career counseling at this stage would be directed reading or course in adult development. The very absence of a standard text on adult career development indicates that much needs to be discovered about this stage of life; yet, until recently, this age group has drawn relatively little attention. Surely, popular books, such as *Passages* (Sheehy, 1976) *Seasons of a Man's Life* (Levinson, 1978), *Transformations* (Gould, 1978), *The Managerial Woman* (Hennig & Jardim, 1976) can stimulate reflection within courses.

Security Pacific National Bank's Counseling Program

To help employees manage their careers, Security Pacific National Bank has a program that includes these four elements: career advisors who act as information brokers, linking employees with resources or information about possible job options; the immediate supervisor who assigns work, reviews potential employee projects with the employee, and provides feedback on performance; a career workshop; and a staff planning unit, which accumulates and reviews information about corporate personnel needs and employee career development needs and plans and proposes and in some cases implements appropriate programs. Through the program, employees may review career goals; pinpoint new ones; and build the confidence, knowledge, skills, personal contact, and commitment needed to improve their careers.

This exposition focuses on the career workshop. Of course, since the workshop is part of a total program, its gains partially reflect the efforts of involved supervisors and career advisors, as well as the ongoing evaluation and support of the planning unit. The workshop described here was fashioned by Mr. Ben Dolin and Ms. Susan Bryant of Security

Pacific National Bank, Dr. Beverly Kaye of Beverly Kaye and Associates, and Dr. Adele Scheele of Social Engineering Technology.

The workshop melds large-group lecture-discussion, reading, small-group self-exploration, guided meditation, fantasy exercises, and homework assignments into an experience that stimulates self and occupational awareness, bolsters motivation, and initiates planning for career renewal or change. Based on the assumptions that adults can direct their careers if they know themselves, compatible opportunities, and strategies for making change happen, the workshop initiates self-asessment and exploration of corporate opportunities and points out acceptable strategies for advancing a career. In the workshop this author observed, the leaders also made special efforts to identify female concerns and advancement obstacles, encouraging women to confront these hurdles.

Underlying Heuristic Principles and Participant Prerequisites

The workshop leaders manifested many of the behaviors described in Chapter 5 under the class of counselor behaviors for involving clients in counseling, and they regularly reinforced constructive career management behavior or intentions to engage in such behavior. Following are three principles that go beyond effective teaching and which underlie the workshop:

1. Constructive career management increases when the repertoire of effective behaviors is clearly and concretely defined.
2. Constructive career management increases when a forum is provided for initiating self-appraisal and planning and for eliciting personal commitment to pursue career advancement.
3. Constructive career management occurs when a person recognizes that employers sanction it, that a peer group approves it, and that peers engage in similar behavior.

Insofar as the workshop involves fantasizing and disclosing personal characteristics and aspirations to obtain feedback, the assumptions concerning discovery group clients on page 507 also pertain to workshop participants, Participants are also expected to be aware of marketing theory and practice or be able to learn about it on their own. In addition, they should have demonstrated good working habits and technical competence in some area of banking.

The Workshop

Organizationally, instruction occurs on two weekends separated by three to four weeks with assigned homework. Eight self-contained instructional units or sessions are delivered in three to three-and-one-half hour blocks with fifteen to twenty-minute breaks. The sessions and their objective are presented here. The following workshop is being modified, however, based on ongoing evaluation.

Session 1. The objectives of Session 1 are to (a) provide an overview of the workshop and introduce technical concepts; (b) establish the credibility of the workshop staff, and (c) initiate the participant in self-exploration.

At the start, leaders distribute a workshop manual and worksheets that will teach the participant concepts to create a successful career and to make one a "winner." Leaders share experiences, which subtly demonstrate their personal success in applying career management principles and describe other professional activities that testify to their expertise in teaching career management. Implicitly, they inform participants that the corporation wants and expects them to develop a proactive approach toward career and that the workshop will review strategies acceptable to the corporation.

In setting the stage for initiating in-depth self-exploration and skill building, the leader reminds participants that their bank careers are a part of their total careers, which in turn are part of their life plans. The counselor explains that since a person's general career skills and goals control bank behavior, they will be the focus of the workshop. Since bank opportunities stimulate expression of the general career and since the person's total personality and life plan affect what is, or might be, in the general career repertoire, the workshop will, at times, stimulate the person to start delving into one's own personality. Participants are cautioned, however, that the workshop is not a psychotherapy or an encounter group.

Next, the workshop introduces the concepts of career, career types, career planning, modes of career enhancement, and career anchors. First, the leader generates a list of definitions of career and career success and notes that all terms are correct, yet distinctive, since every career is unique. Nevertheless, the leader shows that many definitions contain the themes of passage and achievement; that is, career is dynamic, taking the person somewhere. In the words of one presenter, "Career can be a voyage of discovery or it can be just another trip" (Dolin, 1978).

Emphasis moves to explaining that career patterns are transitory (moving randomly and frequently), stable, linear (moving upward or downward), and spiral (changing as a person alters preferences). Linked to this portrayal of career patterns is Schein's (1971) concept of anchors, or supports, that steady the career as it changes.

In regard to career enhancement, the leaders point out the following six kinds of strategies (Kaye & Scheele, 1976):

1. While working, explore the nature of particular activities within one's job or activities in jobs with which one interacts.
2. Increase the challenge or meaning of a job by changing the task or one's ideas about it.

3. Change to a job of comparable level and responsibility to broaden skills.
4. Take a more responsible position to broaden challenges.
5. Relocate to a new firm, industry, or community in order to have new perspective on one's work.
6. Realign downward to reduce unwanted pressure or to gain experience for an acceleration in the future.

Moving from the abstract to the concrete, the leader shows participants how to mold telephone wires to represent the changes in their own careers, and to analyze the transitions to discover the forces that have affected, and may affect, the career and the "anchors" that have supported the person in changing. Participants then mold their wires and explain their production to a peer, attempting to elucidate the causal forces and anchors. Next, each participant displays his or her portrayal to the group, sharing any major reactions or discoveries the rendition might produce.

The leader underscores positive and negative forces and anchors such as divorce, completion of a degree, economic downturn, parents' confidence, and personal tenacity. In closing, the leader promises in upcoming sessions to review strategies for bringing about desirable changes.

Session 2. The objectives of the second session are that clients (a) begin to view their careers as a commodity to be marketed; (b) distinguish among operating-technical skills, general process skills, specialized knowledge skills, and personal strengths (This skill classification parallels Fine's [1974] functional, specific content, and adaptive skills described in Chapter 3, under Career Skills); and (c) start recalling their skills and declaring them publicly.

At the outset, the leaders introduce and illustrate the strategy of operating a career as if one were selling a product. Employees are urged to decide on which skills to market, ascertain the competition and their strengths, identify prospective employers, develop the skills that correspond with the employer's needs, perform well, and assure that prospective employers are aware of their excellent performance. Once employed, workers are to produce good work and consistently confirm that their skills are meeting their employer's needs. Within the context of marketing a career, the leader then illustrates the homework assignment in Figure 12–1 by calling on volunteers to suggest entries that would fit their careers.

Moving on, the instructor presents a four-category classification of skills on a blackboard: (1) technical (filing, editing), (2) general process (planning, analyzing), (3) specialized knowledge (counselor training, mathematics), and (4) personal strengths (assertive, patient). Participants then recall and list their skills in the first three categories.

Continuing the skill discovery phase, the leader explains the self-discovery exercise of telling work success stories to another (reminiscent of Flanagan's [1954] critical incident technique), and demonstrates

Figure 12–1. Homework Assignment: Preparing to Market Your Career

During the next two weeks you are to investigate and then answer the following questions. For some of them you will have to check with other people; for others, you will simply have to do some strenuous soul-searching. BRING THIS SHEET WITH YOU TO THE NEXT MEETING.

A. My Skills

** 1. I will add _____ (number) skills to my present list by the next workshop. I will also note which skills I prefer to use and which ones I believe to be transferable.

** 2. I will check with at least _____ (number) people to see if they agree with my assessment of my strengths and weaknesses. (List the names of those you plan to check with below)

Person I Checked With: *Their Comments:*

B. My Competition

1. Complete this section at home by listing the people or groups of people (eg. other operations officers) you believe to be your primary competition. Then compare what you feel are their abilities/skills with those of your own.

Competition   *Their Abilities/Skills*   *My Abilities/Skills*

C. My Developmental Needs

1. As a result of what I learned from A and B above about my skills, strength, weaknesses and competition (and already knew), some areas or skills which need more development are:

SOURCE: *Career management program manual.* Los Angeles: Security Pacific National Bank Personnel Department, 1978. Reprinted by permission.

Figure 12–1. (*Continued*)

D. My Marketing Effort

   1. Is there a market for the skills I want to use?

   2. Where is that market? (Think of obvious and not so obvious places where those skills are used; use the green package write-ups about types of work in the bank to give you some clues.)

   3. If I am the "seller", is it a buyer's or a seller's market? Are there a lot of other people with my same abilities? What does this say about my chances?

   4. Who are my most likely customers? (Don't forget your boss!)

   5. Why should they choose me over someone else?

   6. Do I look like the type of person who holds the job I would like? Dress?

      Grooming?

      Weight? Posture?

      Attitude? (maturity, confidence, willingness to take on responsibility, showing loyalty, performance, etc.)

Figure 12–1. (*Continued*)

E. My Group and Individual Behaviors

1. What behavior patterns (or roles) do I use most often?

2. Are the behaviors I use appropriate to the situations in which I use them?

   Always   *Sometimes*   *Never*

3. Are there more appropriate behaviors I could use to increase my effectiveness and/or my work-team's effectiveness? What are they?

4. What behaviors/roles do I avoid? Which (if any) of the behaviors I avoid would be required of me in the position I want to hold?

** 5. In the next two weeks I plan to try the following new roles/behaviors.

Behavior/Role   *Where*   *With Whom*   *When*   *Results*

Some examples are: Leader, Team member, Show more support, Show more independence, Speak more often, Speak less often, Validate _____'s positive behaviors/good performance/successes, etc.

how a listener can reflect and probe during the story to assist the presenter in expanding a skills list. Pairs of participants then share success stories to uncover more skills.

In the same vein, participants join into subgroups of three or four to brainstorm the skills of each other's jobs. They display their skill lists, and participants inspect each subgroup's list to be sure they have not omitted one of their skills from their own list. To encourage participants to begin "tooting their own horns," each participant tells his or her skills to a colleague, while holding hands and maintaining eye contact. Finally, lists of skills that are to be reviewed for still further additions to the participant's own growing skill list are distributed.

Session 3. This session enables participants to (a) understand and examine six careering skills, (b) identify at least one way of applying the skills to their own careers, and (c) affirm the legitimacy of advancing one's own career by manipulation.

After reviewing the highlights of day one, the leader reviews the homework assignment of approaching one's career as a marketing problem. The leader guides participants in thinking about their competition (including their number and probable skills), market analysis interpretations and strategies, and methods of locating prospective jobs and employers.

Continuing, the leader pursues the issue of moving ahead in a career, and asserts that proactive and passive careerists differ in their allocations of energy. Proactive careerists give 50 percent to performing their position effectively, 25 percent to establishing connections, and 25 percent to securing recognition. In contrast, passive careerists start out devoting 70 percent to doing their job well and 30 percent to waiting for others to advance them. As their frustration increases because they are not discovered, their working energy begins to be sapped by discontent. Anecdotes underscore the client's need to "toot his or her own horn," to enjoy accepting praise and recognition for accomplishment, and to start connecting with others in the workshop for possible career advantage.

The leader next recounts that Scheele (1979) interviewed many successful careerists and found that many employ most or all of six approaches to career. Scheele conceptualized these approaches as "careering skills" and described them in the following terms, elaborated on and illustrated here with examples:

1. Experiencing: trying out and then reflecting upon actual experiences, noting especially the positive aspects of the experience
2. Risk linking: establishing contacts in spite of risks
3. Show belonging: demonstrating membership in one's firm
4. Exhibit specializing: ascertaining needed specialty role(s) and performing them
5. Use catapulting: using contacts to advance career
6. Magnify accomplishments: assure that successes are recognized.

To make the discovery of these careering skills work for them, participants each fill out a worksheet (Figure 12–2) on which they write an action illustrating their use of the skill, what they have learned or acquired from the experience, and an action for each of the six skills, which they will use in the near future. (Figure 12–2 presents excerpts from different participants' worksheets.) This exercise closes with selected participants sharing intentions and receiving praise, and with the leader's promising to check back with them regarding their successes.

Session 4. The objectives of Session 4 are to (a) initiate a participant in becoming aware of individual task group actions, (b) generate lists of behaviors characterizing effective leader and follower behavior, and (c) enable the participants to practice constructive group behavior.

Clients immediately form subgroups and are asked to brainstorm ten likely changes in banking. About ten minutes into the exercise, the

Figure 12–2. Worksheet of Career Competences

Approach	Have done	Plan to do
Doing	have done part-time grocery clerk; customer contact skills.	analyze political context of current employment in order to function more effectively
Linking	co-host conference—enabled learning promotion and staging skills	propose co-teaching and in-service to broaden knowledge and visibility
Belonging	attend career workshop to show interest in bank career; felt closer to Security Pacific Bank.	assist supervisor with project of special interest to her
Specialization	join speaker's bureau to present specialty; public speaking.	volunteer to brief visitors on specialty
Catapulting	volunteer to serve on charity drive directed by Vice President; acquired prominent friends.	advise manager friend at another branch of my potential for assistant manager because of detailed knowledge of new data processing
Magnify accomplishment	receive award at public ceremony; congratulations from prominent bank officer.	write up my innovation to appear in house organ

SOURCE: *Career management program manual*. Los Angeles: Security Pacific National Bank Personnel Department, 1978. Reprinted by permission.

leader directs each participant to reflect on the role he or she is playing within the group (leader or follower) and to consider playing another role for the remainder of the exercise. At the same time, the subgroups are instructed to devise and execute a strategy by which they can rank the changes in banking from least to most significant.

After the groups struggle with the revised assignment for several minutes, the leader asks the group spokespeople to announce their proposed lists. As they report, they are asked to describe how they arrived at consensus about the order of changes. Everyone also receives lists of innovations generated by other workshop groups.

During discussion of each subgroup's performance, the leader solicits other group members' feelings about being followers and not taking leadership. The dialogue generates lists of leader and follower behaviors; and participants are reminded that leader behavior is often a part of male socialization whereas follower behavior is part of female socialization; and participants are encouraged to become more assertive in expressing their leadership skills. At times, this latter element leads to instructor-participant interactions that are confrontative.

The instructor pushes the participant to tell how he or she could act differently and then publicly to enact the leader role. Generally, the good intention of this activity mollifies the participant's temporary embarrassment, but clearly the counselor must monitor individual participant distress.

Throughout, the leaders also share anecdotes supporting the idea that a manager exercises liaison and coordinating skills, while delegating technical tasks to subordinates. Participants are urged to "risk linking," that is, to join professional or civic or charitable organizations that will provide useful career contacts and information or that will afford opportunities to exercise leadership skills. They are reminded that they must "play to be in the game." They emphasize the legitimacy of initiating such relations primarily for career advancement.

Session 5. The objectives of Session 5 are that participants (a) recall and affirm the legitimacy of their maneuvering and manipulating to advance their careers, and (b) review needed general skills, such as speaking up, taking initiative and assuming leadership, presenting achievement clearly and persuasively, identifying and showing concern about their superiors' needs and objectives, and indicating membership in the organization.

The theme that self-initiative and effort will create a desirable career permeates the session. Where possible, participants who are improving their career are enlisted to tell what they are doing to succeed. At the session this author attended, a participant suggested that the popular song "Be Your Own Best Friend" become the workshop theme song and played the recording by Ray Stevens, to the delight of all.

The leader then focused on creating a marketing strategy and refining it by reviewing sales principles, defending the merits of the strategy against an adversary, and so forth. Such defense, it was noted, could either be in a game wherein the adversary tries to block every step, or in a debate.

Interspersed with this pep talk review of how to advance a career, the leader praises participants for making firm, concise statements. When statements are weak, however, clients are asked to repeat their comments more forcefully and expressively and then receive praise for trying and improving.

Throughout the workshop, but especially in this session, leaders enjoin clients to practice speaking up in order to present themselves more effectively. Clients are told to consider errors as instances by which to learn how to improve, rather than as setbacks. Leaders take turns in sharing personal anecdotes, jokes, and stories illustrating the benefits of taking initiative for such things as making meetings and projects successful. They enumerate the rewards of belonging (opportunity to try out skills, make important contacts, and so forth) to a career-focused group even though membership may require considerable energy and involve some activities that are not enjoyable.

In between stories, a leader reviews the occupational structure of the corporation, as shown in Figure 12–3. In presenting this diagram, the leader points out that one of the promotions at the lower levels requires announcing one's desires, showing one's commitment to the boss, and demonstrating one's competency. Even greater effort, however, is necessary for promotion at the higher levels, for as the figure shows, there are fewer slots. Consequently, for these advancements one must impress strategic people; and it is even desirable to determine expanding areas where the promotions are more likely. Leaders remind participants that they have a license to get acquainted with other bank employees primarily to improve their careers within banking.

Session 6. The objectives of Session 6 are to have employees (1) become aware of their interactions with colleagues and their feelings about behaviors, (b) review principles relating to leadership, and (c) pinpoint irritating work interactions that they can change.

The leader facilitator launches the session with the cube building game. Subgroups are pitted against one another in a contest, which involves teams of blindfolded players stacking sugar cubes to achieve or

Figure 12–3. Occupational Structure of Security Pacific
National Bank: Positions and Officer Level

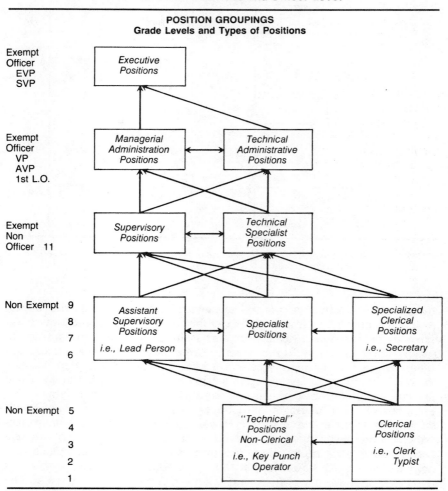

Figure 12–3. (*Continued*)

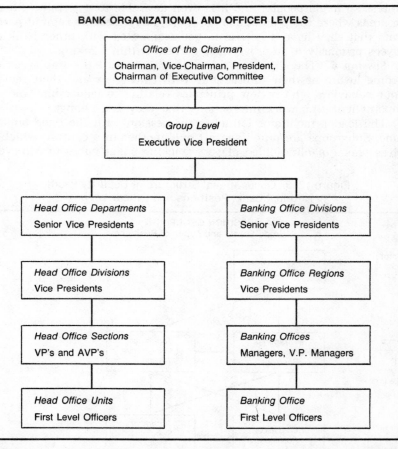

BANK ORGANIZATIONAL AND OFFICER LEVELS

> *Office of the Chairman*
> Chairman, Vice-Chairman, President,
> Chairman of Executive Committee

> *Group Level*
> Executive Vice President

Head Office Departments Senior Vice Presidents	*Banking Office Divisions* Senior Vice Presidents
Head Office Divisions Vice Presidents	*Banking Office Regions* Vice Presidents
Head Office Sections VP's and AVP's	*Banking Offices* Managers, V.P. Managers
Head Office Units First Level Officers	*Banking Office* First Level Officers

SOURCE: *Career management program manual.* Los Angeles: Security Pacific National Bank Personnel Department, 1978. Reprinted by permission.

surpass their estimates. Points are awarded for reaching the quota, which is a player's estimate of the number of cubes he or she can stack; extra points are not awarded for surpassing the quota, and failure to reach the quota results in zero points. After the conferees practice, each subgroup picks a manager who is not blindfolded and who can instruct the other members of the group in setting and achieving its quota. Once the rules are clear and the managers elected, the game begins. After every round, each "manager" announces the group's score, and the facilitator posts it. After three rounds, the leader notes groups that are improving and declining and asks their managers to comment on the performance. Continuing the reflection mode, the facilitator guides participants to ponder how they set their individual goals, how much risk they took and were willing to take, how committed they were to the team's winning as opposed to benefiting themselves, and so forth. Several volunteers share their feelings with the entire workshop.

Continuing, the leader reviews leadership. Members of randomly selected groups are polled about why they chose a peer as manager and how they felt about not being chosen themselves. Predictably, some leaders like leadership and sought it; others claimed it came by default. Similarly, some followers enjoy and want leadership, yet find excuses for not showing their desire. Participants appoint managers whom they know and with whom they are comfortable and like or admire. Rarely are the least competent builders appointed and rarely is the appointment motive purely winning. The facilitator reiterates the reasons, noting the importance of projecting a sense of belonging and an interest in others if one aspires to leadership, at least in a game situation. (Also, a confrontative leader can rouse strong feelings, and attention to participant well being is a leader responsibility.)

To provide more opportunity for participants to practice group behavior, teams choose new managers and the game resumes for two or three more rounds. After play ends and the groups determine and congratulate the winning team, the facilitator leads the participants, especially the women, to reflect further on their feelings and behaviors in leading and following. In closing the review of their game performance, the leader guides the participants to enumerate the qualities they saw exercised by effective leaders and followers. The leader encourages and reinforces women, especially, for expressing their desire for leadership. They list principles, such as leaders talk with conviction and to the point, are enthusiastic, keep to the goal, and so forth.

Following a break, the facilitator presents an anecdote illustrating how men traditionally have been given leader roles, whereas women fill supporter roles. The leader then focuses on how to learn from the workshop interaction: participants inspect seven task roles (initiator, information seeker, information giver, clarifier, summarizer, consensus maker, and nondecider) and seven relationship roles (harmonizer, facilitator, supporter, compromiser, interpreter, cynic, and devil's advocate); they then talk about the advantages or disadvantages they have experienced in each role and ways of playing each. During the dialogue, the facilitator warns clients of the dangers posed to career advancement by assuming the nondecider, cynic, or devil's advocate role too often. The counselor elicits comments about most roles; then participants individually answer questions about roles they like to play, like to have others play, would like to add and to drop, and ways in which they might change their repertoire of roles. After that, some share some of their goals and their reasons for choosing them.

Next, the leader introduces an exercise that emphasizes the negative in contrast to the generally positive thrust of the workshop. Each client is told to map personal interrelationships on the job and to identify the major negative aspect of each. The leader offers examples, such as a colleague whose return call is always late, or a subordinate who manages to crack a joke at the worst time. Once the relationships are mapped, the participant alone, or with the help of peers, considers how he or she can act in the relationship to alter or avoid the negative element. The facilitator shares personal experiences exemplifying negative interactions, emphasizes the need to correct or avoid them, supplies and elicits examples of coping with several unsatisfactory situations, and answers individual participant questions. In closing the session, each client publicly states an action that he or she will take to enhance work interactions.

Session 7. The client objectives of Session 7 are to (a) formulate multiple work goals reflecting long-term aspirations, (b) defend the goals to a workshop colleague, and (c) review the six directions by which one can enhance a career.

A leader initiates the session by reviewing workshop accomplishments, reiterates the necessity of a proactive approach to career in order for the workshop to be effective, and induces a contemplative stance about planning.

The stage having been set, a second leader directs clients to meditate a few moments about what they were doing and hoping for ten years ago. After time for reflection, the leader tells the employees to consider the changes that have occurred since then, and why.

Continuing the contemplative tone, clients project themselves ten years into the future, speculating about what they would like to be doing, expect to be earning, where they will be living, and what will cause such changes. As they ponder these points, the facilitator directs them to consider such general life concerns as the worst thing that could befall them, the people who would be most important to them, and the person who would care most for them. This phase of the session closes with subgroup members sharing their speculations with each other.

Focus now shifts to the difficulties in setting work goals. The leader recalls the six constructive directions a career might take, underscoring with examples the growing acceptability of "realigning downward." He or she then elicits from the entire workshop examples of each of the six career changes and amplifies less common shifts. For instance, the leader tells how job enrichment may result from increasing the percent of a job given to desirable duties, by adding more autonomy, by learning how the job contributes to a total organization or product and how it affects others, and by increasing feedback about its workers' performance.

Once the group reviews these concepts, conferees receive worksheets on which to list specific goals for each kind of career shift. The facilitator reminds them that goals will be more realizable if their statements are specific, involve attainable behaviors, pinpoint time of accomplishment, can be observed, and are related to long-term aspiration. The goal worksheet provides for checking each goal on these criteria. After writing out their goals independently, clients pair off and tell one another about their goals. In sharing, they first read a goal and then say why they set it, how it matches their preferences, whether it is a logical next step for them, whether they have the requisite skills, and whether it fits their long-term aspirations. The listener helps the presenter be more concrete, and if a goal is not defensible tells the client to reconsider it.

The leaders move among pairs, inviting questions and assisting employees in becoming concrete. The session closes with the injunction to reflect on goals and share them with peers during lunch.

Session 8. The primary objectives of Session 8 are for the client to (a) pinpoint the forces likely to support and to thwart goal pursuit, (b) identify means of increasing supporting forces or reducing resistances, and (c) review groups that might support continued career development.

The leader initiates the session by describing how goal pursuit can be graphed as being supported and opposed by internal and external forces, the combination being called a force field. Proceeding, the leader explains how a goal pursuer can anticipate what the forces are and consequently can have more control over them by using a simple graphing procedure such as the one in Figure 12–4.

After introducing the exercise, the leader illustrates the procedure for the situation of a volunteer. Then participants, in teams of three or four, work on the exercise. Each participant writes a goal on a line and then lists restraints on arrows above and perpendicular to the line. First external restraints (lengthy training) and internal restraints (low confidence) are posted. Once the client and his or her peers are satisfied that all restraints are posted, they enumerate the internal supports (desire, resolve) and the external supports (spouse encouragement, appropriate experience). Once all forces are posted, the impact of each is estimated by assigning weights of *ten* (very influential) to *one* (negligible influence). Then the client ponders how to increase the likelihood of goal attainment by adding powerful supports or eliminating, or at least reducing, significant opposition. For example, the employee who had not listed a boss's support for his or her goal would consider how to obtain the boss's approval, or the shy client could be encouraged to delineate steps for reducing shyness.

Figure 12–4. Forces Supporting and Restraining the Goal of Earning a Promotion

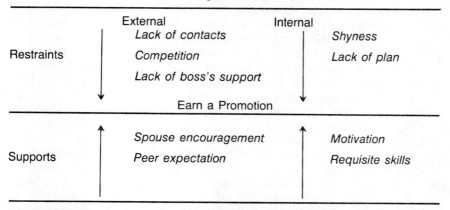

SOURCE: Adapted from Security Pacific National Bank Career Management Workshop presentation of B. L. Kaye.

Once the exercise is over, clients consider how support groups are especially important in any career goal. With the assistance of a list of organizations, they review groups available to them on and off the job. The session and workshop close with clients' sharing their overall reactions in a brief, pointed statement with the entire group. Before sharing, they are reminded that this is another opportunity to practice speaking. Reactions are almost unanimously positive and optimistic, further increasing individuals' enthusiasm for taking action on their plans.

Validity

Evidence is increasing that many people want occupational change but feel trapped in their jobs. This program logically should help such people because its provision and endorsement by the corporation communicate to employees that they need not be trapped and point out some alternatives open to them. By 1981, more than three thousand employees have participated in the workshop, voluntarily and without compensation, many on the recommendation of past participants. Also, this author's positive impression, based on observing the workshop and its participants, supports the efficacy of the procedure.

In terms of more traditional evidence, Townsend (1977) undertook the only experimental study of the Security Pacific Workshop. She contrasted twenty-nine participants with sixteen comparable, no treatment controls in a pre-post test design. All subjects suggested solutions to two career dilemmas involving overcoming obstacles to promotion within the bank. Their responses were scored in terms of how many of the six careering competences taught in the workshop were applied in their answers. Before counseling, there were no differences between groups; whereas after treatment, the workshop participants included careering competences significantly more often. Numerically, the participants averaged one and one-half competences per dilemma after the workshop, in contrast to one-half a competence for the controls. Unfortunately, neither reliability or validity data for the dilemma are available, so the alternative explanation that the workshop cued answers to a paper-pencil test, rather than built career management skills, is also plausible.

Other agencies and firms have reported programs similar to the Security Pacific National Bank Workshop. TRW, for instance, has offered a shorter career achievement workshop based on McClelland's (1967) views, and many employees have expressed satisfaction with it.

Reporting on another corporate program, Pearson (1975) said he had helped three hundred Polaroid employees by teaching them to identify potential employment talents by reflecting upon their successful experiences and by showing them how to pinpoint occupations requiring their talents through publications such as the *Dictionary of Occupational Titles*. His presentation described his methods and included case excerpts. However, he did not specify how he assessed the growth of the 300 employees.

In the only full scale evaluation of a program published, Knowdell (1978) outlined the 37-hour Livermore career planning program and presented follow-up data about 125 participants, which included ratings by their supervisors. The Livermore program is built around a workshop, but it differs from the Security Pacific program because it emphasizes interest and personality testing and individual planning sessions. In addition, it teaches the participants, who are largely engineers and technicians, a variation of McClelland's (1967) achievement motivation paradigm. On the other hand, the program does not promote organizational contacts and public presentation skills as does the Security Pacific program. Interestingly, follow up of 125 clients still in the Laboratory one year later found that the majority of them still believed that counseling had helped to improve the quantity and quality of their work, their peer and supervisor communication, and their morale. Over the year, the clients acted in various ways to improve their careers. Ten percent switched departments; 25 percent changed job titles, and 42 percent job tasks; 50 percent up graded career skills; 42 percent qualified for new jobs; and 66 percent pursued personal growth. Perhaps most impressive was the finding that 100 percent of the supervisors of these employees (more than 90 percent responded) rated the program as useful for the employee and more than 80 percent as useful for the Laboratory and their department.

Hazards

Despite the advantages, employer-provided workshops have the following possible hazards:

1. Stimulating career action might easily lead to focusing on some occupational and industry information, while neglecting other data. For example, in a school district program, one might point out the many counseling and administration positions that have developed since 1960 and the subsequent promotion of many teachers into these positions without noting that most incumbents will not reach retirement age before the late 1990s.

2. The collegial composition of the groups increases the likelihood that a client's self-disclosure eventually will be used to his or her disadvantage, especially when the work milieu is very competitive. Collegial groups, on the other hand, lessen the possibility of taking impulsive action on career plans because colleagues in the same occupation or industry are in a better position than are strangers to judge the feasibility of career action and will have ongoing commitment to their fellow employees.

3. The group's warm, interpersonal atmosphere created to motivate positive feelings about work and to expedite public self-exploration and commitment to career action may be misconstrued as the usual atmosphere surrounding efforts to advance one's career. This misconception may induce people to deflect energy

from other life roles to career in hope of meeting friendship and intimacy needs, which are more likely to be fulfilled in other roles.

Self-exploratory Cognitive Counseling

This author does not know of any published description of an integrated procedure for helping maintenance-stage adults become more aware of how they are expressing themselves through career, although the goal has been recommended often and widely (Sinick, 1977; Walz, 1979).

The procedure described below is a hybrid of actions and objectives derived from the author's limited counseling efforts to further adult career-self-awareness and from writings of Carl Rogers (1961), Albert Ellis (1979), E. C. Thoroman (1968), and others who have detailed procedures for expanding self-awareness. The procedure has not been validated in its entirety and is presented here to promote research. Users should expect that it will require adaptation. Indeed, one should employ the procedure only if one can monitor it within a formative evaluation framework.

The rationale of this counseling rests on several premises:

1. People change over their careers and periodically should systematically update their understanding of who they are and are becoming, in order to retain control of their careers. The changes in people are caused by their career experiences, their maturation, their experiences in other life pursuits, and the changes in work operations and opportunities.

2. An appraisal of self-in-career is likely to be more comprehensive and accurate if undertaken collaboratively with a trusted expert in adult career development.

3. The uniqueness of each career, the possibility of several interpretations and expressions of each career, and the many kinds of careers possible in the educational-work systems support a counseling approach wherein the client retains responsibility for deciding how to portray and to elaborate on his or her relation to work. Systematically reviewing one's career accomplishments and aspirations with a counselor, who actively listens and underscores insights, should help clients to manage their own careers. Proponents of adult learning and client-centered counseling have argued that an adult's comprehension and ownership of counseling insights will be greater when he or she shares control of the process, feeling free to express or not to express himself or herself (Rogers, 1961; Knowles, 1970).

4. A person is able to accept a broader concept fully when he or she feels another understands and accepts him or her.

5. A person is more likely to develop, affirm, and apply realistic principles of action when he or she can review them with a trusted person and obtain feedback about correcting principles that are illogical or not soundly based in experience.

Method

The counseling stage 3 described in Chapter 5 begins after the client and counselor agree that expanding self-awareness is the appropriate career development objective and that a client-directed, shared introspection is a promising strategy to accomplish it. Therefore, the interaction starts with both parties, or the group, affirming that the client has accepted responsibility for developing topics and gathering information, whereas the counselor will clarify communication and perhaps suggest aspects of the self-reconnaissance that need to be amplified to facilitate the self-awareness process.

The counselor describes separately three aspects of the self-awareness process: attributes, goals, and beliefs. Here, they are presented in tandem to aid specification. In counseling, all may be confronted simultaneously.

Throughout self-awareness cognitive counseling, the counselor seeks to be consistent in several actions. He or she listens actively and attentively. Intermittently, the counselor asks the client to elaborate and then paraphrases to be sure his or her understanding matches the client's. Periodically, the counselor mirrors what the client is communicating to expand client awareness and to let the client know he or she is being heard. The tactic is to immerse the client in a shared exploration of who he or she has become and is becoming. All actions described under the counselor behavior category involving client in counseling in Chapter 5 may be undertaken. During their interaction, the counselor prompts the client to bring into focus both the content and the affective aspects of the self-concept. To expand understanding of his or her own communication, at times the counselor may have the client stop and observe posture, gestures, facial expressions, and tone, or may even ask the client to pinpoint feelings in different body parts. The counselor guides the client to review the evidence for self-ascriptions in order to evolve a comprehensive self-concept. To this end, the counselor provides time for them both to digest the client's self-portrait, while communicating acceptance of that emerging self.

To develop client self-understanding, a counselor often must help the person elaborate on the presentation. The excerpt below from an interview with Sid illustrates the importance of focusing on a topic until the counselor clearly understands what is involved for the client. Rogers (1951) noted that the counselor has to develop enough comprehension of what the client's situation is in order to appreciate how he or she is feeling; indeed, the counselor is urged to approach feeling the client's situation as the client does. Achieving this depth of elaboration, however, is difficult, because this fast-paced culture does not encourage taking time to stop and concentrate; and because those aspects of self where elaboration is important often are painful to examine. A counselor will tend to abet the client in moving quickly over a topic, especially one arousing anxiety. Certainly, many novice counselors whom this author has supervised have missed helping a client achieve self-understanding because they did not stay with a topic long enough. Typically, their reaction was that the client had said enough, but usually they did not have sufficient data to explain why the client was manifesting particular feelings.

A second way to expand awareness is to focus on present emotions. In having the client explore the past, a counselor should help the client recognize the feelings that occur while recalling. In the dialogue in Figure 12–5, for example, the counselor spotlights Sid's matter-of-factness in recalling what one would expect to be a depressing episode.

Figure 12–5. Excerpts from Interview with Sid

Counselor: You are saying matter of factly that your move from the auto to the underwater battery project was brought about by the challenge that you felt the underwater battery project offered and by not getting along with the auto group.

Sid: Yeah, the underwater project promised to be exciting. I like challenging jobs. Those guys just seemed to be snooping every time I turned around.

Counselor: You aren't showing upset as you remember how they seemed to be crowding you. You are not feeling what you felt then?

Sid: Naw, it wasn't that upsetting . . . just good to get out of it.

Counselor: In mentioning your move to this new project you said it was riskier and might have led to a lay off. You didn't mention concerns about possible effects on your family. I, uh, wonder . . . ?

Sid: That was it—a big part of it. This affair was going on. It would come out. They'd know. Word would get back to the wife. So I started looking around. When I heard about the underwater project, I moved quickly.

Counselor: An affair stirred you to seek other work?

Sid: Yeah, stirred. More like lit a fire. I didn't want trouble at home. Sally was pretty young. I kind of knew it wouldn't last.

Counselor: Am I right, you sought a move to save your marriage? Family is important in your career.

Sid: As I look back I guess it is. I've always thought about where we'd live—good schools, enough money, before I changed jobs. And it would be a big factor still.

Counselor: And not getting along with coworkers?

Sid: I guess I get along okay. The guys in auto battery never found out—they even had a party for me when I left. We are still friends . . . Sally left for San Francisco about three months later. It really wasn't a serious thing for either of us.

Clarifying that changing jobs was recalled without distress helped Sid to recognize how concern with his family role rather than with the job friendships was influencing his career decisions.

Rogers (1961), Truax and Carkhuff (1967), Carkhuff (1972), Ivey (1971), Brammer (1979), and many others have described actions that research suggests will promote client elaboration. Several scales for measuring counselor empathy, immediacy, and so forth are available. Using these scales can also offer clues about how to promote elaboration.

The client and counselor respect one another's expertise in this procedure, unlike the trait-factor method wherein the counselor assumes the expert position. Both accept or reject material as pertinent to the emerging self-picture, and the counselor assures that both are clear about the affect associated with the decision. Time permitting, the counselor teaches the client to do this independently. Both try to make sure that all evidence is brought to bear, so that the client may be advocate, adversary, and judge about the validity of different attributions.

Throughout the process, the counselor reminds the client to take account of demands typical of the client's position, milieu, or physiology. The teacher, for instance, who is ignoring the feeling of conflict might be asked, "Oh, how did you say you handle challenges about grades or those inconvenient announcements and meetings?" Or the plumber sheepishly concealing a weight gain with loose shirts could be invited to contrast his strength and agility now with what it was five years ago and will be five years from now.

Should client attributions be too generalized or rigid, the counselor alerts the client of the improbability of such ascriptions based on the evidence. The counselor asks the client to review the point again, may jokingly question it, may challenge directly, may have the client apply the illogical leap to another person or situation, and so forth. In offering correction to the client, the counselor also reflects the client reaction to being corrected. When an illogical ascription is not dropped quickly or easily and is important to aspirations and current satisfaction, one should assign related homework. The middle-aged teacher who recently became department chairman, for instance, and who persists in discounting his persuasiveness because he did not succeed in selling insurance twenty years ago and because he was only partially successful in securing the school board's approval of textbook change, could be helped to define a series of increasingly challenging persuasive tasks. Then, with or without rehearsal with a paraprofessional, he might be assigned to try these out and to report his results.

Interviewing has been the primary vehicle for gathering data. Yet a career autobiography, collages, self-portraits, charts and graphs, testing, *in vivo* observation by the counselor, and perhaps an assessment center experience, and ratings from others, can be mentioned to the client as additional sources of information. Of course, the client retains control of what is admitted. Goldman (1971), for one, has shown how to involve clients in the selection of appraisal methods.

Self-attributes

In eliciting elaboration about self-attributes, the counselor proceeds as if taking an oral autobiography, letting the client tell the story, yet seeking trends and influences, carefully identifying critical periods and transactions, and encouraging the client to develop their implications. Both are eager to establish what the experiences have meant and done for and to the client. They join in specifying the skills, interests, values and other attributes acquired and exercised in particular positions, noting how the client is refining some, developing others, while allowing still others to wane. During this review, the counselor takes care to guide the client in considering what led to accepting particular positions, what caused acquisition of specific attributes, and what sustained him or her; that is, what people, internal strengths or external rewards affect him or her. In addition, they elucidate obstructions or diversions, satisfactions and dissatisfactions in different positions and how he or she increased satisfaction and reduced dissatisfaction. Concomitantly, the counselor is attentive to helping the client realize a personal connection with others, inquiring if necessary about the people he or she now spends time with, compared with those at different periods of his or her career. To develop this interpersonal aspect fully, the counselor may have the client reflect on feelings about relationships such as mentor, confidant, colleague, reliable customer, trusted informant, respected supervisor or subordinate, union or professional association representative, and so forth.

As the client's history unfolds, client and counselor strive to induce sound hunches about the what, when, where and what were the results of the major critical periods in the client's work and educational life. They study movement among positions and changes in activities to acquire evidence for predicting future changes, wanted and unwanted.

During this attribute exploration, focus does not remain exclusively on career events. The client reviews, possibly even graphs, how much lifespace has been occupied by career at different times and reflects on how many of life's satisfactions have come and been sought from career. Moreover, the client considers whether some of the attributes developing or waning exclusive of career might be included in career to enrich it or to increase life's overall satisfaction.

Especially important in constructing the self-picture are the feelings that the client has about the attributes. Counselor and client should fully examine strengths and accomplishments, rather than gliding over them. Weigh achievement standards and comparisons, so the client distinguishes the ideal from the feasible and compares himself or herself with peers from school and college, not just with those who are still progressing with him. Gently, the counselor reminds the client to consider how far he or she has come as well as how far he or she might go. The counselor prods the client to recognize accomplishments and to take pride in having accepted setbacks, while persevering. Enumerating the lessons of the failures and the errors to be corrected may be short- or long-term homework assignments.

Goals

In this phase of self-awareness expansion, client and counselor work to bring into focus objectives indicated by the person's attributes and aspirations and career trends. They clarify the feasibility of and paths to these objectives and weigh their value and costs in terms of the person's energy, time, and other resources and commitments.

The client examines career aspirations within the context of other life goals and in terms of goals sought by other people at this stage. The client projects what will be realized at what cost for self, and also for family, and for community. The counselor acquaints the client with human perspectives, such as these presented in Chapter 2, and invites consideration of current and future goals in terms of those models better to appreciate and balance the client's strivings. The counselor prompts the client to recognize how personal heroes and models have changed, to recall the compromises accepted and rejected, and to project accommodations necessary for family and physiological change. When goal inconsistencies appear, the counselor proceeds as an admiring, curious interviewer rather than as a devil's advocate, noting the apparent contradiction. For example, does the principal about to seek the state presidency of the American Association of Secondary School Principals, and also intending to follow up his doctoral research to prepare for an eventual university professorship, view these objectives in conflict with his promise and desire to devote more time to home and children so his spouse can launch her career? If the client will not confront the apparent conflict, the counselor initiates problem-solving activities described under the counselor behavior category of problem solving in Chapter 5. The counselor does not have to resolve each conflict, only to acknowledge it.

Counselors should question the feasibility of specific goals gently, while making sure the client considers available supports and impediments as they review plans. Visualizations, such as Figure 12–4, may help assure consideration of all factors and suggest actions to increase the probability of success. The client, for instance, can lessen obstructions or increase support sources shown in Figure 12–4.

As part of establishing goal feasibility, the counselor also invites the client to enumerate the steps of a personal strategy and to share the reasons for believing he or she can accomplish each step; or the counselor suggests that the client identify how to develop the needed competence.

As this phase of the self-awareness process ends, the client should have specific, feasible goals consistent with personal life goals; he or she should be becoming more selfless in these goals and reflecting more harmony with mankind; should feel pleased with past achievements and be optimistic and enthusiastic about current career goals; should accept limitations and anticipate further obstacles due to age, yet recognize that experiences are equipping him or her for refined development, albeit in a narrower sphere of activities. From Gould's (1978) perspective, the client in the maintenance stage will want to feel and have convincing evidence that he is his "own man," yet a member of an interdependent species.

Beliefs

Client and counselor together scrutinize the client's notions about what he or she ought to be doing at work, what he or she should be earning and accomplishing, and what others should be doing in their relations with her or him. They identify, examine, correct, or note as a future issue to be resolved by the client, the nonsequiturs, overgeneralizations, misinterpretations, and other errors in inducing and deducing careering principles. By verifying that the client is reviewing the full scope of experiences and the conclusions derived from them, the client becomes better able to use personal experience.

Forty to fifty years of living have given the client multiple insights, which counseling helps to assemble and integrate. The client has survived ambiguities and learned to appreciate the relativity of life. The client should have experienced the falsity of absolutes and the value of believing that anything that can be imagined can be realized. The counselor may have to draw attention to these experiences so that the client can fully appreciate them, but doubtlessly he or she has had them. Through counseling, the client assures that overly pessimistic or optimistic beliefs or wishes about career are not thwarting career development. In reflecting on past learning, the client may decide that he or she is reconciled not to learning something because the career has progressed without that knowledge, or the client may ponder alternate approaches, remaining realistic about their costs. For example, he will not assume a spouse's earlier unwillingness to support one or several kinds of career change indicates that she will not support that or another change now. Likewise, his company's denial of a colleague's request for a job redesign will not deter him from formulating a change in his job and preparing to demonstrate its merit. Of course, before he commits extensive energy, the rebuff of his colleague prompts him to obtain soundings about what alterations might be acceptable and to ascertain promising strategies for securing change.

Recognizing that the adult in the maintenance stage is often at the height of occupational status and earnings, the counselor prepares to help him or her to be willing to integrate new perspectives at a stage when some agemates may be resisting new information as a threat to their status. The counselor encourages the client to examine experiences that highlight mankind's continual discovery about its nature and institutions, and the fact that everyone can be enriched by continually incorporating new knowledge and adapting living strategies in light of these changes. The counselor guides the client to feel secure and pleased with career strategies, and, therefore, to be able to alter those strategies to accommodate new challenges or new information. The counselor facilitates client questions about innovation, and supports his or her discovering that one can benefit from weighing possible innovation without moving pell mell to worshipping change for its own sake.

Empirical Evidence

Many of these self-awareness, cognitive counseling guidelines were implemented successfully by counselors at the Western Electric Company from 1936 to 1955. Those counselors conferred with workers at their work stations and in counseling cubicles; they both initiated contacts and welcomed self or supervisor referrals. Dickson and Roethlisberger (1965) reported that the Western Electric counseling staff, which ranged from five to fifty-five over the period, launched the counseling service as observer-researcher-diagnostician and listener-helper operation, but that the listener-helper component gradually overshadowed the observer-researcher-diagnostician aspect.

Dickson and Roethlisberger examined the twenty-year counseling operation at Western Electric in order to clarify factors contributing to its successes and failures, rather than to establish the effectiveness of counseling. Accordingly, their analysis entailed extensive review of copious counseling records and reactions of selected Western Electric counseling staff to the researcher's interpretation of those records, rather than experimental studies of counseling operations. Nevertheless, their description and conceptualization elucidate the kinds of problems for which employees sought help and the extent of services provided. Table 12–1, for instance, shows the relative frequency of concerns that led employees to contact counselors in 1954. Predictably, more than 60 percent of the concerns stemmed from work relations and other job problems, whereas somewhat more than one-third involved personal concerns, such as extra work relations and health. In terms of service, the authors estimated that many of the concerns fell within the five broad, but not mutually exclusive, syndromes of (1) keeping a job, (2) friendship and belonging, (3) felt injuries, (4) authority, and (5) job and individual development.

Examination of the kinds of counselor contact and services offered, moreover, led the authors to estimate the number of employees with access to counseling who benefited from such service and the counseling distribution of service time. In terms of needing help, Dickson and Roethlisberger estimated that as many as 35 percent of the employees had concerns amenable to counseling and were willing to talk to counselors. Of these employees, the counselors helped about one-third (or 10 percent of all employees) during a quarter and devoted about 35 percent of their efforts to this service. Another 40 percent of counselor time was devoted to the remaining two-thirds of the employees requiring help (25 percent of all employees), without manifest benefit during the quarter. Of the remaining 65 percent of employees not expressing assistance needs, 55 percent were willing to talk to counselors, and counselors devoted about 20 percent of their time to interacting with such em-

Table 12–1. Topics of Concern Expressed by 736 Employees
Who Requested Interviews with Counselors
September 1953–December 1954

Reasons	Total No.	Total %	Rank	Men No.	Men %	Rank	Women No.	Women %	Rank
1. Disturbance in outside relationships (fiancé, wife, husband, in-laws, neighbors, etc.)	182	24.7	1	54	16.3	3	128	31.6	1
2. Dissatisfaction with present job or salary	135	18.3	2	61	18.4	2	74	18.3	2
3. Demotion and downgrading (loss in status, reduction in pay, etc.)	84	11.4	3	46	13.9	4	38	9.4	4
4. Disappointed or frustrated over lack of progress in the company	83	11.3	4	62	18.7	1	21	5.2	7
5. Illness or concern over health	81	11.0	5	46	13.9	4	35	8.6	5
6. Disturbance or breakdown in relations with fellow employees	80	10.9	6	20	6.0	7	60	14.8	3
7. Disturbance or breakdown in relations with supervision	57	7.7	7	27	8.2	6	30	7.4	6
8. Employee not measuring up to company requirements (attendance, efficiency, etc.)	21	2.9	8	2	0.6	9	19	4.7	8
9. General personality disturbance (moody, alcoholism, irresponsible, attitude, etc.)	13	1.7	9	13	3.9	8	—	—	9
Totals	736	100		331	100		405	100	

SOURCE: From W. J. Dickson and F. J. Roethlisberger, *Counseling in an Organization: A Sequel to the Hawthorne Researches.* Boston: Division of Research, Harvard University Graduate School of Business Administration, 1966. Reprinted by permission.

ployees in order to establish bases for possible future counseling and to maintain a perspective on the overall work operation. About 10 percent of all employees were not receptive to counseling and attention to them consumed 5 percent of counselor time.

Perhaps of even more interest to those contemplating offering career counseling in an institutional setting, however, is Dickson and Roethlisberger's unique analysis of what led to the expansion and ultimate demise of counseling at Western Electric. Their careful scrutiny of the counseling program in the corporation and how it evolved a posture that interfered with interfacing with traditional corporate functions of supervision, training and, overall management convincingly supports their conclusion that becoming disconnected from the corporate mission, rather than shortcomings in counseling itself, led to the demise of the program. In other words, the facts that employees needed counseling and counseling was enabling some workers to further their self-development and/or to improve their coping did not compensate for the counseling program's inability to help the institution better to address the issue of how workers could produce and develop more constructively. Although Dickson and Roethlisberger acknowledged that counselors may have been forced into the stance of helper-listener for every Western Electric employee in order to be as effective as they were, they surmised that curtailing the observer-researcher-diagnostician functions eliminated the counselors' ability to give research-based advice to management. In so doing, the counselors may have missed the chance for joining other management programs in cooperatively improving the nature of the work so that it would permit fuller worker development. The kind of development such improvement would have permitted was not clearly imagined by employees or counselors and consequently was not sought or offered through the counseling. Their treatise reminds counselors of their responsibility to clarify for the community at large the issues with which clients are wrestling and not to presume exclusive responsibility for helping clients resolve such issues.

Outcomes of Self-Awareness Cognitive Counseling

The intended outcomes of this adult counseling have definite subjective components; but certainly descriptive rating scales, if not cognitive tests, can be created for them. Among the desirable outcomes are the following:

1. The client shows an expanded self-awareness and increased certainty about self-ascriptions; that is, the client is more able to cite evidence for particular ascriptions and presents a more complex description of self.
2. The client interprets career forces in his or her milieu more accurately; that is, if there were an adult version of the Crites *Career Attitude Scales* (1965), the person's score would rise.
3. The client is more efficient in allocating energy and time in career so congruence increases between career actions and valued goals.
4. The client expresses greater satisfaction with the course of the career and reports a greater sense of control over it.

Limitations of Self-Awareness Cognitive Counseling

Counseling usually has removed the client from his or her milieu to aid him or her obtain a perspective on self and one's milieu. Yet the very removal isolates the person from part of the forces propelling and supporting him or her. Too lengthy a removal or too deep an immersion in the counseling can impede the client's normal transactions, perhaps increasing the problems that prompted counseling.

Secondly, counseling depends heavily upon the client to select the data to be reviewed. Since counseling removes the client from his or her milieu without obtaining input from others, it deals only with what the client brings. Certainly this *modus operandi* can easily lead to overlooking important data. Even though the counselor's expertise in adult career development and sensitivity to the client will enable one to ask the client to add some neglected material, other material may be missed either because the client had never attended to it or such data has not been salient for similar clients with whom the counselor had worked.

The third related hazard stems from the limited verification to which material is subjected. Isolation typically precludes the client's obtaining direct testimony from those involved in his or her milieu about interpretations of developments within that setting. Even in group counseling, clients are likely to be from distinct, although perhaps similar, milieus. Therefore, clients may reach conclusions about themselves in their milieus, which seem appropriate for them immediately, but which are inaccurate from the perspective of others. The consequence might well be a deterioration of rather than improvement in managing a career. For example, the project manager, on realizing that he has operated for years with some success under moderately high tension and has indeed sought tension-producing assignments, may be abetted by counseling to conclude that he thrives under moderately high tension and that continuation of his activity pattern is wise. But, the stress suffered by his spouse and children is not manifest because the counselor accepts, without probing, his unequivocal, yet apparently reflective, evaluation that things are going well. His report of subsequent success with subordinates is convincing; but the counselor has not had their testimony about periodic heightened stress and anxiety, nor their view that the project leader increasingly is unable to entertain different viewpoints and is diminishing his own as well as their productivity. The client is not intentionally distorting, but his own elevated tension prevents him from accurately perceiving the true level of stress.

Outplacement Counseling

Employees have always lived under the threat of termination, and perhaps that will always be true in a vital economy. Even the sacrosanct "tenure" of academia and civil service is not an absolute guarantee, for teaching and civil service incumbents can be dismissed if positions become unnecessary. In our twentieth-century work system, many forces contribute to involuntary terminations, including mergers, geographical relocations of firms, technological innovations, foreign competition, increased job stress that exacerbates superior-subordinate or colleague incompatibilities, and relative stability in the percentage of employees working under the protection of union contracts.

Many involuntary terminations occur through no fault of the worker. Advocates of outplacement counseling, such as Morin (1977) and Jameson (1978), therefore, suggest it is only fair, and even in the best interests of the dismissing firm, to provide severance benefits that will enable the terminated employee to resume productive work. Indeed, Morin (1977) even suggests providing outplacement counseling to employees dismissed with cause; for when supervisors realize that the employer facilitates separation, they will be more willing to recommend terminating unproductive personnel. Certainly, corporations providing constructive employee severance can expect considerably more positive public regard than those that do not.

Recently, the dismissal of large numbers of skilled, technical, and professional and managerial employees has made it clear that severance must include more than a formal notice and a severance pay check. Some management consultants, such as Morin (1977), have recommended a so-called "severance" package that includes salary to sustain employee through job search period, a solid reference, outplacement counseling, job seeking training, and office space and secretarial service to support following job leads.

Outplacement counseling minimizes the shock of termination by activating the suddenly jobless worker in seeking a new job, rather than in brooding about the loss. The notion and general operations of outplacement counseling have been presented in several popular magazines and professional journals, but no detailed description has been published. Generally, outplacement counseling is said to involve intensive asset review and résumé preparation, coaching in job seeking, and support. Anxiety reduction activities or assertiveness training appear compatible, but have not been identified by authors whom this author has read. The following description of outplacement counseling is a synthesis of statements about its operation in Morin (1977) and Abramson (1978), and from this author's limited experience as a college placement counselor in assisting alumni who had lost their jobs to find other employment.

Heuristic Principles of Outplacement Counseling

To this author's knowledge, outplacement counseling has not been formally evaluated, but firms, such as Orr, Cuthrell, Fuchs, and Associates, claim that their services result in as many as 88 percent of their clients' achieving jobs of similar or higher pay than those lost (Meyer, 1977). Their claims are impressive because Jameson (1978) has suggested that most management people making job changes take salary cuts. The logic of outplacement counseling—that is, its underlying heuristic principles—provides additional explanation for its probable general benefit. These are its heuristic principles:

1. Timely, expert intervention and support at the point of being fired reduce the anxiety such termination normally arouses. The reduced anxiety makes it easier for the individual to focus energy on the task of obtaining a new job, and the expert guidance makes subsequent job seeking more likely to succeed.

2. Tension from career disruption created by an event, such as job termination, can be repaired with minimal distress if an acceptable replacement job is secured quickly. An employer has an obligation to protect a worker from prolonged tension that employer decisions create.

3. One is most likely to secure acceptable substitute employment by searching systematically before termination, or immediately on termination, under the direction of experts. The longer one delays systematic job search, the less one's chances are of finding equivalent employment.

4. Placement specialists, whose incomes depend on favorable placements, are likely to have linkages to multiple prospective employers and information about current and potential job openings. The professional manager or skilled worker suddenly and unexpectedly expelled from a job is unlikely to have equivalent contacts or information.

5. Employers are likely to look more favorably on job candidates from positions that are discontinued for reasons beyond the candidate's control or from agencies with a reputation for successfully recycling workers in the occupation.

Method

Outplacement counseling has several objectives: to reduce anxiety and tension produced by career disruption; to increase attractive job leads; to assure systematic, constructive job searching; to decrease unemployment time; and to effect a career change, which improves or at least does not reduce the worker's return from working. Although not yet evaluated, these objectives lend themselves to assessment by physiological measures of tension, ratings of job-seeking behavior, counting of job leads and unemployed days, and judgments about the change in job equity using the assessment methods explicated by Super, Kowalski, and Gotkin (1969).

As conceptualized, outplacement counseling is not designed to promote radical career change. Such change would generally require some reeducation or credentialing and would prolong the return to working, which is the opposite objective of outplacement counseling. But, as outplacement services are offered to a wider range of workers, it may become apparent that some very specialized workers would increase their marketability significantly through limited refresher education. Since the essential premise of outplacement counseling is that constructive activity is the best reaction to involuntary termination, engaging in limited, focused education would also seem a fitting outcome for this counseling.

Outplacement counseling might be done in groups, especially for people laid off from the same occupation. Their shared dilemma and similar backgrounds and goals could provide a basis for mutual help. In a tight labor market, however, such a group might not be feasible because its members would properly be competitors. To date, outplacement counseling has been described as a treatment for individuals; therefore, the description here assumes one client. The procedure has the three interrelated phases:

Phase 1: Bolster the Deflated Careerist. Outplacement counseling generally starts on a sour note. The client, who is introduced to the counselor just after being fired expectedly is distressed, probably angry, anxious, confused, and inclined to get away. That natural inclination to withdraw must, however, be redirected by the counselor, for the initial goal of outplacement counseling is that the client channel the energy that has been devoted to the employer's business into the work of finding another employer. One cannot do this if one goes off to brood about his misfortune. Unlike rehabilitation counseling, which assumes that mourning the disabling condition is needed before initiating corrective action, outplacement counseling eschews such mourning as counterproductive. Especially for managers and others expected to perform in spite of stress, delay in effective job search announces deficiency.

The outplacement counselor, therefore, acts immediately. He or she helps the client to recognize that the career has to change, and encourages the client to believe the change can be positive or at least neutral. The counselor shows the client how to "grab the wheel" and steer in this sudden turbulence, rather than to retreat and wait for calmer times.

Counselors help a client to grab and hold control of his or her career in several ways. Initially, they inform the client calmly that they will help secure acceptable work and that they have helped others in similar predicaments. They assure the client that they recognize and will deal with this distress; they are not overwhelmed by it, and indeed, will guide the client to neutralize that distress so that it does not make it harder to resume productive work. They point out the desirability of starting work immediately so that energy is not sapped in brooding, but instead becomes engaged constructively. If the client's anxiey is very high, they point out the benefit of relaxation and show how to relax so they can proceed in preparing for the job search. If the client is concerned about notifying family or friends, counselors develop strategies or even join in announcing the changed status in order to increase the likelihood that family and friends will rally in assisting rather than join in mourning or perhaps in berating the client.

The calmness and take-charge attitude of the counselor should buoy the client, enabling him or her to commit oneself to use the outplacement services. When the client acknowledges that things turn out the best for the people who make the best of the way things turn out, the counselor will know that the first benchmark has been achieved.

Outplacement counselors then immerse the client in the process. Through intensive interviewing, they probe the client's achievements and aspirations, pinpointing with the client the abilities and contacts developed and sustained that might now be used in obtaining a position commensurate with achievements. Together, counselor and client examine the client's situation to identify family and milieu resources that might sustain and help until he or she obtains that new opportunity. Often, coupled with the interview are paper-pencil surveys of client characteristics, perhaps paper-pencil tests, and interest and personality inventories. Following extensive probing, counselor and client scrutinize the accumulating data to generate concrete leads about occupations and positions feasible for the client to seek. This review should produce a list of strengths, alternative occupations, and names of persons who might hire the client, offer leads to jobs and/or a valuable reference. Of course, highlighting achievements, available supports, and prospects uplifts the client. Indeed, the sense of optimism about securing suitable work based on concrete accomplishment is the second benchmark of this phase.

As part of the process, client and counselor may review financial issues. As the minimum, the counselor ensures that the client understands or will be informed about his or her status regarding things such as severance pay, duration of medical and life insurance coverages, eligibility for unemployment compensation, and pension status. Where pertinent, the counselor may join a client and spouse in reviewing provision for long-term obligations such as rents, mortgages, and children's tuitions, and might even recommend consultation with a financial analyst.

Phase 2: Update Career Search Skills. After the client has accepted the need for, and possibility of, altering his or her career, the counselor acquaints the client with the latest approaches to securing his or her type of work. The counselor may also help to generate additional job leads. Typically, this phase includes developing an up-to-date résumé in the latest style and teaching or rehearsing employment interviewing. Some firms even compose and print the résumé for clients; others profess to give their clients an edge in acquiring a job by teaching special employment interviewing tactics, such as not arriving too early, not submitting to interviews with low-ranking personnel, and taking initiative in directing the interview.

Chapter 9 described employment interviewing and résumé preparation. Just as clothing styles change from year to year and by occasion, the style of an appropriate résumé and interview are likely to change over time and to vary from occupation to occupation, and even from employer to employer. As a consequence, a counselor working with clients seeking jobs in a particular occupation and in particular firms may be privy to expected nuances in résumés and interviews.

In terms of new job leads, counselor and client may examine industrial indices such as the *Standard Industrial Classification, Fortune 500, One Hundred Top State Corporations,* and so forth, to identify firms that might have jobs suiting the client. Certainly the client does not limit himself to want ads, but rather initiates contacts with potential employers even though they may not be actively seeking employees. Sheppard and Belitsky (1965) have shown this technique works for blue-collar workers. In addition, counselor and client may use the *Dictionary of Occupational Titles* to locate other occupations that require similar skills and experiences to those the client has gained in the recent occupation.

In the search for new leads, the client is often encouraged to consider relocation. As part of such deliberation, the counselor helps the client obtain information about such things as comparison of prospects at home and in the other specific locations, how to contact out-of-town firms, costs of relocating, the assistance to be expected from a new employer, and how to locate information about new communities. When relocation is being seriously considered, involving the client's spouse directly in the decision and subsequent planning for implementation is sensible.

Phase 3: Sustaining Job Search. Employment decisions about persons at or above the skilled level rarely occur at the time of application or first interview. Test data, background information, references, and other data must be obtained and verified. Even acceptance to the Armed Forces is conditional on passing physical and mental examinations and background checks. Therefore, the job seeker must be ready to sustain enthusiasm while applications are being considered. Occasional conferences about the job search process with an expert, therefore, can help sustain job seeker's enthusiasm, for it enables the client to be reassured that delays and some rejections are normal, but that he or she will succeed by persevering.

Debriefings of the client's efforts may also pinpoint errors and permit corrections. Employers are often reluctant to criticize a prospective employee because they wish to sustain his or her good will. Consequently, they often claim rejection is based on bland reasons, such as "overqualified," or "lack of experience in the job's operation." A debriefing, or sometimes the counselor's contact with the firm, however, can identify problems such as poor presentation of credentials or plans, suggesting low esteem; or inattentiveness to interviewer's communication, suggesting inability to work on a team. These shortcomings can then become the object of corrective training.

The continuation of the commitment to continue reporting about job search may sustain the new job seeker. Just as the client had production deadlines while working, now these are deadlines about making a number of job contacts and follow-ups and analyzing and drawing conclusions about them. Since persevering is a key factor in returning to work, that structure of ongoing contacts should benefit the client by sustaining perseverance.

Finally, as job offers develop, the outplacement counselor guides the client in evaluating whether the position fits or can be modified to meet objectives. The counselor may inform the client about the experiences of similar clients who have entered such positions, can guide him or her in securing and evaluating information about prospective career ladders associated with the proffered position; can help the job seeker acquire up-to-date information about vacancies in the field, and can provide data about the probable latitude in negotiating aspects of a job before and after accepting it. Since outplacement counseling it not fully successful until a client has a job, which bolsters the client's career goals as much as the one from which he or she was expelled, review of the prospective job is very important. This review enables the counselor to help the client avoid settling prematurely and unnecessarily for an unattractive job or rejecting a job that would soon become appropriate, although it is not as immediately attractive as the past job.

Hazards of Outplacement Counseling

Outplacement counseling has two hazards, both of which may have greater consequence for the community than for the fired worker. First, outplacement counseling leads people to accept termination as something the worker, rather than the employer, must correct. This attitude, however, may not always be proper. Since corporations and government agencies use, or benefit from, public resources, knowledge and technology, they have an obligation not only to pursue their established objectives, but also to promote the public welfare. When job terminations are the result of mismanagement or other improper action, the organization shoud be liable. Denial of its liability clearly injures the public at large, as well as the terminated employee. Second, establishment of employment networks that can accept or not accept clients and that can offer persons in the establishment advantage over persons outside such firms can abet discrimination in hiring. Society must ask not only who benefits from outplacement counseling, but also who does it handicap.

Conclusion

During the years from age forty-five to sixty-five, most adults devote more of their waking hours to working than to any other activity. Demographers note that these are productive and stable years. Unemployment is rarer than at other stages, and job changing has diminished considerably. Erikson's (1963) characterization of the time as ego-integrity versus despair suggests that workers either are feeling fulfillment and pride in their accomplishments or are despairing. Past successes and failures weigh more heavily than in any other stage, and though expectations are likely to be high because of the large time commitment to working, expectations may be more limited than at any previous life stage.

Surprisingly, however, knowledge about aspirations and expectations and the impact of work generally on people during these years is very fragmented. Writers such as Toffler (1970, 1981) and O'Toole (1977) point out the discontent and stress occasioned by changing mores and the fluidity of the system. Adult educationists, in turn, claim that many workers in the maintenance stage are taking advantage of the increasingly available educational opportunities to complement work satisfaction as much as to maintain or upgrade work capacity. Major newspapers, such as the *Wall Street Journal*, the New York *Times*, and the Los Angeles *Times*, regularly feature stories about middle agers making dramatic and generally successful career realignments. Yet broad, ongoing surveys, such as those Astin conducts of college students, do not exist to establish the frequency of different accomplishments, plans, frustrations, and aspirations for workers during these years. Likewise, although O'Toole and his task force have hinted that work frustration can cause serious physical and mental debility and although stress management programs are burgeoning, data are not available to indicate the percentage of forty-five-to-sixty-five-year-olds whose health and lifestyles are impaired by work problems.

Not surprisingly, therefore, career counseling programs for this age group are not prolific, nor well differentiated from therapy, and the research on them is sparse. If the promise of these two decades is to be realized, however, broader understanding of the maintenance stage must be obtained. Only then will counseling programs be developed that will respond to tasks, such as mentoring, that are central to the middle age period. Of course, career counselors now serving people in maintenance can contribute substantially by reporting career-related concerns and delineating treatments that are addressing them. Likewise, counselors can discuss adaptations of treatments designed for persons in earlier stages, which facilitate work with maintenance-stage clients. Inasmuch as this area of vocational psychology and career counseling is relatively uncharted, counselors working with this age group have a special responsibility to fulfill the professional role of scientist-practitioner.

CAREER COUNSELING AND THE FUTURE

part four

Part Four points out both propitious and threatening developments likely to affect career counseling in the future. Counselors and their professional associations can embrace the favorable circumstances and take steps to overcome the dangers. Career counseling has helped people to expand their options; if it continues to offer effective, efficient services, this profession will merit societal support.

There is, however, no guarantee that career counseling will be a viable professional service in the year 2000 or even in 1990. In the past, when high school programs have been reduced, counseling has often been one of the first services eliminated. No other industrial nation has the extensive career counseling services that the United States offers in its educational and employment agencies, suggesting that other services can substitute for career counseling or that counseling adds little to career development. Indeed, Walther (1976) has noted, as reported in Chapter 9, that career counseling has not generally been shown to contribute to manpower programs for the disadvantaged. The contribution to manpower development for other groups has yet to be established.

Clearly, the very existence of career counseling as a profession requires counselors that attend to accountability and support means of upgrading the profession. Using the comprehensive career counseling model presented by this text and adopting the formative evaluation posture explicated in Chapter 6 will help counselors increase their accountability and readiness to upgrade service. A prospective counselor should recognize that ongoing formative evaluation of one's career counseling is an arduous task, requiring the hard work, intellectual honesty and discipline, and self-sacrifice that are the hallmarks of a professional. The career counseling profession is not for passive, dependent people who will not risk creating and examining new ways of teaching troubled people or of challenging irrational educational and work practices; nor is it an occupation for those who cannot understand and keep abreast of changes in working and learning. Survival of the profession, indeed, requires bold, energetic, caring, and intellectually able counselors who can work effectively with the community and its troubled members and remain objective about society's work-education system, its people, and the profession's own services. As this final chapter indicates, the challenge is great, but the prospective satisfactions are equally large.

Auspicious Developments and Dark Clouds

13

Careers are causing more concern as they demand less time and energy. Today, very few Americans need to work eighty-four or even sixty hours per week to survive. Yet before this century, such hours were the rule rather than the exception. Work has also become less physically taxing. Indeed, the recreation industry has become mammoth during recent years by providing facilities and materials for workers to play during the hours their forefathers once toiled. The paradox of greater concern as work absorbs workers for fewer hours seems to stem from the multiple options many people now have about career: what to do, when and where to work, for whom to work, how long to work, and the like.

Widespread concern about career can insure that career counseling remains a growth industry. Career is the approved route to the good life in America, and most people want to "make it" by doing honest work. As the work system becomes more complex and jobs more varied and specialized, and as workers are stimulated and sometimes forced to change their career positions, people are likely to want to reflect more about what they have and might become. Career counseling can address this desire, and the profession can further stimulate counseling use by refining its service to enable clients to feel more power over their careers as they meet the challenges of changing work and higher productivity.

This text seeks to stimulate expansion of career counseling. Therefore, it has shown how to describe career counseling procedures so that professionals can improve them through formative evaluation as they use them to help clients. The author has provided a framework for constructing counseling procedures, has illustrated its applicability, has detailed the formative evaluation process to assess counseling, and has suggested objectives and measures to facilitate this assessment process.

In introducing the detailed description of career development procedures, this author explicated the concept of career and the necessity of appreciating different perspectives of human beings as well as the structure and operation of the educational and work system to comprehend how to aid career development.

Clearly, this exposition revealed that much needs to be done to improve career counseling, even as it delineated what has been accomplished. The author will now reflect about developments that promise to aid career counseling and to pinpoint dangers to its growth. In addition, he will touch on counselor preparation and the incorporation of career counseling into existing institutions.

Developments Promising for Career Counseling

Career education, private sector and government assistance to adults in their career development, expansion of legislation guaranteeing equal access to work and training opportunities, expanding research on the nature of career, development of computerized career counseling systems, and refinement of measurement technologies, such as assessment centers, promise to provide supportive milieus, resources, incentives, opportunities, and a quicker access to more current and accurate information about career options and one's own attributes. Each development is reviewed briefly below.

Career Education

Career education encompasses myriad activities to help people, especially youngsters, to have more satisfying and productive careers. Federal financial incentives and research and development projects have influenced career educators to focus on curriculum innovation and collaboration between community and school. As a consequence, curriculum enrichment in the name of career education has exposed many youngsters to multiple experiences wherein they can become aware of career options and the relevance of school-taught skills to those options. More important than increased student career awareness, however, is increased school-community collaboration in addressing career concerns. This bold effort, opposing the trend for society's institutions to remain separate from one another, as noted by Dubin (1976), should enable all to examine more fully how they are relating to and preparing for work. Although a school-based career education program with limited community involvement may be helpful in motivating more students to develop salable skills and to improve their career decision-making, problem-solving, and planning abilities, the lack of broad community collaboration will prevent this education from alleviating workers' concerns about current training and work practices that have provided some of the impetus for career education. These difficulties are not merely a matter of worker attitude and ability; they also are due to the manner of organizing and doing training and work. Only community-school collaboration can hope to overcome such difficulties.

The very nature of career education, a program targeted at assisting maturation continuously during the school years at least, leads to widespread focus on career. Career education compels nearly every teacher's participation, draws periodic parent and community attention, and necessitates coordination among these groups and articulation across schools and with prospective employers. Although the comprehensive career education programs envisioned by the U.S. Office of Education in 1971 and 1972 (Hoyt et al., 1972) had not become widespread by 1975, nearly half the school districts in the United States had undertaken some career education activities by then (McLaughlin, 1976).

Juxtaposing the limited duration and potency of counseling with the continuity of career underscores the need to embed counseling in longer-term, more comprehensive career development programs, especially when the population to be served must operate in an environment that lacks resources to support career development. Hamdani (1977) for example, found that a one-year, one-hundred-plus-hour career guidance program had significant impacts on disadvantaged adolescents, whereas reports about shorter programs for inner-city youth were discouraging. She attributed part of the success to the program's duration. This author found a program, which had previously aided junior college students from generally advantaged circumstances (Healy, 1973b, 1974b), was satisfying to disadvantaged students, but minimally effective in building their career maturity (Healy, 1974c). Clinical impressions suggested that a comprehensive program could have overcome obstructions to career development in their milieu. Unfortunately, there are no recent studies of the long-term impacts of career counseling and career development programs on disadvantaged Americans The limited effectiveness of Manpower Development Training Act programs and compensatory education, however, certainly cautions against believing that duration alone will make a program effective. Evaluators, such as S.B. Sarason (1978), are noting that sound concepts and community involvement are both important for widescale community maturation.

Career Counseling for Employees

Both corporations and governmental agencies are increasingly providing career counseling services for employees. Management hopes to motivate workers to view career accomplishment as self-enhancing and to welcome the challenge of altered job routines and of occupational change. Management's growing affirmation of the wisdom and importance of developing human capital has increased support for career counseling and suggests organizational willingness to consider certain forms of work reorganization to promote employee development.

Increased career counseling of adults at many points over the life span will also clarify obstacles to adult development, strategies effective in overcoming them, and how adults learn these strategies. Currently, many beliefs about what obstructs an adult career and how to remove the obstacles derive from task analysis, not from observation of succeeding adults. This knowledge deficit probably will be corrected quickly, however, when counselors, as employees of the client's corporation or agency, can offer periodic services to a client during his or her tenure with an employer and can obtain information about career progress after, as well as during, counseling.

Better Access to Opportunities

Legislation, affirmative action programs, and more liberal policies for applying life experiences toward degree requirements are insuring fairer, fuller access to career opportunities. If work enhances self and occupations differ in how they enhance self, then a person can express more facets of self by pursuing different occupations. Thus, obstructing access to occupations thwarts individual self-development. Policies, therefore, that expand one's occupational options contribute to counseling's potential effectiveness by rendering the environment more conducive to career development.

Accessible options will increase client motivation for counseling and in turn result in greater benefit. The more possibilities, the more likely that one or several will be attractive. The more options, the less likely that a client will feel he or she is "settling" instead of voluntarily choosing. Likewise, truly accessible opportunities enable the counselor to feel better about the service offered and to be better able to support the client's enthusiasm for the process and the eventual decision.

Upgrading work through occupational professionalization can help occupation's incumbents perform more competently. Their increased competence, in turn, clearly benefits society. The rapid professionalization of occupations through fast enactment of licensing requirements and continuing education requirements, however, may well counterbalance policies to increase job access. Therefore, counselors and other career development professionals should help to ensure that licensure and/or prerequisites are justified.

Federal Career Research

Federal sponsorship of studies of the career behaviors and the attitudes of large random samples of Americans is propitious. Improved career counseling requires the latest information about what people at different stages in their career are doing, have accomplished, and are anticipating, as well as the autobiographical and economic factors that contribute to or hinder particular kinds of career success. The size and diversity of the American population require that extensive, wideranging descriptive data be gathered routinely and continuously and be thoroughly analyzed. Appropriately, the Department of Labor and Department of Education appear to have committed themselves to such research in order to inform manpower and education planners. This author hopes these two departments will also underwrite the intermediate and long-term follow-up research of counseling and other career development interventions that are part of programs such as *CETA* to explain factors that sustain improvements brought about by these interventions.

Computer Counseling Systems

Computer career counseling systems are being used by an increasing number of clients. Computers can administer and then score tests instantaneously; they can furnish accurate, current information about educational and occupational opportunities and immediate estimates of a person's probabilities for different options; they can enable the client to explore the consequences of different actions on career paths; they can store client information for review as his or her career unfolds; and they can collect client input and computer interactions for a data bank that can enable research of career development and formative evaluation of the computer counseling system.

Computers can complement, supplement, and in ways substitute for, counselors. By freeing them from routine information acquisition and exchange, computers enable counselors to focus on organizing an individualized learning program for clients, to gather information, and to interact more with key figures in the client's milieu, to acquire more data by which to evaluate counseling, and to serve more clients. In addition, they enable clients to review elements of counseling without consuming counselor time, while still receiving feedback congruent with the counselor's plan.

As use of computer counseling systems expands, clients can be involved in more beneficial experiences during counseling, thereby enabling counseling to achieve greater impact.

Assessment Centers and Autobiographical Data Blanks

Counseling appraisal will soon be enriched by data from assessment centers and autobiographical data blanks. Both of these assessment practices have been developed for selection of employees, but users have also noted their possible contribution to career counseling.

The limits of paper-pencil assessments and restrospective ratings have long been known. Measurement experts, such as McClelland (1973), have called on psychologists to be more imaginative in measurement. Proponents of naturalistic observation and experimentation, such as S.B. Sarason (1978), have shown the folly of measuring a person independently of his or her milieu. Chapters 2 and 3 of this text point out appraisal's heavy reliance on trait-factor approaches and note that other models call for different kinds of assessment data. Since considerable understanding of assessment centers and autobiographical blanks is accumulating, counselors will soon be able to help clients to understand inferences generated by these methods and to use them in career planning.

The assessment center method was described in Chapter 3; evaluations of it appear in Bray and Grant (1966), Cohen, Moses, and Byham (1974), Howard (1974), and Huck (1973). The autobiographical data blank is described in Anastasi (1976); evaluations of it are included in Muchinsky and Tuttle (1979), Ghiselli (1966), and Owens (1976).

Dangers to Career Counseling

Omissions in current career counseling practice, often caused by time and resource constraints, are jeopardizing the continuation of career counseling as an education, placement or personnel service. Lack of an explicit, articulated rationale leaves clients and community, if not the counselor, confused about what counseling is supposed to do, and how. Therefore, client and community are unclear about what to do to assist the counseling process or how to judge whether the procedure is progressing or incurring obstructions. Isolating counseling from the milieu in which the career problem unfolds may confound, rather than alleviate, the difficulty. Likewise, pursuing nonspecified goals in a casual relationship may reduce client commitment to the counseling process rather than increase his or her sense of responsibility for making counseling work. Certainly, failure to document evaluation, to beware of counseling costs, and to record efforts to improve counseling belies the contention that counseling is a knowledge-based professional, accountable service. Moreover, acknowledging that counseling is individualized teaching for everyday tasks of living; but eschewing instructional aids, such as reading materials, audio visuals, and paraprofessionals, causes the community to wonder about the efficiency and thoroughness of the enterprise. Likewise, heavy reliance on client perceptions, with limited attention to objective information about the person and his or her milieu, contradicts the claim that counseling is quality education.

Rationale

Career counseling procedures are often presented as activities whose rationale and merits are self-evident. Yet, different procedures prompt one to gather different information and to accomplish different objectives. They envision different ways of relating to work, as explicated in Chapter 2. Therefore, the rationale of the methods being used must be presented to the client.

For example, trait-factor counseling prompts the undecided adolescent to acquire self and occupational information that experts deem career-relevant and to select and begin implementing educational and occupational options more congruent with personal attributes. Underlying trait-factor counseling is the belief that there is an oderliness among people and their environments, which can be discovered. When this order is discovered, the trait-factor view presumes people will use it to guide thmselves into compatible activities. In contrast, the adolescent in guided inquiry counseling receives help in deciding what is obstructing his or her choosing. The client is guided to pinpoint whether the obstruction is lack of self or occupational information due to limited experience, lack of reflection, lack of ability or linkages; lack of acceptance by significant others, system faults, and so forth. Then client and counselor devise a plan for overcoming the obstruction or taking a new direction. Proceeding, they carry out their respective parts of the plan, and together they examine the client's success in implementation. Unlike the trait-factor view, the guided inquiry position does not presume that compatibility of person and environment is desirable; instead it posits the importance of the person's deciding for himself or herself.

The counselor who does not articulate the rationale of the treatment cannot defend the treatment as appropriate for the client. An incomplete rationale may mean the counselor does not understand the treatment's likely benefits and dangers or the actions necessary to make it work. If the latter, the counseling actions may thwart the client's growth; if the former, the counselor may be wasting the client's time by achieving an inappropriate goal or may endanger the client by exposure to unnecessary risks.

Clearly, counselors need to dispel the mystery about their craft. They need to publicize the views of human nature underlying their techniques and objectives, and they need to teach clients what to expect from the counselor and what they can do to cooperate fully in their counseling. Sometimes, counselors complain about client's expectations of magic. Yet most clients do not know how counseling operates. Rarely do they have a chance to watch a film, read a description, or listen to a tape of counseling, even though these presentations would help to clarify their expectations and hence their capability of achieving them.

Closely linked with a clear rationale is the empirical evidence behind a procedure. In explicating what and how the client is to do or learn through a procedure, the counselor cannot ignore the evidence for the efficacy of the method. Yet, many counselors use materials and procedures for purposes for which research suggests other techniques are more effective or for which evidence suggests the selected procedure is counterproductive. For example, hundreds of counselors in Southern California now have students complete checklists of preferences resembling the *Self-Directed Search (SDS)*, which produce recommendations about occupations to explore. The checklists are marketed at a lower price than the *SDS*, but this author has not been able to find a statement about why particular items are scored as supporting one occupation rather than others. In other words, counselors are using the checklists without knowing the logic or empirical evidence supporting the recommendations forthcoming from the checklist. Moreover, the checklist materials suggest that completing the inventory and obtaining its recommendations spurs career exploration; but do not suggest actions to realize this objective, nor do the materials allude to evidence supporting the contention. Predictably, the checklist materials do not refer to studies by Holland et al. (1978), Zenner and Schnuelle (1972) or Zytowski (1977), which report that simply completing interest inventories and receiving interpretations decreases, rather than increases, career exploration immediately after being inventoried. Unfortunately, the counselors using these checklists do not believe they have time or resources to verify the impact of this career guidance experience.

Exclusive Relationship

Career counseling obviously must engage the client in exploring self and milieu objectively and thoroughly, without fear. But, making counseling an exclusive relationship removed from the milieu in which the career is being expressed may be counterproductive.

Most career improvements or corrections will occur within the client's milieu and often will require the accession, if not the assistance, of people excluded from the counseling relationship. These people are sometimes part of the problem and should be charged to help in its solution. Even when the difficulty is essentially personal, potent persons, such as parents, spouses, employers, supervisors, teachers, and coaches, may want to help the client. If included in counseling, their efforts for the client can complement and supplement counseling assistance; whereas if they are excluded, their efforts may interfere with counseling.

New counseling approaches are needed to involve affected family, peers, teachers, employers, and community representatives from the outset. These parties will cooperate more willingly if they have helped create the solutions. Too often, counseling launches a client in a direction, but does not help erect supporting structures. Undoubtedly, early involvement of spouses in career planning, retired persons in interpreting work experience, and union officials and supervisors in overcoming on-the-job obstructions to career progress, for example, will increase the time spent in defining problems and generating alternatives. But, the extra effort should be worthwhile, for the analogy of Japanese managerial decision making appears pertinent. According to Drucker (1974), Japanese workers and management who will be affected by a particular decision all participate in examining the problems and in generating possible solutions. The result, Drucker suggests, is swift implementation because the sense of participation in the decision-making process prompts the personnel to commit themselves to a successful execution.

Inclusion of significant others in counseling can be helpful in many ways. The counselor can verify that the counseling goals accord with community-supported career development objectives. Nonclients will better understand the character of counseling and often will become its supporters. Most importantly, many career problems stem from community limitations, such as poor schools and inadequately supervised teachers, unfair job or educational entry requirements and unequal access to opportunities, insufficient jobs, and uneven distribution of community resources, so individuals cannot correct these problems on their own. To ask some person to accommodate to these shortcomings is often unfair and unrealistic. If employers and community leaders were more involved in the career counseling process, they would recognize these inequities and be prompted to correct the community problems. Counselors are unlikely to try to correct community shortcomings themselves, for traditionally counseling has not sought environmental change.

Despite the potential advantage of involving more people directly in career counseling, research has not studied how to integrate significant others and still enable the client to examine personal concerns openly. Clearly, however, the lack of validated procedures should not deter exploration of inclusion. This author's limited experience in involving significant others in counseling suggests the threat to client privacy is often not major, and that the counselors were often more concerned by the involvement of significant others than was the client.

Nonspecific Goals

Client goals should be personalized, reflecting achievements that will bolster the particular client's career and including means suited to his or her special capacities and milieu. Personalized goals should make them more specifiable and verifiable, and thus provide guidance about direction and make accountability easier to achieve.

Current practices suggest, however, that verifiable goals are not always set and used to guide counseling. Often, counseling is initiated in, and proceeds through, informal oral encounters that sometimes cannot be clearly linked to one another. Frequently the client is encouraged to lead the discussion, and is not pressed to commit oneself to particular goals or action, e.g., homework, under the rationale that such direction would deny him or her control over counseling. Professional literature and counseling records offer little documentation that either client or counselor reference benchmarks in directing their interaction or in judging progress. Few counselors use written contracts delineating goals, and most descriptions of career counseling do not specify achievements or counselor-client actions appropriate for different phases of the counseling. The lack of specified, documented goals and operations is surprising in view of research and pressure for accountability. Research of client and counselor perceptions about their mutual interactions suggests frequent disagreements about intentions and meanings. The continued inattention to contracting and to explicating goals and strategies, is unfortunate because studies generally suggest that premature termination of counseling is closely associated with disagreement about what should be, or is, happening in counseling.

Lack of Counseling Evaluation

Few reports in counseling journals, dissertation abstracts, or the ERIC system empirically evaluate career counseling. Even rarer are references to efforts to improve a procedure via formative evaluation methods. These facts suggest that many counselors are rendering services without evaluating them properly, and that only a few are systematically trying to upgrade practice based on their experiences.

There are many reasons exclusive of counselor competence that counseling goals are difficult to realize. Accountability, therefore, does not require constant success. But, lacking evidence of continued success, accountability does demand that counselors demonstrate that they are offering services in accord with professional standards, that they are keeping track of the consequences of their interventions, and are systematically scrutinizing their experiences to improve service. Systematic observation of counselors' practices is especially important because counseling is a developing science, which should be improving through feedback.

Unfortunately, the dearth of detailed written descriptions of career counseling, the lack of agreement about benchmarks for verifying quality counseling, and the inability of many counselors to elaborate systematically on their counseling activities indicate that some, if not many, counselors do not routinely verify that their own or their colleagues' services are professional.

This lack of treatment guidelines doubtlessly also hampers the development of a diagnostic system that would direct clients to different treatments based on their goals and characteristics. Now, diagnosis is often gross, resulting in the prescription of career counseling, no counseling, or personal counseling. If counselors defined treatment, monitored their results with different types of clients and objectives, and reported these, it should soon be possible to create guidelines for assigning clients to different treatment. Clearly, lack of defined treatments and a diagnostic rationale for differential assignment diminishes ability to provide professional caliber service.

An offshoot of career counseling evaluation should be reports to the community about the incidence of different career problems, the resolutions achieved, and the costs of different solutions. When people acknowledge that career problems are community, as well as person, problems and that their solutions can be effected by the community, they will need the above information to judge the seriousness of these problems, the adequacy of investment in counseling, and their need to alleviate the problems directly.

Cost-Benefit of Counseling

Most counseling is now offered in public institutions. Estimates are that the adult services must be heavily subsidized (Walz, 1979). Although one can argue persuasively for the need for counseling, the general public has not yet accepted the need to pay for it (Arbeiter et al., 1978). Although counseling may not have to "pay for itself," it would seem politic for the profession to be showing concern with improving its efficiency in this era of shrinking resources.

This author's suggestions about formative evaluation and using multiple teaching strategies and media directly support a concern for improving the efficiency of counseling. Although counseling outcomes have not been assigned dollar values, suggestions such as those of Krumboltz (1974) show that they might be costed out. Certainly, if the nature of counseling outcomes are delineated, then estimating costs for particular outcomes should soon be possible. At a time when quality of life is being recognized as important, the counseling profession might look forward to realistic appraisal and acceptance of what a counseling benefit costs. For such scrutiny is likely to raise appropriations for counseling and to spur the community to make improvements that will reduce the need for counseling; that is, to modify the milieu to promote career development. Of course, community confrontation with the costs and benefits is also likely to lead to elimination of some services. Yet, prompting counselors to argue the rationale for continuing an inefficient treatment, probably will enhance understanding of the controversial service and eventually lead counselors to offer services for which there is a clear community mandate.

Incomplete Teaching

Career counseling often imparts information, teaches and practices skills, develops new appreciations of the self and the environment, and is frequently acknowledged to be teaching. But, counseling rarely incorporates strategies other than interviewing and test interpretation. The counselor typically functions as the giver of knowledge, rather than as the designer and manager of a learning program. Reliance on only a few strategies reduces efficiency; it probably also prevents counseling from communicating different facts, exercising certain skills, and developing certain appreciations of the counseling problem and solution in the most accurate manner. The fact that various career counseling procedures have encompassed written as well as oral communication, directed reading, films and other audio visuals, paraprofessionally supervised practice, field trips, task tryouts, and homework, indicate that such actions are not incompatible with counseling. Moreover, such innovations challenge the professionalization of those who counsel as if the printing press and more recent communication technology did not exist.

Insight and Reality

Critical to effective counseling is the development of an atmosphere wherein the client can acquire insight into his or her career. Often the counselor must provide the stimulation and support for the client to elaborate on his or her thoughts and feelings. As the exploration proceeds, however, it is counterproductive for the counselor to permit the client to base ascriptions and projections about self in career on erroneous facts or unlikely career events. For example, the handicapped student who has achieved the dictation and typing speeds of thirty words per minute and finds himself far ahead of his peers cannot be allowed to infer that such competence qualifies him for secretarial positions. In aiding self-discovery, the counselor must help the client to reference appropriate norms, confront pertinent experience tables and trends, and distinguish the wish from the reality. Discoveries, such as that of Super et al. (1960, 1969), Gribbons and Lohnes (1968), and Flanagan (1973), that occupational choice during high school is typically unstable, should, for example, prompt the counselor whose adolescent client is intense about making such a choice not only to reflect the importance the client is placing on the choice but also to encourage the client to recognize that choice instability during these years is not an indicator of immaturity and that one's choice is likely to change.

Many new discoveries are being made about careers and the educational-work system in which they unfold. The counselor has an obligation to keep abreast of these findings and to assure that pertinent ones are attended to as the client seeks to expand his or her understanding of his or her career. Moreover, when information about what is successful in the client's environment for people like the client are unavailable, the counselor has a responsibility to examine the milieu directly. Trained in social science observational methods, and not emotionally distracted by forces within the client's situation, counselors often will be more able than clients to discover ingredients of success for that milieu and ways of learning them.

Research Priorities

By encouraging evaluation and other kinds of research related to counseling, this text seeks to help counselors become accountable. Undoubtedly, readers have identified many questions about particular procedures that could be tested and whose answers would help them and others to understand the procedures better. For example, the reader may want to examine certain questions about the nature of career maturity at specific stages in order to serve a particular clientele better. The detailed treatment descriptions will facilitate examining whether replications and modifications of particular procedures would benefit certain clients, and the review of facts and theories pertinent to certain stages show the many gaps in the understanding of career development.

Five elements of counseling research seem most in need of improvement:

1. Counseling treatments must be specified in greater detail, ideally delineating factors such as key concepts and principles; the kinds of materials and exercises used in counseling and as homework; the quality of learning interaction; the total time for counseling and homework;

the client's starting and closing mastery of concepts, principles, and skills; and the degree to which the client voluntarily selected and created the counseling program. Recent reports increasingly specify treatment factors and provide verification about its accurate rendition, but they still omit the starting and closing mastery of the client and the degree to which the client fashioned counseling. Lack of such information, of course, makes it difficult for report readers to judge whether the treatment suits their clientele.

2. Reports need to describe clients more comprehensively at the start and conclusion of counseling, using psychodiagnostic systems such as reported in Chapter 5. Demographics such as age, sex, grade, and previous counseling are useful but insufficient. Replication and transportability require information about strengths and weaknesses of the clients and their environments and data about clients' aspirations and the urgency of their quest. Especially important are information about the achievement of the client's intended goal and avoidance of hazards. Several studies in the 1940s and 1950s evaluated the total client change during counseling; but studies in the 1960s and 1970s have tended to focus on particular changes, such as amount of information seeking, certainty of choice, and satisfaction. Although it would have been helpful if earlier studies had described the starting and closing conditions of their clients succinctly and although the content of counseling records probably varied widely, early studies had the advantage of professional testimony about a person's full progress over counseling. By focusing on one or two specific changes, recent studies often prevent conclusions regarding counseling's benefit to the career. More information seeking or planning or more favorable self-evaluation, for example, do not assure that clients achieve their intended goals. Although specification of outcomes is helpful, reports need to put the particular results into the context of the client's career in order for readers to judge the substance of the findings.

3. Counselors need to examine the modifications of traditional treatments, which may be necessary to serve atypical populations. For example, many displaced and returning homemakers seek direction in entering the labor market and often receive a form of trait-factor, career choice counseling. However, trait-factor counseling was developed and validated for high school and college students and returning veterans, usually in their early twenties. Researchers should study how or whether to adapt such counseling, since these mature women have advantages, such as wider experiences and the resolution of identity conflicts of youth, and disadvantages, such as a nonreceptive labor market, socialization for lesser commitment to career, and more extensive demands from other life roles, than traditional clients.

Closely linked to special adaptations is the issue of differential prescription. Studies have shown several instances in which different procedures help clients to achieve the same or similar goals. Holland (1973), Osipow (1973), and others have noted that typologies, such as Holland's, predict that persons of different types would profit differentially from certain counseling procedures. Relationships between client type and counseling method promises to be an important research concern; and indeed a recent study by Kivlighan (1981) showed that social and enterprising types benefited more from vocational counseling featuring peer interaction, while realistic and investigative types fared better in vocational counseling involving individual problem solving. Certainly, knowing that particular client populations are more likely to benefit from one procedure than from another will improve counseling's efficacy.

4. Counselors need to test whether and how expansion of counseling to include strategies such as assigned reading, extracounseling practice, mastery tests, and securing privileged access to resources for a client contributes to career advancement. Assuming that counseling is teaching implies that a wider range of strategies for facilitating client learning are available than are now being used. Counselors should use their imaginations and examine whether activities other teachers use will help their clients to learn more efficiently. Varying strategies appear to be a way to reach populations with whom counseling has not been effective; therefore, career counseling must become more than test and talk.

5. Counselors need to improve their research designs. Recent studies show improvement with regard to establishing comparable control groups by random assignment or at least by covariate procedures, using several counselors to diminish the possibility that a particular counselor's style produces the effects, and using reliable and valid measures. In spite of such improvement, many recent studies still have design problems. Often they use a very small number of clients from one institution, and frequently these clients are special recruits for counseling or students fulfilling a research obligation rather than clients seeking career counseling. Obviously, counselors in different agencies and schools need to cooperate in evaluation research to increase the N and to demonstrate that the reported counseling effects are not an artifact of the client's institution.

On the other hand, published intensive case studies of career counseling are almost nonexistent, and this author has not located a single study using the adversary or human intelligence models. Yet, as noted in Chapter 6, both designs can complement the traditional factorial design in enriching understanding of career counseling's operation and impact. Both designs, admittedly, are arduous and risky if one hopes to draw conclusions and publish. But does not taking risks to serve others distinguish the professional from the technician?

Other Issues

This text has not examined issues such as changing institutions to accommodate career counseling and methods of training counselors. They will be discussed briefly here.

Implementation

Most counselors ply their trade within educational or health institutions (Shertzer & Stone, 1976). Consequently, they must follow the operating procedures of these institutions; for example, deferring to forty to fifty-minute periods, restricted access to clients, and lack of control over client release. Frequently the institutional operations, although rarely their purposes, pose obstacles to the individual and group procedures presented in this text. Therefore, integrating some of these procedures into existing institutions will be a formidable undertaking.

On the other hand, the procedures presented here should not be dismissed as "elitist" services to be provided only for a few advantaged people, or in well-financed institutions. The efficacy of these sometimes "costly" services is certainly not overpowering; however, to do less has not been shown to be effective. Unfortunately, educators do not scrutinize other services, such as career centers, guidance classes, orientations, field trips, work experiences, directed reading, and the like, as closely as they examine counseling. Nevertheless, data from surveys such as the National Assessment (Aubrey, 1977; Miller, 1977; Mitchell, 1977; Westbrook, 1977) and by Prediger, Roth & Noeth (1973), suggest that guidance services generally are not having major impact. Without doubt, more time and resources must be committed to career counseling before one can expect significant client benefits. Unfortunately, this fact often puts counselors on the defensive.

More and more self-help manuals and career workshops are being sold that imply, if they do not claim directly, that they produce easy and immediate career benefits. Americans raised on "instants" and a "can-do" pragmatism often believe such claims, which occasionally do accrue. In many cases, however, scrutiny of these services and materials indicates they are not likely to yield the benefits claimed. Nevertheless, counselors must keep informed of innovative services in order to be able to use them when warranted and to be prepared to show why ersatz treatments are less likely to boost career development than is a systematic, well-conceptualized career counseling program.

Counselors need to change their standard operations in order to do more professional counseling. There is little chance of establishing accountability unless one renders counseling in a professional manner. Certainly this text's examination of what counseling has and has not done, and what it logically could do, should help to justify the time and resources to do professional counseling. Furthermore, providing a clear, comprehensive rationale for counseling, involving more community people in the counseling, informing the community about problems encountered and progress made in counseling, and improving counseling through systematic evaluation should also build support for professional counseling. But other skills, such as ability to lobby and sell, to analyze an institution's power structure, and to sustain motivation for change, are also needed. Students have learned, or should be learning and practicing, these skills in courses and practicums. Indeed, some counseling programs now offer courses on being a change agent. Texts and manuals, such as Blocher et al. (1971), Abrego and Brammer (1978), and

Benjamin and Walz (1979a, b), explicate the process and provide exercises for building the skills.

Training of Counselors

Counselor training should address these five objectives:

1. To equip counselors with observational skills and knowledge of available tools to enable them to identify client needs and to learn how persons like the client are meeting those needs.
2. To initiate counselors in synthesizing social science understanding into working, but evolving, models of human behavior that they can use to guide data collection and to suggest goals and means of attaining them.
3. To acquaint them with a range of educational strategies and to provide them with practice in organizing and using these strategies to benefit clients.
4. To habituate them to evaluating their own counseling and critically examining the counseling and research reported by others.
5. To engage them in coordinating and cooperating with others in rendering career counseling, and to encourage them to initiate cooperative arrangements.

The desired posture for a professional counselor is that of the collaborating practitioner-scientist. The counselor should be daring enough to join others in trying reasonable strategies to assist clients overcome their problems of everyday living; sufficiently humble to recognize the need to scrutinize one's efforts to assure one is benefiting, rather than harming; and incessantly curious about what is or might benefit the clients.

Since counseling includes the development, administration, and evaluation of a learning program to develop an individual's career, this author believes that the counselor must obtain professional training and continually refresh that training. Logic suggests that extensive training is necessary for such a complex undertaking, but research has not addressed the issue fully. Although studies such as Healy's (1973b, 1974b) and Snodgrass's (1978) show that counseling students without experience and paraprofessionals following explicit guidelines can render phase 3 of counseling effectively, those and most other studies of paraprofessional counseling limit use of paraprofessionals to one or two phases of counseling. Within these phases, the counseling activities are often highly structured, with little room for modification. In other words, research has not tested the capacities of paraprofessionals to construct and to deliver a total career counseling program; and generally has not examined their capacities in phases 1 and 4, that is, in formulating an individualized program based on client appraisal and in designing and implementing an assessment of the counseling program. Judicious assignment of paraprofessionals can enable counselors to serve more clients, but the myriad factors affecting a person's career development necessitate professional supervision of the total counseling operation to maximize the likelihood of quality service.

Conclusion

This exposition has included detailed descriptions of counseling procedures, not to be followed as recipes, but to serve as a starting point for counselors. The author hopes the descriptions will help students and practitioners to better understand what counseling has been and assist them in specifying the counseling they will offer. At times, readers may find parts of a procedure described here are directly applicable to their clientele. But to be ready to select or design treatment components for a client, counselors should first synthesize their own models of a person in relation to work from reflection about their own careers, from careful observation and analysis of the careers of people from the population to be served, and from consideration of the concepts developed in Chapters 2, 3 and 4. With an explicit, yet evolving model of man or woman in career, and ongoing readiness to try to understand another human being, one will be prepared to individualize learning. After all, that is the essence of professional counseling.

APPENDICES

APPENDIX A DESCRIPTIONS OF FIVE CAREER DEVELOPMENT TESTS

APPENDIX B EXCERPT FROM FORESIGHT

APPENDIX C EXCERPT FROM OVERVIEW

APPENDIX D EXCERPTS FROM CAPTAINS INTRODUCTION

APPENDIX E EXCERPTS FROM ALTERNATIVE SPECIALTY

APPENDIX F EXCERPT FROM SELF ASSESSMENT

APPENDIX G EXCERPT FROM CAREER STRATEGIES

SOURCE: Appendices B–G from S. D. Phillips, P. C. Cairo, & R. A. Myers, Career planning modules for the new officer career information and planning system. Unpublished paper. New York: Teachers College, Columbia University, 1980. Reprinted by permission.

appendix A

DESCRIPTIONS OF FIVE CAREER
DEVELOPMENT TESTS

The concept of career maturity became more useful in the 1970s, when several tests of it were introduced. This appendix describes five of the first generation tests that measure aspects of career maturity. They have been used in establishing whether a group has need for particular guidance services and in evaluating whether groups have benefitted from counseling and guidance programs. Critical evaluations of these instruments can be found in O. K. Buros (ed.) *Eighth Mental Measurements Yearbook* (Highland Park, N. J.: Gryphon Press, 1978) and in the journal, *Measurement and Evaluation in Guidance*.

American College Testing. *Assessment of Career Development*. Houghton Mifflin, One Beacon Street, Boston, Ma. 02107.

The *ACD* tests an adolescent's knowledge about common occupations' characteristics and training requirements and knowledge about career planning. On the behavioral dimension, the *ACD* quizzes the student both about formal and informal experiences likely to promote career development and about actions in the career planning process. The norm-referenced feedback enables the adolescent to compare his or her level of career activity with peers. Finally the *ACD* solicits reactions to aspects of the guidance program to assist school faculty in program planning. Testing time is approximately 125 minutes.

Super, D. E., Jordaan, J. P., Lindeman, R. H., Myers, R. A., and Thompson, A. S. *Career Development Inventory*. New York: Consulting Psychologists Press, 577 College Avenue, Palo Alto, Calif. 94306.

This battery builds on the theoretical framework of career development emerging from the classic Career Pattern Study. Its five scales measure the following:

1. The amount of attention a student has given to different aspects of career planning and the amount of information he or she believes he or she has obtained.
2. The perceived usefulness of different information sources.
3. The ability to make career selection for fictitious cases and the ability to identify mature career behavior and attitudes.
4. The ability to match occupations with particular properties such as level of training or frequency of paycheck.
5. The ability to identify features of his or her preferred occupation.

The last scale of the battery should be especially helpful to counselors and program planners because it is the only existing scale in a major career development test that tests a student's knowledge of his or her preferred field. Testing time is approximately 120 minutes.

Crites, J. O. *Career Maturity Inventory (CMI)* CTB/McGraw-Hill, 1221 Avenue of The Americas, New York, New York 10036.

The *CMI* measures students on six characteristics, which career development theory and research indicate are important indices of career maturity in adolescence. Five cognitive tests examine a student's ability to draw conclusions about the appropriateness of different career actions based on a description of the person's attributes, match an occupation with its description, select an occupation that fits one's attributes and experiences, recognize the sequence of steps necessary to realize a career goal, and solve career problems stemming from external impediments or conflicts. The sixth scale, which is attitudinal, assesses the degree to which a student's views about career are similar to the views of students who have reached the twelfth grade. There are 100 test items and 50 attitude items, requiring approximately 150 minutes of testing.

Educational Testing Service. *Career Skills Assessment Program.* The College Board, 888 Seventh Avenue, New York, NY 10019.

This battery assesses adolescent career skill development through sixty-item tests in each of the following six areas:

1. Ability to organize self-information and to synthesize personal data and career facts into career choices
2. Career awareness
3. Career decision making
4. Employment-seeking skills
5. Knowledge of expected on-the-job behavior
6. Personal economic skills.

Accompanying the tests are guidance materials related to them. These materials provide an answer key giving the rationale of the answers for the test.

Healy, C. C., and Klein, S. P. *New Mexico Career Education Test Series.* Monitor, P. O. Box 2337, Hollywood, CA 90028

This experimental battery of six scales (four cognitive, one behavioral, and one attitudinal) is designed to assist program developers and evaluators in assessing junior and senior high school students on six career education objectives. Twenty-to-twenty-five-item scales appraise each of the following career education objectives:

1. The student appreciates the personal and social significance of work.

2. The student can make appropriate decisions about preparing for and selecting an occupation.
3. The student has accomplishd tasks that studies of career development suggest will improve career decision making.
4. The student understands the duties and requirements of a range of occupations.
5. The student knows how to apply and interview for different occupations.
6. The student can identify the work attitudes and behaviors required for holding a job and advancing in responsibility.

Testing takes approximately 20 to 25 minutes per scale. Completion of the total battery requires about 150 minutes.

appendix β

EXCERPT FROM
FORESIGHT

The user has "signed on" to the system, and, given a description of what the module contains, has opted to explore FORESIGHT further. The following frames are presented on the screen:

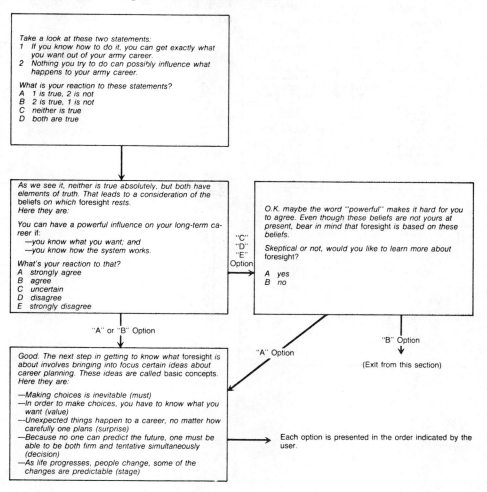

Take a look at these two statements:
1 If you know how to do it, you can get exactly what you want out of your army career.
2 Nothing you try to do can possibly influence what happens to your army career.

What is your reaction to these statements?
A 1 is true, 2 is not
B 2 is true, 1 is not
C neither is true
D both are true

As we see it, neither is true absolutely, but both have elements of truth. That leads to a consideration of the beliefs on which foresight rests.
Here they are:

You can have a powerful influence on your long-term career if:
—you know what you want; and
—you know how the system works.

What's your reaction to that?
A strongly agree
B agree
C uncertain
D disagree
E strongly disagree

"C"
"D"
"E"
Option

O.K. maybe the word "powerful" makes it hard for you to agree. Even though these beliefs are not yours at present, bear in mind that foresight is based on these beliefs.

Skeptical or not, would you like to learn more about foresight?

A yes
B no

"A" or "B" Option

"A" Option

"B" Option

(Exit from this section)

Good. The next step in getting to know what foresight is about involves bringing into focus certain ideas about career planning. These ideas are called basic concepts.
Here they are:

—Making choices is inevitable (must)
—In order to make choices, you have to know what you want (value)
—Unexpected things happen to a career, no matter how carefully one plans (surprise)
—Because no one can predict the future, one must be able to be both firm and tentative simultaneously (decision)
—As life progresses, people change, some of the changes are predictable (stage)

Each option is presented in the order indicated by the user.

appendix C

EXCERPT FROM OVERVIEW

The introductory section of OVERVIEW stresses the complexity of the Army Officer career structure and encourages user to consult additional sources of information for details beyond the scope of OVERVIEW. The following excerpts introduces the user to the offline charts (included here) and begins the explanation and discussion of the career structure.

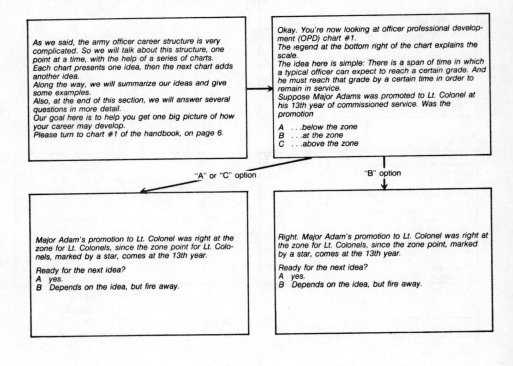

As we said, the army officer career structure is very complicated. So we will talk about this structure, one point at a time, with the help of a series of charts.
Each chart presents one idea, then the next chart adds another idea.
Along the way, we will summarize our ideas and give some examples.
Also, at the end of this section, we will answer several questions in more detail.
Our goal here is to help you get one big picture of how your career may develop.
Please turn to chart #1 of the handbook, on page 6.

Okay. You're now looking at officer professional development (OPD) chart #1.
The legend at the bottom right of the chart explains the scale.
The idea here is simple: There is a span of time in which a typical officer can expect to reach a certain grade. And he must reach that grade by a certain time in order to remain in service.
Suppose Major Adams was promoted to Lt. Colonel at his 13th year of commissioned service. Was the promotion

A ...below the zone
B ...at the zone
C ...above the zone

"A" or "C" option

"B" option

Major Adam's promotion to Lt. Colonel was right at the zone for Lt. Colonels, since the zone point for Lt. Colonels, marked by a star, comes at the 13th year.

Ready for the next idea?
A yes.
B Depends on the idea, but fire away.

Right. Major Adam's promotion to Lt. Colonel was right at the zone for Lt. Colonels, since the zone point, marked by a star, comes at the 13th year.

Ready for the next idea?
A yes.
B Depends on the idea, but fire away.

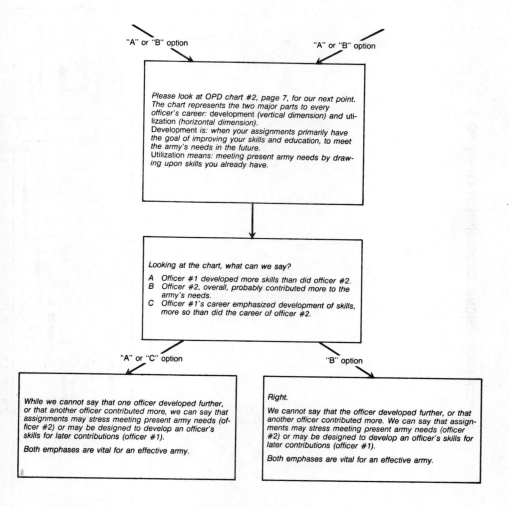

"A" or "B" option   "A" or "B" option

Please look at OPD chart #2, page 7, for our next point.
The chart represents the two major parts to every
officer's career: development (vertical dimension) and utilization (horizontal dimension).
Development is: when your assignments primarily have
the goal of improving your skills and education, to meet
the army's needs in the future.
Utilization means: meeting present army needs by drawing upon skills you already have.

Looking at the chart, what can we say?

A   Officer #1 developed more skills than did officer #2.
B   Officer #2, overall, probably contributed more to the
    army's needs.
C   Officer #1's career emphasized development of skills,
    more so than did the career of officer #2.

"A" or "C" option   "B" option

While we cannot say that one officer developed further,
or that another officer contributed more, we can say that
assignments may stress meeting present army needs (officer #2) or may be designed to develop an officer's
skills for later contributions (officer #1).

Both emphases are vital for an effective army.

Right.

We cannot say that the officer developed further, or that
another officer contributed more. We can say that assignments may stress meeting present army needs (officer
#2) or may be designed to develop an officer's skills for
later contributions (officer #1).

Both emphases are vital for an effective army.

At this point in the module, the computer continues on to present
further concepts and illustrations of the career structure, using the remaining charts in the off-line series.

OFFICER PROFESSIONAL DEVELOPMENT CHART NO. 1

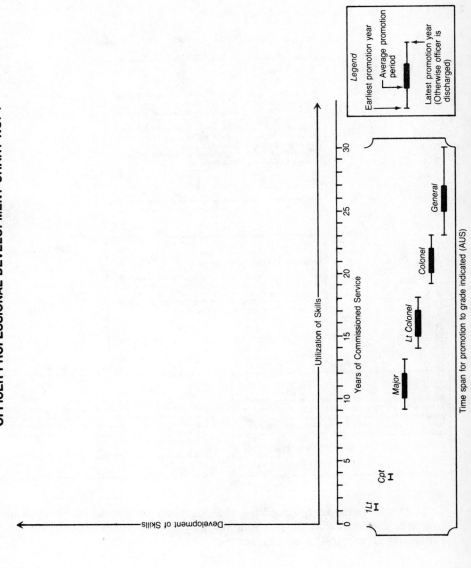

OFFICER PROFESSIONAL DEVELOPMENT CHART NO. 2

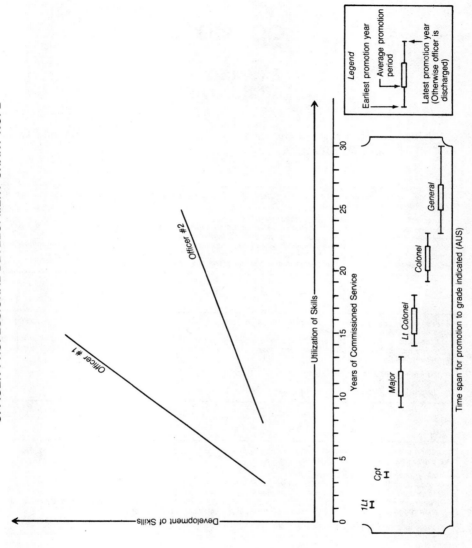

appendix D

EXCERPT FROM
CAPTAINS INTRODUCTION

This module provides the user with an abbreviated version of FORE-SIGHT and OVERVIEW.

The officer career information and planning system (OCIPS) is designed to help you with long-term career planning. It is made up of five separate modules. . . .

—Foresight. . . .deals with basic concepts of career planning.
—Self assessment. . . .helps you create a profile based on your ratings of your skills and values.
—Alternate specialty. . . .includes information and data on alternate specialties.
—Overview. . . .deals with the army's overall plan for the progression of an officer's career, including the factors that influence the way it develops.
—Career strategies. . . .helps you set goals and develop action plans for achieving these goals.

At this point in your army career you may already be acquainted with many of the concepts that are presented in foresight and overview.

Therefore we'd like to give you the choice to begin where you think is most suitable for your experience and interests. You may begin with either the full foresight or with a condensed version that highlights the concepts and leaves off the examples. Choose one:

A I'd like to start with the full foresight
B "   "   "   "   " " condensed form.
C Skip it. Let's go on to alternate specialty.

Option 3

In getting to know what foresight is about involves bringing into focus certain ideas about career planning. These ideas are called "basic concepts". Here they are:

—Making choice is inevitable (must)
—In order to make choices, you have to know what you want (value)
—Unexpected things happen to a career, no matter how carefully one plans (surprise)
—Because no one can predict the future, one must be able to be both firm and tentative simultaneously (tension)
—As life progresses, people change; some of the changes are predictable (stage)

Which concept would you like to look at first?
A Must
B Value
C Surprise
D Tension
E Stage

appendix E

EXCERPTS FROM
ALTERNATE SPECIALTY

This module provides the user with data about the designation of Alternate Specialties in years past and offers suggestions about how to incorporate such data into one's own planning for expressing an Alternate Specialty preference.

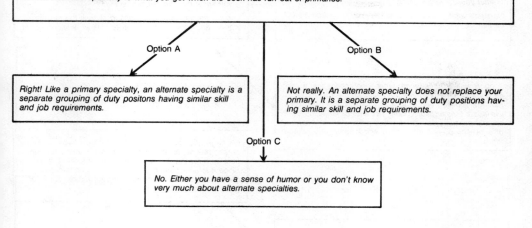

Which of the following is true?

A. An alternate specialty is a specialty in addition to your primary, designated for your professional development and utilization.
B. An alternate specialty is a specialty which takes the place of your primary after your first six to eight years in the army.
C. An alternate specialty is what you get when the cook has run out of primaries.

Option A

Option B

Right! Like a primary specialty, an alternate specialty is a separate grouping of duty positons having similar skill and job requirements.

Not really. An alternate specialty does not replace your primary. It is a separate grouping of duty positions having similar skill and job requirements.

Option C

No. Either you have a sense of humor or you don't know very much about alternate specialties.

Officer Preferences: How many wanted what they got?

Next is a list of some alternate specialties. Beside each one are the percentages of officers entering that specialty who listed it as their first, second, third, fourth, or fifth choice.

For example, of those entering atomic energy, 50% had listed it as their first choice, 25% as their second choice, 5% as their third choice, 7% as the fourth, none as their fifth. And 13% had listed it as their sixth choice or not at all.

Alternate Specialty	1	2	3	4	5	Other
Personnel management	39%	20%	10%	6%	3%	22%
OR/SA	51	22	5	2	1	19
Atomic energy	50	25	5	7	0	13
R & D	43	21	8	5	1	22

appendix F

EXCERPT FROM
SELF ASSESSMENT

The following frames are drawn from values assessment section of the SELF ASSESSMENT module. Prior to viewing this sequence, the user has considered the concept of self-assessment as a career planning tool and has evaluated his or her skills on the basis of preference and performance.

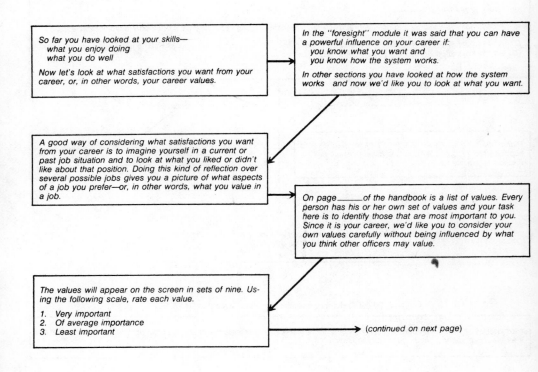

So far you have looked at your skills—
what you enjoy doing
what you do well

Now let's look at what satisfactions you want from your career, or, in other words, your career values.

In the "foresight" module it was said that you can have a powerful influence on your career if:
you know what you want and
you know how the system works.

In other sections you have looked at how the system works   and now we'd like you to look at what you want.

A good way of considering what satisfactions you want from your career is to imagine yourself in a current or past job situation and to look at what you liked or didn't like about that position. Doing this kind of reflection over several possible jobs gives you a picture of what aspects of a job you prefer—or, in other words, what you value in a job.

On page_____of the handbook is a list of values. Every person has his or her own set of values and your task here is to identify those that are most important to you. Since it is your career, we'd like you to consider your own values carefully without being influenced by what you think other officers may value.

The values will appear on the screen in sets of nine. Using the following scale, rate each value.

1. Very important
2. Of average importance
3. Least important

(continued on next page)

606

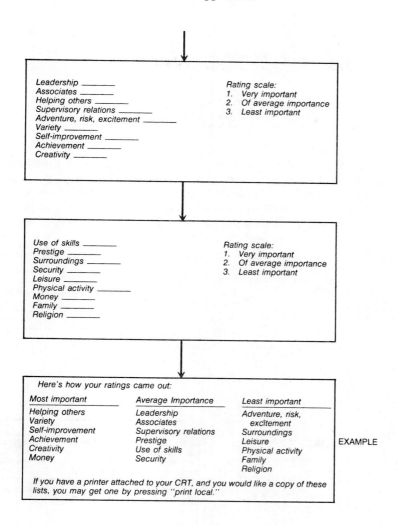

Leadership _____
Associates _____
Helping others _____
Supervisory relations _____
Adventure, risk, excitement _____
Variety _____
Self-improvement _____
Achievement _____
Creativity _____

Rating scale:
1. Very important
2. Of average importance
3. Least important

Use of skills _____
Prestige _____
Surroundings _____
Security _____
Leisure _____
Physical activity _____
Money _____
Family _____
Religion _____

Rating scale:
1. Very important
2. Of average importance
3. Least important

Here's how your ratings came out:

Most important	Average Importance	Least important
Helping others	Leadership	Adventure, risk, excitement
Variety	Associates	
Self-improvement	Supervisory relations	Surroundings
Achievement	Prestige	Leisure
Creativity	Use of skills	Physical activity
Money	Security	Family
		Religion

If you have a printer attached to your CRT, and you would like a copy of these lists, you may get one by pressing "print local."

EXAMPLE

After this rating process, the user is asked to rank those values designated "most important" in order of relative importance and is offered suggestions about using this self-assessment in career planning.

appendix G

EXCERPT FROM CAREER STRATEGIES

The following frames are drawn from the final section of CAREER STRATEGIES. The user has, at this point in the module, played the "SCOR" game, examined questions of interest in the Career Strategies Data Base, revised and set career goals, and is now facing the task of combining these and previous sections of OCIPS into an integrated career Action Plan. This sequence appears on the screen.

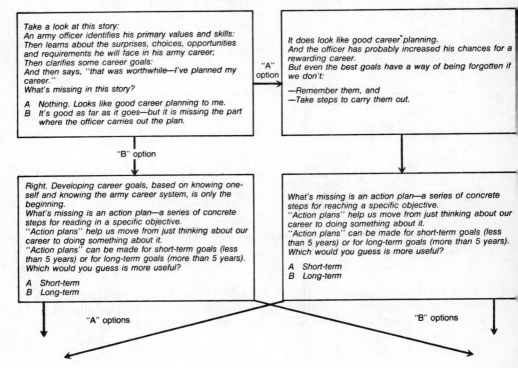

Take a look at this story:
An army officer identifies his primary values and skills;
Then learns about the surprises, choices, opportunities and requirements he will face in his army career;
Then clarifies some career goals;
And then says, "that was worthwhile—I've planned my career."
What's missing in this story?

A   Nothing. Looks like good career planning to me.
B   It's good as far as it goes—but it is missing the part where the officer carries out the plan.

"A" option

It does look like good career planning.
And the officer has probably increased his chances for a rewarding career.
But even the best goals have a way of being forgotten if we don't:

—Remember them, and
—Take steps to carry them out.

"B" option

Right. Developing career goals, based on knowing oneself and knowing the army career system, is only the beginning.
What's missing is an action plan—a series of concrete steps for reading in a specific objective.
"Action plans" help us move from just thinking about our career to doing something about it.
"Action plans" can be made for short-term goals (less than 5 years) or for long-term goals (more than 5 years). Which would you guess is more useful?

A   Short-term
B   Long-term

What's missing is an action plan—a series of concrete steps for reaching a specific objective.
"Action plans" help us move from just thinking about our career to doing something about it.
"Action plans" can be made for short-term goals (less than 5 years) or for long-term goals (more than 5 years). Which would you guess is more useful?

A   Short-term
B   Long-term

"A" options

"B" options

"A" options

"B" options

Right. Action plans are more useful for short-term goals. There are two problems with actions plans for long-range goals:
As our "SCOR" game showed, there are so many surprises, and choices, and so forth, that "long-term" action plans are sure to become obsolete long before the goal is reached; and
A "long-term" action plan would be too long to be manageable—hundreds of concrete steps might make you feel it's not worth taking the first step.
So how do you pick a short-term goal to make this "action plan" for? Here are some ways—choose one.

A Look at one of your long-range goals and see what you have to do within the next 5 years to reach it.
B Pick a goal you know you must reach within 5 years, or else.

While action plans might be helpful for reaching long-term goals, there are two annoying problems:
As our "SCOR" game showed, there are so many surprises, choices, and so forth that "long-term" action plans are sure to become obsolete long before the goal is reached: and
A "long-term" action plan would be too long to be manageable—hundreds of concrete steps might make you feel it's not worth taking the first step.
We suggest that action plans are most useful for "short-term" goals.
So how do you pick a short-term goal to make this "action plan" for?
Here are some ways—choose one.

A Look at one of your long-range goals and see what you have to do within the next 5 years to reach it.
B Pick a goal you know you must reach within 5 years, or else.

Both tactics have merit. Looking at your long-range goals helps make sure that your present endeavors have a long-range payoff. But looking at your short-term "must's" helps make sure you don't neglect anything in the short run, regardless of your specific long-range goals.
The upshot is: good career planning means making more than one action plan.

So now you know that good career planning means:
—Identifying values and skills,
—Recognizing the surprises, choices, opportunities and requirements in an army career,
—Clarifying career goals, and
—Making acton plans for meeting those goals.
One more thing: when should you make your action plans?

A Right now
B Depends on what happens when I monitor my career.
C Hey, hold it a minute—what's this "monitoring my career" business?

At this point in the module, the concept of career monitoring is presented and related to action planning, and the user is offered directions for creating action plans using his or her own data.

BIBLIOGRAPHY

Abramson, M. Recycling the discarded executive. *Trans World Airlines Ambassador Magazine*, 1978, *11* (8), 38–41.

Abrego, P., & Brammer, L. *Developing coping skills for career-related changes.* Monograph 42. Palo Alto, Calif.: American Institute for Research, National Consortium Project, 1978.

Alkin, M. C. Evaluation theory development. *Evaluation Comment*, 1969, 2 (1), 2–7.

Allen, A. R. Peer tutoring: Putting it to the test. *Reading Teacher*, 1978, 32, 274–279.

Allen, G. J., Elias, M. J., & Zlotlow, S. F. Behavioral interventions for alleviating test anxiety: A methodological overview of current therapeutic processes. In I. G. Sarason (Ed.), *Test anxiety: theory, research, and applications.* Hillsdale, N.J.: Erlbaum Associates, 1980.

Allen, R. E., & Keaveny, T. J. The relative effectiveness of alternate job sources. *Journal of Vocational Behavior*, 1980, *16*, 18–33.

Allport, G. W. *Personality.* New York, H. Holt & Co., 1937.

———. *Becoming.* New Haven, Conn.: Yale University Press, 1955.

Allport, G. W., & Odbert, H. S. Trait names: A psychological study. *Psychological Monographs*, 1936, 47, 1–171, No. 211.

Alpert, R., & Haber, R. N. Anxiety in academic achievement situations. *Journal of Abnormal and Social Psychology*, 1960, *61*, 207–215.

American College Testing Program. *Career planning program.* Iowa City, Iowa: Author, 1972.

American College Testing Program. *Assessment of career development.* Boston: Houghton Mifflin, 1974.

American Council on Education. *American universities and colleges.* Washington, D.C.: Author, 1980.

American Institute of Research. *The planning career goals program.* Monterey, Calif.: CTB/McGraw-Hill, 1976.

American Psychology Association. *Standards for educational and psychological tests.* Washington, D.C.: Author, 1974.

———. *Ethical standards of psychologists* (Rev. ed.). Washington, D.C.: Author, 1977 (b).

———. *Standards for providers of psychological services.* Washington, D.C.: Author, 1977 (a).

The American underclass. *Time.* August 29, 1977, pp. 14–27.

Anastasi, A. *Psychological testing* (4th ed.). London: Macmillan, 1976.

Andersen, D. G., & Heimann, R. A. Vocational maturity of junior high school girls. *Vocational Guidance Quarterly*, 1967, *15*, 191–195.

Anderson, E. C. *Promoting career information seeking through group counselor's cues and reinforcements.* Unpublished doctoral dissertation, University of California, Los Angeles, 1970.

Anderson, E. C. Counseling and consultation versus teacher consultation in elementary schools. *Elementary School Guidance and Counseling*, 1969, 4, 43–53.

Anderson, J. A. The disadvantaged seek work through their efforts or ours? *Rehabilitation Record,* 1968, *3*, 5–10.

Angrist, S. S., & Almquist, E. M. *Careers and contingencies*. New York: Dunellen, 1975.

Anton, W. D. An evaluation of outcome variables in the systematic desensitization of test anxiety. *Behavior Research and Therapy*, 1976, *14*, 217–224.

APGA/DOL discuss plans for improved standards. *Guidepost*, 1978, *14*, 1; 5.

Apostal, R. A. Personality type and preferred college subculture. *Journal of College Student Personnel*, 1970, *11*, 206–209.

Arbeiter, S., Aslanian, C. B., Schmerbeck, F. A., & Brickell, H. M. *Forty million Americans in career transition, the need for information*. Princeton, N.J.: College Entrance Examination Board, 1978.

Arnstein, G. E. Trial by jury: The outcome. *Phi Delta Kappan*, 1975, 57, 188–190.

Arterbury, E., Collie, J., Jones, D., & Morrell, J. *The efficacy of career education: Career awareness*. Washington, D.C.: National Advisory Council for Career Education, 1976.

Astin, A. W. Equal access to postsecondary education: Myth or reality? *UCLA Educator*, 1977, *19*(3), 8–17.

Astin, H. S. Preparing women for careers in science and technology. Paper presented at the Massachusetts Institute of Technology Workshop on Women in Science and Technology, Boston, May 1973.

————. Continuing education and the development of adult women. In N. K. Schlosberg & A. D. Entine (Eds.), *Counseling Adults*. Monterey, Calif.: Brooks-Cole Publishing, 1977.

Atanasoff, G. E., & Slaney, R. B. Three approaches to counselor-free career exploration among college women. *Journal of Counseling Psychology*, 1980, 27, 332–339.

Aubrey, R. F. *Career development needs of thirteen-year-olds: How to improve for career development programs*. Washington, D.C.: National Vocational Guidance Association, 1977.

Ausubel, D. P. *Educational psychology: A cognitive view*. New York: Holt, Rinehart & Winston, 1968.

Averich, H. A. *How effective is schooling?* Santa Monica, Calif.: Rand, 1972.

Azrin, N. H. *The job-finding club as a method for obtaining employment for welfare-eligible clients: Demonstration evaluation and counselor training*. Washington, D.C.: U.S. Department of Labor, July, 1978.

Azrin, N. H., Flores, T., & Kaplan, S. J. Job-finding club: A group assisted program for obtaining employment. *Behavior Research and Therapy Journal*, 1975, *13*, 17–27.

Bachman, J. B., O'Malley, P. M., & Johnston, J. *Youth in transition*. Ann Arbor, Mich.: University of Michigan, Institute for Social Research, 1978.

Bailey, L. J., & Stadt, R. W. *Career education: New approaches to human development*. Bloomington, Ill.: McKnight, 1973.

Bakke vs. *Regents of University of California*. 438 U. S. 265 (1978).

Bandura, A. *Principles of behavior modification* (2nd ed.). New York: Holt, Rinehart & Winston, 1976.

Bank, A., Culver, C., McCann, G., Rasmussen, R., & Ruble, T. *The problem solving school: Guidelines for collaborative and systematic problem solving*. Dayton, Ohio: Charles Kettering Foundation Institute for Development of Educational Activities, 1972.

Barahal, G. D., Brammer, L. M., & Shostrom, E. L. A client-centered approach to educational vocational counseling. *Journal of Consulting Psychology*, 1950, *14*, 256–260.

Barbee, J. R., & Keil, E. C. Experimental techniques of job interview training for the disadvantaged. *Journal of Applied Psychology*, 1973, 58, 209–213.

Barkhaus, R. S., & Bolgard, C. W. Experience—key to decision making. *Journal of College Placement*, 1976, 37, (2) 50–63.

Barron's Educational Series. *Barron's profiles of American colleges* (Vols. 1 & 2). Woodbury, N.Y.: Author, 1980.

Bates, G. L., Parker, H. J., & McCoy, J. F. Vocational rehabilitants' personality and work adjustment: A test of Holland's theory of vocational choice. *Psychological Reports*, 1970, 26, 511–516.

Bates, J. C. *Formative evaluation in the development of a counseling mode designed to teach time management.* Unpublishd doctoral dissertation, University of California, Los Angeles, 1971.

Bates, J. C., & Sorenson, A. G. Developing repeatable counseling procedures. Unpublished paper. University of California, Los Angeles, 1973.

Beaumont, A. G., Cooper, A. C., & Stockard, R. H. *A model career counseling and placement program.* Bethlehem, Pa.: College Placement Services, 1977.

Becker, W. C., Englemann, S., & Thomas, D. R. *Teaching: Classroom management.* Chicago: Science Research Associates, 1975.

Bednar, R. L., & Weinberg, S. L. Ingredients of successful treatment programs for underachievers. *Journal of Counseling Psychology*, 1970, 17, 1–7.

Bem, D. J., & Bem, S. L. Training the woman to know her place: The power of unconscious ideology. In M. H. Garskof (Ed.), *Roles women play: Readings toward women's liberation.* Monterey, Calif.: Brooks-Cole Publishing, 1971.

Benjamin, L., & Walz, G. R. *Making change happen: Learning a systematic model for change* (Monograph 51). Palo Alto, Calif.: American Institute for Research, National Consortium Project, 1979. (a)

———. *Making change happen: Overcoming barriers to change* (Monograph 52). Palo Alto, Calif.: American Institute for Research, National Consortium Project, 1979. (b)

Benson, G., & Chasin, J. Entry level positions: Do business schools really give an advantage? *Journal of College Placement*, 1976, 37, (1), 73–77.

Bentler, P. M., & Woodward, J. A. A head start reevaluation: Positive effects are not yet demonstrable. In E. Quellmalz & E. Baker (Eds.), *Proceedings of the 1978 CSE Measurement & Methodology Conference.* Los Angeles: University of California, Los Angeles, Center for the Study of Evaluation, 1979.

Berg, T. *Education and jobs: The great training robbery.* Boston: Beacon Press, 1975.

Bergin, A. E. The evaluation of therapeutic outcomes. In A. E. Bergin & S. L. Garfield (Eds.), *Handbook of psychotherapy and behavior change.* New York: Wiley, 1971.

Bergland, B. W., & Lundquist, G. W. The vocational exploration group and minority youth: An experimental outcome study. *Journal of Vocational Behavior*, 1975, 7, 289–296.

Bergland, B. W., Quatrano, L., & Lundquist, G. W. Group social models and structured interaction in teaching decision making. *Vocational Guidance Quarterly*, 1975, 24, 28–36.

Berlyne, D. E. *Structure and direction in thinking.* New York: Wiley, 1965.

Beyette, B. No light at the end of this tunnel. *Los Angeles Times*, July 15, 1977, Part IV, pp. 1; 6–11.

Bingham, R. P., & Walsh, W. B. Concurrent validity of Holland's theory for college degreed black women. *Journal of Vocational Behavior*, 1978, 13, 242–250.

Bingham, W. *Change of occupations as a function of the regnancy of self concepts.* Unpublished doctoral project, Columbia University, Teachers College, 1966.

Bingham, W. C., & House, E. W. Counselors' attitudes toward women and work. *Vocational Guidance Quarterly,* 1973, *22,* 16–23.

Binet, A., & Simon, T. The development of intelligence in the child. *Anneé Psychologié,* 1908, *14,* 1–90.

Birk, J. M., Cooper, J., & Tanney, M. F. Racial and sex role stereotyping in career illustration. Paper presented at the meeting of the American Psychological Association, Montreal, August 1973.

Birk, J. M., & Tanney, M. F. Career exploration for high school women: A model. Paper presented at American Personnel and Guidance Association Convention, May 1973. (ED–079–662).

Birney, D., Thomas, L. E., & Hinkle, J. E. *Life planning workshops: discussion and evaluation.* Colorado State University, Fort Collins, Colorado Office of Student Development, 1970.

Bishop, L. J. *Staff development and instructional improvement.* Boston: Allyn & Bacon, 1976.

Blaker, K. E. & Sano, J. Communication games: A group counseling technique. *School Counselor,* 1973, *21,* 46–51.

Blau, P. M., & Duncan, O. D. *The American occupational structure.* New York: Wiley, 1967.

Blocher, D. H. Social change and the future of vocational guidance. In H. Borow (Ed.), *Career guidance for a new age.* Boston: Houghton Mifflin, 1973.

Blocher, D. H., Dustin, E. R., & Dugan, W. E. *Guidance systems: An introduction to student personnel work.* New York: Ronald Press, 1971.

Bloom, S. *Peer and cross-age tutoring in the schools: An individualized supplement to group instruction.* Washington, D.C.: U. S. Department of Health, Education, and Welfare, 1976.

Bloss, N. P. *Pima County career development project: Evaluation report.* Tucson, Ariz.: Behavioral Research Associates, 1975.

Bolles, R. N. *What color is your parachute? A practical manual for job hunters and career changers.* Berkeley, Calif.: Ten Speed Press, 1974.

Boocock, S. The life career game. *Personnel and Guidance Journal,* 1967, *45,* 328–334.

Bordin, E. S. Diagnosis in counseling and psychotherapy. *Educational and Psychological Measurement.* 1946, *6,* 169–184.

Bordin, E. S., Nachman, B., & Segal, S. J. An articulated framework for vocational development. *Journal of Counseling Psychology,* 1963, *10,* 107–117.

Bowen, D. B., & Hall, D. J. Career planning for employee development: A primer for managers. *California Management Review,* 1977, *20,* (2), 23–35.

Brammer, L. M. *The helping relationship: Process and skills* (2nd ed.) Englewood Cliffs, N.J.: Prentice-Hall, 1979.

Bray, D. W. Dimensions and group techniques. Paper presented at 85th Annual American Psychology Association Convention, San Francisco, August 28, 1977.

Bray, D. W., Campbell, R. J., & Grant, D. L. *Formative years in business.* New York: Wiley, 1974.

Bray, D. W., & Grant, D. L. The assessment center in the measurement of potential for business management. *Psychological Monographs,* 1966, *80* (17, Whole No. 625).

Brayfield, A. H., & Crites, J. O. Research on vocational guidance. In H. Borrow, *Man in a world at work.* Boston: Houghton Mifflin, 1964.

Brenner, M. H. Use of high school data to predict work performance. *Journal of Applied Psychology*, 1968, 52, 29–30.

Briggs, L. D., & Green, G. L. *Career education in programs for career education: Proceedings of national career education workshops*, Stillwater, Okla.: Oklahoma State University, 1975.

Brim, O. G. Theories of the male mid-life crisis. In N. K. Schlossberg & A. D. Entine (Eeds.), *Counseling adults*. Monterey, Calif.: Brooks-Cole Publishing, 1977.

Broadbent, B. C. *Internal-external control and two modes of counseling*. Unpublished Ph.D. dissertation, University of California, Los Angeles, 1970.

Broadbent, L. A. *The effects of two different belief systems on the perception of two experimental modes of counseling*. Unpublished doctoral dissertation, University of California, Los Angeles, Graduate School of Education, 1968.

Brodine, K. Quota. In *Work Week*. Berkeley, Calif.: Kelsey Press, 1977. (a)

––––––. The receptionist is by definition. In *Work Week*. Berkeley, Calif.: Kelsey Press, 1977. (b)

Bronfenbrenner, U. Toward an experimental ecology of human development. *American Psychologist*, 1977, 32, 513–523.

Browne, J. *The pretender* (album). Los Angeles: Elektra Records, 1976.

Bruner, J. S. *Toward a theory of instruction*. New York: Norton, 1966.

Buros, O. K. (Ed.) *The eight mental measurements yearbooks*. Highland Park, N.J.: Gryphon Press, 1978.

Busby, L. J. Sex-role research on mass media. *Journal of Communication*, 1975, 25, 107–137.

Cairo, P. C. *Annotated bibliography on computer-assisted counseling and guidance*. (Technical Report TR–77–A1), Alexandria, Va.: U.S. Army Research Institute for the Behavioral and Social Sciences, 1977.

Campbell, D. P. A counseling evaluation with a better control group. *Journal of Counseling Psychology*, 1963, 10, 334–339.

––––––. A cross-sectional and longitudinal study of scholastic abilities over 25 years. *Journal of Counseling Psychology*, 1965, 12, 55–61.

––––––. *Handbook for the Strong Vocational Interest Blank*. Stanford, Calif.: Stanford University Press, 1971.

––––––. *Manual for the Strong-Campbell Interest Inventory*. Stanford, Calif.: Stanford University Press, 1977.

Campbell, D. P., & Stanley, J. C. *Experimental and quasi-experimental designs for research*. Chicago: Rand McNally & Co., 1963.

Campbell, R. E. *Vocational guidance in secondary education: Results of a national survey*. Columbus, Ohio: Ohio State University, Center for Vocational and Technical Education, 1968.

Carkhuff, R. R. *Helping and human relations* (Vol. 2). New York: Holt, Rinehart and Winston, 1969.

––––––. *The development of human resources*. New York: Holt, Rinehart and Winston, 1971.

––––––. New directions in training for the helping professions: Toward a technology for human and community resource development. *The Counseling Psychologist*, 1972, 3, 12–30.

Carkhuff, R. R., Berenson, B. G. *Teaching as treatment: An introduction to counseling and psychotherapy*. Amherst, Mass.: Human Resource Development Press, 1976.

Carpenter, R. Mr. Guder. In *Close to you album*. Hollywood: Almo Music, 1968.

Catron, D. W. Educational-vocational group counseling: The effect on perception of self and others. *Journal of Counseling Psychology*, 1966, *13*, 202–207.

Cattell, R. B. *Description and measurement of personality*. New York: World Book, 1946.

———. *16 P.F. Test*. Champaign, Ill.: Institute for Personality and Ability Testing, 1956.

Chase, C. I. *Measurement for educational evaluation*. Reading, Mass.: Addison-Wesley, 1978.

Chang-Liang, R., & Denney, D. R. Applied relaxation as training in self-control. *Journal of Counseling Psychology*, 1976, *23*, 183–189.

Cicourel, A., & Kitsuse, J. *The educational decision makers*. New York: Bobbs-Merrill Co., 1963.

Cloward, R. Studies in tutoring. *Journal of Experimental Education*, 1967, *36*, 14–25.

Clowers, M. R., & Fraser, R. T. Employment interview literature: A prospective for the counselor. *Vocational Guidance Quarterly*, 1977, *26*, 13–26.

Cochran, D. J., & Hoffman, S. G. The vocational exploration group. In R. C. Reardon & H. D. Burck, *Facilitating career developments: Strategies for counselors*. Springfield, Ill.: Thomas, 1975.

Cohen, B. M., Moses, J. L., & Byham, W. C. *The validity of assessment centers: A literature review* (Monograph No. 2). Pittsburgh, Pa.: Development Dimensions Press, 1974.

Cohen, M., & Schwarz, A. *New hire rates—a new measure*. Ann Arbor, Mich.: University of Michigan, Institute of Labor and Industrial Relations, 1979.

Coleman, J. S. *The adolescent society*. New York: Free Press, 1961.

———. (Ed.). *Youth: Transition to adulthood*. Chicago: University of Chicago Press, 1975.

College Entrance Examination Board. *Career skill assessment program*. New York: College Entrance Examination Board, 1977.

Comprehensive Employment and Training Act of 1978, as amended P. L. 95–524, October 27, 1978.

Computerized Vocational Information System (CVIS). Westminster, Md.: Western Maryland College, 1976.

Cooley, W. W., & Lohnes, P. R. *Predicting development of young adults*. Palo Alto, Calif.: American Institute for Research, 1968.

Cooper, J. F. Comparative impact of the SCII and the Vocational Card Sort on career salience and career exploration of women. *Journal of Counseling Psychology*, 1976, *23*, 348–352.

Cory, B. H., Medland, F. F., Hicks, J. M., Castelnovo, A. E., Weldon, J. I., Hoffer, G. L., & Myers, R. A. Army officer career development. Proceedings of panel presented at the annual meeting of the American Personnel and Guidance Association, Chicago, April 1976.

Cory, B. H., Medland, F. F., & Uhlaner, J. E. Developing a research-based system for manpower management and career progression in the U.S. Army Officer Corps. Paper presented at the Conference on Manpower Planning and Organizational Design. Stresa, Italy, June 1977.

Cotton, C. C., & Fraser, R. F. On-the-job career planning: One organization's approach. *Training and Development*, 1978, *32* (2), 20–24.

Counts, D. K., Hollandsworth, J. G., & Alcorn, J. D. Use of electromyographic biofeedback and cue controlled relaxation in the treatment of test anxiety. *Journal of Consulting and Clinical Psychology*, 1978, *46*, 990–996.

Cramer, S. J., Wise, P. S., & Colburn, E. D. An evaluation of treatment to expand the career perceptions of high school girls. *The School Counselor*, 1977, *25*, 125–129.

Crites, J. O. Measurement of vocational maturity in adolescence: I. Attitude Test of the Vocational Development Inventory. *Psychological Monographs,* 1965, 72 (No. 595).

—————. *Vocational Psychology.* New York: McGraw-Hill, 1969.

—————. *The maturity of vocational attitudes in adolescence.* Washington, D.C.: American Personnel and Guidance Association, 1971.

—————. *The Career Maturity Inventory* (Research ed.). New York: CTB/ McGraw-Hill, 1973.

—————. The career maturity inventory. In D. E. Super, *Measuring vocational maturity for counseling and evaluation.* Falls Church, Va.: American Personnel and Guidance Association Press, 1974. (a)

—————. Career counseling: A review of major approaches. *The Counseling Psychologist,* 1974, 4(3), 3-23. (b)

—————. A reappraisal of vocational appraisal. *Vocational Guidance Quarterly,* 1974 22, 272–279 (c).

—————. Career counseling: A comprehensive approach. *The Counseling Psychologist,* 1976, 6(3), 2-11.

—————. Review of the self-directed search. In O. K. Buros (Ed.). *Eighth Mental Measurements Yearbook.* Highland Park, N.J.: Gryphon Press, 1978.

Cronbach, L. J. Evaluation of course improvement. *Teachers College Record,* 1963, 64(8), 102–106.

—————. *Essentials of psychological testing* (3rd ed.). New York: Harper & Row, 1970.

Cronbach, L. J., & Snow, R. E. *Aptitude and instructional methods.* New York: Irvington, 1977.

Daane, C. J. *Vocational exploration group: Theory and research.* Tempe, Ariz.: Studies for Urban Man, Inc., 1971.

—————. *Vocational exploration groups: Theory and research.* Washington, D.C.: U.S. Department of Labor, Manpower Administration, February, 1972.

Daley, M. M. Attitudes toward the dual role of the married professional woman. *American Psychologist,* 1971, 26, 301–306.

Dalkey, N. C. *Toward a theory of group estimation, delphi method: Techniques and applications.* Reading, Mass.: Addison-Wesley, 1975.

Danish, S. J., Graff, R. W., & Gensler, S. A. The self-help vocational decision making booklet: An adaptation of Magoon's effective problem solving manual. Unpublished booklet, Carbondale, Ill.: Southern Illinois University, 1969.

Darcy, R. L. *An experimental junior high school course in occupational opportunities and labor market processes.* Athens, Ohio: Ohio University, 1968.

Darcy, R. L., & Powell, P. E. *Manpower and economic education: Opportunities in American economic life.* New York: Joint Council on Economic Development, 1972.

Darley, J. C. *Clinical aspects and interpretations of the Strong Vocational Interest Blank.* New York: Psychological Corporation, 1941.

Davis, J. A. *Undergraduate career decisions.* Chicago: Aldine Publishing Co., 1965.

Davis, R. G., & Lewis, G. M. *Education and employment: A future perspective of needs, policies, and programs.* Lexington, Mass.: Lexington Books, 1975.

Dawis, R. V., England, G. W., & Lofquist, L. H. *A theory of work adjustment.* Minneapolis, Minn.: University of Minnesota Studies in Vocational Rehabilitation, 15, 1964.

de Charms, R. *Enhancing motivation: Change in the classroom.* New York: Irvington, 1976.

Deffenbacher, J. L., Mathis, H., & Michaels, A. C. Two self-control procedures in the reduction of targeted and nontargeted anxieties. *Journal of Counseling Psychology*, 1979, 26, 120–127.

Deffenbacher, J. L., & Michaels, A. C. Two self-control procedures in the reduction of targeted and nontargeted anxieties—a year later. *Journal of Counseling Psychology*, 1980, 27, 9–16.

Deffenbacher, J. L., Michaels, A. C., Daley, P. C., & Michaels T. A comparison of homogeneous and heterogeneous anxiety management training. *Journal of Counseling Psychology*, 1980, 27, 630–634.

Deffenbacher, J. L., Michaels, A. C., Michaels, T., & Daley, P. C. Comparison of anxiety management training and self-control desensitization. *Journal of Counseling Psychology*, 1980, 27, 232–239.

Deffenbacher, J. L., & Shelton, J. L. Comparison of anxiety management training and desensitization in reducing test and other anxieties. *Journal of Counseling Psychology*, 1978, 25, 277–282.

Deffenbacher, J. L., & Snyder, A. L. Relaxation as self-control in the treatment of test and other anxieties. *Psychological Reports*, 1976, 39, 379–385.

De Nisi, A., & Shaw, J. B. Investigation of the uses of self-reports of abilities. *Journal of Applied Psychology*, 1977, 62, 641–644.

Denney, D. R. Active, passive and vicarious desensitization. *Journal of Counseling Psychology*, 1974, 21, 369–375.

————. Self-control approaches to the treatment of test anxiety. In I. G. Sarason (Ed.). *Test anxiety: Theory, research and applications*. Hillsdale, N.J.: L. Erlbaum Associates, 1980.

Denney, D., & Rupert, P. A. Desensitization and self-control in the treatment of test anxiety. *Journal of Counseling Psychology*, 1977, 24, 272–280.

Dennis, G. A bill of sale. *Los Angeles Times*, November 26, 1978.

DeVivo, E. H. *Student, parent, and student-parent counseling effects on work output and achievement of seventh-grade mathematics students*. Unpublished Ph.D. dissertation. University of California, Los Angeles, 1978.

Dewey, C. R. Exploring interests: A non-sexist method. *Personnel and Guidance Journal*, 1974, 52, 311–315.

Dewey, J. *How we think*. Boston: D. C. Heath & Co., 1910.

Diamond, E. (Ed.). *Issues of sex bias and sex fairness in career interest measurement*. Washington, D.C.: National Institute of Education, 1975.

Dickson, W. J., & Roethlisberger, F. J. *Counseling in an organization: A sequel to the Hawthorne researches*. Boston: Division of Research, Harvard University Graduate School of Business Administration, 1966.

Dinkmeyer, D. *Developing understanding of self and others*. Circle Pines, Minn.: American Guidance Service, 1970; 1973.

Dinkmeyer, D. C., & Caldwell, E. *Developmental counseling and guidance: A comprehensive school approach*. New York: McGraw-Hill, 1970.

Dinkmeyer, D. C., & Carlson, J. *Consulting: Facilitating human potential and change process*. Columbus, Ohio: Charles E. Merrill Publishing, 1973.

Dolin, B. Oral introduction to Security Pacific National Bank career management workshop. Los Angeles, Calif.: Los Angeles Hilton, June 17, 1978.

Dolliver, R. H. *The relationship of certain variables to the amount of agreement in inventoried and expressed vocational interests*. Unpublished doctoral dissertation, Ohio State University, 1966.

Dolliver, R. H., & Will, J. A. Ten-year follow-up of the Tyler Vocational Card Sort and Strong Vocational Interest Blank. *Journal of Counseling Psychology*, 1977, 24, 48–54.

Donahue, T. J., & Costar, J. W. Counselor discrimination against young women in career selection. *Journal of Counseling Psychology*, 1977, 24, 481–486.

Dreger, R. M. Review of State-Trait Anxiety Inventory. In O. K. Buros *Eighth Mental Measurement Yearbook*. Highland Park, N.J.: Gryphon Press, 1978.

Dreikurs, R. *Psychology in the classroom* (2nd ed.). New York: Harper & Row, 1968.

Drucker, P. F. *Management tasks, responsibilities, practices*. New York: McGraw-Hill, 1974.

Dubin, D. *Handbook of work, organization, and society*. Chicago: Rand McNally & Company, 1976.

Dudley, G. A., & Tiedeman, D. V. *Career development: Exploration and commitment*. Muncie, Ind.: Accelerated Development, Inc., 1977.

Duff, W. A. *Counseling disadvantaged parents in the home: Measuring change in parent behavior and its effect upon children's scholastic achievement*. Unpublished Ph.D. dissertation, University of California, Los Angeles, 1972.

Dumphy, P. W., Austin, S. F., & Stone, R. A. *Career development for the college student*. Cranston, R.I.: Carroll Press, 1973.

Dunn, J. A., Steel, L., Melnotte, J. M., Gross, D., Kroll, J., & Murphy, S. *Career education: A curriculum design and instructional objectives catalog*. Palo Alto, Calif.: American Institute for Research in the Behavioral Sciences, 1973.

Dunnette, M. D. *Handbook of industrial and organizational psychology*. Chicago: Rand McNally, 1976.

Dylan, B. Maggie's Farm. In *Bob Dylan's greatest hits* (Vol. II) (album). New York: Columbia Records, 1971.

Eckland, B. K., & Wisenbaker, J. M. *National longitudinal study: A capsule description of young adults four and one-half years after high school*. Washington, D.C.: National Center for Education Statistics, 1979.

Educational Testing Service. *System of interaction, guidance, and information (SIGI)*. Princeton, N.J.: Author, 1972.

————. *National report: College-bound seniors, 1979*. New York: College Entrance Examination Board, 1979. (a)

————. *Preliminary Scholastic Aptitude Test/National Merit Scholarship Qualifying Test student bulletin*. New York: College Entrance Examination Board, 1979. (b)

Edwards, A. L. *Personal preference schedule*. New York: Psychological Corporation, 1959.

Edwards, A. M. *Comparative occupational statistics for the United States, 1870–1940*. Washington, D.C.: Government Printing Office, 1943.

Elementary and Secondary Education Act, as amended, P. L. 89–10 as amended by P. L. 93–380.

Ellett, F. S. A more fair policy and the limits of fair selection. In J. R. Coombs (Ed.), *Proceedings of the 35th annual meeting of the Philosophy of Education Society*. Normal, Ill.: Philosophy of Education Society, 1980.

Ellis, A. Rational-emotive therapy. In R. J. Corsini (Ed.), *Current psychotherapies*. Itasca, Ill.: Peacock, 1979.

Ellson, D. G., Harris, P. L., & Barber, L. A field test of programmed and directed tutoring. *Reading Research Quarterly*, 1968, *3*, 307–367.

Endler, N. S. Review of the *Suinn Test Anxiety Behavior Scale*. In O. K. Buros *Eighth Mental Measurement Yearbook*. Highland Park, N.J.: Gryphon Press, 1978.

Engelhard, P. A., Jones, K. O., & Stiggins, R. J. Trends in counselor attitude about women's roles. *Journal of Counseling Psychology*, 1976, *23*, 365–372.

Englander, M. A psychological analysis of vocational choice: Teaching. *Journal of Counseling Psychology*, 1960, *7*, 257–264.

Equal Pay Act of 1963, as amended. P. L. 88–38, June 10, 1963.

Erikson, E. H. *Childhood and society*. New York: Norton, 1950.
———. *Childhood and society* (2nd ed.). New York: Norton, 1963.
Evans, J. R., & Cody, J. J. Transfer of decision-making skills learned in a counseling-like setting to similar and dissimilar situations. *Journal of Counseling Psychology*, 1969, *16*, 427–432.
Fabry, J. J. An extended concurrent validation of the vocational preferences of clergymen. *Psychological Reports*, 1975, *36*, 947–950.
———. An investigation of Holland's theory across and within selected occupational groups. *Journal of Vocational Behavior*, 1976, *9*, 73–76.
Farmer, H. S. *Formative evaluation of an instructional model of counseling using a case study approach with student teachers in practice teaching*. Unpublished Ph.D. dissertation, University of California, Los Angeles, 1972.
Farmer, H. S., & Backer, T. E. *New career options for women*. New York: Human Science Press, 1977.
Farmer, H. S., & Bohn, M. J. Home-career conflict reduction and level of career interest in women. *Journal of Counseling Psychology*, 1970, *17*, 228–233.
Federal employees part-time career employment act of 1978. P. L. 95–437.
Feldhusen, J., Houtz, J., & Ringenbach, S. The Purdue Elementary Problem Solving Inventory. *Psychological Reports*, 1972, *31*, 891–901.
Feldman, K. A., & Newcomb, T. M. *Impact of college on students*. San Francisco: Josey Bass, 1969.
Festinger, L. *A theory of cognitive dissonance*. Stanford, Calif.: Stanford University Press, 1957.
Fiedler, F. E. A comparison of therapeutic relationships in psychoanalytic, nondirective, and Adlerian therapy. *Journal of Consulting Psychology*, 1950, *14*, 436–445.
Fielding, J., & Fielding, M. *Conducting job development programs*. Palo Alto, Calif.: American Institute of Research, 1978. (a)
———. *Conducting job placement programs*. Palo Alto, Calif.: American Institute of Research, 1978. (b)
Figler, H. E. *Path: A career workbook for liberal arts students*. Cranston, R.I.: Carroll Press, 1975.
Fine, S. A. Counseling skills: A target for tomorrow. *Vocational Guidance Quarterly*, 1974, *22*, 287–291.
Fineman, K. *The influence of field-dependence/independence on mothers' ability to implement behavior therapy with problem children*. Unpublished doctoral dissertation, University of California, Los Angeles, Graduate School of Education, 1972.
Finger, R., & Galassi, J. P. Effects of modifying cognitive versus emotionality responses in the treatment of test anxiety. *Journal of Consulting and Clinical Psychology*, 1977, *45*, 280–287.
Fischer, J., & Cullen, A. The job factory. In R. G. Wegman, Job-search assistance. *Journal of Employment Counseling*, 1979, *16*, 197–228.
Fisher, T. J., Reardon, R. C., & Burck, H. D. Increasing information seeking with a model-reinforced videotape. *Journal of Counseling Psychology*, 1976, *23*, 234–238.
Fitzpatrick, J. *Social issues notes*. Unpublished lecture notes for 1961 class at Fordham University, 1961.
Flake, M. H., Roach, A. J., Jr., & Stenning, W. F. Effects of short term counseling on career maturity of tenth grade students. *Journal of Vocational Behavior*, 1975, *6*, 73–80.
Flanagan, J. C. The critical incidents techniques. *Psychological Bulletin*, 1954, *51*, 327–358.

———. The first 15 years of Project Talent: Implications for career guidance. *Vocational Guidance Quarterly*, 1973, 22, 8–14.

———. *Perspectives on improving education: Project Talent's young adults look back.* New York: Praeger, 1978. (a)

———. A research approach to improving our quality of life. *American Psychologist*, 1978, 33, 138–147. (b)

Flanagan, J. C., & Cooley, W. J. *Project Talent: one-year followup studies* (Cooperative Research Project 2333). Pittsburgh, Pa.: University of Pittsburgh, 1966.

Flanagan, J. C., Davis, F. B., Dailey, J. T., Shaycoft, M. F., Orr, D. B., Goldberg, I., & Neyman, C. A., Jr. *The American high school student.* Pittsburgh, Pa.: American Institute of Research and University of Pittsburgh, 1964.

Flanagan, J. C., Shaycoft, J. F., Richards, J. F., Jr., & Claudy, J. G. *Project Talent, five years after high school.* Pittsburgh Pa.: American Institute for Research, 1971.

Flanagan, J. C., Tiedeman, D. V., Willis, M. B. & McLaughlin, D. H. *The career data book: Results from Project Talent's five-year follow-up study.* Palo Alto, Calif.: American Institute for Research, 1973.

Flanders, N. *Interaction analysis in the classroom.* Ann Arbor, Mich.: University of Michigan Press, 1964.

Fogel, A. J. *Development of a replicable group vocational counseling procedures for use with community college students.* Unpublished doctoral dissertation, University of California, Los Angeles, 1973.

Forgy, E. W., & Black, J. D. A follow up after three years of clients counseled by two methods. *Journal of Counseling Psychology*, 1954, 1, 1–7.

Forney, D. S., & Adams, J. M. Alumni: a resource for career development. *Journal of College Placement*, 1976, 3(7), 11; 48–52.

Frager, S. R. *Achievement change in elementary school children in tutor-free relationship.* Unpublished Ph.D. disseration, University of California, Los Angeles, 1969.

Fretz, B. R. Evaluating the effectiveness of career interventions. *Journal of Counseling Psychology*, 1981, 28, 77–90.

Friedersdorf, N. A. *A comparative study of counselor attitudes toward the further educational and vocational plans of high school girls.* Unpublished manuscript, Purdue University, 1969.

Froelich, C. P., & Hoyt, K. B. *Guidance testing and other student appraisal procedures for teachers and counselors.* Chicago: Science Research Associates, 1959.

Frost, R. The road not taken. In L. Untermeyer (Ed.), *Robert Frost's poems.* New York: Washington Square Press, 1977.

———. Two tramps in mud time. In L. Untermeyer (Ed.), *Robert Frost's poems.* New York: Washington Square Press, 1977.

Gagné, R. M. *The conditions of learning.* New York: Holt, Rinehart & Winston, 1970.

Gallup, G. H. *The Gallup poll: Public opinion, 1972–1977.* Wilmington, Del.: Scholarly Resources, 1978.

Garbin, A. P. *Worker adjustment problems of youth in transition from school to work.* Columbus, Ohio: Center for Vocational and Technical Education, 1970.

Garlington, W. K., & Cotler, S. D. Systematic desensitization of test anxiety. *Behavior Research and Therapy*, 1968, 6, 247–256.

Gelatt, H. B., Varenhorst, B., & Carey, R. *Deciding.* New York: College Entrance Examination Board, 1972.

Gelatt, H. B., Varenhorst, B., Carey, R., & Miller, G. P. *Decisions and outcomes* New York: College Entrance Examination Board, 1973.

Ghiselli, E. E. *The validity of occupational ability tests.* New York: Wiley, 1966.

———. *The self-description inventory.* Unpublished test, University of California, 1971.

Ginzberg, E. Toward a theory of occupational choice: A restatement. *Vocational Guidance Quarterly,* 1972, *20,* 169–176.

———. *The manpower connection—Education and work.* Cambridge, Mass.: Harvard University Press, 1975.

Ginzberg, E., Ginsburg, S. W., Axelrad, S., & Herma, J. L. *Occupational choice: An approach to a general theory.* New York: Columbia University Press, 1951.

Glaser, B. G. (Ed.). *Oragnizational careers.* Chicago: Aldine, 1968.

Goldberg, P. Are women prejudiced against women? *Trans-action,* 1968, *5*(5), 28–30.

Goldfried, M. R. Systematic desensitization as training in self-control. *Journal of Consulting and Clinical Psychology,* 1971, *37,* 228–234.

Goldfried, M. R., & Sobocinski, D. Effect of irrational beliefs on emotional arousal. *Journal of Consulting and Clinical Psychology,* 1975, *43,* 504–510.

Goldman, L. Information and counseling: A dilemma. *Personnel and Guidance Journal,* 1967, *46,* 42–46.

———. *Using tests in counseling* (2nd ed.). Santa Monica, Calif.: Goodyear, 1971.

———. It's time to put up or shut up. *Evaluation and Measurement in Guidance,* 1972, *5,* 420–424.

———. (Ed.). *Research methods for counselors: Practical approaches in field settings.* New York: Wiley, 1978.

Gottfredson, G. D. Career stability and redirection in adulthood. *Journal of Applied Psychology,* 1977, *62,* 436–445.

Gough, H., & Heilbrun, A. B., Jr. *The adjective check list manual.* Palo Alto, Calif.: Consulting Psychologist Press, 1965.

Gould, R. *Transformations.* New York: Simon & Schuster, 1978.

Graff, R. W., Danish, S., & Austin, B. Reactions to three kinds of vocational-educational counseling. *Journal of Counseling Psychology,* 1972, *19,* 224–228.

Graff, R. W., & Maclean, C. G. Evaluating educational-vocational counseling. *Personnel and Guidance Journal,* 1970, *48,* 568–574.

Granovetter, M. S. *Getting a job: A study of contacts and careers.* Cambridge, Mass.: Harvard University Press, 1974.

Gray-Shellberg, L., Villareal, S., & Stone, S. Resolution of career conflicts. The double standard in action. Honolulu, Hawaii: Paper presented at 80th Annual Convention of the American Psychological Association, September 1972.

Greeley, A. M., & Rossi, P. *The education of Catholic Americans.* Chicago: Aldine, 1966.

Gribbons, W. D. Evaluation of an eighth grade group guidance program. *Personnel and Guidance Journal,* 1960, *38,* 740–745.

Gribbons, W. D., & Lohnes, P. R. *Emerging careers: A study of 111 adolescents.* New York: Teachers College Press, 1968.

Griggs v. *Duke Power,* 401 U.S. 424 (1971).

Grinnell, R. M., & Lieberman, A. Teaching the mentally retarded job interviewing skills. *Journal of Counseling Psychology,* 1977, *24,* 332–337.

Gross, N., Mason, W., & McEachern, A. W. *Exploration in role analysis: Studies of the school superintendency role.* New York: Wiley, 1958.

Guilford, J. P. *Personality*. New York: McGraw-Hill, 1959.
————. *The nature of intelligence*. New York: McGraw-Hill, 1967.
Gupta. W. *A factor analytic validation of vocational trait structure with ninth grade boys and girls*. Unpublished doctoral dissertation, University of California, Los Angeles, 1976.
Hagburg, E. C., & Levine, M. J. *Labor relations: An integrated perspective*. St. Paul, Minn.: West Publishing Co., 1978.
Hahn, M. E., & McLean, M. S. *General clinical counseling in educational institutions*. New York: McGraw-Hill, 1950.
Haldane, B. *Career satisfaction and success*. New York: Amacon, 1974.
Hall, C. S., & Lindzey, G. *Theories of personality* (2nd ed.). New York: Wiley, 1970.
Hall, D. T. *Careers in organizations*. Santa Monica, Calif.: Goodyear, 1976.
Hamdani, A. Facilitating vocational development among disadvantaged inner city adolescents. *Vocational Guidance Quarterly*, 1977, *26*, 60–67.
Hansen, J. C., & Putnam, B. A. Improving self-concept and vocational maturity. *Journal of Counseling Services*, 1976, *1*(1), 24–28.
Hansen, L. S. *Career guidance practices in school and community*. (ERIC-CAPS Monograph). Washington, D.C.: National Vocational Guidance Association, 1970.
————. *An examination of the definitions and concepts of career education* (Prepared for National Advisory Council for Career Education). Washington, D.C.: U.S. Government Printing Office, 1977.
Hanson, G. R., & Cole, N. The Career Planning Program—more than a test battery. *Measurement and Evaluation in Guidance*, 1972, *5*, 415–419.
Hanson, G. R., Prediger, D. J., & Schussel, R. H. *Development and validation of sex balanced inventory scales. ACT Research Report 78*. Iowa City, Iowa: American College Testing Program, 1977.
Hanson, J. T., & Sander, D. L. Differential effects of individual and group counseling on realism of vocational choice. *Journal of Counseling Psychology*, 1973, *20*, 541–544.
Hanson, M. C. Career development responsibilities of managers. *Personnel Journal*, 1977, *56*(9), 443–445.
Harmon, L. W., & Zytowski, D. G. Reliability of Holland codes across interest measures for adult females. *Journal of Counseling Psychology*, 1980, *27*, 478–483.
Harren, V. A. The vocational decision making process among college males. *Journal of Counseling Psychology*, 1966, *13*, 271–277.
————. *Preliminary manual for vocational decision making checklist*. Carbondale, Ill.: University of Southern Illinois, 1972.
Harris, S. Sex typing in girls career choices: A challenge to counselors. *Vocational Guidance Quarterly*, 1974, *23*, 128–133.
Harvey, D. W., & Whinfield, R. W. Extending Holland's theory to adult women. *Journal of Vocational Behavior*, 1973, *3*, 115–127.
Hassinger, J., & Via, M. How much does a tutor learn through teaching reading? *Journal of Secondary Education*, 1969, *44*, 42–46.
Havighurst, R. J. *Human development and education*. New York: Longmans, 1953.
————. Youth in exploration and man emergent. In H. Borow (Ed.), *Man in a world at work*. Boston: Houghton Mifflin, 1964.
Hawkins, R. L. *Comparison of three experimental modes of counseling*. Unpublished doctoral dissertation, University of California, Los Angeles, 1967.
Hawley, P. Perceptions of male models of femininity related to career choice. *Journal of Counseling Psychology*, 1972, *19*(4), 308–313.
Hay, N. M., Rohen, T. M., & Murray, R. E. Three approaches to vocational

counseling: A multi factor evaluation. *Journal of College Student Personnel,* 1976, *17,* 475–499.

Healy, C. C. Relation of occupational choice to the similarity between self-ratings and occupational ratings. *Journal of Counseling Psychology,* 1968, *15,* 317–323.

――――. Reducing error variance attributable to social desirability. *Journal of Counseling Psychology,* 1971, *18,* 132–137.

――――. A political role for career counseling. *Personnel and Guidance Journal,* 1972, *51,* 39–44. (a)

――――. Implementing a political role in APGA. *Personnel and Guidance Journal,* 1972, *51,* 45–49. (b)

――――. The relation of esteem and social class to self-occupational congruence. *Journal of Vocational Behavior,* 1973, 3, 43–53. (a)

――――. A replicable method of group career counseling. *Vocational Guidance Quarterly,* 1973, *21,* 214–221. (b)

――――. *Career counseling in the community college.* Springfield, Ill.: Charles C. Thomas, 1974. (a)

――――. Evaluation of a replicable group career counseling procedure. *Vocational Guidance Quarterly,* 1974, *23,* 34–40. (b)

――――. Comparison of the effectiveness of two methods of career counseling with inner-city adolescents. Unpublished project report, University of California, Los Angeles, 1974. (c)

―――― *Career counseling for teachers and counselors.* Boston: Houghton Mifflin, 1975.

――――. *Discovering you.* In C. Winn (Ed.), *Careers in focus.* New York: Mc-Graw-Hill, 1976.

――――. Educators' career development correlates: Their suggestions about career maturity. Paper presented at American Personnel and Guidance Convention, Atlanta, 1980.

Healy, C. C., Bailey, M. L., & Anderson, E. C. The relation of esteem and vocational counseling to range of incorporation scores. *Journal of Vocational Behavior,* 1973, *3,* 69–75.

Healy, C. C., & Klein, S. *The New Mexico Career Education Test Scores.* Los Angeles: Monitor, 1973.

Healy, C. C., & Quinn, J. *Final report of Project Cadre.* University of California, Los Angeles, Graduate School of Education, 1977.

Hedges, J. N., & Bemis, S. E. Sex stereotyping: Its decline in skilled trades. *Monthly Labor Review,* 1974, 97(5), 4–22.

Heller, F. A. Decision processes: An analysis of power-sharing at senior organizational levels. In R. Dubin (Ed.), *Handbook of work, organization, and society.* Chicago: Rand McNally & Company, 1976.

Hendel, D. D., & Davis, S. O. Effectiveness of an intervention strategy for reducing mathematics anxiety. *Journal of Counseling Psychology,* 1978, *25,* 429–434.

Hennig, M., & Jardim, A. *The managerial woman.* New York: Pocket Books, 1976.

Herr, E. L. The outcomes of career guidance: Some current and future perspectives. *Journal of Counseling Services,* 1980, 3(2), 6–15.

Herr, E. L., & Cramer, S. H. *Vocational guidance and career development in the schools.* Boston: Houghton Mifflin, 1972.

Herr, E. L., & Enderlein, T. E. Vocational maturity: The effects of school, grade, curriculum and sex. *Journal of Vocational Behavior,* 1976, 8, 227–238.

Hewer, V. H. Group counseling, individual counseling, and a college class in vocations. *Personnel and Guidance Journal*, 1959, 37, 660–665.
————. What do theories of vocational choices mean to a counselor? *Journal of Counseling Psychology*. 1963, 10, 118–125.
————. Evaluation of a criterion: Realism of vocational choice. *Journal of Counseling Psychology*, 1966, 13, 289–294.
————. Group counseling. *Vocational Guidance Quarterly*, 16: 250–257, 1968.
Hiestand, D. L. *Changing careers after 35: New horizons through professional and graduate study.* New York: Columbia University Press, 1971.
Hilgard, E. R., Atkinson, R. C., & Atkinson, R. L. *Introduction to psychology* (6th ed.). New York: Harcourt Brace Jovanovich, 1976.
Hill, A. W. Career development: Who is responsible? *Training and Development Journal*, 1976 30(5), 14–15.
Hills, D. A., & Williams, J. E. Effects of test information upon self-evaluation in brief educational-vocational counseling. *Journal of Counseling Psychology*, 1965, 12, 275–281.
Hilton, T. E. *Cognitive processes in career decision making.* Carnegie Institute of Technology, Pittsburgh, Pa., 1962.
Hoffman, S. D., & Cochran, D. J. Groups in career counseling. In R. C. Reardon & H. D. Burck. *Facilitating career development: Strategies for counseling.* Springfield, Ill.: Charles C. Thomas, 1975.
Hoffnung, J. J., & Mills, R. B. Situational group counseling with disadvantaged youth. *Personnel and Guidance Journal*, 1970, 48, 458–464.
Holland, J. L. A theory of vocational choice. *Journal of Counseling Psychology*, 1959, 6, 35–45.
————. Exploration of a theory of vocational choice and achievement II. A four-year prediction study. *Psychological Reports*, 1963, 12, 547–594.
————. *Explorations of a theory of vocational choice: One year prediction study.* Moravia, N.Y.: Chronicle Guidance, 1964.
————. *Vocational choice.* Waltham, Mass.: Waltham Press, 1966.
————. *The self-directed search.* Palo Alto, Calif.: Consulting Psychologists Press, 1970.
————. *Making vocational choices: A theory of careers.* Englewood Cliffs, N.J.: Prentice-Hall, 1973.
————. Vocational preference. In M. D. Dunnette (Ed.), *Handbook of industrial and organizational psychology.* New York: Rand McNally & Company, 1976. (a)
————. The virtue of the SDS and its associated typology: A second response to Prediger and Hansen. *Journal of Vocation Behavior*, 1976, 8, 349–358. (b)
————. *Understanding yourself and your career.* Palo Alto, Calif.: Consulting Psychologists Press, 1977.
Holland, J. L., Gottfredson, G. D., & Gottfredson, L. S. Read our reports and examine the data: A response to Prediger and Cole. *Journal of Vocational Behavior*, 1975, 7, 253–260.
Holland, J. L., Takai, R., Gottfredson, G. D., & Hanau, C. A multi-variate analysis of the effects of the Self-Directed Search on high school girls. *Journal of Counseling Psychology*, 1978, 25, 384–389.
Holland, J. L., Viernstein, M. C., Kuo, H., Karweit, N. L., & Blum, Z. D. A psychological classification of occupations. *Journal Supplement Abstract Service*, 1972, 2, 84–85.
Hollandsworth, J. G., Dressel, M. E., & Stevens, J. Use of behavioral versus traditional procedures for increasing job interview skills. *Journal of Counseling Psychology*, 1977, 24, 503–510.

Hollandsworth, J. G., Kazelskis, R., Stevens, J., & Dressel, M. Relative contributions of verbal, articulative, and nonverbal communication to employment decisions in the job interviewing setting. *Personnel Psychology,* 1979, 32, 259–267.

Hollandsworth, J. G., & Sandifer, B. A. Behavioral training for increasing effective job-interview skills: Follow-up and evaluation. *Journal of Counseling Psychology,* 1979, 26, 448–450.

Hollingshead, A. B. *Elmtown's youth.* New York: Wiley, 1949.

Holmes, T. H., & Rahe, R. H. The social readjustment rating scale. *Journal of Psychosomatic Research,* 1967, 11, 213–218.

Holroyd, K. A. Cognition and desensitization in group treatment of test anxiety. *Journal of Consulting and Clinical Psychology,* 1976, 44, 991–1001.

Hoppock, R. *Occupational information* (4th ed.), New York: McGraw-Hill, 1976.

Horner, M. Femininity and successful achievement: A basic inconsistency. In E. L. Walker (Ed.), *Feminine personality and conflict.* Monterey, Calif.: Brooks-Cole Publisher, 1970.

Horowitz, C. *An analysis of the impact of guided inquiry counseling and programmed materials with teachers in an elementary school setting.* Unpublished Ph.D. dissertation, University of California, Los Angeles, Graduate School of Education, 1972.

Horst, P. Educational and vocational counseling from the actuarial point of view. *Personnel and Guidance Journal,* 1956, 35, 164–170.

Horton, J. A., & Walsh, W. B. Concurrent validity of Holland's theory for college degreed working women. *Journal of Vocational Behavior,* 1976, 9, 201–208.

Hosford, R. E. Behavioral counseling: A contemporary overview. *The Counseling Psychologist,* 1969, 1(4), 1–32.

Howard, A. An assessment of assessment centers. *Academy of Management Journal,* 1974, 17, 115–134.

Hoyt, D. P. An evaluation of group and individual programs in vocational guidance. *Journal of Applied Psychology,* 1955, 39, 25–30.

Hoyt, K. B. High school guidance and the specialty oriented student research program. *Vocational Guidance Quarterly,* 1965, 13, 229–236.

———. Toward a definition of career education, In J. H. Magisos (Ed.), *Career education: The third yearbook of American Vocational Association.* Washington, D.C.: American Vocational Association, 1973.

———. Community resources for career education. *Monographs on Career Education,* Washington, D.C.: U.S. Office of Education, 1976.

———. *A primer for career education.* Washington, D.C.: U.S. Government Printing Office, 1977.

———. *National alliance of business and career education.* Washington, D.C.: U.S. Government Printing Office, 1978a.

———. *Rotary international and career education.* Washington, D.C.: U.S. Government Printing Office, 1978b.

———. *Community involvement in the implementation of career education.* Washington, D.C.: U.S. Government Printing Office, 1979.

Hoyt, K. B., Mackin, E. F., Pinson, N. M., & Mangum, G. L. *Career education: A handbook for implementation,* Washington, D.C.: U.S. Government Printing Office, 1972.

Huck, J. R. Assessment centers: A review of the external and internal validities. *Personnel Psychology,* 1973, 26(2), 191–212.

Hughes, H. M. Vocational choice, level, and consistency: An investigation of

Holland's theory for an employed sample. *Journal of Vocational Behavior,* 1972, 2, 377–388.

Hummel, D. L., & McDaniels, C. *How to help your child plan a career.* Washington, D.C.: Acropolis Books, 1979.

Hummel, R. C. Ego counseling in guidance. In K. L. Mosher, R. Carle, & C. D. Kehas (Eds.), *Guidance: An examination.* New York: Harcourt, Brace & World, 1962.

Hunt, J. McV. *Intelligence and experience.* New York: Ronald Press, 1961.

Hunt, R. A. Self and other semantic concepts in relation to choice of vocation. *Journal of Applied Psychology,* 1967, 51, 242–246.

Interpretative Scoring Systems. *Strong-Campbell Interest Inventory Profile.* Minneapolis: Interpretative Scoring Systems, 1976.

Isaacson, L. E. *Career information in counseling and in teaching* (3rd ed.). Boston: Allyn and Bacon, 1977.

Ivey, A. *Microcounseling: Innovations in interviewing training.* Springfield, Ill.: Charles C. Thomas, 1971.

Jameson, R. *The professional job changing system: World's fastest way to get a better job.* Verona, N.J.: Performance Dynamics, 1978.

Janis, I. & Wheeler, D. Thinking clearly about career choices. *Psychology Today,* 1978, *11*(12), 67–76, 121–122.

Jensen, A. R. How much can we boost IQ and scholastic achievement? *Harvard Educational Review,* 1969, 39, 1–23.

Jepsen, D. A. Occupational decision development over the high school years. *Journal of Vocational Behavior,* 1975, 7, 225–237.

Jessee, B. E., & Heimann, R. A. The effects of counseling and group guidance on the vocational maturity of ninth grade boys. *Journal of Educational Research,* 1965, 59, 68–72.

Johnson, N., Johnson, J., and Yates, C. A six-month follow up on the effects of the Vocational Exploration Group on Career Maturity. *Journal of Counseling Psychology,* 1981, 28, 70–71.

Johnson, R. Life planning and life planning workshops. *Personnel and Guidance Journal,* 1977, 55, 546–549.

Johnson, R. H. Individual styles of decision making: A theoretical model for counseling. *Personnel and Guidance Journal,* 1978, 56, 530–536.

Johnson, R. H., & Euler, D. E. Effect of life career game on learning and retention of educational occupational information. *School Counselor,* 1972, *19*(3), 155–160.

Johnson, R. H., & Myrick, R. D. MOLD: A new approach to career decision-making. *Vocational Guidance Quarterly,* 1972, 21, 48–53.

Jordaan, J. P. Exploratory behavior: The formulation of self and occupational concepts. In D. E. Super (Ed.), *Career development: Self-concept theory.* New York: College Entrance Examination Board, 1963.

———. Life stages as organizing modes of career development. In E. L. Herr (Ed.), *Vocational guidance and human development.* Boston: Houghton Mifflin, 1974.

———. Preliminary conclusions about the career pattern boys. New York: Unpublished paper, Columbia University, Teachers College, 1974.

Jordaan, J. P., & Heyde, M. B. *Vocational maturity during the high school years.* New York: Teachers College Press, 1979.

Jordaan, J. P., & Super, D. E. The prediction of early adult vocational behavior. In D. F. Ricks, M. Roff, & A. Thomas (Eds.), *Life history research in psychopathology.* Minneapolis: University of Minnesota Press, 1974.

Kaplan, R. M., McCordick, S. M., & Twitchell, M. Is it the cognitive or behavioral component which makes cognitive-behavior modification effective in test anxiety? *Journal of Counseling Psychology,* 1979, *26,* 371–377.

Katz, M. *You: Today and tomorrow.* Princeton, N.J.: Educational Testing Service, 1958.

Katz, M. R. Can computers make decisions for students? *College Board Review,* 1969, *72,* 13–17.

Katz, M. R., Chapman, W., & Goodwin, W. SIGI—A computer based aid to career decision making. *EDUCOM Bulletin,* Summer, 1972.

Katzell, R. A., & Yankelovich, D. *Work productivity and job satisfaction.* New York: The Psychological Corporation, 1975.

Kaufman, M. A. Alumni: Career advisers. *Journal of College Placement,* 1976, *37,* 53–55.

Kaye, B. L. *Career development programs in organizations: An initial theory.* Los Angeles, Ed.D. dissertation, University of California, Los Angeles, 1976.

———. *Up is not the only way.* Englewood Cliffs, N.J.: Prentice-Hall, 1982.

Kaye, B. L., & Scheele, A. M. *Up and around, a career development manual.* Los Angeles: Privately printed, 1976.

Keil, E. C., & Barbee, J. R. Behavior modification and training the disadvantaged job interviewee. *Vocational Guidance Quarterly,* 1973, *22,* 50–56.

Keith, R. D., Engelkes, J. R., & Winborn, B. B. Employment seeking preparation and activity: An experimental job placement training model for rehabilitation clients. *Rehabilitation Counseling Bulletin,* 1977, *21,* 159–165.

Kellogg, M. S. *What to do about performance appraisal* (Rev. ed.). New York: American Management Association, 1975.

Kelly, D. "The Mason." In *Working* (album). New York: Columbia Records, 1978.

Kelly, E. L., & Fiske, D. W. *The prediction of performance in clinical psychology.* Ann Arbor, Mich.: University of Michigan Press, 1951.

Kelly, E. L., Goldberg, L. R., Fiske, D. W., & Kilkowski, J. M. Twenty-five years later: A follow-up study of the graduate students in clinical psycholoy assessed in the V. A. Selection Research Project. *American Psychologist,* 1978, *33,* 746–760.

Kelly, G. A. *The psychology of personal constructs* (Vols. 1 & 2). New York: Norton, 1955.

Kerlin, B. D. A study of John Holland's theory of careers as it applies to employed adults. (Doctoral dissertation, University of Maryland, 1975). *Dissertation Abstracts International.* 1976, *36,* 6640A. (University Microfilms No. 76-8399, 170)

Kipper, D. A., & Giladi, D. Effectiveness of structured psychodrama and systematic desensitization in reducing test anxiety. *Journal of Counseling Psychology,* 1978, *25,* 499–505.

Kirn, A. *A life work planning workbook and manual* (3rd rev.) Wilton Center, N.H.: Published privately, 1974.

Kivlighan, D. M. The effects of matching treatment approaches and personality types in group vocational counseling. *Journal of Counseling Psychology,* 1981, in press.

Klopfer, W. G., & Taulbee, E. W. Projective tests. *Annual Review of Psychology,* 1976, *27,* 543–567.

Knowdell, R. L. The implementation of a career/life planning program in an industrial setting. *American Society of Engineering Education Conference Proceedings.* Vancouver, British Columbia: American Society of Engineering Education, 1978.

Knowles, M. S. *The modern practice of adult education, andragogy versus pedagogy.* New York: Association Press, 1970.

Knox, A. B. *Adult development and learning.* San Francisco: Josey Bass, 1978.

Kohen, A. I., Grasso, J. T., Myers, S. C., & Shields, P. M. *Career thresholds: Vol. 6* (R. & D. Monograph 16) Washington, D.C.: U.S. Department of Labor, 1977.

Korman, A. K. Toward an hypothesis of work behavior. *Journal of Applied Psychology,* 1970, 54, 31–41.

———. *Organizational behavior.* Englewood Cliffs, N.J.: Prentice-Hall, 1977.

Kourilsky, M. L. An adversary model for educational evaluation. *The Journal of Educational Evaluation: Evaluation Comment.* 1973, 4(3), 3–6.

———. *Beyond simulation: The mini-society approach to instruction in economics and other social sciences.* Los Angeles: Educational Resource Associates, 1974.

Krivatsy, S. E., & Magoon, T. M. Differential effects of three vocational counseling treatment. *Journal of Counseling Psychology,* 1976, 23, 112–118.

Kroll, A. M., Dinklage, L. B., Lee, J., Morley, E. D., & Wilson, E. H. *Career development: Growth and crisis.* New York: Wiley, 1971.

Krumboltz, J. D. Behavioral goals for counseling. *Journal of Counseling Psychology,* 1966, 13, 153–159.

———. *Job experience kits, grades 9–12.* Chicago: Science Research Associates, 1970.

———. An accountability model for counselors. *Personnel and Guidance Journal,* 1974, 52, 639–642.

———. A social learning theory of career selection. *Counseling Psychologist,* 1976, 6, 71–80.

Krumboltz, J. D., & Baker, R. D. Behavioral counseling for vocational decisions. In H. Borow (Ed.), *Career guidance for a new age.* Boston: Houghton Mifflin, 1973.

Krumboltz, J. D., & Schroeder, W. W. Promoting career planning through reinforcement. *Personnel and Guidance Journal,* 1965, 44, 19–26.

Krumboltz, J. D., & Thoresen, C. E. The effect of behavioral counseling in group and individual settings on information-seeking behavior. *Journal of Counseling Psychology,* 1964, 11, 324–333.

———. *Behavioral counseling: Cases and techniques.* New York: Holt, Rinehart & Winston, 1969.

———. (Eds.). *Counseling methods.* New York: Holt, Rinehart & Winston, 1976.

Krumboltz, J. D., Varenhorst, B., & Thoresen, C. E. Non-verbal factors in effectiveness of models in counseling. *Journal of Counseling Psychology,* 1967, 14, 412–418.

Kuder, F. *Vocational Preference Inventory, Form C.* Chicago: Science Research Associates, 1948.

———. *Kuder Occupational Interest Survey.* Chicago: Science Research Associates, 1966.

Kudo, E. I., Lee, W. J., & Ryan, T. A. *Hawaii career development continuum. Curriculum guides 7-9 and 10-12.* Honolulu, Hawaii: Department of Education, Office of Instructional Services, 1974.

Kukic, M. B. *Teachers and student perceptions: Impact on identification of counseling problems.* Unpublished masters thesis, University of California, Los Angeles, Graduate School of Education, 1973.

Lacey, D. Holland's vocational models: A study of work groups and need satisfaction. *Journal of Vocational Behavior,* 1971, 1, 105–122.

Landrum-Griffin Act (Labor-management Reporting and Disclosure Act of 1959).

Lasson, K. *The workers: Portraits of nine American jobholders.* New York: Grossman Publishers, 1971.

Lawler, E. E., III. *Motivation in work organizations.* Monterey, Calif.: Brooks-Cole Publishing, 1973.

Leonard, G. E., & Stephens, E. Elementary school employment service. *Vocational Guidance Quarterly*, 1967, *15*, 13–16.

Levine, M. Scientific method and the adversary model: Some preliminary suggestions. *The Journal of Educational Evaluation: Evaluation Comment.* 1973, 4(2), 1–3.

———. Scientific method and the adversary model. *American Psychologist*, 1974, *28*, 666–677.

Levinson, D. J. *Seasons of a man's life.* New York: Alfred A. Knopf, 1978.

Liebert, R. M., & Morris, L. W. Cognitive and emotional components of test anxiety: A distinction and some initial data. *Psychological Reports*, 1976, *20*, 975–978.

Lin, T. *The interaction effects among counselor, client and counseling setting within the guided inquiry mode: An empirical approach.* Unpublished doctoral dissertation, University of California, Los Angeles, Graduate School of Education, 1970.

Lipman-Blumen, J. How ideology shapes women's lives. *Scientific American*, 1972, *226*, 34–42.

Lofquist, L. H., & Dawis, R. V. *Adjustment to work.* New York: Appleton-Century-Croft, 1969.

Logue, P., Zenner, M., & Gohman, G. Video tape roleplaying in the job interview. *Journal of Counseling Psychology*, 1968, *15*, 436–438.

Long, L. A. Energy conservation and jobs: Old myths give way to new realities. *Los Angeles Times*, July 3, 1977, Part VI, p. 3.

Loughary, J. W., & Ripley, T. M. *Career and life planning: How to choose your job, how to change your career, how to manage your life.* Chicago: Follett, 1976.

Lovejoy, C. E. *Lovejoy's college guide.* New York: Simon & Schuster, 1979.

Maccoby, E. E. Sex differences in intellectual functioning. In E. E. Maccoby (Ed.), *The development of sex differences.* Stanford, Calif.: Stanford University Press, 1966.

Maccoby, E. E., & Jocklin, C. *The psychology of sex differences.* Stanford, Calif.: Stanford University Press, 1974.

Macpherson, D. H. *Selected literature on military career counseling* (Working papers). Alexandria, Va.: U.S. Army Research Institute for Behavioral and Social Science, 1978.

Macpherson, D. H., Eastman, R. F., & Yates, L. G. *Career counseling attitudes and opinions of Army officers (Research Problem Review).* Alexandria, Va.: U.S. Army Research Institute for Behavioral and Social Science, 1977.

Mager, R. F. *Preparing instructional objectives.* Palo Alto, Calif.: Fearon, 1962.

Magoon, T. Innovations in counseling. In J. C. Bentley (Ed.), *The counselor's role, commentary and readings.* Boston: Houghton Mifflin, 1968.

———. Developing skills for educational and vocational counseling. In J. D. Krumboltz & C. E. Thoresen (Eds.), *Behavioral counseling: Cases and techniques.* New York: Holt, Rinehart & Winston, 1969.

Manis, L. G., & Mochizuki, J. Search for fulfillment: A program for adult women. *Personnel and Guidance Journal.* 1972, *50*, 594–599.

Marchant, W. C. Counseling or consultation: A test of the educational model in the elementary school. *Elementary School Guidance and Counseling.* 1972, *7*, 4–8.

Marcon, R. A. *Effect of training and practice on problem solving abilities of inner city children.* Unpublished M.A. thesis, University of California, Los Angeles, Graduate School of Education, 1976.

Markert, L. F. *The use of poetry as a tool in career counseling.* Unpublished Ph.D. dissertation, University of California, Los Angeles, Graduate School of Education, 1980.

Marland, S. P. *Career education.* New York: McGraw-Hill, 1974.

Marsden, G. *Content analysis studies of psychotherapy.* In A. E. Bergin, & S. L. Garfield (Eds.), *Handbook of psychotherapy and behavior change.* New York: Wiley, 1971.

Maslow, A. A. *Motivation and personality.* New York: Harper, 1954.

Mathews, D. F., & Walsh, W. B. Concurrent validity of Holland's theory for non-college-degreed working women. *Journal of Vocational Behavior,* 1978, *12,* 371–379.

Mathews, E., & Tiedeman, D. V. Attitudes toward career and marriage and the development of life style in young women. *Journal of Counseling Psychology,* 1964, *11,* 375–384.

Matulef, N. J., Warman, R. E., & Brock, T. C. Effects of brief vocational counseling on temporal orientation. *Journal of Counseling Psychology,* 1964, *11,* 352–356.

McCleary, E. K. Report of results of tutorial reading project. *The Reading Teacher,* 1971, *24,* 556–560.

McClelland, D. C. *The achieving society.* New York: Free Press, 1967.

———. Testing for competence rather than for intelligence. *American Psychologist,* 1973, *28,* 1–9.

———. Managing motivation to expand human freedom. *American Psychologist,* 1978, *33,* 201–210.

McClure, D. Placement through improvement of client's job seeking skills. *Journal of Applied Rehabilitation Counseling,* 1972, *3,* 188–196.

McGovern, K. B. *The development and evaluation of a social skills training program for college male non-daters.* Unpublished doctoral dissertation, University of Oregon, 1970.

McGovern, K. B., Arkowitz, H., & Gilmore, S. K. Evaluation of social skill training programs for college dating inhibitions. *Journal of Counseling Psychology,* 1975, *22*(6), 505–512.

McGovern, T. V., Jones, B. W., & Morris, S. E. Comparison of professional versus student ratings of job interviewee behavior. *Journal of Counseling Psychology,* 1979, *26,* 176–179.

McGovern, T. V., & Tinsley, H. Interviewer evaluations of interviewee nonverbal behavior. *Journal of Vocational Behavior,* 1978, *13,* 163–171.

McGowan, A. S. Vocational maturity and anxiety among vocationally undecided and indecisive students. The effectiveness of Holland's *Self-Directed Search. Journal of Vocational Behavior,* 1977, *10,* 196–204.

McGreggor, D. *The human side of enterprise.* New York: MacGraw-Hill, 1960.

McKay, C. The Harlem dancer. In L. Wagner & D. Mead (Eds.), *Introducing poems.* New York: Harper & Row, 1976.

McKersie, R., & Ullman, J. Success patterns of MBA graduates, *Harvard Business School Bulletin,* Sept., 1966, 15–18.

McKinley, B. *Developing a career information system: Final report.* Eugene, Ore.: University of Oregon, 1974.

McLaughlin, D. H. *Career education in the public schools 1974–5: A national survey.* Palo Alto, Calif.: American Institute for Research, 1976.

McLaurin, R. A. *A counseling strategy for improving reading proficiency.* Unpublished Ph.D. dissertation, University of California, Los Angeles, 1974.

McMillan, F. R. Attitudes of college men toward career involvement of married women. *Vocational Guidance Quarterly*, 1972, *21*, 8–11.

McMillan, J. R. The effects of desensitization treatment, rational emotive therapy, and a combination treatment program for test-anxious students with high and low levels of generalized anxiety. Unpublished Ph.D. dissertation, University of Maryland, 1973.

Meichenbaum, D. H. Cognitive modification of test anxious college students. *Journal of Consulting and Clinical Psychology*, 1972, *39*, 370–380.

———. *Self-instructional methods: Helping people change*. New York: Pergamon, 1975.

Melnick, J., & Russell, R. W. Hypnosis versus systematic desensitization in the treatment of test anxiety. *Journal of Counseling Psychology*, 1976, *23*, 291–295.

Meltzoff, J., & Kornreich, M. *Research in Psychotherapy*. New York: Atherton Press, 1970.

Meyer, H. E. The flourishing new business of recycling executives. *Fortune*, 1977, *95*(5),328–338.

Meyer, J. *Career guidance through groups: Operations manual*. Houston, Tex.: University of Texas, Center for Human Resources, 1971.

Miller, C. G., & Oetting, E. Barriers to employment and the disadvantaged. *Personnel and Guidance Journal*, 1977, *56*(2), 89–93.

Miller, D. C., & Form, W. H. *Industrial sociology*. New York: Harper, 1951.

Miller, F. W. Evaluating a counseling procedure. *Journal of Educational Research*, 1952, *46*, 61–69.

Miller, J. V. *Career development needs of nine-year-olds*. Washington, D.C.: American Personnel Guidance Association, 1977.

Miller, M. M., & Reese, B. Dramatic TV content and children's sex role stereotypes. *Journal of Broadcasting*, 1976, *20*, 35–50.

Minor, F., Myers, R., & Super, D. E. An experimental computer-based education and career exploration system. *Personnel and Guidance Journal*, 1969, *47*, 564–569.

Mirov, S. S. *Descriptive study of a group vocational model*. Unpublished M.A. thesis, University of California, Los Angeles, Graduate School of Education, 1974.

Mischel, W. *Personality and assessment*. New York: Wiley, 1968.

Mitchell, A. M. *Career development needs of seventeen-year-olds: How to improve career development programs*. Washington, D.C.: National Vocational Guidance Association, 1977.

Mitchell, J. "For Free." In *Ladies of the Canyon* (album). New York, Warner Brothers Records, 1969.

Mitchell, K. R., & Piatowska, O. E. Effects of group treatment for college underachievers and bright failing underachievers. *Journal of Counseling Psychology*, 1974, *21*, 494–501.

Mooney, W. L. *An experiment in the use of two vocational placement techniques with a population of hard to place rehabilitation clients*. Final Report. Washington, D.C.: Department of Health, Education and Welfare, Social and Rehabilitation Administration, 1966. (NTIS No. PB197525)

Moore, W. E. *The professions: Roles and rules*. New York: Russell Sage Foundation, 1970.

Morgan, J. L., & Skovholt, T. M. Using inner experience: Fantasy and daydreams in career counseling. *Journal of Counseling Psychology*, 1977, *24*, 391–397.

Morin, W. J. Outplacement counseling. *Personnel and Guidance Journal*, 1977, *55*, 553–556.

Morley, E. D. The career crisis of losing one's job: Decision making in action. In A. M. Kroll, L. B. Dinklage, J. Lee, E. D. Morley, & E. H. Wilson *Career development growth and crisis.* New York: Wiley, 1971.

Morrill, W., & Forest, D. J. Dimensions of counseling for career development. *Personnel and Guidance Journal,* 1970, *49,* 299–307.

Morrison, R. F., & Arnold, S. J. A suggested revision in the classification of nonprofessional occupations in Holland's theory. *Journal of Counseling Psychology,* 1974, *21,* 485–488.

Morrison, R. L. Self-concept implementation in occupational choice. *Journal of Counseling Psychology,* 1962, *9,* 255–261.

Morrison, R. L. *In-service classroom management training: A consultant model.* Unpublished doctoral dissertation, University of California, Los Angeles, Graduate School of Education, 1973.

Mott, F. L., Sandell, S. H., Shapiro, D., Brito, P. K., Carr, T. J., Johnson, R. C., Jusenius, C. L., Koenig, R. J., & Moore, S. F. *Years for decision* (Vol. 4). (R & D Monograph No. 24). Washington, D.C.: U.S. Department of Labor, 1978.

Mount, M. K., & Muchinsky, P. M. Person-environment congruence and employee job satisfaction: A test of Holland's theory. *Journal of Vocational Behavior,* 1978, *13,* 84–100.

Muchinsky, P. M., & Tuttle, M. L. Employee turnover: An empirical and methodological assessment. *Journal of Vocational Behavior,* 1979, *14,* 43–77.

Murray, H. A. *Explorations in personality.* New York: Oxford University Press, 1938.

———. *Thematic apperception test.* New York: Grune & Stratton, 1949.

Myers, R. A. Research on educational and vocational counseling. In A. E. Bergin & S. L. Garfield (Eds.), *Handbook of psychotherapy and behavior change: An empirical analysis.* New York: Wiley, 1971.

———. Exploration with the computer. *Counseling Psychologist,* 1978, 7(3), 51–54.

Nachmann, B. Childhood experience and vocational choice in law, dentistry, and social work. *Journal of Counseling Psychology,* 1960, 7, 243–250.

Nader, R., Green, M., & Seligman, J. *Constitutionalizing the corporation.* Washington, D.C.: Corporate Accountability Research Group, 1976.

Nafziger, D. H., Holland, J. L., & Gottfredson, G. D. Student-college congruency as a predictor of satisfaction. *Journal of Counseling Psychology,* 1975, 22, 132–139.

National Association of State Boards of Education *CETA/YEDPA Education Policy: Issues and recommendations.* Washington, D.C.: Author, 1979.

National Commission on Working Women, *National survey of working women: Perceptions, problems and prospects.* Washington, D.C. Center for Women and Work, National Manpower Institute, 1979.

Neal, F. Job placement for the bottom 10 percent. *Journal of College Placement,* 1977, *38,* (Winter), 65–66.

Neely, M. A., & Kosier, M. W. Physically impaired students and the vocational exploration group. *Vocational Guidance Quarterly,* 1977, *26,* 37–44.

Nelson, H. Y., & Goldman, P. R. Attitudes of high school students and young adults toward the gainful employment of married women. *The Family Coordinator,* 1969, *18,* 251–255.

Newcomb, T. M. *Persistence and change: Bennington College and its students after 25 years.* New York: Wiley, 1967.

Nicholson, J. A. A comparison of the effects of three career development group techniques on measure of self information and process variables (Ph.D.

dissertation, University of Missouri, 1974). *Dissertation Abstracts International* B, 1975, *35*, 4659B. (Order No. 75–5778)

Niedermeyer, F. C., & Ellis, P. Remedial reading instruction by trained pupil tutors. *Improving Human Performance*, 1971, *1*, 15–21.

Noeth, R. J., & Prediger, D. J. Career development over the high school years. *Vocational Development Quarterly*, 1978, *26*, 244–254.

Nolan, J. J. The effectiveness of the self-directed search compared with group counseling in promoting information seeking and realism of vocational choice (Ph.D. dissertation, University of Maryland, 1974). *Dissertation Abstracts International* B, 1974, *35*, 195A. (University Microfilms No. 14–16, 569)

Nord, W. R. Job satisfaction reconsidered. *American Psychologist*, 1977, *32*, 1026–1035.

Norris, W., Zeran, F. R., Hatch, R. N., & Engelkes, J. R. *The information service in guidance: For career planning and guidance* (4th ed.). Chicago: Rand McNally & Company, 1979.

Obinna, E. S. *Aspirations of black business education students in the California state college and university system.* Unpublished Ed.D. dissertation, University of California, Los Angeles, 1979.

O'Brien, W. F., & Walsh, W. B. Concurrent validity of Holland's theory for non-college-degreed black working men. *Journal of Vocational Behavior*, 1976, *8*, 239–246.

O'Bryant, S. L., & Corder-Boly, C. R. The effects of television on children's stereotyping of women's work roles. *Journal of Vocational Behavior*, 1978, *12*, 233–244.

O'Connell, T. J., & Sedlacek, W. E. *The reliability of Holland's Self Directed Search for educational and vocational planning* (Research Report 6–71). College Park, Md: University of Maryland, Counseling Center, 1971.

Oden, M. H. The fulfillment of promise: Forty-year follow-up of Terman gifted group. *Genetic Psychology Monographs*, 1968, *7*, 3–93.

Oetting, G., & Miller, D. C. Work and the disadvantaged: The work adjustment hierarchy. *Personnel and Guidance Journal*, 1977, *56*, 29–35.

Ogilvie, V. N. *Evaluation of a group career counseling program for women.* Unpublished Ph.D. dissertation, University of California, Los Angeles, Graduate School of Education, 1975.

Ogle, M. G. *The effect of group counseling mode upon internally versus externally oriented counselees.* Unpublished doctoral dissertation, University of California, Los Angeles, Graduate School of Education, 1972.

Oliver, L. W. Evaluating career counseling outcome for three modes of test interpretation. *Measurement and Evaluation in Guidance*, 1977, *10*, 153–161.

Olsen, L. *Lost in the shuffle: A report on the guidance system in California secondary schools.* Santa Barbara, Calif.: Citizens Policy Center, 1979.

O'Neil, J. M., Price, G. E., & Tracey, T. J. The stimulus value, treatment effects, and sex differences when completing the *Self-Directed Search* and *Strong-Campbell Interest Inventory. Journal of Counseling Psychology*, 1979, *26*, 45–50.

O'Reilly, R. H. *Use of differential counseling methods in helping student teachers to cope with interpersonal problems.* Unpublished doctoral dissertation, University of California, Los Angeles, Graduate School of Education, 1968.

Osipow, S. H. *Theories of career development* (2nd ed.). Englewood Cliffs, N.J.: Prentice-Hall, 1973.

Osterhouse, R. A. Group systematic desensitization of test anxiety. In J. D.

Krumboltz & C. E. Thoresen (Eds.), *Counseling Methods.* New York: Holt, Rinehart, & Winston, 1976.

O'Toole, J. (Ed) *Work in America.* Cambridge, Mass.: M.I.T. Press, 1973.

———. *Work, learning and the American future.* San Francisco: Josey-Bass, 1977.

Otte, F. L., & Sharpe, D. L. The effects of career exploration on self-esteem, achievement motivation, and occupational knowledge. *Vocational Guidance Quarterly,* 1979, 28, 63–70.

Otto, H. A. *Human potentialities: The challenge and the promise.* St. Louis: W. H. Green, 1968.

Owens, W. A. Background data. In M. D. Dunnette (Ed.), *Handbook of industrial and organizational psychology.* Chicago: Rand McNally & Company, 1976.

Pace, C. R. *The influence of academic and student subcultures in college and university environments.* Los Angeles: University of California, Los Angeles, 1964. (Cooperative Research Project No. 1083)

Palo, A. J., & Kuzniar, J. Modification of behavior through group counseling and consultation. *Elementary School Guidance and Counseling,* 1972, 6, 258–262.

Parnes, H., Jusenius, C. L., Blau, F., Nestel, G., Shortledge, R. L., & Sandell, S. *Dual careers: A longitudinal analysis of the labor market experience of women* (Vol. 4). Washington, D.C.: U.S. Department of Labor (R & D Monograph No. 21), 1976.

Parsons, F. *Choosing a vocation.* Boston: Houghton Mifflin, 1909.

Paterson, D. G., Schneidler, G. G., & Williamson, E. G. *Student guidance techniques.* New York: McGraw-Hill, 1938.

Patterson, C. H. Counseling: Self clarification and the helping relationship. In H. Borow, (Ed.), *Man in a world at work.* Boston: Houghton Mifflin, 1964.

Paul, G. L. *Insight versus desensitization in psychotherapy: An experiment in anxiety reduction.* Stanford, Calif.: Stanford University Press, 1966.

———. Outcome of systematic desensitization: II Controlled investigations, and current status. In C. M. Franks (Ed.), *Behavior therapy: appraisal and status.* New York: McGraw-Hill, 1969.

Paul, G. L., & Eriksen, C. W. Effects of test anxiety on "real life" examinations. *Journal of Personality,* 1964, 32, 480–494.

Paul, G. L., & Shannon, D. T. Treatment of anxiety through systematic desensitization in therapy groups. *Journal of Abnormal Psychology,* 1966, 71, 124–135.

Pearson, H. G. Self-identification of talents: First step in finding career directions. *The Vocational Guidance Quarterly,* 1975, 24, 20–27.

Pendleton, L. R., Shelton, J. L., & Wilson, S. E. Social interaction training using systematic homework. *The Personnel and Guidance Journal,* 1976, 54, 484–487.

Pepinsky, H. B., & Pepinsky, P. N. *Counseling theory and practice.* New York: Ronald, 1954.

Perry, W. G. *Forms of intellectual and ethical development in the college years.* Cambridge, Mass.: Harvard University, Bureau of Student Counsel, 1968.

Peter, L. J. *The Peter prescription.* New York: Bantam Books,, 1974.

Peter, L. J., & Hull, R. *The Peter principle.* New York: Bantam Books, 1972.

Pfeiffer, W., & Jones, J. *Annual handbook for group facilitators.* La Jolla, Calif.: University Associates, 1972.

Phelps, A. T. *Development and evaluation of an instructional counseling pro-*

gram for the treatment of reticence. Unpublished Ph.D. disseration, University of California, Los Angeles, 1978.

Phillips, L. L. *Mentors and proteges: A study of the career development of women managers and executives in business and industry.* Unpublished Ph.D. dissertation, University of California, Los Angeles, Graduate School of Education, 1977.

Phillips, S. D., Cairo, P. C., & Myers, R. A. *Career planning modules for the officer career information and planning system.* Unpublished paper. New York: Teachers College, Columbia University, 1980.

Piaget, J. Piaget's theory. In P. H. Mussen (Ed.), *Carmichael's manual of child development.* New York: Wiley, 1970.

Pietrofesa, J. J., & Splete, H. *Career development: Theory and research.* New York: Grune & Stratton, 1975.

Platt, J. M. Efficacy of the Adlerian model in elementary school counseling. *Elementary School Guidance and Counseling.* 1971, 6, 88–91.

Popham, W. J., & Carlson, D. Deep dark deficits of the adversary evaluation model. Paper presented at the symposium on the Adversary Evaluation Model: A Second Look. Annual meeting of the American Education Research Association, New York, 1977.

Prediger, D. J. Tests and developmental career guidance. *Evaluation and Measurement in Guidance,* 5, 1972, 426–430.

Prediger, D. J., & Baumann, R. R. Development group counseling: An outcome study. *Journal of Counseling Psychology,* 1970, 17, 527–533.

Prediger, D. J., & Hanson, G. R. A theory of careers encounters sex: Reply to Holland. *Journal of Vocational Behavior,* 1976, 8, 359–366.

Prediger, D. J., & Noeth, R. J. Effectiveness of a brief counseling intervention in stimulating vocational exploration. *Journal of Vocational Behavior,* 1979, 14, 352–368.

Prediger, D. J., Roth, J. D., & Noeth, R. J. *A nationwide study of student career development: Summary or results* (ACT Research Report No. 61). Iowa City, Iowa: American College Testing, 1973.

Psychological Corporation. *Differential Aptitude Test Battery.* New York: Author, 1947.

———. Methods of expressing test scores. *Test Service Bulletin,* 1955, 48, 7–9.

———. *Omnibus Personality Inventory Profile.* New York: Author, 1968.

———. *Differential Aptitude Test Career Planning Program.* New York: Author, 1975.

Pumo, B., Sehl, R., & Cogan, F. Job readiness: Key to placement. *Journal of Rehabilitation,* 1966, 32, 18–19.

Quatrano, L. A., & Bergland, B. W. Group experiences in building planning strategies. *Elementary School Guidance and Counseling,* 1974, 8, 173–181.

Quinn, J. B. *The influence of interpersonal perception on the process of change in two experimental modes of group process.* Unpublished doctoral dissertation, University of California, Los Angeles, Graduate School of Education, 1970.

Quinn, R. R., Levitin, T., & Eden, D. The multimillion dollar misunderstanding: An attempt to reduce turnover among disadvantaged workers. In L. E. Davis (Ed.), *The quality of working life* (Vol. 2). New York: Free Press, 1975.

Quirck, J. Human potential counseling at Ulster Community College. Unpublished paper, Ulster Community College, New York, 1971.

Rabin, M., & Scott, J. *YWCA Vocational Exploration Program.* Los Angeles: YWCA of Los Angeles, 1971.

Bibliography

Raths, L. E., Harmin, M., & Simon, S. B. *Values and teaching* (2nd ed.). lumbus, Ohio: Merrill Publishing, 1978.

Reardon, R. C., & Burck, H. D. *Facilitating career development: strategies for counselors*. Springfield, Ill.: Thomas, 1975.

Redmond, R. E. Increasing vocational information seeking behavior in high school students (Doctoral dissertation, University of Maryland, College Park, 1972). *Dissertation Abstracts International*, 1973, *34*, 2311A–2312A. (University Microfilms No. 73-17, 046)

Renwick, P. A., & Lawler, E. E. What you really want from your job. *Psychology Today*, 1978, *11*(12), 53–65; 118.

Representation of blacks among government contractors. *The Wall Street Journal*, December 7, 1978, p. 2.

Reubens, B. G. Bridges to work. New York: Columbia University, Conservation of Human Resources, 1977. (Mimeographed)

Richardson, F. C., & Suinn, R. M. The mathematics anxiety rating scale: Psychometric data. *Journal of Counseling Psychology*, 1972, *19*, 551–554.

Riesman, D. *The lonely crowd: A study of the changing American character*. New Haven, Conn.: Yale University Press, 1950.

Rimm, D. C., & Masters, J. C. *Behavior therapy: Techniques and empirical findings*. New York: Academic Press, 1974.

Robinson, F. *Studying effectively*. New York: Harper & Row, 1946.

Roe, A. *The psychology of occupations*. New York: Wiley, 1956.

————. Early determinants of vocational choice. *Journal of Counseling Psychology*, 1957, *4*, 212–217.

Roe, A., Hubbard, W. D., Hutchinson, T., & Bateman, T. Studies of occupational history, Part I: Job changes and the classification of occupations. *Journal of Counseling Psychology*, 1966, *13*, 387–393.

Roeber, E. C., Walz, G. R., & Smith, G. E. *A strategy for guidance*. New York: Macmillan, 1969.

Roessler, R., Cook, D., & Lillard, D. Effects of systematic counseling on work adjustment clients. *Journal of Counseling Psychology*, 1977, *24*, 313–320.

Rogers, C. R. *Client-centered therapy*. Boston: Houghton Mifflin, 1951.

————. *On becoming a person: A therapist's view of psychotherapy*. Boston: Houghton Mifflin, 1961.

————. (Ed.). *The therapeutic relationship and its impact*. Madison, Wis.: University of Wisconsin Press, 1967.

Rothman, J. *Planning and organizing for social change*. New York: Columbia University Press, 1974.

Rotter, J. B. Generalized expectancies for internal vs. external control of reinforcement. *Psychological Monographs*, 1966, *80*, (No. 1).

Rounds, J. B., Shubsachs, A. P. W., Dawis, R. V., & Lofquist. A test of Holland's environmental formulations. *Journal of Applied Psychology*, 1978, *63*, 609–616.

Russell, R. K., Wise, F., & Stratoudakis, J. P. Treatment of test anxiety by cue controlled relaxation and systematic desensitization. *Journal of Counseling Psychology*, 1976, *23*, 563–566.

Ryan, T. A. *Effect of an integrated instructional counseling program to improve vocational decision making*. Washington, D.C.: U.S. Department of Health, Education, and Welfare (Ed. 021 132), 1968.

Salomone, P. R., & Salaney, R. B. The applicability of Holland's theory to non-professional workers. *Journal of Vocational Behavior*, 1978, *13*, 63–74.

Sarason, I. G. Test anxiety and intellectual performance. *Journal of Educational Psychology*, 1961, *52*, 201–206.

————. The test anxiety scale: Concept and research. In C. D. Spielberger & I. G. Sarason (Eds.), *Stress and anxiety* (Vol. 5). New York: Hemisphere/ Wiley, 1978.

————. The test anxiety scale: Concept and research. In C. D. Spielberger & I. G. Sarason (Eds.), *Stress and anxiety* (Vol. 5). New York: Halsted-Wiley, 1979.

————. (Ed.). *Test anxiety: Theory, research, and application.* Hillsdale, N.J.: L. Erlbaum Associates, 1980.

Sarason, S. B. The nature of problem solving in social action. *American Psychologist*, 1978, *33*, 370–379.

Sarason, S. B., Sarason, E. K., & Crowden, P. Aging and the nature of work. *American Psychologist*, 1975, *30*, 584–593.

Schaffer, K. Evaluating job satisfaction and success for emotionally maladjusted men. *Journal of Vocational Behavior*, 1976, *9*, 329–335.

Schager, C. R. The efficacy of career education: Other ways of assessing effectiveness. In *The efficacy of career education.* Washington, D.C.: National Advisory Council for Career Education, 1976.

Scheele, A. M. *Skills for success: A guide to the top.* New York: William Morrow & Co., 1979.

Schein, E. H. How to break the college graduate. *Harvard Business Review*, 1964, *42*, 68–76.

————. The individual, the organization, and the career: A conceptual scheme. *Journal of Applied Behavioral Science*, 1971, *7*, 401–426.

Schlossberg, N. K., & Goodman, J. A woman's place: Children's six stereotyping of occupations. *Vocational Guidance Quarterly*, 1972, *20*, 266–270.

Schlossberg, N., & Pietrofesa, J. Career counseling for women. *Counseling Psychologist*, 1973, *4*, 44–53.

Schudt, D. L., & Stahmann, R. F. Interest profiles of clergymen as indicated by the *Vocational Preference Inventory*. *Educational and Psychological Measurement*, 1971, *31*, 1025–1028.

Schwartz, S. It's an art. In D. Kelly, *Working.* (album) New York: Columbia Records, 1978.

Scoggins, W. *Labor in learning: Public school treatment of the world of work.* Los Angeles: Center for Labor Research and Education, Institute for Industrial Relations, 1966.

Scott, A. Underclass: Black youths' job picture still bleak. *Los Angeles Times*, December 24, 1978, Part I, p. 1; 8.

Scriven, M. The methodology of evaluation. In R. Stake (Ed.), *Perspectives of curriculum evaluation.* Chicago: Rand McNally & Company, 1967.

Sears, R. R. Sources of life satisfaction of the Terman gifted men. *American Psychologist*, 1977, *32*, 119–128.

Security Pacific National Bank. *Career management program manual.* Los Angeles: Security Pacific National Bank Personnel Department, 1978.

Segal, S. J. A psychoanalytical analysis of personality factors in vocational choice. *Journal of Counseling Psychology*, 1961, *8*, 202–210.

Serrano v. *Priest*, 5 Cal. 3d 584, 487 P. 2nd 1241 (1971).

Setne, V. L. An educational-vocational development program for adult women. *Vocational Guidance Quarterly*, 1977, *25*, 232–237.

Sewell, W. H., Haller, A. O., Ohlendorf, G. W. The early educational and early occupational attainment process: Replication and revisions. *American Sociological Review*, 1970, *35*, 1014–1027.

Shapiro, B. *Employment and self-esteem: An evaluation of the Cambridge Job Factory, a manpower program under the Comprehensive Employment and*

Training Act (CETA). Unpublished Ph.D. dissertation, Tufts University, 1978.

Shartle, C. L. *Occupational information: Its development and application* (3rd ed.). Englewood Cliffs, N.J.: Prentice-Hall, 1959.

Shaw, T. Blue collar man. In *Pieces of eight* (album). Los Angeles: Almo Music Corporation and Stygean Songs, 1978.

Sheehy, G. *Passages: Predictable changes in adult life.* New York: Dutton, 1976.

Sheppard, D. The measurement of vocational maturity in adults. *Journal of Vocational Behavior,* 1971, *1,* 399–406.

Sheppard, H. L., & Belitsky, A. H. *The job hunt: Job-seeking behavior of unemployed workers in a local economy.* Washington, D.C.: Upjohn Institute, 1965.

Shertzer, B., & Stone, S. C. *Fundamentals of guidance* (3rd ed.). Boston: Houghton Mifflin, 1976.

Sherwood, J. J. Self-report and projective measures of achievement and affiliation. *Journal of Consulting Psychology,* 1966, *30,* 329–337.

Shiner, E. V. *Self-concept and change of occupation.* Unpublished doctoral project, Teachers College, Columbia University, 1963.

Shirts, R. G. *Career simulation for sixth grade pupils.* San Diego, Calif.: San Diego County Department of Education, 1966.

Shoben, J. E. Guidance: Remedial function or social reconstruction. In R. L. Mosher, R. F. Carle, & C. D. Kehas (Eds.), *Guidance: an examination.* New York: Harcourt, Brace & World, 1962.

Shostrom, E. L. *Personal Orientation Inventory.* San Diego, Calif.: Educational and Industrial Testing Service, 1962.

Silberman, H. F. Job satisfaction among students in work education programs. *Journal of Vocational Behavior,* 1974, *5,* 261–268.

Simon, S. B., Howe, L. W., & Kirshenbaum, H. *Values clarification.* New York: Hart Publishing Co., 1972.

Sinick, D. *Counseling older persons.* New York: Human Science Press, 1977.

Skovholt, T. M., & Hoenninger, R. W. Guided fantasy in career counseling, *Personnel and Guidance Journal,* 1974, *52,* 693–696.

Smith, M. L. Influence of client sex and ethnic group on counselor judgments. *Journal of Counseling Psychology,* 1974, *21,* 516–521.

Smith, M. L., & Glass, G. V. Meta-analysis of psychotherapy outcome studies. *American Psychologist,* 1977, *32,* 752–759.

Smith, R. D., & Evans, J. R. Comparison of experimental group guidance and individual counseling as facilitator of vocational development. *Journal of Counseling Psychology,* 1973, *20,* 202–209.

Smith, R. R., Petko, C. M., Jenkins, W. O., & Warner, R. W., Jr. An experimental application and evaluation of rational behavior therapy in a work release setting. *Journal of Counseling Psychology,* 1979, *26,* 519–525.

Snapp, M. I., Okland, T., & Williams, F. C. A study of individualized instruction by using elementary school children and tutors. *Journal of School Psychology,* 1972, *10,* 1–8.

Snodgrass, G. *A comparison of student paraprofessionals and professional counselor trainees in career counseling with university students.* Unpublished Ph.D. dissertation, University of California, Los Angeles, 1978.

Snodgrass, G., & Healy, C. C. Developing a replicable career decision-making counseling procedure. *Journal of Counseling Psychology,* 1979, *26,* 210–216.

Solamon, M. "Who am I?" In L. F. Markert, *The use of poetry as a tool in career counseling.* Unpublished Ph.D. dissertation, University of California, Los Angeles, 1980.

Solmon, L. Rethinking the relationship between education and work. *UCLA Educator,* 1977, *19* (Spring), 18–31.

Sorenson, A. G. *Toward an instructional model for counseling.* Los Angeles: University of California, Los Angeles, Center for Study of Evaluation, 1967.

————. Evaluation for the improvement of instructional programs: Some practical steps. *UCLA Center for the Study of Evaluation: Evaluation Comment,* 1971, *2,* 13–17.

————. Notes for theories of counseling. Unpublished lecture notes. University of California, Los Angeles, Graduate School of Education, 1978.

Sorenson, A. G., & Hawkins, R. *Three experimental modes of counseling.* Los Angeles: University of California, Los Angeles, Center for the Study of Evaluation, 1968.

Sparta, S. N. *A model for follow-up of counseling and psychotherapy.* Unpublished M.A. thesis, University of California, Los Angeles, Graduate School of Education, 1975.

————. *Treatment of helpless children through cognitive interpretations of failure: An examination of some therapeutic influences.* Unpublished Ph.D. dissertation, University of California, Los Angeles, 1978.

Spearman, C. *The abilities of man: Their nature and measurement.* New York: Macmillan, 1927.

Speas, C. M. Job-seeking interview skills training: A comparison of four instructional techniques. *Journal of Counseling Psychology,* 1979, *26,* 405–412.

Spiegler, M. D., Cooley, E. J., Marshall, G. J., Prince, H. J., III, & Puckett, S. P. A self-control versus a counter conditioning paradigm for systematic desensitization: A experimental comparison. *Journal of Counseling Psychology,* 1976, *23,* 83–86.

Spielberger, C. D., Gorsuch, R. L., & Lushene, R. E. *Manual for the State Trait Anxiety Inventory* (Self evaluation questionnaire). Palo Alto, Calif.: Consulting Psychologists Press, 1977.

Splete, H. The elementary school counselor: An effective consultant with classroom teachers. *Elementary School Guidance and Counseling,* 1971, *5,* 165–172.

Splete, H. H., & Sklare, A. R. Career guidance in the elementary school. Career consulting: Utilizing the delphi technique with career education content. *Elementary School Guidance and Counseling Journal,* 1977, *11,* 309–315.

Sprague, D. G., & Strong, D. J. Vocational choice group counseling. *Journal of College Student Personnel,* 1970, *15,* 35–45.

Springstein, B. Factory. In *Darkness on the edge of town.* (album) New York: Columbia Records, 1978.

Squires, G. D. *Education and jobs: The imbalancing of the social machinery.* New Brunswick, N.J.: Transaction, 1979.

Starishevsky, R., & Matlin, N. A. A model for the translation of self-concept into vocational terms. In D. E. Super (Ed.), *Career development: Self-concept theory.* New York: College Entrance Examination Board, 1963.

Stephens, C. But I might die tonight. In *Tea for the tillerman.* (album) London: Irving Music, Inc., 1970.

Stephens, D. B., Watt, J. T., & Hobbs, W. S. Getting through the resume preparation maze: Some empirically based guidelines for resume format. *Vocational Guidance Quarterly,* 1979, *28,* 25–34.

Stephens, R. R. Occupational choice as a crystallized self-concepts. *Journal of Counseling Psychology,* 1961, *8,* 211–216.

Stern, G. C. *People in context: measuring person-environment congruence in education and industry.* New York: Wiley, 1970.

Stevens, R. Be your own best friend. In *Feelings not right again.* (Album.) Burbank, Calif.: Warner Brothers Album, 1978.

Stewart, N. AGCT scores of army personnel grouped by occupations. *Occupations,* 1947, *26,* 5–41.

Stewart, N. R. Exploring and processing information about educational and vocational opportunities in groups. In J. D. Krumboltz & C. E. Thoresen (Eds.), *Behavioral counseling: Cases and techniques.* New York: Holt, Rinehart & Winston, 1969.

Stewart, N. R., Winborn, B. B., Burks, H. M., Johnson, R. R., & Engelkes, J. R. *Systematic counseling.* Englewood Cliffs, N.J.: Prentice-Hall, 1978.

Strong, E. K., Jr. *The Strong Vocational Interest Blank.* Palo Alto, Calif.: Stanford University Press, 1927.

———. *Vocational interests 18 years after college.* Minneapolis, Minn.: University of Minnesota Press, 1955.

Strong, E. K., Jr., & Campbell, D. P. *Strong Campbell Interest Inventory.* Stanford, Calif.: Stanford University Press, 1976.

Strong, S. R., & Matross, R. P. Change process in counseling and psychotherapy. *Journal of Counseling Psychology,* 1973, *20,* 25–37.

Suinn, R. M. The STABS, a measure of test anxiety for behavior therapy: Normative data. *Behavior Research and Therapy,* 1969, *7,* 335–339.

———. *Suinn Test Anxiety Behavior Scale.* Fort Collins, Colo.: Rocky Mountain Behavior Science Institute, 1971.

———. Anxiety management training to control general anxiety. In J. D. Krumboltz & C. E. Thoresen (Eds.), *Counseling Methods.* New York: Holt, Rinehart & Winston, 1976.

Suinn, R. M., & Richardson, F. Anxiety management training: A non-specific behavior therapy program for anxiety control. *Behavior Therapy,* 1971, *4,* 498–511.

Sullivan, H. S. *The interpersonal theory of psychiatry.* New York: Norton & Co., 1953. (a)

———. *The psychiatric interview.* New York: Norton & Co., 1953. (b)

Sullivan Associates. *Sullivan Placement Examination.* Palo Alto, Calif.: Author, 1968.

Super, D. E. *The dynamics of vocational adjustment.* New York: Harper, 1942.

———. A theory of career development. *American Psychologist,* 1953, *8,* 185–190.

———. *The psychology of careers.* New York: Harper & Row, 1957.

———. *Career development: Self-concepts theory.* New York: College Entrance Examination Board, 1963.

———. *The Work Values Inventory.* Boston: Houghton Mifflin, 1968.

———. Vocational development theory in 1988: How will it come about? *Counseling Psychologist,* 1969, *1,* 9–14.

———. (Ed.). *Computer-assisted counseling.* New York: Teachers College Press, 1970.

———. (Ed.). *Measuring vocational maturity for counseling and evaluation.* Washington, D.C.: National Vocational Guidance Association, 1974.

———. How occupational choice occurs. Paper presented at National Career Education Conference, Florida State University, Tallahassee, 1975.

———. *Career education and the meanings of work.* Washington, D.C.: U.S. Government Printing Office, 1976.

———. Vocational maturity in mid-career. *Vocational Guidance Quarterly,* 1977, *25,* 294–302.

————. Adolescent predictors of success and satisfaction in young adulthood. Paper presented at the American Education Research Association Convention, San Francisco, 1979.

Super, D. E., & Crites, J. O. *Appraising vocational fitness.* New York: Harper & Row, 1962.

Super, D. E., Crites, J. O., Hummel, R. C., Moser, H. P., Overstreet, P. L., & Warnath, C. F. *Vocational development: A framework for research.* New York: Teachers College Press, 1957.

Super, D. E., Forrest, D. J., Jordaan, J. P., Lindeman, R. H., Myers, R. A., & Thompson, A. S. *Career development inventory.* New York: Consulting Psychologists Press, 1979.

Super, D. E., & Hall, D. T. Career development: Exploration and planning. *Annual Review of Psychology,* 1978, *29,* 333–372.

Super, D. E., Jordaan, J. P., Bohn, M. J., Lindeman, R. H., Forrest, D. J., & Thompson, A. S. *Career Development Inventory, Form 1,* New York: Columbia University, Teachers College, 1971.

Super, D. E., Kowalski, E. S., & Gotkin, E. H. *Floundering and trial after high school.* New York: Teachers College Press, 1969.

Super, D. E., & Overstreet, P. L. *The vocational maturity of ninth grade boys.* New York: Teachers College Press, 1960.

Super, D. E., Zelkowitz, R. S., & Thompson, A. S. *Career development inventory, Adult Form 1.* Unpublished test. Teachers College, Columbia University, 1974.

Swails, R. G., & Herr, E. L. Vocational development groups for ninth-grade students. *Vocational Guidance Quarterly,* 1976, *24,* 256–266.

Systems Research Incorporated. *In-school youth manpower: A guide to local strategies and methods.* Lansing, Mich.: Systems Research, Inc., 1977.

Szabo, E. M. *Loneliness as the lack of intimacy and behavior patterns associated with interpersonal success and failure.* Unpublished masters thesis, University of California, Los Angeles, Graduate School of Education, 1973.

————. Report of a tryout of translation counseling with an all female group in Santa Monica City College. Unpublished report of fieldwork case study. University of California, Los Angeles, Graduate School of Education, 1974.

Talbot, D. B., & Birk, J. M. *Does the Vocational Exploration and Insight Kit equal the sum of its parts?: A comparison study. Journal of Counseling Psychology,* 1979, *26,* 359–362.

Taylor, J. Millworker. In *Working.* (album) New York: Columbia Records, 1978.

Taylor, J. A. A personality scale of manifest anxiety. *Journal of Abnormal and Social Psychology,* 1953, *48,* 285–290.

Tennyson, W. W., Klaurens, M. K., & Hansen, L. S. *Career development curriculum.* Minneapolis, Minn.: University of Minnesota, Career Development Curriculum Project, 1970.

Terkel, S. *Working.* New York: Pantheon, 1974.

Tharenow, P. Employee self-esteem: A review of the literature. *Journal of Vocational Behavior.* 1979, *15,* 316–346

Thomas, A. H., & Stewart, N. R. Counselor response to female clients with deviate and conforming career goals. *Journal of Counseling Psychology,* 1971, *18,* 352–357.

Thomas, G. P. Feasible alternatives counseling. *School Counselor,* 1972, *19,* 237–242.

Thomas, L. E. *Leader's manual: Life planning workshop.* Fort Collins, Colo.: Colorado State University Center, 1972.

Thompson, A. S. The spectrum of occupational information media. Paper presented to Panel on Counseling and Selection, National Manpower Advisory Committee, May 1967. In W. M. Lifton, *Educating for tomorrow: The role of media, career development, and society.* New York: Wiley, 1970.

Thomson, G. Review of *The description of personality* by R. B. Cattell. In O. K. Buros, *The third mental measurements yearbook.* Trenton, N.J.: Rutgers University Press, 1949.

Thoresen, C. E., & Ewart, C. K. Behavioral self-control and career development. *The Counseling Psychologist,* 1976, 6(3), 29–42.

Thoresen, C. E., & Hamilton, J. A. Peer social modeling in promoting career behaviors. *Vocational Guidance Quarterly,* 1972, *20,* 210–216.

Thoresen, C. E., & Krumboltz, J. D. Similarity of social models and clients in behavioral counseling. *Journal of Counseling Psychology,* 1968, *15,* 393–401.

Thoresen, C. E., & Mahoney, M. J. *Behavioral self-control.* New York: Holt, Rinehart & Winston, 1974.

Thoroman, E. C. *The vocational counseling of adults and young adults.* Boston: Houghton Mifflin, 1968.

Thorndike, R. L., & Hagen, E. *Ten thousand careers.* New York: Wiley, 1959.

———. *Measurement and evaluation in psychology and measurement* (3rd ed.). New York: Wiley, 1969.

Thurstone, L. L. *Primary mental abilities.* Chicago: The University of Chicago Press, 1938.

Tichenor, J. M. Life work planning: A group career program evaluated. *Vocational Guidance Quarterly,* 1977, *26,* 54–59.

Tiedeman, D. V. Can a machine develop a career? A structure for the epigenesis of self-realization in career development. In J. Whiteley & A. Resnikoff (Eds.), *Perspectives on vocational development.* Washington, D.C.: American Personnel and Guidance Association, 1972.

Tiedeman, D. V., & Miller-Tiedeman, A. *Choice and decision process and careers.* DeKalb, Ill.: ERIC Clearinghouse in Career Education, 1975.

Tiedeman, D. V., & O'Hara, R. P. Vocational self-concept in adolescence. *Journal of Counseling Psychology,* 1959, *6,* 292–301.

———. *Career development: Choice and integration.* New York: College Entrance Board, 1963.

Time Share (Career Education Division). *Guidance Information System.* Hanover, N.H.: Author, 1972.

Toffler, A. *Future shock.* New York: Random House, 1970.

———. *The third wave.* New York: William Morrow & Co., 1980.

Tolbert, E. L. *Counseling for career development* (2nd ed.). Boston: Houghton Mifflin, 1980.

Torrance, E. P., & White, W. F. (Eds.), *Issues and advances in educational psychology: A book of readings.* Itasca, Ill.: Peacock, 1975.

Torrez, D. S., Lundquist, G. W., & Bergland, B. W. The effect of the vocational exploration group on career decision making behaviors of high school students. *Journal of Counseling Services,* 1979, *3,* 22–27.

Touchton, J. G., & Magoon, T. M. Occupational daydreams in prediction of vocational plans of college women. *Journal of Vocational Behavior,* 1977, *10,* 156–166.

Townsend, B. *Career planning workshop: An interim evaluation.* Los Angeles: Security Pacific National Bank, October, 1977.

Truax, C. B. Reinforcement and nonreinforcement in Rogerian psychotherapy. *Journal of Abnormal Psychology,* 1966, *71,* 1–9.

Truax, C. B., & Carkhuff, R. R. *Toward effective counseling and psychotherapy.* Chicago: Aldine, 1967.

Trueblood, R. W., & McHolland, J. D. *Self-actualization and the human po tential group process.* Evanston, Ill.: Kendall College, Counseling Center, undated.

Tuddenham, R. D. Soldier intelligence in World Wars I and II. *American Psychologist,* 1948, *3,* 54–56.

Tryon, G. S. The measurement and treatment of test anxiety. *Review of Educational Research,* 1980, *50,* 343–372.

Tyler, L. E. The relationship of interests to abilities and reputation among first-grade children. *Education and Psychological Measurement,* 1951, *11,* 255–264.

————. The development of vocational interests: I The organization of likes and dislikes in ten-year-old children. *Journal of Genetic Psychology,* 1955, *86,* 33–34.

————. Research explorations in the realm of choice. *Journal of Counseling Psychology,* 1961, *8,* 195–202.

————. *The work of the counselor* (3rd ed.). New York: Appleton-Century-Crofts, 1969.

Ullman, J. C. & Gutteridge, T. G. The job search. *Journal of College Placement,* 1973, *3,* 67–72.

U.S. Bureau of the Budget. *Standard industrial classification manual.* Washington, D.C.: U.S. Government Printing Office, 1945.

U.S. Congress, *An Act to develop and promote a national system of employment offices.* 48 Stat. 113, June 6, 1933.

————, *The national labor relations act.* 49 Stat. 449, July 5, 1935.

————, *An Act to amend the national labor relations act to provide additional facilities for the mediation of labor disputes affecting commerce, to equalize legal responsibilities of labor organizations and employers, and for other purposes.* Public Law 101, 80th Congress, 1st Ses., 1947.

————, *An Act to provide for the reporting and disclosure of certain financial transactions and administrative practices of labor organizations and employees, to prevent abuses in the administration of trusteeships by labor organizations, to provide standards with respect to the election of officers of labor organizations and for other purposes.* Public Law 257, 86th Congress, 1st Ses., 1959.

————, *An Act to prohibit discrimination on account of sex in the payment of wages by employers engaged in commerce or in the production of goods for commerce.* Public Law 38, 88th Congress, 1st Ses., 1963. (a)

————, *An Act to strengthen and improve the quality of vocational education and to expand the vocational education opportunities in the nation, to extend for three years the national defense education act of 1958 and Public Law 815 and 874, eighty-first Congress, and for other purposes.* Public Law 210, 88th Congress, 1st Ses., 1963. (b)

————, *An Act to promote equal employment opportunities for American workers.* Public Law 88–352, 88th Congress, 2nd Ses., 1964. As amended by Public Law 261, 92nd Congress, 2nd Ses., 1972.

————, *An Act to strengthen and improve educational quality and opportunities for the nation's elementary and secondary schools.* Public Law 10, 89th Congress, 1st Ses., 1965.

————, Title IX, *An Act to amend the higher education act of 1965, the vocational education act of 1963, the general education provisions act, the elementary and secondary education act of 1965, Public Law 874, 81st Congress, and related acts and for other purposes.* Public Law 318, 92nd Congress, 2nd Ses., 1972.

————, Title IV, sec. 406. *An Act to extend and amend the elementary and secondary education act of 1965, and for other purposes.* Public Law 380, 93rd Congress, 2nd Ses., 1974.

————, *An Act to extend the higher education act of 1965, to extend and revise the vocational education act of 1963, and for other purposes.* Public Law 482, 94th Congress, 2nd Ses., 1976.

————, *An Act to authorize a career education program for elementary and secondary schools, and for other purposes.* Public Law 207, 95th Congress, 1st Ses., 1977.

————, *An Act to amend title 5, United States Code, to establish a program to increase part-time career employment within civil services.* Public Law 437, 95th Congress, 2nd Ses., 1978.

U.S. Department of Commerce, Bureau of Census *Current population reports, Series P-20 No. 335 School enrollment-social and economic characteristics of students.* October, 1978. (Advance Report). Washington, D.C.: U.S. Government Printing Office, 1979.

U.S. Department of Labor. *Counseling and placement services for older workers.* Washington, D.C.: U.S. Government Printing Office, 1956.

————. *Dictionary of occupational titles* (3rd ed.). Washington, D.C.: U.S. Government Printing Office, 1965.

————. *Myths and facts regarding older workers.* Washington, D.C.: U.S. Government Printing Office, 1971.

————. *Manpower report to the president.* Washington, D.C.: U.S. Government Printing Office, 1974.

————. *Manpower report to the president.* Washington, D.C.: U.S. Government Printing Office, 1975.

————. *Occupational information systems grants program: Standards and guidelines.* Washington, D.C.: Author, 1976.

————. *Dictionary of occupational titles* (4th ed.). Washington, D.C.: U.S. Government Printing Office, 1978. (a)

————. *Occupational outlook handbook.* Washington, D.C.: U.S. Government Printing Office, 1978. (b)

————. *The public employment service and help wanted ads: A bifocal view of the labor market* (R & D Monograph No. 59). Washington, D.C.: U.S. Government Printing Office, 1978. (c)

————. *Guide for occupational exploration.* Washington, D.C.: U.S. Government Printing Office, 1980. (a)

————. *Occupational mobility during 1977.* Special Labor Force Report No. 231. Washington, D.C.: Bureau of Labor Statistics, 1980. (b)

U.S. Department of Labor & U.S. Department of Health, Education and Welfare. *Employment and training report of the president.* Washington, D.C.: U.S. Government Printing Office, 1977.

————. *Employment and training report of the president.* Washington, D.C.: U.S. Government Printing Office, 1978.

————. *Employment and training report of the president.* Washington, D.C.: U.S. Government Printing Office, 1979.

U.S. Employment Service. *General aptitude test battery.* Washington, D.C.: Author, 1958.

U.S. General Accounting Office. *A compilation of federal laws and executive orders for non-discrimination and equal opportunity programs.* Washington, D.C.: U.S. General Accounting Office, 1978.

U.S. Office of Education. *An introduction to career education.* Washington, D.C.: U.S. Government Printing Office, 1975.

Valdry, W. W. *The delphi technique as one method to obtain consensus about the utilization of community resources in career education.* Unpublished doctoral dissertation, University of California, Los Angeles, Graduate School of Education, 1977.

Van Nostrand, S. *Generalized computer software for research in Army Officer Career Information and Planning System* (Working paper). Alexandria, Va.: U.S. Army Research Institute for the Behavioral and Social Sciences, 1979.

Varenhorst, B. B. Innovative tool for group counseling: The life career game. *The School Counselor*, 1968, *15*(5), 357–362.

Vaughan, S. *Raising self-esteem through cognitive counseling.* Unpublished doctoral dissertation, University of California, Los Angeles, Graduate School of Education, 1974.

Vaughan, S., & Healy, C. C. *A Cognitive Index of Self-esteem.* Unpublished test, University of California, Los Angeles, Graduate School of Education, 1974.

Vincenzi, H. Minimizing occupational stereotypes. *Vocational Guidance Quarterly*, 1977, *25*, 265–268.

Vivell, S. *Evaluation of a counseling program for teaching time management.* Unpublished M.A. thesis, University of California, Los Angeles, Graduate School of Education, 1972.

———. *An accountability model for research in counseling.* Unpublished Ph.D. dissertation, University of California, Los Angeles, Graduate School of Education, 1975.

Vocational Biographies. Sauk Centre, Minn.: Author, 1979.

Vocational Education Act of 1963, as amended. P. L. 90–576 as amended by P. L. 92–318, 91–230 and 93–380.

Vocational Education Act of 1976, as amended. P. L. 94–482.

The Vogues. Five o'clock world. In *Son of KRLA solid rocks.* (Vol. II) (album). Hollywood: Take 6 Enterprises, 1965.

Vriend, J. Vocational maturity ratings of inner-city high school seniors. *Journal of Counseling Psychology*, 1969, *16*, 377–384.

Wachowiak, D. G. Model reinforcement counseling with college males. *Journal of Counseling Psychology*, 1972, *19*, 387–392.

———. Personality correlates of vocational counseling outcome. *Journal of Counseling Psychology*, 1973, *20*, 567–568.

Wallace, W. G. Incremental effects of modeling and performance feedback in teaching decision-making counseling. *Journal of Counseling Psychology*, 1975, *22*, 570–572.

Wallis, R. T., & Gulkus. S. P. Reinforcers, values, and vocational maturity in adults. *Journal of Vocational Behavior*, 1974, *4*, 325–332. (a)

———. Reinforcers and vocational maturity in occupational aspiration, expectation, and goal deflection. *Journal of Vocational Behavior*, 1974, *5*, 381–390. (b)

Walsh, W. B., Horton, J. A., & Gaffey, R. L. Holland's theory and college degreed working men and women. *Journal of Vocational Behavior*, 1977, *10*, 180–186.

Walther, R. H. *Analysis and synthesis of D. O. L. experience in youth transition to work programs.* National Technical Information, Service No. PB 172435/AS. Springfield, Va., 1976.

Walz, G. Counseling adults for life transitions. Introductory remarks, American Personnel and Guidance Association Convention, Las Vegas, Nev., 1979.

Wagner Act (National Labor Relations Act of 1935) 49. Stat. 449, July 5, 1935.

Warnath, C. F. Vocational theories: Directions to nowhere. *Personnel and Guidance Journal,* 1975, *53,* 422–428.

Warner, R. D., Niland, T. M., & Maynard, P. E. Model reinforcement group counseling with elementary school children. *Elementary School Guidance and Counseling,* 1971, *5,* 248–255.

Warner, W. L., & Abegglen, J. *Occupational mobility in American business and industry.* Minneapolis: University of Minnesota Press, 1955.

Weber vs. *Kaiser Aluminum.* 443 U.S. 193 (1979).

Wegman, R. G. Job-search assistance. *Journal of Employment Counseling,* 1979, *16,* 197–228.

Weinberg, C. *Social foundations of educational guidance..* New York: Free Press, 1969.

Weiner, B. *Theories of motivation: From mechanism to cognition.* Chicago: Markham, 1972.

Wellington, J. A., & Olechowski, N. Attitudes toward the world of work in elementary school. *Vocational Guidance Quarterly,* 1966, *44,* 160–162.

Wesman, A. G. Testing and counseling: Fact and fancy. *Measurement and Evaluation in Guidance,* 1972, *5,* 397–402.

Westbrook, B. W. Items on career development tests which can be used to assess specific instructional objectives in the cognitive domain. Raleigh, N.C.: Unpublished paper, North Carolina State University, 1975.

———. *Career development needs of adults: How to improve career development programs.* Washington, D.C.: National Vocational Guidance Association, 1977.

Westbrook, B. W., & Parry-Hill, J. W. The measurement of cognitive vocational maturity. *Journal of Vocational Behavior,* 1973, *3,* 239–252.

Westbrook, F. D. A comparison of three methods of group vocational counseling. *Journal of Counseling Psychology,* 1974, *21,* 502–506.

Wheeler, C. L., & Carnes, E. F. Relationships among self-concepts, ideal self-concepts, and stereotypes of probable and ideal national choices. *Journal of Counseling Psychology,* 1968, *15,* 530–538.

White, R. W. *Lives in progress.* New York: Dryden, 1952.

———. *Lives in progress* (2nd ed.). New York: Harper & Row, 1966.

Whiteley, J. M. *Research in counseling: Evaluation and refocus.* Columbus, Ohio: Merrill, 1967.

Whitney, D. Predicting from expressed vocational choice: A review. *Personnel and Guidance Journal,* 1970, *48,* 279–286.

Wiggins, J. D. The relation of job satisfaction to preferences among teachers of the mentally retarded. *Journal of Vocational Behavior,* 1976, *8,* 13–18.

Wilkinson, E. G. *Construction and validation of instruments for diagnosing counseling needs.* Unpublished Ph.D. dissertation, University of California, Los Angeles, Graduate School of Education, 1979.

Williams, J. E. Changes in self and other perceptions following brief educational-vocational counseling. *Journal of Counseling Psychology,* 1962, *9,* 18–28.

Williams, J. E., & Hills, D. A. More on brief educational-vocational counseling. *Journal of Counseling Psychology,* 1962, *9,* 366–368.

Williamson, E. G. *How to counsel students: A manual of techniques for clinical counselors.* New York: McGraw-Hill, 1939.

———. *Counseling adolescents.* New York: McGraw-Hill, 1949.

Williamson, E. G., & Bordin, E. S. Evaluating counseling by means of a control-group experiment. *School and Society,* 1940, *52,* 434–440.

———. The evaluation of vocational education counseling: A critique of methodology of experiments. *Educational and Psychological Measurements,* 1941, *1,* 5–24.

Wilms, W. W. *The effectiveness of public and proprietary training.* Berkeley, Calif.: Center for Research and Development in Higher Education, 1974.

————. *Public and private vocational training: A study of effectiveness.* Lexington, Mass.: Lexington Books, 1975.

Wine, J. Test anxiety and direction of attention. *Psychological Bulletin,* 1971, *76,* 92–104.

Winn, C. W. (Ed.). *Careers in focus.* New York: McGraw-Hill, 1976.

Witkins, H. A., Moore, C. A., Goodenough, D. R., & Cox, P. W. Field-dependent and field independent cognitive styles and their educational implications. *Review of Educational Research,* 1977, *47,* 1–64.

Wittrock, M. C. Developmental processes in learning from instruction. *Journal of Genetic Psychology,* 1978, *132,* 37–54. (a)

————. The cognitive movement in instruction. *Educational Psychologist,* 1978, *13,* 15–29. (b)

Wittrock, M. C., Marks, C., & Doctorow, M. Reading as a genetic process. *Journal of Educational Psychology,* 1975, *76,* 484–489.

Wolf, R. E. Trial by jury: The process. *Phi Delta Kappan,* 1975, *57,* 185–188. (a)

————. Trial by jury: A new evaluation method. *Phi Delta Kappan,* 1975, *57,* 185–187. (b)

Wolfbein, S. L. *Occupational information: A career guidance view.* New York: Random House, 1968.

Wolpe, J. *The practice of behavior therapy.* New York: Pergamon, 1969.

Wonderlic, E. F. *Wonderlic personnel test manual.* Northfield, Ill.: Author, 1970.

Wood, R. A., Rogers, N., & Klinge, C. *Planning a career resource center.* Palo Alto, Calif.: American Institute for Research, 1979.

The World Publishing Co. *Webster's New World Dictionary* (College ed.). Cleveland and New York: Author, 1964.

Yabroff, W. Learning decision making. In J. D. Krumboltz & C. E. Thoresen. *Behavioral counseling: Cases and techniques.* New York: Holt, Rinehart & Winston, 1969.

Yankelovich, D. The new psychological contracts at work. *Psychology Today,* 1978, *11*(12), 46–50.

Yates, C., Johnson, N., & Johnson, J. Effects of the use of the vocational exploration group on career maturity. *Journal of Counseling Psychology,* 1979, *26,* 368–370.

Young, D. *Parent counseling and behavior change: A follow-up.* Unpublished master's thesis, University of California, Los Angeles, Graduate School of Education, 1972.

Young, R. A. The effects of value confrontation and reinforcement counseling on the career planning attitudes and behavior of adolescent males. *Journal of Vocational Behavior,* 1979, *15,* 1–11.

Zack, L., Horner, V., & Kaufman, J. Tutoring in a slum school. *Elementary School Journal,* 1969, *70,* 20–27.

Zadney, J. J., & James, L. F. A review of research on job placement. *Rehabilitation Counseling Bulletin,* 1977, *21,* 150–158.

Zenner, T. B., & Schnuelle, L. *An evaluation of the Self-Directed Search* Report 124. Baltimore, Md.: Johns Hopkins University, Center for Social Organization of Schools, 1972.

————. Effects of the Self-Directed Search on high school students. *Journal of Counseling Psychology,* 1976, *23,* 353–359.

Zinar, E. H. *Intervention procedures for classroom management using the guided inquiry mode and programmed materials: A consultant model.* Unpublished Ph.D. dissertation, University of California, Los Angeles, Graduate School of Education, 1975.

Zytowski, D. G. The effects of being interest-inventoried. *Journal of Vocational Behavior,* 1977, *11,* 153–157.

NAME INDEX

Abegglen, J., 14
Abramson, M., 565
Abrego, P., 589
Adams, J. M., 387
Alkin, M. C., 201
Allen, A. R., 284
Allen, G. J., 408–409
Allen, R. E., 382
Allport, G. W., 14, 28, 89–90, 509
Almquist, E. M., 103
Alpert, R., 396, 412
American College Testing
        Program, 93, 250, 418,
        428–429, 434
American Psychological Associa-
        tion, 200, 217
Anastasi, A., 33, 73, 77, 82, 430,
        580
Andersen, D. G., 269, 273, 278
Anderson, E. C., 60, 277, 460
Anderson, J. A., 392
Angrist, S. S., 103
Anton, W. D., 75, 408
Apostal, R. A., 354
Arbeiter, S., 485–487, 585
Arkowitz, H., 351
Arnold, S. J., 354
Arnstein, G.E., 224
Aslanian, C. B., 485–487, 585
Astin, A. W., 98–101
Astin, H. S., 533
Atanasoff, G. E., 356
Atkinson, R. C., 501
Atkinson, R. L., 501
Aubrey, R. F., 66, 104, 246, 271,
        290, 362, 589
Austin, B., 457, 461
Ausubel, D. P., 207
Axelrad, S., 21, 23, 245
Ayrin, N. H., 384

Bachman, J. B., 535
Backer, T. E., 100–101, 107
Bailey, L. J., 293
Bailey, M. L., 60
Baker, R. D., 176–177, 433
Bandura, A., 191
Bank, A., 276
Barahal, G. D., 457–459
Barbee, J. R., 388, 390–391

Barber, L. A., 270, 279–280
Barkhaus, R. S., 451
Bateman, T., 41, 124
Bates, G. L., 354
Bates, J. C., 176, 189, 317, 352,
        359, 502, 505
Baumann, R. R., 378–379
Beaumont, A. G., 380, 382, 390
Becker, W. C., 271
Bednar, R. L., 280
Belitsky, A. H., 151–152, 383
Bem, D. J., 101
Bem, S. L., 101
Bemis, S. E., 100
Benjamin, L., 590
Benson, G., 389
Bentler, P. M., 218
Berenson, B. G., 207–208
Berg, T., 130
Bergin, A. E., 96, 197, 229
Bergland, B. W., 269, 275, 309,
        345, 349–350
Betz, N. E., 338
Beyette, B., 97
Binet, A., 71
Bingham, R. P., 354
Bingham, W. C., 20, 104, 465
Birk, J. M., 267–268, 357
Birney, D., 508, 516, 518
Bishop, L. J., 340
Black, J. D., 457–459
Blaker, K. E., 272
Blau, F., 368, 481
Blau, P. M., 135, 289
Blocher, D. H., 109, 477, 530, 589
Bloom, S., 262, 265–266, 279
Bloss, N. P., 254
Blum, Z. D., 338
Bohn, M. J., 36, 102
Bolgard, C. W., 451
Bolles, R. N., 65, 107, 116, 228,
        383, 385, 532–533
Boocock, S., 322, 342
Bordin, E. S., 64, 209, 232,
        457–458
Bowen, D. B., 521
Brammer, L., 172, 457–459, 589
Bray, D. W., 22, 89, 92, 479, 580
Brayfield, A. H., 197
Brenner, M. H., 14

Brickell, H. M., 485–487, 585
Briggs, L. D., 300
Brim, O. G., 532
Brito, P. K., 481
Broadbent, L. A., 503, 505
Brock, T. C., 460
Brodine, K., 334–335
Bronfenbrenner, U., 227
Browne, J., 335
Bruner, J. S., 207, 351
Burck, H. D., 157, 192, 345
Burks, H. M., 176
Buros, O. K., 77, 82
Busby, L. J., 104
Byham, W. C., 580

Cairo, P. C., 524–528
Campbell, D. P., 30, 64, 83, 465
Campbell, R. E., 27
Campbell, R. J., 479
Canfield, J., 273
Carey, R., 347, 468, 498
Carkhuff, R. R., 60, 199, 207–208,
        221, 377, 557
Carlson, D., 224
Carlson, J., 253
Carnes, E. F., 20, 29
Carpenter, R., 336
Carr, T. J., 481
Castelnovo, A. E., 524
Catron, D. W., 346
Cattell, R. B., 90–91
Chapman, W., 160, 527
Chase, C. I., 74
Chasin, J., 389
Chang-Liang, R., 410
Cicourel, A., 50, 98
Claudy, J. G., 245, 297
Cloward, R., 270, 283
Clowers, M. R., 388
Cochran, D. J., 309–310
Cody, J. J., 347, 359
Cogan, F., 392
Cohen, B. M., 580
Cohen, M., 135
Colburn, E. D., 270, 278
Cole, N., 474
Cole, W. S., 125
Coleman, J. S., 49–50, 248, 289,
        371
College Entrance Examination
        Board, 36, 154
Cook, D., 376
Cook, F. S., 415
Cooley, E. J., 410
Cooley, W. W., 14, 245, 291, 297
Cooper, A. C., 380–382, 390

Cooper, J., 104
Cooper, J. F., 427
Corder-Bolz, C. R., 104
Cory, B. H., 524
Costar, J. W., 102
Cotton, C. C., 521
Counts, D. K., 410
Cox, P. W., 180
Cramer, S., 14, 270, 278, 293, 374
Crites, J. O., 14, 25, 28, 30, 35–36,
        38, 65, 71, 77, 82–85, 87,
        132, 154–155, 197, 226–
        227, 232, 245, 261, 305,
        317–318, 342, 353, 362,
        383, 430, 436, 463, 492,
        563
Cronbach, L. J., 70, 77, 81–82,
        180, 202, 210, 430
Crowden, P., 2
Culver, C., 276

Daane, C. J., 309
Dailey, J. T., 245, 297
Daley, M. M., 102
Daley, P. C., 412
Dalkey, N. C., 258
Danish, S. J., 457, 461
Darcy, R. L., 154
Darley, J. C., 416
Davis, F. B., 245, 297
Davis, J. A., 414
Davis, S. O., 103
Dawis, R. V., 25, 41, 78, 354
deCharms, R., 88
Deffenbacher, J. L., 397, 410–412
De Nisi, A., 362
Denney, D. R., 397, 409–410
Dennis, G., 334
De Vivo, E. H., 270, 279–280
Dewey, C. R., 427
Dewey, J., 31–32, 158
Diamond, E., 104
Dickson, W. J., 51, 561–562
Dinklage, L. B., 415
Dinkmeyer, D. C., 250, 253, 275
Doctorow, M., 180
Dolin, B., 537–539
Dolliver, R. H., 427
Donahue, T. J., 102
Doty, M. S., 338
Dreger, R. M., 413
Dreikurs, R., 276–277
Dressel, M. E., 391
Drucker, P. F., 582
Dubin, D., 25, 120, 132–133, 182,
        576
Dudley, G. A., 365

Duff, W. A., 502
Dugan, W. E., 109, 589
Duncan, O. D., 135, 289
Dunn, J. A., 244
Dunnette, M. D., 30
Dustin, E. R., 109, 589
Dylan, B., 335

Eckland, B. K., 367
Eden, D., 138
Educational Testing Service, 27, 74, 317
Edwards, A. L., 88–89, 350
Edwards, A. M., 131
Ellett, F. S., 70
Elias, L. J., 408
Ellis, A., 208, 377
Ellis, P., 270, 283
Ellson, D. G., 270, 279–280
Enderlein, T. E., 298
Endler, N. S., 412
Engelhard, P. A., 103
Engelkes, J. R., 176, 392
England, G. W., 78
Englander, M. A., 465
Eriksen, C. W., 396
Erikson, E. H., 59, 244, 365, 368, 477, 530
Euler, D. E., 342
Evans, J. R., 347, 359, 457, 462
Ewart, C. K., 4, 5

Fabry, J. J., 354
Farmer, H. S., 100–102, 107, 176, 495, 502, 504
Feldhusen, J., 274
Feldman, K. A., 95
Festinger, L., 183
Fiedler, F. E., 207
Fielding, J., 382
Fielding, M., 382
Figler, H. E., 385
Fine, S. A., 194, 358, 540
Fineman, K., 276
Finger, R., 411
Fischer, T. J., 345
Fiske, D., 5
Fitzpatrick, J., 110
Flake, M. H., 352, 463
Flanagan, J. C., 29, 245, 297–298, 433, 513, 519, 586
Flanders, N., 271
Flores, T., 392–393
Fogel, A. J., 347, 359, 433, 457, 463
Forgy, E. W., 457–459
Form, W. H., 135

Forney, D. S., 387
Frager, S. R., 284
Fraser, R. F., 388, 521
Fretz, B. R., 472
Friedersdorf, N. A., 102
Froelich, C. P., 418, 421
Frost, R., 334, 335

Gaffey, R. L., 354
Gagné, R. M., 351, 374
Galassi, J. P., 411
Gallup, G. H., 23
Garbin, A. P., 27
Gazda, G. M., 272
Gelatt, H. B., 346–347, 469, 498
Gensler, S. A., 461
Ghiselli, E. E., 28, 72, 76, 352, 389, 580
Gilmore, S. K., 351
Ginsburg, S. W., 4, 23, 244
Ginzberg, E., 4, 22–23, 244–245, 386
Glaser, B. G., 10, 44
Glass, G. V., 96
Gohman, G., 391
Goldberg, I., 245, 297
Goldberg, L. R., 4
Goldberg, P., 105
Goldfried, M. R., 397, 409
Goldman, L., 28, 64, 77, 224, 337, 421, 423–424, 430, 473–474, 520, 557
Goldman, P. R., 102
Goodenough, D. R., 180
Goodwin, W., 160, 527
Gorush, R. L., 413
Gotkin, E. H., 14, 22, 71, 87, 97, 137, 191, 245, 365, 586
Gottfredson G. D., 41, 124, 354, 357, 531
Gough, H., 347
Gould, R., 477, 530, 537, 559
Graff, R. W., 457, 461, 467
Granovetter, M. S., 382
Grant, D. L., 89, 92, 479, 580
Grasso, J. T., 360, 368, 482
Gray-Shellberg, L., 101
Greeley, A. M., 85
Green, G. L., 300
Green, M., 114
Gribbons, W. D., 35, 137, 191, 245, 269, 273, 285, 360, 362, 365, 586
Grinnell, R. M., 393
Gross, N., 43, 51
Guilford, J. P., 70, 73, 91
Gulkus, S. P., 492

Gupta, W., 155
Gutteridge, T. G., 394

Haber, R. N., 396, 412
Hagburg, E. G., 153
Hagen, E., 64, 72, 76, 261, 389
Hahn, M. E., 418, 421
Haldane, B., 527
Hall, C. S., 67
Hall, D. T., 20–21, 33, 373, 472, 521
Haller, A. O., 279
Hamdani, A., 359, 362, 364, 577
Hamilton, J. A., 344, 347
Hanau, C., 357
Hansen, J. C., 269, 275, 469
Hansen, L. S., 243, 293, 300, 341
Hanson, G. R., 355, 474
Hanson, J. T., 457, 469
Hanson, M. C., 521
Harmin, M., 374
Harmon, L. W., 353
Harren, V. A., 33, 345–346, 462, 519
Harris, P. L., 270, 279–280
Harris, S., 278
Harvey, D. W., 354
Hassinger, J., 270, 279, 283
Hatch, R. N., 374
Havighurst, R. J., 244, 365, 477, 530
Hawkins, R. L., 176
Hawley, P., 102
Hay, N. M., 347
Healy, C. C., 20, 29, 36, 60, 79, 97, 137, 154–155, 158, 160, 215–216, 221, 252, 254, 316–317, 321, 334, 359, 361, 442–446, 457, 462, 465–467, 577, 590
Hedges, J. N., 100
Heilburn, A. B., Jr., 346
Heimann, R. A., 269, 273, 278
Heller, F. A., 33
Hendel, D. D., 104
Hennig, M., 27, 98, 104–105, 537
Herma, J. L., 4, 23, 244
Herr, E. L., 18, 293, 298, 342, 359, 374
Hewer, V. H., 28, 190, 447, 455, 470, 472
Heyde, M. B., 294–296, 360
Hicks, J. M., 524
Hilgard, E. R., 501
Hill, A. W., 521
Hills, D. A., 460
Hilton, T. E., 33

Hinkle, J. E., 508, 516, 518
Hobbs, W. S., 387
Hoenninger, R. W., 518
Hoffer, G. L., 524
Hoffman, S. D., 309–310
Hoffnung, J. J., 375
Holland, J. L., 14, 29, 65, 83, 92–95, 121, 124–126, 155, 193, 337–341, 348, 354–358, 436, 439, 515, 582
Hollandsworth, J. G., 391, 393
Hollingshead, A. B., 96
Holmes, T. H., 228
Holyroyd, K. A., 410
Hoppock, R., 156–157
Horner, M., 102
Horner, V., 282
Horowitz, C., 276, 495, 502, 504
Horst, P., 424
Horton, J. A., 354
Hosford, R. E., 170
House, E. W., 104
Houtz, J., 274
Howard, A., 580
Howe, L. W., 87
Hoyt, D. P., 461
Hoyt, K. B., 85, 157, 162, 188, 195, 243, 418, 421, 577
Hubbard, W. D. 41, 124
Huck, J. R., 580
Hughes, H. M., 354
Hummel, D. L., 62
Hummel, R. C., 14, 245
Hunt, J. McV., 73
Hunt, R. A., 465
Hutchinson, T., 41, 124

Interpretative Scoring Systems, 452–453
Isaacson, L. E., 121, 157
Ivey, A., 390, 557

James, L. F., 394
Jameson, R., 50, 108, 536, 564–565
Janis, I., 56–57
Jardim, A., 27, 98, 104–105, 537
Jenkins, W. O., 376, 380
Jensen, A. R., 108
Jepsen, D. A., 298
Jessee, B. E., 269, 273, 278
Jocklin, C., 101
Johnson, J., 350
Johnson, N., 350
Johnson, R., 508, 512, 516
Johnson, R. C., 481
Johnson, R. H., 176, 236, 342, 347, 350, 359, 498, 506

Johnston, J., 535
Jones, B. W., 391
Jones, J., 517
Jones, K. O., 103
Jordaan, J. P., 35–36, 261, 391,
    294–296, 317, 348, 360–
    363, 468, 478, 530
Jusenius, C. L., 368, 481

Kaplan, R. M., 392–393, 411
Karweit, N. L., 338
Katz, M. R., 32, 160, 294, 527
Katzell, R. A., 46, 98, 132
Kaufman, J., 282
Kaufman, M. A., 387
Kaye, B. L., 509, 537–539
Keil, E. C., 388, 390–391
Keith, R. D., 392
Kellogg, M. S., 521
Kelly, D., 335
Kelly, E. L., 5
Kelly, G. A., 31, 65, 472
Kerlin, B. D., 354
Kirn, A., 516
Kirshenbaum, H., 87
Kitsuse, J., 50, 98
Kivlighan, D. M., 588
Klaurens, M. K., 293
Klein, S., 5, 36, 317, 344, 365
Klinge, C., 157
Klopfer, W. G., 91
Knowdell R. L., 553
Knowles, M. S., 288, 554
Knox, A. B., 67
Kohen, A. I., 360, 482
Korman, A. K., 20, 60, 66, 88, 479
Kornreich, M., 237
Kosier, M. W., 350
Kourilsky M. L., 150, 154, 224, 322
Kowalski, E. S., 14, 71, 87, 97, 137,
    191, 245, 365, 586
Krivatsy, S. E., 356, 457, 461
Kroll, A. M., 415
Krumboltz, J. D., 40, 61, 176–177,
    197, 206, 211, 219, 305,
    322, 344–347, 359, 419,
    433, 451, 461–462, 585
Kuder, F., 342, 350
Kudo, E. I., 293
Kukic, M. B., 186
Kuo, H., 388
Kuzniar, J., 276

Lacey, D., 354
Lanham, F. W., 415
Lasson, K., 2

Lawler, E. E., 25, 414, 485
Lee, J., 415
Lee, W. J., 293
Leonard, G. E., 322
Levine, M., 223–224
Levine, M. J., 153
Levinson, D., 31, 477–478, 530,
    537
Levitin, T., 138
Liebert, R. M., 396, 411, 413
Lieberman, A., 393
Lillard, D., 376
Lin, T., 503, 505
Lindeman, R. H., 36, 261, 348, 363
Lindzey, G., 67
Lipman-Blumen, J., 102
Lofquist, L. H., 23, 41, 78, 354
Logue, P., 391
Lohnes, P. R., 14, 35, 137, 191,
    245, 269, 273, 285, 291,
    294, 296–297, 360, 362,
    365, 586
Long, L. A., 119
Loughary, J. W., 385
Lovejoy, C. E., 157
Lundquist, G. W., 308, 345, 349–
    350
Lushene, R. E., 413

Maccoby, E. E., 101
Mackin, E. F., 85, 577
Maclean, C. G., 463
Macpherson, D. H., 524
Mager, R. F., 200
Magoon, T., 29, 162, 193, 356, 423,
    455, 457, 461, 515, 517
Mahoney J., 40
Mangrum, G. L., 85, 577
Manis, L. G., 517–518, 520
Marchant, W. C., 277
Marcon, R. A., 252, 269, 273
Markert, L. F., 333–336, 343
Marks, C., 180
Marland, S. P., 365
Marsden, G., 208, 221
Marshall, G. J., 410
Maslow, A. A., 88
Mason, W., 43, 51
Masters, J. C., 408
Mathews, D. F., 102, 354
Mathis, H., 397, 411–412
Matlin, N. A., 465
Matross, R. P., 217
Matulef, N. J., 460
Maynard, P. E., 274, 285
McCann, G., 276
McCleary, E. K., 270, 279, 281

McClelland, D. C., 88, 151, 552–553, 579
McClure, D., 392
McCordick, S. M., 392–393, 411
McCoy, J. F., 354
McEachern, A. W., 43, 51
McGovern, K. B., 311, 351
McGovern, T. V., 391
McGowan, D., 356
McGreggor, D., 46
McHolland, J. D., 517–518
McKay, C., 355
McKersie, R., 382
McKinley, B., 161
McLaughlin, D. H., 29, 64, 341, 433, 577
McLaurin, R. A., 263, 271, 279, 281
McLean, M. S., 418
McMillan, F. R., 101
McMillan, J. R., 401–402, 406
Medland, F. F., 524
Meichenbaum, D. H., 65, 282, 397–398, 406–409
Melnick, J., 410
Meltzoff, J., 237
Meyer, H. E., 565
Meyer, J., 342, 364
Michaels, A. C., 397, 411–412
Michaels, T., 412
Miller, C. G., 14, 75, 96, 370
Miller, D. C., 135
Miller, F. W., 459
Miller, G. P., 347
Miller, J. V., 104, 246, 271, 589
Miller, M. M., 104
Miller-Tiedeman, A., 363, 415
Mills, R. B., 375
Minor, F., 160
Mirov, S. S., 457, 467
Mischel, W., 28
Mitchell, A. M., 66, 104, 241, 290, 362, 366, 369–370, 589
Mitchell, J., 336
Mitchell, K. R., 280
Mochizuki, J., 517–518, 520
Mooney, W. L., 392
Moore, S. F., 180
Moore, W. E., 153
Morgan, J. L., 510
Morin, W. J., 564–565
Morley, E. D., 415, 535
Morrill, W., 163, 192
Morris, L. W., 396, 411, 413
Morris, S. E., 391
Morrison, R. F., 354
Morrison, R. L., 276, 465

Moser, H. P., 14, 245
Moses, J. L., 580
Mott, F. L., 481
Mount, M. K., 354
Muchinsky, P. M., 354, 580
Murray, H. A., 51–52, 88
Murray, R. E., 349
Myers, R. A., 64, 160, 261, 317, 322, 336, 348, 362, 468, 477, 521, 524–528
Myers, S. C., 360, 368, 482
Myrick, R., 347, 350, 359

Nachmann, B., 53, 88, 95
Nader, R., 114
Nafziger, D. H., 354
National Commission on Working Women, 148
Neal, F., 389
Neely, M. A., 350
Nelson, H. Y., 101
Nestel, G., 368, 481
Newcomb, T. M., 95
Neyman, C. A., Jr., 245, 297
Nicholson, J. A., 518
Niedermeyer, F. C., 270, 283
Niland, T. M., 274, 285
Noeth, R. J., 298, 358, 369, 588
Nolan, J. J., 356, 457, 462
Nord, W. R., 132
Norris, W., 374

Obinna, E. S., 107
O'Brien, W. F., 354
O'Bryant, S. L., 104
O'Connell, T. J., 353
Odbert, H. S., 90
Oden, M. H., 60, 479, 533
Oetting, E., 14, 75, 96, 370
Ogilvie, V. N., 457, 466
Ogle, M. G., 503, 505
O'Hara, R. P., 33, 85, 285, 362
Ohlendorf, G. W., 279
Okland, T., 284
Olechowski, N., 156
Oliver, L. W., 474
O'Malley, P. M., 535
O'Neil, J. M., 357
O'Reilly, R. H., 503, 505
Orr, D. B., 245, 297
Osipow, S. H., 87–89, 245, 253, 587
Osterhouse, R. A., 401, 406
O'Toole, J., 4, 5, 15, 23, 115, 130, 194, 373–374, 535, 570–571
Otte, F. L., 274
Otto, H. A., 509, 517–518
Overstreet, P. L., 14, 191, 245, 586
Owens, W. A., 580

Pace, C. R., 95
Palmo, A. J., 276
Paritzky, J., 517
Parker, H. J., 354
Parnes, H., 341, 368
Parry-Hill, J. W., 298
Parsons, F., 29, 64, 174, 416
Paterson, D. G., 416, 418
Patterson, C. H., 213
Paul, G. L., 398–401, 403, 406, 408
Pearson, H. G., 552
Pendleton, L. R., 352
Pepinsky, H. B., 421
Pepinsky, P. N., 421
Perry, W. G., 33, 365
Peter, L. J., 10, 182
Petko, C. M., 376, 380
Pfeiffer, W., 517
Phelps, A. T., 311–316, 351, 359, 502
Phillips, L. L., 105, 531, 533
Phillips, S. D., 524
Piaget, J., 228
Piatowska, O. E., 280
Pietrofesa, J. J., 95, 102
Penson, N. M., 85, 577
Platt, J. M., 277
Popham, W. J., 224
Prediger, D. J., 298, 355, 358, 378–379, 473, 589
Price, G. E., 357
Prince, H. J., 410
Psychological Corporation, 29, 431, 450
Puckett, S. P., 410
Pumo, B., 392
Putnam, B. A., 269, 275, 469

Quantrano, L. A., 269, 275, 345
Quinn, J. B., 157–158, 160, 254, 502–503, 505
Quinn, R. R., 138
Quirck, J., 514, 518

Rabin, M., 267–268, 343
Rahe, R. H., 228
Rasmussen, R., 276
Raths, L. E., 374
Reardon, R. C., 157, 192, 345
Redmond, R. E., 355
Reese, B., 104
Renwick, P. A., 411, 485
Reubens, B. G., 390
Richards, J. M., Jr., 125, 245
Riesman, D., 182
Rimm, D. C., 408
Ringenbach, S., 274

Ripley, T. M., 385
Roach, A. J., 352, 462
Robinson, F., 280
Roe, A., 41, 89, 121–125, 436
Roeber, E. C., 259
Roessler, R., 376
Roethlisberger, F. J., 51, 561–562
Rogers, C. R., 60, 171, 207, 554–556
Rogers, N., 157
Rohen, T. M., 349
Rosse, P., 83
Roth, J. D., 369, 589
Rothman, J., 190
Rotter, J. B., 348
Rounds, J. B., 354
Ruble, T., 276
Rupert, P. A., 409
Russell, R. K., 397, 410
Ryan, T. A., 41, 215, 293, 322–333, 341, 359, 420, 425–426, 461

Salaney, R. B., 354
Salomone, P. R., 354
Sandell, S. H., 461, 481
Sander, D. L., 457, 469
Sandifer, B. A., 393
Sano, J., 272
Sarason, E. K., 4
Sarason, I. G., 396
Sarason, S. B., 4, 412, 577, 579
Schaffer, K., 89
Schager, C. R., 245
Scheele, A. M., 537–539, 544
Schein, E. H., 45–48, 539
Schlossberg, N., 102
Schmerbeck, F. A., 485–487, 585
Schneidler, G. G., 416
Schnuelle, L., 83, 336, 355, 582
Schroeder, W. W., 334
Schudt, D. L., 421
Schwartz, S., 335
Schwarz, A., 135
Scoggins, W., 153
Scott, A., 98
Scott, J., 267–268, 343
Scriven, M., 202
Sears, R. R., 14, 22, 83, 533
Security Pacific National Bank, 541–548, 551
Sedlacek, W. E., 353
Segal, S. J., 53, 88–89, 95
Sehl, R., 392
Seligman, J., 114
Setne, V. L., 517
Sewell W. H., 279

Shannon, D. J., 406
Shapiro, B., 384
Shapiro, D., 481
Sharpe, D. L., 274
Shartle, C. L., 75
Shaw, T., 335, 362
Shaycoft, M. F., 245, 297
Sheehy, G., 27, 194, 537
Shelton, J. L., 352, 410
Sheppard, D., 492
Sheppard, H. L., 151–152, 383
Shertzer, B., 259, 588
Sherwood, J. J., 65, 79, 234
Shields, P. M., 360, 368, 482
Shiner, E. V., 465
Shirts, R. G., 262
Shoben, J. E., 306
Shortledge, R. L., 368, 481,
    517–518
Shostrom, E. L., 459
Shubsachs, A. P., 354
Shudt, D. L., 354
Silberman, H. F., 371, 373
Simon, S. B., 87, 374
Simon, T., 71
Sinick, D., 534–535, 554
Sklare, A. R., 258
Skovholt, T. M., 510, 518
Slaney, R. B., 354, 356
Smith, G. E., 259
Smith, M. L., 96, 102
Smith, R. D., 347, 359, 457, 462
Smith, R. R., 376, 380
Snapp, M. I., 284
Snodgrass, G., 214, 221, 347, 433,
    462, 590
Snow, R. E., 180, 210
Solamon, M., 333
Solmon, L., 104, 333, 415, 488–
    491
Sorenson, A. G., 32, 175–176, 189,
    202, 493–506
Sparta, S. N., 270, 279, 282, 466
Spearman, C., 71
Speas, C. M., 391
Spiegler, M. D., 410
Spielberger, C. D., 413
Splete, H. H., 95, 258, 277
Sprague, D. G., 447, 455, 469
Springstein, B., 334
Squires, G. D., 396
Stadt, R. W., 293
Stahmann, R. F., 354
Stanley, J. C., 376
Starishevsky, R., 465
Stenning, W. F., 352, 363
Stephens, C., 334

Stephens, D. B., 387
Stephens, E., 322
Stephens, R. R., 465
Stern, G. C., 95
Stevens, J., 391, 393
Stevens, R., 546
Stewart, N., 70, 76
Stewart, N. R., 102, 176, 193, 419
Stiggins, R. J., 103
Stockhard, R. H., 380, 382, 390
Stone, R. A., 101
Stone, S. C., 259, 589
Stratoudakis, J. P., 397, 410
Strong, D. J., 447, 455, 469
Strong, E. K., Jr., 14, 29, 83, 124,
    350
Strong, S. R., 217
Suinn, R. M., 397, 412
Sullivan, H. S., 217, 418
Sullivan Associates, 281–282
Super, D. E., 5, 7–9, 14–16, 20,
    22–23, 35–37, 60, 71,
    82–84, 97, 99, 121, 135–
    137, 160, 191–193, 227,
    261, 273, 285, 293–294,
    317, 348, 362–363, 365,
    373, 414, 430, 436, 465,
    468, 472, 475, 478–480,
    492, 529–530
Swails, R. G., 342, 359
Systems Research Incorporated,
    301–303
Szabo, E. M., 166, 466

Takai, R., 357
Talbot, D. B., 357
Tanney, M. F., 104, 267–268
Taulbee, E. W., 91
Taylor, J., 334
Tennyson, W. W., 293
Terkel, S., 4, 27, 194
Thomas, A. H., 102
Thomas, L. E., 508, 516, 518
Thompson, A. S., 36, 158, 261,
    317, 348, 363, 468, 492
Thomson, G., 91
Thoresen, C. E., 5, 40, 61, 206–
    207, 211, 305, 344–347,
    359, 463
Thorndike, R. L., 64, 70, 72, 76,
    97, 261, 389
Thoroman, E. C., 554
Thurstone, L. L., 72
Tichenor, J. M., 516, 518
Tiedeman, D. V., 2, 29, 33, 64,
    102, 285, 362–363, 365,
    415

Tinsley, H., 391
Toffler, A., 120, 570
Tolbert, E. L., 196, 219
Torrance, E. P., 73
Torrez, D. S., 350
Touchton, J. G., 515
Townsend, B., 552
Tracey, T. J., 357
Truax, C. B., 207, 557
Trueblood, R. W., 517–518
Tryon, G. S., 408–409
Tuddenham, R. D., 73
Tuttle, M. L., 580
Twitchell, M., 392–393, 411
Tyler, L. E., 14, 104, 155, 174–
176, 217, 228, 418, 427

Uhlaner, J. E., 524
Ullman, J. C., 380, 394
U. S. Department of Commerce, 97
U. S. Department of Labor, 29, 58,
69–70, 94, 108, 139–149,
154, 235, 261, 307, 381,
415, 435
U. S. Office of Education, 155

Valdry, W. W., 361
Van Nostrand, S., 524
Varenhorst, B. B., 206, 342, 345,
347, 469, 498
Vaughan, S., 251, 269, 359
Via, M., 270, 279, 283
Viernstein, M. C., 338
Villareal, S., 101
Vincenzi, H., 278
Vivell, S., 223, 317, 352, 502, 505
Vocational Biographies, 145
The Vogues, 334
Vriend, J., 298

Wachowiak, D. G., 345–346
Wallis, R. T., 492
Walsh, W. B., 357
Walther, R. H., 379–380
Walz, G., 259, 532, 554, 584, 590
Warman, R. E., 460
Warnath, C. F., 56, 134, 245
Warner, R. D., 274, 285
Warner, R. W., Jr., 376, 380
Warner, W. L., 14
Watt, J. T., 387
Wegman, R. G., 393, 394
Weinberg, C., 48
Weinberg, S. L., 280
Weiner, B., 65, 351
Weldon, J. I., 524

Wellington, J. A., 156
Wells, H., 273
Wesman, A. G., 474
Westbrook, B. W., 66, 298, 360,
484, 589
Westbrook, F. W., 469
Wheeler, C. L., 20, 29
Wheeler, D., 56–57
Whinfield, R. W., 354
White, R. W., 28, 89, 351
Whiteley, J. M., 197
Whitney, D., 83, 125, 515
Wiggins, J. D., 354
Wilkinson, E. G., 105
Will, J. A., 427
Williams, F. C., 284
Williams, J. E., 460
Williamson, E. G., 29–30, 64, 175,
208–209, 211, 217, 232,
416, 418–427, 433, 457–
458, 470
Willis, M. B., 433
Wilms, W. W., 56, 415
Wilson, S. E., 352, 415
Winborn, B. B., 392
Wine, J., 411
Winn, C. W., 145
Wise, P. S., 270, 278, 397, 410
Wisenbaker, J. M., 367
Witkins, H. A., 180
Wittrock, M. C., 180
Wolf, R. E., 224
Wolfbein, S. L., 119
Wolpe, J., 408
Wonderlic, E. F., 409
Wood, R. A., 157
Woodward, J. A., 218

Yabroff, W., 56
Yankelovich, D., 46, 83, 98, 115,
132, 138
Yates, C., 350
Yates, L. G., 524
Young, D., 276
Young, R. A., 347

Zack, L., 282
Zadney, J. J., 394
Zelkowitz, R. S., 492
Zenner, M., 391
Zenner, T. B., 83, 336, 355, 582
Zeran, F. R., 374
Zinar, E. H., 276, 495, 502, 504
Zlotlow, S. F., 408–409
Zytowski, D. G., 83, 336, 353, 359,
582

SUBJECT INDEX

Ability, 66–78, 540, 545
American Personnel and Guidance Association (APGA), 137, 197, 201, 236
American Psychological Association, (APA), 197, 200, 217, 236
Aptitude, 68–70
Assessment center, 92, 579–580
Assessment of Career Development, 154, 250, 595

Career
  and compromise, 4, 23, 497
  definition of, 5–6, 8, 13, 25–26
  effects on person, 14–26
  forces shaping, 9–12, 44–47
  interdependence, 25–26
  ladders, 134
  and organizations, 10, 45–46
  patterns, 134–135
  and satisfaction, 4, 20–25, 130
  as self-expression, 19–20, 22–23, 406
  and social class, 7, 10, 50
Career Assessment Inventory, 81
Career choice style, 498, 506
Career counseling (*see also* Counseling)
  contrasted with career and vocational education, 194–196
  definition, 173–174
  for employees, 520–528, 561–563, 576–577
  group, 192–193, 406
  hazards of, 284–286, 361–364, 394–396, 473–474, 506, 519–520, 528, 553–554, 563–564, 570
  as individualization, 175, 189–190
  logical basis of, 214, 580–582
  models' suggestions for, 29–30, 33–34, 38, 41, 51–52, 54, 56–57, 61–62
  as response to discrimination, 106, 111
  stages of, 175–189

Career counseling procedures
  assessor, 259–262, 278
  check-up, 321
  cognitive anxiety reduction, 406–412
  consulting, 253–259, 269, 275–277
  coordination, 299–305, 340–341
  countering stereotypes, 266–269, 340–341
  desensitization, 398–406, 408–409
  discovery groups, 506–520
  guided inquiry, 493–506
  human potential, 509, 513–514, 517
  life planning, 508–514, 516–517
  Officer Career Information and Planning System, 524–528, 599–608
  outplacement, 565–570
  personnel, 520–528
  placement, 380–394
  reinforcement-modeling, 207, 306–309, 344–349
  rule learning, 311–317, 351–352
  Security Pacific workshop, 538–553
  self-awareness, 247–253, 269–275
  Self-Directed Search, 336–339, 353–358, 462, 473, 518
  self-exploratory cognitive, 554–564
  simulation case study, 322–333, 342–343
  special projects, 262–270, 279–284
  teach the test, 317–321, 352–353
  trait factor, 418–436, 459–465
  translation, 437–447, 465–468
  tutoring, 262–266, 279–284
  values clarification via literature, 333–336, 343–344
  vocational choice case study, 446–456, 468–470
  vocational exploration group, 309–311, 349–350
  work experience, 374–380

Career decision making process, 33, 414–416

Career development
and curriculum, 18, 418
definition of, 14–18, 51–53
models, 35–38
stages of, 14–17
tasks of, 243–244, 291–293, 365, 475–479, 530–536
tests, 595–597

Career Development Inventory, 317, 348, 359, 466, 468, 492, 595

Career Development Study, 295–297

Career education, 18, 157–160, 188, 195–196, 243–244, 246, 248, 576–577

Career information
computer in, 159–160
different strengths, 318–320
dissemination, 156–161
essential facts, 145, 154–156, 426–428
example of a firm's structure, 547–548
for adults, 161–162
human models' suggestions for, 29, 33–34, 36–37, 41, 48–49, 52–55
tests of, 595–597

Career Maturity Inventory (CMI), 154–155, 210, 275, 342, 351, 359, 462, 467, 470, 492, 563, 596

Career Pattern Study, 294–296, 360, 414, 478–480

Career Planning Program, 93, 428–429, 434–436, 474

Career Skills Assessment Program, 81, 596

Client beliefs, 178–179, 560

Client prerequisites, 416–417, 506–508, 493, 521–523, 555

Client reaction typology, 212–213

Comprehensive Employment and Training Act (CETA), 138–143, 234, 236–237, 371

Counseling (*see also* Career counseling)
as teaching, 208–209, 585
content, 189–190, 211–216
contract, 168
cost-benefit of, 584–585
definition of, 166–169
exclusiveness in, 195, 582–583

general techniques, 170–175
implementation of, 589–590
potency of, 192–193
replication of, 210–217
rules of, 212, 213

Counselor, 165, 580

Delphi techniques, 259, 361

Diagnosis, 170–171, 175–185, 208–211

Dictionary of Occupational Titles, 30, 68–70, 93–94, 145–146

Disadvantaged, 283–284, 370, 375, 392–394

Effective Problem Solving, 29, 422, 461

Employment and Training Report of the President, 137, 148–150, 381

Evaluation, 198–206
as a counseling stage, 189
as a counseling technique, 170–171
danger of neglecting, 584
formative, 201–206
summative, 200–204

Fantasy, 245, 515–518

General Aptitude Test Battery, 68–70, 451, 462

Goal impediments, 181–185

Goal setting, 177–178, 494–495, 515, 527, 559

Handicapped, 377, 392

Heuristic principles
definition of, 190–192
for client use, 249, 311–312, 388, 544–545
of counseling procedures, 248–249, 255–261, 262–263, 267, 306, 322, 333, 336, 373–375, 382–384, 398, 417–419, 493–494, 508, 522–523, 538, 554, 565–566

Holland, J. L., career theory of, 29, 83–84, 93, 124

Income, 97, 100

Industry, 8, 118, 133–135

Intelligence, 70–75

Interests, 79–84

Internal locus of control, 516

Inventory, 80–82, 87, 90
  interest, 80–82
  personality, 90

Job redesign, 46, 51, 132, 197–
    198, 537
Job search, 150–152, 383–384,
    392–394, 568–569
Judicial decisions, 72, 107, 183

*Kuder Occupational Interest
    Survey*, 353, 359, 451
Kuder Preference Inventory, 80–
    81, 325, 342

Labor force, 118, 125–127, 150
Labor market, 150
Labor union, 116, 152–154, 564
Legislation, 18, 100, 106–107, 149,
    153, 194, 235, 243, 287
Leisure, 8, 368

Manpower programs, 137–144
Manpower Report to President,
    115, 137, 383
Minorities, 107–111

*National Assessment of Career and
    Occupational Development*,
    66, 246–247, 366–367,
    484–485
Needs, 40, 51–52
Network, 108, 187–188, 382–383,
    416
*New Mexico Career Education
    Test Series*, 154, 269, 344,
    596

Occupation
  definition of, 8, 13, 121
  and differential adjustment,
    486–490
  distribution by gender/race/
    level, 105, 108, 131
  environment/field, 121, 125–126
  forces affecting, 117–121
  level, 121–122, 125–127
  supply-demand, 136–137
  training for, 126–130
Occupational classification, 121–
    125
Occupational Outlook Handbook,
    144, 146–148, 162, 273
Officer Career Information and
    Planning System, 524–528,
    599–608
Ohio Vocational Interest Survey, 81

Omnibus Personality Inventory,
    448, 451
Outcome measurement
  by composite, 232–234
  considerations in, 226–234
  by essay, 460
  for establishment, 505, 518
  for exploration, 359–361
  for growth, 269–272
  immediate, 472
  intermediate, 472
  for maintenance, 536, 563
  for transition between explora-
    tion and establishment,
    457, 470–472

Personal Preference Schedule, 41,
    88, 90, 350
Personal Orientation Inventory,
    516–518
Personality, 89–96
  behavioral view, 39
  developmental view, 34–39
  economic view, 54–58
  intelligent/rational/scientific
    view, 31–34
  psychodynamic view, 51–54
  trait factor view, 28–31
Placement services, 380–382
Planning (*see also* Problem
    solving)
  career direction, 471–472
  guide sheets, 422, 497, 542–543,
    551
  paradigms, 433, 442
  principles of, 417–418
  for problem solving, 495–499
Problem solving (*see also*
    Planning)
  in consulting, 256–259
  general counseling techniques,
    173
  by guided inquiry, 493–500
  guides from past successes, 514
  principles of, 493, 417–418
  steps in, 252, 443
  visual aids for, 57, 551
Professional organization, 152–154
Project Talent, 14, 285, 297–298,
    432

"Q" sort, 346, 460, 519

Readiness for Vocational Planning,
    269, 273, 297–298
Rehabilitation counselor, 146–147
Replication of counseling, 206–216

Research
    deficiencies in, 320–321
    definition of, 198–199
    designs, 222–226
    difficulties in counseling, 221–
        235
    Federal efforts, 578–579
    formulating questions, 197–198
    priorities in, 464–465, 468, 586–
        589
    role of counselor, 197–198
    role of profession, 235–237
Role
    clarification, 51
    definition, 8, 43
    for counselor, 242, 288–289,
        365, 415, 476
    of adolescents, 289–290
    play, 499–500

Self-concept
    and acceptance/self-esteem,
        20–21, 60, 388
    accuracy of, 65, 78–79, 111–
        112, 247–248, 318–320, 362
    agreement of measures, 65
    and career, 11–12, 19–20
    computer exercise for, 527
    definition of, 19–20
    from multiple perspectives,
        58–60
    principles for creating/discover-
        ing, 248–249, 508, 554–555
    rating, 78, 234
    rethinking, 377
    and Self-Observational Gen-
        eralizations (SOGs), 40
Self-Directed Search, 29, 336–339,
    353–358, 462, 473, 518,
    581
Sex, 100–107
Sixteen Personality Factors, 91
Socioeconomic status, 7, 50–51,
    96–99
Strong-Campbell Interest Inven-
    tory, 31, 66, 81, 93, 350,
    353, 447–448, 451–453
Strong Vocational Interest Blank,
    80, 124, 451, 462, 466
Study skills counseling, 280
Super, D. E., theory of, 15–18, 37
System of Interactive Guidance

and Instruction (SIGI), 30,
    32, 58, 160

Test anxiety measures, 412–413
Tests
    ability, 76–77
    and anxiety, 396–398, 412–413
    career maturity, 36, 234, 492,
        595–597
    computer interpretation, 434–
        436
    criterion referenced, 77, 432
    improving scores on, 74
    interpretation of, 421–428, 448–
        451, 453
    norm-referenced, 432
    personality, 92
    presentation of results, 425–
        429, 451–454
    projective, 91–92
    sample/sign, 77, 432
Training programs, 127–129
Trait factor
    counseling, 418–436, 459–465
    theory, 28–31
Tutoring, 262–266, 279–284

Unemployment, of youth, 370–372
United States Employment Service,
    68, 70, 371, 381

Vocation, 8, 13
Vocational card sort, 357, 426–427
Vocational Decision-Making
    Checklist, 33, 345–346,
    463, 519
Vocational education, 194

Women, 100–106, 481–482, 532–
    533
Work
    American view, 115–116
    benefits of, 117
    changes in, 117–120, 369–370
    conditions of, 144–145
    definition, 8
    environments (fields), 121,
        125–126
    ethic, 26, 85
    part-time, 148–150
    satisfaction, 4, 20–25, 130
Work values, 84–88, 373–374